BLOOD ON
THE MARSH

ABOUT DANIEL MCDONALD JOHNSON

I learned to write stories by working at community newspapers for twenty-five years. I worked as a reporter, photographer and editor at newspapers in Charleston, Ridgeland, Walterboro, Barnwell and Allendale, South Carolina, and the newspaper in Sylvania, Georgia. I also have done freelance work for newspapers and magazines, including *Sandlapper: The Magazine of South Carolina*.

I wrote entries on Allendale County, the town of Allendale and the town of Fairfax for *The South Carolina Encyclopedia*, University of South Carolina Press, 2006.

I have published two books on Revolutionary War battles in Georgia: *Brier Creek Battleground*, a guide to a site beside the Savannah River near Sylvania, and *Fort Morris Battleground*, a brief account of the American Revolution in Georgia with emphasis on events at Sunbury on the coast. Both books are illustrated with photographs of Revolutionary War sites.

My poetry has been published in *Lowcountry Weekly* and *Charleston Poetic Review.*

My photography has been used on the 1990 South Carolina Coastal Council tide chart poster and the 1989 Palmetto Rural Telephone Cooperative directory cover. Selections of my photographs are displayed at the Colleton Museum in Walterboro, South Carolina, and the Salkehatchie Arts Center in Allendale, South Carolina.

Please visit my Web site at danielmcdonaldjohnson.com. You may write me at P.O. Box 747, Allendale, SC 29810, or email me at danielmcdonaldjohnson@gmail.com

Blood on the Marsh

The adventures of
Brigadier William Mackintosh
John Mackintosh Mor
Captain Aeneas Mackintosh
Colonel Anne Mackintosh
General Lachlan McIntosh
Roderick McIntosh, Colonel John McIntosh
Flora MacDonald, Sergeant Allen McDonald
and Alexander McDonald of Darien, Georgia

DANIEL McDONALD JOHNSON

Published by Daniel McDonald Johnson

Revised Edition

Copyright 2014
Daniel McDonald Johnson
Post Office Box 747
Allendale, South Carolina 29810

ISBN-13:
978-1500602819

ISBN-10:
1500602817

Available from Amazon.com and other retail outlets

TOO MUCH INFORMATION

Realizing that *Blood on the Marsh* contains too many pages for most people to read, I have extracted a shorter book from it. *Mr. McIntosh's Family,* tells about the Mackintosh clan and the McIntosh family in the Jacobite Risings, the settlement of Darien, Georgia, and the struggle for the colonial American southern frontier; it is available from amazon.com and other retailers.

Another book, now in progress with the working title *This Cursed War*, will explore the effects of the American Revolution on Continental General Lachlan McIntosh and his family.

In essence, *Mr. McIntosh's Family* is Part I of *Blood on the Marsh* and *This Cursed War* will be Part II of *Blood on the Marsh*, but without the information on Clan Donald and my ancestors Alexander McDonald who fought at the Battle of Bloody Marsh and his son Alexander McDonald who served in the 2nd South Carolina Regiment during the American Revolution.

War happens to people, one by one.

– Martha Gellhorn

ACKNOWLEDGEMENTS

I want to thank my wife, my brothers, my sister and my late parents for their love, encouragement and support.

I am grateful to John Mackintosh Mor's descendant Billy McIntosh of Savannah and to Brigadier William Mackintosh's descendant Mattie Gladstone of The Ridge near Darien for sharing McIntosh family stories and for guiding me around the McIntosh stomping grounds in Savannah and McIntosh County.

Alexander McDonald's descendant Isabel Thorpe Mealing, whom my mother called "Cousin Isabel," not only generously shared her vast archives with me but also graciously fixed dinner for me at her home in Darien.

I cherish my memories of conversations with Bessie Lewis of Pine Harbor near Darien and with Dr. Edward Cashin of Augusta, and I continue to admire and enjoy their books.

I also want to thank the staffs of the Georgia Historical Society, the Allendale County Library, the Colleton County Memorial Library, the Screven County Library, the University of South Carolina Library System, and the Interlibrary Loan Department of the Thomas Cooper Library at the University of South Carolina.

CONTENTS

Aeneas Mackintosh perseveres as his regiment suffers attrition in fierce fighting across the Carolinas and is taken prisoner at the Siege of Yorktown.

Allen McDonald performs yet more feats of valor and earns a promotion to lieutenant shortly before dying in battle.

Aeneas Mackintosh sails home to Scotland after nearly two years as a prisoner of war.

Flora MacDonald dies and is given a heroine's burial.

Lachlan McIntosh is regarded as an elder statesman in Georgia, and shows George Washington around Savannah during the President's Southern Tour.

INTRODUCTION

Bards in the Scottish Highlands glorified the heroic deeds of valiant ancestors in terrible battle, and these tales of the Mackintosh and MacDonald men and women fit right into the bardic tradition. Indeed, the historical facts may have been reshaped to make the tales fit right in. When even an eyewitness to the Battle of Bloody Marsh contradicts official records when telling his grandson about it, as William McIntosh did when talking to Thomas Spalding, it is obvious that he doesn't want the facts to get in the way of a good story.

This book is a collection of legends. Legends are neither fiction nor nonfiction; they are based on historical events and feature historical people, but they intertwine mythology, folklore, and creative storytelling with historical facts. I did not invent any of these legends; they have all been published before. In many cases, I quote the authors who published the legends in the past.

I have focused on legends involving Clan Mackintosh in Scotland and its McIntosh progeny in America from 1715 through 1791. I also have included what little information I could find on my immigrant ancestor Alexander McDonald, who was among the Highlanders who founded Darien, Georgia, and information on his son – known in my family as Alexander McDonald Jr. – who served in the 2nd South Carolina Regiment in the American Revolution and presumably participated in the sieges of Savannah and Charleston. His descendants acquired Fairhope Plantation, the former home of Colonel John McIntosh.

My grandfather and namesake Daniel McDonald was born at Fairhope, lived in McIntosh County most of his life, and retired to Pine Harbor, just up the river from Fairhope and in the vicinity of Mallow, the plantation where Roderick McIntosh lived before the Revolution.

I have included good stories about legendary characters who share my family name, including Flora MacDonald – who witnessed both the Jacobite Rising of 1745 in Scotland and the Revolution in America – and the remarkable "Serjt. M'Donald" of Francis Marion's backcountry brigade. And when I came across really good stories about legendary characters such as George

Washington or James Oglethorpe who through no fault of their own were not Scots Highlanders, I couldn't resist retelling the tales.

I have tried to combine the various legends into a single narrative that is told in chronological order. In collecting the previously published legends, I followed the trail blazed by Sir Thomas Malory when he collected the various versions of Arthurian myth, legend and romance into a single narrative in *Le morte d'Arthur*. As in Malory's book, most of the legends in my book are combat tales, and most of the characters are men.

The narrative begins with the adventures of John Mackintosh Mor in the Jacobite Rising of 1715. It then follows the lives of John Mor's children (including Continental General Lachlan McIntosh), John Mor's grandchildren (including Colonel John McIntosh), and the descendants (including Rory McIntosh) of John Mor's uncle, Brigadier William Mackintosh from Borlum. Meanwhile, the adventures of several chiefs of Clan Mackintosh intermingle with the adventures of John Mor's family in Scotland and America.

Daniel McDonald Johnson
Allendale, South Carolina
July 21, 2014

BLOOD ON THE MARSH

THEY SAY THERE ONCE was a lad in the Scottish High-lands who went off to war. His name was John Mackintosh and, because he would grow to a large size, he was distinguished by the Gaelic word for big: "mor."

John Mackintosh Mor was a grandson of the Mackintosh of Borlum and he went off to war with his uncle William the younger of Borlum (Cashin, *McGillivray* 13).

William Mackintosh had served in the French military service and had made friends with a descendant of the Stewart kings of England, Scotland and Ireland. Calling himself James III of England and James VIII of Scotland, and using the French spelling "Stuart" for the dynastic family name, he claimed to be the rightful successor to his father, James II of England and James VII of Scotland. His supporters were called Jacobites, from the Latin word for James.

The last Stewart king had been replaced by a half-sister, Mary, and her husband, William of Orange. Mary's sister Anne succeeded them. When Queen Anne died without an heir, there was a chance that the would-be James III could claim the throne if he converted to the Protestant church but he remained faithful to the Catholic church. Parliament arranged for a German-speaking Hanoverian to be crowned George I – his only qualifications to be King of England were being a great-grandson of James I and, more important, being a Protestant.

When James made a move to reclaim the British crown for the Stuart line of succession, William Mackintosh returned to his homeland in the Scottish Highlands and recruited warriors for the cause. He persuaded Lachlan the 20th Chief of Clan Mackintosh to join the cause and bring out the clan's fighting men – and boys like John Mackintosh Mor, who some people say was 15 years old at the time, but most people say 17 (Mackintosh of Mackintosh 44; Lewis, *Darien* 16; Sullivan 33).

The Jacobite Rising of 1715

The Jacobite rising got underway on September 6, 1715, when the Earl of Mar raised a blue and gold flag at Braemar in the High-lands and proclaimed James VIII to be the rightful and natural king by the grace of God (Aronson 91). The Chief of Clan Mackintosh promptly proclaimed King James at Inverness – the largest town in the Highlands, located in Clan Mackintosh territory – and seized all the public money and arms kept in Inverness.

The Mackintoshes then tried to seize the arms and ammunition at Culloden House, home of Duncan Forbes. "Mrs. Forbes, in the absence of her husband, put her house in a state of defence," writes the official Mackintosh historian, "and sent to Munro of Foulis for help. Munro was coming to her assistance when he was stopped by Seaforth, who was on the Jacobite side. However, Seaforth persuaded Mackintosh not to waste precious time storming a single house against a woman, but to march his eight hundred men south to join the Earl of Mar at Perth" (44-45).

A Jacobite force of twelve thousand men assembled at Perth. Lachlan the Chief of Clan Mackintosh gained the rank of colonel and took command of a regiment while William the younger of Borlum gained the rank of brigadier and took command of a brigade.

"It speaks well for the generosity of the Chief that he was willing to serve under his own clansman," writes Margaret Mackintosh of Mackintosh, herself the lady of a clan chief (45).

Crossing the Forth

Another clan historian tells what happened next:

> [The Earl of Mar] conceived the plan of sending a force under Brigadier MacKintosh into England to encourage the Jacobites there. The Brigadier did not approve of the plan, but finding Mar determined upon it, he went into it with his usual whole-heartedness. The force selected for the expedition consisted of six regiments – Lord Strathmore's, Lord Mar's, Logie Drummond's, Lord Charles Murray's, Lord Nairn's and Mackintosh of Mackintosh's. The Brigadier forthwith pressed into his service all the boats along the Northern shore of the Forth, and chose the nights of the 11th and 12th of October for the crossing. As Argyle was in force at Stirling, several men-of-war were cruising in the vicinity, and from eighteen to twenty miles of water to cross in open boats, the undertaking was a perilous one. Nevertheless he succeeded in getting 1500 men, including MacKintosh's regiment, across, a feat even in the present

day considered remarkable. Having collected his men, who got scattered in crossing, at Haddington, he daringly resolved to march upon Edinburgh. (MacKintosh, "Brigadier" 73)

A nineteenth-century Scottish historian provides some other details of the expedition:

[Mackintosh] was sent to Burntisland with two thousand men to secure boats with which to cross the army, and while here, on the 9th October, he addressed the following curious and ingenuous letter to Captain Pool of H.M.S. Pearl, then employed in guarding the Firth and its shipping from the designs of the Highlanders:

"Sir, - You lying so near a part of the King's army of which I have the honour to command as Brigadier-General, thinks it incumbent upon me to require, command, and summons you in His Majesty King James the Eighth's name, to come in and return your duty, allegiance, and obedience to him, and does promise you that your early appearance will meet with all suitable encouragement from me, and will entitle you in all time coming to receive from His Majesty such favours as so great a service deserves.
If ye incline to hearken to this proposal you'll be pleased to send some officer ashore that I may fully commune with him, and I promise him protection and safety to come and return, and if ye desire I shall send an officer to you upon the like protection granted. The complying with this measure will be just, safe, honourable, and advantageous.
The enclosed is the Earl of Mar and others of the nobility and gentry their manifesto calculate for the kingdom of Scotland, and since it has pleased God to bring His Majesty safely into his own kingdoms, ye may expect that encouragement will be given to the Royal Navy of England."

The reply of Pool to the letter of the "Arch rebel," as he calls him, was a threat to lay the place in ashes, but Highland wit proved more than a match for loyal Pool, for ere the English captain awoke next morning Mackintosh had crossed over with his force, and it was firmly established at North Berwick, Aberlady, and other places along the coast. Ere long they held possession of Haddington for King James. The Lord Justice Clerk writing on 13th October, to Secretary Stanhope of these things, says: -

> "Lord Nairn and two or three other lords are come over, but it is Mackintosh of Borlum that is the principal man that commands at Haddington. Some of the rebels were at the President of the Session's gate before his family was well awake, and his lordship narrowly escaped; two of his sons were taken, but they have let them go again upon their parole of honour, and Borlum, as Brigadier of the Pretender's forces, gives them a pass, which pass I have seen… This landing is the boldest, and perhaps the most desperate, attempt you ever heard of." (Rose 80-82)

Margaret Mackintosh of Mackintosh picks up the story of the expedition:

> Borlum, with fifteen hundred men, including the Mackintosh regiment, succeeded in crossing from Pittenweem and Crail in open boats. The Brigadier promptly marched on Edinburgh, where he hoped to be assisted by the Jacobites within the city. The city magistrates, however, upon hearing of Borlum's approach, had promptly lodged all the leading Jacobites in prison.
> Borlum was too experienced a soldier to waste his little army by attempting to carry a big city by assault without any assistance from within, so he seized Leith instead and fortified himself in one of the forts built there by Cromwell. There he was attacked the following day by Argyll who, failing in his assaults, was compelled to withdraw. Borlum, in obedience to orders received from Mar, thereupon marched his force south to join Lord Kenmore and the Eng-

lish Jacobites under Mr Foster. He found them at Kelso, the Highlanders marching into town playing their pipes. They seem to have inspired the natives with profound terror, and quite a hundred years later the name of Borlum was used as a bogey to frighten children. It must have been merely their wild appearance that produced this effect, for Borlum maintained good discipline.

Lord Kenmure took over supreme command of the army, and Borlum retained command of the Highland division. He advised Kenmure to attack the English under General Carpenter, who was known to be training recruits in cavalry. Kenmure rejected the advice and was to rue his decision...

Borlum was also anxious to join the western clans under General Gordon and so to secure Scotland, rather than to penetrate England, where so far there had been no sign of a rising. His advice was again flouted, as Mr Foster and Lord Widdrington assured Kenmure that all Lancashire, being a nest of Catholics, would rise if the Scots marched in. Kenmure decided to advance into England and march into Lancashire. When the Scots then refused to cross the Border, in loyalty to his General, Borlum personally persuaded about a thousand Highlanders to follow, but five hundred others turned back and went home, though Borlum stood in the Esk swearing at them and calling them "reskels of humanity.' (45-46)

Crossing the Esk

Another clan historian gives a slightly different account of the border crossing:

When they reached the Border some of the men refused to go into England, and an eye-witness describes the Brigadier standing in the middle of the Esk endeavoring with all his authority and eloquence to prevent them from deserting. We can image the beetle-brow darken, and the grey eyes flash, as he thunders at them "Why the ----- not go into England where there are men, meat and money? Those who are deserting me are but the rascality of my men." (MacKintosh, "Brigadier" 74)

Battles decide the Rising of 1715

The Jacobite Rising of 1715 resulted in two major battles fought at the same time, one in Scotland and the other in England. Warriors of the Macdonalds of Clanranald and the MacDonnels of Glengarry served in the Jacobite army that remained in Scotland, while warriors of Clan Mackintosh served in the Jacobite army that invaded England.

The Battle of Preston: November 12-14, 1715

A Clan Mackintosh historian describes events leading up to the Battle of Preston:

> After crossing the Border, the command devolved upon Foster, the English General, who proved himself wholly incapable, and of no military ability whatsoever. When they reached Penrith on the 2nd November they found a force of rustics estimated at 15,000 assembled to oppose them. Those men, however, were not sufficiently trained to resist the little army of 4000 men from the North and they were soon put to flight. After many councils and cross marches, with which the Brigadier was much disgusted, Forster and his force on the 10th November entered Preston. Here they were joined by 1,200 allies, mainly badly-armed recruits. Forster was elated at this accession to his force, but the Brigadier looked upon it with different eyes. "Look you here, Forster," he exclaimed, "are these the fellows you intend to fight Wills with? Good faith, Sir, and ye had 10,000 of them I would fight them all with 1000 of his dragoons." At that very time too several parties of Hanoverian troops under Generals Wills and Carpenter were hastening with all speed to Preston. On the night of Friday, 11th November, Forster received intelligence of the approach of Wills, but instead of making preparations to resist the enemy, he retired to bed, leaving the other leaders to arrange for the defence of the town. Notwithstanding this gross neglect of duty he did not hesitate next morning to change the dispositions that had been made, with the result that neither the bridge nor the fords leading to the town were defended, and the enemy was allowed to cross the Ribble unmolested.

Across the principal streets, however, barricades planned by
the Brigadier were erected. The main barriers were four in
number – one a little below the church, commanded by the
Brigadier; another at the end of a lane leading into open
country, under Lord Charles Murray; a third called the
Wind-Mill, under MacKintosh of MacKintosh; and a fourth
in the street leading towards Liverpool, commanded by Major Miller. The three first barriers were attacked with great
fury, but without success. The attack on the Brigadier's barrier was repulsed with considerable loss to the assailants,
and that on Lord Murray's and MacKintosh's were equally
unsuccessful. In the back part of the town 300 of Wills' men
who tried toward nightfall to enter the "Back Weem," were
repulsed with the loss of 140 men killed. The fight continued throughout the night, although the local Jacobites took
advantage of the cover of darkness to escape. The original
little army was thus left to its fate. (MacKintosh, "Brigadier"
74)

Military historian William Seymour describes the Battle of
Preston in his comprehensive book *Battles in Britain*:

On the night of 9 November the Jacobite horse entered Preston. Two troops of Colonel Stanhope's dragoons, who were
in the town, withdrew without offering any resistance.

On 10 November the foot also arrived in Preston, and
Forster, who had been assured through his local intelligence
system that he could expect ample warning of any enemy
approach, intended resting his army for a day or two before
proceeding to Manchester. It came as a considerable surprise
to him, therefore, to learn on the 12th that General Wills,
who commanded the royalist troops in Cheshire, was at
hand with five cavalry and three infantry regiments. Moreover, General Carpenter, displaying an offensive spirit that
went far to compensate for the inferior material at his dis-
posal, was said to be closing in from the north-east. This information seems to have proved too much for Forster, who
issued a series of orders and counter-orders then retired to
his lodgings. When, a little later, Colonel Oxburgh and

Lords Kenmure and Widdrington reported for orders they found their 'general' in bed.

Preston was a quite unprotected small market town, but a resolute commander could have put up a strong defence. The key point to be held was the bridge over the Ribble and John Farquharson of Invercauld had been sent there by Forster with a small force of picked men. Farquharson had plenty of courage and he and his men would have given a good account of themselves, but at the first hint of danger they were withdrawn to the town. Wills was so amazed at finding the bridge unguarded that he immediately suspected an ambush in the narrow lane with its high hedges that led from the bridge up the hill to the town. He therefore proceeded with caution, which enabled the Jacobites to perfect their dispositions. These were fairly skilfully laid out, and reflect some other hand than Forster's.

Barricades were set up blocking the main entrances to the town and proper use was made of the houses and narrow lanes as points of defence. The Jacobites possessed six cannon, and if these could have been properly manned the royalists, who were without artillery, would have been more severely mauled than was the case: but without trained gunners what little advantage they offered was chiefly psychological. Brigadier Mackintosh of Borlum commanded the barricade set up to the east of the church in the main street, and was supported by the Earl of Derwentwater's troops, who were in position in the churchyard. Another member of Clan Mackintosh commanded what was known as the windmill barrier, which was situated on the Lancaster road, while the one on the Liverpool road was under a Major Mills. Lord Charles Murray blocked a lane leading into fields across which General Carpenter's troops were expected. By midday on 12 November Preston was in a state of adequate defence.

General Wills, having discovered that the approach lanes to the town were clear and that the Jacobites had decided to make a stand, launched a two-point attack. Brigadier Honywood, commanding his own dragoons, and Preston's foot under Lord Forrester, attacked Borlum's post, while Brigadiers Dormer and Munden led a mixed force of infantry and dismounted cavalry against the Lancaster barricade. Little headway was made against this barrier and the attack does not seem to have been a very spirited affair. But on the Wigan side of town the battle was fiercely contested and the Jacobites, firing from the protection of houses, inflicted considerable casualties on Wills' men.

The strength of Borlum's position was that between the double barricade set up to the east of the church there stood two of the largest houses in the town. These belonged to Sir Henry Haughton and Mr Hare; both houses had been occupied by Highlanders. A frontal attack down the road had no chance of success so long as the attackers were subject to enfilade fire from these houses; but when Lord Forrester infiltrated his regiment through the gardens between the church and the two houses the position was dangerous but by no means critical – that is, until the troops in the larger house (Haughton's) were withdrawn. It is not clear from contemporary accounts of the battle why Mackintosh did this, but it was a fatal error. Before nightfall Preston's regiment was in possession of both these houses, although in getting them they suffered the only heavy casualties of the whole battle.

A third attack had also been launched against Lord Charles Murray's barricade, but this had been held after heavy fighting in the course of which Murray had to ask for reinforcements from Derwentwater. As night drew on and the whip-lash sound of close-range bullets became less persistent the Jacobites could be well content with the day's work, for all the barriers were still intact, although the one by the church had become dangerously vulnerable. However, all was not well among the rebel soldiery: royalist prisoners taken in the fighting soon dispelled all hopes that any of their colleagues would desert. Some Jacobites with cool heads, and cold feet, made their way out of the town while there was still time – for the next day General Carpenter arrived and immediately sealed off all exits.

Carpenter claimed the credit for the victory, but at the time he commended General Wills for the fighting on the 12th, and the only serious flaw that he could find in his dispositions was that the bridge and ford across the Ribble had been left unguarded. Once these exits had been closed the rebels were bottled up, but there was little doubt that they could have fought their way out. However, much to the disgust of the Highlanders, caitiff counsels in the end prevailed. (187-90)

Margaret Mackintosh of Mackintosh reports the Highlanders' violent resistance to surrender:

> The Chief of Mackintosh commanded one defence force, Borlum another... Things were not going so badly with the Jacobites at first, until Wills was reinforced by General Carpenter, whom Kenmure had neglected to destroy. This was too much for Foster, who gave up all hope and, without the knowledge of the Scots, sent a secret envoy to Wills to ask for terms. Wills ordered their surrender as rebels and demanded two leaders as hostages – one Scottish and one English. Accordingly the Chief of Mackintosh and the Earl of Derwentwater were placed in Wills' hands.
>
> The Highlanders, on finding the surrender arranged 'were terribly enraged, and declared they would die fighting.' They killed a good many who dared to talk to them of surrender. However, their fury was unavailing, and on Wills threatening with his superior force to kill every man of them the inevitable surrender took place. (46)

British military historian William Seymour resumes his account of the Battle of Preston and its aftermath.

> On 14 November the English marched in and disarmed Forster's men. The number of prisoners taken was about 1,500, of which seventy-five were English noblemen or gentlemen and 143 Scottish. Most of the rank and file taken were Scotsmen and they were treated with considerable savagery. The important prisoners were taken to London and some were sentenced to death... The Jacobite casualties were only eighteen killed and twenty-five wounded, as opposed to about 200 royalists killed or wounded, most of whom were from Preston's regiment.

The Battle of Preston terminated the Jacobite insurrection in England; but at almost exactly the same time as Forster and his officers were negotiating the surrender in Lancashire an even more disastrous blow to James's cause was struck on a lonely moor near Stirling. (187-91)

The Battle of Sheriffmuir: November 13, 1715

On November 13 at Sheriffmuir near Stirling, 3,100 men led by the Duke of Argyll attacked the Jacobite army of 7,100 men under the Earl of Mar. Among the Jacobites with Mar was the chief of the Macdonalds of Clanranald. Clan Donald historian Donald J. Macdonald of Castleton creates a portrait of the chief:

Alan, 14th Chief, succeeded his father at the early age of thirteen. He had a short, but eventful life, was much loved by his clan and greatly respected by others... Educated at Inverness and under private tutors, he became an accomplished young man. At the age of sixteen he began his active life as Chief, taking his clan out to join Viscount Dundee [in a Jacobite Rising that included the battles of Killiecrankie and Dunkeld in 1689 and the enforced pacification of the Highlands starting in 1690; the cruel massacre of MacDonalds at Glencoe in February of 1692 was part of that pacification campaign].

...young Alan was out with 500 of his Clan, but on the failure of the cause, he had to flee to France with his brother, Ranald, and find asylum at the Court of St. Germains...

While in France Alan met and married Penelope Mackenzie... This lady was both beautiful and accomplished. It was a love match of the most romantic kind. At this time Alan was serving in the French Army... On the 21st of July 1696 Mackenzie of Cromartie became surety for his good behavior, and thereupon Alan returned home to resume his duties as Chief.

...The House of Ormiclete was improved and here with the fair Penelope he lived in peace and prosperity for all too short a time. For nine happy years the mansion of Ormiclete became the resort of many visitors to enjoy the hospitality and culture of Alan and his gifted wife. It was a happy time in the best tradition of the House of Clanranald which has always been the repository of all that is best of the ancient culture of the Gael – bardic poetry, music and "seanachas," maintaining and transmitting the historical lore of the ancient Kingdom and Lordship of the Isles. Alan was still at heart a Jacobite, and when the Hanoverian succession rekindled the old flame, he was one of the first to declare for the old House of Stewart. (318)

Alan's participation in the Rising of 1715 would end in tragedy. Military historian William Seymour describes the Battle of Sheriffmuir and its aftermath:

…shortly before midday on this cold November morning, these two armies formed up for battle within a very short distance of each other without either side being perfectly aware of what the other was about.

The Jacobites, confident of victory, were in a mood of exhilaration, tossing their bonnets in the air and emitting loud huzzas…

On the one side of the ridge colourful plaids and kilts, on the other brilliant uniforms with flaunted facings of scarlet and blue; a pageantry of splendor, so soon to become a sorry scene of disarray.

…as soon as the Jacobites topped the crest of the ridge it was seen that the right wings of both armies overlapped the other's left.

…Argyll was in a position to observe the confusion into which the Jacobite left had been thrown and he wasted no time in exploiting it. He went into the attack at the head of five squadrons of dragoons and five battalions of foot, as well as sixty mounted volunteers under the Earl of Rothes. Taken off balance, the Highlanders nevertheless put up an amazingly stout resistance, more especially when the Fife and Angus squadrons had dislocated themselves from the centre and come to their assistance. Wherever the ground was favourable this retreating left wing stood and fought with much stubbornness, but gradually they were pressed back in a two-mile half-circle to the river Allan, which they crossed – still under pressure – in the neighbourhood of Kinbuck.

Sheriffmuir was an inconclusive and untidy battle, for Argyll, though a greatly superior general to Mar, seems to have been guilty of going into the attack before he had assured himself that his left wing was adequately protected... Mar's attack opened with a sharp bout of musketry, both armies firing at almost point-blank range. The ranks shivered like corn in the wind, and among the Highlanders the popular Captain of Clanranald fell, but Glengarry rallied the clan and crying for revenge they discarded their muskets and were quickly among the militia with their broadswords. It was all over in a matter of minutes: Argyll's left was chased from the field and even to the outskirts of Stirling.

The field of battle was now almost deserted... Mar retraced his steps, with his right wing virtually intact, and occupied the high ground... This wing alone was larger than the whole of Argyll's army, and he would have had little difficulty in annihilating the victorious royalist troops... But Mar in his weak, indecisive way lacked the manhood to dare... For the rest of the day the two protagonists, with what was left of their troops, remained passively watching each other. Then, as the early darkness closed in, Mar marched his men back to Ardoch and Argyll camped in and around Dunblane.

If a victory was to be claimed by either side Argyll had that slender right, for on the next day he re-occupied the battlefield and gathered up the spoils – which were considerable. The royalists admitted to 290 killed, 187 men wounded and over 100 taken prisoner, most of whom were shortly released for want of means to accommodate them. Mar owned to the loss of only sixty men and eighty-two prisoners... but certainly the Jacobites lost more than they admitted to – possibly 300-400 – and very probably the royalists did too. Apart from the Captain of Clanranald the Earl of Strathmore was the only Jacobite of importance to be killed, while the government troops lost the Earl of Forfar.

For the Jacobites anything less than a victory was a defeat. Loss of prestige was serious, resulting in many of the clansmen going home – Seaforth's people being hastened on their way by the news that the government had taken Inverness. There was now no chance of joining up with the army in England, and indeed the simultaneous defeat at Preston virtually brought the rebellion to a close, even though James was to arrive in Scotland in just over a month's time. (192-95)

Strange coincidences in Clanranald territory

Strange circumstances surrounded the death of the Macdonalds of Clanranald's chief at Sheriffmuir. Clan Donald historian Donald J. Macdonald explains:

For Clanranald, Alan and his men, the Rising was a disaster. Alan was buried at Innerpeffray, the burial place of the Earls of Perth. By a strange coincidence, his home at Ormiclete, where he and his beloved wife had spent so few years of peace and happiness, was burned down by accident. This strange tragedy took place about the very time Alan was meeting his death, and, still more strangely, the old Castle Tirrim too was burned shortly after Alan had departed to the war. Tradition in Moidart states that the castle was burned by order of the Chief himself, who had a presentiment that he would never return, and did not wish the enemy to find shelter in his ancestral home. Moreover, Fr. Charles Macdonald in his book *Moidart, or among the Clanranalds* states that in his own time the great-grandson of the man who fired the castle at the command of his chief was still alive at a great age and remembered the story quite clearly.

Unfortunately, Alan and his wife left no heir to the estates. So in 1716 Ranald, brother of Alan, who had accompanied him throughout the war, succeeded to the chiefship. …but with others involved in the Rising he had to flee to the Court of St. Germains which was the refuge for so many Jacobites after the collapse of their hopes.

Ranald, 15th Chief, spent all his life in exile in France. (319-20)

Mackintoshes taken prisoner at Preston

Margaret Mackintosh of Mackintosh tells the fate of her clansmen after the collapse of the Jacobite Rising of 1715:

General Wills took possession of Preston with fifteen hundred prisoners – of the rank and file were sixty bearing Clan Chattan names, including thirteen Mackintoshes and sixteen Macgillivrays.

The Chief and Borlum and others of note were sent to London, but many of inferior rank were executed, and others transported to America for slavery, while some were imprisoned in various English towns.

The officers sent as prisoners to London were escorted from Highgate in a mock triumphal procession followed by a jeering mob. Mackintosh is described as 'a brave and handsome gentleman,' and Borlum as 'remarkable for the grim ferocity of his scarred face.' For five months they lay in prison until in April 1716 their trial was to be held. On the night before this trial Borlum and fifteen others overpowered the sentinels and made their escape from prison; seven were recaptured, but the others, including Borlum, got safely away. Foster escaped in a separate venture. The Government issued a description of the Brigadier as 'a Tall Rawboned Man about sixty years old, Fair-Complexioned, Beetle-Browed, speaks Broad Scotch.' They offered one thousand pounds reward for Borlum's capture, but he evaded pursuit and was assisted by his brother-in-law, Thomas Reade, in Oxfordshire, to conceal himself until he was able to find a ship to carry him to France.

The London mob, with whom Borlum was decidedly popular, was highly pleased with his escape. They celebrated his heroism in ballads not flattering to their countrymen. The following ballad is quoted from Hogg's *Jacobite Relics of Scotland*:

> Mackintosh was a soldier brave
> And did most gallantly behave
> When into Northumberland he came
> With gallant men of his own name…
>
> Old Mackintosh he shook his head,
> When he saw his Highland lads lie dead;
> And he wept not for the loss of those,
> But for the success of their proud foes.
> Then Mackintosh unto Wills he came,
> Saying, 'I have been a soldier in my time,
> 'And ere a Scot of mine shall yield,
> 'We'll all lie dead upon the field.'

'Then go your ways,' he made reply;
'Either surrender, or you shall die.
'Go back to your own men in the town:
'What can you do when left alone?'
Mackintosh is a gallant soldier,
With his musket over his shoulder.
'Every true man point his rapier:
'But, damn you, Foster, you are a traitor!'

… Brave Derwentwater he is dead;
From his fair body they took the head;
But Mackintosh and his friends are fled,
And they'll set the hat on another head.
And whether they are gone beyond the Sea,
Or if they bide in this country,
Though our King would give ten thousand pound,
Old Mackintosh will scorn to be found.

…The Chief of Mackintosh was released from prison in
1716, at the intercession of his wife and Lord Lovat and other
friends, who pleaded that Lachlan had been 'trepanned into
the rebellion by the craft of the Brigadier'!

After his release in 1716, the chief devoted himself to
improving his estates and to settling disputes. (46-49)

At least eleven Jacobite prisoners named Mackintosh were
transported from Liverpool to South Carolina in the spring of 1716
(Dobson, *Directory* 162-164).

The Yemassee War
The Highlanders who were banished to South Carolina after
the Jacobite Rising of 1715 arrived in a war-torn colony on the colonial American southern frontier. A strong force of southern Indians sought to exterminate South Carolina and they found allies
among French colonists to the west and Spanish colonists to the
south. Military historian Larry Ivers gives background on the Yemassee War:

South Carolina traders and their caravans of Indian bearers
or pack horses traversed the southeastern forest paths from

Charles Town inland for hundreds of miles to practically every town, exchanging their trade goods for the Indians' deer skins and captive slaves. Indians became so dependent upon English woolens, cutlery, and guns that some nations moved closer to Charles Town, the source of the coveted trade goods. Guarding each of the principal entrances into the colony was a friendly Indian sentry-town, protecting the settlers from attacks by enemy Indians. However, by the first decade of the eighteenth century, South Carolina was taking her Indian allies for granted. The colonial government refused to control the conduct of the traders who extended unlimited credit to the Indian hunters until the debts became impossible to pay, sometimes collected the debts by selling Indian wives and children into slavery, cheated on the weighing of skins with false weights and measures, and conducting themselves like barons in the Indian towns where they were licensed to trade.

By 1715 the Indians would bear no more. A conspiracy of gigantic proportions was formed and in April the Yemassee, whose settlements were then located in South Carolina between the Combahee and Savannah Rivers, began a war by killing the traders in their towns and several scores of settlers living between Port Royal and the Edisto River. Most of the nations and independent towns were members of the conspiracy, but the English discovery of their intentions had caused a premature initiation of the war, resulting in subsequent uncoordinated attacks. In June the Catawba and other northern Indians attacked the Santee settlements north of Charles Town. During July the Creek and Apalachee penetrated South Carolina defenses, destroying the plantations southwest of Charles Town between the Edisto and Stono Rivers. Most of the women and children of the colony were forced to take shelter in Charles Town, but the militia, reinforced with armed slaves and settlement Indians, responded superbly and followed each of the three invasions by defeating the Indians and forcing them to withdraw. A decade of war had well prepared the South Carolinians to defend their colony. The Yemassee retreated to Florida under the protection of the Spaniards, and the former sentry-town Indians along the frontier fled to the interior to live with the larger Indian nations. During the winter of 1715 a South Carolina army, bolstered with Virginia and North Carolina soldiers, marched into the Cherokee nations and compelled their allegiance.

By 1718 the major fighting was over, but the Yemassee and Apalachicola continued to conduct small-scale raids and ambushes against the settlements between the Savannah and the Edisto. (5-6)

Borlum is dead; long live Borlum

In the Highlands of Scotland, William Mackintosh 3rd of Borlum – father of Brigadier William Mackintosh and grandfather of John Mackintosh Mor – died in 1717. The Brigadier, as the elder son, was entitled to the designation 4th of Borlum but not to ownership of the estate. His father, anticipating that the government would seize the property of Jacobite gentry, had arranged in January of 1715 for the estate to pass to the Brigadier's elder son, Lauchlan. When the 3rd of Borlum died, Lauchlan inherited the estate and the designation 5th of Borlum. Lauchlan's uncle Lauchlan Mackintosh of Knocknagael – father of John Mackintosh Mor – served as the young laird's Curator (Ross 186-87).

The Borlum branch of Clan Mackintosh had been founded by a son of Lachlan, known as Mor, the 16th Chief of Clan Mackintosh. Lachlan's oldest son had died – but not before fathering a future chief of the clan – and his remaining adult sons did not abide by his wishes. Margaret Mackintosh of Mackintosh gives the details:

> Lachlan had trouble with his sons, who did not uphold their father's reconciliation with Campbell of Cawdor, and more especially after his eldest son's widow married Donald Campbell. Malcolm and William Mackintosh twice raided Cawdor's lands and disputed their sister-in-law and her husband's liferent for Dunachton. Cawdor's sons were brought as prisoners to the Chief of Culloden, who at once released them. He was very much displeased with his sons, whom he refused to see for a year. William was put in prison and the Clan Mackintosh had to pay a considerable fine as a penalty to the Crown. The fiery William established himself at Borlum about four miles outside Inverness on the east bank of

the River Ness. He thus founded the colourful and important Borlum branch of the Mackintosh clan. A story is told that the wife of one of the early Mackintoshes of Borlum incited her two sons to murder the Provost of Inverness. Her reason was that this gentleman, on seeing her in the town one day, was so shocked by her 'rude and indelicate demeanour' that he had said, 'Oh, fie, fie, fie Lady Borlum' thus rousing her deadly fury! (28-29)

The first Laird of Borlum was succeeded by his son Lauchlan who was succeeded by his "eldest lawful son" William as the 3rd of Borlum. William married Marie Baillie of Dunain. Their first son William would become known as the Brigadier. A clan historian provides biographical details:

William the Brigadier, 4th of Borlum, possessed the estate of Raits, in Badenoch, and married, in 1688, Mary, daughter of Edward Reade, of Ipsden, Oxford, who was, prior to her marriage, a Maid of Honour, to Princess Anne, afterwards Queen Anne, and had issue, Lauchlan 5th of Borlum, Shaw 6th of Borlum, Winwood, Maria Forbes, and Helen. Probably owing to his absence on military service, very little is known of his early life… (Ross 186)

About two years before his marriage, the Brigadier became the father of a natural son, Benjamin (Moncreiffe 128; Sullivan 36).

The third son of William the 3rd of Borlum became known as Lachlan Mackintosh of Knocknagael. He married Mary, daughter of John Lockhart of Inverness. Their first child, born in 1698 or 1700 in Badenoch, was named John and would be known as John Mor. He had a younger brother, Alexander, and a sister, Jane.

In 1713 – two years before John Mor marched off to war with his uncle the Brigadier – his mother died and was buried in the Grey Friars Inverness (Ross 185; Britt and Hawes 110-11).

The quest for a queen and an heir

James Stuart – the Pretender to the British throne – got caught up in rapidly shifting European politics after the Rising of 1715 and had to leave France. A biographer describes his adventures:

Mid-March found him in his mother's childhood home – the ducal palace of Modena. The reigning Duke was his mother's uncle, Rinaldo. James immediately felt at home in this ochre-coloured palace with its elegantly pillared loggias, its beautifully bound books and its priceless works of art. Perhaps it was the atmosphere of the ducal palace, or the joy of being among his family, or the headiness of the Italian springtime, or perhaps, after all, it was the grace of the Duke's eldest daughter Benedicta, that caused James to fall so deeply in love with her.

...His love for Benedicta... had all the ardour of a first love. With her tall, slender figure, her dark beauty and her graceful manner, Benedicta looked very like James' mother. Like Mary Beatrice she was well-educated and well-read. In every way, she would have made James an excellent wife. He certainly thought so for, in a very short time, he had asked her to marry him.

Benedicta's father, Duke Rinaldo, torn between the advantages of his daughter marrying the *de jure* King of England, and the disadvantages of offending the *de facto* King of England, asked James for time to consider the proposal. He also thought it best if James were to leave Modena until such time as the Duke had made up his mind. So, in mid-May, James took to the road once more.

...while James was waiting at Urbino, he heard that the Duke of Modena had turned down his request for the hand of Benedicta. (Aronson 100-01)

Jacobites who wanted to provide James with a queen and an heir searched for a suitable bride. They found Princess Maria Clementina Sobieski; her father James Sobieski was a pretender to the Polish crown just as James was pretender to the British crown. The Sobieski family also was related to the ruling families of Austria, Spain and Bavaria. "Princess Clementina was sixteen years old," a biographer writes, "a petite, piquant-faced, high-spirited creature; fittingly devout, impressively well-connected and gratifyingly rich. Her dowry would be enormous" (Aronson 104).

King George I of England asked Emperor Charles IV to keep Clementina from leaving the Holy Roman Empire. She was imprisoned in a comfortable castle at Innsbrook for six months. A

Jacobite operative – a young Irish captain named Charles Wogan –
came to her rescue on April 28, 1719:

> …Wogan put his plan into action. Leaving the rest of the
> conspirators at the inn, he took a good-natured maid by the
> name of Jeanneton through the black and stormy night to-
> wards Schloss Ambras. With the guards enjoying them-
> selves at a nearby wineshop, Wogan used a stolen key to
> slip into the castle. Having sent the terrified Jeanneton up-
> stairs, he hurried out again. Jeanneton was met by a sympa-
> thetic chamberlain and led into the presence of Princess
> Sobieski and her daughter. Knowing that she was to stand
> in for Clementina but quite unaware of her identity, the
> outspoken Jeanneton hustled her along…
>
> Having said goodbye to her tearful mother, Clementina
> threw Jeanneton's wet cloak about her shoulders and
> slipped downstairs. Jeanneton was then put into Clementi-
> na's bed. Outside, in the deep snow and bitter cold, Wogan
> stood about in an agony of apprehension. When Clementina
> finally appeared, he hurried her to the inn where the others
> were waiting. 'Welcome to you, my brave rescuers,' cried
> out the undaunted Clementina, 'and may God, who has
> brought you to my help, be our guide from now on.'
>
> They certainly needed some help. Their two-hundred-
> mile journey south from Schloss Ambras to the frontier be-
> tween the Empire and the Papal States was fraught with
> danger… On again they lurched, along frightful roads,
> through impenetrable mist and whirling snow, over the
> Brenner Pass and down into Italy. They were forced to eat
> the most unappetising food, to shelter in the filthiest inns
> and to live with the constant fear of discovery.
>
> …A complete collapse of the carriage was the last of
> their major problems and at a half past three on the morn-
> ing of 30 April, travelling in a hired cart, Clementina was
> jolted past the massive wall that marked the border between
> the Empire and the Papal States. With one voice, the group
> cried out 'Alleluia!' Their ordeal was over. The intrepid
> Wogan had safely delivered his sovereign's bride.

But his sovereign was not there to greet her. James was
in Spain, trying, for the third time, to win the crown that

would make Clementina *de facto* Queen of Great Britain. (Aronson 106-07)

The Brigadier participates in the Rising of 1719

Brigadier William Mackintosh, younger of Borlum, found refuge in France for a few years after the Rising of 1715. Some people say that teenaged John Mackintosh Mor "was in France with his uncle, the old Brigadier McIntosh" (Lewis, *Darien* 16; Dobson, *Scottish Emigration* 118). Before long, however, both of them were back in their native country. A pamphlet printed in 1718 explaining the reasons for a standing British army reported "that peril was already looming in Scotland, Brigadier MacKintosh's ghost having been seen in the Highlands" (MacKintosh, "Brigadier" 75). Within a year after his ghost was spotted, the Brigadier appeared in the Highlands in the flesh as part of a renewed attempt to fulfill his friend's desire to rule as James III of England and James VIII of Scotland.

James had formed an alliance with the King of Spain after England had declared war on Spain in 1718. Spanish officials planned an invasion of England with twenty-seven ships and five thousand men while a diversionary force of Spaniards and British Jacobites would go to Scotland to rally the Highland clans to the Jacobite cause.

Storms prevented the Spanish invasion of England, however, leaving the diversionary force to face its fate alone. In the spring of 1719, a force of 307 Spanish soldiers and a few British Jacobites – including Brigadier William Mackintosh of Borlum – sailed to Loch Alsh opposite the Isle of Skye on the west coast of the Scottish Highlands and unloaded their arms, powder and supplies at Eilean Donan Castle. The two Spanish frigates that transported the force returned to Spain. Leaving a few Spanish soldiers to guard Eilean Donan, Jacobite leader the Earl Marischal established his position nearby.

The government took action to keep Brigadier Mackintosh's clansmen from coming out to support him. The "Shirreff principal of the Shirreffdom of Inverness" summoned a number of clansmen – including Angus Mackintosh of Killachy, Lachlaine Macintosh younger thereof, and William Macintosh of Aberarder – to give security for their peaceful behavior (Gailbraith 296-97).

The Rising of 1719 had started inauspiciously and would end ingloriously. In *The Jacobites*, Frank McLynn writes:

> On 9 May 1719 events took an ugly turn. A British squadron sailed into Loch Alsh, overwhelmed the forty-five-strong Spanish garrison, blew up Eilean Donan Castle, captured its store of munitions, and burned the stores. With few provisions, an acute shortage of ammunition and no means of retreat, Marischal had to withdraw inland. No doubt it was his intention to reach Inverness, but the Hanoverian General Wightman advanced down the Great Glen and cornered the Jacobite army at Glenshiel. Although Seaforth's Mackenzies had risen and a handful of MacGregors under Rob Roy, Marischal's force numbered no more than 1,000. Wightman had no great advantage in numbers but he had a formidable battery of cohorn mortars, which tore holes in the Jacobite ranks. The Highlanders melted away into the hills, but the Spaniards were forced to surrender. All the Jacobite commanders made good their escape. Such was the fiasco of the '19. (104)

The Battle of Glenshiel: June 10, 1719

Twentieth-century military historian William Seymour gives details of the Battle of Glenshiel:

> About six miles south-east of Loch Duich the high hills on each side of the present road almost join; here the road, then nothing more than a cattle drove, winds through a pass not fifty yards wide. It was a place where a handful of resolute men might have held up an army for days. The Jacobites arrived at this pass towards the end of May...
>
> ...The Jacobite right, under Lord George Murray, took up a position in the foothills immediately to the south of the drove, with advance patrols some way forward. The 250 Spaniards held the rocky hillside immediately north of the drove, and above them came Lochiel and his 150 clansmen, then forty of Rob Roy's rascals, and further up were men under commanders such as Sir John Mackenzie, Brigadiers Campbell of Ormidale and Glendaruel, and Brigadier Mackintosh of Borlum. Lord Seaforth, with 200 of his best men,

was in a commanding position about half a mile up the steep hill.

Against this Jacobite force of 1,600 Highlanders and 250 Spaniards, General Wightman had 850 foot, 120 dragoons and 136 Highlanders. This was no country for cavalry, so the dragoons had been dismounted on entering the glen. They, together with the six coehorn mortars advanced along the line of the drove. On the extreme right Wightman placed his Mackays from Sutherland, then came some 200 Grenadiers under Major Richard Milburn, the 11th and 15th Foot, and a Dutch contingent. This right wing was commanded by Colonel Clayton, whose own regiment, under Lieutenant-Colonel Reading, formed part of the left wing, which advanced south of the drove with the Monros on the extreme left.

The engagement began on the Jacobite right soon after midday, when Lord George Murray's advance picquets contested ground as they gradually fell back onto the main position, but it was not until after 5 p.m. that the battle proper began. Undoubtedly the mortars played an important part in this short fight. They were used in the first instance against Lord George's men, who promptly withdrew from the very exposed hillock to the south of the drove, thus leaving the pass virtually unguarded. They were then turned upon the Spaniards, and firing at extreme range they probably did little harm, but they set the heather on fire, which must have caused confusion in the ever-narrowing funnel of attack. Meanwhile the Mackays, having made light of the steep and rocky ascent, had got round Seaforth's flank, and in the short bout of musketry that followed the Earl got a ball in the arm. Soon the Jacobite left was in retreat, and although the Earl Marischal and Brigadier Campbell of Ormidale held the centre steady for a while it was not long before these men, and then Lord Tullibardine with the Spaniards, were seen to be scampering up the hillside and away through the pass that leads round the north side of the Sgurr na Ciste Duibhe. Before darkness fell on 10 June 1719 the Jacobite army had disintegrated and the Pretender's troops in Scotland had suffered the last of the repeated blows of fortune.

The surprising ease with which the King's army rolled up the rebels is no indication of the Highlanders' inability to hold an almost impregnable position. The fact is that this was just a face-saving affair. The will to win was lacking, for no one would have known what to do with a victory had it been gained. The battle was chiefly notable in that it was probably the only one in which Highlanders fought without charging or engaging in hand-to-hand grapple. The Spaniards, being unable to melt into the countryside, had to surrender, but the battle casualties were quite insignificant. Wightman lost twenty-one killed and perhaps double that number wounded, while there is no reliable record of any Jacobites being killed. However, some there must have been; and no doubt the figure of less than ten mentioned in Field-Marshal Keith's memoir is about right. Lord George Murray was among those wounded, but he soon recovered and almost thirty years later, when another and more romantic Jacobite prince resolved to venture upon the hazards of invasion, he was to play a most important part. (198-200)

"Captain Downe, of Montague's regiment, was killed," Dr. J.J. Galbraith told the Gaelic Society of Inverness in 1928, "and buried by the river side, where, under the name of the Duitseach he still walks at night. The Spaniards killed are said to have been buried in Clachan Duich under Leac nan Spainteach" (304).

Colonel Jasper Clayton, who commanded the left wing of the government forces, commended the conduct of the Scots Highlanders who served with him. "Lord Strathnaver's and Culcairn's Highlanders behaved perfectly well," he wrote, "but poor Culcairn is shot in the thigh, but not in danger" (Galbraith 306).

Jacobite leader the Marquis of Tullibardine mentioned both "Brigadeer M'Intosh" and "Major McIntosh" in an eyewitness account of the battle:

My Lord Seaforth met us and told me he had brought to the Crow of Kintaile about five hundred of his own men who, it was thought, would heartily defend their own Country. On the eighth Rob Roy's son brought a Company of men who, with some volunteers, made up near Eighty. That night we got accounts the enemy were removed from Gilly whining to the Braes of Glenmoriston, which made us march early next morning, till that part of the pass at Glenshellbegg, which every body thought the properest place for defence, in which we posted ourselves the best way we could…

Next morning [the government troops] were decamp'd and moving slowly forward. About ten a Clock fifty more men joined us, and at twelve Mckinnin came with fifty more which were the last, for tho' several men that were to be with us (were) on top of the mountains on each side, yet they did not descend to incorporate with the rest. I suppose because they thought the Enemy too near us…

We had drawn up to the right of our main body on the other side of the water upon a little Hill about one hundred and fifty men, including the Companys of my Lord Seaforths, besides above four-score more were allotted for that place who was to come from the top of the Hill, but altho' they sent twice to tell they were coming, yet they only beheld the action at a distance. This party was commanded by Lord George Murray, the Lord of MacDougal, Major McIntosh, and John of Auch, ane old officer of my Lord Seaforths people; at the pass on the other side of the water were first on the right the Spanish Regiment which consisted of about two hundred men, about fifty more of them were left behind with the Magazine, several of them being Sick. The next in the line was Locheill with about one hundred and fifty. Then Mr Lidcoats and others, being one hundred and fifty, twenty volunteers, next fourtie of Rob Roy's, fiftie of MacKinnins, and then two hundred of my Lord Seaforths men Commanded by Sr John MacKenzie of Coul; on the left of all at a considerable distance on a steep hill was my Lord Seaforth posted with above two hundred of his best men, where my Lord Marshall and Brigadeer M'Intosh commanded with the Spanish Colonel, Brigadeer Campble of Glenderwell and myself commanded in the center, where we imagin'd the main attack would be, it being by far the easiest Ground, besides the only way through the Glen.

However, it happened otherways, the Enemy placed there horse on the low Ground, and a battalion of them on there left, with there Highlanders on the fare side of the water, all the rest of there foot was on a rising ground to there Right. The first attack they made was on our men with Lord George on the Right, by a small detachment of Red coats and

there Highlanders, who fired several times at each other
without doeing great damage, upon which they sent a second
and third detachment that made most of those with Lord Geo.
run to the other side of a steep Burn where he himself and the
rest were afterwards obliged to follow, where they continued
till all was over, it being uneasy for the enemy to pass the
hollow Banks of that Burn.

When they found that party on our Right give way there
Right began to move up the Hill from thence, to fall down on
our left, but when they saw my Lords Seaforths people, who
were behind the steep rock, they were oblig'd to attack them
least they should be flank'd in coming upon us, upon which
the Laird of Coul (most of whose men began to goe off on
the seeing the enemy) mov'd up with his Battalion to sustain
the rest of the McKenzies, which oblig'd the Enemy to push
the harder that way, on which my Lord Seaforth sent down
for a Reinforcement, and immediately after Brigadeer Campble of Ormondell came likewise, telling it was not certain of
there main body would not just then fall upon our Centre,
which made Rob Roy with the Mcgrigors and MacKinnin the
longer of drawing off to there assistance, but seeing them
give way he made all the dispatch he could to join them. But
before he could get up, so as to be fairly in hands with the
Enemy, Lord Seaforths people were mostly gone off, and
himself left wounded in the Arm, so that with difficulty he
could get out of the place. Rob Roy's detachment, finding
them going off began to retyre. Likewise, that made us still
send off fresh supplys from our left, so that Mr Lidcoats men
and others seeing every body retire before them, did also the
same, and the enemy, finding all give way on that hand, they
turn'd there whole force there, which oblig'd us to march up
the Camerons, who likewise drew off as others had done; at
last the Spaniards were Called and none standing to Sustain
them, they likewise were obliged to draw up the hill on our
left, where at last all began to run, tho' half had never once
an opportunity to fire on the Enemy, who were heartned on
seeing some of ours give way, and our people as much dis-
courag'd, so that they could never be again brought to any
thing. But all went off over the mountains, and next morning

we had hardly any body togeither except some of the Spaniards.

...The Spaniards themselves declared they could neither live without bread nor make any hard marches through the Country, therefore I was oblig'd to give them leave to Capitulate the best way they could, and every body else went off to shift for themselves... (Galbraith 307-10)

When the other Jacobite leaders fled Britain, Brigadier Mackintosh chose to abide in his homeland. He "kept out of the way" of government authorities and remained in Scotland for years (Mackintosh 49).

1720-1739

John Mackintosh Mor, accompanied by his wife and their six children, leads a contingent of Highlanders who establish the town of Darien, Georgia. Alexander and Mary McDonald emigrate to Darien. Brigadier William Mackintosh is captured and imprisoned. Aeneas Mackintosh serves as a ranger in South Carolina and treks through Indian country.

The birth of Bonnie Prince Charlie

They sing a song about a child who was born to be king. He was born on December 31, 1720, and was the son of James Stuart, the Pretender to the throne of Great Britain. James, age 32, had been married to Princess Maria Clementina Sobieski, age 18, for a little more than a year; they had been living near Rome since the failure of the Rising of 1719.

Jacobites welcomed word that the dynasty would continue:

> The birth of a Stuart heir was celebrated by jubilant Jacobites throughout Catholic Europe. In Rome fountains flowed with wine, fireworks seared the night sky and the guns of the Castel Sant' Angelo thundered out a royal salute. Bonfires blazed at St. Germain, Te Deums were sung at Versailles and even in Cartagena, reported an ecstatic Charles Wogan, there was drinking and dancing and *feux de joie*. Some Jacobites event went so far as to claim that a new star had appeared in the heavens at the time of the birth of this Stuart messiah.
>
> The baby was baptized within an hour of his birth by the same Bishop of Montefiascone who had married his parents. He was given the first names of Charles Edward and created Prince of Wales. It was fondly hoped, by all those present and by a great many who were not, that the baby would one day be known as King Charles III of England, Scotland and Ireland. In fact, he was to develop into the most exotic figure of the whole Stuart saga – Bonnie Prince Charlie, the Young Pretender. (Aronson 114-15)

The song they sing about Bonnie Prince Charlie is called "the Skye boat song." It starts like this:

Speed, bonnie boat, like a bird on the wing,
Onward! The sailors cry;
Carry the lad that's born to be King
Over the sea to Skye.

Chief of Borlum goes to America: 1721

Because the Borlum estate was deep in debt, John Mackintosh Mor's cousin Lauchlan Mackintosh, 5th of Borlum, "decided to try his fortune in New England, and left Scotland in 1721 for Darien, where his grand-uncle, Col. Henry, had settled many years before," reports a clan historian. Lauchlan married Col. Henry's daughter, Elizabeth, shortly after arriving in America. Their first daughter, Elizabeth, was born in 1722 (Ross, 187).

Fort established on Altamaha River

On the colonial American southern frontier, Yemassee Indians continued to raid settlements in southern South Carolina. As a defensive measure, Colonel John Barnwell of South Carolina persuaded the British government to post soldiers in the debatable land between the British colony of South Carolina and the Spanish colony of Florida. In 1722 the Independent Company of Foot established Fort King George at the mouth of the Altamaha River. "The ill-conceived fortification was designed to prevent the French from controlling the Altamaha River region and to guard the southern frontier from attacks by Spaniards and Yemassee Indians," writes Larry Ivers in *British Drums on the Southern Frontier*. "However, the French were not then capable of such expansion efforts, and the fort did not prevent the movement of Yemassee war parties from their sanctuary in Spanish Florida to South Carolina" (9).

Borlum is dead; long live Borlum

In the summer of 1723, Lauchlan, 5th of Borlum, planned a visit to Scotland while his infant daughter and pregnant wife remained at their home in New England. Lauchlan drowned at sea; his wife gave birth to their daughter Mary two months later. In

Scotland, Lauchlan's brother Shaw succeeded as 6th of Borlum (Ross 187).

John Mackintosh Mor marries: March 4, 1725

John Mackintosh Mor – a nephew of the Brigadier and a first cousin of Shaw the 6th of Borlum – married Marjory, daughter of John Fraser of Garthmore, on March 4, 1725, at Dores. When their first child was born on January 27, 1726, at Borlum, they named him William – a family name shared by John Mor's grandfather and uncle ("Mackenzie Papers" 111).

Yemassee raids intensify

On the colonial American southern frontier, South Carolinians suffered from unrelenting Indian raids. Military historian Larry Ivers writes:

> Between 1726 and 1728 Yemassee attacks became so severe that South Carolina was forced to a near-war footing. The frontier militia was often on alert, two crews of scouts watched the Inland Passage, and mounted rangers patrolled between the Savannah and Edisto Rivers. In 1727 the British Independent Company of Foot was withdrawn to Beaufort Fort to help protect the Port Royal settlers, leaving only a two-man lookout at Fort King George [on the Altamaha River in the debatable land between Spanish Florida and British South Carolina]. One of the Yemassee Indians' most successful attacks was the ambush of a scout boat on Daufuskie Island; the crew was killed and the commander was carried to Saint Augustine as a prisoner. Finally, a large South Carolina raiding party under Colonel John Palmer, an experienced scout and militia officer, penetrated Florida's defenses in March 1728, burning and pillaging the Yemassee towns nestled near Saint Augustine.
>
> Border warfare slackened following the raid into Florida, but the frontier settlements still lay open to future raids. (9)

The birth of Lachlan McIntosh

The second son of Marjory and John Mackintosh Mor was born on March 5, 1727, in Achugcha, near Raits in Badenoch.

Given a family name – shared by his grandfather Lachlan Mackintosh of Knocknagael and another ancestor Lachlan, known as Mor, the 16th Chief of Clan Mackintosh – the child was destined to become known as Continental General Lachlan McIntosh.

John Mackintosh Mor pursued his career as a gentleman farmer by moving from place to place but never leaving Mackintosh clan territory, as indicated by the birthplaces of his children. The third son – named John like his father – was born in 1728 at Ballochroan near Kingussie in Badenoch (Lawrence, "Lachlan McIntosh" 105; "Mackenzie Papers" 111).

Brigadier Mackintosh imprisoned

In Scotland, Brigadier William Mackintosh of Borlum "lingered for some time in his native land" after the Rising of 1719. "There he was at length captured and imprisoned in Edinburgh Castle" (MacKintosh, "Brigadier" 75). A clan historian writes:

> In 1729, about the time of his incarceration, he published an "Essay on Ways and Means for Inclosing, Fallowing, and Planting in Scotland," and by the manner in which it is written one can judge that not only had he a perfect command of English (Gaelic would have been the language of his childhood), but that he was quite at ease with Latin and Greek from his many references to the classics. That he was a born soldier and a brave gentleman no one will deny. (Ross 186)

The Mackintosh is dead; long live the Mackintosh

Lachlan the 20th Chief of Clan Mackintosh died in 1731 at Moy, the clan seat. The official clan historian describes the succession:

> The funeral was delayed for two months owing to the absence of his successor, and the body lay in state at Dalcross. As with previous funerals of Mackintosh chiefs, the expenses were enormous, and burdened the estate for years. Several thousand persons attended the burial at Petty.
>
> WILLIAM, the twenty-first Chief, succeeded in 1731. He was a second cousin of the late Chief, and a great-grandson of Sir Lachlan, the seventeenth Chief. William had been in the Army, but he now set himself to relieving

the estate of its burdens, and he cleared off some two thousand pounds in debts. For this reason, the Reverend Lachlan Shaw says, 'he did not effect the clannish grandeur, the numerous attendants and servants, common among Highland chieftains. He abridged the number of servants and cut off much of the superfluous expenses of his family.' Shaw also says, 'His life was a pattern of virtue and goodness.' In those days it was the custom to fight duels, and William fought his share. At this time an officer named Graeme had possession of Dundee's sword, which Lachlan had given up to him after the battle of Preston. William challenged Graeme either to give up the sword, or fight a duel, but fortunately Captain Graeme agreed peacefully to return the famous sword, which is still preserved at Moy Hall. (Mackintosh 52)

Mackintosh clansman serves in South Carolina

A high-ranking member of Clan Mackintosh serving in the British military was posted on the colonial American southern frontier in 1732. Known by his Gaelic name Angus in Scotland and by the classical name Aeneas in America, he was a brother of William the 21st Chief of Clan Mackintosh. He was stationed at Fort Prince George, also known as Palachacola Fort, on the Savannah River upstream of the tidewater. Military historian Larry Ivers explains the significance of Palachacola:

> Palachacola had long been a strategic point on South Carolina's southwestern frontier. The name was derived from Palachacola Town, a settlement of friendly Apalachicola Indians, which had served as a sentry-town, guarding the principal crossing site on the lower Savannah River. However, when the Yemassee War began in 1715 those Indians joined the conspiracy against South Carolina and were soon forced to vacate Palachacola Town and flee to their ancient home in present southwestern Georgia. Without a guard on the lower Savannah crossing site, war parties could cross the river and penetrate the settlements at will. The Company of Southern Rangers (1716-1718) built a fort across the river from the abandoned town and patrolled along the east

bank of the Savannah River during the first six months of 1718 in an attempt to secure that portion of the frontier…

For a while Palachacola lay unguarded, but in early 1723 the settlers living north of Beaufort began clamoring for government rangers to protect their plantations from the raids of Yemassee war parties operating from Spanish Florida. In February the South Carolina government ordered a captain, a lieutenant, a sergeant, and nineteen horsemen to be recruited to build and garrison a "small Pallisade Fort" at Palachacola. They were to range east above Beaufort and north to Fort Moore [further upstream on the Savannah River], keeping the Indians west of the Savannah River… (23)

The Palachacola Garrison was instructed to patrol the one hundred miles of frontier between Port Royal and Fort Moore once every two weeks, but it appears very unlikely that they actually covered the terrain that often, if ever. During the period of brutal Indian raids, 1726-28, the garrison's patrols did not discourage all the Yemassee war parties from crossing the Savannah River and penetrating the settlements…

During a Creek Indian scare in August 1732… the Palachacola Garrison went on full alert. Colonel Alexander Glover, the Creek Indian agent, rode to Fort Prince George and assumed command of that section of the frontier. Even though Captain Evans, the commander of the fort, had been too sick to perform duty for some time, he had still been retained in command; however, when war with the Creeks seemed likely Evans was discharged and Lieutenant Parmenter was promoted to captain. Aeneas Mackintosh, a Scottish gentleman and heir to the chieftainship of Clan Mackintosh in Scotland, was commissioned lieutenant. At the end of the first week in September the fear of a major Indian war dissolved when the government discovered that the Creeks had no intention of going to war. (27)

The British colonization of Georgia

In response to French and Spanish threats to British colonies in North America, as well as Indian raids from Florida into South Carolina, the British Board of Trade authorized fortified settlements along the southern frontier. The plan eventually resulted in the founding of Georgia. Larry Ivers explains:

> Two townships were supposed to have been located near the Altamaha River in old Guale, the virtually uninhabited Atlantic coastal area that was hotly claimed by both England and Spain, but their establishment was delayed until the task was undertaken by the new colony of Georgia during the period 1733-36.
>
> The colonization of Georgia was timely for the British defense of the southern frontier...
>
> The Georgia project was the fusing of two requirements into one solution The first requirement was philanthropic. James Oglethorpe, Dr. Thomas Bray, Sir John Percival, and many other Englishmen considered colonization one of the best methods of solving the problems of Britain's debtors, unemployed, and poor. This coincided perfectly with the second requirement, military colonization of the Altamaha-Savannah Rivers region as ordered by the Board of Trade. Slavery was prohibited in Georgia; villages of white protestant yeomen, planting crops and training as soldiers, were to act as a buffer against the Spaniards in Florida and the French in Louisiana. (10)

Aeneas Mackintosh protects new settlement

The rangers on the colonial American southern frontier – including Aeneas Mackintosh, a brother of the Chief of Clan Mackintosh – provided protection for the first settlers of Georgia. In *British Drums on the Southern Frontier*, Larry Ivers describes the role of the rangers:

> About the latter part of January 1733 a messenger from Charles Town rode his horse into Saltcatchers Fort at the head of Combahee River on the South Carolina frontier and delivered a message to Captain James McPherson, the commander. Inside were marching orders from the governor. "You... are hereby order'd immediately with fifteen men to repair to the new Settlement of Georgia, there to Obey orders and directions as you Shall receive from Mr.

Oglethorpe, in order to Cover and protect that Settlement from any insults; of this fail not."

At that moment 113 people, newly arrived from England, were temporarily camped in Fort Frederick at Port Royal, South Carolina, awaiting transportation to the southern bank of the Savannah River where they planned to establish a new British colony called Georgia. South Carolinians correctly viewed the new settlement as a godsend; it would absorb the bloody raids of the Florida Spaniards and their Yemassee Indian allies which had previously been directed against South Carolina. A grateful South Carolina General Assembly had provided the new colonists with boat transportation, breeding cattle and hogs, provisions, and military protection by the provincial scout boat and Captain McPherson's Company of Southern Rangers.

...[Rangers] selected riding and pack horses and strapped provisions and ammunition to pack saddles. Captain McPherson chose six of the company's twenty privates to remain in garrison at Saltcatchers Fort. Within a few days they were reinforced by the temporary assignment of a lieutenant and four rangers from Fort Prince George on the Savannah River...

The company probably began its movement to Georgia at dawn one day during the first week of February 1733. The governor had made preparations for the rangers to ride to the Savannah River, cross on riverboats called piraguas, ride down the western bank, and then rendezvous with the Georgians. The path was a new one, a ride of over forty miles which followed the ridges and crossed a number of creek swamps, perhaps a two-day journey for the rangers and their pack horses. They probably spent a night at Purrysburg, a new frontier "township" of Swiss immigrants on the east bank of the Savannah River. The next morning they pulled and shoved their horses onto the piraguas which had been assembled to transport them down river to the Georgia settlement...

The Georgia colonists had already landed at Yamacraw Bluff on Thursday, 1 February, ...and were laying out a settlement called Savannah. James Oglethorpe, the Georgia trustee who acted as the colony's leader, was proceeding under the advice of Colonel William Bull, a prominent South Carolina frontiersman. When the rangers rode into the Georgians' camp they found them hard at work hacking a town out of the wilderness. A third of the men were clearing trees from the town site, another third were working on a blockhouse, and the remainder were clearing land for the planting season just a month away. Cold rain fell in torrents that February, making working conditions miserable...

Oglethorpe stationed the company up river about five miles northwest of Savannah at a place called the Horse Quarter from where they patrolled the area close around Savannah during the remainder of the winter and spring of 1733. (11-16)

In early February 1733 one of the Southern Rangers from Saltcatchers rode into Fort Prince George [at Palachacola on the Savannah River] with the governor's message concerning the measures to be taken to protect the Georgia settlers. According to the governor's order, Captain Parmenter sent Lieutenant Mackintosh and four men to strengthen the remaining garrison at Saltcatchers Fort, leaving both garrisons with ten men each.

...By March 1734 the South Carolina government realized that the organization of frontier defense would have to be permanently altered because of the settlement of Georgia. The rangers at Saltcatchers were needed in Georgia and were ordered to join McPherson there. Lieutenant Mackintosh and his men demolished Saltcatchers Fort, probably setting fire to the huts and palisade to prevent its being used by hostile Indians.

South Carolina disbanded Captain Parmenter's Palachacola Garrison, but Oglethorpe placed four of his men in Fort Prince George to maintain the buildings and cannons... The South Carolina settlers on the frontier near Port Royal were outraged by the removal of all the soldiers from their portion of the frontier, and to pacify them the government in Charles Town ordered Mackintosh and his ten rangers to station themselves at Fort Prince George [on the South Carolina side of the Savannah River at Palachacola] instead of Fort Argyle [a new ranger fort on the Ogeechee River in Georgia].

Under the new establishment Mackintosh was promoted to captain and his men became known as the Palachacola Rangers. They patrolled the eastern bank of the Savannah River as part of Captain McPherson's Company of Southern Rangers until April 1735... (27-28)

Mackintosh assists Mackay

As the commander of Fort Prince George at Palachacola, Captain Aeneas Mackintosh was called upon to assist Patrick Mackay as Mackay began a journey into Creek Indian territory. Ivers describes the mission:

The Lower Creek were often troublesome to the British, but in the spring of 1734 they were addressing a loyalty of sorts to Georgia because James Oglethorpe had met with some of their headmen during the previous year and had established a treaty of friendship with the help of Tomochichi, the Yamacraw mico (chief), and a large amount of presents. The trustees' Indian policy was initially wise and fruitful. They lavished presents on the Indians, redressed the Indians' grievances wherever possible, and acquired land through treaty rather than appropriation.

Oglethorpe was the perfect man to carry out the trustees' policy. He ate the Indians' food, slept in their houses, sincerely recognized their value as Georgia's allies, and seldom voiced impatience with their alien-appearing customs...

...Oglethorpe wrote a captain's commission for Patrick Mackay, his choice to command the company destined for duty in the Creek nations...

On 15 August 1734, after a summer of frustrating dealings with a hostile Charles Town, Captain Mackay set out overland for Georgia with the herd of horses... On the third day the packhorsemen became so ill that Mackay was forced to camp near the Ashepoo River for two days while they partially recovered. ...two of the packhorsemen had relapses and were left alongside the road to recover. Mackay and his two remaining men had considerable difficulty in driving the herd, which probably consisted of about fifty horses of the tough breed raised by the Cherokee. During the week it took to travel from the head of the Ashepoo River to Palachacola on the Savannah River, several horses escaped and drifted into the swamps.

Finally, on 26 August, Captain Mackay rode into Fort Prince George at Palachacola with his horses. Captain Aeneas Mackintosh, the garrison commander, lent Mackay two of his rangers to help corral the herd and tend it until the packhorsemen were well enough to rejoin Mackay. The piragua arrived soon afterward and its cargo of presents and equipment was secured in the fort. (31-37)

After Mackay left Palachacola to join the company of men allocated for his mission, he discovered that all of them suffered from a fever. Mackay himself became delirious with fever and lay in bed for two weeks in Savannah. In October he went to Beaufort, suffered a relapse and "lay near death for twenty days." His expedition into Creek territory finally got underway in November (Ivers 37-39).

John Mackintosh Mor faces family responsibilities
In the Highlands of Scotland, John Mackintosh Mor cared for a growing family and mourned the death of his father. His wife Marjory gave birth to Phineas while the family – including sons William, Lachlan and John – lived at Ardo. About two years later the twins Lewis and Janet were born on November 4, 1734. John Mor's father Lachlan died January 29, 1735, and was buried at Grey Friars Inverness (Gladstone, "Family Group Record;" "Mackenzie Papers" 111).

Recruiter entices clansmen to Georgia
When Oglethorpe determined to establish a fortified settlement on the Altamaha River in the debatable land claimed by both England and Spain, he sent recruiters to Clan Mackintosh country. Oglethorpe had other links to the Mackintosh clan in addition to his dealings with Captain Aeneas Mackintosh in America. Oglethorpe's mother, Eleanor Wall Oglethorpe, was a Jacobite sympathizer. Oglethorpe's sisters married into the French Catholic aristocracy and had connections with the Stuart court. Oglethorpe himself may have met Brigadier William Mackintosh of Borlum and

his nephew John Mackintosh Mor when the three of them were in France (Dobson, *Scottish Emigration* 118).

McIntosh County local historian Bessie Lewis says that Oglethorpe chose Highlanders to defend the southern frontier because of their reputation as fierce fighters:

> In January, 1734, James Edward Oglethorpe, his Savannah settlement well on its feet, made a journey down the coast. He carefully inspected the mouth of the Altamaha and its environs, saw the ruins of old Fort King George and the need for a fortified town at this place. It was then that he decided Scottish Highland warriors – men whose willingness to "face cold steel" was legend – were the settlers he wanted there.
>
> Under his orders, Captain Hugh Mackay and Captain George Dunbar spent the next few months in the Highlands near Inverness, recruiting men and families for this settlement. (*Darien* 11)

Georgia historian Edward Cashin describes the recruitment process in *Lachlan McGillivray, Indian Trader*:

> The summer of 1735 was an opportune time for Captain George Dunbar and Hugh Mackay to come to Inverness to recruit men for Georgia in America. A succession of poor crops had reduced gentlemen and tenants alike to poverty. The town council of Inverness thought so well of the idea of sending a hundred or so hungry men to Georgia that it made Georgia's founder, James Oglethorpe, an honorary burgess of the town. The authorities were even more pleased that the emigrants were Jacobites. Dunbar was wise to the ways of his native shire. He obtained the support of William Mackintosh, chief of Clan Chattan [a confederation of clans led by the Mackintoshes], for the venture. The chief was called Mackintosh of Mackintosh, and he lived at Moy Hall… He borrowed money on his lands to assist the gentlemen who should go to Georgia. Most of them were chosen for their leadership qualities. Outstanding among them was John Mohr Mackintosh, who had gone off to fight in 1715 with his uncle Brigadier [William] Mackintosh of Borlum… Dunbar's tactic, as Oglethorpe explained it to his fellow Trustees of Georgia,

was "to bring the enterprise into vogue with the chief gentlemen" so as to secure their tenants. He was fully aware that these gentlemen "were unused to labour," and therefore each had to bring a man capable of working. John Mackintosh of Holme, aged twenty-four, with the chief's money and his own, paid for himself and sixteen-year-old Lachlan McGillivray. Lachlan's aunt Magdalen was married to William Mackintosh of Holme, brother to John. Seventeen gentlemen paid their own passage on Dunbar's ship the *Prince of Wales*, and the Georgia Trustees paid for 146 others.

Among the emigrants was a confusion of Mackintoshes. Besides John Mohr Mackintosh of Borlum and John Mackintosh of Holme, there were John Mackintosh of Kingussie, John Mackintosh of Dornes, John Mackintosh Bain, and John Mackintosh Lynvilge. The McGillivrays were represented by Lachlan, his cousin Farquhar, aged thirty, and Archibald, aged fifteen.

Why would the Mackintosh of Moy Hall pay to speed the departure of his clansmen? For one thing, his brother Aeneas Mackintosh was already in Georgia in the service of James Oglethorpe. In 1735 this Aeneas was stationed at a fort on the Carolina side of the Savannah River to protect the new German settlement at Ebenezer, forty-five miles above Savannah. The agricultural depression undoubtedly was a factor in the migration of so many from the same district. It has been suggested that Mackintosh would never have been able to enclose his lands for sheep raising if the likes of John Mohr Mackintosh still occupied the estates.

In going to Georgia, Lachlan McGillivray was not running away from home... He was going with his clan to join others already in Georgia and Carolina. He must have felt a touch of nostalgia as the blue-green hills faded from view, but he must also have felt the quickening flush of adventure. (12-14)

Like Cashin, the official historian of Clan Mackintosh stresses that the exodus to Georgia was a clan affair rather than a series of individual choices:

During William's chiefship an important emigration took place. General James Oglethorpe, the English philanthropist, had obtained a royal grant of lands in what is now the Savannah area of Georgia in order to colonise it with distressed persons such as debtors or sufferers from religious persecution, both from England and continental Europe. After founding the colony in 1733 Oglethorpe was soon in difficulty with the Spanish in neighbouring Florida, who claimed the land. To stiffen his colonists he decided to recruit Highlanders with strong military potential. In 1735 he… carefully selected men of good character willing to go to America. These men were led by John Mor Mackintosh, a nephew of Brigadier Mackintosh of Borlum and thus related to the Mackintosh Chief, described as a gentleman farmer. Also in the party were Roderick and John Mackintosh, grandsons of the Brigadier, and many other Mackintoshes. They took their whole families with them, and the better off also took their servants. Their willingness to go at all may be partly accounted for by the depressed state of the Highlands and it seems likely that William encouraged his clansmen to go. On 18th October 1735 the good ship *Prince of Wales* commanded by Captain George Dunbar sailed from Inverness with 200 Highlanders, 50 women, and some children. On arrival they called their settlement New Inverness, but later changed it to Darien in memory of the ill fated Darien expedition of the end of the seventeenth century. (52-53)

Going to Georgia with the grandsons of Brigadier Mackintosh – John and his younger brother Roderick, probably about 20 years old – were their younger sister Winnewood and their father Benjamin, about 50 years old. Lady Mackintosh may be too polite to mention Benjamin because he was a natural son of the Brigadier born two years before the Brigadier was married (Moncreiffe 128; Sullivan 36). Benjamin, being a son of the Brigadier, was a first cousin of John Mackintosh Mor.

John Mackintosh Mor was about 37 years old when the emigrants set sail and his wife Marjory was about 34. Of their nine children, six remained alive in 1735: William, age 9; Lachlan, 8; John, 7; Phineas, 3; and 11-month-old twins Lewis and Janet (Gladstone "Family Group Record").

Highlanders settle in Georgia

The emigrants who set out to sea from Inverness in mid-
October of 1735 made landfall at Savannah in early January of
1736. Local historian Bessie Lewis imagines the arrival of Scots
Highlanders in the lowcountry of coastal Georgia as "Scene I" in
They called their town Darien:

A chill wind blew over the marshes of the Altamaha delta as
the small boats – manned by sturdy Scottish Highlanders and
a few of Tomochichi's Indians – came up the river to Barnwell Bluff that 19th day of January, 1736. As they rounded
the last bend before the high bluff they saw just ahead the ruins of Old Fort King George and all that was left of the landing used by the Independent Company nine years before.

Pulling close to the point, they tied up the boats and disembarked. Here the land was low, and the kilted Highlanders
with their Indian friends walked to the high bluff adjacent,
where they could look out over the vast Altamaha delta. In
Savannah they had been told by would-be troublemakers that
at this place Spaniards would shoot them upon the ground
from their houses in the fort. And the Highlanders had replied, "Why, then, we will beat them out of their fort and
shall have houses ready built to live in."

But there were no houses in sight, only that vast expanse
of marsh interlaced with the waters of the Altamaha – they
would have to build their own houses.

This group was the vanguard of the "177 heads" of Scottish Highlanders... The women and children, with the older
men, were left in Savannah while the able bodied men and
the indentured servants went on down the Inland Waterway
to the site selected by James Edward Oglethorpe for their settlement. There they were to build huts and shelters for the
comfort and protection of their families and a chapel in
which their minister, the Rev. John McLeod, would hold divine services on Sundays and teach the children on week-
days.

First they mounted their "great guns" on the ruins of Fort
King George in case Spaniards or enemy Indians should ap-

proach. Then they set to work to build accommodations for families.

The work went on – soon the huts and shelters were ready and the rest of the Highland embarkation came to join the settlement at Barnwell's Bluff. Already they had named their town Darien.

On Sunday, the 22nd of February, 1736, James Edward Oglethorpe made his first visit to the Highlanders who had been recruited under his special orders for this settlement. They met him in full military regalia, and in their honor he wore the kilt. In a letter to the Trustees for the Establishment of the Colony of Georgia, reporting on that visit, he wrote, "I arrived at the Scotch settlement, which they desire may be called Darien. They were all under arms and made a most manly appearance, with their Plads, broad Swords, Targets [a type of shield used by Highlanders was called a targe or a target] and Firearms."

There on the bluff the Highland Company paraded before him, in the first formal military review in the colony of Georgia.

Thus was founded the town the Highlanders called Darien...

Oglethorpe spent but one day and night in Darien on his first visit, but it was long enough to convince him that he had been wise in his selection of Highlanders for this strategic point on the Altamaha. He found them to be what he had requested and expected, "the Freemen of Gentlemen's families... Industrious, laborious and Brave; speaking the Highland language."

They were the McIntoshes, led by John McIntosh Mohr; the Mackays, headed by Hugh Mackay; the McDonalds, Morrisons, Sutherlands, and others. They were soldiers, schooled in war and ready and willing to fight. Hugh Mackay held a commission in the British army, as did James Mackay; John McIntosh Mohr had been in battle at the age of fifteen.

As Oglethorpe was pleased with the settlers of Darien, so they were with him, giving him on that first visit a warm affection and fierce loyalty which was to endure throughout his stay in Georgia... He asked nothing of his men but what he would himself endure.

This was proven on his first night in Darien. Hugh Mackay offered him a bed in his own tent, with sheets, but Mr. Oglethorpe refused, and wrapping himself in his plaid lay down by the guard fire outside. Mackay and the other officers joined him, though the night was cold.

Before Oglethorpe left Darien on the occasion of his first visit, Mr. McPherson, with a detachment of the rangers, arrived overland from Savannah, pleasing the Highland settlers with the knowledge there was communication for horsemen between the two towns. (1-2, 11-12)

Another account says that Oglethorpe slept beneath "a great tree;" consequently, a huge live oak tree in Darien became known as the Oglethorpe Oak (Sullivan 19).

"Oglethorpe arrived at Darien, so well coached by Dunbar that he wore a plaid. Kilts had not yet been introduced to the Highlands," points out Georgia historian Edward Cashin, "and the men wore a fourteen-foot-long swath of cloth gathered at the waist and falling freely to the knees, the loose ends pinned at the left shoulder to leave the right arm free to brandish a sword" (*McGillivray* 16). Cashin continues:

Captain Hugh Mackay had the nominal military command, but the real authority figure in Darien was John Mohr Mackintosh. Oglethorpe soon discovered that he could deal with the Gaelic-speaking indentured servants only through their leaders. Because they spoke no English, they could not be dispersed among the other settlements. John Mackintosh set them to work clearing fields and planting corn before he let them build houses...

Although the Highlanders managed to raise enough corn that first year to supply themselves, farming was not their long suit. They were not good at it in Scotland, and they were less proficient in America, where they had more excuses for leaving off such disagreeable labor. They much preferred cutting down trees and sawing wood for their own houses and for their sister settlement, Frederica, on St. Simon Island. They must have wondered at the number and size of the tall sea pines and the girth and spread of the giant oaks. There were more trees in Darien than in all of Invernesshire in Scotland. (16-17)

Indians and Highlanders form friendships

In *Lachlan McGillivray, Indian Trader*, Edward Cashin explores the bonds that developed between Scots Highlanders and American Indians on the colonial American southern frontier:

> A party of curious Creek Indians went to see the Highlanders even before Oglethorpe arrived in Darien. The Indians and the Scots got along famously from the start. They discovered that they shared the same values. The clan system was not unlike the tribal divisions. Status was the product of kinship and prowess. The manly arts were esteemed in both cultures, both had their war songs, their traditional dances, their reciters of the great deeds of the past. The Gaels and the native Americans were born storytellers, given to flights of imagery and metaphor. The world of spirits was real to both cultures. The mutual respect led to friendly competition in an American version of the Highland games as Scots vied with Creeks in feats of swiftness, strength, and dexterity.
>
> [John Mackintosh Mor's son] William Mackintosh… recalled in later life that a quick friendship developed between the visitors and the men of Darien. We can picture the Scottish lads engrossed in their efforts to communicate with the young warriors, first in sign language and then in sound recognition. We can only guess at the wonder they felt as they were introduced to a culture as rich and proud as their own. Both William [McIntosh] and Lachlan [McGillivray] learned the language of the Creeks. William later became a planter on the Georgia coast, but Lachlan was intrigued by the glimpses into the world of the Creeks. He had relatives [in South Carolina] already engaged in the Indian trade. He would join them as soon as he had satisfied his obligations to his patron, John Mackintosh of Holme.
>
> The Highlanders learned more about their situation from the Indians than they did from the busy Oglethorpe. They were aware of the threat from the Spanish in St. Augustine and from their Indian allies. Some of the Darien men accompanied Oglethorpe on his reconnaissance through the debata-

ble land below the Altamaha River. Highlanders were posted on Amelia Island at the entrance to the St. Johns River. They called their fort St. Andrews [after the patron saint of Scotland] and the island Highland and bid defiance to the dons. They knew that Oglethorpe was preparing Frederica as his garrison town for the inevitable war. (17-18)

John Mackintosh Mor's son Lachlan was "of athletic form and great activity," an early Georgia historian writes, and "when a lad at New Inverness, there was not an Indian in all the tribes that could compete with him in the race." This information came from the historian's grandfather William McIntosh, Lachlan's older brother (Spalding, "Lachlan McIntosh" 110).

Highlanders raise black cattle

Raising and raiding cattle provided money and excitement for Highlanders in Scotland. Following their ancient custom, the Highlanders in Darien raised black cattle to provide beef to the soldiers at Fort Frederica on St. Simons Island. Captain James McPherson – who was born in South Carolina but still bore a Highland name – drove the first herd of cattle to Darien from South Carolina (Rowland 141; Ivers 17).

In addition to raising cattle, McPherson served with Aeneas Mackintosh as a ranger on the southern frontier. While stationed at Saltcatchers Fort in southern South Carolina, McPherson established a five-hundred-acre cattle ranch near the fort. When Georgia was founded, McPherson and Mackintosh were sent to protect the new settlements; McPherson's wife managed the cattle herd and the corn crops while McPherson was away on assignment (Ivers 12).

McPherson "spent a large amount of his time purchasing beef cattle in South Carolina and driving them to Georgia where they were butchered for the settlers," reports Larry Ivers. "Oglethorpe and the trustees were well satisfied with his performance of duty and showed their appreciation by presenting him with a silver watch" (74).

Nieces of Laird of Borlum settle in Georgia

John Mackintosh Mor's cousin Shaw 6th of Borlum sailed from Scotland to New England in 1736 to visit the two daughters of his late brother Lauchlan, who had emigrated to New England and started a family before his death at sea. Shaw tried to persuade his nieces to come to Scotland. His nieces, however, found husbands in America and settled in Georgia (Ross 187).

The birth of Ann McIntosh

A child was born to John Mackintosh Mor and his wife Marjory a little more than a year after they arrived in Georgia. Their daughter Mary Ann, called Ann, was born on April 18, 1737 ("Mackenzie Papers" 111). Their family now contained five sons – William, Lachlan, John, Phineas and Lewis – and two daughters – Janet, the twin sister of Lewis, and newborn Ann.

Alexander and Mary McDonald emigrate to Darien

General Oglethorpe authorized additional efforts in the Highlands of Scotland to recruit fighting men for fortifications and watchposts along the Georgia coast and to obtain servants for the colonists. About forty Highlanders, representing twenty-six different clan names and perhaps including a piper or two, arrived at Darien in November of 1737 aboard the *Two Brothers* (Parker 66-67).

Another ship, the *Mary Ann*, sailed to Georgia in 1737 carrying five recruits for the Independent Company of Foot. One of the recruits, Alexander McDonald, brought along his wife Mary. William Stephens, an official with the Georgia Trustees who was a passenger in the cabin, reported that rough weather delayed their departure for nine days.

"The Wind holding still in our teeth, we lost as much by the Flood tide as we gained by the Ebb" Stephens wrote on August 19. The next day, he wrote, "Wind increased to a perfect Storm: so finding we could not reach Portland as we meant, we bore away; & about 9 in the morning we got into Studland Bay; where we anchored under the High Land in good ground, waiting for the first favourable Spurt of a Wind to put to Sea again." When the *Mary Ann* finally left Great Britain for Georgia, Stephens drew the conclusion, based on hard-earned experience, "I think we have a tight Ship, for She has been pretty well tryd in the late weather, & no Pump has worked yet. Our company are all well; but were a little too much ruffled (as is usual wth such Strangers to the Salt water) when the Sea ran high" (*Colonial Records of Georgia* 21: 443-46).

Alligator kills son of John Mackintosh Mor

Marjorie and John Mackintosh Mor's twin children died shortly after the family settled on the colonial American southern frontier. A note in the family Bible simply said Janet died young at
Darien. Her twin's death was reported in 1738 by an official in Savannah: "And at Darien, a most unhappy Accident befell Mr.
McIntosh's Family, whose two Sons (young Lads) being swimming in the River, an Alligator snapped one, and carried him quite
off" (*Colonial Records of Georgia* 4: 165). The official did not
name the two children who were swimming, but the alligator's victim had to have been 3-year-old Lewis because the other sons were
still alive after 1738. Based on the statement that both boys were
"young lads," 6-year-old Phineas may have experienced the horror
of watching Lewis being dragged away in an alligator's jaws. If
William, age 12, Lachlan, 11, or John, 10, witnessed Lewis's gruesome demise, the older brother certainly would have felt that he
had failed in his responsibility to protect his little brother.

Highlanders oppose slavery: 1739

Oglethorpe and his fellow trustees forbade slavery in Georgia
for humanitarian and military reasons. Georgians who envied the
wealthy slave-owning planters of South Carolina agitated for a
change in the trustees' policy. Local historian Bessie Lewis describes John Mackintosh Mor's role in supporting the trustees:

> ...As a leader of his people, an arbitrator of disputes and one
> whose opinions were respected, he must take a strong part in
> this controversy. If nothing else, his loyalty to Oglethorpe
> demanded he do so. On a night in January [1739], he sent his
> eldest son, William, a lad of twelve, out to the houses of the
> town, calling a meeting at his home. Eighteen men respond-
> ed, and their names are affixed to a unique document... It is a
> petition against the importation of Negro slaves. The men of
> Darien gave their reasons for this protest – all were sound
> and practical. There were five paragraphs in the petition –
> and the fifth reads like a prophecy: "It's shocking to human
> Nature, that any Race of Mankind, and their Posterity, should
> be sentenced to perpetual Slavery; nor in Justice can we think
> otherwise of it, that they are thrown amongst us to be our

Scourge one Day or another for our Sins; and as Freedom to them must be as dear as to us, what a Scene of Horror must it bring about! And the longer it is unexecuted, the bloody Scene must be the greater."

...We who look back through the pages of history and read the tragedy which came to Darien in the 1860's, cannot but wonder if the Highland Scots who signed that petition possessed the second sight that is legend among the Gaels. (16-17)

The "sound and practical" arguments against slavery in Georgia mentioned in Bessie Lewis' narrative are:

I.   The Nearness of the Spaniard, who have proclaimed Freedom to all Slaves who run away from their Masters, makes it impossible for us to keep them without more Labour in guarding them, that what we would be at to do their Work.

II. We are laborious, and know that a White Man may be by the Year more usefully employed than a Negro.

III. We are not rich, and becoming Debtors for Slaves, in case of their running away or dying, would inevitably ruin the poor Master, and he become a greater Slave to the Negro Merchant, than the Slave he bought could be to him.

IV. It would oblige us to keep a Guard-duty at least as severe as when we expected a daily Invasion; and if that was the Case, how miserable it would be to us, and our Wives and Families, to have an Enemy without, and more dangerous ones in our Bosom!

The fifth paragraph continues after the section quoted by Bessie Lewis: "We therefore, for our own sakes, our Wives and Children, and our Posterity, beg your Consideration, and intreat, that instead of introducing Slaves, you'll put us in the way to get us some more of our Countrymen, who with their Labour in time of Peace, and our Vigilance, if we are invaded, with the Help of those, will render it a difficult thing to hurt us, or that Part of the Province we possess. We will ever pray for your Excellency, and are, with all Submission..."

The leader of the Highlanders signed his name as John Mackintosh Moore. Other signers are: John Mackintosh Lynvilge;

Ranald M'Donald; Daniel Clark, First; Alexander Clarke, Son to the above; Donald Clark, Third, his Mark; HM Hugh Morrison's Mark; John McDonald; John Macklean; John Mackintosh, Son to L.; John McIntosh Bain; James McKay; Jos. Burges, his mark; Donald Clark, Second; Archibald AMB McBain, his mark; Alexander Munro; William Munro; John Cuthbert (*Colonial Records of Georgia* 3: 427-28).

The birth of George McIntosh

Marjory, the wife of John Mackintosh Mor, gave birth to a boy on May 24, 1739. He was their first son born after they arrived in Georgia and they named him George. Their family now contained five sons – William, Lachlan, John, Phineas and George – and their 1-year-old daughter Ann.

Aeneas Mackintosh treks across Creek Country

Ranger captain Aeneas Mackintosh accompanied Oglethorpe on a three-month, five-hundred-mile journey to and from Creek Indian towns on the Chattahoochee River. Military historian Larry Ivers describes the expedition:

> On 8 July [Oglethorpe] left Frederica accompanied by a few officers of the Forty-second Regiment and some Scottish gentlemen including Lieutenant George Dunbar, Adjutant Hugh Mackay, Jr., and Aneas Mackintosh. After traveling by boat to Ebenezer they transferred to horseback and rode north to the Uchee town where Lieutenant John Cuthbert and his party of six rangers were waiting to act as the expedition's escort. The rangers had just finished blazing a trail from Augusta to the Uchee town along the west bank of the Savannah River. The expedition now consisted of Oglethorpe, twelve officers and gentlemen, Cuthbert and his rangers, about five servants, and an unknown number of Indians who served as hunters and guides. Oglethorpe also hired an additional ranger, probably Thomas Hunt, to accompany him as a bodyguard-servant...
>   They left the Uchee town on 24 July... On 8 August the expedition arrived at Coweta and received a very cordial welcome from Chigelley, the principal mico of the Lower Creek. Chigelley was a warrior to be reckoned with.

Twenty-four years earlier he had led a war party of several hundred Creek and Apalachee to within twelve miles of Charles Town, South Carolina, leaving ashes and death behind him. During the next two and a half weeks Oglethorpe was treated as a very important guest of the towns of Coweta and Kashita where he held several councils during which he passed out presents and exchanged speeches with the headmen of both Creek nations. Even the men of his expedition served as diplomats. On one occasion while they were watching the Indians dance, traders' rum or the primitive beat of the drums induced some of them to compliment the Indians by joining in the rhythmic stomping. The visit was extremely timely and may have been partially responsible for the Creek maintenance of neutrality during the subsequent war with Spain and France. The results were probably disappointing to Oglethorpe, however, for he had hoped that the Creek would provide him with large war parties for use in raiding Florida.

On 25 August Oglethorpe and his expedition began their return to the coast, initially setting out on the Lower Trading Path toward the Savannah River, arriving at Augusta eighteen days later. Even though Oglethorpe became sick with a fever he inspected Fort Augusta, …visited with Captain Daniel Pepper of South Carolina's nearby Fort Moore, and talked with several Cherokee headmen who came down from their nations to receive presents.

On 13 September, a rumor arrived at Augusta that war had been declared against Spain. Four days later, after Oglethorpe and his expedition had started down river toward Savannah, they met a trading boat whose crew was carrying the terrifying news that some Negro slaves in South Carolina had revolted a few days before. South Carolinians, outnumbered by their slaves and living in fear of a revolt for more than a quarter of a century, had taken elaborate but ineffective measures over the years to keep the slaves unarmed, uneducated, and unorganized. The slave insurrection took place west of Charles Town on Stono River where Angola-born slaves who lived in that neighborhood had banded together, armed themselves, and killed twenty-three people. The local militia quickly cornered them, killed about forty, despite their brave stand, and scattered the remainder in the swamps.

…When Oglethorpe arrived at Fort Prince George, or Palachacola Fort, across the river from the Uchee town he found thirty South Carolina militiamen from Purrysburg in garrison. The obvious objective for the rebellious slaves was Saint Augustine – the Spanish governor had promised freedom for all slaves who escaped to Florida – and the principal route to Saint Augustine crossed the Savannah River at Palachacola. In fact, some of Captain James McPherson's slaves had recently escaped on stolen horses from his Saltcatchers plantation, crossed the river at Palachacola, and ridden nearly unhindered through Georgia to Florida. Oglethorpe ordered Captain Aneas Mackintosh, the former commander of the fort and a member of the expedition, to recruit and command a new ten-man garrison of rangers for Fort Prince George. (86-88)

A ranger who accompanied Oglethorpe on the journey to the Lower Creek towns of Coweta and Kashita recorded the day-to-day progress of the expedition:

His Excellency Genl. Oglethorpe making a Tour into the Indian Nations to Establish Peace between them and the English ordered me to attend him it being about four Hundred Miles through the Woods...

July the 24th. The General set out with about twenty Five Persons in Company and some Indians all well Armed, it being very Necessary so to be, for not long before a Party of the Choctau Indians came down to the General who gave them Presents and they staid amongst the English as Friends, but did not prove so, for in their Return home, they met two English Men who traded among the Indians, one of these they killed and shot three of the others Fingers off, however he made his Escape to a Town of the lower Creeks, Who upon hearing his Relation of what the Choctau's had done, immediately charged them, killed a great many and took the rest Prisoners. The General had also at this time two of the Choctau Indians with him who had put themselves under his Protection for fear of the People of the Creek Nation who would have killed them for the Barbarity of their Countrymen to the two English Traders. But now I return to our Journey, which we Continued being Supplied with Venison by the Indian Hunters, and also Wild Honey of which they took Plenty.

July 27th. We arrived at Great Ogeechee River which we Swam our Horses over and The Packhorse Man got his Things over in a Leather Canoe which they carry for that Purpose and at every River where they are to use it, they stretch it with Stakes made on Purpose.

July the 28th. The Things being all got over the River we set forward, The Indians killing plenty of Deer and Turkeys for our Refreshment, also several Buffaloes, of which there is great Plenty and they are very good Eating. Though they are a very heavy Beast they will out Run a Horse and Quite Tire him.

July 31st. We Travelled over many Hills from which we had a very Pleasant Prospect of the Valleys which abounded with fine green Trees and abundance of Grapes and other Fruits, but which were not Ripe. From the Top of one of these Hills we perceived a great Smoke at a Distance from us, which we Imagined to be at the Camp of a Party of Spanish Horse which were sent out on Purpose to hinder us if possible from going to make this Treaty of Peace with the Indians and which has since been of so great Service to us, the Friendly Indians annoying the Spaniards very much. We encamped at Occomy River where we found a Horse belonging to one of the Spaniards; We crossed the River and killed two Buffaloes of which there are abundance, We Seeing Several Herds of sixty or upwards in a Herd. We Camped at Ocmulgas River where there are three Mounts raised by the Indians over three of their Great Kings who were killed in the Wars.

August the 6th. We came to Dollus Rivulet where we Encamped; In the Night came to us Capt. Wiggin, Mr. Gudell, and two of the Chief Indians, before they came to us they hooped which our Indians Answered, then they came to our Camp and saluted the General in a very friendly Manner which he Returned.

August the 7th. We set forward and on our way we found several strings of Cakes and Bags of Flower etca. which the Indians had hung up in Trees for our Refreshmt.

August the 8th. We Encamped about two Miles from the Indian Town, The Indians sent Boys and Girls out of their Town with Fowls, Venison, Pompions, Potatoes, Water Melons, and Sundry other things. About ten of the Clock we set forward for the Indian Town and were met by the Indian King And some of their Chiefs, the King had English Colours in his hand. We Saluted them and they Returned our Salute, and then shaking Hands with the General and Company the King very gracefully taking him by the Arm led him towards the Town, and when we Came there they Brought us to Logs which they had placed for that purpose Covered with Bear Skins and desired us to sit down which when we had done The head Warriours of the Indians brought us black Drink in Conkshells which they presented to us and as we were drinking they kept Hooping and Hallowing as a Token of gladness in seeing us. This Drink is made of a Leaf called by the English Casena (and much Resembles the Leaf of Bohea Tea) It is very Plenty in this Country.

Afterwards we went to the Kings House or rather Hut where we Dined, at night we went to the Square to see the Indians dance, They dance round a large Fire by the beating of a Small Drum and Six Men singing; their Dress is very wild and frightfull their Faces painted with several sorts of Colours their Hair cut short (except three Locks one of which hangs over their Foreheads like a horses fore Top) they paint the Short Hair and stick it full of Feathers, they have Balls and rattles about their Waist and Several things in their Hands, Their Dancing is of divers Gestures and Turnings of their Bodies in a great many frightfull Postures.

The Women are mostly naked to the Waist wearing only one short Peticoat which reaches from their Waist a little below their Knees, they are very nice in Smoothing and putting up their hair, it is So very long when untied that it reaches to the Calves of their Legs.

Their Houses or Hutts are built with Stakes and plais-
tered with Clay Mixed with Moss which makes them very
warm and Tite.

They dress their Meat in Large pans made of Earth and
not much unlike our Beehives in England. They do not
make use of Mills To grind their Corn in, but in lieu thereof
use a Mortar made out of the Stock of a Tree which they
cut and burn hollow and then Pound their Corn therein, and
when it is pounded sufficiently they seperate the husks
from the Meal by sifting it thro' a Sieve made of Reeds or
Canes.

The Chief Business of the Women is Planting Corn
and other things and minding the Business of the House,
The Men Hunt and Kill Deer, Turkeys, Geese, Buffaloes,
Tygers, Bears, Panthers, Wolves and several other Beasts
whose Skins they sell to the Traders for Powder Ball and
what other Necessaries they want.

August the 12th. We set out from this Town which be-
longed to the Couettaus to go to a Town of the Causettaus;
As we drew near the Town the King came with English
Colours in his Hand attended by his Chief Men, We saluted
them and they returned the Salute; The King and his Chief
Men conducted the General to their Square where he dined
and after Dinner the General went to Captain Wiggins
House where he lay that Night.

August the 17th. The Indians went into the Square to
Dance and some of the English Danced with them which
pleased them very well.

August the 21st. His Excellency General Oglethorpe
went to the Square to give the Indians the Presents he had
Caused to be brought for them, and to Establish that Peace
with them which has since been so Beneficial to the English; He also settled the Trade between the Indians and the
Traders. ("Ranger's Report" 218-21)

The Highlanders on the expedition witnessed orders from
Oglethorpe protecting Creek lands from encroachment by colo-
nists. Aeneas Mackintosh signed his name to the document as
"Eneas Mackintosh, Esq., Brother to the Laird of Mackintosh."
Other Highlanders signing beneath the statement "Made in the

square at Coweta Town and in the square at the Cussita Town and translated by a sworn interpreter in the presence of the within mention Indians and under mentioned Britons, and by me" included "Mr. Robert McPherson, brother of Thomas McPherson of Darhade; Mr. John Mackintosh, son of John Mackintosh of Holmes; Mr. James Mackqueer, son of James Mackqueer of Corsbrough; Mr. Kenneth Bailie, son to John Bailie of Balbrobart; Mr. John Mackintosh; Mr. John Cuthbert of the County of Inverness, North Britain" ("Oglethorpe's Treaty" 8).

War erupts on the southern frontier
General Oglethorpe returned to Savannah from his trek across Creek territory. On September 27 he received a letter from King George announcing that war was imminent between England and Spain and instructing Oglethorpe to "annoy" the Spanish forces in Florida and to defend the English colonies of South Carolina and Georgia. After taking measures to implement the king's instructions, Oglethorpe moved south to his military headquarters at Frederica on St. Simons Island. Larry Ivers, who developed an understanding of military issues while serving as an infantry officer and living "in a primitive earthen walled fort with Vietnamese provincial soldiers," describes the opening incidents of the war that erupted on the southern frontier of colonial America (xi):

> Before dawn on 13 November 1739 about a dozen Yemassee Indians silently beached their dugout canoes on the west side of Amelia Island. The warriors cautiously advanced through the woods and thickets to the northwestern end of the island until they were looking across a space of cleared ground at the silhouette of Amelia Fort's stockade and house. The war party concealed itself inside the woods near the path that led from the fort and hoped a man would stray into their ambush.
>
> Garrisoning Amelia Fort were sixteen Highland indentured servants who belonged to the trustees and served as scouts aboard Francis Brooks's scout boat Amelia, a sergeant's guard of twelve men from Oglethorpe's Forty-second Regiment, and about ten women and children. Adjutant Hugh Mackay, Jr., the commander, was temporarily at Frederica. After sunup two Highlanders, John Mackay

and Angus Macleod, left their warm beds to gather wood for the breakfast fire. Although neither man was feeling well they had not shirked their duty. Unarmed and unsuspecting, they walked out of the fort's gate and up the sandy path into the pines where the war party was hidden. They probably had little time to react before they were shot down by a volley from the Indians' trade muskets. The war party hacked off the Highlanders' heads and carried them off, scalping them as soon as time permitted. Startled from their slumber by the gunshots, the Highlanders and regulars attempted to pursue the Indians, but they were too late. The Indians escaped in their dugouts and paddled safely toward Saint Augustine with their trophies.

Five days after the raid Oglethorpe surrounded Amelia Island with several small boats while he and a detachment of soldiers searched the woods, thickets, and dunes for skulking Indians. They found none. An officer and a platoon of regulars reinforced the fort and Oglethorpe returned to Frederica to continue preparations for the invasion of Florida.

Two weeks after the first raid on Amelia Fort, Spanish Indians repeated their performance and may have killed two more men… In the style that became typically Oglethorpe, he gathered about two hundred regulars, rangers, militia and Indians under his personal command for a raiding and reconnaissance thrust into Florida.

The rangers who were ordered to accompany the raiding force were members of a new unit, the Troop of Highland Rangers, which had been raised on 19 November 1739. The troop numbered about a dozen men commanded by Adjutant Hugh Mackay, Jr., who thus held commissions in both the Forty-second Regiment and the Georgia provincials. The rangers had been recruited from the Highlanders at Amelia Fort and Darien.

The raiding party embarked in fourteen boats on 1 December 1739. During the ensuing two and a half weeks they inflicted very little material damage on the Spaniards; two lookout huts were burned, several cattle were destroyed, and one man was killed. However, Oglethorpe and his officers did familiarize themselves with the terrain immediately south and east of the Saint Johns River and they gained confidence as a result of the Spaniards' timid reaction... (90-91)

The British raiding party returned to Frederica on December 18, but two scout boats continued to harass Spanish outposts along the St. Johns River.

General Oglethorpe, meanwhile, planned a full-scale attack on the Spanish stronghold at St. Augustine.

1740-1743

John Mackintosh Mor and his eldest son William participate in the Battle of Mosa and John Mor is taken prisoner. William serves in the regiment at Frederica. John Mor's second son Lachlan is placed in an orphanage, and John Mor's wife seeks refuge with a kinsman at Palachacola. Lachlan joins William at Frederica shortly before the Battle of Bloody Marsh, where Highlanders play a major role in a victory against Spanish forces. John Mor rejoins his family after three years as a prisoner of war. Aeneas Mackintosh returns to Scotland, succeeds to the title of 22nd Chief of Clan Mackintosh and marries beautiful and accomplished Anne Farquharson.

Aeneas Mackintosh departs for Scotland

Captain Aeneas Mackintosh learned in February of 1740 that his older brother had died or was dying and Aeneas would inherit the estate at Moy, the title of Chief of Clan Mackintosh, and the leadership of a confederation of clans called Clan Chattan. He went from Palachacola to St. Simons Island to inform Oglethorpe that he was going to Scotland. Oglethorpe gave the commission to succeed him as commander of the fort at Palachacola to Aeneas's brother John Mackintosh. Aeneas returned from Savannah to Palachacola, turned over command to his brother, and then left Georgia for Scotland (Ivers, *Colonial Forts* 70; *Colonial Records of Georgia* 4: 511, 522).

Lachlan McIntosh placed in orphanage

John Mackintosh Mor and his wife Marjory placed their son Lachlan and their daughter Ann in the orphanage at Bethesda near Savannah in February of 1740. Lachlan was on the verge of turning 13, and Ann was no older than 3. Records do not explain why children who weren't orphans were placed in an orphanage. An obvious reason is that John Mackintosh Mor anticipated going off to war at any time. He commanded the militia at Darien, and war had erupted between British and English forces on the colonial American southern frontier. While he was away on military service, his wife would be solely responsible for raising four sons, ranging from 14-year-old William to the infant George. The Mack-intoshes may have sent Ann to safety because she was the only girl in the family. Since family tradition holds that Marjory wanted her sons to be well educated, she may have viewed Bethesda as a boarding school for Lachlan (White 334-35; "Lachlin M'Intosh" 103).

A report from the Orphan House dated June 4, 1740, gives an idea of Lachlan's daily routine:

> They [the orphans] rise about five o'clock, and each is seen to kneel down by himself for a quarter of an hour, to offer up their private prayers from their own hearts; during which time they are often exhorted what to pray for, partic-ularly that Jesus Christ would convert them, and change their hearts.
>
> At six all the family goes to church, where a psalm is sung and the second lesson expounded by Mr. Whitefield, or in his absence an exposition of it is read out of Henry or Burkitt by the president.
>
> …Between seven and eight we go to breakfast in the same room with the children, who sometimes sing a hymn before, sometimes after and sometimes both before and af-ter every meal, as well as say graces.
>
> During breakfast the business of the day is talked of and each appointed his station and perhaps some useful questions are asked the children, or exhortations given them.
>
> From eight to ten the children go to their respective employs, as carding, spinning, picking cotton or wool, sew-ing, knitting. One serves the apothecary, who lives in the house, others serve in the store or kitchen; others clean the house, fetch water, or cut wood. Some are placed under the tailor, who lives in the house; and we expect other trades-men, as a shoemaker, carpenter &c. to which others are to be bound.
>
> As the grace of God appears in any, together with suit-able abilities, they are to be bred to the ministry, and we have already one or two in view for that purpose.
>
> At ten they go to school, some to writing, some to reading. At present there are two masters and one mistress,

who in teaching them to read the scripture, at the same time explain it to them, and sing and pray with them more or less as they think fit, not by form, but out of their own hearts, whereby they teach both themselves and children much knowledge in the scriptures, exercise their talents and build each other up in our most holy faith.

At noon we go to dinner all in the same room, and between that and two o'clock every one is employed in something useful, but no time is allowed for idleness or play, which are Satan's darling hours to tempt children to all manner of wickedness, as lying, cursing, swearing, uncleanness &c., so that though we are about seventy in family yet we hear no more noise than if it was a private house.

From 2 'till 4 they go again to school, as in the morning, and from 4 to 6 to work in their respective stations as before mentioned. At six the children go to supper, when the master and mistresses attend to help them, and sing with them, and watch over their words and actions.

At seven the family all goes to church, where is a psalm sung and exposition after the second lesson, as in the morning service. And at our return about 8 many of the parishioners come in to hear Mr. Whitefield examine and instruct the children by way of question and answer, which perhaps is as edifying to all present, as any of his sermons or expositions. His main business is to ground the children in their belief of original sin, and to make them sensible of their damnable state by nature, and the absolute necessity of a change to be wrought on their souls by the power of God, before they can be in a salvable state, or have any real right to call themselves Christians; for this purpose they are ordered to get by heart the excellent articles of *Original Sin,* of *Free Will* and of *Justification.*

At nine o'clock... the children [go] up to their bedroom, where some person commonly sings and prays again with them. Before they go to bed, each boy, as in the morning, is seen to kneel by his bedside, and is ordered to pray from his own heart for a quarter of an hour, some person instructing them how to pray...

On the Lord's Day we all dine on cold meat, prepared the day before, because all may attend the worship of God, which we have that day four times at church, which fills those hours employed at work on the other days. And thus is our time all laid out in the service of God, the variety of which is a sufficient relaxation to a well-disposed mind and obviates idle pretenses for what is called innocent (though in reality damnable) recreations… (Lane 2: 437-39)

Highlanders defeated at Mosa: June 15, 1740

They say that a boy once went off to war on the southern frontier of colonial North America. His name was William McIntosh and was 14 years old when he went off to war with his father Captain John Mackintosh Mor, the leader of Scots Highlanders who had founded Darien, Georgia.

In 1740 war was brewing between England and Spain and spilling over into the Spanish colony of Florida and the English colonies of South Carolina and Georgia. General James Oglethorpe, the commander of English forces in South Carolina and Georgia, was preparing to attack the Spanish stronghold at St. Augustine. The invasion would be supported by a fleet of British vessels: five ships were assigned to blockade St. Augustine and several privateers were authorized to plunder the Spaniards.

In *British Drums on the Southern Frontier,* Larry Ivers describes the preparations for war:

> On 2 May, Oglethorpe ordered John Mackintosh, commonly called John Mohr (Big John), the forty-year-old commander of the Darien militia, to recruit the Highland Independent Company of Foot. Captain Mackintosh returned to Darien from Frederica on 6 May and recruited his company of warlike Highlanders within about five hours. The company was authorized 115 officers and men, but only 70 men could be recruited; there were not enough Highland men to fill up a 35-man ranger troop, a 115-man foot company, and still have enough left to protect the women and children of Darien. The men of the Highland Independent Company of Foot were dressed and armed in the Highland fashion. Their skirt-like plaids were wool tartans about ten to twelve yards long, part of which was gathered and belted around the waist, making a knee-length kilt. The remainder of the material was draped over the left shoulder and fas-

tened with a brooch. It was a practical garment that also served as a blanket. Some of the men probably wore little kilts (similar to modern kilts). Scotch plaids were sold in the trustees' store and seem not to have been any particular pattern. (101)

Oglethorpe assigned four hundred soldiers of the 42nd Regiment stationed at Frederica to prepare to invade Florida, while the rest of the regiment remained on garrison duty at forts and outposts along the coastal frontier. About two hundred Indians agreed to accompany the British troops.

Oglethorpe moved south of the St. Johns River with an advance party and captured Fort Diego, a fortified plantation house belonging to a Spanish colonist. The Highlanders, meanwhile, were on their way to join Oglethorpe. Local historian Bessie Lewis picks up the story:

> Soon the Highland Company, with some of the Indians, were marching from Darien up the River Road toward the pass where later Fort Barrington would be built. There they would cross the Altamaha and go on to join the regiment.
>
> Young William McIntosh, son of Captain John McIntosh Mohr, was with them. He had run away from home and was with the Indians, who would keep him hidden from his father until they crossed the Altamaha, when it would be too late to send him back to Darien (*Darien* 18-19).

The source of this story was presumably William himself, because his grandson Thomas Spalding would later write this version of it:

> William McIntosh, the eldest son of John More McIntosh, named after his grand-uncle, Brigadier General William McIntosh, who commanded the Highlanders in the rising of 1715, was not quite fourteen years of age when his father marched from Darien. He wished to accompany his father, but was refused. He pursued the moving columns, and overtook them at Barrington. His father sent him back the next day with an armed guard. He then took a small boat

and passed up to Clarke's bluff, on the south side of the Altamaha. He intended to keep in the rear until the troops had crossed the St. Mary's river. He soon fell in with seven Indians who knew him (for Darien was then the great rendezvous of the Indians) and he had acquired something of their language. The Indians were greatly attached to the Highlanders, not only as being the soldiers of their beloved man, General Oglethorpe, but because of their wild manners, of their manly sports, of their eastern costume, so much resembling their own. The young soldier was received and caressed by them. They entered into all his views. Following after the advancing troops, they told him every thing that passed in the white man's camp; but carefully concealed his presence among them, until after the passage of the St. Mary's, when, with much triumph they led him to his father, and said, "that he was a young warrior, and would fight; that the great Spirit would watch over his life, for he loved young warriors." ("Oglethorpe" 271)

The Highlanders, the 42nd Regiment, and troops from South Carolina joined Oglethorpe's advance party on the south bank of the St. Johns River on May 15. Ivers picks up the story:

In the cool of that evening Oglethorpe set out with a detachment of rangers and the Highland Company to resupply his garrison at Fort Diego seventeen miles to the south-southeast. The following morning, as the tired soldiers pulled the supply carts within sight of Fort Diego, an ambush was suddenly triggered by a party of Yemassee Indians. Gabriel Baugh, a Salzburger serving as an English Ranger and one of Oglethorpe's servant-bodyguards, was immediately killed. The Spanish allied Indians took advantage of the confusion to cut off Baugh's head and escape through the woods. Oglethorpe began an immediate pursuit of the Yemassee toward Saint Augustine through thickets and swamps. The regulars and Highlanders probably fell behind, but Oglethorpe and his rangers continued a hot pursuit on horseback for several miles, causing the Indians to drop Baugh's head. During the chase Oglethorpe had a horse shot from under him and his coat was reportedly torn by the Indians' musket balls. That night the weary pursuers returned to Fort Diego, having rounded up thirty badly needed Spanish horses. The most effective result of the pursuit was the Yemassee Indians' refusal to ambush Oglethorpe again. (106-07)

Oglethorpe and his detachment of rangers and Highlanders returned to the main camp on the St. Johns River, and he continued to plan an attack on St. Augustine. Ivers explains that Oglethorpe did not plan to lay siege to St. Augustine; he planned to capture the town by an assault of land forces and naval forces. Once he had captured the town, he planned an artillery bombardment against Castillo de San Marcos, the Spanish stronghold at St. Augustine.

The invasion force moved to Fort Diego on May 20. Oglethorpe and some of his officers, escorted by a detachment of the Highland Company and some Indian allies, explored the coast around St. Augustine. "Oglethorpe and his officers," Ivers reports, "set such a fast pace that the independently minded Indians and the already tired Highlanders, on foot, dropped behind. ...long, fast marches through deep sand under a hot sun with full equipment is extremely exhausting... and death by sunstroke was not uncommon during the campaign" (107-08).

In early June, Oglethorpe placed the South Carolina Regiment, a detachment of the 42nd Regiment, and an artillery battery on a peninsula on the north side of the harbor at St. Augustine. Oglethorpe led two hundred soldiers, two hundred seamen and about two hundred Indians to capture Anastasia Island on the south side of the harbor.

To keep the Spaniards in St. Augustine from foraging for food and gathering cattle, Oglethorpe established a force to patrol the mainland north of the Spanish town. Ivers tells the story:

On 9 June, Oglethorpe assembled the flying party and gave its officers their orders. The Troop of Highland Rangers, commanded by Captain Hugh Mackay, Jr., took ten men on the mission, half of whom were officers. The Troop of English Rangers, under Lieutenant Robert Scroggs, counted only eight men... The Troop of Carolina Rangers, composed of South Carolina volunteers... mustered nine men. This troop, commanded by Captain William Palmer, had been formed after landing in Florida. The Highland Independent Company of Foot, under Captain John Mackintosh, included only fifty-seven men since several were sick and left behind. Thirty Uchee Indians served under a white trader named James Hewit, and ten Yamacraw and Creek followed the leadership of the half-Indian, Thomas Jones... In order to provide a disciplined core around which the party could be bolstered during battle, a regular red-coated detachment including a sergeant and twelve privates was added from the Forty-second Regiment of Food. The entire flying party apparently consisted of 137 men of all ranks.

Oglethorpe gave the ill-defined operational control of the party to Colonel John Palmer... but actual command of the soldiers was retained by Captain Mackay. (114)

...The flying party left Fort Diego on 10 June and marched to a place between Saint Augustine and Fort Diego called the "Grove," where they camped the first night. They arrived at Fort Mosa about noon the following day. The fortification was described as "four Square with a Flanker at each Corner, banked round with Earth, having a Ditch without on all Sides lined round with prickly Palmetto Royal and... a Well and House within, and a Look Out." The British had partially demolished the structure during their previous visit a few days before. The gate had been carried off, a large breach had been battered in each of two walls, and the house within had been burned, making the structure no longer useful as a fortification.

General Oglethorpe had instructed the flying party to range west and east across the narrow strip of land between the Diego and Saint John Rivers, taking advantage of their mobility... They were to spend no more than one night in any one location, hiding in the thickets by night and moving into the open during the day to intercept Spanish foraging parties... Nevertheless, most of the officers chose to ignore the general's instructions by establishing a semipermanent camp at demolished Fort Mosa. (115-16)

...On Saturday, 14 June, three hundred Spanish infantry, dragoons, militia, and Yemassee Indians were assembled and briefed. Captain Antonio Salgado was appointed as the commander and ordered to conduct a predawn assault.

At about eleven o'clock that night the Spanish raiding force quietly moved out of Fort San Marcos and began a cautious advance toward the sleeping camp. The ranger patrol and the Spanish raiders apparently missed making contact by only a few minutes. Salgado's force arrived near Fort Mosa at about two o'clock on Sunday morning, 15 June. A small reconnaissance party was sent forward to ascertain the positions of the British, and the dragoons were dispatched in a half circle around the fort to station themselves astride the route of escape to Fort Diego. An hour later the reconnaissance party returned with information concerning the British positions and strength. Their details of the British flying party's unpreparedness bolstered Spanish confidence.

About three o'clock, when Colonel Palmer had the drums "beat to arms," the majority of the Carolina and British Rangers left their blankets and dressed. Palmer then walked into the fort and found most of the soldiers asleep. After he berated them for their laziness and inefficiency nearly all got up and dressed; however after standing to arms for a few minutes most of the soldiers within the fort and some of those outside crawled back into their bedrolls.

Captain Salgado's soldiers deserve praise for their stealth and discipline. They were divided into three parties and apparently attacked from as many directions. They were able to move unseen to within almost one hundred yards of the fort before one of the sentries, a Carolina Ranger, discovered them moving forward in the first light of dawn. The frightened sentry ran back to the fort crying that the Spaniards were upon them.

Colonel Palmer and Thomas Jones were standing in the gateway talking when they heard the sentry's warning. Palmer immediately called for everyone to stand to their arms and to hold their fire until the Spaniards had fired first. No sooner had he spoken than a detachment of the Highlanders stationed in the nearest bastion opened fire. With curses Palmer ordered the Carolina and English

Rangers into the moat. The Spaniards began pouring volleys on the fort.

Jones ran inside to assemble his Indians who were just waking from a sound sleep. He found the entire party in a state of confusion. Half-dressed soldiers were searching frantically for weapons. Shouting officers and sergeants were vainly trying to gather their men in their appointed bastions.

Captain Mackay had probably been wakened by the commotion. He was dressed only in a shirt, a pair of linen breeches, [and] stockings, and was carrying a small sword and a musket. Mackay ordered the officer of the guard, Cornet Baillie, to defend the gate with his guard of eighteen men, but within a short time the Spaniards began pushing them back. Mackay then ordered his cousin, Ensign Charles Mackay of the Highland Company, to support the guard with twelve men.

Outside in the moat the rangers were holding their own. Lieutenant Scroggs and the English Rangers were separated from Captain Palmer's Carolina troop. Captain Palmer had just finished pulling his boots on and buckling his spurs when he heard the warning shouts. He grabbed his brother and another ranger and ran to the moat about twelve yards away, believing they were in more danger from the Highlanders' fire to the rear than from the Spaniards' fire to the front. A short distance away Colonel Palmer, William Steads, and another ranger kept firing at the Spanish party that was trying to enter the gate. The rangers outside the fort do not appear to have been in much danger at that moment; the Spaniards were more interested in getting inside.

Inside the fort Captain Mackay and Jones met while moving from bastion to bastion, each trying to rally the men and improve their dispositions. Jones reported he had killed the Spanish officer who had led the first assault. He suggested that Mackay reinforce those Highlanders who were trying to hold the gate.

The Highlanders repulsed the first two charges, but a considerable body of Spaniards finally forced their way in by sheer weight of numbers. Captain Mackay hurriedly dispatched what men he could find to reinforce the gate, but it was too late. The fighting became hand to hand. The Spaniards had the advantage in that their numbers were greater and they were using bayonets to cut the British to pieces. The Highlanders had left their bayonets and targets (shields) behind to make them lighter on foot. Without a target a broadswordsman was no match for a trained soldier with a bayonet. They began to give way. The Spaniards from the other two assault parties were now hacking their way into the fort through the two breaches in the walls.

Colonel Palmer was loading his gun when he was hit by a musket ball. Bleeding at the mouth, he finished loading his gun and died. (119-22)

Among the Highlanders at Mosa was Roderick "Rory" McIntosh, a grandson of Brigadier William Mackintosh of Borlum. "I am a scoundrel, sir," he told a military officer decades later. "At Musa, a Captain of the Spanish Grenadiers was charging at the head of his company, and, like a vermint, sir, I lay in the bushes, and shot the gallant fellow" (White 470).

Although "the Highlanders and Indians fought bravely," local historian Bessie Lewis writes, "there was no hope from the first. Many were killed, others were captured, only a few survived. Young William McIntosh, fighting like the soldier he was, saw his father wounded and captured by the Spaniards. Among others taken prisoner that day were Ranald MacDonald, Joseph Burges, Alexander Cameron and John Mackintosh Bain. James Mackay was among those who were killed" (*Darien* 19).

John Mackintosh Mor described the battle in a letter to Alexander Mackintosh, a merchant in Lothbury:

> ...about an hour before day light, we were Attacted by Seven hundred of the Enemy, as we were Credibly Inform'd afterwards, where they met with as Hot a Reception as might possibly be Expected from So Small a Party against Such a Number, keeping a Closs fire uppon them for about an hour, and afterwards Attacting them Sword in hand – Where we hade the Misfortune being overpower'd by Numbers, to be Cut to pieces; Twenty Eight of us taken prisoners, If any Escaped it is more than I Can tell, but My Self a Cornet, and Quartermaster belonging to Capt.

Mckays Troop was Stript of our Cloaths, our hands bound behind our backs And So Carried in Captives to the Town, where we Remaind in Confinement four Months, dureing Which time we were Civily us'd by the Governour of Said town…(*Colonial Records of Georgia* 35: 336-37)

Military historian Larry Ivers continues his account of the battle:

Two thirds of the men of the Highland Company were casualties. The detachment of regulars were all dead, wounded, or captured. Almost half of the Highland Rangers had been killed or taken prisoner. One fourth of the English Rangers were dead. The majority of the Yamacraw and Creek were dead or captured.

Captain Mackay scrambled to the top of the earthen wall and called to those below to follow. He and William Mackintosh, the fourteen-year-old son of Captain Mackintosh, jumped off the wall into the moat below.

Shortly afterwards Jones and everyone who was able also climbed over the wall. Jones met Captain Palmer and his brother near the moat and, in the company of six Indians, they began to force their way through the Spaniards under the cover of thick clouds of gunsmoke. A Yemassee Indian lunged at Jones, but Captain Palmer turned and shot him. Jones and Palmer broke through and ran to the stream near the fort, wading down to its junction with the Diego River where they met Captain Mackay, Lieutenant Scroggs, and the men they had been able to bring from the fort. The appearance of Scroggs suggests that he had also been caught napping. He wore only a shirt and was armed only with a pistol. Mackay had a wound across two fingers and two other wounds, "in his Breech and the Top of his Yard." He said he had been wounded while defending the gate, but the Carolina officers suspected he must have received his wounds from the prickly palmetto royal that had been planted in the moat around the fort. (122)

Thomas Spalding describes his grandfather William McIntosh's escape from the deathtrap at Mosa:

He followed his father's footsteps until he saw him fall,
covered with many wounds, at fort Moosa. But the great
Spirit did watch over him most miraculously. For when he
saw his father fall, he was so transfixed with horror, that
not until a Spanish officer laid hold upon his plaid, was he
roused to action. Light and elastic as a steel bow, he slipped
from under the grasp of this officer, and made his escape
with the wreck of the corps. It was from the lips of this gentleman (my aged grandfather) I learned much of what I
know respecting General Oglethorpe, and the times and the
things of that day. ("Oglethorpe" 271)

Ivers describes the aftermath of the battle:

The remains of the party were in a perilous state. At any
moment the Spaniards might find them and add them to the
list of casualties. One man was ordered to swim across the
river to Point Quartell and ask Colonel Vanderhussen to
send over a boat. A short time later the scout boat *Georgia*
was sighted coming down the river. The boat was hailed
and twenty-five thankful survivors boarded and were taken
to Point Quartell and safety. Other survivors made their
way to safety by ones and twos.

      At Fort Mosa, the Spaniards were surveying their vic-
tory in the early Sunday morning sunlight. Their prisoners
included Captain Mackintosh and about a dozen men of the
Highland Independent Company, Cornet Baillie and Quartermaster McQueen of the Highland Rangers, four or five
men of the Forty-second Regiment, and an unknown number of Indians. The Spaniards stripped them, bound their
hands behind their backs, and began marching them to
Saint Augustine. Two prisoners who were too badly
wounded to walk were killed and their heads and genitals
were chopped off. One of the severed, dripping heads was
sadistically rubbed in the face of Edward Lyng, a soldier of
the Forty-second Regiment. A total of sixty-three British
dead, including both whites and Indians, were left lying in
and around the fort. Determining Spanish casualties is difficult. British estimates placed Spanish losses at between

sixteen and three hundred. Governor Montiano admitted to losing ten men. (122-23)

The loss at Mosa thwarted Oglethorpe's strategy for capturing St. Augustine, and on July 4 he called off the attack. The results of the battle, however, did not shake his faith in Highlanders as warriors. "The Georgia Rangers, the Highlanders and some of the Creek Indians had but too fatal an occasion of giving proofs of their resolution at Moosa," Oglethorpe wrote, "where most of those who died fought with an obstinacy worthy of the Greeks or Romans" (Lane 2: 536).

John Mackintosh Mor's role in the war on the southern frontier ended abruptly in defeat and imprisonment, eerily similar to his fate in the Jacobite Rising of 1715. By 1740, he had much more to lose. He was a husband and a father. He had established himself as a high-ranking gentlemen in Scotland and he had become the leader of a strategically important settlement in the New World. When he was captured at Mosa he was cut off from everything he cherished and he could only wonder what would become of his family, the settlement at Darien, and his own future.

Darien dwindles after Highlanders defeated

Bessie Lewis describes the aftermath of the ill-fated offensive at St. Augustine and the disaster at Mosa:

> The invasion failed, and the town of Darien bore the greatest loss. The bagpipes skirled the clan dirges as the men came up the river to Darien to tell the widows and orphans the sad news. Most of them expecting the Spaniards to invade the frontier, fled to Fort Argyle [between Darien and Savannah] and some obtained shelter in the orphanage. So many Highlanders had died in the battle; their leader, John McIntosh Mohr, was in a Spanish prison with his comrades. The fields at Darien lay fallow, black cattle ran wild, the pit saws were idle – the servants who would have attended to these matters of every day living were manning the scout boats or in the regiment of the Rangers, patrolling the woods or training for the invasion that was daily expected.

The women and children were afraid to come home – there were those who said the Scottish town of Darien was dead, that it would never recover. (19)

John Mackintosh Mor's family seeks refuge

After John Mackintosh Mor was taken prisoner his family was fragmented. His 14-year-old son William, who had escaped from Mosa, joined Oglethorpe's regiment at Frederica across the marsh from Darien. John Mor's 13-year-old son Lachlan and daughter Ann, who was no older than 3, remained in the orphanage at Bethesda near Savannah (White 334-35).

"The Spirit of the Lord I hope is beginning to blow among the dry bones here," Lachlan wrote while staying at Bethesda. "The House was never since I came thither likelier to answer to the end of its Institution than now: Little Boys and Little Girls, at this and that corner, crying unto the Lord, that he would have Mercy upon them" (qtd. in Sullivan 34).

John Mackintosh Mor's wife Marjory took the other children – John, age 12, Phineas, 8, and George, less than a year old – to Palachacola fort on the South Carolina side of the Savannah River. Marjory sought refuge with her husband's distant kinsman John Mackintosh, who had been given command of the fort when his brother Aeneas had returned to Scotland.

Marjory Mackintosh also received protection and sustenance from William Stephens, the secretary to the Georgia Trustees (Parker 82-83; Jackson 4).

Oglethorpe suffers

Larry Ivers describes the physical and psychological effect of the failure of the Florida invasion on General James Oglethorpe:

> During August and September 1740 General Oglethorpe isolated himself in his house at Frederica. Long marches, lack of sleep, bad water, and tainted food had sickened him. His most serious illness, however, resulted from the psychological shock that his extraordinary pride and self-confidence had suffered because of his defeat in Florida.
>
> About October, Oglethorpe overcame his fever and the shame of his failure and began thinking about his responsibilities to Georgia. During the following twenty-one

months he worked unceasingly to bolster Georgia's defenses with the knowledge that Florida's Governor Montiano would invade Georgia and South Carolina as soon as he could amass enough men and ships. (133)

The Mackintosh is dead; long live the Mackintosh

The official Clan Mackintosh historian tells of the death of William the 21st Chief of Clan Mackintosh following the death of his wife Christian Menzies of Castle Menzies:

> Christian died before her husband, who was much upset by her death. William was a delicate man, who to improve his health went to the South of France, but returned to Edinburgh, where he died in 1740. He was buried at Holyrood, his funeral expenses were very moderate and none of the usual extravagance was allowed. (Mackintosh 52)

Since William and his wife did not have children, his younger brother was next in line to the chieftainship. Georgia historian Edward Cashin discusses the new leader of Clan Chattan, a confederation of clans led by the Chief of Clan Mackintosh:

> The most important member of Clan Chattan to leave Georgia in 1740 was Captain Aeneas Mackintosh, commander at Fort Palachacola. His reasons had nothing to do with the dissolution of the Darien community. His brother William, chief of the Clan of the Cat, died on September 24, 1740, and Aeneas succeeded to the title of Mackintosh of Mackintosh. Captain Aeneas had served James Oglethorpe faithfully and well, and Oglethorpe wrote a generous recommendation to Duncan Forbes, lord president of the Court of Sessions at Inverness. "His long absence from his Country is the only reason that makes it necessary for me to recommend him, for otherwise his birth, being the Laird of Mackintosh's Brother, is such as would have made recommendation entirely needless." (*McGillivray* 35)

The ranger captain known as Aeneas Mackintosh in Georgia was sometimes called by his Gaelic name Angus in Scotland. He succeeded as the 22nd Chief of Clan Mackintosh (Mackintosh 54).

Benjamin Mackintosh goes to Charleston

Some of the Highlanders who had founded Darien relocated to Charleston to seek their fortunes. By moving to South Carolina they escaped the Georgia Trustees' policies restricting land owner-ship and prohibiting slavery. John Mackintosh of Holmes and Ben-jamin Mackintosh – a natural son of Brigadier William Mackintosh of Borlum – moved to Charleston in October of 1740.

Lachlan McGillivray, a young settler at Darien who had learned the language of the Creek Indians, went to Charleston in 1740 to work in an Indian trading company operated by Archibald McGillivray.

John McLeod, the Presbyterian minister at Darien, moved to South Carolina to serve as the pastor of a church on Edisto Island not far south of Charleston (Parker 83; Cashin, *McGillivray* 36).

John Mackintosh Mor languishes in prison

At that time both John Mackintosh Mor and his uncle Briga-dier William Mackintosh of Borlum were imprisoned due to mili-tary misfortune but their circumstances were different. The Briga-dier was more than 70 years old and passed his time in Edinburgh Castle writing learned treatises. John Mackintosh Mor was about 40 years old and languished in a jail cell in Spain worrying about his wife and young children.

After the Battle of Mosa on the American frontier between British colonies and Spanish colonies, the victorious Spaniards took John Mackintosh Mor and their other prisoners to their stronghold at St. Augustine. Then they transferred him to Havana, and later transferred him to Spain.

He wrote a letter dated May 1, 1741, and signed "John Mack-intosh Moore" asking Alexander Mackintosh, a merchant in Loth-bury, to provide credit for obtaining food, clothing, and other ne-cessities while he was imprisoned (*Colonial Records of Georgia* 35: 335-37).

Afraid that the first letter may not have been delivered, he sent a second letter dated June 20, 1741. Emphasizing his clan connec-tion with Alexander Mackintosh, he reported that he had no way of knowing what had become of his wife or children; he was not even aware that his eldest son William had escaped from the battlefield of Mosa. He wrote:

Sir

You being my Friend and Namesake, staying nigh the Court makes me presume to write you in my Necessity. That you may know who gives you this Trouble, my name is John Mcintosh Son to Lachlan Mcintosh who was Brother to Brigadier Mcintosh of Borlom. Now I will inform you what my case is and how I came here, no doubt you have heard of General Oglethorpe's disappointment at Florida and how the Highlanders were cut to pieces except a few had the bad fortune to be taken Prisoners, of which number I was one, and what compleats our Misery and makes it worse than others of his Brittanick Majesty's Subjects is that we were never enquired for, by any person what came of us, nor do I know whom to apply to. I had the Command of the above Highlanders since their Settlement in Georgia. When the War began the General sent for me and presented me with a Captains Commission, told me he had Authority to raise Troops and that my Company should be independent under the Kings Pay. With that encouragement and all of us being willing and forward to serve our King and Country, I listed Seventy Men, all in Highland Dress, marched to the Siege, was ordered to scout nigh Augustine and molest the Enemy while the General and the rest of his little army went to an Island where we could have no succour of them. I punctually obeyed my orders untill Seven Hundred Spaniards sallied out from the Garrison one hour before day light, they did not surprise us for we were all under arms ready to receive them, which we did briskly, keeping a constant firing for a quarter of an hour, when they prest on us with numbers was obliged to take our Swords, untill the most of us was shot and cut to pieces. You are to observe we had but Eighty Men, and the engagement was in view of the rest of our Army, but could not come to our assistance by being in the 'foresaid Island under the Enemy's Guns. They had Twenty Prisoners, a few got off, the rest killed As we were well informed by some of themselves they had 300d. killed on the spot besides several wounded. We were all stripp't naked of Cloaths, brought to Augustine where we remained three

months in close confinement, afterwards sent to the Ha-
vannah, where the Governor was so civil to all called Officers, that we had the Liberty of the City for our confinement. After staying three months here, was ordered on
board a Ship for St. Sebastians in old Spain. Tho' the Ha-
vannah Governor recommended me as Captain of foot, my
treatment was to be put in close confinement in the Common Town Jayl, and my Allowance Bread and Water. If it
was not for six pence a day his Brittanick Majesty allows
all Prisoners we might starve. You are to know I left a Wife
and seven Children in Georgia for ought I know starving
there for all my Servants was listed to make up the Company. There is a son of Corebrough Mcqueens and a Nephew
of Duncan's here who was an Ensign in a troop of Rangers
belonging to the Trustees As also one Mcdonald who has a
Family in Georgia. I hope when this comes to hand as there
is a great many Spanish Prisoners in England, by your endeavors you'll get some of them to be exchanged for us
four, if not a little Credit to help us in Cloaths and a better
living which we want much. In Justice and for the Credit of
the Country I ought to be maintained conformed to the Station I am Prisoner. I do not doubt your Diligence in apply-
ing the proper persons whom I believe to be the Secretary
of War and the Trustees. I wrote to them both but no Answer, begs pardon for this Trouble... (*Colonial Records of
Georgia* 35: 340-43)

While imprisoned in Spain, John Mackintosh Mor sent at least
two letters to an official with the Georgia Trustees. He wrote on
June 24, 1741:

> ... We were sent... to this place to our Misery. ...to be con-
> fined in the common Jayl and allowed no more than bread
> and water. I thought proper to acquaint you with this that it
> might be made Publick. The reason I trouble you is, the lit-
> tle correspondence I had with You by writing when at Dar-
> ien. And what Compleats my Misfortune and makes it real-
> ly worse than any other of his Brittanick Majesty's Subjects
> is, that there was no Inquiry made concerning me whether
> Dead of Alive, nor do I know whom to apply to, therefore I
> expect you'll please be so good as to Inquire and apply to

the proper persons for my Releasement and a little Credit to my self, and the other two Gentlemen who has served the Trustees in the Troop of Rangers these five Years, to support us in our Necessitys here, I having faithfully Served the Honble. the Trustees for five Years, besides the Love I had for my King and Country made me forsake my Wife and Children and all my Effects, so that now I hope by your good Endeavors in Representing my case I shall have no reason to complain if God spares me to see England. I am

Sir with great Esteem

Your most Obedient humble Servt.

John Mackintosh Moore (*Colonial Records of Georgia* 35: 345-46)

The Chief of Mackintosh marries

Once upon a time a man who was a veteran soldier and prestigious clan chieftain fell in love with a beautiful young lady. He was Aeneas Mackintosh, who had served as a ranger captain in Georgia before returning to Scotland as heir to the chieftainship of not only Clan Mackintosh but also a confederation of clans called Clan Chattan. She was Anne Farquharson, the eldest daughter of John Farquharson of Invercauld, the chief of that branch of Clan Chattan; her father had fought under the command of Brigadier William Mackintosh of Borlum in the Rising of 1715 and had been taken prisoner with the other Clan Chattan soldiers at Preston.

Men described Anne as both beautiful and accomplished, "a somewhat delicate-looking girl, with a retiring, modest look, elegant figure, and rather high forehead" (MacKintosh, "Lady MacKintosh" 45; McGillivray, "Colonel Anne" 72-73).

A clan historian describes the marriage:

> In 1741, at the age of 18, Anne married Aeneas Mackintosh of Mackintosh. The marriage contract, dated at Aberdeen 2 February 1741, was witnessed by her brother, several Farquharsons and Alexander MacGillivray of Dunmaglass. Aeneas had succeeded as 22nd Chief of his Clan only a few months earlier. He was considerably older than his bride, as much as 20 years perhaps, but from all accounts it was a happy and contented union. As Charles Fraser-Mackintosh was to observe, her letters show that "she threw herself...

heart and soul into everything tending to the honour and prosperity of Mackintosh, and the haill Clan Chattan."

The newly-weds set up home in Moy Hall, built about 1700... (McGillivray, "Colonel Anne" 72)

New settlers arrive at Darien

To revive depopulated Darien, the Georgia Trustees conducted another recruiting drive in the Scottish Highlands. Captain Hugh Mackay played a major role in the recruitment effort, historian Anthony Parker points out: "Of the forty-three emigrants from the Highlands, twelve were surnamed Mackay and two other men, who had families, were connected directly to the Mackay clan through marriage. Almost half the new emigrants were known Mackays and the other names represented included MacDonald, Munroe, Douglas and Grant" (85-86). The new settlers arrived at Darien in December of 1741.

Lachlan McIntosh joins the Frederica regiment

Lachlan McIntosh, who had lived in the orphanage at Bethesda since February of 1740, left the orphanage on April 26, 1742. Lachlan, who had turned age 15 in March, "Was ordered by Gen. Oglethorpe to his regiment at Frederica, being a cadet there." Lachlan's duties with the regiment included standing guard and herding cattle, but he apparently did not engage in combat. At Frederica, Lachlan reunited with his brother William, age 16, who had been taken into the regiment after the Highland Company was decimated at Mosa, where William escaped after seeing his father taken prisoner (White 334; Jackson 4-5).

Spaniards invade Georgia: May-July, 1742

The King of Spain ordered forces from Cuba and Florida to attack South Carolina and Georgia in the spring of 1742. Nearly two thousand infantrymen, dragoons, artillery gunners and scouts, including sixty Indians, sailed from St. Augustine to the Georgia coast on a fleet of fifty-two vessels. The British defensive force under General James Oglethorpe consisted of fewer than a thousand men stationed at posts along the coast supported by an inadequate amount of artillery. As the Spanish fleet approached, British recruiters sought volunteers in Savannah. The Highland Independent Company of Foot at Darien – commanded by Lieutenant

Charles Mackay while John Mackintosh Mor was a prisoner of war in Spain – was ordered to join Oglethorpe's forces at St. Simons Island. The Troop of Highland Rangers commanded by Captain Hugh Mackay, Jr., also reported for duty at St. Simons. Small parties of Chickasaw, Creek, and Yamacraw Indians came to support their friend Oglethorpe. By the time the Spanish fleet anchored at the mouth of St. Simons Sound, about five hundred British soldiers had assembled on St. Simons Island (Ivers 152-59).

On July 5 the Spanish fleet forced past the guns of small British vessels and the artillery of Fort St. Simons on the south end of St. Simons Island. As soon as the fleet entered the Frederica River, about fifteen hundred Spanish soldiers conducted an assault landing throughout the evening and the night, sweeping aside resistance from Georgia Rangers and their Indian allies. British troops abandoned Fort St. Simons and began marching after midnight along the trail to Frederica on the north end of the island (Ivers 159-61).

"On the Georgia mainland the settlers panicked" Ivers reports. "Women and children fled from Darien to Fort Argyle [between Darien and Savannah] and beyond, while those from Savannah hastily sought refuge in Abercorn and other outlying settlements in an attempt to somehow evade the rape and pillage that they believed was imminent. Fear was only slightly less prevalent in South Carolina, for the real prize for any enemy fleet would have been the sacking of Charles Town" (161).

British rangers patrolling the trail to Frederica encountered a Spanish reconnaissance party on July 7. The rangers raced to Frederica to inform Oglethorpe, who decided to attack the Spaniards while they were confined on the narrow trail through the semitropical forest. Ivers describes the encounter:

> The Highland Company, mustering between thirty and forty men, was the only infantry unit in formation prepared to march. Oglethorpe commandeered a horse and began leading the Highlanders out of the town gate and down the trail at a run. He was quickly joined by Captain Thomas Jones with his rangers, Toonahowi and a party of Yamacraw and Creek, Lieutenant Scroggs and a detachment of English Rangers, and Captain William Gray of South Carolina with a party of Squirrel King's Chickasaw from near Augusta.

Running a long distance on a July day in Georgia is exhausting, especially if you are carrying about twenty-five pounds of weapons and equipment; nevertheless, six Highlanders and most of the Indians managed to keep up with the galloping rangers.

About a mile southeast of Frederica, as the disordered body of provincials and Indians rounded a slight bend in the wood-enclosed trail, they saw the Spaniards' lead element on the other side of a small open savannah to their front. Captain Sanchez was moving his reconnoitering party toward a nearby creek bed that he intended to use as a defensive position. Without hesitating, Oglethorpe spurred his horse toward them. For the Chickasaw, Yamacraw, Creek and Highlanders, all warlike by tradition, the charge represented life at its best. If the rangers felt the rising temperature of fear they had little time to reflect upon it; they swept the lead element aside and collided with the main body of Spanish regulars, scouts, and Indians. Oglethorpe and his followers never relinquished the momentum they gained from their surprising charge. Two Spaniards threw down their weapons and surrendered to Oglethorpe who was at the head of his men. Toonahowi, wounded in his right arm, drew a pistol with his left hand and killed a Spanish officer who was threatening him. Lieutenant Scroggs plunged his horse into the milling Spaniards and forced the surrender of their commander, Captain Sanchez. Captain Hernandez was captured shortly afterward. The Spaniards' resistance disintegrated and they began stumbling wildly into the woods and back along the trail. Oglethorpe and the rangers pursued a party of fleeing Spaniards about three and a half miles before calling a halt to wait for Mackay's Highlanders and Demere's regulars to catch up. The Creek, Chickasaw, some Highlanders, and a few rangers remained near the battle site, running down the terrified survivors. The Spaniards suffered thirty-six men killed, captured, or missing, and most of the remainder were temporarily lost in the woods and thickets. The British lost one man, a Highlander, from heat exhaustion. (163-65)

A ranger serving with Oglethorpe identified the Highlander who died from heat exhaustion: "Mr. Maclane a Highland Gentleman who running very hard in pursuit of the Enemy spoiled the Circulation of his Blood and died Soon after he was brought to Town" ("Ranger's Report" 235).

The Battle of Bloody Marsh: July 7, 1742

Soldiers – including William McIntosh and Alexander McDonald – from the regiment at Frederica went out to support the Highlanders, rangers and Indians led by General Oglethorpe who had driven off a Spanish reconnaissance party. Expecting a counter-attack, Oglethorpe posted the combined force to guard the trail leading to Frederica. (Ivers 165; Spalding, "Oglethorpe" 284; Redfearn 26). Ivers describes the situation:

> The position Oglethorpe selected to block the trail was between four and a half and five miles south-southeast of Frederica on the western edge of present Bloody Marsh. He placed Captain Demere and his company of about sixty regulars, who had just arrived from Frederica, on the left (east) side of the trail and the Highland Company and the rangers, about forty-five to fifty men, on the right (west) side. A branch of Bloody Marsh, an open savannah perhaps a hundred yards wide, lay perpendicular to their front (south). The trail crossed this spongy marsh on a narrow causeway of brush and logs and led into the dense woods between the British positions. While Oglethorpe returned to Frederica the regulars and provincials prepared their blocking position by building several small piles of fallen logs and limbs in the tree line as protection from Spanish musket balls.
>
> Meanwhile, a few Spaniards of the defeated reconnoitering party arrived at Fort Saint Simons about noon and reported the clash. Montiano reacted quickly by ordering Captain Antonio Barba to take three companies of grenadiers, probably between 150 and 200 men, and march to the battle site in order to protect the withdrawal of the members of the reconnoitering party, most of whom were scattered in the dense woods. The relief force set out and began picking up stragglers from the reconnoitering party as they marched

north. Clouds had been gathering and now a light steady rain began to fall.

About three o'clock in the afternoon Captain Barba's grenadiers began crossing a narrow causeway spanning a marsh. A few survivors of the defunct reconnoitering party, who were acting as guides, noticed some piles of brush and logs situated in the woods on the far side of the marsh which they could not remember having seen before. Barba called a halt and sent a few men forward to investigate. When they drew near the far side of the marsh the brush and trees on both sides of the trail suddenly erupted with the blasts and smoke from dozens of muskets. Several Spaniards were cut down while running to the rear. Barba formed his three companies inside the cover of the trees on the south side of the marsh and began placing a disciplined fire on the British positions. A steady drizzle of rain held the smoke close to the ground, obscuring the scene. The Spaniards were shouting and their drummers were loudly beating Barba's commands. Demere's regulars became excited and a few turned and fled. They were soon followed by some more. Finally, three whole platoons broke and ran along with Captain Demere and another officer.

At Frederica, Oglethorpe... heard the distant firing. After ordering the units to follow, he spurred his horse toward the battle. About two miles north of the marsh he met Captain Demere and the three fugitive platoons who informed him that the entire force had been routed; however, Oglethorpe could still hear the firing and ordered them to return with him to the marsh...

Half of the British force had held courageously. To the left of the trail Lieutenant Patrick Sutherland and Sergeant John Stewart of Demere's company had somehow managed to hold a platoon of about fifteen men in place. To the right Lieutenant Charles Mackay's Highland Company and the rangers seem not to have ever considered leaving the battle. For about an hour Sutherland's and Mackay's outnumbered soldiers continued firing steadily across the marsh at the Spanish grenadiers.

The Spaniards were unaware that almost half of the British force had fled. About four o'clock, after firing all

their ammunition, Captain Barba formed the three companies into marching order and began an orderly retreat to
Fort Saint Simons. They reported an officer and six men
killed, probably in the first few seconds of the fight, and
two wounded men had been captured.

The Spaniards had just completed their withdrawal
when Oglethorpe arrived. His elation is easy to imagine, for
if the entire British force had been routed the effect on the
morale of both regulars and provincials could have been
disastrous. Instead, the brave stand by the soldiers under
Sutherland and Mackay made the Spaniards seem less omi-
nous and gave Oglethorpe's army new-found courage.
(165-67)

The British victory at Bloody Marsh contrasted sharply with
the British defeat two years earlier at Fort Mosa, where some of
the same Spanish military units had crushed some of the same British units, particularly the Highlanders. "We have some Satisfaction
for the Blood at Mosa," Oglethorpe declared in a letter to a friend
(Ivers 172).

A ranger serving with Oglethorpe recorded his somewhat mis-
taken impression of the battle:

The Spaniards hearing of the Fate their first Party met with
sent out another 300 Men under the Command of Don Antonio Barbara Captain of a Company of Grenadiers; about
three o' th' Clock in the afternoon the Spaniards advanced
up to the Place where we were Posted and some of them
being Come within our Lines a Sharp Fire continued on all
hands and betwixt both parties for some time. The Spaniards fell in great Numbers amongst which was Several Officers and also that Famous Captain of Grenadiers; the
Number of the Spaniards was so great and their Fire so
brisk, that some Platoons of ours gave way and were Retiring in Confusion but the timely presence of the General
prevented their Retiring far. He immediately ordered them
to Rally, riding himself up to the Place where he found
Lieutt Sutherland and Lieutt Charles Mackay with the
Highlanders and Rangers had Entirely defeated the Spaniards. ("Ranger's Report" 234-35)

As a soldier in the Frederica regiment, William McIntosh may have been among the fifteen regulars who did not flee or he may have been among his fellow Highlanders. When he described the Battle of Bloody Marsh fifty years later to his grandson Thomas Spalding, William McIntosh did not let historical facts interfere with a good Celtic tale. He apparently blended several events from the Spanish invasion of Georgia into one story. And, as in all legends, his account combines elements of folklore with historical events. Describing the scene when Oglethorpe hurried from Frederica to the battleground, Spalding writes:

> ...at the last bend of the marshy way, a scene opened upon him, which his proudest expectations could not have looked for; a scene to himself of glory and security; to his enemy of shame and defeat.
>
> The last bend of the marsh was covered by two hundred grenadiers, who lay dead or dying upon the field, while not an enemy was in sight. All was still, save sometimes at intervals a Highland shout or an Indian yell proclaimed that another and another had been found and dragged from his covert. But how rose that shout, how rang that yell, when the actors stood around their chief to hail him victor of the day. And we have seen the eye glisten, and the voice rise, fifty years afterwards as we fondly listened to the tale by one who had mingled in the strife and been partner in the scene.
>
> But we will detail the little that remains to be told. While the troops were attacked in the wood by the Spanish forces from their camp, they were overwhelmed by superior numbers, and became, as is sometimes the case with even veteran troops, seized with a panic, lest the Spaniards, pushing on, should take possession of the defile, and cut off their retreat. They therefore made a precipitate retreat, the Highlanders following in the rear reluctantly. After passing through the defile Lieut. McKay communicated to his friend Lieut. Southerland (who commanded the rear guard of the retreating forces, composed also of Highlanders) the feelings of his corps, and they agreed to drop behind, and as soon as the whole had passed the defile, as there were no

Spaniards in view, to return through the brush and take post at the two points of the crescent. Four Indians that were with them, and particularly attached to the corps, remained with them. They had just taken post and concealed themselves in the woods when the Spaniards, having made all their arrangements for an advance, their grenadier regiment, the *elite* of their troops, advanced into the defile, where, seeing in the foot-prints the rapid retreat of the broken troops, and observing that their right was covered by an open morass, and their left, as they supposed, by an impracticable wall of brush-wood, and a border of dry white sand, they stacked their arms and sat down to take the refreshment that had become necessary after having been under arms many hours, believing as they did that the contest for the day was over. Just at that moment, a Highland cap was raised at either point, and the scene of death began. All was terror – no resistance was made – sometimes they attempted to fly along the marsh. The pass was too narrow. They were met and slaughtered by the broad-sword. Those that did escape, had at last to make their way to and through the brush-wood, where many wounded perished, and their bodies were only found when all that remained of them were their whitened bones.

The young soldier of Fort Moosa, just then sixteen years of age, was there. No shout rose higher, no sword waved quicker than his upon that day. But his heart was as soft as it was brave, and there was melancholy in his mood, when standing upon the ground and pointing to where the victor stood, and where the vanquished fell, he told to his daughter's son this tale of other times. ("Oglethorpe" 283-84)

Local historian Bessie Lewis uses details from Spalding's account in her vivid telling of the Battle of Bloody Marsh:

Taking a party of Indians, the Rangers and the Highland Company, and ordering the regiment to follow, Oglethorpe advanced to meet the enemy, coming upon them in the deepest part of the woods, where there was neither time nor room for battle formation. Claymores flashing, muskets spitting fire, the eerie battle cry of the Highlanders with the skirling of bagpipes mingled with the war whoop of the Indians while the Scots and redmen took vengeance for comrades who fell at Moosa. Rangers galloped to right and left, their muskets taking bitter toll of Spanish lives. Completely routed, the Spaniards fled in disorder, with the British forces in pursuit.

Oglethorpe halted his men on the edge of an open meadow or savannah. There he posted three platoons of the regiment with the company of Highland infantry. Completely hidden in the thick woods, these forces commanded a full view of the savannah over which any fresh Spanish forces must pass going from their camp to Frederica.

The trap worked. Three Spanish captains, with one hundred grenadiers and two hundred foot soldiers, besides Indians and Negroes, marched into the savannah. Without suspicion of ambush they advanced into the meadow, marching boldly to the rhythm of drums. They halted, stacked their arms and prepared to cook a meal.

Suddenly a horse gave a snort of fright. Pandemonium broke loose – the Spaniards ran to their arms and tried to form for action. The Highlanders and soldiers of the regiment, shooting from ambush, brought down man after man, while the desperate Spaniards, unable to see their targets and untrained in woods warfare, fired wildly with little effect. Spanish officers were killed and their men scattered in all directions.

The air was filled with the smoke of black powder, settling low in the rain, and two platoons of the regiment became confused and began to retreat. Oglethorpe, galloping his horse toward the noise of battle, met and stopped them. They reported the British forces routed and Lieutenant Sutherland killed. With the noise of the battle still going on, Oglethorpe could not believe this, and he ordered them back to the savannah. His report to the Trustees tells the story: "I found the Spaniards entirely routed by one Platoon of the Regiment under the command of Lieut. Sutherland and the Highland Company under Lieut. Charles Mackay ...An officer whom the Prisoners said was Capt. Don Antonio Barba was taken prisoner but desperately wounded, and two others were prisoners dead on the spot. Lieut. Sutherland, Lieut. Charles Mackay and Sergt. Stuart having distinguished themselves, I appointed Lieut. Sutherland Brigade Major and Sergt. Stuart Second Ensign."

The Battle of Bloody Marsh was over... (*Darien* 22-23)

The legend of Bloody Marsh became a staple in the bardic repertoire of descendants of Scottish Highlanders. In a presidential address to the St. Andrew's Society of Savannah in 1936, Alexander R. MacDonell told this version of the tale:

The highland soldier has always had a military character for valor. Taught to consider courage as the most honorable virtue, cowardice the most disgraceful feeling, he was ready to follow wherever honor and duty called him, and to devote himself to his native country and to his clan.

With such principles and regarding any disgrace he might bring on his clan and district as the cruelest misfortune, the highland private soldier had a peculiar motive to exertion, and he knew that every proof which he displayed, either of bravery or cowardice, would find its way to his native home, and that he had a separate and individual reputation to sustain, which would be reflected on his family and clan.

The character of ardor belongs to the highlander; he acts from internal sentiment and possesses a kind of honor which does not permit him to retire from a danger with a confession of inferiority. Close charge was his ancient mode of attack, and it is probably from the impression engrafted in his nature that he still sustains the approaching point of a naked weapon with a steadier eye than any other man in Europe.

...A famous English General once said that in all his experiences of war the Scotch soldier was the only one who did not flinch from an assault with cold steel, but that, on the contrary, the Scotch Highlander delighted in a close hand to hand conflict, a delight which must have been hereditary in his blood... (251)

The youthful Scotch Highlander, his imagination fired by the martial reputation of his race, often burned with zeal to bear arms and fight shoulder to shoulder with the other members of his clan, and many instances of such youthful warriors are to be found in the records of those battles in which the Scotch clans engaged. Young William MacIntosh presents a typical example of such warlike precocity. At the age of fourteen, desiring to join his father, John Mohr, in the invasion of Florida... he determined to follow anyhow... He followed his father until he saw him fall at Fort Moosa, covered with wounds... (256)

...an armada of forty vessels and between three and four thousand troops from the West Indies engaged the defenses which Oglethorpe had thrown up, entered the inner passage and landed. A great crisis had come. For the Scotchmen, it was to be a great victory, a Bannockburn of the new world. The battle which ensued was known as the Battle of Bloody Marsh. It was one of the decisive battles of the world.

Carlisle said that half the world was hidden in embryo under it. The Yankee nation itself was involved, the greatest phenomenon of the ages.

Whitfield said that it determined that North America should be left to the exploitation of the Anglo-Saxon, the Celtic and the Teutonic. By it North America remained English instead of becoming Spanish.

The decisive blow of the battle was struck by the Highlanders under Lieuts. Sutherland and Mackay... The Spaniards marched into the defile and, supposing the contest over for the day, stacked arms and began to partake of refreshments. Sutherland and Mackay, who, from their hiding places, had watched the movements of the Spaniards, now from either end of the line, raised the Highland shout and signaled the work of death to begin. Immediately, the Highlanders poured into the unsuspecting enemy a well delivered and most deadly fire. Volley succeeded volley and the sand was soon strewed with the dead and dying. Terror and dismay seized the Spaniards, who, making no resistance, attempted to fly along the marsh. Discipline was gone; orders were unheeded; safety alone was sought; and when, with a Highland shout of triumph, the hidden foes burst among them, with level muskets and flashing claymoors, the panic stricken Spaniards fled in every direction; some to the marsh, where they were mired and taken; others along the defile, where they were met by the broad sword; and still others into the thicket, where they became undiscovered and perished; and only a few succeeded in escaping to their camp. In these actions William MacIntosh, already mentioned, was conspicuous, although he was only sixteen years old at the time. No shout rose higher and no sword raised quicker than his on that day... He was avenging the capture of his father, John Mohr MacIntosh, by the Spaniards at Fort Moosa. (257-58)

Spanish invasion force withdraws

Late in the day of the Battle of Bloody Marsh, Oglethorpe led his army southward to within two miles of the Spanish army. The British army spent the night on the trail. The next morning, the British army marched back to Frederica while rangers and Indian allies stayed behind to harass the Spanish camp (Ivers 165-67).

One of the rangers reported an incident that may have contributed to the legend that the Spanish soldiers at Bloody Marsh had stopped to cook a meal: "The Spaniards after this never ventured out beyond their Centinels who were also Fortified. I having been out by order observing their Motions and within Musquet shot of them, The Rangers and Indians were always so near them that nine Spaniards were shot in their Camp as they were Eating" ("Ranger's Report" 235).

A few days after the battles on the trail, three Spanish vessels explored the Frederica River to see whether infantry and artillery could approach Fort Frederica by water instead of by marching along the trail. Artillery fire from Frederica forced the vessels to turn around. Oglethorpe pursued them with his scout boats.

A British seaman who had been captured by the Spaniards escaped and told Oglethorpe that Spanish morale was low. Oglethorpe planned a night raid to inflict more consternation on the invaders. On July 12 he led five hundred men, including the Highland Company, toward the fort occupied by the Spanish army. In the middle of the night, a French seaman with Oglethorpe's force fired his musket and alerted the Spaniards. The Frenchman fled into the woods, and later entered the Spanish camp. Oglethorpe's force returned to Frederica.

Oglethorpe sent a letter to the French seaman, knowing it would be intercepted by the Spanish commander. The letter made the French seaman seem to be in a conspiracy with Oglethorpe to deliver the Spaniards into an ambush. Once the letter was intercepted, the Spaniards lost trust in the French seaman's information.

When five ships from South Carolina appeared to the north of St. Simons Island, the Spanish forces sailed away before their avenue of escape could be cut off.

As the Spaniards moved southward toward Florida, they threatened the British garrison at Fort Prince William on Cumberland Island. Oglethorpe sent the garrison's commander a message ordering him to hold out until Oglethorpe could get there with reinforcements. The Spaniards thought the fort was defended by more men than the garrison actually contained, and called off their assault. Oglethorpe arrived two days later with a flotilla of scout boats. Oglethorpe's flotilla followed the Spanish fleet as far as northern Florida before returning to Frederica.

By August, Oglethorpe received support from ships of the Royal Navy and ships from South Carolina. Oglethorpe took the fleet to St. Augustine and attacked six Cuban half-galleys in the mouth of the harbor. A cannonball knocked the boom off the scout boat carrying Oglethorpe. A man in the boat was killed in the naval battle and two men were wounded. The battle ended at nightfall. Three days later, faced with strong winds and high surf, Oglethorpe's fleet left Florida (Ivers 168-72).

Oglethorpe returns to England

General James Edward Oglethorpe left Georgia forever on July 23, 1743, two years before the Jacobites would launch a final effort to restore the Stuarts to the throne of Great Britain. This coincidence of timing has inspired a bit of McIntosh family lore.

As preparations were underway for Oglethorpe's ship to set sail, so the story goes, William and Lachlan McIntosh were discovered hiding in the hold of another vessel. William and Lachlan were the teenage sons of John Mackintosh Mor, a nephew of Brigadier William Mackintosh of Borlum. The Brigadier had commanded a portion of the Jacobite forces attempting to restore the Stuarts to the throne of Great Britain in 1715. Now his great-nephews wanted to return to their birthplace in Scotland to assist in the next Jacobite rising. They wished not only to restore the Stuarts to the throne but also restore the Borlum branch of Clan Mackintosh to prominence. William McIntosh's grandson Thomas Spalding tells the story of what happened when Oglethorpe discovered that the boys were aboard:

> General Oglethorpe sent for the two young lads into his own cabin; he spoke to them of the friendship he entertained for their father, of the kindness he entertained for themselves, of the hopelessness of every attempt of the house of Stuart, of their own folly in engaging in this wild and desperate struggle, of his own duty as an officer of the house of Brunswick; but if they would go ashore, be hereafter quiet, and keep their own secret, he would forget all that had passed; – he received their pledge, and they never saw him again. ("Lachlan McIntosh" 103)

John Mackintosh Mor returns to Georgia

Marjory Mackintosh and three of her children remained at Palachacola – where their relative John Mackintosh commanded the garrison – while her husband John Mackintosh Mor was a prisoner of war and their eldest sons William and Lachlan served in the regiment at Frederica. After nearly two years at Palachacola, Marjory went back to Darien in anticipation that her husband would return. She retrieved her daughter Ann from the orphanage at Bethesda in September of 1742. John Mackintosh Mor was released from a Spanish jail in a prisoner exchange and arrived in Georgia late in 1743. Retaining his rank as captain, John Mackintosh Mor resumed command of the Highland Independent Company of Foot at Darien. When John Mackintosh Mor reunited with his wife and children, his son Lachlan left Frederica to live in the family home (Parker 82-83; Jackson 4-5; Ivers 186, 193-94; White 335).

Macdonald clansmen rally around Bonnie Prince Charlie in the Jacobite Rising of 1745. Aeneas the 22nd Chief of Clan Mackintosh serves in the government army while his wife Anne rallies the clan for the rebels. Both Clan Donald and Clan Mackintosh suffer horrible casualties in the Battle of Culloden. Flora MacDonald helps Bonnie Prince Charlie elude government pursuers.

The Rising of 1745

Once upon a time a handsome prince sought to restore his family to its rightful place in the world. His name was Charles Edward Stuart and he would become known as Bonnie Prince Charlie. His father claimed the titles King James III of England and James VIII of Scotland although he was in exile in Europe, and Charles was next in the line of succession of the historic dynasty. Their allies were called "Jacobites" from the Latin word for "James."

Clan historian Margaret Mackintosh of Mackintosh tells how Bonnie Prince Charlie set off on his grand adventure:

> News of the discontent in Scotland was carried to Rome where the so-called James VIII and his son, Prince Charles Edward, were living. It is important to know that the enthusiasm for the Stuarts or for actual rebellion in the Highlands was, over a long period, grossly exaggerated to the Old Pretender, the Prince, and the French by the various Jacobite emissaries with subsequent fatal results. However, the Prince declared his intention of overthrowing King George II and of placing his father on the throne, and moved to France with great secrecy in January 1744. Delayed and disappointed by lack of support from King Louis XV, the Prince eventually set out for Scotland in a French ship, landing in the Western Highlands in July 1745. (54)

Macdonalds rally around Bonnie Prince Charlie

Prince Charles arrived in Scotland with only seven followers and plans to raise an army of Highlanders. The Highlanders themselves were not enthusiastic about the Prince's plans. Military historian William Seymour writes:

> …When Alexander Macdonald of Boisdale, almost the first chief to meet him, advised the Prince to go home, Charles replied, 'I am come home, sir, and I will entertain no notion at all of returning to that place from whence I come; for that I am persuaded my faithful Highlanders will stand by me.' And in the event a great many of them did. By 19 August, when the huge white, red and blue silk standard was broken at Glenfinnan, there had gathered some 200 Clanranald Macdonalds, and Alexander Macdonald of Keppoch was on his way with 300 more men. And we can readily imagine what joy there must have been in that little valley flanked by mountains of timeless antiquity when the sound of the Cameron pipers could be heard in the distance leading 700 of their clansmen towards the royal standard. Donald Cameron of Lochiel had been one of those who advised the Prince to return, but when he saw the spirit of the man he declared, 'I'll share the fate of my prince; and so shall every man over whom nature or fortune hath given me any power.' (203-04)

Prince Charles led his army of Highlanders toward Edinburgh, the capital city of Scotland. A history of the MacDonells of Glengarry describes their arrival:

> On September 16th the Highlanders reached the outskirts of Edinburgh and after failure to come to terms with the magistrates for the surrender of the city, "betwixt ten and eleven at night" detachments from Glengarry's Regiment "Keppoch's, Clanranald's and Lochiel's" some 900 strong were sent under Lochiel accompanied by Murray of Broughton, and O'Sullivan to seize the capital. Lochgarry commanded the Glengarry detachment. The accident of opening the gate to allow the exit of the carriage that had carried back the deputation of the magistrates from the Prince permitted the Highlanders to rush in and make themselves masters of the city "without the strok of a sword, and not the least opposition made within the town."

While the Prince was settling in at Holyrood, the ceremony of proclaiming his father [as king] was taking place at the Mercat Cross in the High Street of Edinburgh. The wild looking Highlanders after their successful exploit of the previous night stood in their ranks chatting in their native Gaelic and totally incomprehensible to the Edinburgh public. The heralds and pursuivants who had been secured earlier in the day now appeared in their colourful robes on the Cross balcony where they were joined by the Duke of Perth, Lord Elcho, Coll MacDonell of Barrisdale and several others. (MacDonald 88)

A French officer serving with the Jacobites described the scene when Charles proclaimed that his father James Stuart was the rightful king of Scotland and England:

...the Prince was conducted to Holyrood House, the palace of his ancestors, at the end of the suburbs, amidst the acclamations of an immense crowd, whom curiosity had brought to meet him a quarter of a league from the city. It was a new sight, Scotland having been deprived of the presence of its kings since the Revolution; and indeed they had seldom visited it since the union of the two crowns under James the First, son of the unfortunate Mary Stuart. The next day king James was proclaimed at Edinburgh, and the Prince named Regent to govern the kingdom, in the absence of his father, at Rome. (Johnstone 11)

Led by Ewan, younger of Cluny, the Macphersons – part of the confederation called Clan Chattan – joined the Jacobite army at Edinburgh (Mackintosh 55).

The Battle of Prestonpans: September 21, 1745

Sir John Cope, the government commander in Scotland, transported an army by ship from Aberdeen to the coast near Edinburgh. The army totaled 2,300 men and included cavalry and artillery.

The Highlanders who marched out to meet General Cope's army were about equal in number but were less well-armed. Some of them had various sorts of firearms such as muskets and fowling pieces but did not have swords, others had both firearms and broadswords, others had only swords, and about fifty of them had only a scythe blade attached to a pitchfork handle. Four regiments – Glengarry, Clanranald, Keppoch and Glencoe – represented Clan Donald. Two priests accompanied the Highlanders: Aeneas Mac-Gillis, the chaplain to the Glengarry clan, and Allan MacDonald of Clanranald; the priests wore the Highland dress and carried a sword and a pistol (MacDonald 88).

General Cope established a strong strategic position near Prestonpans with defensive features including the sea, a marsh, and a boundary wall around the Preston House park. Military historian William Seymour describes the maneuver that penetrated the defenses:

> The Jacobite army, having passed… round the front of the enemy, still had to cross the marsh before reaching suitable ground over which to attack. One of their number, a local man called Robert Anderson, volunteered to show them a track that he knew well from snipe-shooting, and in the early hours of the morning he led the way. The mist swirled up from the bog as the wraith-like army wound its silent way through a defile near Riggonhead Farm and on through the morass. …as day was breaking Anderson had the army safely across the bank that divided the marsh from an open stubble field.
>
> …The royalist infantry now had the unenviable task of facing the full fury of a Highland charge. …as was their wont, having discharged a volley the Highlanders threw away their muskets and relied upon their broadswords, which, wielded with accuracy and vigour, bit deeply into the heads and limbs of the badly shaken redcoats. General Cope and Lords Loudoun, Drummore and Home did their best to rally the terrified royalists… But all was chaos and confusion, and in a white heat of undisciplined passion the Highlanders laid about them, scattering the English army, until eventually the few officers and men who had tried to stem the flood joined the broad stream of fleeing men. (206)

Six Jacobite officers and about forty fighting men died in the battle. The Highlanders killed about three hundred English soldiers, took more than a thousand prisoners, and captured all the English baggage.

Even the Highlanders who carried only homemade weapons "did great execution with their scythes," an officer observed. "They cut the legs of the horses in two; their riders through the middle of their bodies" (Barthorp 12; Seymour 208; Johnstone 16).

General Cope fled to Berwick, inspiring the song "Johnnie Cope:"

> *Chorus:*
> Hey, Johnnie Cope, are ye wauking [waking] yet?
> Or are your drums a-beating yet?
> If ye were wauking I wad wait
> To gang to the coals i' the morning.
>
> Cope sent a challenge frae Dunbar:
> 'Charlie, meet me an' ye daur,
> An' I'll learn you the art o' war
> If you'll meet me i' the morning.'
>
> *Chorus*
>
> When Charlie looked the letter upon
> He drew his sword the scabbard from:
> 'Come, follow me, my merry merry men,
> And we'll meet Johnnie Cope i' the morning.'
>
> *Chorus*
>
> 'Now Johnnie, be as good's your word;
> Come, let us try both fire and sword;
> And dinna rin like a frichted bird,
> That's chased frae its nest i' the morning.'
>
> *Chorus*
>
> When Johnnie Cope he heard of this,
> He thought it wadna be amiss

To hae a horse in readiness,
To flee awa' i' the morning.

Chorus

Fy now, Johnnie, get up an' rin;
The Highland bagpipes mak' a din;
It's best to sleep in a hale skin,
For 'twill be a bluidy morning.

Chorus

When Johnnie Cope tae Dunbar came,
They speired [asked] at him,
'Where's a' your men?'
'The deil confound me gin I ken,
For I left them a' i' the morning.'

Chorus

'Now Johnnie, troth, ye werena blate [shy]
To come wi' news o' your ain defeat,
And leave your men in sic a strait
Sae early in the morning.

Chorus

'I' faith,' quo' Johnnie, 'I got sic flegs [frights]
Wi' their claymores an' philabegs [kilts];
If I face them again, deil break my legs!
Sae I wish you a' gude morning.'

Chorus

Invasion of England

In an echo of Brigadier William Mackintosh's invasion of England in the Rising of 1715, Charles Edward led the Jacobite army toward London. In early November, the Jacobite army of 1745 crossed the Esk – where the Brigadier had stood in the middle of the river and cursed deserters as "reskels of humanity."

William Augustus, the Duke of Cumberland – King George II's third son – took command of the Royal army to oppose the army of Prince Charles. If Cumberland's army triumphed, his father would remain on the throne of Great Britain. If the army of Prince Charles triumphed, the Prince's father would reclaim the throne of his ancestors as King James III of Great Britain.

Rumors reached the Jacobites that many residents evacuated London carrying only their most valuable possessions and that King George II had ordered his yachts readied to carry him away at a moment's notice. "It was at this juncture that King George and his court were said to be as struck with panic as if the wild McGillivrays were in the Strand," writes Edward Cashin ("McGillivray 53). A detachment of the Jacobite army feinted toward Wales, drawing Cumberland's army away from London. The two wings of the Jacobite army rejoined at Derby, 120 miles from London.

In Scotland, meanwhile, government forces regained control of Edinburgh and Inverness. Highland clans loyal to the government formed regiments and independent companies that launched attacks on clans loyal to Prince Charles. Under those circumstances, the clan leaders participating in the invasion of England defied the Prince's wish to proceed toward London and demanded that the Jacobite army return to Scotland. This reversal of fortune threw the Prince into low spirits and caused the troops to lose morale. As the Jacobites retreated from England, the Duke of Cumberland gave a mission to James Oglethorpe, who had named Cumberland Island off the coast of Georgia in the duke's honor.

Oglethorpe leads troops against Jacobites

After returning to England from Georgia, Oglethorpe had married Elizabeth Wright in 1744 and had moved from his family home to her estate in Cranham. He raised a volunteer unit for local defense that was named General Oglethorpe's Royal Foxhunters (Barthorp 28). During the Jacobite Rising of 1745, Oglethorpe found himself at war with relatives of the Highlanders he had recruited to settle Darien in Georgia. Oglethorpe intended to do battle with relatives of the Highlanders he had led into battle at Bloody Marsh. "It was an ironic destiny that linked Oglethorpe's career with the Highland Scots," observes Georgia historian Edward Cashin. "They had been his best allies in Georgia; now they were his enemies... Among the clans that marched to the bagpipes were the Mackintoshes and Clan Chattan. Oglethorpe's friend Aeneas Mackintosh, chief of the clan, was not with them because he was a captain in the first royal Highland regiment" (*McGillivray* 53).

Military historian Larry Ivers explains how Oglethorpe was called upon to resist the Rising of 1745:

> Oglethorpe was commissioned a major general in March 1745. During the fall of that year he was in northern England with a volunteer regiment of horsemen and a few Georgia rangers, the latter having been recruited for duty in Georgia but temporarily diverted to help fight the Scottish rebels.
>
> When the rebels began their retreat toward the Scottish border in early December 1745 Oglethorpe was ordered to lead his horsemen in an encircling movement to cut them off. He pushed his soldiers over one hundred miles of unimproved roads that were covered with ice and snow in less than three days. They apparently arrived in a position from where they could block the rebels' escape; however, that night Oglethorpe withdrew to a distance of five miles and did not begin his movement toward the enemy until about eleven o'clock the following morning. By then Prince Charles and his rebels had escaped. Criticism of his failure to halt the enemy's retreat began almost immediately. He and his horsemen were not allowed to accompany the army as it pursued Prince Charles...
>
> ...Two accusations were being voiced. First, it was suggested that he had not possessed the necessary courage to meet the Scots in battle. Second, it was rumored that he was in sympathy with the Jacobites, some of whom had been his active correspondents. Adding to the suspicion was the fact that the Oglethorpe family had previously exhibited Jacobite leanings. But he certainly did not lack courage, and his principal biographer was convinced that he had no political affiliation with the Jacobites. Oglethorpe's reasons for not setting out in pursuit until eleven o'clock were that his soldiers were exhausted, they had to forage for food, and they were outnumbered four to one. (*British Drums* 200-01)

Edward Cashin adds some details about the attempt to block the retreat of the Jacobite army:

> Oglethorpe, at the head of a regiment that included a company of Georgia rangers and accompanied by the faithful George Dunbar, now his aide-de-camp, was ordered to intercept the invaders at a village called Shap. The light-footed Scots got away. When the Duke of Cumberland learned about it he called out to Oglethorpe, "General Oglethorpe, had you done what I ordered you to do, few of these People would have escaped."
>
> Oglethorpe demanded and received a court-martial. The testimony of Dunbar and others revealed that Oglethorpe had not slept for five nights before he reached Shap, that he was so ill that night that his officers feared for his life, that the duke's orders reached him late, and that weapons had to be put in order as the result of rain and sleet the previous day. Besides, the Scots slipped out at 4:30 in the morning before any attack could have been launched. Oglethorpe was acquitted...
>
> The exoneration and promotion did not improve Oglethorpe's status in the opinion of the Duke of Cumberland. As long as the duke lived, Oglethorpe would never again command British troops. When Oglethorpe offered to raise a regiment in America during the Seven Years' War, he was ignored by Cumberland. (*McGillivray* 53-54)

A history of the MacDonells of Glengarry adds another detail: "An unfortunate incident during the retreat was the capture of the 21 year old Captain John MacKenzie, son of Hilton, of the Grenadier Company of the Glengarry Regiment along with 20 stragglers, by the country people, near Preston, by whom he was handed over to General Oglethorpe" (MacDonald 93).

Two government armies, one under the Duke of Cumberland and another under General George Wade, continued to pursue the fleeing Jacobites. Wade tried to intercept the Jacobites at Wigan, but like Oglethorpe did not succeed. The Highland rear guard – including Cluny Macpherson's regiment and the MacDonells of Glengarry – fought off Cumberland's advance guard at Clifton.

A French officer serving with the Jacobites described the army's return to Scotland:

> We left Carlisle on the 20th of December, at three o'clock in the morning, and arrived on the bank of the river Esk, which separates Scotland from England, about two o'clock in the afternoon. This river, which is usually shallow, had been swelled by an incessant rain of several days, to a depth of four feet. However, we were obliged to cross it immediately, lest a continuation of the rain, during the night, should render the passage altogether impracticable. Our position was become extremely critical. We had not only to encounter all the English troops, but likewise the Hessians and Swiss, with six thousand Dutch, of the garrisons of Dendermonde and Tournay, who had been landed in England.
>
> Nothing could be better arranged than the passage of the river. Our cavalry formed in the river to break the force of the current, about twenty-five paces above that part of the ford where our infantry were to pass; and the Highlanders formed themselves into ranks of ten or twelve a-breast, with their arms locked in such a manner as to support one another against the rapidity of the river, leaving sufficient intervals, between their ranks, for the passage of the water. Cavalry were likewise stationed in the river below the ford, to pick up and save those who might be carried away by the violence of the current. The interval between the cavalry appeared like a paved street through the river, the heads of the Highlanders being generally all that was seen above the water. By means of this contrivance, our army passed the Esk in an hour's time, without losing a single man; and a few girls, determined to share the fortune of their lovers, were the only persons who were carried away by the rapidity of the stream. Fires were kindled to dry our people as soon as they quitted the water; and the bagpipers having commenced playing, the Highlanders began all to dance, expressing the utmost joy on seeing their country again; and forgetting the chagrin which had incessantly devoured them, and which they had continually nourished ever since their departure from Derby.

We entered England on the 8th day of November, and left it on the 20th of December, the birth-day of the Prince, without losing more than forty men, either from sickness or marauding, including the twelve at the affair of Clifton-hall.

...As there is no town nearer than eight or ten miles from the ford of the Esk, we were obliged to march all night, though it had never ceased raining since the affair at Clifton-hall. Highlanders alone could have stood a march of two nights of continual rain in the midst of winter, and drenched as they were in crossing the river, but they were inured to fatigue, and of a strong and vigorous constitution, frequently marching six or seven leagues a-day, our ordinary marches in England, without leaving any stragglers behind... (Johnstone 43-46)

The Duke of Cumberland returned to London at the end of December, assigning General Henry Hawley the task of pursuing the Jacobites into Scotland. Hawley and Wade joined forces at Edinburgh (Barthorp 13).

The Jacobite army, swelling to nine thousand men upon its return to Scotland, laid siege to the government garrison at Stirling Castle in January of 1746.

General Hawley set out from Edinburgh to relieve Stirling. Jacobite General Lord George Murray left a thousand men at Stirling and led most of the Jacobite army to oppose Hawley's advance. The government army and the Jacobite army were destined to do battle at Falkirk (Barthorp 13).

Conflicting loyalties divide Clan Mackintosh

The horns of a dilemma gored Aeneas the 22nd Chief of Clan Mackintosh during the Rising of 1745. Both his clan and his wife's family had a heritage of loyalty to the Stuarts, while he also felt the pull of duty as an officer in the British army. Aeneas had commanded a fort on the colonial American southern frontier and he received another commission when he returned to Scotland. As a witness to treaties with the Creek Indians, he would have observed their strategy of exploiting the rivalry among the colonial powers. Highland clans adopted a similar strategy during the Jacobite Risings. "A favorite tactic was for the clan chiefs to remain at home, officially loyal to the government, while a son brought out the clan for the Stuarts," writes Frank McLynn, PhD. "Another was for a family to send one son to fight with the Hanoverians and another with the Jacobites" (66). Referring to Aeneas Mackintosh by his Gaelic name, McLynn reports "In 1745 Angus, chief of the Mackintoshes, was on the Whig side, in the service of Lord Loudoun, but in his absence his young wife, Anne, raised the clan for Charles Edward" (65-66). "As soon as her husband, a Hanoverian loyalist, departed to raise a company of militia for King George, 'Colonel Anne' raised the Mackintoshes for the prince," McLynn continues. "She then rode at their head in her tartan riding habit, with a clansman's blue bonnet on her head" (155).

Bruce Lenman, a professor of modern history at the University of St. Andrews, describes the situation:

> ...the Mackintoshes made a shamblingly indecisive entry onto the stage of the '45. Aeneas Mackintosh of Mackintosh held a captain's commission from George II... and he was married to a Jacobite spitfire of a wife, Anne, daughter of John Farquharson of Invercauld. Mackintosh during the early stages of the rising seemed on the surface to be pursuing an ambiguous course. However, it is clear in retrospect that his main aim was to hinder the raising of recruits for the Jacobite army by potential rivals for the leadership of the Clan Chattan [a confederation of clans led by the Chief of Clan Mackintosh] and that he was throughout hand-in-glove with Duncan Forbes of Culloden. When, under the influence of the Lord President and MacLeod of MacLeod, he finally made it clear that he would not raise his clan for Prince Charles, his formidable lady raised it herself, making free use of force on reluctant tenants and earning the immortal title of 'Colonel Anne.' (126-27)

Clan Mackintosh and Clan Chattan historian Margaret Mackintosh of Mackintosh places the dilemma facing the Laird and Lady of Mackintosh in the context of military events in the Rising of 1745:

> ... at Derby it was decided in a Council of War to return to Scotland, and the army sadly retraced its steps. A party of

Clan Chattan supporters joined the Prince at Stirling on his return. Cluny Macpherson attempted to enlist other Mackintoshes in Badenoch. However, the Chief of Mackintosh did not join the Prince, but continued to hold his commission under King George II and to command a company of the Black Watch. The Chief's wife, Anne Farquharson of Invercauld, though only twenty years old, took up the Prince's cause, and raised the clan without any hindrance from her husband. In his absence she inspected the clan regiment before it left for Stirling, selecting MacGillivray of Dunmaglas as Colonel. (55)

When Cluny Macpherson attempted to enlist men of Clan Mackintosh in the Jacobite cause, the Chief of Clan Mackintosh insisted on the privileges of rank. The Chief wrote to Cluny:

> Dear Sir, – As I am determined to command my own people and to run the same fate with them, having yesterday received a letter from the Prince, and another from the Duke of Atholl, I hope, notwithstanding the order you got from the Prince, you will not offer to meddle with any of my men, as we are both designed on the same errand. I am resolved to maintain the rank due to my family, and if you think proper to accept the next rank to me you will be very welcome... (qtd. in MacKintosh, "Lady MacKintosh" 45)

Clan Chattan historian Robert McGillivray views the predicament of Aeneas and Anne Mackintosh sympathetically:

> During their first years together, Anne was "amusing herself at Moy Hall"...
> This idyllic period came to an end in July 1745, however, with the arrival in Scotland of Prince Charles Edward Stuart. The previous year Aeneas Mackintosh had raised a Company for the Black Watch and had been commissioned to command it by the Government. His position, like that of many of the Clan chiefs, was a difficult one. He decided to stand aloof from the Jacobites, causing historians to speculate as to his motives.

[In the words of their nephew Sir Aeneas Mackintosh]: "Pitying the prince for his misfortunes which he had not brought upon himself, she resolved to exert all her influence in his behalf. She therefore took steps, soon after the commencement of the Rising, for embodying her husband's clan."

Calling on her close friend Alexander MacGillivray of Dunmaglass, she quickly formed a strong well-armed battalion which she placed under Dunmaglass' command. Perhaps because of this action in choosing a leader from outwith her immediate clan, or perhaps because they chose to follow the example of their Chief, the leading men of Clan Mackintosh were absent. Nonetheless it was a fine force, perhaps 800 strong, and Lady Mackintosh had earned her soubriquet "Colonel Anne."

Subsequent accounts described her in wildly romantic terms as riding at the head of her men, dressed in semi-masculine attire, pistols at her saddle-bow. Sir Walter Scott named her "a gallant Amazon"…

…While General Stewart, an obvious admirer, observed "Of all the ladies who testified their Jacobite tendencies, few were more accomplished, more beautiful, or more enthusiastic than the Lady Mackintosh."

But it had taken time to make her decision and to raise the Clan. It was December before the Mackintosh Regiment was despatched south to join the Prince on his return from the venture into England. It was ready to take its place in the centre of the front line at the Battle of Falkirk on 17 January 1746, fighting with distinction alongside the Clan Macpherson Regiment and next but one to the Farquharsons under James of Balmoral. Colonel Anne's father, having given his pledge to the Government and finding himself unable to persuade his own clansmen to refrain from rising, had left the Highlands and taken up residence in Leith. ("Colonel Anne" 73-74)

The Battle of Falkirk: January 17, 1746

Jacobite forces laid siege to Stirling Castle for two weeks before General Henry Hawley approached in an attempt to relieve the government garrison. Military historian David Smurthwaite tells what happened when the opposing armies came to grips:

Hawley's force of 8000 men advanced toward Stirling on 13 January 1746 and Charles, leaving 1000 Highlanders to screen the Castle, concentrated his army on Plean Muir. For the Jacobites the key position was a ridge of moorland rising steeply to the south-west of Falkirk about a mile from Hawley's camp. The forward slope of this ridge would provide an ideal springboard for a Highland charge, and on 17 January [Jacobite General Lord George] Murray advanced to occupy the ridge south-westwards and crossed the River Carron at Dunipace. Meanwhile a deception force under [Lord John] Drummond marched toward Falkirk on the main road from Bannockburn.

As Murray's Highlanders wound their way up the ridge from the west, Hawley at last realised the seriousness of his position and dispatched his three regiments of dragoons... up the eastern face. Both armies reached the crest in the midst of a rain storm and immediately deployed for battle. The Jacobites formed two lines with the first company, from left to right, the Appin Stewarts, Camerons, Frasers, MacPhersons, Mackintoshes, Farquharsons, and Macdonalds, and the second two battalions of the Atholl Brigade.

...Before his infantry had time to order its ranks, Hawley launched the dragoons... in a charge against the Jacobite right. A shattering volley of musketry delivered when the dragoons were within ten yards of the Highland line brought down eighty horsemen and most of the survivors turned and fled. Careering from the field pursued by the Macdonalds, the dragoons crashed into the Hanoverian left wing and the Glasgow Volunteers, scattering men in every direction. Having already discharged their muskets and being unable to reload because of the lashing rain, the Highland centre drew swords and charged. Equally hampered by damp powder, the Hanoverian centre fired a desultory volley at the approaching clansmen and then ran for their lives. Only on the right, where the infantry were protected from a charge by the ravine, did any regiments hold their position.

Here Ligionier's, Price's, and Barrel's Regiments joined forces and advanced up the hill to enfilade the advancing Highland line. So effective was this fire that the pursuit stopped and the Highland ranks began to waver, with many clansmen leaving the field convinced they had been defeated. The situation was reversed by the arrival of the Irish picquets who obliged the three Hanoverian regiments to follow the rest of their army along the road to Linlithgow.

Night was falling and Murray, with his own regiments dispersed over the countryside, was content to occupy Falkirk and the enemy camp where quantities of arms, provisions and wines quickly found new owners. The Jacobite loss had been small with not more than 50 dead and 80 wounded, but Hanoverian casualties were substantial with perhaps 350 dead and over 300 taken prisoner. The battle had lasted little more than twenty minutes. (205)

Glengarry's son killed

A tragic accident befell the MacDonells of Glengarry a few days after the Battle of Falkirk. Jacobite General Lord George Murray described it in a letter: "Colonel Angus Macdonell, Glengarry's son, who was a modest, brave admirable lad, was mortally wounded by an accidental shott of a miserable fellow of Clanranald's Regiment out of a window upon the street, of which he died this day, vastly regreated; it is more loss to us then all we suffer'd at the Batle" (qtd. in MacDonald 95). Glengarry clansmen dragged the "miserable fellow" to a park outside town and executed him by firing squad that included his own father, who hoped a well-placed bullet would cause instantaneous death.

When Charles learned of the death of Colonel MacDonell, the Prince "showed the most respectful attentions," writes a clan historian, "to console the Clan for their loss. He caused the grave of Sir John Graham, the close comrade of the National Hero, Sir William Wallace, to be opened to receive the young warrior, as the only part of Falkirk churchyard worthy of the honour and himself attended the funeral as chief mourner" (MacDonald 95).

After the English army retreated to Edinburgh, the Jacobites resumed the siege of Stirling without success. At the beginning of February, the Jacobites abandoned the siege and moved into the Highlands to spend the winter.

Meanwhile, the Duke of Cumberland resumed his pursuit of his rival Prince Charles. Cumberland's army moved as far as Perth before being stopped by wintry weather (Barthorp 14).

The Rout of Moy: February 16, 1746

As Prince Charles traveled from Stirling toward Inverness, he stopped along the way at Moy Hall, the seat of Clan Mackintosh. With the Chief of Clan Mackintosh away on service in the government army, Prince Charles could count on being hospitably received by Lady Anne Mackintosh, who had raised her clan in support of the Prince. She provided supper for ten people at the Prince's table, eight aide de camps at another table in the same room, and at least seventy servants in the Prince's household. The master of the Prince's household called the supper "exceedingly genteel and plentiful" (McGillivray, "Colonel Anne" 74).

Meanwhile, twelve miles away in Inverness, government officials learned that Prince Charles was at Moy. At evening, they sent out Lord Loudon with at least fifteen hundred troops on a mission to capture the Prince. Margaret Mackintosh of Mackintosh describes the result in *The History of the Clan Mackintosh and the Clan Chattan:*

> … The Lady Mackintosh sent out Donald Fraser, the Smith at Moy, with four other men to watch the road from Inverness. About midnight, when they became aware of the approach of a body of troops, Fraser posted his men among a number of peat-stacks which might be mistaken in the darkness for groups of men. When Loudon's troops came near, Fraser and his men fired their guns and ran in various directions shouting loudly for the Mackintoshes, Camerons and Macdonalds to advance. The ruse was successful, and the army fell back in alarm to Inverness. At the same time a small boy was smuggled out of Inverness by old Lady Mackintosh, who was Anne Duff, widow of the twentieth Chief, to warn the Prince of Loudon's approach. The boy was secretly carried out on horseback under the cloak of a dragoon, and once outside the town he slipped off the horse to make his way by short-cuts to Moy. He gave the alarm, the Prince was aroused and left Moy Hall to join Lochiel's men, who were preparing to make a stand, when a messen-

ger came to tell them of the Smith's success, which came to be known as the Rout of Moy. The Smith's sword and anvil are still kept at Moy Hall, and so are Prince Charles' bonnet and the bed he slept in.

Lord Loudon, thinking the Jacobite army much larger than it actually was, withdrew his troops immediately from Inverness. Accordingly, Prince Charles took possession of the town as his headquarters, staying for two months in the house of the dowager Lady Mackintosh, in Church Street. (55, 57)

Robert McGillivray, who calls the Rout of Moy "part of Clan lore" describes the commotion when the Prince learned of the approaching enemy:

...In the small hours of the morning of Monday 17th February, the whole household at Moy Hall was awakened; the Prince by one of his guards. James Gib [who served as "Master-Household in the Prince's service] observed the scene: "and in the close he saw the Prince walking with his bonnet above his nightcap, and his shoes down in the heels; and Lady Mackintosh in her smock petticoat running through the close, speaking loudly and expressing her anxiety about the Prince's safety." Lady Mackintosh and her sister issued hurried orders to the servants as they sought to make provision to safeguard the Prince. He was escorted by thirty Highlanders down to the side of Loch Moy for about a mile where they joined up with the Camerons, ready to make a stand if necessary. James Gib said he "went along with the Prince down the side of the loch, and left several covered wagons and other baggage at Moy, about which Lady Mackintosh forbad Mr. Gib to be in the least anxious, for that she would do her best to take care of them. And indeed she was as good as her word: for upon the Prince's return to Moy, Mr. Gib found all his things in great safety, the most of them having been carried off by Lady Mackintosh's orders into a wood, where they would not readily have been discovered, though Lord Loudon and his men had proceeded to Moy."

Alexander Stewart, who was in the kitchen that evening, described what was happening in Moy Hall itself. "My
Lady McIntosh and her sister and me went to the rooms
where he sleept and took all the most valuable things that
were in the roome where he lay and went upe to the garrats
and hide them in fether stands that was almost full of feathers, and my Lady was always calling at me to follow with
the curtains for I would stay till they would take me by the
neck, for by this time the Prince was more than a mile towards the southwest of the loch thorrou a wood."

Welcome news of the rout of the Government troops in
the pass was enough to send a messenger after the Prince,
advising him to return to Moy Hall. He was glad to do so.
He was suffering from exposure to the early morning frost
and contacted a very bad cold from which he was to suffer
for some time. Nonetheless he spent the rest of that day
gathering his army together and the following morning advanced and occupied the town of Inverness from which the
Hanoverians had fled. ("Colonel Anne" 75-76)

Being part of clan lore, the tale of the Rout of Moy has been
told many times, many ways. In an article in *The Celtic Monthly*
published in 1902, Angus MacKintosh tells the tale in a dramatic
style:

[Lady Mackintosh] sent Donald Fraser, a doughty blacksmith, and five other men on whom she could rely to watch
the road between Inverness and Moy. There were Hanoverian troops in Inverness, and also clans who supported the
Hanoverian Government. Lord Loudon was there with
1700 men, eager to distinguish himself, and he was kept
well informed of the Prince's movements by the Grants of
Strathspey and others. On the very day on which the Prince
arrived at Moy, Loudon heard that he was there, and
promptly made arrangements for a surprise.

Having placed sentinels round the town to prevent
any Jacobites from giving the alarm, he waited until nightfall, and then went forth with 1500 men. The night was
dark, with frequent flashes of lightning. MacLeod of Mac-
Leod was amongst those in front, with his trusty piper

MacCrimmon (who played when they were leaving Dunvegan the prophetic Lament that shall ever be associated
with his name "Cha till mi tullidh") by his side.

When they reached Faillie Bridge, the blacksmith and
his men who were watching, fell back unobserved, and stationed themselves among some peat stacks beside the road
near the Pass of Crag-nan-eoin. Silently the 1500 marched
on, never doubting but success would crown their lordly
leader's plan, until out of the darkness flashed tongues of
flame, and a few of them fell, amongst whom was Mac-
Crimmon. Then the war-cries of Lochiel, MacKintosh,
Keppoch, and other Jacobite clans rang in their ears. Thinking that the Prince's whole army was in front of them they
wheeled round and in great confusion fled. Their opponents, however, were only the blacksmith and his little
band, who, when they had fired their muskets, separated
and ran hither and thither shouting the war-cries of the
clans, and giving orders as if they were leading men to battle.

Meanwhile a messenger from Inverness reached Moy
with the intelligence that Loudon was on his way to take
the Prince by surprise. Accounts differ as to who the messenger was. Once is that the Dowager Lady MacKintosh,
who resided in Inverness at the time, sent a youth named
Lachlan MacKintosh, who knew the short byways from Inverness to Moy, with the message; another is that the bearer
of the alarm was a young girl from Moy, serving in a tavern
in Inverness, who overheard some of Loudon's officers
talking about the intended surprise over their cups, who
succeeded in eluding the sentinels and with all speed made
her way to Moy: and that when she told Lady MacKintosh
her story she fell down dead from over-exertion. The incident, according to the latter version, has been put into excellent verse by Miss Alice MacDonell, the gifted bardess
of Keppoch. The commotion into which Moy was thrown
by this intelligence did not last long, for the blacksmith arrived shortly after with an account of the rout.

On the 18th February the Prince, whose men had then
arrived at Moy, marched to Inverness, but only to find that

Loudon had retired into Ross-shire. ("Lady MacKintosh"
46-47)

Sir Fitzroy Maclean of Dunconnel, author of the splendidly illustrated *Highlanders: A History of the Scottish Clans*, elaborates
on the fate of the ill-starred piper:

> Almost the only casualty in the Rout of Moy, as it came to
> be called, was MacLeod of MacLeod's personal piper,
> Donald Ban MacCrimmon, of the famous family of pipers
> from Skye, whose Chief had sent him against his will to
> serve against Prince Charles and who, having the second
> sight and foreseeing his own death in a cause which he ab-
> horred, composed for the occasion the haunting lament *Cha
> till, Cha till, Cha till MacCraimein,* MacCrimmon will not
> return. (213)

The tale about the girl who ran to warn the Prince originated
in the memoirs of the Chevalier de Johnstone, translated from a
French manuscript:

> Whilst some English officers were drinking in the house of
> Mrs. Bailly, an innkeeper in Inverness, and passing the time
> till the hour of their departure, her daughter, a girl of thir-
> teen or fourteen years of age, who happened to wait on
> them, paid great attention to their conversation, and, from
> certain expressions dropped by them, she discovered their
> designs. As soon as this generous girl was certain as to their
> intentions, she immediately left the house, escaped from the
> town, notwithstanding the vigilance of the centinels, and
> immediately took the road to Moy, running as fast as she
> was able, without shoes or stockings, which to accelerate
> her progress, she had taken off, in order to inform the
> Prince of the danger that menaced him.
>   She reached Moy, quite out of breath, before Lord
> Loudon; and the Prince, with difficulty, escaped in his robe
> de chamber, night-cap, and slippers, to the neighbouring
> mountains, where he passed the night in concealment.
>   This dear girl, to whom the Prince owed his life, was
> in great danger of losing her own, from her excessive fa-

tigue on this occasion; but the care and attentions she experienced restored her to life, and her health was at length reestablished. (66)

Mackintosh versus Mackintosh

Even after Lord Loudon's forces withdrew northward they continued to harass the Jacobite army under Prince Charles at Inverness. Meanwhile, the Duke of Cumberland had advanced to Aberdeen, so that the Jacobite army was threatened by government armies in two directions. Prince Charles sent a detachment to pursue Lord Loudon's Regiment of Foot, in which Aeneas the 22nd Chief of Clan Mackintosh served as a captain. The Jacobite detachment pursuing Lord Loudon included the Mackintosh regiment, according to the clan historian. Other clans participating in the expedition included Glengarry, Clanranald, Stewart of Appin, the Frasers, MacGregors, MacKinnons and MacKenzies.

Loudon retreated as far north as Sutherland, and eluded the pursuers by crossing and recrossing the Dornoch Firth. He had commandeered all the boats, and the Jacobites had to march around the firth. The Jacobites collected boats at Findhorn and took them northward past British warships in a heavy fog. On March 20, about a thousand Jacobites commanded by the Duke of Perth landed in Sutherland in pursuit of two thousand government troops. The Jacobites marched on Dornoch, where Loudon had set up headquarters (Mackintosh 57; MacDonald 96).

The stage was set for a civil war not only among the Mackintosh clan but also among other Highlanders who served in Loudon's Regiment and their fellow clansmen in the Jacobite army. Donald of Scotus, a MacDonell clansman, was usually cheerful but as his detachment prepared to attack Lord Loudon he had tears in his eyes. "A son whom I adore is an officer in his regiment," Donald told a friend. "I thought myself fortunate in being able to procure such a situation for his youth, being unable to anticipate the landing of the Prince in Scotland. Perhaps tomorrow I may be so unfortunate as to kill my son with my own hand; and thus the same ball which I fire in my defense may give to myself the most cruel death. However, in going with the detachment I may be able to save him; and if I do not go he may fall by the hands of another" (Johnstone 73-74).

The Jacobite forces captured Loudon's headquarters at Dornoch on March 30, taking three hundred prisoners. Lord Loudon withdrew to the Isle of Skye and the Jacobites returned to Inverness (Barthorp 14; MacDonald 96).

Aeneas the 22nd Chief of Clan Mackintosh was among several Highlanders in Lord Loudon's regiment who avoided battle against their kinsmen by surrendering, according to Donald MacDonnell of Lochgarry:

> The laird of McIntosh, capt. in Loudon's regiment, and Major McKenzie of the same, with several other officers (including Ranald MacDonnell, son of Donald of Scotus whom his own father had the good fortune to take prisoner) came and surrendered themselves prisoners, with all the men under their command ... Capt. Stack of Laly's regiment and I received the arms of the whole prisoners. (qtd. in MacDonald 96)

Aeneas Mackintosh's surrender give rise to a legendary belief that "Colonel Anne" Mackintosh led the soldiers who "captured the Hanoverian captain who happened to be her husband" (Lenman 127). Ranald MacDonnell's surrender gave rise to a scene recorded in the memoirs of the Chevalier de Johnstone:

> ...I heard a loud knocking at my door; and running to it, I perceived this good father [Donald of Scotus], holding a handsome young man by the hand. He instantly called out, with eyes sparkling with joy, "Here, my friend, here is he, who caused me yesterday so much anxiety. I took him prisoner myself, and, having secured him, I troubled myself very little about taking others." He then shed tears of joy; very different from the tears of the preceding evening. We supped all three together in my apartment, and I scarcely ever enjoyed more satisfaction than in witnessing this tender scene between the father and son. (74)

After Aeneas the 22nd Chief of Clan Mackintosh was taken prisoner, a Clan Chattan historian writes:

The Prince released him into the care of his wife, saying he could not be more secure or more honourably treated. Chambers, incorrectly describes Anne as "then acting a semi-military part in the chevalier's army", and goes on to tell how when she encountered her husband: "She said, with military laconism: 'Your servant, Captain!' to which he replied, with equal brevity, 'Your servant, Colonel!'" A nice little anecdote, whether true or not. (McGillivray, "Colonel Anne" 76)

Another keeper of clan lore, Angus MacKintosh, states that Aeneas Mackintosh was held prisoner in Inverness although "the Prince is said to have jocularly remarked that he had better make MacKintosh's wife his custodian" ("Lady MacKintosh" 47) .

The Battle of Culloden: April 16, 1746

At Aberdeen, the Duke of Cumberland spent February and March drilling his troops in tactics designed to counter the Highland charge. The infantrymen were trained to engage the enemy soldier to their right rather than the enemy directly ahead. The Highlanders, with their sword in one hand and their shield, called a target, in the other hand could not defend themselves against a bayonet attack from the side (Harrington 44).

In April, when the roads were free of snow and the River Spey was low enough to ford, Cumberland moved toward Inverness. Prince Charles led his army out of Inverness to make a stand near Culloden House. When Cumberland reached Nairn, the Jacobites decided to launch a surprise attack. After the Highlanders marched all night to reach Nairn, the attack was called off and they marched back to Culloden. Because their supplies had been left in Inverness, they had nothing to eat. Starved of both sleep and food, some of them lay down on the ground and some went foraging. When Jacobite officers told Prince Charles that the men were not fit for battle, he observed that they were too fatigued to conduct an orderly retreat.

Cumberland's troops, meanwhile, had slept through the night. Early in the morning, they ate breakfast, sipped brandy, and marched toward Culloden. Heavy showers were falling when the opposing armies – about eight thousand government troops against about five thousand Jacobites – came within sight of one another across two miles of open moor. For the first time in the Rising, the armies exchanged artillery fire. The Jacobite artillery nearly knocked the Duke of Cumberland off his big gray horse, while the government artillery aimed at Prince Charles, killing his groom and some cavalrymen. Many of the Jacobite artillerymen fled when the government artillery opened fire, and within a few minutes all but one of the Jacobite guns had ceased firing. The English guns, however, roared on. Gunpowder blew in the faces of the Highlanders as shot plowed through their ranks. Without an order to launch their famous Highland Charge, the clansmen huddled in ranks and endured the English cannonade for nearly half an hour. Hundreds of them fell dead or wounded, others lay on the ground to avoid the artillery shells, and some ran away seeking safety (Harrington 52-60).

Military historian Peter Harrington describes the battle in *Culloden 1746: The Highland Clans' Last Charge:*

> Shortly before 1:30 p.m., with a squall of hail and rain lashing the clansmen, the order to charge was given. Lord George Murray, who described the regiments in the front rank as 'so impatient that they were like to break their ranks', had been approached by several clan leaders anxious for a decision and fearful that they would be unable to hold their men much longer amidst the terrible slaughter. The restive Mackintoshes urged their leader, Lochiel, to persuade Murray to order the charge. Murray sent Kerr of Graden to the Prince who consented to the attack. By now the Jacobite line was skewed, the right wing being well in advance of the left, so Kerr directed the Duke of Perth on the left to move to the attack. Laclan MacLachan, one of Charles's aides-de-camp, was sent to Murray, who was with the Athollmen on the right, to order the attack, but was killed by round shot before he got to the front. Further delay ensued, while more and more casualties were sustained. Charles then sent Sir John Macdonald to the left and Brigadier Stapleton to the right with orders for the line to advance. The order was received, but the Macdonalds refused and were urged on only a few paces level with the other regiments in the front line.

In rage and despair the Mackintoshes of the Clan Chattan in the centre 'scrugged' their bonnets over their heads, broke the ragged line and darted forward through the wet heather, spurred-on by the pipes and by their commander, the yellow-haired Colonel MacGillivray. Grape-shot continued to pepper the oncoming clansmen. At their heels came the men of Atholl and the Camerons who had been positioned on the right of the Clan Chattan, but the direction of their charge changed suddenly towards the left to avoid some walls and toward the firmer ground of an old moor road. At the same time, the Mackintoshes veered right to avoid the boggy ground between the two armies, and possibly forced by the heavy musketry which opened up from the centre of the Royal ranks. Confused and blinded by smoke, many were lost in the mêlée, or fell to the brisk firing from the Royal centre. Survivors later stated that they were caught in thick smoke and became disoriented. The Clan Chattan lost eighteen officers and hundreds of men before getting within twenty yards of the Royal lines. Similarly, the Athollmen were cut down before they had a chance to engage. They had run broadsides to Wolfe's men lining the wall who decimated them with accurate musket fire. The walls on each flank had a funneling effect, forcing the charging clansmen into an area little more than 300 yards wide. Undeterred, the dense mass now crammed into this narrow corridor against the park wall and the Leanach dike, and moved towards the left of the Duke's army to engage the men of Barrell's, Munro's and Wolfe's Regiments. In the few seconds it took to cover the distance, many of the Highlanders, unable to fire their customary volley because of the congestion, discarded their primed muskets and pistols and resorted to the broadsword, scythe blades or axes. For a moment the Prince's soldiers were shrouded in cannon smoke, but as it lifted they saw an orderly line of Redcoats, 30 yards away, who leveled their muskets and fired an accurate and deadly volley; a distinctive counterpoint to the monotonous pounding of [English artillery commander Brevet-Colonel William] Belford's guns which continued to fire. The troops in the front ranks knelt to fire while two other ranks stood behind with mus-

kets raised to shoulder, providing continuous firing as one
line after another reloaded. The enfilade fire from Wolfe's
men in front of the Leanach dike was now beginning to
take effect, but the shouting Highlanders came on pell-mell
towards the left.

...Towards the centre and left, the Highlanders were
faring little better. The advance of the Clan Chattan and
others on the right had inspired others to follow. The
MacLeans and MacLachlans charged, but – the rebel lines
being skewed – they had further open ground to cover and
none reached the Royal lines; the musket fire from the
Royals and Pulteney's was so deadly that no living thing
could survive. Of the 200 MacLeans, whose boast it was
that they never gave ground, 150 were killed. Keppoch and
Macdonnell of Scothouse [Donald of Scotus] died in the
thick of the action, the latter only twenty paces from the
enemy. The dead ground between the two armies was lit-
tered with dead and dying clansmen. Less enthusiastic were
the Farquharsons and the Macdonalds. Since early morning
the Macdonalds of the Glengarry Regiment had been complaining about their placement on the extreme left of the
Jacobite line, and the Duke of Perth had tried to placate
them. When the Regiment saw the Highlanders' charge on
the right and centre they advanced a few paces and began
to run towards the Royal lines, firing pistols and waving
their swords in the vain hope of tempting the Royal troops
to attack. Some fell into knee-deep water and could advance no further because of the swampy ground. They were
swept back by musket fire, it being said by Cumberland
that his infantry 'hardly took their firelocks from their
shoulders' and, seeing activity amongst the Royal cavalry
suggesting a flanking movement, started to retrace their
steps, just as other clans in the rear began to flee the field.
Some officers charged with Keppoch, but many including
the leader were felled by musket balls. A number of the
Macdonalds were brought off by picquets before they could
be surrounded by Kingston's Horse. The guns of the Royal
artillery continued to fire relentlessly and stragglers were
still being killed by grape-shot. To add to the slaughter
Cobham's 60 troopers and Kingston's Horse moved off

from the Royal lines and rode in amongst the fugitives, hacking at them without mercy. The Jacobite lines were in complete disarray, with gaps left by the fleeing clansmen. The battle had been raging for less than half-an-hour, but the left and centre of the army no longer existed. (Harrington 60-68)

Realizing that the cause was lost, Prince Charles was escorted from the field by remnants of two Highland regiments. The English artillery ceased firing for the first time in an hour. Government troops crossed the field and bayoneted wounded Jacobites. Saber-wielding cavalrymen pursued fleeing Highlanders, hacking to death any clansmen who stood their ground. The cavalrymen also killed noncombatants, including two men plowing a field. Some of the fleeing Highlanders were killed by fellow Highlanders, Campbell clansmen of the Argyll Militia in the government army.

The government reported casualties of fifty killed and 259 wounded. An estimated two thousand clansmen died – including Alexander MacGillivray of Dunmaglass, the commander of the Mackintosh regiment – and 558 Jacobites were taken prisoner (Harrington 78-83; McGillivray, "Colonel Anne" 76).

Margaret Mackintosh of Mackintosh describes the battle from the perspective of her clan:

> The Jacobite leaders, thinking that the Duke of Cumberland would celebrate his birthday, decided on a night attack while the Duke's men would be sleeping off the effects of the festivity. The Jacobites had about ten miles to travel, and as they started at eight o'clock in the evening they should have been there by midnight. However, they had not come up with the enemy by two o'clock in the morning, and all hope of a surprise attack was abandoned. The weary and half-famished Highlanders were led back to the fatal moor of Culloden, which they reached about five o'clock in the morning. News came that the enemy was advancing, and the Jacobite army was at once drawn up in battle array. They were nearly starving, and the only food they obtained was one biscuit per man. Some others had gone into Inverness to find food for themselves. The enemy consisted of

eight thousand fresh, well-fed troops, supported by plenty of cavalry and cannon.

The battle began at one o'clock on the 16th April. The Camerons were placed on the right, with the Mackintoshes in the centre and the Macdonalds on the left. Charles had unfortunately selected for their battlefield the open moor where Cumberland's horse could make good use of the ground. Another blunder was that Charles kept his little force waiting to be attacked. For some time they stood firm and were raked by a terrible cannon fire, while to add to their misery a snowstorm beat mercilessly on their faces. The Mackintosh regiment, unable to refrain, broke from the front line and charged, to be followed by the rest of the line.

What followed was a foregone conclusion. The Highlanders rushed ahead in a last despairing charge; regardless of their hunger, regardless of their frozen limbs, driven to a frenzy by their misery and inspired by their hatred of their English foes, the little band swept forward to its doom. Not once did it falter though three lines of steady muskets, and cannon loaded with grape-shot made cruel gaps in its ranks. Forward it rushed. It reached its goal, broke through the first line of English, whom it swept aside like chaff; almost reached the second line, and then it melted, literally mown down. All that loyalty, all that heroism could do was done that day, and done in vain. Unsupported by the rest of the army the first forlorn hope could do no more. The Mackintosh regiment which led the fatal charge suffered the most severely, and more Mackintoshes were killed than any other clan. Out of seventeen officers only eight were surviving. The day after the battle the Highlanders were found lying in heaps three to four deep, so eager were those behind to reach their foes. ...so numerous were the Mackintosh casualties that their massed graves are commemorated by three grave-stones. (59-61)

Angus MacKintosh hints at legends arising from "feats of prowess and valour" performed by his clansmen during the battle:

But the dark day of Culloden with its sad tale of mismanagement, hunger, jealousy, pride and disaster drew near. In
the futile night march to Nairn the MacKintoshes were in
the front and on the moor the next day they were the first to
close with the foe. Galled with the enemy's fire they rushed
forward before the order was given, and bravely they acquitted themselves. Out of 22 officers and 700 men, they
left 19 officers and 400 men dead on the field. To tell of the
feats of prowess and valour performed by many of them in
that wild charge – from Gillies MacBean defending the
breach in the wall, to Donald MacKintosh saving the ban-
ner, when all else was lost – would take too much space.
("Lady MacKintosh" 47)

Military historians Brigadier Peter Young and Professor John
Adair describe horrid hand-to-hand combat:

...Barrel's regiment was borne backwards by the sheer
weight of the mass of charging men. Captain Lord Robert
Kerr received a Cameron on his spontoon, as his men gave
way, and was cut down by Major Gillies MacBean of the
Mackintosh regiment, his head 'cleft from crown to collar-
bone'. Lt.-Colonel Robert Rich of Barrel's was terribly
wounded, six cuts in the head, his left hand lopped off, and
his right arm nearly severed above the elbow. Ensign
Brown was wounded defending a colour. But Barrel's
fought back like heroes. Michael Hughes, a volunteer in
Bligh's regiment, could see the officers, 'some cutting with
their swords, others pushing with their spontoons, the sergeants running their halberts into the throats of the enemy,
while the soldiers mutually defended each other... ram-
ming their bayonets up to the socket.' (267)

Donald J. Macdonald of Castleton emphasizes the role of Clan
Donald in the Battle of Culloden:

The Clan Chattan were the first to charge, followed by the
Frasers and the Appin Stewarts, and then by the whole right
wing. Contrary to their orders, most of them threw away
their muskets and flung themselves upon the enemy with

their swords and dirks, advancing in a headlong rush against the disciplined fire of line after line of seasoned troops. The Camerons and Stewarts penetrated as far as the second line before they were forced back with heavy casualties, and the whole of the right, now suffering the full weight of the Campbell flanking assault, was soon in retreat. Meantime on the left wing the Macdonalds of Glengarry and Clanranald, with Keppoch in their centre, had been suffering the enemy fire without flinching while they awaited his attack. They realized that the distance between them and Cumberland's right destroyed all possibility of success for their own characteristic method of attack, and hoped that by withholding their fire they would provoke the enemy to advance.

The evidence of officers in Cumberland's army suggest that the Macdonalds made three taunting moves forward with the object of drawing their attack which, of course, did not take place because Cumberland was quite content with the results being achieved with his artillery. They continued to hesitate after the clans on their right had launched their charge, and it was at this point that Alexander of Keppoch advanced alone to face the enemy, exclaiming in frustration "Mo Dhia, an do threig clan mo chinnidh mi?" (My God, have the children of my clan forsaken me?). Rushing forward with pistol and drawn sword, he was almost at once hit by a musket ball which shattered his right arm. Now followed by his clansmen, he continued to advance, but was shot again in the chest, and fell never to rise again. His last words were an exhortation addressed to his kinsman Donald Roy Macdonald, who was close behind him as he fell: "God have mercy on me, Donald. Do the best for yourself, for I am gone." He was later carried by Angus Ban, his natural son, to a hut off the field in which other wounded and dying had sought refuge. But he was dead before they reached it – as it happened, fortunately for him because it saved him from the slow agony suffered by the other poor victims who perished in its flames on the orders of Cumberland.

The Macdonald regiments suffered heavily. Many of the officers followed Keppoch's example and charged headlong at the enemy. Young Clanranald escaped with a head wound, but among the many killed were Keppoch's own brother Donald, and old Donald of Scotus. They had reached within a few paces of the enemy when the right wing crumbled, leaving the Macdonalds without support, and the flanking movement of Kingston's Horse on their left finally forced them into retreat and a merciless pursuit along the road to Inverness. Only by the exertions of the Irish picquets of Lally's and Dillon's French regiments, who gallantly covered their retreat, were the Macdonalds saved from a much heavier toll being exacted by the blood-thirsty victors. (391-93)

The memoirs of Jacobite officer the Chevalier de Johnstone give gruesome details of the burning of the barn where wounded soldiers huddled:

> ...the road from Culloden... was every where strewed with dead bodies. The Duke of Cumberland... ordered a barn, which contained many of the wounded Highlanders, to be set on fire; and, having stationed soldiers round it, they with fixed bayonets drove back the unfortunate men who attempted to save themselves into the flames, burning them alive in this horrible manner, as if they had not been fellow-creatures. (85)

According to Culloden lore, Clan Donald refused to fight after being denied a position of honor on the right side of the line. (Seymour 218, 222). Norman H. MacDonald dispels the claim:

> Maxwell of Kirkconnel's account shows the Glengarry Regiment on the extreme left of the front line with the Duke of Perth. Next to them were Keppoch's and Clanranald's. There is no contemporary authority whatsoever for the allegation that the Clan Donald refused to fight and no such charge appeared in print until over seventy years after the battle.
> The distance between the two armies was between 400 and 500 yards of broken and marshy ground. The ground in front of the Jacobite left wing where the Clan Donald regi-

ments were placed, was the most marshy of all. The Jacobite right flank was protected by a stone dyke, but the left
flank had no protection at all and Cumberland, observing
this, sent Kingston's Horse and a squadron of Cobham's to
threaten it. The Jacobite left wing was therefore dangerously exposed and they were further from the enemy than the
rest of the line.

The Jacobite centre, galled by the enemy fire charged
before the order was given and were followed by the right
wing. The heavy fire and the marshy nature of the ground
caused those in the centre to deflect to the right leaving a
gap between the centre and the left wing. In spite of this
and the heavy fire of grape-shot they advanced in good order, and Cumberland, on his own right observed them come
down "three several times within 100 yards of our men, firing their pistols and brandishing their swords, but the Royals and Pultney's hardly took their firelocks from their
shoulders, so that after these faint attempts they moved off,
and the little squadrons on our right were sent to pursue
them."

...The writer of the anonymous tract published in Andrew Lang's *Highlands of Scotland in 1750* says that Donald of Scotus: "Carried 50 Men to the Battle of Culloden
and was Reckoned the most Valiant man of all the McDonalds, together with his Lieutenant, Ensign, Sergeant and
Corporal and 18 Private men were all Killed upon the
Spot."

When the Jacobite line gave way Scotus was carried
off the field by two of his men but observing their pursuers
coming too close, he requested the men to leave him, as his
wound was mortal, and save themselves. The agreed to do
so after receiving from him his watch, purse etc. and, according to family tradition a silver snuff box presented to
him that very day by the Prince, to take home to his wife.
He then asked them to turn his face to the enemy, that they
might not think he was running away. After retreating some
distance the men looked back and saw the dragoons dispatch him.

Glengarry's brother, William, was also killed in the
battle, as were Keppoch and his brother Donald. Lochgar-

ry's brother, Major Angus MacDonell of Greenfield, was
wounded. (98-99)

The Chevalier Johnstone, a French officer serving in the Jacobite army, mourned the death of his friend Donald of Scotus:

> ...the English... fired with grape-shot on our right wing.
> Their fire, from the circumstance of their being quite close
> to the right, was so terrible, that it literally swept away, at
> once, whole ranks. From the inequality of this marshy
> ground, our right and centre came first up with the enemy,
> our first line advancing a little obliquely; but, over-powered
> by a murderous fire in front and flank, our right could not
> maintain its ground, and was obliged to give way, whilst
> our centre had already broken the enemy's first line, and at-
> tacked the second.
>
> The left wing, where I was with Scothouse, was not
> twenty paces from the enemy, who gave their first fire at
> the moment the flight began to become general, which
> spread from the right to the left of our army with the rapidi-
> ty of lightning. What a spectacle of horror! The same High-
> landers, who had advanced to the charge like lions, with
> bold determined countenances, were, in an instant, seen fly-
> ing like trembling cowards, in the greatest disorder...
>
> ...My unfortunate friend Scothouse was killed by my
> side; I was not so deeply affected at the moment of his fall,
> as I have been ever since. It would almost seem as if the
> Power that presides over the lives of men in battles, marks
> out the most deserving for destruction, and spares those
> who are more unworthy...
>
> As the Highlanders were completely exhausted with
> hunger, fatigue, and the want of sleep, our defeat did not at
> all surprise me; I was only astonished to see them behave
> so well. (82-84)

The Dowager Lady Mackintosh jailed

Cumberland's army occupied Inverness in the afternoon after
the Battle of Culloden. The victors, after releasing Argyll militiamen and other loyalist captives from prison in Inverness, promptly
placed captured Jacobite soldiers in the prison. In what must have

been more than coincidence, the Duke of Cumberland – the third son of King George II – set up headquarters at Inverness in the same house that Charles – the son of the would-be King James III – had used as his quarters. Margaret Mackintosh of Mackintosh writes:

> …Cumberland pursued his victorious march to Inverness, which he entered without opposition. There he stayed in the house of the Dowager Lady Mackintosh, in the very room and the same bed which Prince Charles had so lately occupied. The old lady, speaking afterwards of those events, was wont to remark: 'I've had two King's bairns living with me in my time, and to tell you the truth I wish I may never have another.' She was confined for fourteen days in the common guard as were also several other ladies attached to the Jacobite cause. (62-63)

Prince Charles seeks refuge

After he was led away from the battlefield at Culloden, Prince Charles sought refuge in the bens and glens of Clan Donald country. A history of the MacDonells of Glengarry reports:

> In his retreat the Prince crossed the River Nairn with a few companions and riding past Fort Augustus halted at Gortuleg house. After supper he and his companions left for Glengarry where they arrived about 2 a.m. on April 17th at the house of MacDonell of Drynachan on the west side of Loch Oich. After resting there they proceeded to Invergarry Castle which they found deserted and "without meat, drink, fire and candle, except some firesticks!" Fortunately, their guide, Ned Burke spotted a fishing net and "catched two salmons", which provided an agreeable breakfast. The Prince and his companions spent the rest of the day at Invergarry Castle resting and in the evening rode on by Loch Arkaig to the house of Cameron of Glenpean where they spent the night. (MacDonald 99)

Lady Anne Mackintosh imprisoned

The victorious government forces soon systematically persecuted the Jacobite clans. It wasn't long before government troops

made the short trip from Inverness to the Mackintosh clan seat at
Moy. Angus MacKintosh describes the scene:

> ...On the 17th of April a detachment of Col. Cockayne's
> regiment was sent to Moy to bring in all the cattle they
> could find there, and another detachment of the same regi-
> ment was sent the same day to take Lady MacKintosh to
> Inverness. Some of the men, who seem to have reached
> Moy Hall in advance of the main body, behaved brutally. In
> her zeal for the Prince's cause Lady MacKintosh sent every
> man about the place who could wield a sword to Culloden,
> and those who survived of them were scattered on the
> mountains. There only remained a few women and one or
> two infirm old men. The soldiers at first took her for a girl,
> and inquired for "the ------ rebel Lady MacKintosh."
> Mr. Lesley, the minister of Moy, who saw the men ap-
> proaching Moy Hall, hastened thither, thinking he would be
> able to prevent them from committing acts of rudeness, but
> they heeded him not. He took out his watch and one of the
> men snatched it from him. Seeing this Lady MacKintosh
> offered the man a guinea to return the watch. He took the
> coin and then snatched the purse, which contained fifty
> guineas, all the money she had, from her. Another soldier
> insisted that she had more money, and struck her with his
> bayonet. It was then that another of the soldiers recognised
> her as the young lady who in Perth years before saved him
> from a flogging. He immediately showed his gratitude by
> seizing her cowardly assailant, and threatening his life if he
> did not desist. On the main body coming up another recog-
> nition took place. Sir Everard Falconer, Cumberland's sec-
> retary, found the "Amazonian Colonel Anne" they were
> sent to make prisoner, was in reality the slim, beautiful, and
> accomplished Miss Farquharson whom he once knew and
> greatly admired, slim and beautiful as in her maiden days.
> He wanted to apprehend the brutal soldiers, but she begged
> him to do nothing further in the matter.
> She was then mounted on the only horse left at Moy
> and taken to Inverness. Great was the curiosity of the Eng-
> lish soldiers to see the lady of whom such extraordinary ta-
> les, which they believed, were told. When near Cumber-

land's camp, the old war-horse she rode pricked up his ears, and much against her will carried her to where the drummers were beating their drums. "O!" said they, "that is the horse on which she charged at the head of her men at Falkirk and Culloden."

She was kept in custody at Inverness for six weeks, and this is how the arch-coward Hawley expressed his wishes concerning her at the Duke of Cumberland's table: "D--- that rebel Lady Mackintosh, I shall honour her with a mahogany gallows and a silken cord," language well befitting the craven of Falkirk, and not out of place at the table of the Butcher. ("Lady MacKintosh" 47-48)

Another clan historian, Robert McGillivray, picks up the thread of the tale:

Colonel Anne was placed in custody by order of the Duke of Cumberland and kept under guard in her own room. She seems to have been reasonably well treated herself, but was extremely concerned for the well-being of fellow prisoners, who were kept in appalling conditions. While there she heard that enemies of her husband, also on the Government side, had gone to Moy. She was able to alert him to the danger and he arrived with his men in time to protect the house. "Colonel Anne" 77)

Margaret Mackintosh of Mackintosh continues the narrative:

In consequence of a Government order to deprive the Jacobites of their arms, a party was sent to Strathdearn to seize all the weapons. Grant of Dalrachny went to Moy and took the famous swords, which were heirlooms, to wit, the swords of Charles I and of Dundee, and two dating from the battle of the North Inch, 1396. Mackintosh [the 22nd Chief of Clan Mackintosh] at once got Lord Loudon to ask the Duke to have them restored. This was granted, but Mackintosh got word that his family papers were being destroyed. He hastened to Moy, where he found the Grants had seized many Charters and documents which he had placed for safety in the Castle on the island. The Grants were already burning the precious papers, but Mackintosh had a force of two hundred men and dispersed the evil-doers and saved most of his valuable records. (63-64)

After six weeks of imprisonment, Lady Mackintosh was released into the custody of her husband (McGillivray, "Colonel Anne" 77).

Prince Charles eludes pursuit

"The months," writes Theo Aronson in *Kings over the Water: The Saga of the Stuart Pretenders*, "that Prince Charles spent in Scotland as a hunted fugitive are generally regarded as the most praiseworthy of his life. This has become his finest hour. Sometimes alone, sometimes with a handful of companions, he survived a series of extraordinary adventures. He endured hardships, ran incredible risks, affected disguises, achieved hair's-breadth escapes, commanded touching loyalty and revealed a daring and a vigour and an optimism that was to become legendary. Although he had a price of £30,000 on his head, he was never once betrayed. The story of that great adventure is as much a testimony to the loyalty of the Scottish people as to Charles's heroism" (158).

Hoping to rendezvous with a French ship on the west coast, Charles arrived at Arisaig where he had landed in Scotland nine months previously. Sir Fitzroy Maclean of Dunconnel tells what happened next:

> ...at Borrodale in Arisaig he [Charles] encountered Donald MacLeod, an old seaman from Skye with Jacobite sympathies... Donald offered to carry him in an eight-oared boat to the Outer Islands... ...after a stormy crossing, Charles and his companions landed at dawn on Sunday 27 April at Rossinish on Benbecula, just across the island from Nunton, the house of the older MacDonald of Clanranald, whose son had fought for him throughout the Rising.
>
> After consulting old Clanranald and his half-brother MacDonald of Boisdale, the Prince and his companions now left Benbecula for Stornoway in Donald's boat under the guise of shipwrecked merchants in search of a sizeable vessel with which to carry on their trade. Next day they were driven ashore on the Island of Scalpay, off Harris,

where they were hospitably entertained by Donald Campbell, the tenant of Scalpay. Meanwhile from Benbecula the
Rev. John Macaulay, who had happened to be dining with
Clanranald when news of the Prince's arrival was brought
to him, had sent an urgent message to his father, the Rev.
Aulay Mac-aulay, Minister of Tarbert in Harris, urging him
to have the Prince seized on his arrival there. But when the
Rev. Aulay made his appearance with a boat-load of parishioners keen to seize the Prince and claim the reward of
£30,000 offered for his capture, they were chased away by
Donald Campbell who, although a Whig and a Campbell,
put the laws of hospitality before mere political expediency. In the end, after an arduous journey by land and sea, the
Prince reached Stornoway, only to learn from old Donald
MacLeod, who had gone on ahead in search of a larger vessel, that his attempts to hire a ship had been unsuccessful
and that a company of the local Mackenzie militia were by
now already on the look out for him.

There was clearly no time to be lost and so, piling back
into old Donald's little boat, they headed south again for
Benbecula. After a hair-raising journey and a narrow escape from enemy warships, they eventually landed on a little island off the east coast of Benbecula, just to the south
of Rossinish, where they found shelter in a bothy. Here
they were visited next day by Old Clanranald, bringing
with him from Nunton his family's tutor, Neil McEachain.
Neil, he said, would guide them to Glen Corrodale in South
Uist, where, under Clanranald's protection, they would for
the time being be safe from enemy visitations.

Setting out on the night of 14 May, the Prince and his
companions walked the fifteen miles across rough country
to Glen Corrodale, where they found "a famous palace" in
the shape of a forester's bothy, lying in an idyllic spot between two sizeable hills, Ben Hella and Ben More. Here
they spent three weeks undisturbed. (216-18)

MacDonells of Glengarry suffer

The Battle of Culloden in 1746 not only was the last gasp of
the Stuart claim to the British throne but also proved to be the last
infantry battle on British soil. To prevent the Stuart claim from ris-

ing yet again, the British government inflicted harsh punishment on the Highlanders who had supported the lost cause, including the MacDonells of Glengarry. A clan historian reports:

> ...efforts to persuade the Glengarry men to surrender were hampered by the news that on May 4th, 68 of the men of Glenmoriston and 16 of Urquhart had surrendered their arms to Ludovick Grant who had promptly marched them to Inverness and handed them over to Cumberland to be imprisoned and later transported to the American Colonies; few of them ever to see their native land again. Glengarry eventually succeeded in persuading most of the common people to deliver up their arms, which they did at Inverness on May 26th, and after receiving from Lord Loudon, "Certificates of their Surrendry" were sent home.
>
> Notwithstanding "in a few days after the King's Army came from Inverness to fort Augustus" all the houses in Glengarry, with the exception of Invergarry Castle, were burnt and all the cattle and other effects carried off by the "red soldiers." Finally, on May 29th a party of soldiers under the command of Captain Loftus of the Buffs arrived at Invergarry and "first pillaged the Memorialist's dwelling house of Glengarry, burnt it and all his office houses down to the Ground and by the indulgence of the Officers who Commanded, there were only given to the Memorialist's Lady and Nine Children Two small highland Cows, one Chest of Drawers and six pair of Blankets for their maintenance and Support and not so much as a Hatt left to Cover them, and upon this occasion the Memorialist's whole furniture, plate, books, Charter Chest, and other writes, Cloaths, a great Stocking of Cattle of different kinds the Memorialist's riding horses and in short everything he had was Carried away by the Army" and "the Memorialist was threatened with imediat Death if he would not prevail on his Tennants of Morar and Knoidart... likewise to Surrender." (Glengarry's Memorial of 1750).
>
> ... The horses, cattle, sheep, goats and other livestock which were brought into Cumberland's army at Fort Augustus were sold to dealers from the south and the profits distributed as prizes. "Last Wednesday," wrote a gentle-

man..., "the Duke gave two prizes to the soldiers to run heats for, on bare back gallowayes [ponies] taken from the rebels... Yesterday his Royal Highness gave a fine holland smock to the soldiers wives, to be run for on these gallowayes, also bare-legged, and riding with their limbs on each side of the horse, like men..."

"These races were said to have been attended with circumstances of even grosser indecency than is acknowledged by these Whig writers. According to the gossip of the time, the female camp-followers who took part in them were as destitute of raiment as was Godiva in Coventry during her famous ride" wrote Alexander MacKay in *Urquhart and Glenmoriston.*

...Lieutenant-Colonel Cornwallis marching through Glenmoriston with his corps, observed two men *leading* dung to their lands, and shouted to them to come over to him. The men having Gaelic only and not understanding his order continued with their work; whereupon they were instantly ordered to be shot.

...A party of Lockhart's men in the Braes of Glenmoriston ravished a gentlewoman, Isabel MacDonell, wife of Alexander MacDonell of Aonach while here husband, skulking in the heather on a nearby hillside, watched helplessly. Flora MacDonell, wife of John MacDonell, of the same neighbourhood was also ravished by the same party and at the same time. The two women thereafter resolved, with the consent of their husbands, not to lie with them until after the expiry of nine months "lest they should have been with child." Fortunately for them neither became pregnant nor did they contract any disease as a result of their ordeals. (101-03)

...A few days after the surrender of the Knoydart and Morar men Colonel Watson, Cumberland's Quarter-Master-General paid a visit to Glengarry who with his family were then occupying "a poor pitiful Hutt belonging to the Millart in the midst of an oak wood" and informed him that the Duke wished to see him. Glengarry thereupon hastened to Fort Augustus where the Earle of Albermarle transmitted to him Cumberland's orders which were that he was immediately to join Colonel Conway and Lieutenant-

Colonel Cornwallis at the head of Loch Arkaig and proceed with them to Knoydart, presumably as their guide.

The Edinburgh Evening Courant... reports... "Lord George Sackville and Major Wilson are marched to the Barrack of Bernera with 500 Foot from whence they are to proceed Southwards through the Countries of the MacDonalds of Moidart and Knoydart, while Capt. Scott with the old Garrison of Fort William... will advance from the South to meet them." This operation was carried out to the letter and the marauding bands of Hanoverian soldiers, encouraged by their officers burned, pillaged, bayoneted, shot and raped as they went. (104-05)

Prince Charles flushed out of hiding

Prince Charles, evading pursuit on the west coast of Scotland, found a brief respite at Glen Corrodale under the protection of the Chief of Clanranald. Sir Fitzhugh Maclean writes:

> ...But it was not long before even Corrodale became unsafe for the fugitive. There were disturbing stories of militia companies in the vicinity and enemy warships off the coast, and on 6 June the Prince set out once more on his travels. After a couple of days in a cave on an island off Benbecula and a few more near Rossinish, he made his way south to Loch Boisdale, where he had barely installed himself in the ruins of an old tower on the islet of Calvey, when a party of the enemy landed within a mile of him. Alarmed by this, he at once sent a messenger to the nearby house of MacDonald of Boisdale, only to find that Boisdale himself had been carried off by the enemy.
>
> By this time it was all too clear that the Prince could no longer safely remain on the Long Island and, with the help of Lady Clanranald, a plan was made for him to go to Skye, en route to the mainland where, it was hoped, he would have a better chance of hiding until a ship could be found to take him to France. (218-20)

Flora MacDonald rescues Bonnie Prince Charlie

Once upon a time a vivacious young woman rescued a charming but ill-starred prince from terrible peril. The young woman be-

came known in history and legend as Flora MacDonald or Macdonald although she called herself Flory McDonald (Toffey 34-35;
Vining 103). The prince was Charles, son of the would-be James
III of England and Scotland, known in legend as Bonnie Prince
Charlie. Flory's adventures with Bonnie Prince Charlie started, as
legends often do, with a coincidence. Although she lived on Skye
with her mother and step-father – who was a captain in the government military service – 24-year-old Flory happened to be vising
her friends and relatives on the Long Island at the same time that
26-year-old Charles was hiding on the Long Island from government forces seeking to capture him after his attempt to restore his
family to the throne ended in disaster.

Nineteenth-century author Alexander Macgregor, who incor-
porates copious amounts of folklore in his *The Life of Flora Macdonald*, tells the following version of Flory's adventures with Bonnie Prince Charlie:

> The family at Ormiclade, with whom Flora principally re-
> sided [while on a visit to the Long Island], were grievously
> perplexed at the aspect of existing events. Old Clanranald
> was night and day in deep distress, on account of the part
> which his son had taken in embracing the Royal adventur-
> er's cause, so directly in opposition to his father's will, and
> Lady Clanranald was nothing less so, but Flora, with her
> natural vivacity and geniality of temper, mightily soothed
> them in their grief...
>
> ...Already about two thousand regular troops and mili-
> tiamen were posted in suitable localities all over the island.
> Every avenue was guarded, every ferry had its watch, and
> every highway and hill-road was protected by soldiers. The
> lochs and bays, and the sea-coast all round, were so studded
> with the sloops of war and cutters of all sizes, that no craft
> could possibly leave the island or come to it unknown, ex-
> cept perhaps under the dark shade of night... Lady Clan-
> ranald and Miss Flora were continually engaged devising
> schemes for the immediate protection and ultimate release
> of the unfortunate Prince, whom, however, as yet they had
> never seen. Twelve powerful and trustworthy men, who
> could acquit themselves by sea or land, were selected by
> Lady Clanranald to be in readiness by night and day,

should their services be required. Flora very frequently conversed with these gallant Islanders… They had seen the Prince on several occasions, but she had not.

One morning as two of them had come to Ormiclade to give intelligence as to how he had passed the night in his rocky cave, Flora met them at the door and asked them, "Am bheil e laghach? Am bheil e aoidheil? Am bhiel e idir iriosal agus taitneach?" (Is he nice? Is he cheerful? Is he at all humble and pleasant?)… (81-83)

Although there is no historical record of Flory's conversations with her associates in 1746, Macgregor frequently quotes what he imagines her to have said, such the questions about Charles and a statement that supposedly sums up her philosophy. Flory's statement came in response to an exchange between the Chief of Clanranald and Donald Macleod, who had accompanied Charles to Benbecula:

…The worthy chief was sorely perplexed, and as he paced up and down the room he addressed the faithful Donald, "Och! a's och! a Dhomhnuill, the egal mor orm, gu'm bheil grian Thearlaich, a bha aon uair co dealrach, gu dol fadha ann un uine ghearr ann an fuil, agus ann un tiughchorchadas" (Alas! alas! Donald, I am greatly afraid that the sun of Charles, which was at one time so brilliant, is about soon to sink in blood and in darkness). …she smartly addressed him, "Tha do bhriathra ri Domhnull a' cur iongantais orm, or fhad's a mhaireas beatha, mairidh dochas… (I am astonished at your expressions to Donald, for while there is life there is hope…) Clanranald could not help smiling at his amiable protégé's confident remarks… (91-92)

…She was no doubt greatly influenced by the principles of sympathy and pure humanity in contributing to the safety of the Prince apart from any political views. She had now learned all about his miserable state; the cold, damp cave in which he had taken refuge; his gaunt, haggard, and half-famished appearance; his clothes in tatters from his solitary wanderings for so many weeks amid the caves and recesses of those sterile mountains. The pure sympathy of her nature yielded to the pressure of the demand now made upon her... (102)

...Flora, in the hearing of the military present, subsequently addressed her step-father and informed him that she had a strong desire to go to Skye and visit her mother at Armadale, to avoid all these unpleasant encounters with the soldiers, who then ransacked every dwelling, and creek, and corner of the Long Island. To this natural request the Captain readily assented, and promised to transmit to her by a trusty messenger that evening the necessary passports for herself, her man-servant (Niel MacEachainn), an Irish spinning-maid, named Betty Burke, and six for a crew. It is needless to say that Betty Burke, the smart Irish girl, was none else than Prince Charles Stuart... (106)

...As the hut in which Charles had been hitherto concealed was within a short distance of a military station, he deemed it prudent to shift his quarters to Rossinish, in doing which he and [Colonel Felix] O'Neil nearly lost their lives. ...owing to the darkness of the night, they had almost fallen over a precipice... (107)

An excellent six-oared boat, the best that could be had, and six stalwart and experienced seamen, were already selected and secured, and sworn-in to be faithful... A great portion of the evening was spent in procuring from Lady Clanranald's wardrobe suitable habiliments for the poor, ragged Irish girl. The difficulty experienced was not from any scarcity of every variety of garments in the good Lady's possession, but from the uncommonly awkward, masculine-like   stature   of   that   half-famished   maiden! ...However, the dress finally decided upon was one almost made up that same evening by all who could handle a needle in the house. ...Lady Clanranald, Flora, and Niel MacEachainn, the latter of whom carried Betty Burke's dress in a well-packed bundle, were cautiously conducted... to the miserable abode where the Prince was concealed... ...and found his Royal Highness alone at the time in his wretched cave. The elegant youth, the descendant of a line of kings stretching back to the remotest antiquity, was here found roasting kidneys and the heart and liver of a sheep for his humble repast. The sight, which was most affecting, moved the party to tears; but the natural, cheerful, and affable demeanor of the Prince soon restored his affected visitors to calm composure of mind. At his request, they all sat down to partake of his cookery. The table was a flat stone resting on a pillar of turf, while the seats on which they sat were bundles of heather closely packed and tied together. Though the fare consisted of no great variety, yet it was very substantially supplemented by a large supply of prepared meat and roasted fowls, as well as by an abundance of wine, brandy, and other acceptable eatables and viands that had just arrived from Ormiclade, as requisites for the intended voyage. While thus seated at his primitive and rude table, the Prince greatly amused his guests by racy anecdotes and facetious remarks. Indeed he made himself so agreeable that all present were charmed with his affability and pleasant manners.

...When the homely Royal repast was over, Lady Clanranald suggested that it was now time to begin the business for which they had met, and to get the Prince robed in his new habiliments. To the no small amusement of all present, Flora unloosed the parcel, and produced the newly-made-up antique dress of Betty Burke. She explained to the Prince that he must now assume the character of that Irish spinning-maid, to suit the passport which she had procured for him. He laughed heartily at the idea... ...though he greatly appreciated the ingenuity of the contrivance...

His Royal Highness then retired... to the cleft of a rock in the neighbourhood to get robed in his new vestments. [When he returned] to the no small merriment of the ladies, he stood before them as a tall, awkward, Irish servant. (107-10)

About ten o'clock the following evening, being Friday, the 27th June, 1746, the Prince, Flora, and Niel MacEachainn proceeded to the sea-shore, to the place where it was previously arranged they should meet the boat. On their arrival, wet and weary, as the rain fell in torrents, they observed to their horror several small vessels or wherries, filled with armed men, sailing within gunshot of the spot where they lay concealed. Fortunately, however, these objects of terror tacked in an opposite direction, and soon disappeared in the hazy gloom. In about an hour after, their own boat, which lay concealed in a neighboring creek, rowed up gently with muffled oars to the spot where they were so anxiously awaiting it. With all possible speed they embarked on their perilous voyage across the Minch to Skye, a distance of between thirty-five and forty miles...

...The wind blew in terrific gusts, the billows rolled mountains high... and when less than two hours at sea, the storm increased to such a terrific degree, that the ocean was lashed into deep, foaming waves! At that moment, as if to add to their already indescribable terror, thunder rolled in rattling peals over their heads, while the lightning flashed from cloud to cloud in the murky atmosphere! The crew had to steer before the wind, which frequently shifted, and for hours they were entirely at the mercy of the raging elements...

...At break of day they were greatly perplexed at seeing no land in any direction – nothing visible but the azure horizon all round, and without a compass they did not know how to direct their craft. The storm had by this time fortunately moderated, and while the seamen had been steering at random for so many hours, their hearts were at last cheered, by beholding in the dim distance the lofty headlands of Skye... But who can judge of their dismay, when, on drawing near the land, they beheld a large party of the Macleod Militia on the beach waiting their arrival! ...with a few desperate pulls the boat was soon rowed beyond the reach of the red-coats on shore. The militia, sadly disappointed, and having no boat fit to pursue, fired a shower of bullets after them, which fortunately did no injury, though the balls struck and riddled their sails. ...The Prince stood up and cheered the crew...

During the rapid firing of the militia, he was endeavoring to persuade Flora to recline in the bottom of the boat; but the heroine... refused, unless the Prince himself, whose life she considered far more valuable than her own, would take the same precaution. Eventually as the danger increased, and as the bullets whizzed past close to their ears, the Prince, Flora, and Niel squatted down all three on the ballast flags…

Early on the afternoon of Saturday they landed safely at a place called Kilbride… (112-15)

The Skye Boat Song

The voyage of Flory and Charles to Skye inspired the ballad "Skye Boat Song:"

Chorus:
Speed, bonnie boat, like a bird on the wing,
Onward! The sailors cry;
Carry the lad that's born to be King
Over the sea to Skye.

Loud the winds howl, loud the waves roar,
Thunderclouds rend the air;
Baffled, our foes stand by the shore,
Follow they will not dare.

Chorus

Though the waves leap, so soft shall ye sleep,
Ocean's a royal bed.
Rocked in the deep, Flora will keep
Watch by your weary head.

Chorus

Many's the lad fought on that day,
Well the Claymore could wield,
When the night came, silently lay
Dead in Culloden's field.

Chorus

Burned are their homes, exile and death
Scatter the loyal men;
Yet ere the sword cool in the sheath
Charlie will come again.

Macdonald of Kingsburgh shelters the Prince

Charles stayed in a cave on the shore, Macgregor says, while Flory made arrangements for him to stay at the home of Alexander Macdonald of Kingsburgh. The Prince, still dressed as a woman, accompanied Kingsburgh on an all-day trek along "the more unfrequented tracks across the moors" while "the rain fell in torrents." Kingsburgh's wife and Flora, accompanied by Niel MacEachainn and two other young men, made their separate way to Kingsburgh House, although "unceasing rain fell in such torrents as to swell the mountain streams to overflowing, and render most of the usual fords almost impassible." They reached the house about midnight, and Lady Kingsburgh prepared a meal because her cook was asleep (116-132). After eating, the Prince drank many bowls of toddy, even though Kingsburgh urged him to get some sleep in preparation for the next day's tribulations:

> "Charles as eagerly pressed the necessity of more drink; and after some good-humoured altercation, when Kingsburgh took away the bowl to put it by, his Royal Highness rose to detain it, and a struggle ensued, in which the little vessel broke in two pieces, Charles retaining one in his hands, and Kingsburgh holding the other. The strife was thus brought to an end, and the Prince no longer objected to go to bed.
>
> He slept soundly until two o'clock in the afternoon, when Kingsburgh entered his bedroom, and told him that it was high time to get up, get breakfast, and prepare for the journey to Portree, a distance of about eight miles. (132-33)

Charles arose and donned Betty Burke's clothes. Lady Kingsburgh gathered the sheets from the bed Charles had slept in and pledged to preserve them until her dying day when the relics would be used as winding-sheets for her burial.

Flory and Niel MacEachainn accompanied Charles to Portree. Along the way, the Prince found a private space between two rocks and changed into men's clothes (134-35). At Portree they met young Raasay and Captain Donald Roy, who would convey Charles to the island of Raasay:

When the Prince and his attendants arrived, they went to the only inn in the village with young Raasay and Donald Roy to procure refreshments. Donald suggested the propriety of the Prince's retiring to a place of safety, as there was great danger in remaining longer in a public hostelry, when so many spies and suspicious characters were moving about. He told him that he knew of a cave where he could find shelter until removed under night to Raasay, and that the sooner he resorted to it the better. They all left the inn immediately, except Flora, under a drenching rain.

The time had now come when Charles had to part for ever with his true and faithful protectress, the gallant Flora. With tears in his eyes he laid hold of the heroine's hands, and bade her a tender and affecting farewell...

Such were the adventures of three days, and of only three days – but adventures which have immortalised the name of our heroine, and for ever shed a halo of glory over the devotedness of the female heart.

...During the darkness of that night he was conveyed from his cave to Raasay, and thence through Skye to the mainland, where for nearly three months he had to undergo terrible trials and severe hardships. His home was in rocks and in caves, and in mountain recesses, where he passed his weary time hourly exposed and liable to be seized by his vigilant pursuers. (135-37)

Flory McDonald imprisoned

Government officials quickly realized that they had been duped and apprehended the offenders. They arrested Colonel Felix O'Neil, Father Allan MacDonald, Lady Clanranald and MacDonald of Kingsburgh.

In mid-July they arrested Flory. "Giving her no chance to go home and tell what had happened or to get a change of clothing, they carried her off to the *Furnace* in Applecross Bay, where she was at once taken before General Campbell and questioned," writes biographer Elizabeth Gray Vining (75-76).

Vining continues:

General Campbell, who must have been impressed by the gentle self-possession of this steadfast young woman, did not release her, but he gave orders that she was to be treated with respect.

John McKinnon of Elgol was taken and questioned the same day, and two days later MacLeod of Talisker went to Raasay, where Ferguson's men had already burned 300 houses, including the laird's mansion, and 32 boats and slaughtered 280 cows and 700 sheep, and hunted down his friend Malcolm MacLeod in the cow byre where he was hiding, and brought him to the *Furnace*. The old laird of MacKinnon and his wife were captured several days later.

On the day after Flora was taken prisoner, Donald Roy MacDonald and Hugh of Armadale burned the incriminating letters in their possession and took to the hills. (79)

After three weeks aboard the *Furnace*, Flory was transferred to the *Eltham*. The captain of the *Eltham* allowed Flory to visit her family for two hours and to get some clothes. She came back to the ship with a maid, Kate MacDonell, who accompanied her for a few months.

Prince Charles skulks on the mainland

Sir Fitzroy Maclean gives a summary of the travels and travails of Bonnie Prince Charlie after he bade Flory McDonald adieu:

…Charles, believing he could count on help from MacLeod of Raasay, now crossed to that island, recently sacked by the Red Coats, but, finding it offered no real cover, returned immediately to Skye, where this time he took refuge near Strathardle in the south of the island with the staunchly Jacobite Mackinnons, whose old Chief John readily escorted him back across stormy seas from Elgol to Mallaig on the mainland. In Morar, after yet another narrow escape from some militiamen, the Prince had a disheartening encounter with old Clanranald, who happened to be in the neighbourhood. "What muckle devil has brought him to this country again?" exclaimed the old Chief, whose enthusiasm for the Prince and his cause was by now beginning to wane. Nor was he much better received by Mac-Donald of Morar, Lochiel's brother-in-law, who, on meeting him, "became very cool and backward". But Mackin-

non remained staunchly loyal, staying with him until he
could hand him over to Angus MacDonald of Borrodale,
who had helped him when he landed in Morar the year before, and since his own house had been burned down, had
been sulking nearby in a hut in the woods. Almost immediately after this came the news came that old Mackinnon,
whose clan had been out in the Fifteen as well as the Forty-
five, had been taken. The pursuit was closing in on every
side. In the knowledge that to landward side they were by
this time cut off by a regular line of militia posts, while out
at sea naval vessels patrolled the coast, the decision was
now taken to try somehow to break through to the East.
Guided by Borrodale's son and by MacDonald of Glenaladale who had served as a major in Clanranald's regiment,
the Prince in the end somehow managed to slip between
two enemy posts and reach the neighbourhood of Loch
Arkaig. There they were joined by Lochiel's brother, Dr.
Archibald Cameron, who led them through Chisholm and
Fraser territory to Strathglass, some twenty miles to the
west of Inverness. In Strathglass the Prince took shelter in a
cave, where he was joined by young Clanranald, who from
the first had shown himself a stauncher Jacobite than his father. It was now, at Corriergoe, in the hills between Loch
Cluanie and Glen Affric, that the Prince first met the Seven
Men of Glenmoriston, as they were called, all of whom had
fought in his army and who now became his devoted body-
guard, foraging for him and guiding him from hiding-place
to hiding-place...

On 14 August the Prince and Glenaladale and some of
the men of Glenmoriston went by Glengarry to Achnausaul
at the eastern end of Loch Arkaig, where they were joined
by MacDonald of Lochgarry. Thence they made their way
to the neighbourhood of Achnacarry, where they received a
message from Lochiel by his brother Dr Archie to say that
the Prince would be safe where he himself was now hiding
in Badenoch, to the east of the Great Glen. Glenaladale
now took his leave of the Prince, handing over to Lochgarry and Dr Cameron. On 30 August, by Loch Ericht on the
south-eastern slope of Ben Alder, some twenty-five miles
east of Fort William, they finally met Lochiel, who enter-

tained them there and then to a much needed meal of mutton and whisky and minced collops.

Two days later, on 1 September, they were joined by Cluny Macpherson and with him moved two days after that higher up Ben Alder to "a romantic comical habitation", a kind of hut, built into the hillside in a wood on the upper slopes of Ben Alder and known as Cluny's Cage. Here the Prince was to spend a week in relative comfort in the company of Cluny, Lochiel, Lochgarry and Dr Cameron...
(221-23)

Norman H. MacDonald reports the adventures of Bonnie Prince Charlie from the perspective of the MacDonells of Glengarry:

The Prince, after giving his pursuers the slip in the Hebrides, arrived at Little Mallaig on Loch Nevis in the early hours of July 5th and lay for three nights in the open. He then rowed up Loch Nevis and, after eluding his pursuers, took refuge on Eilean na Glaschoille, "a little island about a mile from Scotus' house," until nightfall, when he moved on to Morar.

On the 10th he arrived early in the morning at Borrodale, and on the 19th reached the Braes of Loch Arkaig. The following day he went to "a fast place" at the head of Loch Quoich, and from there on the 21st he broke through the cordon surrounding Moidart and reached the head of Loch Hourn in company with MacDonald of Glenaladale and Cameron of Glenpean. The following day the Prince and his companions reached Glen Shiel, where on learning that the only French ship at Poolewe had gone, they abandoned their intention of going there.

In Glen Shiel, they met Donald MacDonell, a Glengarry man who had been chased by soldiers who, the day before, had killed his father. Glenaladale immediately recognised Donald as one who had served in the Glengarry Regiment and, knowing him for "a trusty fellow," recommended that he be made their guide.

They set out on July 27th but, after proceeding a quarter of a mile, Glenaladale found his purse, in which that of the Prince had been put for safekeeping, was missing. Leaving the Prince in a hiding place, Glenaladale and Borrodale's son John MacDonald returned to the house from which they had set out and, fortunately, retrieved the purse. When they returned, they were informed by the Prince that he had observed a Hanoverian officer and two private men under arms pass by. Their little mishap had, in fact, enabled them to slip past the patrol which otherwise must inevitably have taken them.

They continued their journey by night, led by their Glengarry guide, to Strath Cluanie, where they rested on the 20th but, being alarmed by the sound of firing, they made for the mountain range between Glen Moriston and Glen Affric.

The Glengarry guide, being unfamiliar with the country beyond Strath Glas, conveyed his precious charge to the celebrated Men of Glenmoriston at their cavern retreat in Corrie Dho. They had no bread to give their royal visitor but a hearty meal of their mutton, butter, cheese and whisky. They agreed to swear the following oath of fidelity and secrecy, which was administered to them by Glenaladale: "That their backs should be to God and their faces to the Devil, and all the curses of the Scriptures did pronounce might come upon them and all their posterity if they did not stand firm by the Prince in the greatest dangers, and if they did discover to any person – man, woman, or child – that the Prince was in their keeping, till once this person should be out of danger." Charles remarked after the ceremony, that they were the first Privy Council that had been sworn to him since the Battle of Culloden. (107)

...Passing through Glen Moriston and Glen Lyne to Glen Garry, they forded the River Garry, which was in spate, with difficulty and spent the night in the open in heavy rain. The following morning they continued their journey, again in heavy rain, to Achnasaul, where... they "passed the day in a leaking habitation." They were joined that night by Lochgarry... (108)

The Chief of Lochgarry, in a narrative of his experiences, wrote: "We travell'd in this manner three days and nights without much eating or any sleep, but slumbering now and then on a hillside. Our indefatigable Prince bore this with greater courage and resolution than any of us, nor ever was there a Highlander born cou'd travel up and down hills better or suffer more fatigue. Show me a king or prince in Europe cou'd have born the like or the tenth part of it" (qtd. in MacDonald 109).

Flory McDonald held prisoner at Leith

In early September, Flory McDonald's captors transferred her from the *Eltham* to the *Bridgewater* in the port of Leith near Edinburgh. Jacobite ladies from Edinburgh came to call on Flory, bringing her a Bible, linen, a thimble, needles and thread to help her pass the time of her imprisonment.

The ladies reported that Flory sang well and was charming at the tea-table (Vining 87).

Prince Charles leaves Scotland

Sir Fitzroy Maclean describes the departure of Charles from Scotland after dodging pursuers through the bens, glens and islands for six months:

> ...on 13 September they at last received the news that there were French ships at anchor in Loch nan Uamh.
>
> Setting out that same night, they marched north between Ben Alder and Loch Ericht, then west through the Ben Alder forest and past the south end of Loch Laggan towards Glen Roy and the River Lochy. Crossing the Lochy by moonlight in a leaky old craft, they came again to Achnacarry, where they stopped for a day, continuing the following night by Loch Arkaig to Borrodale and Loch nan Uamh, where Charles had landed fourteen months before. There at long last the Prince boarded the French ship *L'Heureux*, which soon after weighed anchor and set sail for France. With him went Lochiel, Dr Archie Cameron and Lochgarry. Cluny, for his part, did not accompany the Prince, but continued for the next eight years to skulk undisturbed in his cage before in his turn finally escaping to France. (223)

"With all due respect to… the other loyal clans, the Mac-Donells of Glengarry contributed most to Charles' Cause," writes Norman H. MacDonald. He quotes the Chief of Lochgarry, who referred to Prince Charles by an abbreviation of his Royal Highness: "Now, you may observe what number of McDonells were at each battle; and I dare say without any selfishness, that none of the battles cou'd have been won without them; and further, I say that these and their followers, under God, had the good fortune to save his Royll. Hs. person" (111).

Flory McDonald pardoned: 1747

Flory McDonald spent about three months as a prisoner aboard the *Bridgewater* until it sailed from Leith to London in November of 1746. She was held for a few days aboard a prison ship and then was lodged with other Highlander prisoners in the home of a government official (Vining 89-91).

The British government pardoned Flory McDonald in 1747 for her role in helping Bonnie Prince Charlie escape to France after his defeat at Culloden. Freed from imprisonment in London, she traveled to Scotland by coach, staying about three weeks in Edinburgh and about ten days in Inverness. Her stepfather on the Isle of Skye sent a horse and saddle to her at Inverness; when she reached her home on Skye after a year of imprisonment, she complained only that her fingers were blistered and bleeding from holding the bridle as she rode the rough trails of the Highlands. She stayed with her mother for two months, and then went off to visit friends and relatives on the Western Isles who welcomed her with joy. Her clan chief gave a splendid banquet in her honor with "festivities extended over four days, when high and low were entertained in a manner that did credit to the friendly generosity and hospitality of the great *Mac Dhomhnuill* of the Isles" (Macgregor 149-57).

Lady Anne dances with Duke of Cumberland: 1748

A few Highlanders remained loyal to the Stuart dream and were willing to suffer the consequences. Among them was Lady Anne Mackintosh, the wife of the 22nd Chief of Clan Mackintosh. She had been imprisoned for six weeks for her role as "Colonel Anne" in the Rising of 1745 but she never relinquished her combative spirit. In 1748, Lady Anne visited London and attended a ball given by William Augustus, the Duke of Cumberland, who had commanded the British forces that had quelled the Rising. He asked her to dance when the musicians played a song in his honor: "Up and waur them a' Willie." After dancing with him to his tune, she asked him to dance with her to her tune. He gallantly complied and she asked for the tune "The auld Stuarts back again" (MacKintosh, "Lady" 48).

Highland Company at Darien disbanded

To save money, the British government drastically cut its military forces in Georgia. "About four hundred unemployed veterans, perhaps more than one-quarter of the Georgia labor force, were suddenly and unexpectedly released upon the already distressed economy," reports military historian Larry Ivers. "Georgia's principal industry ceased to exist. Many of the veterans who had originally abandoned their land grants to join the provincial army now applied for charity" (203).

When the Highland Company of Foot was disbanded in 1747 its commander, John Mackintosh Mor, was commissioned as a lieutenant in the 42nd Regiment of Foot and became acting commander of a company garrisoning the fort at Darien (Ivers 206). In addition to his military duties, John Mackintosh Mor continued his lifelong occupation as a gentleman farmer and also operated a store. His son Lachlan, who was a veteran of the regiment at Frederica, probably worked on the family farm and in the store (Jackson 5).

Lachlan McIntosh moves to Charleston: 1748

When Lachlan McIntosh turned 21, he asserted his independence by moving away from his family in the Darien district. McIntosh's biographer Harvey H. Jackson gives the facts:

> … After the treaty of Aix-la-Chapelle in 1748, British wartime aid to Georgia ended. A recession resulted which caused such an exodus that it seemed the colony "became almost entirely depopulated." Twenty-one-year-old Lachlan McIntosh took his eleven-year-old brother George and joined other immigrants who went to Charleston.
>
> South Carolina's capital made a lasting impression on the young McIntoshes. The major trading center of the Southern colonies, its businesslike bustle and crowded

commercial district showed them just how provincial Georgia was. In addition, the charm and grace of Charleston society set a standard which few American cities were able to match. Its example was not lost on the young men from Darien. George was put in a grammar school and later apprenticed to an architect. Lachlan found employment in a counting house, and though he did not "make his fortune" he at least prospered and was soon able to supply his brother with 100 pounds in Carolina currency as "pocket money" and buy a young Negro to assist him. The brothers were close and the elder always felt protective toward his younger charge, a feeling which characterized their relationship the rest of their lives.

Nearly six feet tall, athletic, described by one friend as the "handsomest man he had ever seen," and possessing a ready wit that in later, more reserved years would be seen only by close associates, young Lachlan McIntosh began to make friends and slowly wind his way through the labyrinth of Charleston society. His efforts found an influential ally when, during his third year in the city, he met Henry Laurens. A rising member of the merchant elite and a man of considerable political promise, Laurens took a genuine liking to the Georgian, invited him into his home, and, though only three years McIntosh's senior, became a guiding force in his career. It was a relationship which grew into a long business association, produced a political alliance, and, most importantly, gave Lachlan McIntosh one of the most loyal friendships he was to experience outside his family.

For nearly eight years Charleston was the center of McIntosh's life. He served Laurens well, made the most of the connections he developed, and generally seemed to impress those with whom he dealt… (Jackson 5-6)

A nineteenth-century writer offers a more romantic interpretation in *The National Portrait Gallery of Distinguished Americans*:

Lachlin M'Intosh and his brothers were well instructed in English under their mother's care, and after they were received under the patronage of General Oglethorpe, were instructed in mathematics, and other branches necessary for their future military course. But when General Oglethorpe left Georgia, all hope, and perhaps all wish, for remaining longer attached to his regiment, ceased in the young men. William became an active and successful agriculturist, and Lachlin, in search of a wider field of enterprise, went to Charleston in South Carolina, where his father's gallantry, and his father's misfortunes, drew upon him the attentions of many; and his fine and manly appearance, his calm, firm temper, his acquirements for his opportunity, procured for him first the acquaintance, and then the warm friendship, of Henry Laurens, the most distinguished and most respectable merchant at that time in Charleston, afterwards president of congress, and first minister from the United States to Holland. Mr. Laurens took the young M'Intosh into his counting-house and into his family, and with him he remained some years. In association with this enlightened and respectable gentleman, Mr. M'Intosh had an opportunity of studying men and books, and of filling up the blanks in his education. From some repugnance to commerce, arising probably from his early military propensities, he did not adopt the pursuit of his friend and patron, but after spending some years in Charleston, he returned to his friends still residing on the Altamaha... ("Lachlin M'Intosh" 103-04)

South Carolina historian George C. Rogers points out: "As a merchant, Henry Laurens trained many boys as clerks in his counting house. His wharf on Cooper River with its auxiliary buildings was an early business school" (269-70).

The end of an era: 1749
While Lachlan and George McIntosh were in Charleston, their brother Phineas died in Darien in about 1749 at about age 17.

In April of 1749 the Frederica regiment was disbanded and the company that had been garrisoning the fort at Darien was disbanded; as a result John Mackintosh Mor was no longer needed as a lieutenant in the company. Military historian Larry Ivers analyzes the historical significance of the occasion:

The year 1733 began a military era on the southern frontier, and the year 1749 brought that era to a close. The War of Jenkins's Ear-King George's War was over, Georgia's career as a military buffer colony was ended, and the drums of the British regulars and Georgia provincials were silent. Naïve visions of fortified frontier villages populated with free yeomen farmers, carrying a hoe in one hand and a musket in the other, evaporated forever in July 1749 when the Georgia trustees legalized the use of Negro slave labor. No longer were settlements strategically located for defense; of all of the towns settled during the military era, only Savannah, Augusta, and Darien survived. The military no longer served as Georgia's principal industry. Regimental and provincial officers no longer exercised excessive influence in civil affairs. Military command of the southern frontier was transferred from the commander of the forces in Georgia to the governor of South Carolina, and Georgia became a military backwater; only a few regulars and a single crew of boatmen were maintained on duty.

The sixteen years between 1733 and 1749 were also James Edward Oglethorpe's personal era. During most of that period he was the dominant personality, both politically and militarily, on the southern frontier. By utilizing varying degrees of diplomacy and armed force, he worked to carry out Britain's imperialistic policy, much of which he had formulated...

In 1749, at the age of fifty-three, Oglethorpe abandoned the social and professional seclusion that he had entered in 1746 as a result of public criticism concerning his actions during the Jacobite Rebellion, and he began devoting his energies to Parliamentary work. Over one-third of his life still lay ahead of him, and he would enjoy additional successes and suffer new failures. However, he severed all contact with Georgia, attending his last trustees' board meeting on 16 March 1749. (214-15)

1750-1774

Lachlan McIntosh and his brothers take an active role in the independence movement in Georgia. Flory McDonald emigrates from Scotland to North Carolina with her family. Aeneas the 22nd Chief of Clan Mackintosh dies and his nephew, also named Aeneas, succeeds as the 23rd Chief.

Flory McDonald marries: November 6, 1750

In the Western Isles of Scotland, 29-year-old Flory McDonald married Allan McDonald, son of Alexander Macdonald of Kingsburgh. Allan "is said to have been one of the most handsome and powerful Highlanders of his clan, and possessed of all the qualities of body and mind which constitute the real gentleman" (Macgregor 160). Flory and Allan had been attracted to one another since they were teenagers. The wife of the chief of Clan Donald observed "that Allan and Flory resembled one another in tempers, characters, and ages" and "that they were no doubt intended for one another" (Macgregor 157). Flory's biographer describes the wedding:

> At length the time appointed for her marriage arrived, and this event, so important to her, took place at Flodigarry, on the 6th of November, 1750. It is almost superfluous to say that the wedding festivities were conducted on a grand scale, and lasted for the greater part of a week. The company was unusually numerous, and consisted of almost all the gentlemen in Skye and the Long Island, many of them with their ladies. The bride, robed in a dress of Stuart tartan, with which she was presented when in London by a lady friend, on condition that she would wear it at her marriage, looked remarkably well. All present admired her calm, modest demeanor, appropriately described by the bard: –

> A Fhionnaghail chaoimh chaoimheil,
> 'S tu sgathan gach maighdinn,
> 'S an reul iuil tha 'toirt soillse
> Dhoibh dh' oidhche 's do lo,
> 'S oigh uasal air chinnte,

An ribhinn ghlan og;
De Chlann Domhnuill do rireadh,
An ribhinn ghlan og;
'S gur ailleagan ciatach
An ribhinn ghlan og.

The means adopted to furnish accommodation for such a vast assemblage was both amusing and romantic. An immense barn was fitted up for gentlemen's sleeping berths, and a similar place for ladies, while a temporary pavilion was reared, and roofed with heather, to serve alike as a banqueting-hall and a ball-room.

...On occasions of such festivities, even when the parties interested were well-to-do, the practice was that the guests privately contributed, as each thought proper, to the cellars and larders of the parties about to be married. In this way all creature comforts of every description, both solid and liquid, were furnished on a scale of abundance which was indeed extravagant, and more than sufficient to serve the company, should it be requisite, three times over! (Macgregor 158-60)

Allan rented Flodigarry on the north end of Skye while his father occupied the hereditary estate of Kingsburgh about sixteen miles away. Flory's biographer describes the newlywed couple's home as "a beautiful and romantic place:"

The scenery around it is exceedingly grand. The low grounds are studded with small natural tumuli, grass-covered and green, probably the result of ancient glaciers or convulsions of Nature. Above it are the serrated towering cliffs of the far-famed Quiraing, frowning in their stern majesty. To the east, the broad Sound of Gairloch, with Loch Staffin and its little Isle, lie fully in view; while on the opposite coast, the Gairloch hills, in successive vistas, and the projecting *Seann-Rudha*, are seen stretching away in soft and distant perspective. Close at hand, the Bay of Steinscholl presents itself, with its rough boulder-strewn shore to resist the fury of the Atlantic waves, while a little farther on the eye rests upon the basaltic walls of Garafad, shivered into ghastly shapes, and cloven into huge gorges and fissures, which resound by the thundering roll of the dashing waves. (Macgregor 155-56)

Ann McIntosh marries Robert Baillie: 1751

At Darien, John Mackintosh Mor's daughter Ann married Robert Baillie, a Highlander who had emigrated to Darien under John Mor's leadership and who had commanded Fort Barrington on the Altamaha River. After the Independent Company of Foot was disbanded and Fort Barrington was abandoned, Robert and Ann Baillie grew rice on her land at the headwaters of the Sapelo River (Cashin, *Bartram* 33).

John Mackintosh goes to Jamaica

John Mackintosh Mor's third son, John, moved from Georgia to Jamaica in around 1752. Although he never returned from Jamaica, he corresponded with his family (Sullivan 34-35).

Highlanders want Gaelic-speaking minister

Gaelic remained the language of the Highlanders at Darien for many years. Sixteen years after Darien was founded, a memorial of the inhabitants of Darien requested a Gaelic-speaking Christian minister from Scotland because many of them did not speak English.

John McLeod, the Presbyterian minister who accompanied the first emigrants to Georgia, had moved to South Carolina after five years in Darien. After he left, Darien residents depended on the Rev. Thomas Bosomworth, an assistant chaplain to the regiment at Frederica, to officiate at occasional religious services. A chapel that had been built in Darien when the Highlanders first arrived was replaced by a meeting house eight miles north of Darien before 1750. When Bosomworth returned to England in 1752, the inhabitants of Darien were left utterly destitute of any minister of the gospel. The nearest minister was in Savannah.

"I assure you the people here will miss your absence very much, having no other clergyman to apply to," wrote John Mackintosh Mor to Bosomworth. "A good many souls here lay under for want of one to teach them the way of salvation … I assure you, there is not a place in America wants it more" (*Colonial Records of Georgia* 27: 258-60).

The great hurricane of 1752

As residents of Charleston, Lachlan McIntosh and his younger brother George McIntosh would have witnessed what was called "the great hurricane." South Carolina historian Dr. Walter Edgar describes the experience:

> … the hurricane of 15 September 1752 was remembered by all who lived through it. Late in the afternoon of 14 September the wind began to below from the northeast with ever-increasing force. By the morning of the 15th it was "irresistible." The eye of the storm crossed the coast on an incoming tide, right at Charleston harbor. The storm surge was ten feet above the highest spring tides and tossed all but one of the ships in the harbor onto Charleston's streets. The city's eight wharves were destroyed and dozens of structures were swept away. Those that remained suffered heavy damage: toppled chimneys, blown-out windows and doors, and missing roofs. In the countryside for forty miles around Charleston, there was wide-spread damage. Barns and outbuildings were flattened, one-half the rice crop destroyed, bridges and roads washed out, and trees mowed down as if by a scythe. At least twenty-eight people were reported killed, but the total was probably much higher. While the populace was trying to clean up and rebuild, another hurricane on 30 September dealt the province a glancing blow.
>
> The Hurricane of 1752 became a part of the collective memory of the colonists. It and other weather phenomena were recorded in residents' diaries, journals, plantation books, daybooks, and letter books… Henry Laurens maintained letter books with copies of… business correspondence (which often included local news) addressed to individuals throughout the Atlantic world. (161)

Highlanders own large plantations

Many Highlanders received land grants in the District of Darien as rewards for their service in the Battle of Bloody Marsh and other action against Spanish forces on the southern frontier of America. John Mackintosh Mor was granted property along the

Sapelo River known as the "Borlum lands" because he was related to the Mackintoshes of Borlum in Scotland. His sons William, Lachlan and George and his daughter Ann also received land grants, and one of William's plantations was named Borlum. When large-scale slaveholding was allowed in Georgia in the 1750s, Highlanders who had opposed slavery in 1739 became slave owners. Taking advantage of slave labor, landowners in coastal Georgia became prosperous planters.

Alexander McDonald requests more land

Alexander McDonald – who had been recruited in the Scottish Highlands to serve in the Independent Company of Foot– filed a petition for a large tract of land in 1753. A fifty-acre farm a mile from Darien that had been given him when he first arrived in 1737 was "wore out and unfit for Cultivation." Another fifty-acre tract eight miles from Darien that had been given him when the regiment was disbanded was too small for his "large Stock of black Cattle and Horses." The Georgia government gave him 150 acres on a branch of the Sapelo River "on Condition of his resigning the two Tracts aforesaid of fifty Acres Each, which he readily complyed with" (*CRG* 6: 413). By this time, Alexander McDonald and his wife Mary were parents: a son named Alexander had been born in 1750 (Moss, *South Carolina* 615).

John Laurens born: October 28, 1754

Lachlan and George McIntosh were living in the Henry Laurens household in Charleston when John Laurens was born on October 28, 1754, and left when John was two years old. Lachlan McIntosh and John Laurens would serve together on several occasions during the American Revolution, including Valley Forge and the Siege of Charleston.

Lachlan McIntosh and Henry Laurens remained lifelong friends and business partners, and maintained their correspondence during the American Revolution while Henry Laurens rose to exalted political and diplomatic offices.

Mr. and Mrs. Lachlan McIntosh go to Georgia

While living in South Carolina, Lachlan McIntosh met Sarah Threadcraft of Williamsburg. He married her on New Year's Day of 1756, and they relocated to the Darien District later that year.

When Lachlan's younger brother George finished his apprenticeship to an architect in Charleston, Lachlan "brought him back to Georgia and got him appointed commissary of supplies for Troops in garrison at Frederica, and other ports dependent thereon." Lachlan also "instructed him in geometry and surveying and furnished him with books for those purposes, in order that George might by those means acquire a more perfect knowledge of his own Country and have an opportunity of getting the most valuable lands at that early period for himself" under Lachlan's advice and direction. When George showed inclination to be a planter, as Lachlan recalled later in a legal deposition, Lachlan was "his security in Charleston for the first parcel of Negroes said George ever purchased, with which and his own industry he acquired all the property he ever possessed. Of all these advantages he made the best use and became one of the most thriving planters in this State, uniformly ascribing all his successes to [Lachlan's] steady friendships to him, and always declaring and looking upon [Lachlan] in the light of a father and a tryed friend, rather than a brother" ("Case" 136).

Biographer Harvey Jackson reports a blessed event in 1757:

> Shortly after the new year began, Sarah McIntosh gave birth to her first child, a healthy son. The boy was named John after his grandfather, an ancient name for a new and promising generation. Now a man with new family responsibilities, Lachlan McIntosh's activities took on an added sense of purpose. (Jackson 8)

Lachlan and Sarah's second son – named Lachlan and called Lachlan Jr. or Lackie – was born about a year later. Over the years, their marriage would produce eight children.

In 1758 Lachlan McIntosh acquired a thousand acres on an island across the north branch of the Altamaha River from Darien; the tidal flow of the waterways of the island made the property suitable for growing rice. Starting with sixteen slaves, he developed the land into a plantation (Sullivan, Appendixes 1). Later that year, he and his older brother William McIntosh acquired a thousand acres on Broughton and Doboy Islands. Eventually acquiring fourteen thousand acres of land and sixty slaves, Lachlan McIntosh experienced success as a rice planter.

McIntosh and Laurens form partnerships

In 1763 Henry Laurens – Lachlan's mentor in Charleston – acquired nine hundred acres on Broughton Island adjacent to the McIntosh property. As an absentee landowner, Laurens depended on Lachlan to help manage the Broughton Island property. Laurens and Lachlan made other joint investments in various enterprises in coastal Georgia. Lachlan sent his oldest son John to school in Charleston under Laurens' supervision (Cashin, *Bartram* 34, 37; Sullivan, Appendix 1).

While ventures with McIntosh enriched Laurens' business life, a remarkable daughter enriched his home life. An account written years later by David Ramsay, who was by then Lauren's son-in-law, reports:

> Martha Laurens Ramsay was born in Charleston, S.C. on the 3d. of November, 1759. She was the daughter of Henry Laurens and Eleanor Ball, and born in the ninth year of their marriage…
>
> In the first year of her life she had the small pox so severely that she was supposed to be dead, and as such was actually laid out preparatory for her funeral. This was done under an open window, instead of the close room in which she had been kept, according to the absurd mode of treating the small pox in 1760. Dr. Moultrie, coming in at this crisis, pronounced her to be still alive, probably recalled to life by the fresh air of the open window. Under other circumstances she would have been buried, as was then commonly done, with persons who died of the small pox in that year of extensive mortality. A valuable life was thus providentially saved for future usefulness.
>
> Martha Laurens early discovered a great capacity and eagerness for learning. In the course of her third year she could readily read any book, and, what is extraordinary, in an inverted position, without any difficulty. In youth her vivacity and spirits were exuberant. Feats of activity, though attended with personal danger, were to her familiar; great exertions of bodily labour; romantic projects; excesses of the wildest play were preferred to stagnant life; but

from all these she could be turned off in a moment to serious business. (12)

Tales about Rory McIntosh

Roderick "Rory" McIntosh, the son of John Mackintosh Mor's first cousin Benjamin, became a legendary character. Rory's plantation Mallow adjoined Fairhope, home of John Mackintosh Mor's son William McIntosh.

ON ONE OCCASION, Rory and William went together to Charleston. Along the way, they stayed several days at a house near Jacksonborough. Rory fell in love with a young woman who lived there, and assigned William to seek permission from the girl's father for Rory to marry her. The father thanked William for the honor, but reported that the girl was already engaged to a local man.

When Rory got the bad news, he declared, "I will beat him and spit on her intended."

William asked, "But why? He has not injured you."

Rory answered, "He is my rival, and I will disgrace him."

William argued with Rory for a long time before convincing him to continue on their journey.

DURING A SLAVE INSURRECTION near Savannah, Rory led a party who attacked the slave's fortification. One of his men fired his musket and stepped behind a tree to reload.

Rory asked him, "And can't you, like a brave man, load your musket in the road?"

Rory was wounded during the skirmish, and for the rest of his life one of his shoulders was disfigured. The attackers succeeded in taking the slaves prisoner.

ANOTHER ADVENTURE ENSUED when Rory went to apprehend a Creek Indian who had committed murder. Armed with a Scottish dirk, Rory intimidated a group of the murderer's friends, seized the murderer, and brought him to justice. In an alternate version of the tale, Rory killed the murderer on the spot.

ALTHOUGH NOT WEALTHY, Rory made a comfortable living by raising cattle at Mallow. Once, when Florida was still possessed by Spain, he conducted a cattle drive to St. Augustine. He was paid in dollar coins, which he put in a canvas bag on his horse. On his ride home over rough paths, he had almost reached Mallow when the canvas tore and some of the dollars fell onto the ground. He secured the dollars left in the bag but did not look for the coins that had fallen. When he needed money several years later, he went to the spot where the bag had broken, and picked up as much money as he needed. Later, when he needed money again, he used the same resource.

WHEN RORY LEARNED that a new acquaintance was fond of shooting birds, Rory said, "My young friend, I see you are a sportsman and I love you for it."

Rory hunted game not only for "amusement," according to his friend John Couper, but also for "business," which "supplied a bountiful table." Rory often told tales of shooting on Blackbeard Island near Darien, where the huge flocks of ducks and geese made so much noise on a frosty morning that the hunters could hardly hear each other talk.

RORY LOVED DOGS and owned hounds and setters, including a dog named Luath. (The Scots Gaelic word "luath" is an adjective meaning "quick, fast"). One time, Rory made a considerable bet that Luath could follow his trail three miles and retrieve a gold doubloon that Rory had hidden under a log. Luath set off on Rory's trail but returned without the doubloon.

Rory rushed to the hiding spot and found that Luath had scratched under the log. Rory turned over the log, but the doubloon was no longer there.

Then Rory noticed a man in the distance splitting rails. Rory approached the man, drew his dirk, and swore he would kill him unless the man returned the doubloon. The man gave Rory the doubloon, and explained that he had seen Rory put something under the log and had gone to investigate and had found the gold.

Rory then tossed the doubloon back to the man. "Take it, vile caitiff," said Rory. "It was not the pelf, but the honor of my dog I cared for."

HIS SCOTS HIGHLANDER heritage was important to Rory. He carried a dirk, went about attended by bagpipers, and spoke

Gaelic. When he met a Scots immigrant who was ignorant of Gaelic, Rory told the immigrant, "I pity you, but you may be an honest man for all that."

Being a grandson of the illustrious Jacobite Brigadier William Mackintosh of Borlum, Rory kept alive romantic notions of the royal Stuarts and Bonnie Prince Charlie, surreptitiously referred to as "The Young Gentleman" (White 470-74).

John McIntosh moves to Indian country

Rory McIntosh's brother John McIntosh married Margaret McGillivray, whose family was involved in trading with the southern Indians. John and Margaret and their teenage son William went to live in Indian country in the 1760s. John established a trading post called McIntosh Bluff on the Tombigbee River ("Captain William McIntosh;" Sullivan 34-37).

John Mackintosh Mor dies: 1761

In his later years John Mackintosh Mor concentrated on his farming operations. He had returned to a lifelong occupation: he had been "a gentleman farmer" in Scotland and his uncle Brigadier William Mackintosh had published a treatise on agriculture. Local historian Bessie Lewis gives the location of John Mackintosh Mor's farm and assesses the family patriarch's social status:

> John McIntosh Mohr, returned at last from Spanish prison, settled on Black Island, near where the highlanders landed when they came to Barnwell's Bluff... He was appointed Conservator of the Peace for Darien, and continued to be leader and mentor of his people. (24)

Another Georgia historian, Alexander Lawrence, gives this interpretation of John Mackintosh Mor's final years:

> Eventually Captain Mackintosh returned to Georgia after long confinement in the "common Jayl" at San Sebastian where his fare, he complained, was "no more than bread and water." Broken in health, the Highland chief lived out his remaining years at Darien, passing most of his time, tradition tells us, beneath a great oak along the salt creek that flowed by his home (104-05).

John Mackintosh Mor died in 1761 at his farm Essick on the Sapelo River. A contemporary observer wrote that the 63-year-old patriarch died "prematurely… by the quackery and ignorance of the first Doctor who ever tried to make his fortune amongst the honest patriarchs" (Sullivan 46). He was buried in the old city cemetery in Darien along with his wife Marjory, who died "after May 1741" (Gladstone, unpublished Family Group Record).

McIntosh family takes part in politics: 1764

In 1764, two members of Lachlan McIntosh's extended family were elected as delegates from St. Andrews Parish to the Commons House of Georgia. One of them was his younger brother George McIntosh. His brother-in-law Robert Baillie, husband of his only sister Ann, was the other delegate.

Lachlan himself served as tax collector and justice of the peace. He also supervised an effort to rebuild Fort Frederica, where he had been stationed as a cadet at the time of the Battle of Bloody Marsh. He used his surveying skills on road projects and to lay out a new plan of the town of Darien based on Oglethorpe's original concept.

Ebenezer MacIntosh protests Stamp Act: 1765

British emigrants and the descendants of British emigrants gradually developed an identity as Americans even while insisting on their rights as subjects of the British king. Conflicts between Americans and British rulers started in the oldest colony, Massachusetts, and spread to the youngest colony, Georgia. As early as 1741, Bostonians beat up British officials who forced Americans to serve in the British navy.

In August of 1765, riots erupted throughout the colonies expressing rage over the British Stamp Act. In Charleston, two thousand protestors lamented the loss of American liberty. In Boston, thousands of rioters packed the streets and destroyed the stamp collector's personal property. People's historian Ray Raphael reports that a prominent rioter in Boston was named MacIntosh:

> … the leader of the Boston Stamp Act rioting was Ebenezer MacIntosh, a debt-ridden shoemaker from the South End whose father, one of the strolling poor, had been warned

out of Boston when Ebenezer was in his teens. Appointed a fireman for Engine Company No. 9 in 1760, MacIntosh rose to prominence in the annual Pope's Day riots. Every year on November 5, to mark the anniversary of an aborted Catholic conspiracy to blow up Parliament in 1605, Boston's artisans and laborers staged dramatizations depicting the pope beside a giant effigy of the devil, suitably coated with tar and feathers. Early in the day, working-class youths solicited money for feasting and drinking from more prosperous inhabitants throughout Boston, who dared not refuse. As the day and the drinking progressed, competition between the North Enders and the South Enders turned violent, with paramilitary street gangs fighting for the honor of torching the stage sets in giant bonfires. On the surface, this fighting served no great purpose – and yet, every November 5, lower-class Bostonians owned the town while genteel society huddled indoors.

Seventeen sixty-five was different. During the Stamp Act riots in August, North Enders and South Enders had worked side by side, destroying mansions in their wrath. Upper-class citizens nervously awaited the approach of November 1, the day the Stamp Act was supposed to take effect, with its close conjunction to November 5. What might happen if the mob ceased to expend its destructive energy upon itself? Boston called out a military watch.

On November 5, 1765, Boston's working class marched en masse past the statehouse to display its power, with Ebenezer MacIntosh firmly in command. Refraining from the usual street brawls, the combined North Enders and South Enders, two thousand strong, appeared as a formidable political force. While royal authority quivered, however, affluent Whigs relaxed: MacIntosh and other leaders had been bought. With the avowed intention of uniting the North and South Ends, the Whigs had provided a feast for the street leaders at a popular tavern, carefully dividing the guests into five different classes according to rank. For the Pope's Day parade they furnished pompous military regalia and bestowed official-sounding titles on key men. When MacIntosh marched at the head, he wore a blue and gold uniform, gilded armor, and a hat laced with gold. There were no riots on Pope's Day in 1765. (Raphael 15)

Creek chief tries to shoot Rory McIntosh: 1768

In Georgia, Roderick McIntosh narrowly escaped death in 1768. He antagonized an Indian while he was on an assignment with Edward Barnard and George Galphin to mark the boundary between Indian territory and lands open to settlement. Georgia historian Edward J. Cashin, who says Roderick was "known as Old Rory for his ferocious temper," tells what happened:

> ...Three Creek chiefs – the Young Lieutenant, Salechee, and Blue Salt – led the wary Creek contingent. The Indians argued that Upton Creek at the proposed town of Wrightsborough should be the boundary set by the 1763 treaty. "Old Rory" contended with increasing vehemence that the south fork some twenty-five miles upstream should be the source of the line. One of the chiefs took a decided aversion to McIntosh, pointed his gun at the Scotsman, and pulled the trigger. Fortunately for the cause of peace along the frontier and to the enormous relief of Galphin, Barnard, and presumably McIntosh, the gun misfired. Galphin calmed the hot heads, and they settled on Williams Creek by way of compromise. (*Bartram* 33, 60)

Political intrigue engulfs Georgia

When George McIntosh and his brother-in-law Robert Baillie attempted to take their seats in the Commons House in 1768, their election was challenged. Before the controversy was resolved, the royal governor of Georgia dissolved the Assembly because the Georgians had supported their fellow colonists in Massachusetts against British policies. In 1770, Lachlan McIntosh was elected as a delegate to the Commons House. Once again, the Georgians flexed their political muscle and the royal governor dissolved the Assembly. Later, George McIntosh was elected as a delegate from St. Mary's parish, where he had recently purchased property.

The Mackintosh is dead; long live the Mackintosh

In Scotland, the chieftainship of Clan Mackintosh went through a succession when Aeneas, 22nd Chief of Clan Mackintosh, died in 1770. His nephew Aeneas Mackintosh succeeded as the 23rd Chief of Clan Mackintosh

Lady Anne Mackintosh – the legendary "Colonel Anne" of the Rising of 1745 – moved to Edinburgh after the death of her husband the 22nd Chief. "There," clan historian Angus MacKintosh writes, "far from Moy, she doubtless often mused on the stirring days she had seen, and the brave clansmen that rose round her to fight and die for Bonnie Prince Charlie" ("Lady" 49).

Borlum is dead; long live Borlum

John Mackintosh Mor's cousin Shaw the 6th of Borlum died about 1770 and was succeeded by his only son Edward as 7th of Borlum. By that time the estate of Borlum had been sold to satisfy creditors, so Edward lived at Raits in Badenoch.

Kingsburgh is dead; long live Kingsburgh: 1772

On Skye, Flory McDonald's father-in-law Alexander Macdonald of Kingsburgh died in 1772 and her husband Allan inherited the estate. Flory and Allan left Flodigarry where they had lived for twenty years and moved into the comfortable thatched house at Kingsburgh (Jolly 238).

George McIntosh marries into influential family

In 1772, John Mackintosh Mor's son George McIntosh married Ann Priscilla Houston, whose family was among the social elite in colonial Georgia. Shortly afterwards, George McIntosh and his brother-in-law Sir Patrick Houston were elected to the Commons House as delegates from St. Andrew's parish. At least one of them continued to serve until the American Revolution brought an end to British government in Georgia. In 1774, George McIntosh was among the citizens who met in Savannah to protest British policies.

Lachlan McIntosh befriends William Bartram

Lachlan McIntosh offered his hospitality to naturalist William Bartram in the spring of 1773, and they continued to correspond throughout their lifetimes. Georgia historian Edward J. Cashin tells the tale:

Traveling alone on horseback, he [William Bartram] followed the high road south from Midway. After ten miles
the plantations became fewer and the road worse... With
the poor road and the gathering dusk, William managed to
lose his way completely and blundered along through
swamps and creeks, characteristically unafraid and trusting
to Providence. Sure enough, he saw a light glimmering
through the darkness and followed it to a house, where he
stayed the night...

    ... [The man] whose "glimmering light" rescued Bar-
tram had his overseer guide the botanist through a dangerous swamp and point him in the direction of Darien. He
rode through a forest of pines, crossed a branch of the Sapelo River and arrived at a small plantation on the South
Newport River, the home of Donald McIntosh, one of the
original emigrants from Inverness. Bartram described how
the "venerable grey headed Caledonian" came out to welcome him to his home and hospitality. He admired the
primitive simplicity of the household. A furious storm
broke out while they were at a meal of venison; a bolt of
lightning set a tree ablaze less than forty yards away... Although William may have never visited Donald McIntosh
again, he never forgot him. Writing to Lachlan McIntosh in
1796, he said, "Give respects to Good Old Don'd McIntosh
at the Swamp between Sapello and the great swamp where
I had shelter during the tremendous thunder storm" (31-35).

After delivering a message from Governor Wright to Robert
Baillie – the husband of John Mackintosh Mor's daughter Ann – at
the headwaters of the Sapelo River, Bartram proceeded to Lachlan
McIntosh's home on the banks of the Altamaha River at Darien
(Cashin 35, Sullivan 56). William Bartram and Lachlan McIntosh
had an acquaintance in common: Henry Laurens of Charleston,
who was something of a father figure to both of them.
    Cashin continues the tale:

Of the many people he met and friends he made, with the
exception of Mary Lamboll Thomas, William Bartram
liked Lachlan McIntosh best. They hit it off from the first.
Many years later Bartram's heart filled with sentiment

when he recollected that meeting: "When I came up to the door, the friendly man, smiling, and with a grace and dignity peculiar to himself, took me by the hand and accosted me thus, 'Friend Bartram, come under my roof and I desire you to make my house your home as long as convenient to yourself; remember, from this moment that you are part of my family, and on my part I shall endeavor to make it agreeable.'" There were already ten in the McIntosh household so the invitation to Bartram represented a triumph of hospitality over housekeeping. The eight children paraded by to be introduced to their guest: John, at sixteen the oldest, then in chronological order, Lachlan, William, George, Henry, John Hampton, Hester and Catherine. William [Bartram] got along famously with them, and the warmth of their regard drew him to Darien for prolonged visits during his explorations. William later recalled "those happy scenes, happy hours which I enjoyed with your family." He especially liked the conversations he had with McIntosh in the evenings, the "improving Philosophic conversation," as he phrased it. The discussions touched on William's favorite theme, the working out of the designs of Providence. He exclaimed, "O my Friend, what a degree of intellectual enjoyment our nature is susceptible of when we behold and contemplate the Moral system impressed on the Human Mind by the Divine Intelligence" …

William encountered so many McIntoshes that he had difficulty sorting them out. The Scots compounded the problem by insisting on using the names of fathers and grandfathers. For example, Lachlan and Sarah named their sons John, Lachlan, William, George, Henry and John Hampton. Lachlan's older brother William, and his wife, Jane Mackay, also named their sons John, William, Lachlan, and George… [William McIntosh's children] Lachlan and Hester both married Baillies. Margery had recently married James Spalding… and the couple lived on nearby St. Simons Island… Barbara, the youngest daughter, compounded the confusion by marrying yet another William McIntosh. Even Bartram, who knew them well, could get confused. Years later, when a young man approached Bartram at his home in Kingsessing, William recognized him as a McIntosh but could not place him. "Lachlan," the young man answered. That narrowed the possibilities but remained imprecise. "Lachlan's or William's?" "William's," came the answer. William Bartram paid him a nice compliment: "His countenance and manners bespeaks the Gentleman."

Sixteen-year-old Jack [Lachlan and Sarah's oldest son John] expressed keen interest in Bartram's expedition. The idea of exploring a vast and mysterious wilderness appealed to his sense of adventure. Would William permit Jack to accompany him on his trip to the interior of Georgia? William expressed his entire satisfaction at the idea... Proud father Lachlan was all for it; Sarah McIntosh needed further gentle persuasion. (35-37)

Jack McIntosh travels with William Bartram

After pondering Jack's request while Bartram was off exploring along the Altamaha for about a week, Sarah McIntosh gave Jack permission to accompany Bartram on his travels. Jack and Bartram set out from Darien on May 1, 1773. As they rode across Georgia, Bartram jotted notes on the farms they passed and the herds of deer and flocks of turkeys they saw. In a few days, beautiful springtime weather turned terribly hot and dry. They came across Governor Wright on his way to a congress in Augusta and learned that several fine horses belonging to the group escorting the governor "died in the Road by reason of the Heat and drouth." They stayed a few days at Indian trader George Galphin's post at Silver Bluff on the South Carolina side of the Savannah River. On May 14 they crossed the river to Augusta and joined a large expedition sent to survey lands recently ceded to Georgia by the Creek and Cherokee nations. Edward Barnard led the group of at least eighty men, including contingents of Creek and Cherokee warriors, along the main Creek trading path out of Augusta. Two days of traveling brought them to Wrightsborough in the Georgia piedmont. As they followed the old Cherokee trail westward out of Wrightsborough to a camp on Williams Creek in June, Bartram noted outcroppings of rock (Cashin 41-60). Cashin describes the botanist's activities:

After caring for his horse and pitching his tent, Bartram liked to roam about in hopes of discovering new plants, a joy shared by few others as he admitted. At times the agreeable young McIntosh would go along. They found the yellow root plant at the Williams Creek camp. The next morning after Young Warrior's daily ritual, they saddled up and resumed their deliberate pace along the south side of the Little River. They crossed numerous small streams, thought by Bartram to be branches of the Ogeechee but most likely tributaries of the Little River...

The next day they crossed the north fork of the Little River and entered a region described by the surveyors as heavily timbered in oak, hickory, walnut, chestnut and tulip poplar, interspersed with pine and canebrakes. The dark topsoil of six to seven inches covered a bed of red clay. Bartram expressed awe at the most magnificent forest he had ever seen. He measured several oaks that had a circumference of thirty feet...

They passed a buffalo lick... on the way to their destination, the Great Buffalo Lick. Bartram called the latter "an extraordinary place" [covering] an acre and a half with some depressions five and six feet deep. Buffalo had roamed this region as recently as Oglethorpe's time. By 1773 they were gone... Deer and other animals kept the ground clear [because] sodium sulphate in the soil appealed to animals...

The significance of the Great Buffalo Lick, as Bartram's contemporaries knew, was that it lay in a gap of the ridge that divided the waters of the Savannah River from those of the Oconee-Altamaha basin. Bartram referred to it as the Great Ridge, probably because of its cartographical importance rather than its topographical elevation. In truth, there is little to distinguish this ridge from the innumerable long hills of the piedmont. However, the treaty writers regarded the ridge as a crucial dividing place... [As the surveyors tried to mark the boundary of the land ceded by the Creeks] the question led to a lively dispute between Young Warrior and Philip Yonge that must have reminded Barnard of Rory McIntosh's near-fatal dispute [in 1768]. Bartram witnessed the surveyor pointing in one direction and the chief in another… The angry Creeks said this was a trick to cheat them out of their lands… Barnard… respected the Native Americans' intimate knowledge of the region. He decided to follow the direction of Young Warrior rather than that of his professional. Bartram approved the decision and praised "the complaisance and prudent conduct of the Colonel." (61-63)

When the expedition divided into two teams, Bartram and Jack McIntosh accompanied Barnard's team as it explored the northern line of the ceded lands. When they reached a marked tree that showed where Creek hunting grounds ended and Cherokee hunting grounds began, the contingent of Creek warriors left the expedition. Barnard and the contingent of Cherokee warriors continued to follow the boundary of the ceded lands to the junction of the Tugaloo and Keowee rivers. The beautiful landscape impressed Bartram: "A pleasant morning attended by the feather'd inhabitants of these shady retreats, with joyful song invites us forth, the elevated face of this Hilly country breathes an elastic pure air, inspiring health and activity" (Cashin 64). After traveling for two days, the team made camp on a tributary of the Broad River while the Cherokee warriors hunted deer and turkey. Cashin reports that Bartram went looking for new plants and when he returned to camp:

> …he found Jack McIntosh, his "philosophic companion," raptly engaged in the study of little hills of gravel here and there in the shoals of the swift, flowing stream. He thought the hills were made by crawfish as tiny citadels against the numerous predatory goldfish. The swift-darting, beautifully colored goldfish so fascinated Bartram that he drew a picture of one… The little hills in the water are made by minnows hatching their eggs. (65)

Bartram and Jack McIntosh rode with Colonel Barnard over rolling hills to the Tugaloo River and to the Indian town of Tugaloo in the foothills of the Cherokee mountains. In July, they reached the junction of the Tugaloo and the Savannah rivers, where Bartram commented on the flourishing rhododendron, mountain laurel and hydrangeas. Two young Indians harpooned dozens of trout and bream; one trout was two feet long and weighed about fifteen pounds, Bartram said. The Indian and white members of the expedition shared a meal of barbecued fish to celebrate the success of their mission. The next morning the Indians went their way and the white men headed back toward Augusta. Barnard and Bartram continued to Savannah. News soon reached them that two young Indians from their expedition had been murdered by settlers on the Broad River, disrupting the colonial governor's plans for developing the ceded lands (Cashin 66-67).

Laurens family travels abroad

Lachlan McIntosh's longtime friend and business partner Henry Laurens spent the early years of the 1770's abroad. His wife Eleanor Ball Laurens had died in the spring of 1770 shortly after giving birth to their daughter Mary Eleanor. In the fall of 1771 he and his sons Henry, John and James sailed for England. He and his sons stayed in London awhile before touring through Britain and Europe. He left his sons John and Henry in Geneva to be educated, and he continued to tour. He paid attention to the political issues of the time and strongly expressed opposition to tax policies and other attempts to impose British authority over the American people. In a letter to his son John he predicted war between Britain and the colonies. After visiting his sons in Paris in the summer of 1774, Henry Laurens returned without them to South Carolina at the end of 1774. His son James died in an accident in London shortly before turning 10 years old (Hamer, v. 1, xv-xvii; v. 9, xxiii-xxiv). At about that time his daughters Martha and Mary Eleanor traveled to England accompanied by their aunt and uncle.

> Martha Laurens was received on her landing by her elder brother, John Laurens, from whom she had been for some years separated. Being older, he had taken great delight in forwarding her education, and particularly, in forming her mind to be superior to the common accidents of life, and the groundless fears of some of her sex. To ascertain whether his labours had been successful or not, he bribed the postillion to drive very rapidly, and at the same time, without discovering his views, narrowly watched her countenance, to observe whether there were any changes in it expressive of womanish fears at the novel scene, so totally different from all her former travelling in the low, flat,

stoneless country of Carolina. On the termination of the ex-
periment to his satisfaction, he announced to his unsuspecting sister his congratulations, that "he had found her the
same Spartan girl he had left her." (Ramsay 16-17)

The last Laird of Borlum

In the Highlands of Scotland, Edward Mackintosh 7th of Borlum became known as the last laird of Borlum. "The heir male of
the line of Borlum may be found in the descendants of John Mhor
Mackintosh and his wife, Mary Fraser, in the State of Georgia,"
clan historian William Fraser Ross reports and then points out,
"Raigmore is generally looked upon as head of the family of Borlum."

Ross acknowledges that Edward was a controversial figure.
"Tales of his wrongdoing are legion, many of them, no doubt, pure
fiction," Ross writes. "It is a fact, however, that in 1773, Edward
had to flee the country for an armed attack on a Ross-shire drover
of the name of McRory, but his illegitimate brother, Alexander,
was apprehended, tried, found guilty and suffered the extreme pen-
alty of the law in 1773. It is believed that Edward made his way to
America, and that he made some atonement for his past crimes in
the ranks of the Army of his adopted country" (188).

An article in *The Celtic Monthly* tells the legend of the last
laird of Borlum in gruesome detail. The writer refers to the laird's
brother by both his Gaelic name Alister and the classical name Alexander:

> At Raitts, or, as it is now called, Belleville, the last laird of
> Borlum, Edward Mackintosh, resided. In many respects he
> excelled most of his forefathers in ferocity, and was one of
> the most daring robbers that ever lived in the Highlands of
> Scotland. Within a mile and a half of the mansion house
> there is an artificial cave in which he and his band found a
> convenient and secure lurking-place from which to sally
> forth to rob travellers of their purses, and sometimes of
> their lives...
>
>   In the now thriving village of Kingussie, in the imme-
> diate vicinity of the haunt of the Mackintoshes and their as-
> sociates, there were at the time of which we write, but a
> few miserable, straggling huts, whose proximity to the cave

imposed no check upon Borlum's movements, but rather aided, than obstructed him in his bad and bold career...

A warrant was... issued and placed in the hands of an officer, for the apprehension of Edward Mackintosh and his brother Alexander... Edward contrived to get information of the warrant for his apprehension having been issued... when he summoned a full attendance of his companions in crime to the house at Raitts, where he entertained them to a sumptuous supper and a splendid ball, and early next morning took his departure for the south, escorted a number of miles by his comrades.

He remained in private for some weeks in the house of a friend in Edinburgh, and afterwards made good his escape to France...

...yet his illegitimate brother, Alexander, was apprehended and conveyed to Inverness, and, in due time, tried for robbery and other crimes... Mackintosh produced several witnesses to prove that... he never in his life accompanied Edward in his lawless pursuits – his habits being quiet, peaceful, and honest... ...the jury, after some deliberation, returned a verdict of *Guilty*. The prisoner heard the verdict with the same calm and decent composure which he manifested throughout the trial. The court was crowded to suffocation, and great sympathy was manifested by the majority of the audience for the prisoner, whom they believed to be innocent. The most death-like silence pervaded the Court – every countenance reflected the awful solemnity which all felt, and, in slow and impressive language, the Judge pronounced the

DREADFUL SENTENCE OF THE LAW

the most awful it can inflict – death. ...even in this dreadful hour the prisoner flinched not – no weakness such as might have been expected on such an occasion manifested itself, and his fine handsome form, clad in the humble gray *thickset*, or home-spun corded cloth, stood erect and firm, with the dignity so characteristic of the Highlanders on great and solemn occasions. ... [Mackintosh] solemnly and emphatically denied his guilt... This declaration... produced a strong impression on the audience, which was increased by pity and commiseration for his wife and family. His wife was a mild and gentle creature, and in every respect, a most amiable woman. The prisoner was removed from the bar amidst the prayers and blessings, both loud and deep, of the greater portion of the audience.

At length the day of Mackintosh's execution arrived. How solemn was that dreadful day! Such as could leave their avocations did so in the morning, and paraded the streets in gloomy silence, or, if they spoke, it was only in whispers. By twelve o'clock the streets were almost entirely deserted, and nearly half the population of the town and neighbourhood was collected round the gibbet. It was erected at Muirfield, a little above the town, upon the top of the hill...

At length the culprit, accompanied by two clergymen (the Rev. Messrs. Fraser and Mackenzie), the magistrates, and a strong *posse* of constables, appeared. Mackintosh ascended the fatal ladder with a steady and firm step, and stared vacantly around – he appeared overwhelmed by internal agony – his face was pale, and large drops of perspiration rolled down his cheeks. The Rev. Murdo Mackenzie almost immediately commenced to discharge his sad duty. He began with prayer, to which the prisoner listened with the utmost attention, and his countenance became more settled, as if communing with his Maker and composing his soul. After prayer a psalm was sung, the voices of the assembled multitude rising in solemn consonance into the air...

THE EXECUTIONER

slowly adjusted the noose and pulled down the white cap over his face. ...the culprit's voice broke in accents of piercing agony upon the ear, and sunk into the heart – the last words he uttered were – "Oh, Father, Son, and Holy Ghost, I come." The sound was still murmuring in the breeze when the crowd were startled by a short, sharp knock, or jerk, a something falling, but not distinctly seen... and the culprit's lifeless body was swinging in the wind, and his soul winging its flight into the mansions of eternity. With mingled feelings of sorrow and horror, the multitude slowly and silently dispersed, many, if not most of the company, placing a small piece of bread under a stone, which, according to a superstitious tradition, would prevent after-dreams of the unfortunate Alexander Mackintosh.

After hanging the time required by law, the body was cut down, and according to the sentence, was placed in an iron cage, which was suspended from the top of a post near the gibbet, in order to be a warning and terror, in time coming, to evildoers…

…Highlanders… still secretly, and sometimes openly, maintained their attachment to their chief, and their friendly and brotherly feeling to their namesakes and clansmen…

THE CLAN MACKINTOSH,

in particular, had preserved with the utmost tenacity that spirit of clanship… …a few of them, resident in and about Inverness, came to the determination of preventing any long continuance of the exposure of the body by cutting it down and interring it. Amongst the number was William Mackintosh, a dyer, better known by the name of "Muckle Willie the Dyster," who from his daring and great strength was looked upon as a leader. The day… had been cold and cloudy, and towards evening showers of drizzling rain began to fall, the wind gradually increased, and about seven o'clock, when the dyer and his companions thought it safe to put their purpose into execution, it swept along in strong gusts. The night was very dark – not a star was to be seen – and as the Mackintoshes stole cautiously out of the town, they, in an undertone congratulated each other that the night was so favourable for their design. They walked circumspectly and slowly until they reached the burn of Aultnaskiach, when they proceeded up the bed of the burn until they arrived at the bridge which crosses it… From that place they crept, rather than walked, over the barren heath, in the direction of the gallows. … [The Mackintoshes] were almost transfixed with fear, by hearing a short, hard, screeching sound at no great distance from them… For upwards of a minute, the whole party stood fixed and mute – nothing was to be seen – nothing heard, save the whistling of the wind and the grating sound produced by the swinging of

THE IRON CAGE WHEREIN THE BODY

was suspended. The party, however, seeing it like a black cloud hanging in the horizon above their heads, became irresolute and discouraged, and were on the eve of returning home, when Willie broke the silence by a very unceremonious "Pooh, you heard nothing but the wind..." On this they feebly and slowly followed Willie, who sprang to the post, and climbing up with the agility of a cat, was speedily sitting on the top undoing the fastenings, and in a few minutes the cage, with its contents, fell at the feet of his companions with a crash, which they afterwards solemnly declared shook the earth under them. The body was taken out of the cage with the utmost dispatch, and carried across the moor to the bank of the burn. Here they made a hole in the sand with their hands, in which the body was deposited, and covering it over, returned to their dwellings, inwardly congratulating themselves that so disagreeable and dangerous a piece of business was ended... In the morning, when it was discovered that the body of Alister Mackintosh had been taken away during the night, a reward of five pounds was immediately offered to any person who should discover the perpetrators of this daring act... Towards evening, a claimant appeared in the person of Little Tibbie, the wife of Archy the waterman. She had been at Aultnaskiach burn for sand, and to her amazement discovered the stolen body of Mackintosh. She, with great speed repaired to the town to claim the reward, and... roared out as she ran – "Oh, sirs, sirs, Saunders Mackintosh's body!" ...

ANOTHER PARTY OF THE CLAN headed by the ever ready dyer, proceeded with the greatest expedition to Aultnaskiach burn and removed the body to Campfield, where it was again interred, and allowed to remain...

The widow and children of Alister were amply provided for in every respect by the humane and patriotic Bailie Inglis...

The eldest son, James, entered the Gordon Fencibles... Edward, the second son, entered the navy... There was also a daughter, who, after being educated in all the branches of education suitable for a lady of rank, repaired to the south...

The estate of Raitts subsequently became the property of James Macpherson, Esq., the celebrated translator of the poems of Ossian, who changed its name from Raitts to Belleville – the original name being in his, as well as in the estimation of others, obnoxious. This property he highly cultivated and improved, whereon he built an excellent mansion-house. ("Traditions" 165-68, 187-89)

Flory McDonald entertains Johnson and Boswell

On Skye, England's distinguished man of letters Samuel Johnson, age 64, and his biographer James Boswell visited Flory and Allan McDonald in 1773. By this time, the Macdonald estate named Kingsburgh was mired in money problems, causing Flory and Allan to plan to emigrate to America.

Johnson wrote, "We were entertained with the usual hospitality by Mr. Macdonald and his lady, Flora Macdonald, a name that will be mentioned in history, and if courage and fidelity be virtue, mentioned with honour. She is a woman of middle stature, soft features, gentle manners, and elegant presence" (50).

Boswell wrote in his journal:

> [September 12]: It was a beautiful day… We were resolved to pay a visit at Kingsburgh, and see the celebrated Miss Flora Macdonald, who is married to the present Mr. Macdonald of Kingsburgh… [John MacLeod of Raasay, who had sheltered Bonnie Prince Charlie in 1746] himself went with us in a large boat, with eight oars, built in his island. We had a most pleasant sail between Rasay and Sky; and passed by a cave, where Martin says fowls were caught by lighting fire in the mouth of it… But it is not now practiced, as few fowls come into it… (228-29)
>
> …In the evening, Dr. Johnson and I remounted our horses… It rained very hard. We rode what they call six miles, upon Rasay's lands in Sky, to Dr. Macleod's house… The doctor accompanied us to Kingsburgh, which is called a mile farther; but the computation of Sky has no connection whatever with real distance.
>
> I was highly pleased to see Dr. Johnson safely arrived at Kingsburgh, and received by the hospitable Mr. Macdonald, who, with a most respectful attention, supported

him into the house. Kingsburgh was completely the figure of a gallant Highlander, – exhibiting "the graceful mien and manly looks," which our popular Scotch song has justly attributed to that character. He had his Tartan plaid thrown about him, a large blue bonnet with a knot of black ribband like a cockade, a brown short coat of a kind of duffel, a Tartan waistcoat with gold buttons and gold button-holes, a bluish philibeg, and Tartan hose. He had jet black hair tied behind, and was a large stately man, with a steady sensible countenance.

There was a comfortable parlor with a good fire, and a dram went round. By and by supper was served, at which there appeared the lady of the house, the celebrated Miss Flora Macdonald. She is a little woman, of a genteel appearance, and uncommonly mild and well bred. To see Dr. Samuel Johnson, the great champion of the English Tories, salute Miss Flora Macdonald in the isle of Sky, was a striking sight; for though somewhat congenial in their notions, it was very improbable they should meet here. (232)

[Boswell described the meal in his manuscript but not in his published book: We had as genteel a supper as one would wish to see, in particular an excellent roasted turkey, porter to drink at table, and after supper claret and punch. But what I admired was the perfect ease with which everything went on. My *facility of manners*, as Adam Smith said of me, had fine play (Pottle 159).]

Miss Flora Macdonald (for so I shall call her) told me, she heard upon the main land, as she was returning home about a fortnight before, that Mr. Boswell was coming to Sky, and one Mr. Johnson, a young English buck, with him. He was highly entertained with this fancy. Giving an account of the afternoon which we passed at *Anock*, he said, "I, being a *buck*, had miss in to make tea." [In his manuscript, Boswell put it: …speaking of the afternoon which we passed at Anock, he said, "I, being a *buck*, had Miss in to make tea," or some such expression about Macqueen's daughter (Pottle 159-60).] – He was rather quiescent tonight, and went early to bed. I was in a cordial humour, and promoted a cheerful glass. The punch was excellent… Yet in reality my heart was grieved, when I recollected that

Kingsburgh was embarrassed in his affairs [was under a load of debt], and intended to go to America. However, nothing but was good was present, and I pleased myself in thinking that so spirited a man would be well every where. I slept in the same room with Dr. Johnson. Each had a neat bed, with Tartan curtains, in an upper chamber. (Boswell 232-33)

Monday, 13th September
The room where we lay was a celebrated one. Dr. Johnson's bed was the very bed in which the grandson of the unfortunate King James the Second lay, on one of the nights after the failure of his rash attempt in 1745-6, while he was eluding the pursuit of the emissaries of government, which had offered thirty thousand pounds as a reward for apprehending him. To see Dr. Samuel Johnson lying in that bed, in the isle of Sky, in the house of Miss Flora Macdonald, struck me with such a group of ideas as it is not easy for words to describe, as they passed through the mind. He smiled, and said, "I have had no ambitious thoughts in it." – The room was decorated with a great variety of maps and prints...

Upon the table in our room I found in the morning a slip of paper, on which Dr. Johnson had written with his pencil these words:

"Quantum cedat virtuitibus aurum."

[With virtue weigh'd, what worthless trash is gold!]

What he meant by writing them I could not tell. He had caught a cold a day or two ago, and the rain yesterday having made it worse, he was become very deaf. At breakfast he said, he would have given a good deal rather than not have lain in that bed. I owned that he was a lucky man, and observed, that without doubt it had been contrived between Mrs. Macdonald and him. She seemed to acquiesce; adding, "You know young *bucks* are always favourites of the ladies." He spoke of Prince Charles being there, and asked Mrs. Macdonald, "*Who* was with him? We were told, madam, in England, there was one Miss Flora Macdonald with him." – She said, "they were very right;" and perceiving Dr. Johnson's curiosity, though he had delicacy enough not

to question her, very obligingly entertained him with a re-
cital of the particulars of which she herself knew of that escape, which does so much honour to the humanity, fidelity,
and generosity, of the Highlanders... (233-34)

Kingsburgh conducted us in his boat, across one of the
lochs, as they call them, or arms of the sea, which flow in
upon all the coasts of Sky, – to a mile beyond a place called
Grishinish. Our horses had been sent round by land to meet
us. By this sail we saved eight miles of bad riding. Dr.
Johnson said, "When we take into the computation what we
have saved, and what we have gained, by this agreeable
sail, it is a great deal." He observed, "it is very disagreeable
riding in Sky. The way is so narrow, only one at a time can
travel, so it is quite unsocial; and you cannot indulge in
meditation by yourself, because you must be always attending to the steps which your horse takes." (247)

...As soon as we reached the shore, we took leave of
Kingsburgh, and mounted our horses. We passed through a
wild moor, in many places so soft that we were obliged to
walk, which was very fatiguing to Dr. Johnson. Once he
had advanced on horseback to a very bad step. There was a
steep declivity on his left, to which he was so near, that
there was not room for him to dismount in the usual way.
He tried to alight on the other side, as if he had been a
young buck indeed, but in the attempt he fell at his length
upon the ground; from which, however, he got up immediately without being hurt. During this dreary ride, we were
sometimes relieved by a view of branches of the sea, that
universal medium of connection amongst mankind. A
guide, who had been sent with us from Kingsburgh, explored the way (much in the same manner as, I suppose, is
pursued in the wilds of America,) by observing certain
marks known only to the inhabitants.

We arrived at Dunvegan late in the afternoon. The
great size of the castle, which is partly old and partly new,
and is built upon a rock close to the sea, while the land
around it presents nothing but wild, moorish, hilly, and
craggy appearances, gave a rude magnificence to the scene... (248-49)

Flory McDonald emigrates to America: 1774

Flory McDonald – who had helped the fugitive Bonnie Prince Charlie escape from the British Isles after the failure of the last Jacobite rising – emigrated to America in 1774. The reason that she agreed to "begin the world again, anewe, in another Corner of it" as she put it was purely economic. On "this poor miserable Island" of Skye in the Scottish Highlands, she said, "we cannot promise ourselves but poverty and oppression, haveing last Spring and this time two years lost almost our whole Stock of Cattle and horses; we lost within these three years, three hundred and twenty-seven heads, so that we have hardly what will pay our Creditors which we are to let them have" (qtd. in Vining 118).

At the time of emigration, she had been married to Allan McDonald of Kingsburgh for more than twenty years, and they had five sons and two daughters. Their oldest son Charles – named in honor of Bonnie Prince Charlie – was a lieutenant serving with the East India Company. Their son Ranald was a lieutenant in the Marines. Their youngest son John remained in Edinburgh, where he attended school, and their youngest daughter Frances stayed in Scotland with family friends. Their sons Alexander and James emigrated with them. Their daughter Anne and son-in-law Alexander McLeod also emigrated at the same time (Toffey 119).

Flory and Allan McDonald settled among fellow Highlander emigrants in the Cross Creek country near the North Carolina coast. Their daughter Anne and her husband settled nearby. An early biographer who interviewed Anne tells the tale:

> At that period, many respectable families from Skye emigrated to America, owing to a general depression in the price of cattle, and other untoward circumstances. Allan determined to follow his countrymen across the Atlantic, with his wife and family, in the hope of repairing his fortune, and of rendering himself independent. The embarrassments of her husband only tended to show the true nobleness of Flora's character. She who had risked her life with her Prince was ready and willing to sacrifice everything for a husband's comfort, and to accompany him to whatever quarter of the world it might be expected that fortune might yet smile on the ruined family. Consequently, in the month

of August, 1774, Kingsburgh and family sailed in the ship *Baliol*, from Campbeltown, Kintyre, to North Carolina.

They had a very favourable passage to the Western World. The time of their departure from Scotland became known among their countrymen in Carolina where they were anxiously expected and joyfully received on their arrival. Flora's fame preceded her for years; and her countrymen of whom there were hundreds in the colony, felt proud of the prospect of having her presence among them. Various demonstrations, on a large scale, were made to welcome her to American territory. Soon after her landing, a largely attended ball was given in her honour at Wilmington, where she was gratified by the great attention paid to her daughter Anne, then entering into womanhood, a young lady of surpassing beauty. An American gentleman, speaking of Flora's reception on this occasion, says, that "on her arrival at Cross-Creek she received a truly Highland welcome from her old neighbours and kinsfolk, who had crossed the Atlantic years before her. The strains of the *Piobaireachd* and the martial airs of her native land, greeted her on her approach to the capital of the Scottish Settlement. In that village she remained for some time visiting and receiving visits from friends, while her husband went to the western part of Cumberland in quest of land." Many families of distinction pressed upon her to make their dwellings her home, but she respectfully declined, naturally preferring a settled place of her own. She spent about a half-year at Cameron's Hill, in Cumberland, where she and her family were regular worshippers in a Presbyterian Church on Long Street, under the pastoral care of a countryman, the Rev. Mr. Macleod. (Macgregor164-65)

A twentieth-century biographer who describes the early biography as "full of errors and decorated with pious observations" casts doubt on the story that Anne was the belle of the ball. "Anne at this time had been married three years and was the mother of two children, possibly pregnant with her third," the later biographer points out, and "there is furthermore no record of such a ball" (Vining 9, 138).

The later biographer describes Flory's new home:

The North Carolina coastal plain spread more than a hundred miles inland from the sea. The soil was a light, sandy loam, productive when it was cleared and fertile along the rivers and creeks. The planters in the lower Cape Fear region raised indigo, rice, corn and wheat, though not enough of the last even for their own needs. Their chief source of wealth was the miles of pine forest from which they took the naval stores, the pitch and tar and turpentine, the lumber and the shingles, which they shipped to England and to the West Indies. In the pine-covered sand hills and rich valleys of the upper Cape Fear, people raised black cattle, horses, hogs and grain, which they sent overland to Charles Town in South Carolina or down the river to Wilmington. They did not tap the trees for turpentine, for that was tedious work best performed by slaves, and few of the Scotsmen of the sand hills owned slaves, though they made use of indentured servants

Cross Creek and Campbelltown at the head of navigation on the Cape Fear were twin villages a mile and three quarters apart. Campbelltown stood on the flat and swampy land on the river itself, Cross Creek on a bluff over the creek for which it was named, at the beginning of the sand hills which rolled away to the west behind it... In 1774, when the MacDonalds arrived, both were thriving trade centers with mills, shops, dwelling houses, a pharmacy and a courthouse, thronged with people and with wagons from the back country laden with goods to be sent to the coast by road or river.

... The Highlanders continued to pour into the country in waves which reached a crest in 1774 and 1775, when there were, it has been estimated, about ten thousand of them in the region...

... they raised black cattle, as they had done in Scotland. The former tacksmen lived much as they had lived at home, but the small farmers found life considerably richer and easier here. They raised corn and hogs for their staple food; fished in the rivers and creeks; shot deer, wild turkeys, pheasant, quail, ducks, wild geese and wild pigeons, with no complaint from anyone about poaching; and got

just for the picking all the wild grapes, strawberries, black-
berries, apples, mulberries, cherries and persimmons that
they could eat. The former crofters who had subsisted on
oatmeal and milk must have felt themselves in clover. (Vining 139-141)

Flory's husband Allan bought more than five hundred acres
with fields already in cultivation, peach orchards, a gristmill, a
corn crib, a keeping house, a barn and a stable in addition to a
dwelling house and a kitchen. Flory and Allan, their sons Alexander and James, and eight indentured servants settled on the plantation. They set up house with the books, plate and furniture they had
brought from Kingsburgh House. Their daughter Anne and her
husband Alexander MacLeod and twelve indentured servants settled about twenty-five miles away from Flory and Allan. In addition to silver, china, tablecloths and apparel, Alexander brought
324 books from Scotland to North Carolina. Flory's stepfather
Hugh MacDonald settled about five miles away from her new
home, and his daughter Annabella's family also settled in the area.
Flory had left the Scottish Highlands behind, but she was still surrounded by family and fellow Highlanders (Vining143-144)

As fate would have it, Flory and her family arrived in North
Carolina when America was on the cusp of a revolution. The Highlanders' reputation as fierce fighters attracted recruiters from both
revolutionaries and loyalists. The maze of relationships and conflicting loyalties that had engulfed Flory and her fellow Highlanders in Scotland would once again engulf them in America.

1775-1776

In Georgia, Lachlan McIntosh, age 48, assumes command of Continental troops; several members of the McIntosh family join his battalion. In North Carolina, Flory McDonald's husband leads loyalist Highlanders in one of the earliest battles of the American Revolution. In South Carolina, Alexander McDonald serves in the 2nd South Carolina Regiment as it defends Charleston from a British assault. In New York, Aeneas the 23rd Chief of Clan Mackintosh, age 25, arrives with the 71st Regiment and engages in a campaign that drives out George Washington's army.

Darien Committee supports Continental Congress

When the first Continental Congress met in Philadelphia in 1774, Georgia did not participate. By 1775, friction between the American colonies and the English government had reached a crisis. Although Boston was the center of attention, Georgia played a supportive role. McIntosh County historian Buddy Sullivan describes the situation:

> On January 1, 1775, several months before Lexington and Concord, the Darien Committee gathered at the Meeting House on the Broad Road north of Darien and appointed Lachlan McIntosh as their leader and spokesman. The group expressed full support for their defiant colonial brethren in New England. The Darien Committee met again on January 12 to reaffirm its support of the revolutionary cause as well as choose local delegates to the Provincial Congress which was to be convened in Savannah. (57)

Biographer Harvey Jackson gives context to McIntosh's decision:

> Because of his well-known reluctance to intervene in colonial politics, McIntosh's role as leader of the Darien committee comes as something of a shock…
>
> Still, it would have been difficult for him to have done otherwise. The McIntoshes had come to Georgia, as refu-

gees from English-dominated Scotland, to serve the Trustees, not the crown. After royalization, that allegiance was
transferred to the colony, Georgia; and there is nothing to
indicate that, in the process, they developed a similar attachment to George III. (25)

Apparently referring to his Mackintosh forebears' role in the
Jacobite risings, Lachlan McIntosh told a fellow Georgian "Neither
we or our fathers could Bear, or even understand aright, that Med-
ley of all Governments the British, with its numberless Offices and
Pomp" (qtd. in Lawrence, "Suspension" 107).

Darien Committee opposes slavery
The Darien Committee's most remarkable declaration was a
call to free the slaves in Georgia, an eerie echo of the petition
against slavery signed by the Scots at Darien in 1739. John Mackintosh Mor had led the generation who opposed slavery in 1739,
and his son Lachlan McIntosh led the generation who opposed
slavery in 1775.

Even though Lachlan McIntosh owned about sixty slaves and
his brother George owned about forty slaves, Lachlan recognized
that slavery was untenable. The Darien Committee called slavery
"an unnatural practice… founded in injustice and cruelty, and
highly dangerous to our liberty (as well as our lives) debasing part
of our fellow creatures below men, and corrupting the virtue and
morals of the rest, and is laying the basis of that liberty we contend
for… upon a very wrong foundation" (Sullivan 57).

The shooting begins: April 19, 1775
The first skirmishes of the American Revolution erupted in the
vicinity of Boston, Lexington and Concord, Massachusetts, on
April 19. Close to four thousand Massachusetts militiamen participated at different times during a day-long series of engagements
against 1,800 British soldiers. American losses were forty-nine
killed, forty wounded and five missing. British casualties were
nineteen officers and 250 rank and file killed or wounded.

Before midnight, news of the battle reached 32-year-old Nathanael Greene at his home in Rhode Island sixty miles from Boston. Although raised a pacifist Quaker, Greene had become a student of military strategy. He had purchased books on military his-

tory from Henry Knox, a bookseller in Boston who studied books on artillery. Greene had helped form a militia company in 1774. That same year, he had married a beautiful young woman named Catherine but called Caty or Kitty. A biographer describes her as "small, with blue-gray eyes, and vivacious. A graceful dancer, she possessed a lively wit and contributed brightly to the repartee at any social gathering" (Bailey 19). Upon learning of the fighting in Massachusetts, "Greene saddled his horse, kissed Caty good-bye, and rode to East Greenwich to take his place as a private in the Kentish Guards;" the Royal Governor, however, ordered the Guards to halt (Bailey 27). When the Rhode Island General Assembly formed a brigade, Greene was commissioned as the Brigadier General on May 8.

The Second Continental Congress assembled in May of 1775 as the American confrontation with Great Britain became more warlike. Greene led the Rhode Island brigade of 1,500 troops into Massachusetts, reaching Cambridge on June 3. "Greene at once set about molding the three regiments into what soon were recognized as the best disciplined and best equipped units of all the raw troops sent by the colonies to the aid of the beleaguered town of Boston" (Bailey 30). In the middle of June, Greene returned home briefly to set his affairs in order in anticipation of a long absence on military duty.

The Battle of Bunker Hill: June 17, 1775

On the night of June 16, American militiamen established a military position on Breed's Hill overlooking the British stronghold at Boston. The next day, after British warship bombarded the position, two thousand British troops crossed the Charles River and attacked the position defended by about three thousand Americans. The British charged uphill in a series of assaults and fought the Americans hand to hand. When the Americans withdrew to Bunker Hill, the British continued to attack until they drove off the Americans. British losses were 1,150 killed or wounded. One of the wounded British soldiers probably was Charles McDonald, son of Flory McDonald – famous for having rescued Bonnie Prince Charlie (Vining 179). American losses were 140 killed and several hundred wounded. On the evening after the battle, Nathanael Greene learned of it and rode all night to return from Rhode Island to Cambridge.

Washington chosen as commander

The Continental Congress formed a Continental Army and appointed 43-year-old George Washington as commander in chief on June 15. Washington received his commission on June 20 and left Philadelphia the next day to take command of the American forces outside Boston. He arrived at Cambridge on July 2, and soon met Nathanael Greene. They developed a close friendship; when Nathanael and Caty's first child was born later that year the baby was christened George Washington Greene.

Flory McDonald dragged into conflict

Among the far-reaching effects of the fighting around Boston was the involvement of Flory McDonald – legendary for having rescued Bonnie Prince Charlie – in efforts to strengthen British forces in America. Flory and her husband Allan McDonald of Kingsburgh had recently emigrated from Skye to the Cross Creek country where numerous Highlanders were settled. A biographer describes how Flory's family fell into the conflict:

> In June, the month of the Battle of Bunker Hill and of the appointment of Colonel George Washington to the command of the new continental army by the Congress in Philadelphia, Allan MacDonald called a meeting of the "leading Highlanders." That would include, certainly, Alexander MacLeod, his son-in-law, who was still a lieutenant on half pay; Alexander MacDonald of Cuidreach; Hugh MacDonald of Armadale; Alexander Morrison of Cross Hill, who had come to Cumberland County from Skye in 1772, bringing with him 300 of his neighbors; Murdoch MacLeod, the surgeon of Cross Creek and Anson County; and others: Stewarts, MacRaes, MacArthurs, Camerons, Campbells, MacNeils...
>
> Many of the Scots, like Allan himself, had come to North Carolina too recently to have developed firm ties to the land. All of them looked on monarchy as the form of government ordained by heaven and considered republicanism horrid and unnatural. And finally they had, even those who were not new arrivals, that lasting and romantic feeling for Scotland characteristic of Scotsmen every-

where... Of the humbler Scotsmen, "the common Highlanders," many spoke only Gaelic and obeyed without
question the call of their leaders, as they had done from
time immemorial.

...the leading Highlanders of North Carolina agreed
that they would raise companies to defend the King's interests by force... Everybody there no doubt intended to be an
officer. They delegated Allan – or he offered – to go... to
see the Governor and inform him of their meeting and the
readiness of the Highlanders to rise.

So Flora, still in the process of getting settled in the
unfamiliar wooden house among the melancholy pines,
saw, with what sinking of the heart we can imagine, her
husband set out for the distant coast... (Vining 148-51)

An early biographer who says he "was furnished, to a great
extent, with the facts here given, from the lips of Flora's daughter,
the said Mrs. Major-General Macleod," gives a flowery description
of the recruitment process:

Unfortunately for Flora and her family, on their arrival in
the New World the American war was about its commencement, and young Kingsburgh soon became involved
in its troubles. In 1775, Governor Martin determined to
raise among the Scotch Highlanders a body of men to be
sent to Boston, and mustered them into the Royal Highland
Emigrant Regiment, the better to enable General Gage to
look down all opposition in that quarter. Seeing the distinction and honour which all classes of Highlanders awarded
to Flora and her husband Kingsburgh, the crafty Governor
resolved to invest him with the chief command... "In order
to assemble the Scots," says an American writer, "balls
were given in different parts of the settlement, some of
which Flora attended, with her daughter, Mrs. Major Macleod... Upon these occasions, Anne... reigned supreme, and
bore off the honours of the ball-room." (Macgregor 165-66)

South Carolina prepares for war
During the time when the shooting started in Massachusetts
and the Continental Congress formed an army, South Carolinians

also prepared for war. In April, 1775, organized parties of patriots took control of the gunpowder magazines in the Charleston area. Lachlan McIntosh's friend Henry Laurens was among the patriots who removed muskets and ammunition from the State House armory in Charleston. In June, the South Carolina Provincial Congress created a Council of Safety with Laurens as its president, and authorized two Continental infantry regiments and a mounted ranger squadron. Colonel William Moultrie served as commander of the 2nd South Carolina Regiment and Francis Marion served as a captain in Moultrie's regiment. The regiment sent recruiters not only through South Carolina but also through Georgia, and William Jasper joined the regiment in Halifax County, Georgia, in July.

Georgians move toward revolution

Georgians opposed to British rule called a Second Provincial Congress in the summer of 1775. Lachlan McIntosh remained the leader of the Darien Committee that elected delegates to the Provincial Congress. The committee selected Lachlan and his brothers William and George as delegates. On July 4, 1775, the Provincial Congress declared support for the Continental Congress and established itself as Georgia's revolutionary government.

The Georgia Provincial Congress set up a Council of Safety to operate the government when the Provincial Congress was not in session. George McIntosh served on the Council of Safety.

British army recruits Allan McDonald

In July, the British army recruited Allan McDonald – the husband of the legendary Flory McDonald. Allan had already informed the royal governor of North Carolina that he and other leaders of the Highlanders in the Cape Fear were willing to raise companies to fight for their king. A biographer of Flory McDonald describes the recruitment effort authorized by the commander of British forces in America:

> In the back country the slow hot summer wore on. The grain was harvested and their neighbors brought it to the MacDonalds' mill to be ground. The cattle drowsed in the shade of the trees and the July flies sent up their hot rasping drone till midnight. Anne MacLeod, having been delivered

of one daughter, was pregnant again. Cuidreach's son Donald, who had reached North Carolina the previous year, was given a plantation on Mountain Creek in Anson County by his grandfather. The family gathered in [Flora's stepfather] Hugh's house to witness the signing of the deed.

...In the height of the summer two Highland officers sent by General Gage arrived at Glendale...

They were already known to the people from the islands. Major Donald MacDonald was a cousin of Allan's who had grown up on the tack of Knock, on the east coast of Skye between Portree and Armadale. He had fought at Culloden – and at Bunker Hill. Captain Donald MacLeod, his companion, was of the St. Kilda MacLeods.

They had come to recruit three companies of Highlanders for the Royal Highland Regiment which was then being formed in Boston. Allan's Staten Island cousin, Alexander MacDonald, having... "fled to Boston in the Nick of time when a parcel of low lived rebellious rascals were about to take possession of him and his house," was a captain in the second battalion of this regiment. Major MacDonald offered both Allan MacDonald and Alexander MacLeod captaincies. This put them in something of a quandary, for the Governor had already promised them higher rank in his own regiment, which he had not yet got official permission to raise. They accepted Major MacDonald's proposal on condition that [North Carolina Governor] Martin's plan did not go through. (Vining 155-56)

Mackintosh Chief joins British army

On August 23, 1775, King George III of Great Britain and Ireland proclaimed that the colonies were in rebellion and ordered his military men to suppress the rebellion. As Great Britain built a larger army to put down the rebellion in America, the Highlands of Scotland seemed a fertile recruiting ground. Simon Fraser raised a regiment of two battalions, officially named the 71st Regiment of Foot and commonly called Fraser's Highlanders or the 71st Highlanders. Aeneas the 23rd Chief of Clan Mackintosh recruited a company for the 71st Regiment and was awarded the rank of captain in the regiment's 2nd Battalion.

Alexander McDonald joins 2nd Regiment

Alexander McDonald of St. Andrews Parish – the area formerly called the Darien District – enlisted as a sergeant in the 2nd
South Carolina Regiment on November 4, 1775. When he went off
to war he left his wife Christine at home with two young children,
their elder son Alexander and 3-year-old William. While Alexander served with the patriots, Christine's father Murdoch McLeod
remained a loyalist throughout the war. Alexander – whose father
Alexander McDonald had been recruited in the Scottish Highlands
to serve in the Independent Company of Foot when Darien was
founded – shared the McDonald name with twenty-seven men in
the 2nd South Carolina regiment (Moss, *South Carolina* 615; *American Revolution Roster: Fort Sullivan* 238-240; Redfearn 29, 78).

Wives join officers for winter

In Massachusetts, Continental Commander in Chief George
Washington's wife Martha joined him at his quarters in Cambridge
before Christmas of 1775 and stayed for the winter. She was accompanied by her son Jack Custis and his wife.

Nathanael Greene's wife Caty and their newborn son also
came to Cambridge. Other officers' wives arrived as well, contributing to a lively social scene. Martha Washington and Caty Greene
developed a lasting friendship.

Lachlan McIntosh leads Continental battalion

Congress elected Lachlan McIntosh to lead the first Continental battalion in Georgia in January of 1776. He held the rank of
Colonel and his teenage sons William, Lackie, and John were subalterns. Lachlan's older brother William McIntosh led a troop of
Light Horse. William's son John McIntosh, who had become an
officer in the Continental army in 1775 at age 20, was promoted to
the rank of captain in the 1st Georgia Regiment.

Battle of the Riceboats

A British fleet including four men-of-war arrived at the mouth
of the Savannah River early in 1776. The royal governor of Georgia explained that the ships had come to collect supplies of rice and
other provisions. The Council of Safety did not allow the British to
obtain provisions because of the Continental non-exportation
agreement. The Council arrested the governor and other royal offi-

cials to keep them from communicating with the British fleet. The governor and several other officials sneaked out of Savannah during the night of February 11 and boarded a British ship before daylight the next morning.

A few weeks later, the British decided to take the rice by force. A British schooner and a sloop sailed up the Savannah River and crossed behind Hutchinson Island. Three hundred men disembarked and seized about twenty riceboats anchored beside the island. The warships then sailed around to escort the riceboats downriver.

Lachlan McIntosh, as a Colonel in the Continental army and also the commander of Georgia militia, led the patriot resistance to the British operation. He ordered an artillery battery at Yamacraw to open fire on the British ships. The ships returned fire, and the artillery battle raged throughout the afternoon.

As night fell, McIntosh decided to burn the riceboats to keep them from falling into enemy hands. The Georgians coated the mast, spars, and rigging of a confiscated ship with pitch, set the pitch ablaze, and sent the fireship drifting toward the riceboats. The fireship ran aground and became a beacon in the evening sky. The Georgians prepared a smaller fireship and sent it toward the riceboats. The British cut ten riceboats free from their anchors and escorted them to safety. The Georgians' fireship rammed two of the riceboats that the British had left behind. Throughout the night, the burning boats drifted up and down the river with the tide, passing Savannah in one direction and later passing the town in the opposite direction (Jackson 37-38).

When morning came, McIntosh arranged for the riceboats that had not been damaged during the battle to be moved to a location where they could be closely guarded. The British fleet abandoned Georgia a few days later, leaving only two ships to observe the Savannah harbor.

Lachlan McIntosh's friend William Bartram happened to be in Savannah, and accompanied Lachlan to Darien shortly after the battle of the riceboats (Cashin, *Bartram* 230).

Threats from the southern frontier

Unlike any other Southern state, Georgia bordered on British-held territory. British troops, loyalists and Indians operating out of British East Florida raided the sparsely populated plantations and villages of South Georgia almost with impunity. Among the British soldiers stationed in Florida was a captain in the 3rd Battalion of the 60th Regiment named George McIntosh (Searcy 33).

The Georgia patriots were not in a position to protect the frontier, because they had managed to raise only 286 men for their Continental battalion, supplemented by about six hundred militiamen. As the Continental commander in Georgia, Lachlan McIntosh entrusted the defense of the frontier to two sixty-man troops of horse militia commanded by his older brother William.

On February 27, recognizing that Georgia could not defend itself, Congress created a Southern Military Department covering Virginia, North Carolina, South Carolina and Georgia. Congress placed Major General Charles Lee in command of the department. Congress named James Moore of North Carolina to serve as one of four brigadiers in the new department.

On that same day, as fate would have it, Moore led Continental troops and North Carolina militia in defeating a loyalist army of immigrants from the Scottish Highlands.

Cross Creek Highlanders rally to the king's cause

British strategists assumed that Southern loyalists would rally to support British troops. Under the British plan, forces under Lord Cornwallis would set sail from Ireland, forces under General Clinton would set sail from New York, loyalists would march from settlements in North Carolina, and they would all rendezvous on the coast near Cape Fear. From there, they would attack Charleston and bring the South under British control.

The job of recruiting loyalists among emigrant Highlanders in the Cape Fear Valley was given to a veteran British officer, 80-year-old Donald McDonald. Encyclopedia editor Mark Boatner describes McDonald's effort:

> Donald McDonald raised the standard at Cross Creek (now Fayetteville) and on 5 Feb. '76 called for an assembly of armed supporters. Because of his own reputation as a veteran of Culloden and the work of others including the legendary Flora Mcdonald, 1,000 Highland Scots gathered by 18 Feb. They came with bagpipes, broadswords, dirks, drums, and many wore kilts and tartans. Most of them were recent immigrants and were motivated not so much by loy-

alty to George III (from whom they held their land) as by their dislike for the Lowlanders and Ulstermen so prominent in the rebel camp… (732).

The loyalists marched toward the coast for their rendezvous with the British regulars sailing from New York and Ireland. A biographer who interviewed Flory's daughter writes that Flory set off on the march with her husband Allan McDonald of Kingsburgh:

> When the royal banner was unfurled at Cross Creek in 1776, and the loyalist army marched towards Brunswick, under the command of General Donald Macdonald, Allan of Kingsburgh had his own duties allotted to him as Brigadier-General. Flora, with the due devotion of an affectionate wife, followed her husband for many days, and encamped one night with him in a dangerous place, on the brow of Haymount, near the Arsenal of the United States. For a time she would not listen to her husband's earnest entreaties that she should return home, as his own life was enough to be in jeopardy. Next morning, however, when the army took up its line of march, midst banners streaming in the breeze, and martial music floating on the air, Flora deemed it high time to retrace her steps. She affectionately embraced her husband, and her eyes were dimmed with tears as she breathed to heaven a fervent prayer for his safe and speedy return to his family and home. (Macgregor 167).

After saying goodbye to her husband, some people say, Flory "mounted her snow-white horse, rode along the columns of the army, encouraging the men," and returned home (Maclean 50). Some people say that Flory "mounted on a white pony, addressed the troops in Gaelic… . She appealed to their love of the old land whence they came. She rallied them by memories of Highland heroism and Highland devotion. The clansmen, wild in their enthusiasm, answered her in fierce Gaelic oaths of loyalty… As the Highlanders passed… she called out to each clan its Gaelic battle-cry" (qtd. in Toffey 51-52).

Moore's Creek Bridge: February 27, 1776

Colonel James Moore led the 1st North Carolina Continentals to intercept the advancing loyalists. He was joined by several militia units, including a hundred Volunteer Independent Rangers commanded by his brother-in-law John Ashe. The patriot units engaged the loyalists at Moore's Creek Bridge on February 27.

Highlanders practice traditional warfare

James Hunter, a historian from Skye, focuses on Highland traditions in his account of the Battle of Moore's Creek Bridge:

> … That long and slightly curving mound near the crest of the low ridge which overlooks Moore's Creek was then a freshly constructed embankment, smelling strongly of raw earth. The ridge's defenders sprawl full-length behind this all too scanty piece of cover. Their muskets are cradled to their cheeks, each musket barrel pointing towards the bridge not very many paces down below.
>
> The visibility is poor. But it is not poor enough to shelter those other troops who are known to be just north of Moore's Creek and who are seen suddenly to be getting to this side of it. One of those attackers, shouting something in a language none of the waiting men can understand, is far before the rest. Clutching in one hand an upraised sword, he comes running full tilt up the gentle incline from the creek… Fingers tighten on a score of triggers. The swordsman, it seems probable, is dead before he falls…
>
> … He was called Donald MacLeod and he was in charge that February morning of several hundred troops whose names, like their commander's, were redolent of Scotland. MacLean, MacNeil, MacDougall, … Campbell, Stewart, MacEachen, … Cameron, MacPhail, MacLennan and MacRae.
>
> These men were not full-time soldiers. Mostly, in fact, they were farmers. But they were also Gaelic-speaking Scottish Highlanders. And so they had been turned out to fight in the familiar Scottish Highland manner. This meant that they had been pressed or persuaded, by Donald MacLeod and by others of their officers, to leave behind their

homes, their wives, their families and to march away to war.

Such had been the pattern in their homeland for a dozen or more generations. Such, so far at least, remained the pattern here in their new country. For all this country's distance from the glens and islands where the largest number of them had been born, it was as if the men who mustered here beside Moore's Creek felt still that matters of this kind ought to be ordered in accordance with tradition...

And there was now, for just a moment, a glimpse of what had been experienced at Prestonpans, at Killiecrankie... Among the long-leaf pines... the polished blades of broadswords glinted in the first, faint light of morning. There was the sound of bagpipes. Not since Scotland's final Jacobite rebellion, thirty years before, had an army quite like this prepared for battle. No such army ever would exist again (Hunter 11-12).

...The bridge, which was the one sure way to get across a channel much too deep and treacherous ever to be forded, had been partially demolished... All that remained were the three squared timber beams... ...they had also been smeared with home-made soap and tallow...

... what was left of the bridge had been so treated... as to make it impossible for the Highlanders to make one of those massed, screaming charges which were their favorite tactic. Being unable to advance at speed and in large numbers, MacLeod's troops were equally prevented from engaging in the close-quarter, hand-to-hand fighting in which Scotland's clans had long excelled.

... Running on to the remnants of Moore's Creek Bridge, MacLeod set out across one of its slippery wooden beams, digging his sword point into the beam's surface to retain his balance, yelling at his men to hurry.

... Then, just as the Highlanders began in more substantial numbers to attempt the crossing of Moore's Creek, a volley of small arms fire rang out – followed, a few seconds later, by the deeper and more alarming din of the several artillery pieces which the Americans had just had time to get dug in behind their earth embankment.

Donald MacLeod, one of the few Highlanders to get clear across Moore's Creek that morning, was also the first to die, nine musket balls and twenty-four pellets of swanshot afterwards being taken from his mangled body. Several dozen of MacLeod's soldiers, struggling to maintain some sort of foothold on the greasy bridge supports which had been so efficiently transformed into a deathtrap, were quickly killed in the ensuing chaos. Then, a mere two or three minutes after the first shots had been heard and seeing that they were quite literally lining up to be slaughtered, the dead men's surviving comrades took precipitately to their heels, throwing away both their swords and their muskets... (Hunter 20-21).

An American writer tells the story from a different perspective:

About twenty miles north of Wilmington the road on the eastern side of the Cape Fear crossed Widow Moore's Creek on a narrow bridge in the middle of a swamp...

The Americans got there first... They built earthworks and set up two cannon, known as Mother Covington and her daughter. They then took up the planks in the center of the bridge, greased the sleepers with tallow and poured soft soap on them, and retired behind their fortifications to wait.

The Highlanders stopped six miles from Moore's Creek Bridge for a council of war. Their elderly general was worn out and ill; he could go no farther. They put him to bed in a tent and the remaining leaders conferred...

At one o'clock on the cold, cloudy morning... the advance began, led by seventy-five picked men with broadswords, Colonel MacLeod at their head. They plunged and floundered through the swamp in silence. When the sky was turning gray, they came on the smoldering fires near the bridge, and thinking that [American commander] Caswell had abandoned his camp, they took heart and rushed forward, not sure in the dark just where the bridge was. Suddenly MacLeod shouted, "King George and broadswords!" and the pipers and drummers broke into shrill and stirring sound.

MacLeod led the charge on the bridge; others crowded on his heels. After the first few planks the bridge was nothing but two slippery poles and a gaping hole. The Americans behind their earthworks opened fire. Mother Covington and her daughter spoke. Donald MacLeod got across the bridge by digging the point of his sword into the greased sleeper but fell as he struggled up the bank. Fifty others sliding and stumbling in the morning twilight, tumbling headlong into the creek, were shot or drowned. In three minutes of noise, confusion and anguish, the Highlanders fought – and lost – the Battle of Moore's Creek Bridge. Those Scots who had not got onto the bridge turned and ran; those who could get hold of horses, it was said, went off helter-skelter, three on a horse.

...With General MacDonald ill in a tent six miles away and Colonel MacLeod lying dead on the creek bank, [Flora's husband] Allan [MacDonald] succeeded in command. When the officers managed to stop the flight of the soldiers and hold a council, it must have been Allan's voice that gave the orders to march up the river again to Smith's Ferry, beyond Cross Creek, and from there let each man get home as best he could. He paid for food for them on the march back.

The Americans did not pursue them immediately, being much too busy gathering up the baggage and plundering the wagons that had been left behind. When [American Colonel James] Moore joined them a few hours later he ordered pursuit. One detachment took General MacDonald prisoner; the rest caught up with the fleeing Highlanders near Black Mingo Creek, only a few miles away. They held the officers but set free the common soldiers, after administering the oath of allegiance to them. Allan was taken prisoner, with both his sons; so were Alexander of Cuidreach and his brothers, James and Kenneth, the aide-de-camp to General MacDonald. [Flora and Allan's son-in-law] Alexander MacLeod escaped into the swamps and so, after a few days, did Allan's younger son James.

In the three-minute battle the 1,500 Highlanders lost 50 killed or wounded, 850 prisoners; the 1,100 Whigs had one man killed, one wounded. (Vining 165-67)

Allan McDonald imprisoned

The captors imprisoned Allan McDonald and many of the other loyalist officers in the jail at Halifax, North Carolina. Allan McDonald was paroled within the bounds of Halifax on April 11 due to ill health, and his son Alexander was paroled a few days later. After the local Committee of Safety decided to transfer the prisoners of war out of North Carolina, Allan and Alexander began marching to Philadelphia on April 25 (Vining 173-75).

Defeat represses loyalist participation

The calamity at Moore's Creek Bridge intimidated many thousands of loyalists who otherwise would have helped British troops restore royal reign over North Carolina.

Loyalist support for British military operations lagged not only in North Carolina but also throughout the South for the entire course of the war, undercutting British strategies that required support from the local population.

Flory McDonald suffers

Referring to herself in the third person, Flory McDonald wrote about her suffering after the battle:

> Mrs. Flora MacDonald being all this time in misery and sickness at home, being informed that her husband and friends were all killed or taken, contracted a severe fever, and being dayly oppressed with straggling partys of plunderers from their Army, and night robbers, who more than once threatened her life wanting a confession where her husbands money was – Her servants deserting her, and such as stayed, grew so insolent, that they were of no service or help to her. When she got better of her fever, she went to visit & comfort the other poor Gentlewomen whose Husbands were prisoners with Mr. MacDonald, as they blamed him as being the outher of their misery, in the riseing the highlanders and in one of those charitable visits, fell from her horse and brock her right arm, which confined her for months; the only phisishtian in the colony being prisoner with her husband in Philadelphia Gaol having no comforter

but a young boy her son, the oldest Alexr., being prisoner with his father. (qtd. in Toffey 125-26).

The British abandon Boston: March 17, 1776

Continental Commander in Chief George Washington besieged Boston for nearly a year. He sent artillery commander Henry Knox to transport captured cannon from Fort Ticonderoga on Lake Champlain across the wilderness to the Massachusetts coast. On he night of March 2, Knox emplaced cannon on Dorchester Heights overlooking Boston. British commander Sir William Howe realized that he could no longer defend Boston. The British left by sea on March 17.

Washington chose General Nathanael Greene to take command of Boston for the Americans. Two weeks later, Washington ordered Greene to lead his brigade to Brooklyn in anticipation of a British offensive against New York.

Aeneas Mackintosh fends off privateer

The 71st Regiment of Foot – in which Aeneas the 23rd Chief of Clan Mackintosh served throughout the war – set sail from Glasgow in April. Colonel David Stewart describes the voyage:

The transports with the 71st sailed in a large fleet, having the 42d and other troops on board. A violent gale, however, scattered the fleet, and several of the single ships fell in with, and were attacked by, American privateers. A transport having Captain, now Sir Aeneas Mackintosh, and his company on board, with two six-pounders, made a resolute defence against a privateer with eight guns, till all the ammunition was expended, when they bore down with an intention of boarding; the privateer, however, did not wait to receive the shock, and set sail, the transport being unable to follow. (48)

Georgians raid Florida

In May of 1776 the Georgia Council of Safety ordered William McIntosh's troop of horsemen to raid Florida. Their objectives were to destroy a loyalist fort and carry the loyalists and their slaves as well as their provisions and arms to Georgia. Further objectives were to capture vessels in the St. Marys River and drive cattle from Florida into Georgia.

The Council also instructed William McIntosh to build forts on the Altamaha and the St. Marys. Lachlan McIntosh visited the Georgia border at that time on what he called important business and may have joined his older brother in the endeavor (Searcy 37).

The governor of Florida, Patrick Tonyn, and the commander of regular British troops in Florida, Colonel Augustine Prevost, responded by sending a military unit to guard the crossings on the St. Marys, arming the loyalist settlers on the border, and stationing a schooner in the St. Marys. Cattle in southern Georgia and northern Florida were moved out of the raiders' reach south of the St. Johns.

Raiders from Georgia succeeded in capturing several loyalists, burning their plantations, destroying provisions, and carrying off slaves and cattle. British pursuers caught up with the raiders as they returned across the St. Marys to Georgia. The opponents exchanged fire across the river, wounding three Georgians and killing one British soldier. Three of the loyalist plantation owners escaped during the fight. Later that night, a British party crossed the river in a small boat and rescued three more loyalist planters.

Both the Georgians and the Floridians built up defenses against border raids. The Georgians established a stronghold at the southern port of Sunbury with a fort, ditches and earthworks, artillery, twenty men from the Georgia Battalion and forty residents designated as minute men. Another detachment from the Georgia Battalion was stationed on the Altamaha.

The British authorized a troop of rangers to operate along the border. Thomas Brown, a loyalist who had fled Georgia after being tortured by patriots in Augusta, recruited the rangers from the backcountry of Georgia and South Carolina. The British also sought assistance from Indian trading partners.

The Georgia Council of Safety panicked when rumors arose that British troops and Indian allies were advancing from Florida toward the Georgia border. The president of the Council, Archibald Bulloch, ordered all detachments of the Georgia Battalion to rush to the defense of Savannah, leaving parish militia to defend the border. Bulloch pleaded with Colonel Lachlan McIntosh to stop the invaders at the Satilla River if possible and to fall back to the Altamaha only if absolutely necessary. As it turned out, the rumored invasion did not materialize (Searcy39).

As raiding continued, thousands of cattle were driven across the border. When four thousand cattle were stolen from a plantation in south Georgia, the caretaker accused Scots settlers of assisting the British (Searcy 46).

Henry Laurens visits Georgia

Lachlan McIntosh's friend and business partner Henry Laurens of Charleston checked on his investments in coastal Georgia as warfare swept through the area. Laurens spent the month of May at his New Hope plantation and at his plantation on Broughton Island adjoining William and Lachlan McIntosh's property (Cashin, *Bartram* 231).

Allan McDonald arrives at Philadelphia

Allan McDonald – husband of the legendary Flory McDonald – and his son Alexander marched for a month as prisoners of war being transferred from North Carolina to Philadelphia. The long march over bad roads caused permanent injury to Allan's legs. In late May Allan and Alexander were confined in a newly-constructed jail across the square from the State House (Vining 176-77).

Southern headquarters established in Charleston

Continental General Charles Lee arrived in Charleston in the summer of 1776 to take command of the Southern Military Department. Colonel Lachlan McIntosh led a delegation from Georgia to meet with Lee to devise a defensive strategy. While the delegates were in Charleston, they witnessed a British assault on the city.

The first Battle of Charleston: June 28, 1776

General Sir Henry Clinton – the commander of British forces in North America – planned to seal off Charleston harbor – the principal port in the South – with an amphibious assault employing a fleet commanded by Admiral Sir Peter Parker. The fleet of fifty vessels, including troop transports, anchored near Charleston in early June.

Two forts protected Charleston harbor, one on James Island to the south and the other on Sullivan's Island to the north. About a thousand American troops – including about eighty Peedee,

Waccamaw, Cheraw and Catawba Indian riflemen – were stationed on Sullivan's Island. Fort Sullivan – which was still under construction when the British fleet appeared – was garrisoned by the 413 men of the 2nd South Carolina Regiment and two dozen men detached from the 4th Regiment's artillery. Colonel William Moultrie of the 2nd Regiment commanded the garrison. Francis Marion was a major in the 2nd Regiment. Alexander McDonald – the son of a Highlander who had settled at Darien – was a sergeant in the 2nd Regiment; he was one of four soldiers named Alexander McDonald at Fort Sullivan (*American Revolution Roster: Fort Sullivan* 239).

On June 9, Clinton began landing troops on an island to the north of Sullivan's Island; the islands were separated by a narrow tidal inlet called the Breach. Over several days, 2,500 British troops went ashore. The British troops launched an attack on Sullivan's Island on June 19 but few troops could cross the Breach because it had holes too deep to wade through and shoals too shallow to row across. The American defenders put up a spirited defense and drove the British back. Clinton abandoned plans for an amphibious assault and put his faith in a naval assault.

On June 28, the fleet attacked Fort Sullivan. Moultrie described the action in his memoirs:

> …I immediately ordered the long roll to beat, and officers and men to their posts: We had scarcely manned our guns, when the following ships of war came sailing up, as if in confidence of victory; as soon as they came within reach of our guns, we began to fire; they were soon a-breast of the fort… let go their anchors, with springs upon their cables, and begun the attack most furiously about 10 o'clock, A.M. and continued a brisk fire, till about 8 o'clock, P.M.
>
> THE ships were, the Bristol, of 50 guns, Commodore Sir Peter Parker: The captain had his arm shot off, 44 men killed and 30 wounded.
>
> THE Experiment, 50 guns: the captain lost his arm, 57 men killed and 30 wounded.
>
> THE Active, 28 guns: 1 lieutenant killed, 1 man wounded.
>
> THE Sole-Bay, 28 guns: 2 killed, 3 or 4 wounded.
>
> The Syren, 28 guns.
>
> THE Acteon, 28 guns: burnt; 1 lieutenant killed.

THE Sphinx, 28 guns: lost her bowsprit.

THE Friendship, 26 guns; an armed vessel taken into service.

THE Thunder-Bomb had the beds of her mortar soon disabled; she threw her shells in a very good direction; most of them fell within the fort, but we had a morass in the middle, that swallowed them up instantly, and those that fell in the sand in and about the fort, were immediately buried, so that very few of them bursted amongst us...

...when the action begun, (it being a warm day) some of the men took off their coats and threw them upon the top of the merlons, I saw a shot take one of them and throw it into a small tree behind the plat-form, it was noticed by our men and they cried out 'look at the coat.' Never did men fight more bravely, and never were men more cool; their only distress was the want of powder; we had not more than 28 rounds, for 26 guns, 18 and 26 pounders, when we begun the action; and a little after, 500 pounds from town, and 200 pounds from Captain Tufft's schooner lying at the back of the fort.

THERE cannot be a doubt, but that if we had had as much powder as we could have expended in the time, that the men-of-war must have struck their colors, or they would certainly have been sunk, because they could not retreat, as the wind and tide were against them... They could not make any impression on our fort, built of palmetto logs and filled in with earth, our merlons were 16 feet thick, and high enough to cover the men from the fire of the tops: The men that we had killed and wounded received their shots mostly through the embrasures.

Footnote: Twelve men were killed and 24 wounded. When Sergeant M'Donald received his mortal wound, he, addressing his brother soldiers who were carrying him to the doctor, desired them not to give up, that they were fighting for liberty and their country. [This Sergeant M'Donald was not Sergeant Alexander McDonald of the Darien area, who survived the war.]

...It being a very hot day, we were served along the plat-form with grog in fire-buckets, which we partook of very heartily: I never had a more agreeable draught than that which I took out of one of those buckets at the time; it may be very easily conceived what heat and thirst a man must feel in this climate, to be upon a plat-form on the 28th June, amidst 20 or 30 heavy pieces of cannon, in one continual blaze and roar; and clouds of smoke curling over his head for hours together; it was a very honorable situation, but a very unpleasant one.

DURING the action, thousands of our fellow-citizens were looking on [from Charleston, about six miles away from Fort Sullivan] with anxious hopes and fears, some of whom had their fathers, brothers, and husbands in the battle; whose hearts must have been pierced at every broadside. After some time our flag was shot away; their hopes were then gone, and they gave up all for lost! supposing that we had struck our flag, and had given up the fort: Sergeant Jasper perceiving that the flag was shot away, and had fallen without the fort, jumped from one of the embrasures, and brought it up through a heavy fire, fixed it upon a spunge-staff, and planted it upon the ramparts again: Our flag once more waving in the air, revived the drooping spirits of our friends; and they continued looking on, till night had closed the scene, and hid us from their view; only the appearance of a heavy storm, with continual flashes and peals like thunder; at night when we came to our slow firing (the ammunition being nearly quite gone) we could hear the shot very distinctly strike the ships: At length the British gave up the conflict: The ships slipt their cables, and dropped down with the tide, and out of reach of our guns. When the firing had ceased, our friends for a time, were again in an unhappy suspense, not knowing our fate; till they received an account by a dispatch boat, which I sent up to town, to acquaint them, that the British ships had retired, and that we were victorious. (174-80)

Congress declares independence: July 4, 1776

The Continental Congress voted to declare independence from Britain on July 2 and approved the wording of the Declaration of Independence two days later. Two days after that, Congress adopted a Declaration of the Causes and Necessity of Taking Up Arms.

Allan McDonald paroled

Allan and Alexander McDonald – the husband and son of the legendary Flory McDonald – spent seventeen months and twelve days in a prison in Philadelphia after being captured at the Battle of Moore's Creek Bridge. Allan and Alexander were paroled July 9.They waited in Reading, fifty-five miles from Philadelphia, to be exchanged for American prisoners of equal rank (Vining 177).

Attention shifts to southern frontier

The commander of the Southern Department of the Continental army, General Charles Lee, recognized the strategic importance of the southern frontier and knew that Georgia did not have the resources to protect the border with British East Florida. Lee asked Congress to send more troops to Georgia and proposed that a cavalry force be created. He also sent the 2nd South Carolina Regiment to Purrysburg on the South Carolina side of the Savannah River just upstream from Savannah. Congress authorized two more battalions, four row galleys, two artillery companies and a regiment of rangers for the defense of Georgia.

Young Lackie McIntosh defends family at home

They say a boy on the southern frontier of America defended his family's home from marauders. The boy was Lackie McIntosh, the second son of Continental General Lachlan McIntosh. Because duties in Savannah and Charleston consumed nearly all of General McIntosh's time and attention, 18-year-old Lackie became responsible for protecting the family home and property around Darien, as well as protecting his mother, three of his younger brothers and his two sisters. Lackie's 17-year-old brother William was stationed in Savannah as an ensign in the Fifth Regiment, while Lackie commanded a company of the Georgia Battalion that was stationed at Darien in mid-July (Cashin, *Bartram*235). Lackie described the situation in letters:

> Darien July 22d, 1776
>
> DEAR FATHER. I received your Orders by Ensign Morrison Dated July 13th. with a Command of 24 Men with the Sergeant and two Corporals. Two of the Men By name Gray and Martin, Deserted from Morrison on the Road. I arrived home the Second Day after I left you, and

found all the family in perfect Health, Plantation Business going on very well. Osburn [Captain George Osborne, a privateer based in St. Augustine who conducted raids into South Carolina and Georgia] has not been to Visit us yet, nor am I the least afraid of him now, as I am sure our 20 Men can Cope with his Co. at any time. James Baillie before I came home, had moved all the Wenches, and Children up to Cathead and makes the fellows at night sleep over at new hope. I fancy Osburn can do him no other Damage than Burning the Houses upon the Island, which I shall endeavor to hinder, if I have the least Warning of his being there.

The Children comes on very fast indeed with their Schooling. Geor[g]e mends Dailey in his writing and reading. Henry, and Hetty can spell pretty well. They are very much in Want of some Spelling Books, or Primers. it went entirely out of my Head, when I was comeing out of Town, or I should have Supplyed them with that article; if you would send Billey to one Mills's on the Bay he may get some Primers, as for Spelling Books there is none to be had in Town. Wee have a verry fine Crop of rice upon the ground, the field below the House is under Water, and all Shooting out. wee have not let Water into the other field yet, but shall in a couple of Days. The Corn is pretty good, but the potatoes are but poor. The Negros are now getting Stuff for a Barn. Squared Loggs 20 feet by 30. long. I have got Camil Laciter to put them up for me he will begin about the latter end of the Week. I have no more to acquaint you of at present. I am

> Your affectionate Son
> Lachn McKintosh Junior

Darien July 27th. 1776
DEAR FATHER. I received your Letter Yesterday Evening by Sergeant Law, Express... I am sorry to hear by your Letter that Osburn has got safe over the Barr. I was in hopes Captain Bowen if he did not take him, would damage his Vessels very much. He has not been up this river yet. However I shall keep as strict a Guard as If I expected him Hourly, and I shall endeavor to get some trusty [word torn

off] down at Frederica that will inform me if he should come that Way. I am sorry you can't take a step home at this time, however it was a thing impossible as you expected General Lee, and another Battalion of Continental Troops. I should like much to be there, at the time of their comeing in, they will make a fine show. The family are all verry hearty.

    I remain Dr. Father

    Your affectiote Son

    Lachn. McKintosh Jr.

    P.S. The Command are all very satisfied quite contented with their rations. I have given them half a pint of Rum every other Day since they came here, but I intend for the future to give them but every third day. They were sent of here without Catridge Boxes, they are obliged to put their Catridges in their pockets which makes it very inconvenient.

Encounter with Indians on the St. Mary's

In late July William McIntosh's force encountered British soldiers from St. Augustine and their Indian allies on the St. Mary's River. Some people say that the botanist William Bartram, a longtime friend of the McIntosh family, acted as a volunteer scout for William McIntosh at the time but would not enlist as an officer because of his Quaker beliefs (Cashin, *Bartram* 233). Bartram wrote a letter about the British raid on the southern frontier:

They advanced to the Banks of St. Mary's, possess'd themselves of it, and took Shelter in the old Indian trading house. A few Indians were in company. A Small party of the Georgians marched from the Altamaha to oppose them and they gain'd the banks before the enemy had passed the Flood. Hostilities commenced by the parties firing at each other across the River. The British were under cover of the evacuated trading houses, and the Georgians shielded themselves behind the Trees, on the River Banks. The conflict had continued for some time when the Chief of the Indians threw down his Gun and boldly stepping out from the corner of a House he took off his Hat and whirling it up in the Air as he advanced to the River Side, amidst showers of

Bullets, he spoke aloud to the Georgians, declaring that
they were Brother's and friends and that he knew not any
cause why they should spill each others Blood. Neither I
(said he) nor my Companions the Red Men, will fire another Gun. He turned about, shouted, and immediately le'd off
the Indians. (qtd. in Cashin, *Bartram* 232)

In *William Bartram and the American Revolution*, Edward J.
Cashin writes:

The chief in question was almost certainly Bartram's friend
Ahaya, the Cowkeeper of Cuscowilla, who had given him
the name Pug Puggy... His story excites the imagination.
Did the Cowkeeper recognize his friend across the river?
Something of that sort caused the chief to stop fighting on
this occasion. The Cowkeeper had no qualms about
fighting in subsequent battles. In February 1777 the
Cowkeeper and his band followed Thomas Brown to the
fort on the Satilla River built by and named after Lachlan
McIntosh. The Cowkeeper's war whoops, as much as the
actual shooting, frightened the Georgia garrison into surrendering. Throughout the war the Cowkeeper remained
Governor Tonyn's best ally; however, on this occasion,
perhaps, the chief decided not to shoot at Pug Puggy. (232-
33).

As commander of Continental forces in Georgia, Lachlan
McIntosh reported the 1776 skirmish on the St. Mary's River to the
commander of the Southern Department. He said that two hundred
Indians had intercepted patriots led by his brother William, who
"obliged them to desist." When the patriots dropped back to the
Satilla River, the Indians did not pursue them (Cashin, *Bartram*
233).

Americans invade Florida
General Charles Lee, the Continental commander in the South,
led about fifteen hundred Continental troops from Charleston to
Savannah early in August and prepared to invade British East Florida. Lee placed General William Moultrie of the 2nd South Carolina Regiment in charge of the invasion. Georgia failed to support

the invasion with equipment, clothing and shoes for the invading force, inspiring Lee's caustic comment that the Georgians would propose "mounting a body of Mermaids on Alligators" (qtd. in Searcy 56). Lee, however, respected Lachlan McIntosh and described the 1st Battalion of Foot under McIntosh's command as one of the best battalions in America.

Lackie McIntosh reports problems at home

Lachlan McIntosh's teenage son Lackie maintained responsibility for the families and the property in the Darien area. Letters to his father show that so much responsibility on such a young man took a toll:

> Darien, Alatmaha 14th. August 1776
> DEAR FATHER. I received Your Letter of the 10th. Instant I am sorry to find you are disappointed in coming home, as wee have been expecting you for this Week past. however wee shall look for you dailey. I am happy to find the Colonys have at last proclaimed a Free and Independent States – let us have no more of British Tyranny.
> As it is inconvenient for you to send a command to relieve me, I am verry well satisfied as I find all the Command excepting three or four are quite contented to stay another month. The only thing I have to complain of, is that a Detachment of Men should be sent to so dangerous a post as this, without a plenty of Ammunition. I have but a small Kegg of Catridges. Lieut. Handley Brought here, not more than 5 or 6 rounds at most apiece for the men and not one single man has a Catridge Box. Wee had an alarm a few days ago. they were obliged to carry their Ammunition in their pockets, which was verry unhandy in case they had been engaged. however I shall endeavor to make out another month with what amuni[tion] I have. I believe wee shant be in Want as I may get some powder from Captain Thredcraft belonging to the militia in case of necessity.
> I suppose you heard before now that Colonel Laurens's overseer at N. hope George Aaron has run away carryed 5 of Colonel Laurens's Negroes, Uncle Williams Negroe fellow Oskar, and 5 or 6 of his best Horses, robbed poor James Baillie of every ragg of his wearing apparel. James

Baillie with eight or ten of the militia went immediately in persuit of him, but it answered no affect. he got safe into Florida. Baillie is now moving the rice from New hope up to Darien, and I believe he will move the Negroes likewise. I advised him to do it, as I thought Colonel Laurens's Inter[es]t not at all safe there, since Aron went away and it would be impossible for Baillie to give me timely notice in case he would attempt to robb a second time. I shall consult with the Commissioner, and get the Negroes doing something about the Fort. is better than they should be Idle. I shall endeavor to put a guard at Billey Clarks or Creightons Island.

My Mother and all the Children are verry well, excepting Hetty she has had the fever for some days past, but is getting better again. Inclosed I send you some of George's writing. he and Henry comes on verry fast in their Schooling, their Master takes great pains with them.

Wee have as fine a Crop of rice as you wou'd ever desire to see, wee shall have some fit to cutt in less than three Weeks. Since I wrote you last wee have had most of the Negroes employed in getting stuff for a Barn. I have got Camil Laciter to Build it, he will finish in a Week or ten Days more. I am at a Loss what to put the Negroes about now, without it is to clear a new Corn field betwixt this and Darien. I have nothing to acquaint you of more. I remain Dr. Father

Your affectionate So[n]

Lachn. McKintosh Jr.

I delivered the two necklesses to my Mother and Hetty they are verry fond of them being American produce.

P.S. The White Maire Serjeant Law rode here, took the stagers a few Days after he went away and died. I wish you could send [my] Horse home as he is much wanted.

Alatamaha August 24th.1776

DEAR FATHER   The Unhealthy Situation of my Command Just now, obliges me to send an Express to acquaint you. I have now Six or Seven Extreem ill with a verry Violant kind of fever, they have no I[n]termission at all Scarcely and last night one of them a little Scotch Boy died.

I can assure you Sir it was not the want of care occasioned his Death; I spare no pains or Expence attending the poor fellows when they are Sick, and I keep Doctor Blunt, continually with them. I excuse him from all duty on that Account. They seem to cry out now for to be relieved, I think a change of air will be of Service to them. However I am in hopes no more of them will die, as I give them to Day plenty of Dogwood Bark, they seem to be more lively than they were yesterday.

 I remain Dr. Father
 Your affectte.
 Lachn. McKintosh Jr.
 My Mother and the Children are all well and desires to be remimber to you.
 If you cant relieve them they say if they cou'd get some Cloths they would be satisfied some of them and indeed almost the whole I can assure you have not wherewith to hide their Nakedness
 I am as before
 L.M.

 [August, 1776]
 The Gray maire the Express rode, fagg'd very much by the time she got here. I did intend last night to let my Horse go in her rome [room], but was obliged to do it this morning as she got out of the Way and as the Express has been almost three Days coming from Savannah. I could not think of keeping him longer than last night. I shall look up the mair this morning & acquaint you by my next Letter how I like her. I believe her to be a verry good Creature.
 I am yours, &ca.
 L. Mackintosh Jr.
 (Hawes, *Collections* 52-56)

Battle of Long Island: August 22–27, 1776
British Major General Sir William Howe determined to wrest New York from the possession of Continental Commander in Chief George Washington. Convoys of transports and warships brought twenty thousand troops from Canada and Britain to Staten Island. General Sir Henry Clinton and General Earl Charles Corn-

wallis returned from their expedition against Charleston and placed another 2,500 troops at Howe's command. A fleet arrived on August 12, bringing the force to 32,000 British and Hessian soldiers and ten thousand seamen. At the time, it was the largest expeditionary force ever sent from Britain. Among the British forces was the 71st Regiment of Foot – in which Captain Aeneas Mackintosh served.

On August 22, fifteen thousand British troops led by Lord Cornwallis crossed from Staten Island to Long Island in flat-bottom boats and landed without resistance. The British seized Flatbush and challenged the American outposts at Long Island Heights. Five thousand Hessian troops reinforced the British on Long Island, while the main army remained on Staten Island.

Because Continental General Nathanael Greene was ill with fever, Washington sent General Israel Putnam to command the American forces on Long Island. Washington stayed in Manhattan with half of the American army and stationed more than ten thousand troops on Long Island. General William Alexander – who claimed the Scottish title Lord Stirling – commanded the Continental troops on the right of the American defenses.

The British army went into action on the night of August 26. Historian Christopher Ward describes the 71st Regiment's role:

> At nine o'clock in the evening a column of march was formed… General Henry Clinton led the van, made up of the 17th Light Dragoons and a brigade of light infantry. General Lord Cornwallis came next with the reserve – that is to say, the 1st Brigade of four battalions of grenadiers, two regiments of foot, and the 71st (Fraser's Highlanders), with fourteen pieces of field artillery. After them fell in General William Howe and General Lord Percy with the main body – the Guards and three brigades of infantry comprising twelve regiments, with ten guns. Bringing up the rear were one regiment and the baggage train with its guard and four guns. In this column were 10,000 soldiers and twenty-eight pieces of artillery. (216)

Shortly after midnight on the unusually cool morning of August 27 British forces advanced in the dark against the American defenses. Americans at an outpost near the Red Lion Inn on the

Gowanus Road opened fire on the British, and fighting spread across the American outposts. British artillery pounded key points in the American defenses. General Alexander – Lord Stirling – led two regiments to support the outpost on the Gowanus Road. Despite British infantry attacks and cannonading, Stirling's regiments held their position (Dupuy and Dupuy 122-31).

In the British strategy for the battle, the attack on Lord Stirling's position on the right flank was a diversion. The main British army and its generals – Howe, Clinton, Cornwallis and Earl Hugh Percy – marched through the night toward the left flank of the American defenses. By 9 a.m. they were in position to attack the barricades at the Flatbush Pass commanded by General John Sullivan. Military historians Colonel Ernest Dupuy and Colonel Trevor Dupuy describe the attack:

> In vain did Sullivan attempt to rally his troops. Caught between the inexorable pressure of the British and German professionals, the raw Americans broke and fled, despite individual and unit exceptions of gallantry. Sullivan was last seen by some of his fugitive men caught between the two lines of converging foes with a smoking pistol in each hand. In fact, although the Hessians were mercilessly bayoneting many of the cowering Americans, Sullivan and several hundred of his surviving troops were taken prisoner and sent to the rear. Clinton and Heister [a Hessian officer] pursued the fugitives to within musket shot of the Brooklyn fortified line. (133)

While the main British army was overrunning the Flatbush Pass, the diversionary force under General James Grant resumed its attack on the American position on the Gowanus Road near the marsh along Gowanus Creek. Lord Stirling's fifteen hundred men staunchly held their position against an advance by Grant's seven thousand men. When Lord Stirling heard the sounds of battle at Long Island Heights, he realized the British had cut off his route of retreat to the American fortifications at Brooklyn.

Cornwallis, meanwhile, advanced with a force including the 71st Highlanders from the Flatbush Pass toward the Gowanus Road (Boatner 653). "It was clear that the American position could not be held much longer," Ward writes. "Nor was the direct way of retreat to the rear open. Cornwallis was there with the 71st Regiment" (225).

Dupuy and Dupuy describe Lord Stirling's remarkable escape:

> Stirling seems to have made an estimate of the situation, and reached a decision, in less than a minute. About an hour earlier he had noticed a detachment of his men carrying some wounded back to the Brooklyn fortifications by a trail through the marsh. Here was the only possible line of retreat – but even this would be cut off unless Cornwallis could be stopped. He ordered two of his three regiments to fall back slowly in front of Grant, and then to withdraw across the marsh as best they could. At the same time Stirling led Colonel William Smallwood's Maryland Continentals – some 500 men – in a spirited charge to the northeast against the advancing British [under Cornwallis]. He apparently hoped to cut his way through to reach the Flatbush Road and the center of the Brooklyn fortifications, while gaining sufficient time to enable the other two regiments to get back across the marsh.
>
> Five times Stirling's and Smallwood's men attempted to cut their way out, and five times they were thrown back. Finally, as Grant came up from the south, [Stirling, who was wounded] and the survivors of his command were completely surrounded and forced to surrender. Meanwhile, from hills inside the Brooklyn fortifications, Washington saw Stirling's main body fall back across the marsh. He immediately rushed some troops to the high ground overlooking the creek and marsh, to cover the withdrawal. This musketry and artillery fire forced Grant's left wing units to halt their pursuit of the withdrawing Americans. It was evidently while observing this withdrawal, and Stirling's gallant charges against Cornwallis, that Washington made the statement attributed to him: "Good God, what brave men must I lose this day!"

This virtually ended the Battle of Long Island, at about noon. Though reports are conflicting, it seems that the Americans lost about 1,500 men – Washington's subsequent report of less than 1,000 was due to poor American records. About 1,100 were captured; many of them wounded. Another 100 wounded had been evacuated to the Brooklyn fortifications. Probably 300 had been killed. British losses were about 370 killed and wounded, plus 23 men captured by Stirling's brigade, and brought back in that remarkably steady withdrawal across the Gowanus Marsh. (133-34)

Americans withdraw from Brooklyn Heights

During the night of August 28, the British began to dig siege works in front of the American fortifications at Brooklyn Heights. Knowing that he could not defend the position against British land and sea forces, Washington decided to abandon the fortifications. Dupuy and Dupuy describe the evacuation:

> Were the British to learn of the withdrawal before it was complete, a determined attack could break through the thinly-manned defenses and annihilate that portion of Washington's army still on the Long Island side.
>
> Consequently, although Washington made up his mind early on the morning of the 29th, he did not reveal his decision even to his most trusted subordinates until late that afternoon. Too much secret information had already reached the British through unsuspected Loyalist spies. Meanwhile all the many measures he took, and the activities which he started, were for the ostensible purpose of moving still further reinforcements to Brooklyn. Every available boat was assembled on the New York side of the East River, and units there were alerted to move. To man the boats collected, Colonel John Glover's regiment of Marblehead men, seamen all, were assembled.
>
> ...He ordered that the troops manning the lines were to be informed that reinforcements were arriving to take their places in the line, and that therefore they should expect to be relieved during the night. At the same time, all supplies and all the artillery (save for five old and very heavy pieces) were to be prepared for evacuation.
>
> To hold the defenses after all the other units had withdrawn, and to cover the embarkation, Washington selected five units of proven discipline, commanded by reliable

leaders... In command of this picked group was Brigadier General Thomas Mifflin.

The evacuation began at dark, and – thanks to Washington's preparations – moved with amazing speed and smoothness. A rising wind threatened to interfere with the boat movement, but this soon subsided. Continuing rain, while making the troops uncomfortable, tended to dull British alertness.

[General Mifflin received an inaccurate message to withdraw the units holding the defenses] ...Mifflin ordered his units to move quietly from their trenches and report to the ferry. When he arrived there, he found great lines of troops still waiting to get on the boats.

Washington, as close to despair as he ever came during the war, stalked up to Mifflin and said, "Good God, General Mifflin, I am afraid you have ruined us by withdrawing the troops from the line!" Briefly explaining how the mistake had occurred, Mifflin ordered his units to return to their trenches. That they did so, under the circumstances of the time, was a tribute to their own courage and discipline, as well as the care of their selection by Washington.

Finally, shortly after 4:00 A.M., Mifflin received the authentic message to withdraw. Pulling back quickly and silently, the troops reached the river, and began to embark, just as dawn was breaking. Fortunately the aftermath of the storm had left a heavy fog over Brooklyn. Though the British had already begun to suspect that the American lines were unusually quiet, they could not observe what was going on.

British patrols probed forward, and soon after 4:30 discovered that the American lines had been abandoned. Moving ahead cautiously, they reached the ferry shortly before 7 o'clock, to find the last boat just pulling away. They opened up with muskets, and with a light field piece, but they scored no hits.

This was fortunate for the rebel cause, since the last man to get onto the last boat had been General George Washington. Sleepless for more than 48 hours, he had given the closest possible personal supervision to every detail of the brilliantly planned evacuation, and had by his calm presence and deliberate energy, inspired, calmed, and reassured his men.

The skill and brilliance of the withdrawal could not undo the damage caused by Washington's earlier strategical and tactical mistakes in attempting an impossible task, and by his failure to exercise adequate command supervision and control of the forces on Long Island. But it did demonstrate that Washington could learn from his mistakes, and that he possessed potentialities for higher military leadership...

Thanks to him alone, Long Island, instead of being the final battle of the war – which it might well otherwise have been – became merely another setback to the Revolutionary cause.

As British military historian Trevelyan has well put it, the evacuation was "a master stroke of energy, dexterity and caution, by which Washington saved his army and his country." (136-38)

Invasion of Florida collapses

In the South, the advance guard of the American expedition against British East Florida reached the St. Johns River, wiping out plantations and settlements as it went. The hungry soldiers took food wherever they could find it.

The invasion, however, was doomed to fail. When the Continental troops sickened in coastal Georgia's semi-tropical climate, the Georgians did not provide medical supplies; as a result, the death rate at Sunbury was fourteen or fifteen a day. The main body of American troops had advanced no farther than Sunbury when the invasion collapsed in mid-September. The departing troops left Sunbury in shambles (Searcy 56, 61-62;Coleman 102).

In the midst of the invasion, Congress gave Lee a new assignment. Brigadier James Moore of North Carolina, who had defeated a force of loyalist Highlanders in the Cross Creek country early in the war, was named commander of the Southern Department. General Robert Howe was given command of Continental forces in South Carolina and Georgia. When Lee left Georgia, he took some of the South Carolina units with him. Georgia historian Edward J. Cashin reports:

Before the Carolina troops left Georgia, they devastated Sunbury and Darien in their foraging. Ironically, friendly troops, not the enemy, destroyed Lachlan McIntosh's plantation and put an end to William Bartram's visit there. Lachlan later appealed to Congress for compensation for the loss of his crop of rice, corn, peas, and potatoes, all "taken and destroyed by our own troops who burnt my fences and turned their horses into the fields." Eventually, McIntosh suffered worse losses. He did not make clear whether Americans, following a scorched earth policy, or British invaders caused the damage, but he lost his residence, barn and outbuildings, all his livestock, and twenty-four slaves. Presumably the slaves escaped to Florida. McIntosh did say that as a result of the damage to his property, he had to remove his family to Savannah. (*Bartram* 238-39)

Sarah McIntosh, children move to Savannah

Because his wife and younger children faced constant danger at Darien, Lachlan McIntosh purchased a large house on St. James Square in Savannah for his family. He also moved his slaves from Darien to Savannah (Lawrence, "Suspension" 133). William Bartram followed his friends from Darien to Savannah and stayed for about a month.

Lachlan McIntosh promoted to Brigadier General

Congress continued to take steps to defend the southern frontier by authorizing more Continental forces in Georgia. Because of the added responsibility, Lachlan McIntosh was promoted to Brigadier General on September 16, 1776.

The authorization of additional manpower in Georgia, however, was more theoretical than actual. The 538 men in the 1st Battalion of Foot were dispersed in small groups on guard duty around the state.

Recruiters strove to fill the ranks of the 2nd and 3rd battalions. About three hundred horsemen patrolled the frontier and garrisoned Fort Barrington on the Altamaha. The troops lacked barracks, clothes, blankets, medicine, entrenching tools and axes (Searcy 64-65).

Washington protects his army

In the North, as the British army and navy maneuvered into positions around New York, Washington decided to evacuate the city before the British blocked all escape routes. Washington refused to risk the destruction of his army because he realized that without the army there would be no revolution. He told Congress, "We should on all occasions avoid a general action, or put anything to Risque, unless compelled by necessity, into which we ought never to be drawn" (qtd. in Dupuy and Dupuy 140).

Washington began moving the army's supplies out of New York on September 12, three days before the British launched attacks on the American defenses. Lord Cornwallis led four thousand British and Hessian troops in an advance division that soon received reinforcements as flatboats carried troops from Long Island. The Americans abandoned New York and took positions around Harlem Heights. Although casualties were light, the British captured ammunition, supplies, dozens of cannon and more than 350 American soldiers.

The Battle of Harlem Heights: September 16, 1776

Shortly before dawn on September 16 an advance British unit encountered American defenders along a depression called "the Hollow Way." Soon more than five thousand troops on each side engaged in battle. The Americans withdrew after a six-hour fight known as the Battle of Harlem Heights. British casualties were seventy killed and two hundred wounded; American casualties were 30 killed and 90 wounded (Dupuy and Dupuy 139-146).

Fire broke out in New York on September 20 and the British struggled for two days to put out the flames.

On September 21 the British captured Captain Nathan Hale and the next morning they hanged him as a spy. His last statement was, "I only regret that I have but one life to lose for my country" (qtd. in Dupuy and Dupuy 148).

On October 12 the British moved ten thousand men toward the American positions on Manhattan Island. Cornwallis led an advance unit of four thousand English and Hessian light infantrymen in assault across a causeway through the marsh that was stopped by about eighteen hundred American defenders covering the causeway with rifle fire from behind piles of wood.

On October 16 Washington decided to abandon Harlem Heights and withdraw to White Plains on the mainland. He left two thousand men at Fort Washington on Manhattan and sent three thousand men to Fort Lee on the Jersey shore. Washington gave command of the troops at the two forts to General Nathanael Greene. The British, meanwhile, established a base at New Rochelle (Dupuy and Dupuy 148-50).

Fighting in South Georgia

In the South, British forces from Florida continued to threaten Georgia. General Lachlan McIntosh ordered a troop of horsemen commanded by his older brother William McIntosh to cross the Altamaha and confront the British. Acting on reports in early October that the British were planning to invade Georgia by land and sea, Lachlan McIntosh arrayed his troops in defensive positions along the coast. The South Carolina navy and a detachment of the 2nd South Carolina Regiment helped protect the Georgia coast.

William McIntosh, who had been promoted to lieutenant colonel, continued to patrol the border with a light horse regiment of about three hundred men (Jackson 49). In late October, William McIntosh's troops attacked a British party on the Satilla River, killing one member of the party and capturing two. General Lachlan McIntosh ordered the Georgians to fall back to Georgia's strongest natural barrier, the Altamaha River. He envisioned a system of forts along the Altamaha connected by horse patrols.

On October 27, a party of loyalists and Indian allies destroyed a plantation south of the Altamaha, crossed the river, and attacked Fort Barrington, upstream of Darien. Other attacks were reported at Midway, Beards Bluff, and St. Simons Island. About twenty Chiaha Indians attacked forty Georgia Rangers, killing four and wounding two (Searcy 67-68).

The Battle of White Plains: October 28, 1776

In the North, British forces including the 71st Highlanders – the regiment that Aeneas Mackintosh served in throughout the war – continued to advance against American positions near New York and George Washington continued to save the revolution by saving his army. Military historians Colonel Ernest Dupuy and Colonel Trevor Dupuy describe the Battle of White Plains on October 28:

Again [British commander General Sir William] Howe avoided a frontal assault. His reconnaissance... having convinced him that Chatterton's Hill was the key to the American position, he sent a combined British and Hessian force of more than 4,000 men west of the Bronx River to take it.

Momentarily checked by determined American small arms fire from Chatterton's Hill, the British and Hessians, with intense artillery support, pressed ahead. They crossed the stream and slowly started up the south slope.

Meanwhile, Colonel Johann Rall's Hessian regiment and a small force of British cavalry had moved further to the west, and began to climb the west slopes, taking the Americans in the flank. The militia regiments immediately ran. The Continentals attempted to hold the crest for a while, but as the British and Hessians pressed forward, extending their flanks around the base of the hill, they too fell back, covered by the slow and deliberate withdrawal of Haslet's regiment.

The Hessians and British now hastened to the crest and began to organize for further advance while artillery was being dragged up behind them.

In the face of this threat, Washington ended the battle by withdrawing his right flank north of White Plains, to a position between the Bronx River and St. Mary's Lake.

American losses in this battle of White Plains were probably slightly more than 250 men, of whom some 50 were killed. British losses were approximately 240, with 50 killed. The Hessian troops suffered about one third of these casualties. (150-52)

British reinforcements arrived over the next three days. In the dark of night, Washington withdrew to higher ground on North Castle Heights. Four days later, the British withdrew to the lower Hudson.

Washington divided his army, leaving seven thousand men at North Castle and leading about two thousand men to join the two thousand men protecting Fort Lee on the west bank of the Hudson River across from Fort Washington.

William Bartram leaves Georgia

The botanist William Bartram, a friend of the Lachlan McIntosh family, left Savannah in November on his way to the Bartram family's ancestral home on the Cape Fear River in North Carolina. Historian Edward J. Cashin describes Bartram's departure:

> The muted wildflowers of autumn decorated the low country marshlands as William Bartram crossed the Savannah River at Zubly's Ferry and made his way to Charleston. He commented on how the climbing asters flourished in the low, moist land. (*Bartram* 241)

The birth of Chief William McIntosh

Rory McIntosh's brother John had gone to live among the Creek Indians in the decades before the American Revolution, and John's son William became a captain in the British army.

In 1776, Captain William McIntosh visited the Lower Creek towns to recruit warriors for the British. During the recruiting mission, Captain McIntosh met Senoya Henneha – known in McIntosh family lore as a Creek princess – and they had a son who would grow up to be known as Chief William McIntosh.

The superintendent of the Southern Indian Department for the British government, John Stuart, appointed Captain William McIntosh a deputy to the Lower Creeks. By early November, Captain William McIntosh had recruited thirty Hichitas to support the British forces at St. Augustine (Searcy 75).

Lachlan's son John goes to Jamaica

Lachlan McIntosh's son John, called "Jack," left for Jamaica sometime before November. He stayed with his uncle John Mackintosh in Jamaica throughout the war (Lawrence, "Suspension" 108-09; Cashin, *Bartram* 258).

Assault on Fort Washington: November 16, 1776

In New York, British General Sir William Howe decided to push the Americans off the northern tip of Manhattan Island. Dupuy and Dupuy describe the British assault on Fort Washington on November 16:

Fort Washington, located on a bluff 230 feet above the Hudson, was formidable principally because of its location, and the extremely rugged, rocky slopes which it over-looked. It was a simple, open pentagonal earthwork, with a bastion at each corner...(153)

Howe had assigned 8,000 troops to assault the fort. The main effort was to be made from the north, by some 3,000 Germans under Knyphausen. To the east, two small columns totaling 3,000 men, under Generals Edward Mathew and Cornwallis, were to make assault crossings over the Harlem River, and then drive westward against the face of the fort. Lord Percy was advancing from central Manhattan with a mixed British-Hessian force of 2,000 men.

Percy had opened the action shortly after dawn with an intensive bombardment across the Hollow Way, followed by a general advance all along the line. The thinly spread out Americans were quickly pushed back, but Percy halted when he discovered that Cornwallis and Mathew were hav-ing troubles getting started on the other side of the Harlem River. Meanwhile, shortly before 10 A.M., Knyphausen's Germans had begun their assault through the wild and rocky area in the northern portion of Manhattan. Despite stubborn resistance the Germans pushed forward aggres-sively. For more than three hours, the hardest fighting of the day raged amidst the boulders and ravines north of Fort Washington.

Shortly before noon Mathew and Cornwallis overcame the administrative difficulties which had delayed their movement, and successfully assaulted over the Harlem River, despite heavy American fire from the west bank heights. Now all four British columns began to forge ahead, and by early afternoon Rall's Hessian regiment was close to the fort itself, on the crest above the Hudson. As the oth-er three columns continued to close in, Rall now demanded [American commander] Magaw's surrender.

From the ramparts of Fort Lee, Washington and his companions had heard the firing grow in volume, and ap-proach the fort from both directions. From the sound, it was apparent that other British forces were advancing against the fort from the east, having crossed the Harlem River. By early afternoon it was obvious that the British were within musket range of the fort itself, and action could be observed near the river banks. Washington, now convinced that the fort could not be held, sent a message to Magaw, ordering him to cling to his remaining positions until nightfall, and then to evacuate to the other side of the river…

Meanwhile Magaw, to gain time, had attempted to discuss surrender terms with Rall…

The German, refusing discussion, insisted that Magaw… surrender at once… Magaw, fearful of the casualties which artillery fire would cause amongst the crowd of troops huddled in the fort, now agreed to surrender. It was at this moment, probably near 3:00 P.M., that he received Washington's message to hold on until nightfall. Magaw responded to Washington that he had so committed himself to surrender that he could not with honor obey the order. So fell Fort Washington.

American losses were 53 killed, 96 wounded, and 2,722 unwounded captured. The British lost 77 killed, 374 wounded and 7 missing; nearly three-fourths of these casualties were Hessians. They captured 43 artillery pieces, and great quantities of artillery and small arms ammunition.

The loss of nearly 3,000 men was serious to Washington, while the relatively easy capture of the supposedly impregnable fortress by the British struck another sharp blow at American morale. (155-57)

Americans abandon Fort Lee

British General Lord Cornwallis led four thousand troops in a nighttime crossing of the Hudson River on November 19-20. Landing about five miles above Fort Lee, the British advanced on the fort at dawn. American General Nathanael Greene organized a hasty evacuation of the fort, leaving behind thirty cannon and stores of ammunition and provisions.

Greene's division joined Washington's division at Hackensack, and the two divisions withdrew to Newark. Washington expected General Charles Lee's division to join him there, but Lee remained on the east side of the Hudson for three weeks.

Cornwallis waited a week at Hackensack and then advanced toward Washington at Newark. Washington withdrew to New Brunswick, and Cornwallis occupied Newark on November 28 (Dupuy and Dupuy 158-60).

Cornwallis pursues Washington

Cornwallis continued to pursue Washington's army, which had dwindled to 3,400 men after the battles in New York, the surrender of Fort Washington, and the departure of two thousand men whose enlistments expired. British and American troops skirmished at New Brunswick on December 1 as Washington fell back toward Philadelphia, located across the Delaware River from New Jersey.

Meanwhile, American General Charles Lee's division of four thousand men crossed to the west side of the Hudson River on December 2 and moved slowly across New Jersey without taking any offensive action.

As Cornwallis approached Princeton on December 7, Washington led three thousand men from Princeton toward Trenton on the east bank of the Delaware. As the Americans withdrew, they destroyed bridges and blocked roads to delay the British pursuers. Washington's army crossed to the Pennsylvania side of the Delaware River on December 8. Cornwallis arrived at Trenton while the last Americans to cross were still in boats on the river; American artillery on the west bank kept Cornwallis from harming the men in the boats. The British could not pursue the Americans across the river because Washington had arranged for all the boats in the region to be moved to the west side.

Lee's division, meanwhile, camped near Morristown on December 12 and Lee spent the night at a tavern three miles away from the encampment. Early the next morning, Lieutenant Banastre Tarleton led a British cavalry detachment in a raid on the tavern and captured Lee.

With winter setting in, the British commander called a halt to the campaign on December 14. The British had 23,000 troops in the region; about half of them stayed in winter quarters in New York and the other half occupied posts in New Jersey. Advanced posts were placed at Princeton, Trenton, and Bordentown

On December 19, an essay by Thomas Paine was published in Philadelphia. "These are the times that try men's souls," Paine wrote. "The summer soldier and the sunshine patriot will, in this crisis, shrink from the service of his country; but he that stands it *now* deserves the love and thanks of man and woman" (qtd. in Dupuy and Dupuy 164).

The remnants of Lee's division joined Washington on the west side of the Delaware River on December 20. The American army gained strength when Congress ordered two thousand Pennsylvanians to join the three thousand men remaining with Washington and the two thousand men who had been in Lee's division. But with enlistments due to expire on January 1, Washington could expect to field less than fifteen hundred men at the beginning of the new year (Dupuy and Dupuy 160-62). Military historians Colonel Ernest Dupuy and Colonel Trevor Dupuy describe the gloomy mood enveloping Washington at midwinter:

> Washington's depression following his defeats in and around New York, and the humiliating retreat across New Jersey – combined with the frustration he felt in the face of the prospective dissolution of his small army – were revealed in the letters which he wrote to Congress, and to others, during those dark days of December. On the 17th he wrote: "The unhappy policy of short enlistments and a dependence on militia will, I fear, prove the downfall of our cause... Our only dependence now is upon the speedy enlistment of a new army. If this fails, I think the game will be pretty well up, as from disaffection and want of spirit and fortitude the inhabitants instead of resistance are offering submission and taking protection from [British forces] in Jersey. Three days later he bluntly added, "Ten more days will put an end to the existence of our army." (163)

Raids continue on the southern frontier

In Georgia, American General Lachlan McIntosh received reports in December that British forces and Indian allies were planning raids across the frontier. He issued orders to his brother Colonel William McIntosh to report to Fort Barrington – now named Fort Howe in honor of General Robert Howe – and to build stockades on the Satilla and the St. Marys and at Beards Bluff on the Altamaha. Before Colonel William McIntosh received the orders, Indians killed a trooper of the Light Horse on the frontier. Colonel

William McIntosh and Major Leonard Marbury promptly set out for Fort Howe to hunt the killers. Shortly afterwards, General Lachlan McIntosh himself led reinforcements to Fort Howe and took command of the operation. Colonel William McIntosh captured three Indians who were accused of killing the trooper.

The McIntosh brothers worked to improve defensive positions along the frontier, although the Georgia convention did not provide funding for adequate fortifications. General Lachlan McIntosh ordered an infantry attachment to establish positions on the Sapelo River and at several locations along the Altamaha in the vicinity of Darien. Still, British raiding parties continued to steal slaves and plunder property.

When raiders from Florida drove off a herd of cattle, a party of the Georgia Light Horse pursued them but could not catch them; while on the Florida side of the St. Marys River, the Georgians did some plundering of their own (Searcy 76-78).

Colonel William McIntosh leads troops on border

Captain Charles Middleton kept a journal that describes the tedious day-to-day operations on the border. Among the misspellings in the journal is "Malberry" for Marbury. The journal gives insight into the leadership shown by Colonel William McIntosh:

DECEMBER 20, 1776
The men all got over the river on our march southwardly. Colonel McIntosh, Major Malberry and Lieutenant Dogharty sat off from the river to join Captain Caldwell...

SUNDAY, December 22, 1776
...Adjutant Fash waited on the Colonel to know whether the Carolinians were to take the front or rear; the Colonel did not choose to determine, as he did not know which was the oldest Regiment, but, in order to satisfy both parties, gave order that the officers and men were to fall in promiscuously and no distinctions made – which was agreeable to both parties until it was known which had the rank. On our march some one discovered, as he thought, a party of men running from us; a party pursued but could make no discovery of them. ...the main party proceeded to pursue the tracks, following them some distance, found them to be cattle tracks.

Judged the man who had thought he saw people made a mistake... ...rendezvoused at Middleton's that night.

MONDAY, December 23, 1776

...We arrived at the old ferry; I was ordered with a party to reconnoiter the landing, but could make no discovery of the enemy. Ordered that every officer mounting a guard should sleep at the main guard, and visit the sentinels at least three times a night. Placed a lance sergeant and four men as a guard at the river.

Sergeant Warren, who was ordered from head-quarters to bring provisions round to us, arrived in the night; hailed the sentry, but was made no answer, came past them, landed and came up to the Colonel's camp; the Colonel immediately ordered the sentry under the main guard.

TUESDAY, December 24, 1776

Major Malberry arrived with his detachment at the other side; a boat was sent for him immediately; he had seen no signs of the enemy. Lieutenant Dogharty came over the river; says he saw very fresh signs of four or five men crossing the river. Ordered that a Court Martial be held upon Abner Islands for being caught sleeping on his post. Lieutenant Fitzpatrick returned; says he followed the tracks up to Mr. Inglis' plantation; they appeared to have run off from there; they followed the tracks until they got intermixed with ours in such a manner that they could follow them no longer. The Court Martial were opinion that the prisoner should receive twenty lashes on the bare back, but my writing a note to the Colonel, informing him of the character of the soldier, of its being his first offence committed in the service, the Colonel thought proper to forgive the prisoner. The Regiment was drawn up and some of the articles of war I read to them. Ordered that every man hobble and bell his horse and have him ready to cross the river early in the morning.

WEDNESDAY, December 25, 1776

The whole detachment crossed the river, all to a small guard at the river of a subaltern and twenty men. The detachment proceeded as far as Lee's Hill. I was detached to

McGirth's as a reconnoitering party; could make no discovery of any sign fresher than three or four days; joined the party. (Gibbes 2: 47-49)

Washington crosses the Delaware

In the North, Continental Commander in Chief George Washington was desperate to salvage the revolution after being driven out of New York in a string of humiliating defeats. Military historians Colonel Ernest Dupuy and Colonel Trevor Dupuy describe Washington's response to his dilemma:

> Washington had decided to cross the Delaware and to strike one or more blows against the British in their winter quarters in New Jersey. Without some sort of dramatic success to electrify the country, and to inspire his troops, he had no hope of holding an army together during the winter, or of recruiting more men before the next spring campaign. If successful, a blow at Trenton, possibly followed by a raid on the main British supply depot at New Brunswick, would gain supplies of clothing and ammunition for his men, and give them some concrete and tangible basis to hope for the eventual success of their cause. Failure, of course, as Washington well knew, would mean the end of the Revolution, as well as complete disaster for himself... (165-66)

Washington's troops assembled on Christmas afternoon for their expedition across the Delaware. They reached McKonkey's Ferry as midwinter dark descended. Chunks of ice careened down the swift current of the Delaware River and slammed into the fifty-foot-long boats that transported the troops.

Snow fell steadily throughout the evening and before midnight sleet pelted the troops. The wind rose as the night went by, complicating not only the crossing but also the loading and unloading of men, horses and artillery.

The expedition was hours behind schedule when the crossing was completed. The troops marched through the stormy night, and shortly after dawn reached the town of Trenton, where Hessian troops in the service of the British army had established winter quarters.

The American army of 2,400 men – with General Nathanael Greene commanding the left wing – attacked the Hessian quarters in the early morning of December 26. Captain William Washington and Lieutenant James Monroe led a company of Virginia riflemen in a charge that succeeded in capturing two Hessian cannons although both Captain Washington and Lieutenant Monroe suffered wounds. After Greene led a brigade to block the route to Princeton, the Americans hemmed in the Hessians on three sides while Assunpink Creek trapped the Hessians on the fourth side. Soon after the Hessian commander died leading a counterattack, the Hessian troops soon surrendered.

In a battle lasting a little over an hour, the Hessian losses were twenty-two killed and 948 captured; about 430 Hessian and British troops escaped. Four Americans were wounded in the fighting, and two Americans froze to death shortly after crossing the Delaware. The Americans captured ammunition, arms and artillery (Dupuy and Dupuy 166-74). Dupuy and Dupuy describe the aftermath:

> … herding their prisoners along – accompanied by several wagonloads of booty, plus the captured cannon – the indomitable little army retraced its steps through the continuing storm to its boats at McKonkey's Ferry. The return river crossing was as bitter as that of the previous night, save that it was in daylight. Even so, three more men froze to death. During the late afternoon and early evening, the troops reached their old bivouacs. They were exhausted by a march of nearly 30 miles, in abominable weather; yet at the same time they were as happy as only men can be who have tasted victory after months of defeat.
>
> The results of the battle have been summed up by Trevelyan, the British historian: "It may be doubted whether so small a number of men ever employed so small a space of time with greater or more lasting results upon the history of the world." The country was galvanized; the Revolution reprieved. (174)

Colonel William McIntosh patrols the frontier

In the South, Colonel William McIntosh's troop of horsemen continued to patrol the frontier through the short, cold days of midwinter. Captain Charles Middleton kept a journal:

THURSDAY, December 26, 1776

I was ordered to take a subaltern and twenty-three privates, volunteers, to cross the river St. Mary's in search of the Florida scouts; the men turned out, and we crossed the river that night and went as far as Taylor's.

FRIDAY, December 27, 1776

We proceeded, and in about an hour afterwards came upon fresh signs of cattle, imagined them to have been drove along late last night. I gave the necessary orders, as in all probability we might expect to come upon them every minute. However we did not come up with them until we got to Cornelious Rains', where they had just gone from, but discovering a house we made three different parties to surround the houses.

Unluckily, Joseph Rains was going over to his brother's and discovered us creeping up; he immediately ran and gave the alarm at the house; and then proceeded after the men who were driving the cattle and alarmed them also.

We surrounded the house and came in; the men were all gone; though I could not learn that there were more than Cornelious Rains there at that time; the cattle drivers had been gone about half an hour before; Mrs. Rains and her daughter informed me that one Captain York, with a party, was with the cattle, and that James Moore and Sampson Williams were each to have been there the night before with each of them a company. We had several times information that there was a strong party of whites and another of Indians coming out, though I did not put much faith in the report. I thought if it was true, and any strong party came against us and we should be defeated, I should be much blamed, my order being very particular to be as careful as possible what number I was to engage.

Again our retreat was very bad no conveniency for crossing the river St. Mary's, we thought proper to retreat as fast as possible over St. Mary's and there ambuscade on the river bank, on the Georgia side, as there we might give them battle, be their number what they would. We took two negroes and three horses from Rains', and retreated. About two

miles from there we met a party that was detached to join me
on coming up with the sign where the cattle had crossed the
river. Lieutenant Gooden commanded the party, fifteen
strong, which made the command forty, officers included.
We then thought we were strong enough for anything on this
side St. John's, and returned and surrounded Rains' houses a
second time, but there was no appearance of the enemy.

We then began to collect what intelligence we could. We
were informed that one Capt. Jeffres had been there that
morning, and went off with a party to William Mills'; that
Colonel William McIntosh's fellow, Osker, was with them.
Lieut. Gooden and Lieut. Daughty, and a number of the men,
knew this Jeffres to be a noted tory, and had been among the
Cherokee Indians endeavoring to, and did, bring them against
us. I was very anxious to catch him... I took the men off immediately to Loughton's, and surrounded the house.
McGuire, who was in the yard, spied us, and ran for the bush,
which was not above twenty yards from the house – very
thick. In his flight two of my men fired at him, but I believe
with no success. We made a strict search in the bushes, but
could not find him. Our horses were much jaded. Jeffres had
not been that way. I was at a loss to think what was become
of them. Our horses were not able to proceed any farther, as
some of the men were obliged to walk on foot. We remained
there that night; put all the men on guard. About break of day
one of the sentry fired twice. We all ran out, thought the Indians and scouts were come up. I ordered the men to possess
themselves of the houses, and detached a party to know the
reason of the guns firing. The sentry says he shot a man that
was walking up within ten steps of him; he fired first with his
pistol, then with his rifle. On his firing his rifle, the man
stumbled very much; he believes he hit him. I thought it
could be no one but McGuire, who was endeavoring to steal
our horses. I sent parties all round the plantation, but they
could discover no signs of any body there... (Gibbes 2: 49-
50)

Indians attack fort on southern frontier
As night fell on December 27, Indians wounded a man outside
the Georgia fort at Beards Bluff, forty miles upriver from Fort

Howe/Barrington. At daybreak, Lieutenant Jeremiah Buggs led twelve men out of the fort to find the attackers. The Indians killed four of the men and shot Buggs' horse out from under him.

The surviving men raced back to the fort. Buggs was left behind, but managed to reach safety on foot. The Indians scalped the four dead men and stuck arrows in them.

All of the men stationed at Beards Bluff deserted from their post except for one who accompanied Buggs to Fort Howe (Searcy 76-78).

Colonel William McIntosh remains on patrol

Captain Charles Middleton of Colonel William McIntosh's troop of horsemen kept a journal of events on the southern frontier:

SATURDAY, December 28, 1776
We got from McGuire a negro boy, who he had taken from Captain Anderson, and a mare, saddle and saddle-bags, and his rifle, and some of his cloth, and returned. Crossed the river that night.

SUNDAY, December 29, 1776
Proceeded and joined the main body at Sattillie, and informed the colonel of our proceedings.

MONDAY, December 30, 1776
Sergeant Warren informed me that one of my men, George Hall, had a fall from his horse, and was dangerously hurt. I went to see him immediately, and believe he will die. A court-martial was summoned to hold and try Levi Coleman and John Bilbo, two soldiers, for sleeping on their posts. The court-martial were of opinion that Levi Coleman should sit down, and have one gun under his hams, and another over his neck, and brought as close together as possible, and tied fast, there to remain for the space of ten minutes, and at the expiration of the time the upper gun to be fired off – the whole detachment to be drawn up at the same time. John Bilbo, who had some favorable circumstances on his side, was to stand up alongside of Levi Coleman, with a gun across his head, and to remain ten minutes. Some of the plunder was sold.

Ordered that every man be ready to march. We marched about six miles that night.

TUESDAY, December 31, 1776
Several horses missing. We were obliged to wait until late in the afternoon. There were two sergeants and twenty men left to hunt the horses, and to follow. We proceeded as far as Red Cap that night. (Gibbes 2: 50-51)

Washington crosses the Delaware again

In the North, Continental Commander in Chief George Washington led his army once again across the Delaware River into New Jersey on December 29. General Nathanael Greene with three hundred picked men led the van of the American expedition. The Americans reoccupied Trenton, where they had won a victory three days earlier.

During the next two days Washington conducted personal visits to each of his regiments to urge the men to extend their enlistments past the end of the year. More than half of the Continental soldiers who had served with him in the campaign across New York and New Jersey agreed to remain in his army for another six weeks. Washington faced the new year with an army of nearly five thousand men (Dupuy and Dupuy 176).

1777

Rory McIntosh leaves Darien and finds refuge in British-held Florida. In February, Lachlan McIntosh mounts a rescue expedition to Fort McIntosh near the Georgia-Florida border and is wounded in the fighting. In May, Lachlan McIntosh engages Button Gwinnett in a duel, and Gwinnett dies of his wounds. Aeneas Mackintosh fights at Short Hills in the summer and in the Battle of Brandywine in the fall. Lachlan McIntosh joins George Washington's army and endures the winter at Valley Forge.

Colonel William McIntosh defends border

On New Year's Day of 1777, a troop of Continental horsemen led by Colonel William McIntosh arrived at a strategic location on the Satilla River where they intended to build a stockade to protect Georgia against raids from British East Florida. The troop had been on a defensive expedition through the semi-tropical wilderness for nearly two weeks. Captain Charles Middleton described the mission in his journal:

WEDNESDAY, January 1, 1777

We got to the Bluff, where we were to build the fort that night

THURSDAY, January 2, 1777

Nothing particular.

FRIDAY, January 3, 1777

Ordered, that a court-martial be summoned to try Josiah Clark for sleeping on his post. The court-martial ordered him to ride the wooden horse ten minutes. The colonel thought proper to take off five minutes. The major and myself viewed the Bluff, in order to point out a proper plan for a stockade. The tools were got in order to begin.

Ordered, that thirty men be set aside as a guard in the day. The whole are to be on duty to guard the workmen and horses – that is, twenty-two as a guard around the workmen and eight as a grass guard, to go out by turns, and at night fifteen men on duty, who will be relieved the next night by other fifteen.

That thirteen men, with an officer, be kept as a scouting party continually.

That the remainder be kept at work on the stockade, except a sergeant and six men, to be sent out occasionally to bring in cattle, or any other necessaries that should be wanting, as there is no commissary to supply them.

In case the scout or any other party discover any of the enemy, the commanding officer will act as he thinks best for the good of the service.

That John Bilbo act as sergeant to the first company.

That William Goold and [blank space] act as sergeants to Capt. Cade's company.

John Gray, one of my troop, arrived express to the colonel the purport of which was, that there were four men of the third troop killed, and the rest had evacuated the fort on Beard's Bluff, saving two men, which were all that Lieut. Bug could get to stay with him. These two men and himself went to Fort Howe. (Gibbes 2: 51-52)

The Battle of Princeton: January 3, 1777

In the North, a British army led by Lord Cornwallis opposed about five thousand Americans under George Washington who had crossed the icy Delaware River into New Jersey. "Confronting Washington's gaunt, footsore, exhausted veterans, and his unreliable militia, Cornwallis had 5,500 regulars in hand," Colonels Ernest Dupuy and Trevor Dupuy note, "with two additional brigades, some 2,500 men, disposed in reserve a few hours away" (177). Washington executed a silent midnight maneuver around the left flank of the British forces toward Princeton. Shortly after dawn on January 3, an American brigade led by Brigadier General Hugh Mercer encountered two British regiments led by Colonel Charles Mawhood. After General Mercer suffered a mortal wound, his brigade retreated with the British in pursuit. Washington sent a militia unit from Philadelphia into the fray; when the British fired a volley the militiamen fled. Washington ordered his rear guard commanded by Colonel Daniel Hitchcock to move into battle position while he himself rallied the fleeing Americans. Dupuy and Dupuy write:

...Washington dashed into the mob of militia to help [Colonel John] Cadwalader, who was vainly trying to re-form his men. Raising his voice, Washington shouted: "Parade with us, my brave fellows. There is but a handful of the enemy, and we shall have them directly."

The effect was almost miraculous. Washington's presence was all that Mercer's leaderless men needed to restore them to order. Their example, and the sight of the imposing figure on his big horse, quickly shamed the Philadelphia militiamen also to turn around and form ranks again. Mawhood's troops, now firmly established behind a fence on the ridge, saw the men they had just routed turn and begin to re-form beside Hitchcock's fresh troops. Then galloping across the fields between the two forces came the American general, waving his men forward with his hat. Across the field his stentorian voice carried: "Follow me! Hold your fire!"

As though drawn by a magnet, the militiamen and Continentals advanced behind their imposing Commander-in-Chief. About 30 yards from the British line, the General drew rein and cried: "Halt!" His men raised their muskets, awaiting his command to fire. But before he could speak, a volley rang out from the British troops, spontaneously answered by the ready American muskets. Washington, between the fire, was swallowed in billowing smoke. Frantic aides, dashing forward, fearful of what they would find, discovered their chief untouched and unruffled. "Bring up the troops!" he called. "Bring up the troops, the day is ours!"

And so it was. ...Mawhood abandoned his guns and ordered a withdrawal. ...Washington, sensing an opportunity to turn this retreat into a rout, ordered a troop of Philadelphia Light Horse to follow them. ...the general himself clapped spurs to his horse to clatter across the bridge after the Philadelphia cavalrymen. He shouted to his aides as he left: "It is a fine fox chase, my boys!"

The unexpected cavalry charge had the effect Washington desired. Mawhood's infantrymen scattered, and ran for the woods, while the small group of British cavalry galloped down the road...

...Washington reluctantly gave up the pleasure of the chase to reassume the responsibilities of command. Realizing that Cornwallis would soon be coming… he ordered the Philadelphia cavalrymen to turn back, and he led them towards Princeton, where [Continental General John] Sullivan was now engaged. On the way he took time personally to chase away a thief who had begun to rob a helpless wounded British soldier lying on the battlefield. After a word of comfort to the surprised redcoat, he galloped on to Princeton, to find the town in Sullivan's control.

…Quickly Washington ordered his troops to collect what they could carry from the British stores, and to destroy the rest. Most of his ragged, barefoot men were able to refit themselves with new shoes and blankets, and to gorge themselves on British rations.

…The Battle of Princeton, which lasted less than half an hour, was only a skirmish insofar as numbers engaged and casualties suffered were concerned… Actually, however, this small engagement was the magnificent conclusion of one of the most brilliant, and one of the most significant, military campaigns in history.

Strategically and politically, the effects were enormous. The British had been driven from western and central New Jersey. The dying embers of an almost lost cause flamed anew; the War of the Revolution would continue. (180-83)

Colonel William McIntosh relieved

On the southern frontier, Colonel William McIntosh completed his role in establishing a stockade on the Satilla River, a natural boundary between Georgia and British East Florida. Captain Charles Middleton recorded McIntosh's departure in his journal:

SATURDAY, January 4, 1777

Lieut.-Colonel McIntosh, Major Marbury, Capt. Caldwell and Lieut. Daughty, left us. Lieut. West, with fifteen men, went as a scouting party as far as the Altamaha, and on their return to bring provisions. The command now fell upon me, the Colonel and Major being absent. We had a great deal of difficulty to get the men to work on the stockade; however, promising them that they and their horses should be exempt from guard duty, they went to work.

...MONDAY, January 6, 1777

The men continued on the stockade. The grass guard reported that there were many horses missing. Sent men in search of them all day, but could not find any...

TUESDAY, January 7, 1777

Copy of a letter sent to the commanding officer at Fort Howe:

... "I shall be much obliged to you to procure a few tools for the stockade, as they are much hindered for the want of them; also, two or three sets of wedges are very much wanted, and a cross-cut saw, file, one or two chisels, and some nails... We get on very well with the stockade, considering the want of tools. Some axes are also wanted...

"Our provisions are out. I hope though before this reaches you, the supply will arrive..."

...THURSDAY, January 9, 1777

Copy of a letter wrote to the commanding officer at Fort Howe:

"Lieut. Beams and his attachment arrived here 7th inst. I was a good deal alarmed that they brought no provisions, at least not enough to last two meals round to each man. We have here, including Lieut. Beams' party, near one hundred souls. I sent out Lieut. Fitzpatrick and fifteen men yesterday, with orders to scout as far as the Old Ferry, on Sattillie, round by Middleton's plantation, to answer two purposes – first, as a scouting party; second, in hopes they might meet with the lost horses... I hope there will be some method fallen upon to supply this place with provisions. The men seem eager to have an opportunity of complaining; they are coming to me every moment enquiring what they should eat. I have had hunters out since yesterday morning; they have not come in yet, so that we are out of beef as well as rice.

"The hunters have just come, and brought beef, which is some satisfaction. Pray, don't omit sending me as much salt as possible, as we shall be obliged to keep a good deal of beef salted up, the cattle being very hard to get here unless it is breeding cattle. Some chisels are very much wanted to finish the fort gate. The horses are very troublesome, as they incline much to ramble."

FRIDAY, January 10, 1777

...Lieut. Fitzpatrick and his party arrived; had discovered signs of Moccosins, very fresh, supposed to have crossed Sattillie about three or four hours, and signs of four horses, supposed to be the four that was lost on our march from the Old Ferry to the Bluff. There appeared by the signs of the tracks to have been about fifteen men. They crossed at Lemmons' ferry. (Gibbes 2: 52-54)

At age 50 and beset with illness, Colonel William McIntosh decided he could no longer ride horseback through the semitropical wilderness of the southern frontier, where he had been involved in raids and counter-raids sporadically over thirty-five years. As a teenager, he had served with colonial British forces that raided into Florida when it was a Spanish colony. Young William had seen his father John Mackintosh Mor taken prisoner in a battle at Fort Mosa near St. Augustine; William himself managed to escape through enemy lines along with his relative Roderick "Rory" McIntosh and a few other soldiers. A few years later, William and his younger brother Lachlan were in the English garrison at Fort Frederica on St. Simons Island that repulsed a Spanish invasion of Georgia in the Battle of Bloody Marsh. When the American Revolution began, William McIntosh had been given command of a Continental troop of horsemen that patrolled the southern frontier and established forts along the Georgia-Florida border. For a full year, William McIntosh had been conducting raids into British East Florida and fending off counter-raids. Early in 1777, General Lachlan McIntosh relieved his ailing older brother of duty by sending Colonel Samuel Elbert to take command at Fort Howe (Searcy 79).

Armies establish winter quarters

In the North, George Washington established winter quarters at Morristown, New Jersey. From there, he kept a watchful eye on the seat of American government at Philadelphia. Morristown was both protected against attack from the coast and near farmland that provided food for the soldiers. Washington found comfortable lodging in a former tavern, but missed his wife and worried about his home in Virginia; unlike the first years of the war, Martha Washington was not able to join her husband at winter quarters because the campaign had lasted into January and the roads had become impassable in winter weather.

American officers resided in houses while common soldiers occupied buildings or constructed huts. Still struggling to enlist and re-enlist soldiers, Washington scattered his men throughout hamlets around Morristown to give the impression that his army of three or four thousand men was ten times that size.

The British army in the North – including Captain Aeneas Mackintosh and his fellow Highlanders in the 71st Regiment – placed posts at Amboy and New Brunswick in addition to head-quarters at New York, where the officers enjoyed a vibrant social scene.

Foraging parties from American and British encampments of-ten engaged in skirmishes. The raids pitted American cavalryman Henry Lee against British cavalryman Banastre Tarleton; they would contend against one another throughout the war (Chernow 285-86, Thane 102).

Rory McIntosh joins loyalists in Florida

During the American Revolution, Roderick "Rory" McIntosh parted ways with his relatives in Georgia. While his neighbor William McIntosh and William's brother Lachlan served as Continental officers, Rory remained loyal to the king. Rory accused his relatives with trying to deceive him at the beginning of the war by saying that their design was to bring in "The Young Gentleman" to reign in America. Like many other Georgians who remained loyal to Great Britain during the American Revolution, Rory found refuge in the British territory of East Florida. When he arrived in St. Augustine in 1777, a British officer congratulated him on having made his escape from the rebels. Rory replied, "My escape, sir! No! I despised them too much to run away, but sent them a message that I should leave Mallow for East Florida at twelve o'clock and to come and stop me if they dared."

A resident of St. Augustine, John Couper, gave this description of Rory: "In 1777, he must have been about sixty-five years of age, about six feet in height, strongly built, white, frizzled, bushy hair, and large whiskers (then uncommon) frizzled fiercely out, a ruddy McIntosh complexion, handsome, large and muscular limbs. In walking, or rather striding, his step must have been four feet. I have seen him walking along, and a small man trotting by him.

One of his shoulders was rather, depressed, the effect of 'an inglorious wound' received from a slave."

While in St. Augustine, Rory engaged twenty fellow loyalists who had evacuated from the Darien district to serve as mariners on a privateer ship. He resented with great indignation a report that he was after prize money, and he made a deed to another man's children of any prize money he might be entitled to. As the ship was leaving St. Augustine, it struck a sand bar. Rory drew his dirk on the pilot and accused him of being bribed by the rebels. The pilot succeeded in getting the ship over the bar, but the privateers did not succeed in taking any prizes.

Struggle for the southern frontier

Rory McIntosh's adventures were part of a larger struggle between the British in East Florida and the Americans in South Carolina and Georgia. Raiding parties crossed back and forth along the Georgia-Florida border, inflicting a few casualties and plundering property, including Lachlan McIntosh's plantations at Darien. The McIntosh property had been "more in danger, & exposed by Land & Water to Enemys of every collour & kind," Lachlan McIntosh observed, "than any other Citizen perhaps in the United States." His losses included not only all his crops but also all his hogs and about four hundred head of cattle (Lawrence, "Suspension" 133).

A planned invasion of Florida to be led by General William Moultrie had fallen apart when Georgia had failed to provide adequate supplies and the men had sickened in the semi-tropical climate.

As the year 1777 opened, the situation on the border remained unsettled. A fort at Beards Bluff on the Altamaha had been abandoned after an Indian attack. General Lachlan McIntosh, the highest-ranking Continental officer in Georgia, assigned forty men to reoccupy the fort at Beards Bluff and sent reinforcements to Fort Howe, formerly Fort Barrington, on the Altamaha. Georgia did not provide enough money to pay the soldiers and provide supplies, prompting some of the men to steal civilian property and some of their officers to resign.

Political fissures develop in Georgia

Georgia adopted its first state constitution in February of 1777. Debate over the constitution highlighted tension between old-guard conservatives and backcountry populists. Lachlan McIntosh mentioned that he was not fond of several provisions in the constitution, a foreshadowing of political struggles that would bedevil him for the rest of his career.

Lachlan McIntosh wounded

British East Florida officials authorized cattle raids into Georgia to provide food for the soldiers and civilians in St. Augustine. Early in the morning of February 17, Florida Rangers and their Indian allies attacked Fort McIntosh on the Satilla River. In seven hours of fighting, one American was killed and three were wounded. General Lachlan McIntosh sent out a relief force that halted when Florida Rangers fired upon it. The fort surrendered on February 18 as regular British troops arrived to reinforce the Rangers. The British burned Fort McIntosh and proceeded toward Fort Howe on the Altamaha.

Lachlan McIntosh responded by stationing a galley in the Altamaha and sending reinforcements to Fort Howe and to Beards Bluff, forty miles upriver. In subsequent fighting against a British force led by Colonel L.V. Fuser in late February, Lachlan McIntosh was wounded and twelve of his men were killed.

The British regulars retreated to St. Augustine. The Rangers and Indians drove two thousand head of cattle into Florida.

To assist in Georgia's time of need, a detachment of the 2nd South Carolina Regiment led by Colonel Isaac Motte and Lieutenant Colonel Francis Marion arrived in Georgia with artillery, naval vessels and provisions. General Robert Howe, the Continental commander in South Carolina and Georgia, came to Savannah in early March to survey the situation. The 2nd South Carolina Regiment returned to Charleston in mid-March, but two hundred troopers in the Third Regiment of South Carolina Horse commanded by Colonel Thomas Sumter remained in Georgia (Searcy 84-88; Lawrence, "Suspension" 112).

Gwinnett faction resents McIntosh status

During the emergency on the border, Georgia's Council of Safety gave all executive power to its president, Archibald Bulloch. When Bulloch suddenly died, Button Gwinnett was elected to be the new president and to control the state's military forces.

George McIntosh was the only member of the Council of Safety who voted against Gwinnett (Jackson 55).

Since the beginning of the war, Gwinnett had wanted military command and had envied Lachlan McIntosh's position as commander of Georgia's Continental forces. Lachlan McIntosh believed that Gwinnett's allies were attempting to discredit him by attacking the character of his older brother William (Searcy 88-90; Lawrence, "Suspension" 111).

Gwinnett orders arrest of George McIntosh

In mid-March, Gwinnett ordered the arrest of George McIntosh for treason. American authorities suspected that George McIntosh had sold rice to British colonists in the West Indies. George McIntosh was incarcerated in the common jail and put in irons. The Georgia government confiscated his estate in the Darien area and housed soldiers there who destroyed much of his property (Searcy 235). The incident infuriated Lachlan McIntosh, who felt fiercely protective of his younger brother. Lachlan had taken young George with him to Charleston, where the two of them lived in the same household for eight years before they both returned to their family territory in coastal South Georgia.

His family arranged for George McIntosh to be released on bail and he set out to defend himself before the Continental Congress. He was in North Carolina by the time guards from Georgia caught up with him and escorted him the rest of the way to Philadelphia.

Washington suffers illness

In New Jersey, Continental Commander in Chief George Washington remained in winter quarters at Morristown well into the spring. In early March, he became so ill that he was not able to attend to official business. Fearing that he might not recover, he recommended that Nathanael Greene take over as commander in chief after his death (Burke Davis 197). After suffering for more than a week, Washington regained enough strength to resume his duties. His mood improved even more when his wife Martha arrived in mid-March. Other officers' wives and female relatives created an air of festivity in the rural town. Nathanael Greene's wife Caty was unable to leave her home in New England; on March 11 she had given birth and suffered a difficult recovery.

Caty named her newborn daughter Martha Washington Greene in honor of her friend (Bailey 47).

Gwinnett launches invasion of Florida

In Georgia, Council of Safety President Gwinnett hatched a plan to invade British East Florida without consulting Lachlan McIntosh, the commander of Continental forces in Georgia. Their relationship was tangled not only because they hated one another but also because Gwinnett was the highest-ranking civil official and McIntosh was the highest-ranking Continental officer in Georgia. Unable to raise enough state militia for his invasion of Florida, Gwinnett finally asked McIntosh in late March for the support of Continental troops. Although McIntosh called the operation the "Don quixot Expedition to Augustine," he complied with Gwinnett's request. "Whatever my opinion of the Expedition may be," McIntosh told his friend Henry Laurens, "I am resolved to go and do all in my power to forward it & bring it a happy issue" (Lawrence, "Suspension 113).

Officials recall both Gwinnett and McIntosh

The Georgia forces reached Sunbury by the middle of April. Sickness took its toll just as it had the year before. McIntosh and Gwinnett argued for weeks over who should be in command of the expedition. The Council of Safety asked both of them to return to Savannah, leaving Colonel Samuel Elbert of the 2nd Georgia Battalion to lead the invasion. McIntosh said he turned the command over to Elbert "For peace sake" (Lawrence, "Suspension 114).

Also in April, General Robert Howe was named commander of the Southern Department of the Continental Army following the death of General James Moore of North Carolina.

Americans invade by land and water

Elbert loaded his men on transports escorted by two sloops and three row galleys and, on May 1, floated down the inland waterway toward Florida. Meanwhile, a mounted force under Colonel John Baker rode southward, planning to rendezvous with Elbert's men at the mouth of the St. Johns River. For Baker's men, crossing the Altamaha was difficult and time-consuming because the river floods in the spring. When they finally got across the big river, Indians attacked their camp and wounded two soldiers. Baker's men spent the rest of the day chasing the Indians without success. The next day they resumed their trek southward, where the spring-swollen Satilla and St. Marys rivers awaited them. They managed to reach the rendezvous point according to schedule on May 12 and discovered that Elbert's flotilla had not yet arrived (Searcy 92-94).

Assembly holds hearings on invasion

Problems with Georgia's invasion of Florida damaged the prestige of the man who proposed the invasion, Button Gwinnett. When a new Georgia constitution called for a governor rather than a president as chief of state, Gwinnett ran for the post but was defeated.

The assembly under the new constitution held hearings on Gwinnett's conduct during preparations for the invasion. As the hearings concluded, Lachlan McIntosh accosted Gwinnett, calling him a scoundrel and lying rascal. Gwinnett responded to the insult by challenging McIntosh to a duel (Coleman 87-89, Coulter 134-35, Jackson 64-65).

McIntosh kills Gwinnett in duel

A witness gave a sworn statement describing the duel between Lachlan McIntosh and Button Gwinnett:

> State of Georgia:
>
> Personally appeared before me, John Wereat, Esqr. of Richmond County of the State aforesaid, who being duly sworn upon the Holy Evangelists of Almighty God, maketh Oath and Saith -----
>
> That late on the Evening of Thursday, the 15th of May instant [1777], a written challange was brought to Genl. McIntosh, signed Button Gwinnett, wherein the said Mr. Gwinnett charg'd the General with calling him a Scoundrel in public Conversation, and desir'd he would give satisfaction for it as a Gentleman, before Sunrise next morning in Sir James Wright's pasture, behind Colo. Martin's house; to which the General humorously sent in answer to Mr. Gwinnett, that the hour was rather earlier than his usual, but would assuredly meet him at the place and time appointed

with a pair of pistols only, as agreed upon with Mr. Gwinnett's second, who brought the Challange.

Early the next morning Mr. Gwinnett and his second found the General and his Second waiting on the Ground, and after politely saluting each other, the General drew his pistols to show he was loaded only with single Balls, but avoided entering into any other conversation but the business at hand. It was then proposed and agreed to, that they shou'd go a little lower down the hill, as a number of spectators appear'd, and when the Ground was Chose the seconds ask'd the distance. Mr. Gwinnett reply'd "whatever distance the General pleases." The General said he believ'd Eight or ten feet would be sufficient, and they were immediately measur'd, to which the General's second desir'd another step might be added. It was then proposed to turn back to back. The General answer'd "By no means let us see what we are about" ----- & immediately each took his stand, and agreed to fire as they cou'd. Both pistols went off nearly at the same time, when Mr. Gwinnett fell, being shot above the Knee, and said his thigh was broke. The General, who was also shot thro' the thick of the Thigh, stood still in his place, & not thinking his antagonist was worse wounded than himself ----- as he immediately afterwards declar'd – asked if he had enough or was for another shot, to which all objected, and the seconds declar'd they both behav'd like Gentlemen and men of honor. Led the General up to Mr. Gwinnett and they both shook hands – further this Deponent Saith Not.

[Note: This is endorsed: George Wells' Affidavit respecting B.G. and L.M. June 1777.] (qtd. in Williams 3-4)

McIntosh expressed his emotion, according to family lore, by smashing his pistol against a tree, breaking the stock. McIntosh and Gwinnett left the dueling field for their homes. McIntosh recovered from his wound, but Gwinnett died three days later (Jackson 65-66, Holland 7A).

Invasion force defeated

While politicians in Savannah weighed the wisdom of invading Florida, the men actually involved in the invasion were fighting for their lives. Colonel Thomas Brown's Florida Rangers discovered the camp of Colonel John Baker's invasion force on May 14. That night, Brown's Indian allies stole forty of Baker's horses. When morning came, Baker followed the tracks for four miles and found the horses hobbled beside a swamp. Baker believed the Indians were waiting in ambush in the swamp. He left a party of men in plain sight to divert the Indians and sent two other parties to cut the hobbles and drive the horses away from the swamp. When his tactic succeeded, the Indians came out of ambush and pursued Baker's men for a mile. Although Baker's men outnumbered the Indians sixty to fifteen, Baker could not make his men stop and face the Indians in battle. During the pursuit, a young Indian was killed and two of Baker's men were wounded. The Indians called off the chase and burned the woods so that they could not be tracked. Baker's men scalped and mutilated the dead Indian (Searcy 94).

Because the British knew the location of his camp, Baker moved inland. The British intercepted his line of march and prepared for battle. The British forces totaled about two hundred, while Baker had 150 to 180 horsemen. Historian Martha Condray Searcy describes the battle:

> About ten o'clock the next morning (17 May) at Thomas Creek, a tributary of the Nassau River, the Americans were ambushed. Brown had left a small party in a branch of the swamp on the American flank. Then, his main body fired at the oncoming rebels at fifty yards' range. The Americans had no alternative but to retreat directly into the force of Major Mark Prevost's one hundred regulars, who were advancing rapidly with fixed bayonets in three columns. Surrounded by the Rangers, Indians, and regulars, twenty or thirty of the Americans fled at the first fire.
>
> After a five-minute skirmish, the rest of Baker's force began retreating through the swamp. The British almost captured Colonel Baker himself; one of his men stole his horse and rode away upon it. Three Americans were killed, including Lieutenants Frazer and McGowen; nine wounded, including Lieutenant Robeson; and thirty-one taken prisoner, including Captains Few and Williams. Baker and his men straggled northward in small parties. Thomas

Coleman drowned crossing the Satilla. The king's troops were too exhausted by the heat and too ill shod, many of them being barefoot at the battle, and the Rangers' horses were too jaded for the British to pursue the rebels. (95)

Flotilla stops at Amelia Island

On May 18, Elbert's flotilla stopped at Amelia Island to gather provisions for the invasion force. Loyalists killed a lieutenant and badly wounded two men who were rounding up cattle and pigs. In retaliation, Elbert ordered that every house on Amelia be burned and all the livestock killed. Elbert's forces also seized at least seven slaves from plantations on Amelia.

While Elbert was at Amelia Island, fifteen of Baker's men arrived and told of their defeat. Three more of Baker's men arrived a few days later and reported that Indians had killed five of the Americans who had been taken prisoner in the battle at Thomas Creek.

Elbert attempted to continue the invasion down the inland waterway, but the flotilla was unable to navigate the narrow passage between Amelia Island and the mainland despite six days of effort. The invasion force had dwindled to about three hundred men healthy enough to fight. The men were running out of provisions and subsisted on rice for five days. With British forces guarding the river crossings and British vessels patrolling the coast, Elbert decided to withdraw. Most of the force embarked on the flotilla to return northward, while a hundred men marched overland, destroying settlements and farms along the way (Searcy 93-96).

Invasion ends ignominiously

The famished men of Georgia's invasion force reached Fort Howe/Barrington on June 9 and proceeded to Darien the next day. At Darien, Elbert ordered Colonel Screven of the 3rd Regiment to take several hundred men to the Satilla to protect Georgians who were driving cattle out of the disputed land. Once the Georgians succeeded in driving about a thousand cattle north of the Altamaha, Screven's regiment returned to Fort Howe (Searcy 95-97).

George McIntosh arrives in Philadelphia

George McIntosh – who had been arrested in March by Georgia Council of Safety President Button Gwinnett and had departed to defend himself before Congress – arrived in Philadelphia in late June, according to a journal kept by a fellow Georgian. Raymond Demere of St. Simons Island – who had served on the Georgia Provincial Council in 1775 and had been taken hostage by British sailors during the Battle of the Riceboats in Savannah in 1776 – was serving in 1777 as an aide-de-camp to the Continental general known as Lord Stirling. Demere wrote in his journal:

> May 31st. Arrived at headquarters; waited on Gen. Washington… Dined with Gen. Washington…
>
> June 5th. Spent the day with Lord Stirling. Gen. Washington having reason to think the enemy intended a sudden movement from Brunswick to New York, ordered Col. Martin, with a detachment of 500 men, to watch his movements and check him. Lord Stirling acquiescing, I joined the detachment and was appointed second in command. We left the parade at 12 o'clock at night. The road to Quibble town was rough and uneven and in many places so narrow we were obliged to march in files… But the Brigade Major had been so negligent in supplying provisions, the weather rainy and the troops hungry and fatigued, we were obliged to make three divisions and quarter them in different farms. When we were refreshed we commenced our march. Col. Martin went forward to gain intelligence and we appointed to meet on a hill near Woodbridge. When there, I formed the battalion and, to rest the men, ordered them to ground arms. It began to rain violently; I formed into platoons and marched to gain shelter from the weather. I was soon joined by Col. Martin who had discovered a strong encampment of the enemy near Woodbridge. As the houses in the neighborhood were so small that the troops could be only in separate detachments, where they could be easily surprised, we were determined to approach the enemy and cut off his picquets. Accordingly, we quickened our pace, but within a mile of their camp, on examination, our arms were found damp with rain, the officers wet to the skin, the men overcome with fatigue and several really sick. …a countermarch was ordered, but we had not proceeded four miles when it rained so hard and the men became so weary we were compelled to quarter them in small detachments in

different houses, about a mile from Woodbridge… among people disaffected to our cause and whom we knew would give intelligence to all our movements. However, we made the best of it, appeared cheerful and satisfied and gave out we were to remain all night, planted sentries, and appointed a place of rendezvous. After the men had rested a little, issued private orders and we then marched eight miles to the Scotch plains, where we did not finish quartering the troops until two o'clock. The excessive fatigue I endured for two nights and one day (for even when the men were reposing, our situation required such constant vigilance that I could not rest) had so overcome me that I was completely exhausted and sleep and refreshment were absolutely necessary.

June 9th… We received advice to return to our camp this evening. About six miles from it we learned from a Sergeant there was a Hessian guard 200 yds. off. We halted, and I was allowed to make an attack (though contrary to orders) if the men would volunteer. Only forty offered, then twenty more joined. I made three divisions and attacked the redoubt at three points. The Hessians deserted at first fire and eight prisoners were made. We marched off in the face of a thousand of the enemy who began to beat arms, returned to camp and made a report to Lord Stirling then at headquarters…

June 24th… In company with Mr. Roche from Carolina went to Philadelphia… Dined with Col. Laurens [Col. John Laurens was a son of Henry Laurens, who was President of Congress and also was a business partner with Lachlan McIntosh; at the time of John Laurens' birth, Lachlan and his brother George were residents of the Laurens household in Charleston] and several members of Congress…

George McIntosh and Capt. Scott are just arrived from Georgia. Neither of them brought me letters which is a great disappointment. (qtd. in Cate 179-81)

Congress releases George McIntosh

When George McIntosh defended himself against charges lodged by former Georgia Council of Safety President Button

Gwinnett, the Continental Congress released him for lack of evidence.

The mistreatment of George McIntosh was cited by South Carolinian William Henry Drayton as one in a series of blunders committed by the Georgia government. In a letter to a Georgia official, Drayton wrote:

> I am bound to proclaim to your people... their property is not secure under your Government – a disgrace and detriment to the American cause – that the life and liberty of the subjects are in the greatest danger under your management, or we would not, among many other enormities, have seen George M'Intosh, Esq., who I consider as an abused gentleman, arbitrarily ordered into a distant State, to be tried by those who have no such jurisdiction in such a case... circumstances of tyranny, and total disregard to the most valuable rights of the people, that not only ought to alarm every honest and sensible man in Georgia, but fill such with indignation against you... (Gibbes 2: 86)

John McIntosh promoted

In Georgia, the latest attempt to invade Florida had failed as usual and the invasion force was on its way home. Georgia officials then adopted a defensive strategy. In early June the assembly approved two battalions of minute men to defend the frontier, and General Lachlan McIntosh renewed recruiting efforts to bring the Continental regiments to full strength. To encourage the officers doing the recruiting, he ordered numerous promotions. As a result, his nephew John McIntosh rose from captain to major of the First Battalion (Searcy 101). Lachlan's son William was promoted to captain in 1777 (Hawes, *University* 6).

During the summer in coastal Georgia, many of the soldiers became ill, so General McIntosh moved most of them inland to healthier locations with better water, leaving a detachment at Sunbury. The 2nd Regiment under Colonel Elbert was stationed on the Savannah River and the 3rd Regiment under Colonel Screven was stationed on the Ogeechee River.

McIntosh's feud and duel with Button Gwinnett complicated his relationship with Colonel John Baker. When petitions for removing McIntosh from command were circulated after the duel,

Baker reportedly told his whole regiment to sign. When McIntosh reassigned Baker's regiment of light horse from the western frontier to the southern frontier, the orders were not carried out. Baker's men were dispirited because they had lost their horses and they had not been paid for their military service. The officers complained that their financial accounts had not been certified. Feeling that he had been unjustly criticized, Baker resigned in late August.

The Georgia government tried to go over McIntosh's head by giving Elbert command of the Continental troops on the western frontier, but Elbert abided by the chain of command that placed McIntosh in charge of all Continental troops in Georgia.

Intrigue in Indian country

Hundreds of miles inland from the British in St. Augustine and the Americans in Savannah and Charleston, agents representing the two rivals tried to persuade the Creek Indians to take sides. The Creeks, for the most part, followed their time-honored diplomatic strategy of remaining neutral while white factions fought among themselves.

By the time of the American Revolution nearly three hundred Scots and Englishmen lived among the Creeks (Searcy 20). One of the British agents was William McIntosh, the son of Rory McIntosh's brother John McIntosh. Living among the Creeks for long periods, William McIntosh was the father of two boys who were raised by their Creek mothers.

The leading American trader among the Creeks was George Galphin of the Augusta area. During a meeting at Ogeechee Old Town on June 17, Galphin urged his Indian allies to expel William McIntosh and another British agent, David Tait. Encouraged by Tait, a few Creek parties raided into Georgia from time to time. In the period from 1776 through 1778, Georgians suffered more casualties from the Creeks than from regular British troops (Searcy 109-13, 177).

The British capture Ticonderoga: July 6, 1777

In the North, British General John Burgoyne led close to ten thousand British and Hessian troops, French Canadian militia, loyalists, allied Indian warriors and camp followers in an invasion from Canada into the United States. The invaders easily captured an American stronghold at Ticonderoga on Lake Champlain on

July 6. Burgoyne then proceeded into eastern New York with the intent of joining forces with General William Howe at Albany.

Continental Commander in Chief George Washington sent General Benjamin Lincoln and General Benedict Arnold to assist the Northern Department of the Continental Army in resisting Burgoyne. Congress, meanwhile, appointed General Horatio Gates as commander of the Northern Department.

Allan McDonald arranges his own exchange

Allan McDonald – husband of the legendary Flory McDonald – waited for more than a year as a prisoner of war on parole waiting to be exchanged. He had been captured at the Battle of Moore's Creek Bridge early in 1776 and had been paroled in the summer of 1776. Since British prisoners were exchanged for American prisoners of equal rank, a question about Allan's rank delayed the process; he was a lieutenant colonel in the North Carolina militia but a captain in the regular army. He petitioned the Continental Congress to allow him to meet with the British commander in New York and arrange his own exchange. His petition dated July 18, 1777, mentions Flory's circumstances:

> Now, sir, permit me to say: when you'll know the dispersed and distress't state of my family you will at least sympathize with me and pity my oppress'd mind. I am here with one of my Sons – seventeen months a Prisoner.
>
> My wife in North Carolina 700 miles from me in a very sickly tender state of health, with a younger Son, a Daughter, & four Grand Children.
>
> Two Sons in our Service of whom I heard little or nothing since one of them had been wounded in the Battle of Bunkers hill – and two in Britain, of whom, I heard no account since I left it.
>
> Them in Carolina I can be of no service to in my present state, but were I Exchanged I would be of service to the rest if in life. (qtd. in Vining 178-79)

Congress agreed on August 21 to allow Allan to go to New York to discuss his exchange with the British commander (Vining 179).

Lachlan McIntosh acquitted and reassigned

In Georgia, the wheels of justice ground slowly after the duel between Lachlan McIntosh and Button Gwinnett. Official reaction awaited the next meeting of the Georgia assembly, when McIntosh was arrested for killing Gwinnett. He was acquitted at trial, but that did not quell a political firestorm raging around him. As he fought for his honor and his career, his old friend and business partner Henry Laurens came to his aid. Laurens, who held a powerful position in the Continental Congress, arranged for McIntosh to report to General George Washington for reassignment. As fate would have it, Laurens' son John served as an aide to General Washington, and so the paths of Lachlan McIntosh and John Laurens would cross once again. Washington issued the order reassigning McIntosh on August 6. Colonel Samuel Elbert assumed command of Continental forces in Georgia.

British capture Fort Frederica

Throughout August the East Florida Rangers and their Indian allies continued to raid into Georgia, coming within five miles of Savannah and passing through Augusta. The East Florida Rangers captured Fort Frederica on St. Simons Island, where the young McIntosh brothers William and Lachlan had served under General Oglethorpe in the colonial era.

A loyalist and Indian force ambushed twenty Georgia recruits in a dense swamp near Fort Howe on the Altamaha River, killing fourteen. Lieutenant Colonel John McIntosh led a detachment from Darien to bury the mutilated bodies of the Georgia recruits. The attackers crossed the Altamaha at Reid's Bluff and withdrew to St. Augustine (Searcy 113).

The Battle of the Brandywine: September 11, 1777

In the North, the British continued to pursue a two-pronged attack on American positions. General John Burgoyne maintained an invasion that had begun in Canada while Sir William Howe and Lord Cornwallis maneuvered by water out of their stronghold in New York toward the Continental Congress's seat in Philadelphia. Continental Commander in Chief George Washington detached some of his most reliable units – including Daniel Morgan's rifle corps – to reinforce the Northern Department in its resistance against Burgoyne. When Howe and Cornwallis landed nearly fifteen thousand troops at the upper end of Chesapeake Bay on August 25, Washington positioned less than ten thousand Continental soldiers and a few thousand militiamen at a crossing of Brandywine Creek on the main road to Philadelphia.

The British advanced on Washington's position at dawn on September 11. A biographer describes the battle from General Nathanael Greene's point of view:

> Greene was given command of the left center, with Sullivan on the right. In Greene's division was Colonel George Wheedon with his stalwart Virginia regiment
> ...Before Washington, who rode with Greene on the left center, knew what was happening the British were forcing Sullivan backward. Heavy cannonading and musketry fire... gave the alarm. The commander in chief sent Greene and his division... at the double quick through the late September afternoon to the rescue of Sullivan. They would try to bolster the panicked troops. The reinforcement was too late, Greene suspected, to save the battle, but his men might keep the army intact if they could reach Sullivan in time.
> Sullivan's force had broken under the unexpected British attack and rapidly was becoming disorganized when Greene's sprinting troops came up. There was no time now to try to stop Sullivan's fleeing men. Greene's soldiers fixed bayonets and plunged into the charging British line. Smoke and the thickening haze of late afternoon in the river valley made the distinction between friend and foe difficult as Greene's men, on order, opened their ranks, allowing Sullivan's men to pass quickly through to the rear. Then the American ranks closed, and a relentless barrier of steel and musket fire halted the British charge.
> The battle swayed back and forth as the sun slowly sank. Cornwallis, watching from nearby, wished that he could have just one more hour of daylight. Time after time the enemy's cold steel pressed forward, but the American line under Greene held compact and firm, pouring a steady fire into the ranks of Grenadiers, Hessians, Ansbachers, and light infantry. Soon Greene's enfilading artillery under [General Henry] Knox began to take a heavy toll, causing

the enemy's lines to quiver and bend like a cornfield in a whirlwind.

...the battle became one of bayonet against bayonet... Thrust for thrust, men matched their strong arms, skill, wits, and trickery against each other. Charge followed charge as the sun sank slowly behind the trees.

Brigadier General Anthony Wayne... long since had re-formed his brigade behind Greene's division and was helping valiantly to repulse the British attempt to break through.

Then the gallant Wheedon, overborne at last by sheer weight of numbers, was forced to draw off behind [Continental Brigadier General Peter Gabriel] Muhlenberg's rear. Greene, driven back to a narrow pass on the Chester road, slowly began to draw off his men, who fired in deliberate volleys as they retired. He had accomplished his mission and given the broken divisions time to retreat in good order. Twilight deepened and drew a swift curtain across the battlefield. Cornwallis broke off the action. Then slowly Greene led his exhausted men back toward their camp in Chester. His calm intervention and masterly rear guard action had saved the army. The battle was a defeat and a bad one, but Washington's men would live to fight another day. (Bailey 52-56)

The 71st Regiment – in which Aeneas Mackintosh served as a captain in the 2nd Battalion – played a role in the Battle of the Brandywine. The regiment's 1st Battalion "spearheaded the attack across the ford" (Boatner 109, Ward 353).

After the battle, reports historian George C. Rogers Jr., Continental Congress President Henry Laurens "picked up the wounded LaFayette and carried him in his own carriage to the Moravians at Bethlehem, a kind and gentle gesture amidst the chaos of war" (274).

The Battle of the Clouds: September 16, 1777

After the battle of Brandywine, American commander George Washington moved into position to protect his sources of food and supplies. One of the roads Washington watched led from Philadelphia to Wilmington, Delaware. On September 13, British commander Sir William Howe sent the 71st Highlanders to occupy Wilmington. The Highlanders traveled so swiftly and arrived so unexpectedly that they captured Delaware President and Commander in Chief John McKinley. Howe then sent wagons full of sick and wounded soldiers to a hospital established in Wilmington.

Late in the night of September 15, British General Charles Cornwallis set out to confront Washington's troops. Darkness and muddy terrain slowed the march. A storm of wind and rain slowed the march even more, and the mud got even deeper as infantrymen, artillery carriages, horses, livestock and supply wagons churned the dirt (McGuire 29, 30; Ward 355).

When Washington learned early the next morning that the British were coming, he arrayed the main army on high ground and sent forward a vanguard under General Anthony Wayne. The American vanguard met an advance force of Hessians early in the afternoon; Wayne's men steadily fired their rifles while crouching behind walls and fences until the Hessians escaped. The next wave of British forces, the 1st Battalion of British Light Infantry, chased back a force of Pennsylvania militia. Washington, meanwhile, withdrew his main army to more advantageous ground two miles away (McGuire 31-35).

As the armies maneuvered, a violent storm pelted the troops. One of the Hessian officers involved in the fighting against Wayne's force reported: "I believe that it was about five o'clock in the afternoon, an extraordinary thunderstorm occurred, combined with the heaviest downpour in this world." Another Hessian wrote, "I wish I could give a description of the downpour which began during the engagement and continued until the next morning. It came down so hard that in a few moments we were drenched and sank in mud up to our calves" (McGuire 35). The storm gave the skirmish the name "the Battle of the Clouds." Other than American backwoodsmen in General Daniel Morgan's force who covered their rifles with bearskins and Hessian hunters known as Jagers who also knew how to protect their firearms, most of the men in both armies found that the rain had ruined their muskets and rifles. The Hessians drew their hunting swords and expected the Americans to use their bayonets. With powder soaked, visibility cloaked, and roads choked with mud, however, the British army commanders decided to hunker down. The British had been traveling light, without tents, so they sought shelter in farm sheds or built huts with fence rails, tree limbs and brush. Washington's troops, meanwhile, withdrew six miles away from the British because the rain had ruined their ammunition. Normally small creeks were so swollen that the men had to swim across. Moving artillery carriages up muddy hills required repeated changes of horse teams. Dripping-wet men shivered in the cold night.

Washington's aide Colonel John Laurens later informed his father Henry Laurens – a lifelong friend and business partner of Lachlan McIntosh – that the heavy rain "half drown'd us on our march to Yellow Springs, (and which by the bye spoilt me a waist-coat and breeches of white Cloth and my uniform Coat, clouding them with the dye wash'd out of my hat)" (McGuire 37). A Pennsylvania historian writes:

> Night fell amid relentless sheets of rain as the Continental Army inched forward, slogging over steep hills and raging streams through a quagmire of Chester County mud. For over eight exhausting hours they marched, the soldiers pushing and pulling the horses and wagons, the artillery pieces, and each other, on bottomless roads to the Yellow Springs, a place known for rest and healthful waters. (McGuire 37)

The storm continued to rage until the afternoon of September 17. The Schuylkill River rose eight feet, and when riders tried to ford creeks the water lapped against their horses' bellies. Leaving a division under General Nathanael Greene at Yellow Springs to cover the main army, Washington moved out toward a supply of fresh powder to replace what the rain had ruined. The wagons and artillery lurched through the flooded countryside, and the men walked single file on logs laid across creeks. Although the lack of powder left the American army defenseless, pursuit by the British was frustrated by boggy ground and ravaged roads.

Lachlan McIntosh joins Washington's army

Lachlan McIntosh and his son Lackie traveled together from Georgia through South Carolina and North Carolina. In Virginia, Lachlan left Lackie to be inoculated against smallpox (Hawes, *University* 21). Lachlan McIntosh reached George Washington's army in the north, according to Pennsylvania historians, shortly after Washington's retreat from Brandywine (Williams 4; Lamdin 396).

The Battle of Freeman's Farm: September 19, 1777

Further north, Burgoyne's invasion force encountered American forces led by Daniel Morgan, Benjamin Lincoln and Benedict Arnold – under the overall command of General Horatio Gates. On the crisp morning of September 19, Morgan ventured forth from American fortifications near Saratoga. Military historians Dupuy and Dupuy describe the ensuing battle:

> The impetuous Morgan and his equally impetuous riflemen plunged into the woods, badly extended, seeking their enemy. Just south of Freeman's Farm they ran into a left flank packet of Fraser's – Canadians, Indian and Tory irregulars – most of whom were at once shot down. The riflemen, whooping in pursuit of the survivors, ran smack into the right regiment of Hamilton's brigade, drawn up in the clearing. Its volley fire broke up the riflemen, who scattered in all directions, leaving Morgan alone, twirping on his turkey call to rally them. While Morgan slowly regathered his shame-faced brush-war fighters, Arnold, closely watching, pushed in Cilley's 1st and Scammell's 3rd New Hampshire on his left. They fell afoul of Fraser's light infantry and grenadiers, were roughly handled and in turn thrown back.
>
> ...Alternate waves of assault washed the fifteen-acre clearing of Freeman's Farm for the rest of the day, with Burgoyne's silent guns – the gun crews successively picked off by sharpshooters – the focal point. Several times the accurate fire of the riflemen, many of them in the tree-tops, drove the British infantry into the surrounding woods, but each time the American infantry rushed the guns the British came back with bayonet and drove them off...
>
> ...Arnold, with his entire division now engaged, went whirling back to Gates, impetuously demanding reinforcements. He was sure he could break the British line with additional men. Gates, snug in his headquarters hut, refused; it would not, he said, be prudent to "weaken his line." Sharp words passed between the pair... Gates... perempto-

rily prohibited Arnold from returning to the field... (248-50)

Hessian infantry and artillery drove back the Americans, who withdrew from the battlefield at dusk. Burgoyne lost six hundred men killed, wounded or captured, while the Americans lost sixty-five killed, 218 wounded and thirty-three missing.

The British occupy Philadelphia
In Pennsylvania, British and American armies maneuvered around the countryside for three weeks without finding an opportunity for a decisive battle. British forces under Cornwallis occupied Philadelphia on September 26.

Rangers raid Georgia
In Georgia, Continental troops halted a raid by fifty East Florida Rangers in late September. The Continentals found the Rangers on the north side of the Altamaha and killed one or two of the Rangers. The Continentals captured some of the Rangers' horses and saddles and recovered some cattle (Searcy 113).

Indian affairs involve agent William McIntosh
During the summer and fall of 1777, Americans tried to persuade the Creek Indians on the southern frontier to turn against the British. When a group of Creek warriors visited Charleston, the South Carolina council demanded that they kill British agents John Tait and William McIntosh, the nephew of Rory McIntosh.

On August 13 Colonel Samuel Elbert, the commander of Continental troops in Georgia after Lachlan McIntosh left the state, told Creek leader Handsome Fellow that Georgia would not make peace with the Creeks unless they assassinated agents Tait, McIntosh and Alexander Cameron. Regardless of whether Handsome Fellow agreed to the conditions he could not implement them because he died on the way back to the Creek town of Okfuskee.

When Handsome Fellow's companions returned to Okfuskee, William McIntosh was making plans to attack the Georgia frontier with a force of Creeks, Cherokees and white loyalist refugees. In the Upper Towns of the Creek nation, Cameron also assembled a force of Cherokees and white loyalists. British strategy called for the forces under William McIntosh and Cameron to create a diversion along the frontier while British forces in St. Augustine moved up the coast to conquer Georgia.

The faction of Creeks who had been turned against the British planned to kill William McIntosh and all the other British agents, and confiscate their supplies and trading goods. Creek leader Alexander McGillivray protected his friend Cameron and his relative by marriage Tait, who was the husband of one of McGillivray's sisters.

McGillivray's mother was the daughter of a French man and a woman from the powerful Wind Clan. McGillivray's father was a Scot who had emigrated to Darien with other Highlanders before becoming an Indian trader among the Creeks, much like William McIntosh's father. McGillivray also had ties to the patriot faction: his father had sent him to Charleston for an education, and he had worked in a counting house in Savannah operated by Samuel Elbert, who would become the commander of Continental forces in Georgia. McGillivray turned against the patriots when they seized the property of his loyalist father who, as a result, returned to Scotland (Searcy 224).

Warriors from factions of the Creek nation who remained friendly toward the British guarded William McIntosh. The faction that had turned against the British succeeded, however, in confiscating goods from the British traders. All of the British agents and traders fled from Creek territory to refuge at Pensacola (Searcy 114-16).

Allan Macdonald exchanged

The legendary Flory McDonald's husband Allan arrived at British headquarters in New York in September. He had been captured at the Battle of Moore's Creek early in 1776 and Congress allowed him to go to New York to arrange his exchange for an American prisoner of equal rank. After he successfully negotiated his exchange, he sent for Flory to join him in New York (Vining 179-80).

Attack at Billingsport: October 2, 1777

In order to hold Philadelphia, the British had to bring supplies up the Delaware River. Washington tried to thwart the British by placing obstacles in the river and establishing defensive posts along the banks. On October 2, the British 42nd Regiment and part of the 71st Regiment attacked a redoubt at Billingsport. The garrison of the redoubt fled (Ward 373).

Battle of Germantown, October 4, 1777

While the British held Philadelphia, the main British army encamped five miles away at Germantown. Washington launched a surprise attack against the encampment on the morning of October 4. A biographer describes the battle from General Nathanael Greene's viewpoint:

> [Washington] sent Greene in command of the left and Sullivan the right in two flanking columns. Each had the job of rolling up the British from his side. Washington... rode with Sullivan...
>
> Greene had two miles farther than the others to march, and, because of heavy fog that settled over the area, his guide lost the way. Thus Sullivan engaged the enemy three quarters of an hour before Greene's left wing could come into action. This delay threw the burden of the initial engagement on Sullivan's division and Wayne's brigade. By the time Greene reached the scene the battlefield was in great confusion. Shortly afterward, in the fog and smoke, Wayne's men became entangled with the brigade of General Adam Stephen, sent forward by Greene to their aid. Sullivan's and Wayne's men, their ammunition nearly gone, thought they were surrounded, broke, and ran.
>
> Meanwhile, the British had rallied their forces around the strongly built Chew House in the center of Germantown. Artillery failed to knock out the building, and the battle for some time swirled around this temporary fort.
>
> With Sullivan's and Wayne's lines broken and retreating in panic, and Muhlenberg's eager Virginians so far ahead of the line that most of them were taken prisoner by the British in Howe's overrun camp, Greene suddenly found himself the pivot on which the safety of the entire army depended. The British had taken refuge inside stone dwellings, encircled by high garden walls, which made excellent breastworks. Even Knox's cannon were of little use. Smoke from gunpowder and burning hay, mixed with thick

fog, limited the visibility to forty yards. Distinguishing friend from foe was difficult.

Greene found himself between two fires as Howe wheeled his line and Cornwallis came up with fresh troops from Philadelphia. Washington, Sullivan, Wayne and their officers rallied the panicked troops, restoring some semblance of order, while Greene threw his men in front of the again advancing British.

Greene's officers watched anxiously as he recklessly exposed himself amid the thick hail of musket balls. But he knew where men looked for encouragement in danger... Greene in his blue uniform with buff facings seemed to be everywhere, utterly disregarding the danger.

There came a renewal of enemy musket fire. Seemingly it intensified as Cornwallis with his fresh troops tried to end the struggle quickly...

...a musket ball... snipped off one of the curls on Greene's powdered white wig. The general smiled broadly...

The American cannon were making even more smoke than the British guns as Knox's cannoneers had time to load and fire their fieldpieces behind the American lines holding firm with musketry fire. Every effort Cornwallis make to break the solid defense line Greene had formed split on the stubborn resistance of the Rhode Islander's inspired men. They fought like demons with ever greater confidence. Their line had held under Greene at Brandywine against the cream of the British and Hessian armies. Surely they could hold it again – and they did. Even the precious American cannon were saved, including a dismounted gun that Greene ordered onto a farm wagon, to be trundled to the rear.

For five miles the men slowly retreated under the heaviest fire the British could concentrate on Greene's exhausted division, while the main army fell back. Then came a lull in the fighting. Cornwallis, realizing that he could not break Greene's retreating line, had called a halt. His men had taken a terrible beating from Knox's cannon and the deliberate marksmanship of Greene's men.

...There still was a weary march of fifteen miles back to the American bivouac... Although they had been beaten, ...they had demonstrated real courage. [The battle had shown] that disciplined American troops, properly and bravely led, could stand up against the best the British Army could send against them. (Bailey 58-62)

Lachlan McIntosh, according to a local historian, "participated in the Battle of Germantown where, General Nash being mortally wounded, McIntosh succeeded to the command" of the brigade Nash had led (Williams 4).

Burgoyne surrenders at Saratoga: October 17, 1777

At Saratoga, the balance of power between British General John Burgoyne's invasion force from Canada and Continental Northern Department commander General Horatio Gates tilted in favor of the Americans. Burgoyne's force had dwindled to fewer than six thousand men and they were running out of rations. As American reinforcements and new recruits flowed northward, Gates mustered about eleven thousand men who had plenty of food and ammunition. The Americans occupied a strong defensive position at Blemis Heights. The chief difficulty in the American camp was an ongoing feud between Gates and Benedict Arnold, whom Gates had ordered off the battlefield at Freeman's Farm the previous month. On October 7, Burgoyne conducted a reconnaissance in force to seek a weakness in the American fortifications. Gates sent three brigades – including Daniel Morgan's men – to meet the British advance. Dupuy and Dupuy describe the action:

> ...And then a little man on a big bay horse raced toward the field: Benedict Arnold bound into battle. Gates had seen him gallop out of camp, had sent an aide to halt him, but the aide never caught up.
>
> Arnold, assuming command of the attack, led Learned's men across Mill Creek and up to Riedesel's line, only to be repulsed. A second effort forced the Germans back, as Morgan's men on their right and Poor on their left came swarming in to threaten their flanks. The stubborn Brunswickers withdrew towards the earthworks, among Balcarres' men.

There [Brigadier General Simon] Fraser, leading the thin files of his own 24th Foot, tried to turn the tide, or at least slow down the retreat. Conspicuous on a gray charger, Fraser drew the fire of one of Morgan's men, urged by Arnold to pick him off. Three times the rifleman – one Tim Murphy – drew bead, and the third shot found the mark. Fraser, mortally wounded, was carried back to the British entrenchments with the tide, and the first phase of the engagement was over, 50 minutes from the time it started.

But Arnold was not through. By this time the remainder of Gates' army, in an apparently spontaneous advance, was in the field and moving to join the attack... Behind their entrenchments, the British regulars stiffened... With Morgan, on the extreme left flank, and regiments of both Poor's and Learned's brigade closing in, the redoubt was surrounded. Arnold, impetuous, put spurs to his mount, led cheering Continentals through the sallyport. A jager's bullet knocked him from his horse with a fractured thigh... But his men weren't stopped. They swarmed over the redoubt...

This second battle of Saratoga – often called Bemis Heights or Stillwater – had cost Burgoyne another 600 men in killed, wounded and captured, against an American loss of 150. All the ten guns accompanying the British gamble were lost.

Like a wounded snake, Burgoyne's army coiled up at Saratoga...

...an agreement was signed and Burgoyne's army laid down their arms on the 17th, wiping one quarter of King George's forces in America off the slate.

...The surrender of an entire army of disciplined, regular soldiers to the makeshift Americans astounded Europe. Seven general officers were included in the bag of more than 5,700 prisoners. Twenty-seven guns, five thousand stand of small arms and quite a quantity of other materiel had been garnered.

Strategically, the results were most important. All British posts to the north were withdrawn into Canada. The King's men held only the New York City area, Rhode Island, and Philadelphia.

Psychologically, the effect was enormous. In America, confidence in the patriot cause – shaken by the results of the Brandywine and Germantown – soared again. Abroad, France's Louis XVI recognized the United States, and moved inevitably towards war with England. (259-62)

Armies encamp for winter

In Pennsylvania, the British and American armies encamped for the winter. British commander Sir William Howe withdrew from Germantown into Philadelphia on October 18 and constructed strong fortifications around the city.

To hold the British in check, Continental commander George Washington chose a defensible location twenty miles from Philadelphia and encamped for the winter at Valley Forge.

Henry Laurens runs government

The town of York, Pennsylvania, served as the temporary seat of the United States government while the British occupied Philadelphia. With members of Congress scattered before the British onslaught, the responsibilities of the Congress fell on its President, Henry Laurens. George C. Rogers, Jr., notes, "Laurens with no more support than a few clerks ran the whole apparatus of national government, often staying up until midnight to accomplish his job" (274).

Allan McDonald waits in New York

Allan McDonald – husband of the legendary Flory McDonald – received good news in October. Allan, who had been captured at the Battle of Moore's Creek Bridge, had gone to New York to negotiate his exchange for a prisoner of equal rank. While in New York, he contacted his cousin Captain Alexander MacDonald in Nova Scotia.

His cousin wrote that he was extremely happy to hear and Allan and Allan's son Alexander were safe in New York. Captain MacDonald reported that Allan's sons Ranald and Charles were in Nova Scotia and were "very happy at the Thoughts of seeing you soon." Captain MacDonald urged Allan to leave New York before winter descended and take a position with the British forces in Nova Scotia. Allan, however, waited in New York for Flory to join him. In the meantime, he raised a company described as "Gentle-

men Volunteers, all scotsh Refugees from Carolina & Virginia;
with them (all dressed in Scarlet & blew)" (Vining 179-80; Toffey
134).

Women suffer in war zone

Flory McDonald and her daughters, like other women in
America at the time, suffered the consequences of living in a war
zone:

> Mistreatment and indignity, the more frightening because
> the threat of rape was always present, were possible wher-
> ever armies roamed. Examples are easy to find, but difficult
> to quantify; they form a substantial segment of the memoir
> material compiled by both sides. The murder of Mrs.
> Caldwell in Connecticutt Farms, New Jersey, by a British
> sharpshooter in 1780 took on the proportions of a patriotic
> myth; likewise, the loyalists made a legend of Flora Mac-
> Donald's daughters, whose rebel captors in the fall of 1777
> put "their swords into their bosoms, split down their silk
> dresses and, taking them out into the yard, stripped them of
> all their outer clothing." The loyalist Ann Hulton reported
> that "at Roxbury Mr. Ed. Brinleys wife whilst lying in, had
> a guard of Rebels always in her room, who treated her with
> rudeness & indecency, exposing her to the view of their
> banditti, as a sight 'See a tory woman' and stripd her & her
> Children of all their Linnen & Cloths." The king's troops
> were even more cruel to Hannah Adams, the wife of Dea-
> con Joseph Adams of Cambridge, Massachusetts: on their
> retreat from Concord, three soldiers broke into her room
> where she was lying in bed, "scarcely able to walk … to the
> fire, not having been to [her] chamber door … [since] being
> delivered in child-birth." They forced her outside with bay-
> onets and set the house on fire while her five children were
> still inside.
>
> Women were made refugees by the war. The war was
> so disruptive to family life that one begins to wonder
> whether the cult of domesticity – the ideological celebra-
> tion of women's domestic roles – was not in large measure
> a response to the wartime disruption and threat of separa-
> tion of families. (Kerber 46-47)

Flory's husband Allan received a letter from his cousin Captain Alexander MacDonald asking, "Pray for God's sake is it possible to Gett Mrs. McDonald & the other poor women from N. Carolina?" (Vining 180)

Pro-British Creeks raid Georgia

With the Creek nation on the verge of civil war, Chief Alexander McGillivray convened the headmen to devise a unified strategy for dealing with the British and American governments striving for their allegiance. The Americans lost favor when they were unable to provide trade goods. The British, meanwhile, had cut off trade with the Creeks out of concern for the traders' safety. Hoping to restore trade with the British, the Creeks sent delegations to Pensacola during the fall and winter of 1777. A few pro-British war parties raided Georgia in the fall, and on November 19 Georgia Continentals killed five Creek warriors and wounded seven who were then taken prisoner (Searcy 114-16).

Plantation plundered

In December troops stationed at Darien plundered the plantation of Colonel William McIntosh, the former commander of the Light Horse who had resigned due to ill health. Throughout the war, plantations around Darien had been plundered by invading armies passing back and forth between Georgia and Florida. The plundering of an American officer's property by American troops during a period of relative stability enraged the Continental commander in Georgia. Samuel Elbert declared, "Those unhappy men whose conduct has held them up as enemies to the state will be dealt with…" (qtd. in Searcy 121).

Lachlan McIntosh endures winter at Valley Forge

Lachlan McIntosh reported for duty at George Washington's winter encampment at Valley Forge on December 17. Washington quickly gave McIntosh an assignment, as he mentioned in a letter to General Robert Howe: "I had the pleasure of receiving your favours of the 2d. and 3d. November by Genl. McIntosh who arrived very opportunely to take command of the North Carolina Brigade, which had wanted a Brigadier very much since the Fall of Genl.

Nash" (Fitzpatrick 10: 300-01). The official assignment was reported in the General Orders for December 20:

> Genl. McIntosh is appointed to the command of the North Carolina brigade.
>
> The Major Generals accompanied by the Engineers are to view the ground attentively, and fix upon the proper spot and mode for hutting so as to render the camp as strong and inaccessible as possible. The Engineers after this are to mark the ground out, and direct the field Officers appointed to superintend the buildings for each brigade where they are placed.
>
> The soldiers in cutting their firewood, are to save such parts of each tree, as will do for building, reserving sixteen or eighteen feet of the trunk, for logs to rear their huts with. In doing this each regiment is to reap the benefit of their own labour.
>
> All those, who in consequence of the orders of the 18th instant, have turned their thoughts to an easy and expeditious method of covering the huts, are requested to communicate their plans to Major Generals Sullivan, Greene, or Lord Stirling, who will cause experiments to be made, and assign the profer'd reward to the best projector.
>
> The Quarter Master General is to delay no time, but use his utmost exertions, to procure large quantities of straw, either for covering the huts, if it should be found necessary, or for beds for the soldiers. He is to assure the farmers that unless they get their grain out immediately, the straw will be taken with the grain in it, and paid for as straw only.
>
> The Quarter Master General is to collect, as soon as possible, all the tents not now used by the troops, and as soon as they are hutted, all the residue of the tents, and have them washed and well dried, and then laid up in store, such as are good for the next campaign, the others for the uses which shall be directed; the whole are to be carefully preserved. The Colonels and Officers commanding regiments are forthwith to make return to the Qr. Mr. General, of every tent belonging to their corps.

The army being now come to a fixed station, the Brigadiers and officers commanding brigades, are immediately
to take effectual measures, to collect, and bring to camp, all
the officers and soldiers at present scattered about the country.

All officers are enjoined to see that their men do not
wantonly, or needlessly burn and destroy rails, and never
fire their sheds or huts when they leave them. (Fitzpatrick
10: 180-81)

Biographer Harvey Jackson describes Lachlan McIntosh's ordeal during the notorious winter at Valley Forge:

What happened in Valley Forge that winter has become so
deeply embedded in the saga of this nation's birth that there
is a tendency, in this cynical age, to treat the accounts of
suffering, privation, and courage as romantic tales, embel-
lished with each new telling. But Valley Forge was real –
as the men whom McIntosh found cramped in unfinished
huts or huddled for warmth in tattered tents knew all too
well. Fully a third of the approximately 10,000 soldiers in
Washington's army were incapacitated for want of clothing, shoes, and blankets. The men were tired, discouraged,
and restless. If the army was to exist when spring came, it
would take a monumental effort, and its leaders knew it.

On December 20 Washington placed McIntosh in
charge of the North Carolina brigade, the sickliest and
worst-clothed unit in an army that was characterized by illness and exposure. Troop returns showed that of the 2,700
men who manned the brigade at full strength, only 928
were in camp. Of those, 327 were sick and 164 were "unfit
for duty for want of cl[othin]g." So short of manpower was
McIntosh's new command that he was forced to enlist the
"walking sick" to erect shelters, but it seemed to do little
good. As the snows deepened, casualty lists lengthened,
though not a shot was fired by the enemy. (71-72)

Lachlan McIntosh and George Washington had corresponded
on military matters throughout the war. While serving at Valley
Forge together they developed a sense of camaraderie. Not only

were they both Continental generals, but in civilian life both of them were planters and both of them had worked as surveyors. They also had a common friend in high places: Henry Laurens, President of the Continental Congress, not only had been a business partner with McIntosh for decades but also became Washington's most powerful supporter in Congress; his son John Laurens served as one of Washington's aides at Valley Forge. Washington consistently supported McIntosh and always spoke highly of him. Washington described McIntosh as "an officer of great worth and merit" and praised his "firm disposition and equal justice; his assiduity and good understanding" (qtd. in Jackson 74). Their friendship lasted throughout the rest of their lives.

1778

Lackie McIntosh serves as an aide to Baron von Steuben, the officer who molds George Washington's army into an efficient military force at Valley Forge. Lachlan McIntosh takes command of the Western Department, based at Fort Pitt, and mounts an expedition into the frontier. Colonel John McIntosh of the Continental Army defends Fort Morris at Sunbury, Georgia, and – according to legend – his relative and former neighbor Roderick "Rory" McIntosh accompanies the British troops laying siege to the fort. Aeneas Mackintosh sails southward as part of a new British strategy and participates in the British capture of Savannah.

Rebirth at Valley Forge

The Continental army commanded by George Washington suffered tremendously during the harsh winter of 1777-1778 at Valley Forge, Pennsylvania, but emerged as a more formidable military force than ever. Biographer Harvey Jackson describes the condition of the North Carolina brigade under Lachlan McIntosh's command:

> During January and February 1778, the North Carolina brigade averaged 88 sick in camp, 219 sick in hospitals, and 199 unfit for lack of clothes; not once during that season did the unit record over 564 able-bodied men available for duty. Any decline in the number of sick was usually accompanied by the grim notion that death, not recovery, had ended their suffering. In view of the "skeleton" medical corp (at one point only a doctor and his assistant), it is remarkable that the record was not worse, but it was bad enough. As his men crouched around their fires and hoped for warmer days, McIntosh exhausted every means of bettering their situation.
>
> In the end, his efforts produced scant results. North Carolina Governor Richard Caswell tried to help, but the scarcity of money, the cost of supplies, and the distance between Valley Forge and the brigade's home state all but negated his attempts... Surprisingly, the army's desertion

rate had been lowest among the North Carolina troops. Distance from home and lack of proper clothing for the trip were surely primary factors, but one must give credit to the officers who supported their men through the ordeal. (72-73)

In late January an artilleryman stole Lachlan McIntosh's horse. A court martial ordered half of the artilleryman's pay forfeited each month until McIntosh was reimbursed for the value of the horse (Fitzpatrick 10: 404).

Lackie McIntosh serves with Steuben

Continental Commander in Chief George Washington used the wintertime break in fighting to mold a motley assembly of men into an organized army. His efforts were enhanced by Friedrich von Steuben, an experienced European military officer who called himself Baron de Steuben and would become known as the Drillmaster of Valley Forge. Steuben arrived at Valley Forge on February 24 accompanied by his secretary – 17-year-old Pierre Duponceau, who served as a translator because Steuben did not speak English – two aides, a German servant, and a greyhound.

Lackie Lachlan McIntosh Jr. – the general's 20-year-old son who was called Lackie – was assigned as an aide to Major-General Steuben (Sullivan 34; Hawes, *University* 6). A coincidence of timing may have had something to do with Lackie's assignment. After a stopover in Virginia to be inoculated against smallpox, Lackie had arrived at Valley Forge on February 13, just eleven days before Steuben arrived (Hawes, *University* 21). The long-standing relationship between the McIntosh family and the Laurens family may have been a factor in Lackie's assignment. Steuben had met Henry Laurens – the President of the Continental Congress and a longtime business partner with Lachlan McIntosh – at York, Pennsylvania, where the Congress resided while the army was at Valley Forge. Steuben biographer Paul Lockhart describes the result of that meeting:

> As Steuben was preparing to leave York, Henry Laurens had suggested that he seek out his son, Lt. Col. John Laurens. Twenty-three-year-old Colonel Laurens, an aide on Washington's staff, had much in common with the older

Baron: he was an avid student of the art of war; he embraced the progressive political and social thought of the Enlightenment; and he spoke the Baron's language, and not just in terms of ideals...

The president had judged right. John Laurens fell in love with the Baron on sight. So, too, did Laurens's best friend and fellow aide, Lt. Col. Alexander Hamilton. And the Prussian was equally smitten with them. Here were two impressionable young men who understood his speech and who hung on his every word as he regaled them with tales of bloody battles decided by massive cavalry charges and the point of the bayonet, of warrior-kings and glittering courts. He could converse with them on topics ranging from infantry tactics to the works of Seneca, Cervantes, and Voltaire. He represented a touch of Enlightenment sophistication – something for which the young Laurens and Hamilton were starved... (76-77)

Conditions at Valley Forge were somewhat better for officers – presumably including Lachlan and Lackie McIntosh – than for common soldiers. While the enlisted men barely survived in huts and tents, General Washington lived in a stone farmhouse in one corner of the encampment. Many of the officers' wives joined them for the winter respite in fighting and brought touches of refinement. Steuben's biographer describes the situation:

...Steuben was not content with merely being accepted by his new comrades. He had to immerse himself in the social scene at camp, too, which was surprising vibrant. Officers of all grades made the best of their unpleasant circumstances, hosting dinner parties and "carousals" in the evenings, and the presence of so many generals' wives in the camp lent the whole an air of almost surreal gaiety amid the army's sufferings.

The Baron fit right in. Like most of the European-born officers, he became a regular guest at the table of Caty Greene, the vivacious spouse of Maj. Gen. Nathanael Greene. Mrs. Greene, an incurable flirt who was fluent in French, took an immediate shine to Steuben. So, too, did

Martha Washington and Kitty Alexander, the daughter of Maj. Gen. William Alexander, Lord Stirling…

At the request of his aides [presumably including Lackie McIntosh], the Baron hosted a party exclusively for their lower-ranking friends. .. and never was there "such a set of ragged, and at the same time merry fellows" at Valley Forge. Duponceau led the group in singing a few raucous American songs he had learned, while the captains and lieutenants – including Lord Stirling's aide-de-camp, the future President James Monroe – indulged in the feast put together by Carl Vogel: "tough beefsteak and potatoes, with hickory nuts for our dessert." Over this rough fare, and several rounds of a flaming high-proof concoction dubbed "Salamanders," the Baron quickly earned a reputation as a bacchanalian lord of mirth. It was not the kind of behavior that the Continentals expected out of a Prussian nobleman, and they liked it. Only a couple of weeks into his stay, Steuben had already made himself a legend. (Lockhart 84-85)

Using the techniques he had learned in Europe, Steuben drilled the American army in military procedures. Historians George F. Scheer and Hugh F. Rankin describe the army's progress:

In spite of cold and hunger, sickness and death, it was at Valley Forge that new spirit entered the army. There the army mastered for the first time the manual of the musket, and charged an imaginary enemy by platoons, firing and advancing and rushing with bayonets; no longer was that weapon merely a tool for cooking or an encumbrance to throw away…

The army learned to march in column and to deploy from column into line. At last, it marched in compact masses. The columns of files gave way to marching in double rank and in columns of four. No longer would it string out so long on the roads that discipline broke, scores straggled, and precious minutes were lost forming to the front to meet the enemy; each battalion learned to occupy on the road no more space than it would in line of battle. (308-09)

An aide to Steuben described the drillmaster's vigilant and animated watch over the soldiers:

> When some movement or maneuver was not performed to his mind he began to swear in German, then in French, and then in both languages together. When he had exhausted his artillery of foreign oaths, he would call to his aides, "My dear Walker and my dear Duponceau, come and swear for me in English. These fellows won't do what I bid them." A good-natured smile then went through the ranks and at last the maneuver or the movement was properly performed. (qtd. in Scheer and Rankin 308)

Nathanael Greene named Quartermaster

Washington rebuilt his army not only by instituting rigorous drilling under Steuben but also by reorganizing the Quartermaster and Commissary departments, which shared much of the blame for the men's lack of food, clothing, blankets, shelter, supplies and pay. Washington asked his friend General Nathanael Greene to serve as Quartermaster General. Greene, who had distinguished himself in combat, agreed to accept the post although he complained "Who ever read of a quartermaster in history" (qtd. in Scheer and Rankin 311). Spring brought not only better weather to Valley Forge but also adequate provisions to the men stationed there.

Lachlan McIntosh guards cattle drive

Like Greene, General Lachlan McIntosh was willing to accept assignments lacking prospects of glory. A biographer describes McIntosh's duties with the North Carolina brigade:

> As spring came, the unit, still undermanned, was given the responsibility of collecting intelligence on enemy movements... The enemy, it turned out, was not moving, and so the assignment mainly involved protecting a herd of cattle that was brought in as provisions for the army. The animals were important, especially to men on short rations, but it was not the type of duty from which military careers are

made. Still, McIntosh gave it his full attention and delivered the beef as ordered. (Jackson 73)

In addition to the account by McIntosh's biographer Harvey Jackson, another historian describes the cattle herding assignment at Valley Forge:

> Washington tried with mixed success to coordinate the efforts of regular army and militia forces east of the Schuylkill... Washington sent small army detachments across the river on missions of assigned duration with limited objectives...
>
> This new policy of increased but restricted Continental involvement east of the Schuylkill was underlined by the choice of Lachlan McIntosh to lead one of the detachments into the area. This marked the first time since the army came to Valley Forge that a general officer was sent across that river. McIntosh was not, however, given broad responsibility for military operations in the area. Instead, he was directed to meet a large drove of cattle coming through the district and to fend off a British detachment reportedly on its way to intercept it... McIntosh found the cattle, after probing a neighborhood whose people were, he concluded, both aware of and inimically disposed toward his presence there. (Bodle 214)

Washington's orders to McIntosh took into account that McIntosh was not familiar with the Pennsylvania countryside:

> Head Quarters, Valley Forge, March 21, 1778.
> Sir: Having received information that a considerable number of the Enemy, both Horse and Foot, have advanced as far as Hickory Town upon the Wissahicken Road, you are immediately to cross the Schuylkill with the detachment of your command and endeavor to discover the Number, situation and intention of the Enemy.
> I have received information that a large drove of 500 Cattle are upon their way from Sherrard's Ferry upon Delaware and it is more than probable that the intention of the Enemy may be to carry them off. Colo. Nagle who will be

with you, knows the Country well and will provide a number of good officers likewise well acquainted with it. It will be proper to send an officer to meet the Cattle and to order them to be kept pretty high up and by observing the Route of the Enemy it will be easy to keep between them and the Cattle. If you should find their numbers and situation such that you can attack them to advantage, I expect that you will do it, but that I will leave to your judgement (and the Intelligency you shall rce.)

As this is the time of one of the Quakers general Meetings, it is more than probable that many of that Society will be going into Philadelphia. If you fall in with any of them, I desire they may be stopped and turned back and their Horses taken from them. Be pleased to inform me of your proceedings. I wish you success and am, etc.

P.S. There is a Gentleman on the other side of the River, Colo. Curry, perfectly acquainted with every Road. Send to him and he will attend you instantly, and will be very useful to you. (Fitzpatrick 11: 120-21)

Head Quarters, March 24, 1778.

Sir: I have received your letter of Yesterday by Major Duvall. As the principal object of your detachment is the protection of the Cattle said to have been expected to cross at Sherard's Ferry, all your movements and operations are to be directed to that end, and you will take the best means to answer it effectually.

The intelligence which you may receive concerning the motions and number of the Enemy's parties, from intelligent persons that may be depended on, will enable you best to judge of their real designs, and to counteract them, if their views are turned to intercepting the supply which you are to cover.

Mr. Chaloner D.C. of Purchases has sent expresses to inquire the Route of the Cattle and direct them by the upper Road from Sherard's ferry to Potts Grove, it will facilitate your business, perhaps to send an express and discover where they really are at present. I am etc. (Fitzpatrick 11: 135-36)

Although not a glorious military achievement, cattle herding was part of McIntosh's heritage. As a native of the Scottish Highlands, he came from a culture where cattle herding and cattle raids were the stuff of legend. After his family emigrated to Georgia, a fellow Highlander drove a herd of black cattle from South Carolina to Darien, and selling beef became a mainstay of Darien's economy. Even during the American Revolution, much of the border war between Georgia and Florida involved stealing cattle or protecting cattle from raiders

Flory McDonald joins husband

Flory McDonald – legendary for having rescued Bonnie Prince Charlie – remained in North Carolina after her husband was taken prisoner at the Battle of Moore's Creek Bridge early in the war. When Flory refused to take an oath of allegiance required by the North Carolina Congress, her family's plantation was confiscated. Some people say the McDonald house was burned. Referring to herself in third person, Flory wrote:

> She remained in this deplorable condition for two years, among Robers, and faithless servants, Untill her husband and son in law, major Alexr. McLeod obtained a flag of truce from Sir Henry Clinton and Admirall How, which brought me, my daughter, and her Children, from wilmingtown in N. Carolina to New York. (qtd. in Toffey 126)

On the voyage from North Carolina in March of 1778, she and her daughter Anne were "in danger of our lives by a constant storme" (Jolley 134).

In April she reunited with her husband Allan and their son Alexander in New York, the British stronghold in America. Their daughter Anne was also in New York at the time with her husband Alexander MacLeod and four children (Vining 181).

Lachlan McIntosh inspects hospitals

At Valley Forge, Lachlan McIntosh faithfully carried out General George Washington's orders. After conducting an operation that amounted to cattle herding, McIntosh was given another assignment lacking in glamor. McIntosh's biographer explains:

In April, Washington removed the Georgian from his brigade command and ordered him to inspect all Continental hospitals in New Jersey and Pennsylvania... Washington had long been dissatisfied with the medical corps and McIntosh was chosen as the "discreet Field Officer" who was capable of carrying out what was, in reality, a housecleaning. Although the new assignment lacked the glamor of a field command, the discretionary instructions gave him the most personal authority he had enjoyed since he left Georgia. Setting out as soon as he received his orders, the general spent almost two months traveling from hospital to hospital. Few significant changes resulted from his visits... Yet his conduct impressed General Washington... (Jackson 73)

Washington's army gathers strength

As the winter lull in fighting came to an end, Washington concentrated on recruitment efforts to bring his army to fighting strength. Washington approved Lachlan McIntosh's suggestion to consolidate the North Carolina brigade from nine regiments into three battalions, resulting in a surplus of former regimental officers who could be sent on recruitment missions. The army at Valley Forge grew from about four thousand fit for duty in February to more than eleven thousand fit for duty in early May.

Washington ceremoniously displayed his army's newfound ability with a Grand Review on May 6. The ceremony began with a worship service, proceeded to salvos from thirteen cannon, and climaxed with an intricate military salute involving choreographed musket fire. Washington's aide John Laurens wrote to his father Henry Laurens:

> The order with which the whole was conducted, the beautiful effect of the running fire which was executed to perfection, the martial appearance of the Troops, gave sensible pleasure to every one present... Triumph beamed in every countenance. (qtd. in Lockhart 116)

British rangers raid Georgia

In the South, the pattern of raiding into Georgia from British East Florida persisted in 1778. When the East Florida Rangers drove off a herd of cattle from the Georgia side of the Altamaha, the Liberty County militia was ordered to pursue the raiders. Although some of the Liberty County men refused to join the expedition, two of the raiders were captured and another raider deserted.

As spring approached, Thomas Brown led a hundred East Florida Rangers and ten Indians into Georgia. The Rangers and Indians swam a quarter of a mile across the dangerously cold Altamaha River and surprised the garrison at Fort Howe – formerly Fort Barrington – on March 13.

British casualties were one killed and four wounded, and American casualties were two killed, four wounded and twenty-three captured.

The fort's two pieces of artillery and two swivels fell into British hands. The Rangers could not spare enough men to garrison the fort so they burned it and abandoned it (Searcy 130-31).

The loss of Fort Howe left the Georgia border undefended except for a small force near the coast downriver from Darien. The Rangers plundered South Georgia at will. As historian Martha Condray Searcy puts it, "Their raids on Georgia cattle herds were peaceful roundups" (131).

Loyalists recruited in South Carolina

In addition to seizing provisions for the British, the East Florida Rangers sent intelligence-gathering missions into not only Georgia but also South Carolina. In April, Thomas Brown presented a detailed description of patriot fortifications in the two states and reported that six thousand Carolinians were loyalists willing to fight for the British. Several bands of loyalists traveled to East Florida and were organized into the South Carolina Royalists (Searcy 131-32).

William McIntosh meets with Creeks

Captain William McIntosh, a nephew of Rory McIntosh who served as a British agent among the Creek Indians, had withdrawn to Pensacola because Creeks allied with the Americans had threatened to kill the British agents. By the spring of 1778, the Creeks were so desperate for trade goods that they begged the British agents to return. McIntosh returned under the personal protection of Hycutt of Cussita. McIntosh met with the Lower Creek leaders at the Hitchitas in early April. They promised that warriors would go to St. Augustine in May to join a British invasion of Georgia (Searcy 133).

Americans plan invasion of Florida

Despite their earlier failures, American military leaders planned yet another invasion of East Florida. The plan called for coordination among Georgia state troops, the Georgia navy, Continental troops from the Georgia line, Continental troops from South Carolina's 1st Regiment, 3rd Regiment and 6th Regiment, South Carolina militia, and Continental troops from the Southern Department.

The expedition began when Georgia Continentals marched southward, spending April 12 at Lachlan McIntosh's much-misused plantation at Darien and arriving on April 14 at the ruins of Fort Howe, where they planned to rendezvous with the other bodies of troops (Coleman 107; Coulter 135-36; Searcy 134).

The next day General Samuel Elbert, the commander of the Georgia Continentals after Lachlan McIntosh's departure from Georgia, detached a party to attack three British ships anchored near St. Simons Island. The detachment boarded three galleys and a flatboat at Darien and proceeded by water to St. Simons. Most of the detachment disembarked and captured the British garrison at Fort Frederica, while the Georgians remaining on the galleys captured two of the British ships. Cargo on the captured ships included uniforms for South Carolina Continental troops; the uniforms previously had been captured by the British in naval action off Charleston (Searcy 135).

Continental troops from the Southern Department under General Robert Howe marching southward met minor opposition near Midway from the fierce loyalist Daniel McGirth. On May 9, General Howe reached the fort on the Altamaha named in his honor (Coulter 136; Searcy 136, 139).

John McIntosh promoted

While the Georgia Continentals were at Fort Howe, several changes were made in their command structure. John McIntosh – the 23-year-old son of Colonel William McIntosh and nephew of General Lachlan McIntosh – was promoted from major to lieutenant colonel and was transferred from the 1st Regiment to the 3rd Regiment (Searcy 139).

Lachlan McIntosh leads Western Department

As Commander in Chief, General George Washington was responsible not only for the army he commanded but also for the patriot effort across America. While Washington and General Lachlan McIntosh were stationed at Valley Forge in the spring of 1778, commissioners from Virginia and Pennsylvania met at Fort Pitt to make plans for defending the western frontier. They suggested an expedition against the British western headquarters at Fort Detroit. Congress approved the plan on May 2 and authorized the formation of two regiments for the expedition. Biographer Harvey Jackson explains the significance of the mission and the appointment of Lachlan McIntosh to lead it:

> Washington had been interested in the Ohio Valley (whose security was the object of the Detroit expedition) since his involvement in the Ohio Company prior to the French and Indian War. Plans to ensure that it remained free from foreign control were to occupy his thoughts throughout the Revolution. But the capture of Detroit promised to create as many problems as it solved. Both Virginia and Pennsylvania claimed the area and their conflicts (which predated the Revolution) had so hampered the efforts of General Edward Hand, commander of the Western Department, that he had asked to be relieved. Congress accepted his resignation; then on the same day it approved the Detroit expedition, it authorized Washington to appoint a replacement. The man he selected was Lachlan McIntosh.
>
> In recommending McIntosh, Washington stressed the Georgian's "firm disposition and equal justice; his assiduity and good understanding," which made him "an officer of great worth and merit," with whom his commander parted "with great reluctance." Washington also "imagined" that previous experiences had given McIntosh "knowledge of negociation in Indian affairs," which would be useful on the frontier. But these qualifications, though excellent in themselves, could have been duplicated in other commanders. Washington was looking for something more, and Lachlan McIntosh was judged able to provide it.

The expedition was filled with pitfalls, the major one being the participants themselves. Fort Pitt was to serve as headquarters, but three-quarters of the troops were to be drawn from Virginia. Thus, it was hoped, neither state could use the anticipated victory to reinforce its claims. But since almost all who were involved, with the exception of McIntosh, had some interest (usually personal) in who owned the land, there was little reason to believe that the balance struck by Congress would overcome the differences. The Georgian was about to step into a maze of state claims, land-company schemes, colonization enterprises, and speculators which confuses historians to this day. To do nothing more than prevent conflicts with the American forces promised to be a major undertaking.

Clearly, such a joint effort could succeed only if its commander kept peace between all parties and held himself above charges of favoritism. Washington believed, or at least hoped, that McIntosh could perform the task, and later informed Pennsylvania officials that it was primarily for his "disinterested concern" that the Georgian was selected. And so, for the second time in his career, Lachlan McIntosh was chosen to keep quarreling parties' energies directed against the British. His record in the previous attempt offered little encouragement for success.

McIntosh realized that it was the most prestigious assignment he had yet undertaken, but it is doubtful that he, or anyone else, anticipated how important it would be. The operations of the next year would go far toward deciding which nation would permanently occupy the territory beyond the Appalachian Mountains, and the part the Georgian played was essential to fulfillment of the American dream of being more than a nation of small states crowded between those mountains and the Atlantic Ocean. Territorial expansion was second, and remained second only to independence in the minds of American leaders, especially Washington. In a very real sense, their hopes rested on Lachlan McIntosh. (Jackson 74-75)

Washington informed the President of the Continental Congress of his choice of a Western Department commander in a letter dated May 12, 1778:

> ...After much consideration upon the subject, I have appointed Genl McIntosh to command at Fort Pitt and in the Western Country for which he will set out, as soon as he can accommodate his affairs. I part with this Gentleman with much reluctance, as I esteem him an Officer of great worth and merit, and as I know his services here are and will be materially wanted. His firm disposition and equal justice; his assiduity and good understanding, added to his being a stranger to all parties in that Quarter, pointed him out as a proper Person, and I trust extensive advantages will be derived from his command, which I could wish was more agreeable. He will wait on Congress for their instructions... (Fitzpatrick 11: 379)

On May 15, Washington transferred command of the North Carolina Brigade from McIntosh to Colonel Thomas Clark of the 1st North Carolina Regiment while McIntosh prepared for his new assignment (Fitzpatrick 11: 388-89). Washington officially gave command of the Western Department to McIntosh in a letter dated May 26, 1778, at Valley Forge:

> To Brigadr Genl McIntosh
> SIR: The Congress having been pleased to direct me, to appoint an Officer to command at Fort Pit and on the Western Frontiers, in the room of Brigadier General Hand, I am induced, but not without reluctance, from the sense I entertain of your merit, to nominate you, as an Officer well qualified from a variety of considerations...
>
> I have only to add, that I shall be happy to hear from you, as often as opportunity will permit, and my warmest wishes, that your services may be honorable to yourself and approved by your Country.
>
> I am Sir with great esteem & regard Yr most Obed Sevt
>   GE WASHINGTON
> (Kellogg 60; Fitzpatrick 11: 460-61)

In another letter, dated May 27, 1778, Washington directed Lackie McIntosh to accompany his father:

> Captain Lachlan McIntosh of the first Georgia Regiment is to attend Brigadier General McIntosh in the Western Department while he shall have occasion for him, acquainting his commanding officer in Georgia of the same when opportunity offers.
>
> The Captain's stay in camp this winter for improving himself in discipline is approved and while he remains with the General he is to act as Brigade inspector to the Troops under his command. His rank in the line of the Army is not to be prejudiced by this appointment or his absence on the command on which he is now ordered. (Kellogg 60-61; Fitzpatrick 11: 461-62))

In a letter dated May 29, 1778, Washington informed Colonel William Russell of the 13th Virginia Regiment that McIntosh was on the way to the West:

> Sir: I received yours of the 28th. ulto. inclosing a Return of that part of your Regiment that is at Fort Pitt, and giving me an account of the situation of matters to the Westward.
>
> The Commissioners had made a representation to Congress a good deal similar to that of yours and therefore in consequence of their direction to nominate a proper Officer to succeed Genl. Hand, I have appointed Brigr. Genl. McIntosh. I have great expectations from his prudence, good sense and knowledge of negociation in Indian Affairs, which I imagine he has been conversant during his long residence in Carolina and Georgia.
>
> Congress have ordered two Battalions to be raised expressly for the purpose of defending the Frontier or carrying on an expedition against the Enemy should it be found practicable. It is my wish to have Regiments united, and I would for that reason send the remainder of yours to Fort Pitt could I spare them at this time. When the intentions of the Enemy are more fully known and our arrangements for the Campaign are made, I will endeavor to send them up. I

shall, as soon as possible, fill up the Vacancies of Field Officers in the Virginia line, when a Lieutt. Colo. Major will be appointed to the 13th. I am &ca. (Fitzpatrick 11: 422)

McIntosh did not have formal experience in negotiating with Indian tribes in 1778, but he was familiar with the ways of Southern Indians. When he was a child in Darien, native tribes inhabited the area and he competed in foot races with the Indian children. His brother William learned to speak the local Indian language. Some of their relatives such as their father's cousin Benjamin McIntosh moved from Darien to Charleston and became involved in the Indian trade; Lachlan may have associated with them while he lived in Charleston as a young man. In his role as Continental commander in Georgia during the opening years of the American Revolution, McIntosh monitored not only American attempts to recruit Indian allies but also attempts by British officials such as his relative Captain William McIntosh to coordinate Indian attacks on the southern frontier with maneuvers of the British garrison at St. Augustine.

General Lachlan McIntosh and Captain Lachlan "Lackie" McIntosh headed west together. In late May they arrived at York, Pennsylvania, where Congress was meeting. Lachlan McIntosh had an opportunity to visit his longtime friend and business partner Henry Laurens, who was then President of the Continental Congress. McIntosh handed over to Laurens a letter written by Washington on May 21:

General McIntosh will have the Honor to deliver you this. He is now on his way to take the command at Pitsburg and in the Western Frontiers, and waits on Congress for their instructions.

I would also take the liberty of submitting to Congress the inclosed account of expences incurred by the General in his Journey from Georgia to join this army, and which he presented to me and to the auditors for payment. I did not know how far I might be authorized to comply with his request, and therefore lay the matter before Congress. At the same time I would observe, that nothing appears to be more equitable, than that claims of this sort, where they are not immoderate, should be satisfied by the public. If this were not the case, the expences of an Officer when ordered from one post to another, especially where they are distant would sink the whole or a very large part of his pay. The charges attending the General's journey from hence to Pitsburg, will require equal attention, and the whole I am persuaded will meet with a just and suitable provision. (Kellogg 57; Fitzpatrick 11:429-30)

McIntosh discovered that the Board of War had not recruited the two regiments that Congress had authorized for the expedition against Fort Detroit and also had not secured supplies for the expedition. Since part of the 13th Virginia Regiment was already at the Western Department's headquarters at Fort Pitt, General Washington designated the entire regiment to serve in the expedition; the commander of the 13th Virginia Regiment, Colonel John Gibson, knew the language and culture of the Indians on the western frontier. Although Washington needed as much strength as possible in his own army at Valley Forge, he also ordered the 8th Pennsylvania Regiment under Colonel Daniel Brodhead to participate in the expedition. The assignment of regiments from both Virginia and Pennsylvania fit into the American plans to prevent either Virginia or Pennsylvania from claiming ownership of the western territory due to military conquest by either of the states alone. Other troops joined the expedition, including Colonel George Morgan, the Indian Agent for the Middle Department who also was a land speculator eyeing the Ohio Valley (Jackson 75-76).

Patriots invade Florida yet again

An American force in Georgia under General Robert Howe intent on invading British East Florida began crossing the Altamaha on May 26. The regular British troops opposing the invasion fell back across the St. Johns, leaving only the East Florida Rangers to impede Howe's advance. On June 17 a patriot scouting party skirmished with East Florida Rangers near Cowford on the Satilla; the patriots took one prisoner and captured eight horses and five saddles, bridles and blankets. On June 28 the patriots nearly captured Thomas Brown, the commander of the East Florida Rangers, but he escaped into a swamp. By the end of June, Howe had reached the St. Marys, where he occupied Fort Tonyn.

Georgia militia fought East Florida Rangers and British regulars on June 30 at the Battle of Alligator Creek. At least thirteen patriots were killed and several were wounded; patriot Colonel Elijah Clarke was shot through the thigh. One of the British regular troops was killed, two officers and three soldiers of the Rangers were wounded, and one loyalist officer was taken prisoner.

The 1778 invasion of Florida met many of the same problems that plagued previous invasions. Shortages of tents, medicine, canteens and cooking utensils were reported. The soldiers sweltered in unseasonably warm weather. Many hundreds of men suffered from tropical illnesses; half of the men in the South Carolina Brigade became ill. Loyalists and their Indian allies harried the patriot troops. Many Americans deserted; some escaping and some being captured and hanged or shot. A chain of command was never established among the various state and Continental units. Supplies of provisions were delayed and the Continental troops ran out of rice and bread. Their horses also were starving.

General Howe called a halt to the invasion. The Georgia Continentals under Elbert joined the Continentals under Howe in withdrawing from Florida on July 14. The Georgia and South Carolina militia troops soon followed (Searcy 139-47).

William McIntosh urges Creeks to aid British

The British response to the American invasion included recruiting Indian allies. The British Superintendent of Indian affairs in the South ordered agents David Tait and William McIntosh to send parties of Creek warriors to reinforce St. Augustine and to raid the Georgia-Florida border region. The Creeks, however, decided to postpone action until late summer so they could harvest their crops and observe a harvest ceremony known as the Green Corn Dance. British authorities in St. Augustine expected 1,700 Creeks to come to their aid, but only a hundred warriors actually arrived.

Darien abandoned, McIntosh family scattered

Constant raids across the Georgia-Florida border by soldiers on both sides of the conflict and Indians allied with the British, as well as by opportunistic bandits, devastated the plantations and settlements near the border. The town of Darien – seat of the McIntosh family in Georgia for three generations – was uninhabited by late June of 1778 (Searcy 152). Lachlan McIntosh had moved his family and slaves to a large house on St. James Square in Savannah when the Darien area became too dangerous (Lawrence, "Suspension" 133); his wife and younger children remained in Savannah while he and his son Lackie served at Valley Forge and subsequently in the Western Department. Lachlan's nephew John McIntosh was a lieutenant colonel in the Georgia Continentals. Roderick "Rory" McIntosh had left his family's plantation adjoining John McIntosh's plantation in the Darien area and had joined the British forces at St. Augustine. A Georgia historian later reported that a woman whose married name was Ann McIntosh temporarily left the Darien area for the only time in her 100-year-long life:

> ...Her parents came to this country with General Oglethorpe, and she was born shortly after at Darien, where General Oglethorpe had a military post. She spent her life within ten miles of that place, ninety-five years within two miles of it, and eighty-six on the same spot, never having left it but once, when she was expelled by the British. Mrs. M. possessed her voice and animation to the last hour, was a woman of good character, and highly esteemed by her friends. (White 546)

The Battle of Monmouth: June 28, 1778

Sir Henry Clinton replaced William Howe as commander of British forces in America. The British strategy called for Clinton to abandon Philadelphia and maintain a defensive posture at New York. Continental Commander in Chief George Washington displayed confidence in his army, which had been reshaped at Valley Forge, by attacking the British forces as they were on the move. Washington ordered General Charles Lee to lead the attack as soon as the British began marching on the morning of June 28. When American troops under Anthony Wayne and Charles Scott encountered the British column, however, Lee declined to issue any orders and the American forces fell into confusion. Military historians describe the consequences:

> Clinton, who had promptly faced Cornwallis to the rear, now saw an unexpected opportunity to inflict a sharp defeat on a major portion of the American army. Directing Corn-

wallis to attack, he sent orders to Knyphausen to halt [on the march toward New York], and to send back about 3,000 troops toward Monmouth Courthouse. Pressing closely after the withdrawing Americans, the British soon turned the retreat into a rout. Only Wayne's brigade, falling back in good order from one delaying position to another, prevented total disaster.

It was now noon, or after. Washington, approaching Freehold Meeting House at the head of the remainder of his army, had for some time been worried because he had not heard the expected noise of battle... [Washington] found stragglers fleeing down the road. Since there had been no sustained firing, it was obvious to Washington that there could have been no serious engagement. Thus this confused retreat was incomprehensible to him. Putting spurs to his horse, he galloped through the thickening crowds of refugees, until, less than a mile east of Freehold Meeting House, he met Lee, riding calmly to the rear with a group of staff officers.

"What, Sir," asked the angry Washington, "is the meaning of this? Whence came this disorder and confusion?"

"Sir, Sir?" stammered the embarrassed Lee, who either did not understand, or was disconcerted by the glint in his commander's eye. Washington repeated his question in an icy tone of voice.

The remainder of the conversation between the two generals has been reported with many discrepancies by the several eyewitnesses who were there. Some have asserted that after hearing Lee's halting excuses, the usually composed Washington exploded in a rage as had never been seen before by his associates. Of his fury, there can be no question, though there is serious doubt whether he called Lee a "damned poltroon," or otherwise used what one observer called "a terrific eloquence of unprintable scorn." Whatever he said, he left Lee cowering and sputtering, as he plunged ahead into the motley, retreating mob to attempt to restore order...

"I never saw the General to so much advantage," Alexander Hamilton wrote later. "His coolness and firmness were admirable. He instantly took measures for checking the enemy's advance, and giving time for the army, which was very near, to form and make a proper disposition."

Lafayette, who had apparently been endeavoring to rally the fugitives, unexpectedly found himself joined by Washington. The Marquis has also given us a description of the General's actions during these critical minutes:

"His presence stopped the retreat... His fine appearance on horseback, his calm courage, roused to animation by the vexation of the morning, gave him the air best calculated to excite enthusiasm... I thought then, as now, that never had I beheld so superb a man."

Washington rallied two regiments, just as Wayne and a few steadfast men pulled back to join him, a mere 200 yards from the redcoat skirmishers. Turning the covering force over to Wayne, Washington immediately galloped a few hundred yards to the rear, where a low ridge overlooked a meandering stream flowing through a gentle, marshy depression, locally called a "ravine." Here he was rallying fugitives when Greene arrived, with the head of the army's main body. Ignoring the fact that Greene was now a staff officer, theoretically ineligible to command, Washington immediately placed him in command of the right wing. He ordered Stirling, whose division was bringing up the rear, to move as rapidly as possible on Greene's left, while he himself, with the assistance of Lafayette, attempted to organize Lee's refugees to form a reserve...

Washington and von Steuben – who was helping the Commander-in-Chief direct the arriving units to their posts – could now see the results of the months of training at Valley Forge. The troops already in line, though greatly outnumbered at first, stood steady as they threw back one attack after another...

...Clinton realized at last that he could not drive the Americans from their positions. Accordingly he broke off the fight, calling his men back to a strong position a few hundred yards from the American line, out of musket range.

...Washington meanwhile had tested the mettle of his army, and was satisfied that they were every bit as good as the British regulars. He decided to counterattack. But only two of his brigades had not been engaged, and even these had marched more than fifteen miles in 100° heat. The troops on both sides were simply incapable of further offensive effort.

...During this hard-fought Battle of Monmouth, the records show that the Americans suffered 360 casualties, of whom 40 were deaths from sunstroke. British returns list 358 men killed and wounded, 59 being sunstroke deaths. Other, apparently corroborating, reports show, however, that the Americans buried between 217 and 249 British dead. The losses on each side were probably about twice as heavy as admitted in official reports. (Dupuy and Dupuy 281-86)

The British army proceeded to New York. Washington deployed his forces around New York to keep the British from leaving their stronghold except by sea.

Expedition against Fort Detroit stalls

On the western frontier, General Lachlan McIntosh prepared to lead an expedition against Fort Detroit, the British headquarters in the west. Congress authorized a force of three thousand Continental troops and up to 2,5000 Virginia militia and appropriated nearly $933,000 for provisions, amounting to the largest command ever led by General McIntosh. Virginia authorities, however, failed to provide the militia force and would not send the supplies requested by Congress. Plans for the expedition ground to a halt as the month of June came to an end (Jackson 77).

Indians attacked settlements in western Pennsylvania in mid-July, throwing settlers across the western colonial frontier into a panic. McIntosh detached the 13th Virginia Regiment to protect the settlements that had been attacked (Jackson 77).

McIntosh finally got the expedition against Fort Detroit underway, crossing the mountains west of York and marching to the fork of the Ohio River. He reached the Western Department headquarters at Fort Pitt on August 6. There he was disappointed to learn that Congress had decided to abandon the expedition against Fort Detroit. His new orders from Congress were to attack the Indian towns in western Pennsylvania (Jackson 78).

As commander of the Western Department, McIntosh devised a plan for protecting the western frontier that resembled his previous plan for the southern frontier. He proposed a network of forts along the frontier and a mobile force of horsemen. Local officials, however, clung to their established system of small stockades located near settlements (Jackson 78).

Meanwhile, logistical problems bogged down preparations for attacking the Indian towns. Food for the army was lost or spoiled during transport across the mountains. McIntosh's queries into the problems created hard feelings in the supply corps (Jackson 79). Local farmers claimed they barely had enough grain in storage to provide for their own families and livestock and could not spare any provisions for the army or feed for its pack-horses and cattle (Kellogg 148-49). The Virginia Council countermanded McIntosh's order to raise militia units for his expedition (Kellogg 176).

War separates Flory and Allan McDonald

In New York, the legendary Flory McDonald's husband Allan was ordered to join the 84th Regiment in Nova Scotia, separating him from Flory once again. For six months Allan and Flory had been together in New York along with a son, a daughter, a son-in-law and four grandchildren. When Allan left for Nova Scotia in late August, Flory planned to follow him as soon as possible even though she "was very nigh death's door, by a violent disorder" that she blamed on "the Rough sea and long passage" from North Carolina to New York the previous spring (Vining 182-83).

The British defend Newport

In the North, the American army and the French navy attempted in August to expel the British from Newport, Rhode Island, which the British had seized in an amphibious assault nearly two years earlier. Although the attempt failed, it provided an opportunity for General Nathanael Greene to return briefly to his home state and spend precious moments with his wife Caty.

William McIntosh recruits warriors

On the southern frontier, Indian agent Captain William McIntosh recruited Creek Indians from the Chiaha and Hichata bands in August of 1778 to reinforce the British at St. Augustine.

American allies among the Cussita band of the Creeks issued threats against McIntosh personally and against loyalist settlers in the Pensacola area.

Creeks allied with the British raided along the Satilla, Altamaha and Ogeechee rivers and across the Georgia backcountry, killing eight Georgia soldiers, slaying about thirty settlers, burning buildings, destroying plantations and taking horses. Continental forces dispatched from Savannah and Ebenezer joined South Carolina and Georgia militia to quell the raids (Searcy 154-55).

Lachlan McIntosh negotiates with Indian allies

On the western frontier, as General Lachlan McIntosh prepared to attack the towns of hostile Indians he negotiated an alliance with the Delaware tribe. The Treaty of Fort Pitt, concluded in mid-September, became the first Indian treaty signed in the name of the United States. The Delaware agreed to help the Americans fight the British, and the Americans promised not only to provide protection—including a military post to protect their territory – and trading privileges but also guarantee that the Delaware would keep their land forever (Jackson 79-80; Kellogg 138-45).

McIntosh recognized the assistance of a Delaware leader named White Eyes by giving him a promotion dated September 21, 1778:

> As Capt. White-Eyes of the Delaware Nation, has distinguished himself by his solid & sound judgement, his steady and unalterable attachment to the interests of the United States & humanity, amidst the general disaffection, prejudice, & corruption of his countrymen, was the principal instrument of our alliance with his tribe, & is likely to be of considerable service by his knowledge, understanding, & influence: Genl McIntosh therefore thinks proper, in the name of the United States, to confer upon the said Captn White Eyes the title of Lieut. Colonel of all the Indian Nations between the rivers Ohio, Mississippi & the Lakes, expecting Congress will confirm it, and orders him to be distinguished hereafter by the name of Coll. White-Eyes. (Kellogg 433)

A Pennsylvania historical magazine describes the fate of White Eyes after the treaty was concluded:

> White Eyes, Delaware chief, was one of the great Indian statesmen. He envisioned the time when his tribe should become civilized, live in peaceable trade relations with their white neighbors. The Treaty of Fort Pitt, 1778, was largely his work. While attempting to carry out the provisions of this treaty, White Eyes was perfidiously murdered by renegade whites. His body was quickly buried, and the story was told that he had died from smallpox. All feared the consequences. The officers entered into a solemn pact to keep the secret and it was many years till the truth was known. (Williams 17)

A soldier's recollection of the death of White Eyes seemed dubious about the small pox claim: "Capt. White Eyes at Fort McIntosh was taken with the Small-pox and was sent to Pittsburg where he soon died… None others had small pox" (Kellogg 157).

Fort McIntosh established on the western frontier
While negotiating the treaty with Indian allies, McIntosh made plans for subduing the hostile Indians. Instead of simply raiding the Indian towns, which would allow the Indians to reorganize as soon as the raid ended, he decided to build a series of forts as bases for operations inside Indian territory. The forts would extend along the route toward Detroit, which would be helpful if Congress again authorized an expedition against the western British headquarters at Fort Detroit (Jackson 80-81).

The plan got underway in the autumn of 1778 when McIntosh marched thirty miles west of Fort Pitt to a bluff over the Ohio River about a mile below the junction with Beaver River. Construction of Fort McIntosh atop the bluff marked two historic milestones: first, McIntosh's army of more than 1,300 troops was the largest force ever gathered on the western side of the Appalachians throughout the course of the Revolution and, second, the United States established its first military post on the northern side of the Ohio River, which until then had been Indian territory (Jackson 80-81). The Chevalier de Cambray-Digny, chosen by Washington as the artillery commander and engineer officer in the Western De-

partment, designed Fort McIntosh in the shape of a four-pointed
star with bastions projecting from the points (Williams 5-6).

McIntosh transferred the headquarters from Fort Pitt to Fort
McIntosh on October 8 (Williams 5). On October 11 he appointed
his son Lackie to serve as the Deputy Adjutant General for the
Western Department, as recorded by a clerk in the army's orderly
book:

> As a Deputy Adg^t Genl is absolutely necessary for the Good
> Order and Decipline of the Army in this Department Since
> the junction of the Militia brigade ---- Major McKintosh
> who Has heatherto Done ye Duty ----- is appointed to that
> office with the pay and subsistence of Lt. Col^o And without
> Any prejudice to his Rank in the line of the Army (Wil-
> liams 165).

Flory McDonald goes to Nova Scotia

Flory McDonald left New York in October to join her husband
Allan, who was stationed at Windsor, Nova Scotia, with the 84th
Regiment. Their son Alexander may have been with her. Their
daughter Anne left New York at about the same time; Anne's husband Alexander MacLeod wanted to clear up confusion about his
commission in the British army and he brought his wife and four
children with him (Vining 182).

Because of rough autumn weather, Flory's voyage northward
stretched out over at least two weeks. After disembarking at Halifax, she stayed there eight days because of her poor health. Then
she set off on a five-day trek across the snowy wilderness to Windsor in the midst of "one of the worst winters ever seen there." At
Windsor, she said, she and Allan nearly starved during the harsh
winter. Some people say "despite ill health, she followed him in
Canadian engagements" Flory and Allan's sons Alexander and
Charles were also at Nova Scotia at the time, along with other acquaintances from Scotland and North Carolina ("Flora MacDonald;" Schafer 990; Moss 33; Toffey 134, Vining 182, 183).

Lachlan McIntosh marches west

In the West, with Fort McIntosh firmly established, General
McIntosh attempted to implement his plan to construct another fort

farther west. The second fort would fulfill the treaty obligation to establish a defensive post in Delaware tribal territory.

His grand plan continued to be undermined by mundane matters of supplies and provisions for the Western Department. The orderly book for October 22, 1778, noted:

> ...The General having unsuccessfully endeavored to engage the wholesome & useful article of beer for the soldiers of this Department on reasonable terms, & finding Agnus Labatt, brewer, taking every advantage of the necessities of the public, & extorting unmercifully upon the soldiers upon all occasions... [McIntosh forbids dealing with Labatt] until he retails his beer upon reasonable terms...
>
> The General wishes to see all the Staff with their stores, &c. removed [from Fort Pitt to Fort McIntosh] as soon as possible... where they are wanted immediately to receive & provide convenience for their stores, & render inexcusable persons who neglect their duty... (Kellogg 437)

McIntosh asked the magistrates of Westmoreland County, Pennsylvania, to find a way to provide "forage" – feed for the horses and cattle – for the expedition. Addressing the political problems plaguing the expedition, he wrote, "I have the more reason to expect your assistance in this, as the people of Virginia think me Partial to your State, for allowing all your militia to remain home at this time, to defend your own frontiers... whoever attempts to foment or revive these old Jelousys which I could wish to be buried in oblivion, have some sinister designs of their own and are no friends to their Country" (Kellogg 148).

On October 27, McIntosh reminded the soldiers at Fort McIntosh that they were in dangerous territory:

> The General is extremely sorry to find the unmilitary practice of firing guns in & about camp... on pretext of a trifling deer, which might have been sent by a cunning & vigilant enemy (& we know to be practised in such deceptions... (Kellogg 438)

Leaving 150 men at Fort McIntosh under the command of Colonel Richard Campbell, General McIntosh led about 1,200 men westward on November 4. The march was slowed by lack of supplies for the men and lack of forage for the horses in the harsh climate of western Pennsylvania in late autumn.

Robert McCready, a militiaman who had signed on to serve four months at Fort Pitt, kept a journal of the expedition. Like McIntosh, McCready had been born in Scotland. McCready came to America at age 20 and had eventually settled on the western Pennsylvania frontier. He was a farmer, a school teacher, and a leader in his community's Presbyterian church. At Fort Pitt, McIntosh appointed McCready to serve as an adjutant to Colonel John Stephenson, who commanded a militia regiment and happened to be a friend of George Washington (Williams 6-7). McCready's journal for November 7 gives some gruesome details of the march:

> The [Army] detained as usual by the horses and Cattle squandring out of the lines until the day was far spent ----- About one mile from Camp on their march Capt Steel of the Thirteenth Virginia Regiment who had Advanced somewhat in the front of the Army was alarm.d by the fireing of Two Guns in his front and Advanceing forwards found A Soldier Viz –   Ross of said Regiment ----- killed and Scalped by the Indians ----- the Army proceeded on to the Second fork of little Beaver running nearly South about four perches wide Advancing forwards about a mile further found Lieu^t Parks killed and Scalped likewise. they having both gone out to hunt in opposition to General orders fell a dishonorable and in Some measure unlamented prey to the Enemy   The Army Proceeding arriv.d at Camp N° 4 an hour by sun in the evening ----- this camp is likewise Situate on a small Branch of little Beaver running S.E. this is call.d Camp cruelty taken from the Instances of cruelty Aforementiond... (Williams 12)

In response to the two deaths, McIntosh severely punished soldiers who hunted or fired guns, traded with Indians, or left camp without permission. Such discipline angered the soldiers, who counted on hunting to augment the army's meager supplies (Jackson 84-85).

McIntosh wrote a letter to Campbell at Fort McIntosh reporting that the journey was going slowly because the pack horses procured for the expedition were unfit for the task. Since each extra
day on the trail required additional food for the men and the animals, the slow pace would have serious consequences:

> CAMP PLEASANT 18 MILES FROM FORT M^{C}INTOSH
>   7th Novm^r 1778
>   tell Mr Lockhart, Steel and Brady, they have used me
> extremely ill in sending such Horses upon this Journey,
> they detain us unaccountably. – they are tiring every day
> and Cannot Travel above four or five miles a day altho I
> find their loads upon an average does not exceed 100^{lb}
> weight each which will also make us exceeding Short of
> Provisions and will require a supply from you soon and re-
> quest you to have it ready for us as soon as Possible, we are
> also in great want of forage now – which you will push
> Steel to get soon. (Kellogg 167-68)

Harsh weather afflicted the marchers late on the afternoon of
November 10 and continued throughout the night and the next day.
The orderly book for November 11 reported that the feed supply
for the livestock had been exhausted:

> …Since the weather will not allow the Army to march this
> Day And food All Eat out within the lines One half of the
> Pickets Are to Guard the Drivers Wherever they Carry
> there Cattle And horses where the Best food Can be Got the
> rest of the picket Are to Guard the lines until reliev.d in the
> Evening as Usual (Williams 272-73)

The orderly book also reported that McIntosh rewarded his
soldiers for following his orders not to fire guns nor to go hunting:

> for the Good Behavior of the men in there Strict Obedience
> to Orders, which the General Saw himself A remarkable In-
> stance of yesterday when the deer ran through the lines and
> for which he Publickly returns them his thanks he allows
> An Officer and Twelve men from Each line to hunt Du-
> reing this Day for the Benefit of the whole, Observing that

the men of each party are to keep within Sight of Each Other and Report every Discovery they make of the Indians (Williams 273)

The supply situation improved that afternoon when about seventy men arrived from Fort McIntosh with what McCready called "a small Brigade of pack-horses And some Stragling Bullocks" (Williams 14).

The trek westward resumed at noon the next day. The marchers passed a large spring and saw a tree marked with an Indian war pole and two scalps, assumed to be the scalps of the soldiers killed five days earlier. McIntosh warned the soldiers to be ready for battle and to perform military maneuvers quickly and precisely because, the orderly book said, "the General is Ever Anxious for the honour as well as the Safety of An Army of such Brave men... Especialy A Gainst Such enterprising An Vigelant Enemies as Indians are, who take every Advantage and Attack with Savage furry" (Williams 273).

Snow began falling at sunset on November 13 and continued the next day, forcing the army to remain in camp. A court martial convened and punished two soldiers for firing their guns unnecessarily. The orderly book reported "the General highly approves the Sentences of the Court on those too men & thanks the Gentlemen for the attention and desire they Have shown to brake the vile practice of Shooting which besides the waste of ammunition where we cannot get supplied is extremely dangerous in our present Situation" (Williams 274).

McIntosh sent a letter dated November 13 to Campbell at Fort McIntosh, describing the obstacles besetting the trek:

This is the 10th day I have been upon my march. I am not 50 miles from your fort yet owing to the scandelous Pack Horses that were imposed upon me, notwithstanding the many Charges I gave old Brady and the Q. Masters several days before I set off, above one half of them tires every day before we Travel two or three miles, and the woods is Strewed with those that have given out and dyed. I have now but Sixteen Miles to Tuscorawas yet I much fear I shall not be able to Carry our Provisions and Stores that length. I have put Elliott under arrest for his neglect and In-

solence and expect you will do the same with Brady. I find
there is no other way to manage this Gent[n] upon whom our
all depends and on whom all our disapointments Should be
charged. &ca (Kellogg 172-73)

Messengers from the Delaware tribe came to the American
camp and told McIntosh that their warriors would join his army at
the Tuscarawas River. McIntosh ordered his soldiers to be "ex-
ceeding cautious to distinguish well whether any Indians they meet
are friends are enemies before they fire upon them... at the same
time every precaution is Necessary and to be used against treach-
ery no man or party of Men must be suffered to come in or go out
of Camp without the Generals approbation" (Williams 274).
    On the afternoon of November 15, the men marched six miles
before sunset and set up camp. They marched six miles farther the
next day. As they neared the meeting place with the Delaware warriors, McIntosh ordered his soldiers not to conduct personal business with the Indians:

> Every person without Exception is positively forbid to Buy
> Or sell Or have Any kind Of Barter Or Dealing whatsoever
> with An Indian Or Indians. without the Generals Special
> leave in Writing And any Officer Soldier Or Other person
> who Buys A single Article or Articles hereafter if ever so
> trifeling Contrary to this Order Shall forfeit such Article
> with whatever he Give for it. And Three months pay Be-
> sides Such Other punishment as a Court Martial shall inflict
> for Breach of Orders. (Williams 274-75)

Incessant rainfall kept the army in camp all day November 17.
As each passing day depleted the expedition's supplies, the daily
ration dwindled to four ounces of half-spoiled flour and eight
ounces of poor-quality beef (Jackson 85, Williams 16).
    The next day the orderly book reported:

> The General is informd that some Enemy Indians have
> Been seen near Our Camp, therefore Cautions All Officers
>   Be Verey Carefull that none of their men Stragle or Go
> Out side of their lines by Night or Day unless they are Or-
> dred upon some Duty and Call there Roles Often as the

Repeted [orders] issued Against firing Guns wantonly is Shamefuly Neglected...

And also that The Centinels have No fires At Night. all Officers and Soldiers Are desired to Colect and save all the Deers Tails they Can Get and wear them in their hats which may Induce our friend Indians to do the same & Distinguish Ourselves and them from Our Enemies. (Williams 275-76)

The army reached its destination on the Muskingum River – formed by the confluence of the Tuscarawas and the Walhonding – on November 18. When the soldiers arrived, they met representatives of their allies among the Delaware tribe. Robert McCready described the scene in his journal:

The Army march.d about twelve OClock and Arriv.d at the banks of Tuskarawas by two hours of up Sun. as soon as Our Stock and Baggage had passed the River the Army was form[d] in the usual Order of marching and continued passing through an Extensive plain into a Scattering wood where Ordred to halt for the Reception of the Indians &c who were fully apprised of Our Coming and held themselves in Readiness to receive us in great taste. they Formed themselves with great regularity. And when Our front Advanced near theirs they began the Salute with Three Indian Cheirs. from thence A Regular fire which was Returned By A hasty Running Fire round Our whole lines which being done we Ecamped round our Brethren... (Williams 16)

On the second day after the army reached the Muskingum, according to McCready's journal, the Indians gave gifts to McIntosh:

The Indians made A present to the General of A Quantity of Venison And Skins, and Expressed their great Grief for the loss of White Eyes their Chief but assurd the General there was Yet many Among them that Would render him as much Service as White Eyes Could Do was he then Alive. And keep the Chain as Bright. they likewise Insisted much on the Generals going down to their Town to Build A fort for their Defence And Safety ----- (Williams 17)

McIntosh told the Delaware that the fort not only would defend their tribe but also would be part of a path to Detroit. McIntosh appointed the Delaware to spread the word among neighboring tribes that he wanted to meet with them. He would consider any tribes that refused to meet with him to be enemies of the United States and his army would conquer them. Looking around at McIntosh's underfed, ill-equipped troops, the Delaware delegates couldn't help but laugh (Jackson 85-86; Kellogg 178-80).

As McIntosh was meeting with his Indian allies, his soldiers began building what he envisioned as the second fort on a route to Detroit. He named the new fort after his longtime friend and business partner Henry Laurens, who was serving as president of the Continental Congress. The Western Department engineer, the Chevalier de Cambray-Digny, followed nearly the same four-pointed design for Fort Laurens that he had implemented for Fort McIntosh (Williams 8)

The orderly book entry for November 21 bears bad tidings:

> As the weather Begins Already to Set in Very Severe And we have Experienced the pack horses to be Exceeding Sorry which will make Our Suplies Uncertain the General is Sorry he is Obliged To Curtail the Rations to One pound Of flour per man p^r Day untill A suply Arrives here. And hopes the Brave men of his Army will Content themselves with it for A short Time And see the Necessity and Propriety of, to make up for the Dificency Each man is to be Serv.d with 1-1/2 lb of Beef per Day which the Commisary must Strictly Observe Untill farther Orders---
>
> After Orders-------
>
> As the General is Anxious to have the Fort Finished and Try if we Can Do any thing Against the Enemy this Season he Desires Each Reg^t to take there Share Of it in proportion to there number of men off Duty Imeadatly as the pickets are Now Cut and he hopes they will Exert themselves to Shew who will be Done first (Williams 276-77)

A few days later a court martial laid the blame for the shortage of provisions on the men who were entrusted with the job of delivering supplies. McIntosh, who had suffered from insufficient supplies when he served on the southern frontier and at Valley Forge, observed that the problem plagued all the American states:

> William Eliot (Elliott) A superintendant Or A director of pack horses for this division tried by the same Court for Neglect of duty the Court were of the Opinion Every Blame of the delay of Our Army Ought to have fallen upon Braidy And Eliot Should be Discharged. the General in Compliance with their Opinion releases both these Gentlemen And Disolves the Court but at the Same time As the States have Sufred so Amazin[g]ly Already in this department And Every Expedition and plan hitherto set On foot has fallen through By the Neglect of those Employ.d on it which is well known to every person in this Army. the General Expects more from the Directors of it in the future. And desires Such Careless persons as Mr Eliot will not be Employ.d hereafter as he finds laying the Blame Upon any others will be deem.d a suficient Excuse And no Examples Can be made Of such delinquents and plunderers of the publick------- (Williams 277)

One of the measures McIntosh took to make delivering supplies to the western outposts faster and safer was to build a road from Fort Pitt to Fort McIntosh (Agnew 36, Kellogg 294). The Americans continued to have problems, however, in getting supplies from the east across the mountains to Fort Pitt. Resulting shortages at Fort Pitt caused problems in sending supplies to Fort McIntosh and Fort Laurens. A commissary official at Fort Pitt wrote:

> I fear that the Salting our Beef at Fort McIntosh will be greatly retarded by the demand of 100 Bushels of Salt made by the General – Which I am sure will not leave 20 Bushels behind. I am endeavoring to borrow about 50 Bushels at this place [Pittsburgh] which I intend taking down with me the Morrow or Next Day at furthest, as also a hand Mill for Grinding it, if it can be Possibly procured &c^a I find that we will be Universally distressed for want of Salt, there is not half enough in Store here, for Curing the Quantity of Beef. …it appears to me that in a few Weeks more our

Beeves in every Quarter will be wasted to mere Skeletons. I am really very much distress'd on the thoughts of this very great misfortune, the want of Salt &c[a] (Kellogg 175)

Unto Alexander McDonald a son is born

In the South, Alexander McDonald of the Darien area was promoted to sergeant major in the 2nd South Carolina Regiment on November 16, 1778 (Moss, *South Carolina* 615).

An even more important event in his life occurred in 1777 or 1778: his son Daniel was born. Family historian Daniel Huntley Redfearn, after citing evidence that Alexander's son may have been born in New York and noting that Alexander's father-in-law Murdoch McLeod remained a loyalist throughout the war, provides an explanation:

> As Alexander McDonald was in the Revolutionary Army, it is possible that his wife, Christine, was staying with her father and that he took her with him to New York, then in control of the British. One tradition is that Daniel was born there; that his mother died when he was born; that the McLeods kept him until they themselves returned to South Carolina. Another tradition is that his mother did not die but returned to Georgia and joined her husband after the Revolution. Another tradition is that she remained in Georgia and never left. There are variations to these traditions in every branch of the family.
>
> Exhaustive research has failed to substantiate any of the traditions with reference to the early life of Daniel McDonald... The pioneers had hard lives; most of them were uneducated; transportation and communication were slow and difficult. The result is that too few authentic records of rural, American families have survived the primitive conditions existing in the 17th and 18th centuries. (Redfearn 77-78)

The defense of Midway: November 24, 1778

On the southern frontier, forces from British East Florida invaded Georgia in the autumn of 1778 primarily to gather provisions (Searcy 179-80). A force under Lieutenant Colonel Mark

Prevost marched toward Georgia by land and a force under Lieutenant Colonel L.V. Fuser sailed up the waterway.

Colonel Prevost entered Georgia on November 19, destroying plantations, confiscating property, and taking all able-bodied men prisoner. Local militia skirmished with Prevost at Bulltown Swamp and at Riceboro Bridge but could not stop his advance toward Savannah.

All of the American officers opposing the British invasion were under orders of Colonel Samuel Elbert, who had taken post at the Great Ogeechee crossing.

John McIntosh, who had been promoted to Lieutenant Colonel at age twenty-three, was stationed with the Continental troops at Sunbury. The commander at Sunbury, Colonel John White, marched about a hundred men with two pieces of artillery to intercept Prevost at Midway, which is midway on the road between Darien and Savannah. While White was absent, McIntosh was the ranking officer remaining at Sunbury.

When White's men reached Midway, they hurriedly constructed a breastwork across the road. On November 24, General James Screven with twenty militiamen joined White at Midway. The Patriots then relocated to a stronger defensive position a mile and a half below Midway. Soon afterward, the British force under Colonel Prevost arrived and a battle began. During the fighting, General Screven suffered a fatal wound.

When Colonel Prevost's horse was shot from under him, the Americans thought they would win the battle, but Prevost mounted another horse and continued to press the attack.

White retreated several miles past Midway. He wrote a false letter saying that Colonel Samuel Elbert was coming to reinforce the Patriots with a large body of cavalry and left the letter in the road. When the British found the letter, Prevost apparently thought it was genuine.

A British scouting party sent to Sunbury reported to Prevost that Colonel Fuser's force had not yet arrived. Prevost, considering his own lack of reinforcements and White's prospect of reinforcements, decided to return to St. Augustine. On the way back, Prevost's men burned the church known as the Midway Meeting House and burned all homes and barns in the area. The men plundered the plantations and took all the valuable items they could carry.

A laconic reply: 'Come and take it'

Fuser's ships had been delayed by storms. While Prevost's unit was leaving Midway, Fuser's foot soldiers were disembarking on Colonel's Island, seven miles south of Sunbury. As the infantry marched toward Sunbury, the ships sailed up the Midway River to positions where they could shell Fort Morris.

Inside the fort, Colonel John McIntosh commanded 127 Continental troops as well as some militia and local volunteers.

On November 25, Fuser sent a letter to McIntosh:

> You cannot be ignorant that four armies are in motion to reduce this Province. One is Already under the guns of your fort, and may be joined, when I think proper, by Colonel Prevost who is now at the Medway meetinghouse. The resistance you can, or intend to make, will only bring destruction upon this country. On the contrary, if you will deliver me the fort which you command, and lay down your arms and remain neuter until the fate of America is determined, You shall, as well as all the inhabitants of this parish, remain in peaceable possession of your property. Your answer, which I expect in an hour's time, will determine the fate of this country, whether it is to be laid in ashes, or remain as above proposed.

McIntosh replied:

> We acknowledge we are not ignorant that your army is in motion to endeavor to reduce this State. We believe it entirely chimerical that Colonel Prevost is at the Meeting-House: but should it be so, we are in no degree apprehensive of danger from a junction of his army with yours. We have no property compared with the object we contend for that we value a rush; and would rather perish in a vigorous defense than accept your proposals. We, Sir, are fighting the battles of America, and therefore disdain to remain neutral till its fate is determined. As to surrendering the fort, receive this laconic reply: Come and take it.

His reply earned John McIntosh the nickname "Come and Take It." The Georgia legislature was so impressed with his conspicuous gallantry that it presented him a sword with the words "Come and Take It" engraved on it (Massey 241-242).

Fuser maintained the siege while awaiting reports of Colonel Prevost's activities. When Fuser learned that Prevost was returning to St. Augustine, he called off the siege and sailed back to Florida.

Rory McIntosh accosts John McIntosh

Years after the Revolution, a friend of Rory McIntosh recorded a legendary encounter between Rory McIntosh and John McIntosh during the siege of Sunbury. This legend is at least half true, because historical documents indicate that Rory McIntosh participated in the capture of Sunbury by British forces in January of 1779 and John McIntosh led the defense of Sunbury in November of 1778. Rory McIntosh was related to John McIntosh and had been his neighbor in the Darien district. Rory had left Georgia during the war and had served with the British troops stationed at St. Augustine. As a grandson of Brigadier William McIntosh from Borlum in the Highlands of Scotland, Rory was very proud of his heritage. The tale of Rory McIntosh's encounter with his relative and neighbor John McIntosh was told in a letter written in 1842:

> In 1778, a part of the garrison under General Prevost marched by land to join a force from New York to attack Savannah. Rory accompanied them, and attached himself particularly to the light infantry company (4th Battalion, 60th Regiment) commanded by Captain Murray. In their advance, a part of them beleaguered a small fort at Sunbury, commanded by Captain (afterwards General) John McIntosh. The British opened lines, in which Captain Murray's company was placed.
>
> Early one morning, when Rory had made rather free with the "mountain dew," he insisted on sallying out to summon the fort to surrender. His friends could not restrain him, so out he strutted, claymore in hand... and he approached the fort, roaring out, "Surrender, you miscreants! How dare you presume to resist his Majesty's arms?"

Captain McIntosh knew him, and seeing his situation, forbid anyone firing, threw open the gate, and said, "Walk in, Mr. McIntosh, and take possession."

"No," said Rory, "I will not trust myself among such vermin; but I order you to surrender."

A rifle was fired, the ball from which passed through his face, sideways, under his eyes. He stumbled, and fell backwards...

Someone shouted out "Run! They'll kill you!"

Rory replied, "I come from a people who never run."

Rising from the ground, Rory put his hand to one cheek. By looking at his hand he could tell that his cheek was covered with blood. He then put his hand on the other cheek, and found that it also was covered with blood.

Continuing to face the enemy and still flourishing his sword, Rory stepped backwards to the British lines (White 472-74).

As a local historian puts it, "He lost one eye, but he kept his dignity and his honor" (Lewis 34).

Construction of Fort Laurens continues

On the western frontier, General Lachlan McIntosh's army worked to complete Fort Laurens on the Muskingum River in the heart of Delaware tribal territory. The orderly book entry for November 29 reported:

> The Militia have behaved so well this two days past that they are allowed this day to rest themselves from any Fatigue Duty and to send four Men from each Regiment every day to hunt deer for the Benefit of their respective Corps under the direction of Captain Prator as he was the first to put a stop to the unmilitary practice of wasting ammunition and firing guns wantonly those who work at or near the Fort for the future are to lodge their Arms in the Bastions & a Guard of a Subaltern one Serjeant one Corporal and 19 Privates to mount there every morning for the Protection of them, the provisions & & & & --------------
>
> As we cannot be too Wary of the artful enemy we have to deal with, notwithstanding their chiefs are expected to come in it is hoped the Field Officers of the Day always see

the whole line up in good Order with their Accoutrements & the Rolls, called at day light. & that the Centinels & Picquets be always Vigilant & Elert agreeable to former Orders. As the General observes by cutting the Timber that the Lines are mostly in the Clearing whereby the enemy have a great Advantage the Adjutant General is ordered to Visit them often with the Field Officers of the Day and make such Alterations as they find Necessary & no person is to go out or to come in hereafter without leave -----

On November 30, McIntosh appointed Captain Abraham Lincoln of the Virginia militia to serve as Deputy Commissary of Hides West of the Mountains and ordered all commissaries, butchers and others who dealt with public hides, leather or shoes to keep Lincoln informed of "their proceedings and the present state of that business" (Kellogg 448). As history continued to unfold, Captain Lincoln would become the grandfather of President Abraham Lincoln (Williams 287-88).

The Southern strategy

The Continental Congress and its commander in the Southern Department contemplated yet another invasion of East Florida to stop raids into Georgia and South Carolina by the East Florida Rangers and Indian war parties allied with the British. Learning from the failure of the previous expeditions, the Americans planned the next invasion for late fall and early winter when the semi-tropical climate would be less dangerous. American plans were thwarted, however, when the British launched a major campaign in the South (Searcy 157-61).

The war in the North reached a stalemate in 1778, and British authorities devised a plan to restore British sovereignty over the colonies of Georgia and South Carolina. If this plan succeeded, England would gain the economic advantage of access to commodities such as indigo, rice, tobacco, and naval stores, and Washington's army would suffer the disadvantage of losing access to food and other supplies from the South.

The strategy called for sending invasion forces from British strongholds in the North. Smaller forces in British East Florida would assist the large invasion forces.

British fleet sails south

The full-scale invasion of the South began when three thousand British, Hessian, and loyalist soldiers set sail from New York on November 27, 1778. Lieutenant Colonel Archibald Campbell of the 71st Regiment commanded the force, which included both battalions of the 71st Regiment –Aeneas Mackintosh was a captain in the 2nd Battalion.

The force also included two battalions of North Carolina and South Carolina Provincials. The commander of the North Carolinians was Colonel John Hamilton, who had fought at the Battle of Culloden in Scotland in 1746 before emigrating to North Carolina and becoming a successful planter. Another emigrant from Scotland to North Carolina, Flory McDonald's brother-in-law Alexander MacDonald of Cuidreach, also was with the British forces sailing southward.

A wintry trip down the Atlantic coast meant rough sailing. Although the sailors tried to tie down everything, "trunks and portmanteaus were hurled helter-skelter," an officer reported. "The sea was composed of terrific mountains and valleys; the foam looked all the time as if snow were floating about" (qtd. in Lawrence, "Capture" 307).

The return to Fort McIntosh

On the western frontier, General Lachlan McIntosh's army had not yet completed construction of Fort Laurens when the enlistment period of the soldiers began to expire. McIntosh refused to leave the job undone, as the entry for December 1 in the orderly book recorded:

> as all the field officers and Cap^{ts} of the whole Army or a majority of them AGreed that no person S[h]ould Go home until the Indian Treaty should be over this Fort Compleatly Finished and in Good Order -------------------- and four Good Blockhouses Built on the Road Between this and Fort M'Intosh. the General AGreed to these Conditions and promises that none Shall be Detaind longer then they are Complied with that they may be all upon a footing at the Same time he thanks the Spirited Officers who Engaged the men for A longer time and in which they Could Expect to be of some Service to there Country The General himself

proposeth Going with the Militia to Fort M'Intosh in Order
to See them paid off For their Services And Expects every
man will appear their To be Mustred for that purpose without which they Cannot Receive any. And Orders no person
to Go out side of the lines without his permision. Except 4
hunters from each Reg^t By Capt Prethors live and under his
Direction...

    The officers Commanding each Regt and Company are
to be Accountable for All the Amunition there men Recd at
Fort M'Intosh as it will be wanting at this place (Williams
279)

The entry for December 3 showed that Fort Laurens was nearly completed:

    The General assures the Militia that if they Exert them-
selves and will finish the Two Sides Rows of Cabins laid
out for them by monday night with what they have Already
Begun they Shall have but One Block-house upon the Road
to fort M'Intosh where are to remember they most all Appear To be mustred before they Can be paid off... (Williams 280)

On December 5 the soldiers were "Served with A Gill of
whisky each and the General is Sorry horses Could not be procur.d
to bring more of that Necessary Article. They who Came up with
the whiskey are not to have any as Two keggs are missing To
make every One more Carefull in future of what they have in
Charge" (Williams 281).

When construction was completed, most of the men prepared
to return to Fort McIntosh while 150 men garrisoned the new Fort
Laurens. The orderly book entry for December 8 reported: "all the
Troops are to be Serv.d with Two days more Flour Except Col^o
Gibsons Reg^t who Remains in the fort and prepare Imeiadately to
march without any Stope or delay until they reach Fort M'Intosh
all persons are alowd to go out and in without passes To day to
hunt there horses." (Williams 282)

As the army returned eastward, some of the militiamen left the
main army and traveled in small groups. A Virginia militiamen
experiencing his first military service on McIntosh's expedition

later recalled that some of the men were so eager to return home that they traveled day and night, "some stopping and making a camp fire, sleep a while, and then push in to Fort McIntosh, not in much order, except each company kept together and all were scattered along, perhaps over half the whole distance" (Kellogg 160-61).

Provisions remained in short supply, and some of the desperate men ate roasted cowhide. The Virginia militiaman recalled coming across "one poor young fellow named John Bell, sitting by the roadside, crying, saying he was so weak he could not proceed any further." The militiaman shared his meager supply of bread with the young man and "encouraged him to renew the march, which he did, and got in, and finally reached the region of the South Branch of Potomac where he belonged" (Kellogg 161).

A frontiersman escorting supplies from Fort McIntosh to Fort Laurens remembered meeting the army coming the opposite way:

> ... on the head of yellow creek, the escort began to meet parties of the Militia, rushing on toward the ohio with all possible speed, the company of Militia composing fully one third of the escort Joined their Companions and returned, leaving two companies of regulars (of which I was one) to Guard the provisions to the fort. Some distance down Sandy creek, we met General McIntosh Co^l Brodhead and Co^l Crawford, with the regular troops, and a few Militia. (Kellogg 185)

The orderly book indicates that the expedition had returned to Fort McIntosh on December 13:

> The General congratulates the troops upon their return to this post on their way home after establishing two important posts in the enemy's country, by which he hopes the safety of the frontiers [will be] secured hereafter, by keeping the savages in awe at home, & preparing the way for further enterprises against them; and the General expects that the most of the Gentlemen here will have the honor of finishing in the spring what they have so well began under many difficulties, as the enemy had not the spirit

to engage us this time near Tuscaraway as they had promised.

> The General returns his hearty thanks to the brave militia of Virginia for a conduct during this campaign which would do honor to the best regular troops, except a few individuals who, he hopes will stay at home the next time, & never come here again to poison & corrupt an army so determined to serve their country. That they may not be detained, he desires they may be all mustered this morning... to enable them to make out their pay rolls properly...

> As a farther mark of the General's satisfaction with the behavior of the militia he orders them to be served with a pint of whiskey each man, and be discharged immediately after they are mustered, although the time of very few of them is expired yet... (Kellogg 451-52)

McIntosh celebrated by giving the soldiers not only extra food but also a half pint of whiskey. According to a ranger from Pennsylvania:

> ... the men generally poor and emaciated, the liquor flew to their heads, and some 2000 (of about 25 or 26 hundred) were quite inebriated in a few minutes. Gen. M. said "a hair of the same dog was good for the bite, & to-morrow morning you shall all have double rations & another half pint." But none were seen drunk the next day. (Kellogg 163)

The militiamen soon went their various ways. One of the reasons McIntosh had discharged them a short while before their enlistment periods ended was that he did not have enough provisions at Fort McIntosh to continue feeding them. They were not given food for the journey home, so many of them "had to beg supplies, and not unfrequently plunder the fowls of the settlers along the route." A Virginia militiaman reported that he reached his home on the south branch of the Potomac "in good health, on Christmas eve, 1778" (Kellogg 161).

Considering the scarcity of provisions, McIntosh left only one regiment commanded by Colonel Daniel Brodhead at Fort McIntosh for the winter. McIntosh himself returned to the Western Department headquarters at Fort Pitt (Jackson 86; Kellogg 197).

From Fort Pitt, McIntosh wrote a letter to the vice president of Pennsylvania describing "a good strong Fort for the Reception and Security of Prisoners & stores, upon the Indian side of the Ohio below Beaver Creek, with Barracks for a Regiment; and another upon the Muskingam River, where Colo. Bocquette had one formerly near Tuscarawas, about one hundred miles from this place, which I expect will keep the savages in awe, and secure the peace of the frontiers effectually in this quarter hereafter, if they are well supplied; and will also facilitate any further enterprises that may be attempted that way" (Williams 17, Agnew 33-35, Kellogg 188-90).

In a report on December 21, Gibson reported that fourteen soldiers in the garrison at Fort Laurens were sick and another fourteen were "Unfit for Duty for Want of Clothing." The report also mentioned that five women were in the fort (Kellogg 409). "The distressed situation of the men for clothing prevents the work from going on so briskly as otherwise it would," Colonel Gibson informed McIntosh, "if any supply of that article should have arrived, please order it forward" (Kellogg 186). Despite the hardship, Gibson told McIntosh, "the men who formerly attempted to mutiny, have behaved extremely well, and unanimity prevails amongst us" (Kellogg 186).

British fleet arrives at Savannah

The British fleet that had sailed from New York in November arrived at Tybee Island near Savannah on December 27. The ships crossed the bar into the mouth of the Savannah River on a rising tide and dropped anchor.

The first troops came ashore at the boat landing of Girardeau's plantation on the morning of December 29. To move from the landing to high ground, the troops had to cross a ricefield on a narrow bank edged by ditches full of water. The light infantry of the 71st Regiment advanced along the bank. A small band of Americans guarding Girardeau's landing fired a volley that wounded five Highlanders and killed three – one of the dead was Captain Charles Cameron, an officer of "high spirit and great promise" (qtd. in Lawrence, "Capture" 315).

The Highlanders launched a bayonet charge and forced the Americans to retreat. The full British force then landed and marched toward Savannah.

The capture of Savannah: December 29, 1778

Fewer than a thousand Americans commanded by General Robert Howe faced the three thousand British invaders. Howe had been in charge of the Southern Department, but Major General Benjamin Lincoln replaced him in September of 1778 because Howe had quarreled with Christopher Gadsden, an influential South Carolinian. Gadsden and Howe fought a duel in August of 1778 during which Howe's bullet grazed Gadsden's ear and Gadsden fired into the air. A British wit commemorated the duel with this verse:

> He missed his mark, but not his aim,
> The shot was well directed;
> It saved them both from hurt and shame,
> What more could be expected? (qtd. in Stokes 156)

Some said the reason for replacing Howe involved a little ridiculous matter with regard to a woman in South Carolina (Lawrence, "Capture" 313).

While Lincoln was on the way to assume control of the Southern Department, Howe went to Georgia to deal with threats from Tories and Indians. Lincoln arrived in Charleston a week before the British fleet reached Georgia.

As the British approached Savannah, Howe hoped that Lincoln would bring reinforcements from South Carolina. British commander Archibald Campbell understood the advantage of attacking Savannah before American reinforcements arrived, and kept the British force on the march toward town.

Howe called a council of war and abided by its decision to defend the city despite being outnumbered four to one. Howe arranged his small force in a defensive position protected by natural barriers. A lagoon separated Howe's position from the advancing British force. The marshes of the Savannah River secured Howe's left. A wooded swamp lay on his right. The town with its fortifications along the Savannah River sat behind him.

The American defenders included about 650 Continental troops, a hundred Georgia militiamen and a small artillery unit. General Isaac Huger commanded a brigade of South Carolina Continental troops stationed on the right wing of the American defensive position.

On the left wing, General Samuel Elbert commanded what remained of the Georgia brigade after a series of disastrous attempts to invade British East Florida (Lawrence, "Capture" 311).

An engineer achieves victory

The British commander devised a way to thwart the American defensive strategy, perhaps because he was an engineer by training. Campbell had started his military career as an ensign in the Royal Corps of Engineers during the Seven Years War. Then he had served as the chief engineer in Bengal for the British East India Company for seven years. He had rejoined the British army when the American Revolution began. At Savannah, he conducted a reconnaissance of the terrain and found a path through the swamp on the right of the American position.

British troops including the 71st Regiment held Howe's attention with a feint on his front lines. The British light infantry under Sir James Baird – who often "indulged the propensity of the Highlanders to close upon the enemy" (qtd. in Lawrence, "Capture" 307) – conducted a secret flanking movement.

An old Negro named Quamino Dolly led the light infantry through the swamp to the rear of the American defenses. Once Baird was in place, British artillery opened fire on the Georgia brigade. Campbell ordered a direct assault across the lagoon on the American front line. Baird's troops then attacked the Americans from the rear. Howe ordered the Americans to retreat. The South Carolina brigade moved out quickly and cleared the British flanking movement; Howe and a few hundred men eventually found refuge in South Carolina.

As the South Carolinians headed homeward, the Georgia brigade came under enemy fire and discovered that British troops had blocked the escape route. While Elbert sought an alternative route, many of the Georgians broke ranks and fled through the streets of Savannah.

The men who remained with Elbert became trapped between the British troops and the waters of Musgrove Creek at high tide. Elbert and a few followers escaped by swimming across the swollen creek, but most of the Georgians refused to go into the water. Major John Habersham, who could not swim, raised a white flag and the Georgians surrendered to Lieutenant Peter Campbell.

Aftermath of battle
Americans casualties were reported as 83 killed and 11 wounded in battle, 30 drowned while trying to escape, and 488 taken prisoner. On the British side, seven men were killed and nineteen were wounded.

Savannah historian Alexander Lawrence describes a "little vignette of Savannah's past" featuring a "Scottish chieftain in Yamacraw summoning the Highland clan about him:"

> ...Sir James Baird came up. Mounting a ladder placed against the side of the house, he blew upon his brass bugle horn whereupon his Highlanders gathered about him. He proceeded to address them in their Gaelic tongue. ...as soon as Baird finished, his men dispersed and resumed the plundering of such of the Americans as had not been searched already. ("Capture" 322)

A teenage girl who lived in Savannah at the time reported:

> ...the Americans as they retreated wantonly fired on the 71st Regiment of Highlanders, without attempting a regular stand. This exposed the inhabitants to the fury of the British soldiers, who then felt as though they were taking the place by storm. In consequence, before the officers could have time to stop them they committed much outrage, ripped open feather beds, destroyed the public papers and records, and scattered everything about the streets. Numbers of the enemy were taken in a swamp a few miles from Savannah. While Mr. Johnston was with his [loyalist] company in the pursuit he saw his father at his own door, and had only time to go up to Colonel Maitland [of the 71st Regiment] and request that he would put a guard at his father's house to secure his safety from the enraged troops, who knew not friend from foe. Colonel Maitland had been the early friend and college companion of my father-in-law Dr. Johnston, in Edinburgh, and meeting with his son at New York was like a father to him and did all he could to serve him. He, of course, placed a guard there.
>
> My father in a few days sent a passport for myself and my aunt to come to town. I was then in my fifteenth year,

and new to scenes of the kind, and having to stop within a mile of Savannah that the Hessian officer on duty there should examine our pass, I was dreadfully frightened. He soon allowed us to go on; and what a sight did the streets present of feathers and papers!

The meeting with my father I scarce need add was joyful… (Johnston 48-49).

Although the British commander reported that "few or no depredations occurred," other witnesses claimed that British soldiers stabbed defenseless Americans repeatedly with bayonets, stole property, destroyed public records, and smashed fine furniture (Lawrence, "Capture" 323-324).

Lawrence points out the crucial consequences of the capture of Savannah:

The battle fought that day was not a great one as battles go. Indeed, the main forces of the two armies never really came to grips. Casualties were small. Yet the results were to be far reaching. The victory restored the Province to George III in almost a single stroke. It all but obliterated Georgia's Continental establishment. It exposed the long under belly of Carolina to British invasion. The taking of Savannah was the first step in the train of events that followed – the capture of Charlestown, the overrunning of South Carolina and parts of North Carolina, and the three years of bloody civil war that ensued in those regions. ("Capture" 303-04)

McIntosh family trapped behind enemy lines

One consequence of the British capture of Savannah was that Lachlan McIntosh's house on St. James Square was plundered and his wife, two daughters, and three youngest sons found themselves living in territory ruled by the enemy (Lawrence, "Suspension" 122). Lachlan and Sarah McIntosh's youngest child Hampden was only 6 years old when the British occupied Savannah.

Captain Aeneas Mackintosh and Colonel John McIntosh op-
pose one another in the Battle of Brier Creek, a crucial contest in
the campaign to regain British reign over Georgia. Lachlan McIn-
tosh leads a relief expedition to Fort Laurens in the heart of Indian
territory on the western frontier. After returning to the South to
serve with American forces trying to regain control of Georgia,
Lachlan McIntosh frets over the safety of his own family inside
British-held Savannah. Alexander McDonald of Darien and Allen
McDonald of the Cross Creek country serve in the 2ⁿᵈ South Caro-
lina Regiment, which suffers heavy casualties in the assault on Sa-
vannah. Meanwhile, Captain Aeneas Mackintosh and Captain Ro-
derick McIntosh are among the British and loyalist forces defend-
ing Savannah against the American attack.

The British establish control over Georgia

Once Savannah was under British control, most of the residents of coastal Georgia came in and took an oath of allegiance to
the king. The commander of the forces that captured Savannah,
Lieutenant Colonel Archibald Campbell, organized the loyalists
into rifle and musket companies and dragoon squadrons. Henry
Lumpkin, author of *From Savannah to Yorktown: The American*
Revolution in the South, gives this evaluation of Campbell's ac-
complishments:

> In establishing the British position strongly in Georgia,
> Archibald Campbell proved to be an equitable and just
> conqueror. If he had remained in command, the war in the
> south might have had different and far more serious results
> for the American cause. Fortunately for the Americans, he
> was relieved and succeeded by less honorable, exemplary,
> and intelligent men. (29)

Major General Augustine Prevost, who had invaded from British East Florida late in 1778 and had laid waste to south Georgia
on his retreat, outranked the lieutenant colonel as overall commander of British and loyalist forces in Georgia and Florida. After

Campbell captured Savannah, Prevost sailed north with two thousand British soldiers, loyalists, and Indians.

The British capture Sunbury: January 1779

As Continental General Robert Howe fled from Georgia after the capture of Savannah, he ordered Major Joseph Lane to evacuate the American troops from Sunbury and join Howe at Zubly's crossing on the Savannah River. The citizens of Sunbury, however, persuaded Lane to remain at Fort Morris. As a result, Lane later was court-martialed for insubordination and was dismissed from military service.

A contingent of Prevost's troops landed at Colonel's Island below Sunbury on January 6. By this time, John McIntosh was no longer stationed at Fort Morris. Prevost debarked with his light infantry, circumvented Fort Morris, and captured the town of Sunbury on January 7. His main force arrived a day later. Three vessels sailed past Fort Morris despite heavy fire from the fort. The British unloaded artillery from the vessels and aimed the guns toward Fort Morris.

The next day Prevost demanded the unconditional surrender of the fort. Major Lane refused to surrender. The British artillery opened fire, and the guns of Fort Morris returned fire. Four Americans and one British soldier died in the fighting. Lane realized the fort could not survive the bombardment, and asked Prevost for better terms than unconditional surrender. Prevost refused to negotiate. On January 10, Lane surrendered the fort and its garrison of seventeen officers and 195 men.

The crews of two American naval vessels guarding Sunbury beached their galleys on Ossabaw Island and burned them. A third vessel, the armed sloop *Rebecca*, escaped to Charleston.

Thousands of destitute women and children fled Georgia. Sunbury never recovered from the exodus, and eventually became known as one of the dead towns of Georgia.

After capturing Sunbury, Prevost continued to Savannah to join forces with Campbell and take control of British operations in the South.

Rory McIntosh appointed captain of fort

The historical record indicates that Rory McIntosh's exploits at Sunbury took place during the second siege of Sunbury in January of 1779 rather than during the first siege two months previously. A British officer who was at Sunbury in January of 1779 mentioned Rory in a memoir:

> …Mr. Roderic Mackintosh accompanied by his faithful Negro Cyrus, disdaining the counsel of Cyrus, walked under the musketry of the Garrison, setting them at defiance, when they shot him down and disarmed him so quickly that Lieutenant Baron Breitenbach and Sergeant Supman of the 4th. Battalion Light Infantry who with alacrity ran to his rescue could only carry him in wounded in the face. As soon as our men seized him the Americans ceased firing…
>
> …a shell fell upon a building where the rebel officers messed, and killed and wounded 9 of them, and shattered about 50 stand of arms; upon which they proposed to capitulate; which being refused and 2 more shells falling into the fort, they hauled down their colours and surrendered at discretion… The Garrison with their Commander Major Lane embarked for Savannah… Lieutenant Colonel Allen was left at Sunbury with the Jersey Volunteers. Mr. Mackintosh was appointed Captain of the Fort, he lost the use of his eye. (Murray 310-11)

The British expand from base in Savannah

From their base in Savannah, British forces pursued a plan to extend control over Georgia and, eventually, the entire South.

The Americans responded by sending a force of about nine hundred North Carolinians to reinforce the army in South Carolina; the North Carolinians were led by Brigadier General John Ashe. Benjamin Lincoln, commanding the American forces in the South, marched from Charleston and set up camp at Purrysburg on the Savannah River early in January.

Across the river, British forces including the 71st Regiment marched from Savannah toward Augusta. About half way between Savannah and Augusta the route crosses Brier Creek, a tributary of the Savannah River. The light companies of the 71st Regiment reached Brier Creek on January 25 and defeated a party of militia attempting to burn the bridge. The British entered Augusta on January 31.

Feuding in Western Department

In an echo of his feuds on the southern frontier, General Lachlan McIntosh's tenure on the western frontier erupted in political rivalries among Virginians and Pennsylvanians along with personal resentment toward McIntosh. His chief critic, Indian agent Colonel George Morgan, referred to "the ignorant, absurd and contradictory conduct and orders of General McIntosh, throughout the whole campaign" (Kellogg 210). A settler who wanted McIntosh to be replaced by an officer with a record of accomplishment in the Western Department told Congress:

> ...But we will say the public has been at great Expense for two years past and we are no nearer now than we was when we first set out, but what is the Reason? it is because there was people sent that knew nothing of the Matter. The General told me that he was brought up by the Sea Shore, and that he knew nothing about Pack Horseing in this Wooden [wooded] Country... I think that ought to be enquired into before there was thousands spent, but now it is too late to recall. The Horses & Bullocks are dead, the provisions is eat, the Men must have their Pay it is sunk, lost gone, & here we are still going on in the same way. The General has likewise got the Ill Will of all his Officers, the Militia in protickaler which I am very sorry for as they are the only people that We have to depend upon to do any thing in this Department. (Kellogg 208-09)

A high-ranking officer under McIntosh's command, Colonel Daniel Brodhead, brought complaints about McIntosh to the attention of Commander in Chief George Washington in a letter dated January 16, 1779:

> Nothing but a love for my Country brought me into the Service and the same principle makes me ever anxious for its good.
>
> I trust I shall utter nothing that has the least appearance of detraction & will not even mention particulars But beg leave only to inform your Excellency that General McIntosh is unfortunate enough to be almost universally Hated by every man in this department, both Civil & Military.

Therefore whatever his Capacity may be for conducting another Campaign, I fear he will not have it in his Power to do any thing Salutary – I wish my fears may prove Groundless but I have no reason to think them so.

There is not an Officer who does not appear to be exceedingly disgusted, and I am much deceived if they serve under his immediate Command another Campaign. I am ever oblidged to your Excellency for offering me another Reg^t last Spring & I am sorry I did not accept it. (Kellogg 200)

Washington waited nearly a month before sending a noncommittal, politically astute reply to Brodhead:

I have received your letter of the 16th Ult^o Its contents give me that concern which ever arises in my mind from any indication of a want of that harmony and mutual confidence between officers, which the public interest requires.

As it is my duty to remedy every abuse of which I am authorized to take cognizance – if any charge were brought against General McIntosh I should immediately give it proper attention. But a moments reflexion will make you sensible that your general assertion and opinion with regard to the dissatisfaction of his officers is by no means a foundation for any measures on my part respecting him, that will either convey or imply censure.

Impartial Justice as well as that delicate regard which is due to the character of an officer, and which you and everyone in a similar case would expect, requires something more positive and definite to proceed upon.

If there are discontents among the officers – the motives of them must be known before their merits can be judged of and they alone can furnish grounds for an investigation.

The sole reason for appointing General McIntosh to his present command was an opinion of his being in every view qualified for it, and I must observe that while the General was immediately under me, his conduct gave the most favorable impressions of him in every respect.

I have only to add that the honorable the Congress having put this command immediately under my direction, and thereby created a degree of responsibility in me, I am particularly called upon to watch over its success.

And as it is my duty and wish on the one hand to redress every just complaint – so it will be expected of me on the other to discountenance every ill founded uneasiness that may prejudice the service.

Upon the whole it is my earnest desire that every one will as far as depends on him – cultivate and promote that good understanding, which is indispensable to the general interest.

And I entreat that you will do all in your power to accomplish this desirable end. (Kellogg 230-31)

Dire straits at Fort Laurens

The garrison of Fort Laurens on the western frontier suffered from harsh January weather, incessant danger from Indians allied with the British, and inadequate supplies. The commander of the fort, Colonel John Gibson, informed Lachlan McIntosh "the Weather has been very Cold and the Rivers very high... unless a Supply of Cloathing soon Arrives, I shall not have fifty men fit for duty in a short time, which are by no means Adequate" (Kellogg 190).

The soldiers nicknamed the post "Fort Nonsense." A letter written by a soldier inside the relative safety of Fort McIntosh on January 29 reports:

Last night there was Two Indians Come in with an Express from fort Noncence which informed us that Capt. Clark of our Reg[t] and the Men that was Left there was Comeing Home to Join there Reg[t] was Atacted on the Road within Two Miles of Tuskeyraways & had two Killed on the spot And four wounded & one a Missing the[y] fought them till the[y] was Reinforced from the fort and then to Return with the party Back Again there is know Account of any of the Indians Being killed as I Can Lerern... But wright to me any opertunity & tell me how Afares goes on their gave My Love to the family & Inquireing friend & well wishers But in Particular to the prity Girls. (Williams 162-63)

General McIntosh reported the same incident to Colonel Archibald Lochry, who helped defend the Pennsylvania frontier throughout the Revolution:

> I am just informed that Capt. Clark, of the 8th Pennsylvania Regiment who was sent to command an escort to Fort Laurens as he was returning with a sergeant & 14 men, three miles this side of that post, was attacked by Simon Girty, & a party of Mingoes, who killed two of our men, wounded four, and took one prisoner.
>
> I am also informed that a large party of the same people are set off to strike the inhabitants about Ligonier & Black Leg Creek, and send you this express to inform you of it, that you may acquaint the neighborhood and be upon your guard. (Kellogg 210)

Action at Port Royal: February 3, 1779

With coastal Georgia under their control, the British made plans to march into South Carolina. A detachment of British and Provincial soldiers from the Savannah garrison made an amphibious landing at Port Royal Island, South Carolina, to establish an advanced base. A British naval squadron supported the detachment. General William Moultrie and Brigadier General Stephen Bull brought the Beaufort militia and other American troops across the saltwater streams surrounding the island to thwart the British operation. Two of the American companies were led by signers of the Declaration of Independence, Thomas Heyward and Edward Rutledge. Three hundred Americans drove three hundred British from their beachhead on February 3.

The Battle of Kettle Creek: February 14, 1779

British General Augustine Prevost sent two hundred mounted infantry under Colonel John Hamilton, a loyalist, toward Augusta to encourage loyalists and potential loyalists to support the British cause. Loyalists from North Carolina led by Colonel James Boyd intended to join Hamilton at the Savannah River. The Americans countered with five hundred militiamen from Georgia and South Carolina commanded by Colonel Andrew Pickens, known as the fighting Presbyterian elder. Boyd and Pickens had known each other before the war.

Pickens' men attacked Boyd's men at Kettle Creek, Georgia, on February 14. During an hour of sharp fighting, forty loyalists were killed, seventy were captured, and the rest were scattered.

Boyd suffered a mortal wound. When Pickens told Boyd he was sorry to see him suffering, Boyd said he proudly gave his life for his king. Boyd handed Pickens a brooch he had been wearing and asked Pickens to take it to Boyd's wife. Boyd also asked that two men stay with him until he died. Pickens demonstrated his integrity by honoring both requests.

The seventy loyalists who were captured were later tried for treason and convicted. Five were hanged and the others were pardoned.

American forces gather at Savannah River

The American commander in the South, Benjamin Lincoln, countered British maneuvers along the Georgia side of the Savannah River by sending a force to the South Carolina side of the river opposite Augusta. The force, which slightly outnumbered the British in Augusta, consisted of Continental troops from North Carolina, Georgia troops under Colonel Samuel Elbert, and militiamen.

The commander of the force was General John Ashe of North Carolina. Three years earlier, Ashe had participated in a fight at Moore's Creek Bridge near Wilmington, North Carolina, against a loyalist force of immigrants from the Scottish Highlands; the immigrant community included Flory McDonald, who had aided Bonnie Prince Charlie after the Battle of Culloden in Scotland in 1746.

Sergeant MacAlister cruelly killed

While the British held Augusta, Sergeant Hugh MacAlister of the 71st Regiment was stationed at the home of a patriot officer who was a prisoner of war. MacAlister's chief duty was to protect the patriot from reprisals by local loyalists. A party of patriots shot MacAlister and cut up his dead body with hatchets.

Colonel Campbell, the British commander at Augusta, reported in his journal: "The British Troops... were greatly exasperated by this shameful Act of Injustice; especially the Light Infantry, who had determined to revenge MacAlister's Murder on the first favourable Occasion" (Campbell 58).

On February 13, Campbell withdrew the British troops from Augusta and marched back toward Savannah.

Attacks directed at Fort Laurens

On the western frontier, British officials at their headquarters in Detroit directed attacks against American outposts. Loyalists and Indian allies sporadically besiege Fort Laurens, the westernmost fort constructed by Lachlan McIntosh in his role as commander of the Western Department of the Continental Army. The 150-man garrison at Fort Laurens under the command of Colonel John Gibson faced not only enemy warriors but also harsh wintry weather, the threat of starvation, and a debilitating lack of shoes and clothing.

McIntosh made plans to send supplies by boat to the desperate men at Fort Laurens in the heart of Indian territory. On February 8 he instructed Major Richard Taylor to transport two hundred kegs of flour from Fort Pitt, fifty barrels of beef and pork from posts at Wheeling and Beaver Creek, "as much whiskey as the Commissary of Issues can spare, some medicines from the Surgeon of the Hospital, and a Black smith with his Tools, and some Iron and steel for the use of that Garrison, with any other articles, which you know them to stand in need of." McIntosh added a personal note to Taylor: "As your health and private affairs required your Going home and this necessary business, has disapointed you now, You have leave of absence for three Months when you return here again, provided the situation of our affairs then will admit of it. I wish you Success" (Kellogg 221).

With no way of knowing that supplies were on the way, Gibson wrote letter to McIntosh dated February 13 begging for relief at Fort Laurens:

> Recommend sending, if not a reinforcement, a supply of provisions and other stores, without delay to this place. You may depend on my defending it to the last extremity, and of my care to prevent surprise. The officers and men here think it is rather hard they should be curtailed in their rations when the troops at the interior posts draw full ra-

tions. I am not the least afraid they will forsake me, let what will happen. (Kellogg 226)

John McIntosh attacks British garrison

In the South, troops from Georgia and South Carolina under Colonel John McIntosh, Colonel Leroy Hammond and Colonel John Twiggs tried to delay British troops returning toward Savannah after pulling out of Augusta. The patriot troops killed or captured most of the small British garrison at Herbert's on the Savannah River (Davis, *Georgians* 90).

Cannon falls into Brier Creek

The British force leaving Augusta detoured to reach a party of loyalists and crossed Brier Creek on a pontoon bridge at Odom's Ferry. General William Moultrie, who was downstream on the Savannah River at Purrysburg at the time, described the situation in a letter dated February 27, 1779:

> … the enemy retreated so precipitately from Augusta, as to leave twelve beef killed and skinned upon the ground;… a panic seized them, and they pushed for Brier-creek, which they accomplished before our horsemen could destroy the bridge, and they passed it, they burnt it down to prevent our pursuit, they lost one field-piece in crossing, by the boat sinking: Gen. Ash has sent to have it taken up and brought to his camp… (Moultrie 317-18)

American army camps at Brier Creek

With the crossing at Augusta uncontested, Continental General John Ashe led his force across the Savannah River and marched down the River Road to Brier Creek at its junction with the river. The army of about 1,200 men camped near one of the bridges that had been destroyed and waited from February 27 until March 3 for reinforcements to arrive. Ashe complained that only 207 mounted soldiers from South Carolina joined him, and only 150 of them were fit for duty. Ashe had General Bryan's brigade of nine hundred men, Lieutenant Lytle's light infantry of about two hundred fit for duty, about seventy Georgia Continental troops, a four-pound field piece and two two-pound swivels mounted as field pieces.

On the other side of the Savannah River, Major John Grimke's South Carolina artillery and General Rutherford's North Carolina regiment of 700 infantry arrived at Matthews Bluff. The American plan called for them to cross the river and march three miles to General Ashe's camp. Fifty men began building bridges and clearing a road across the swamp to Ashe's camp, but they did not complete the job in time for the plan to work.

The Battle of Brier Creek: March 3, 1779

After the British withdrew from Augusta, they stopped at Hudson's Ferry. While there, Colonel Archibald Campbell received permission to go to England for reassignment. He turned over command of the campaign to James Marc Prevost, a brother of General Augustine Prevost, who was the British commander in Georgia. Before leaving, Campbell suggested that Prevost maneuver around Ashe's camp and launch a surprise attack.

On March 2, nearly four hundred men of the 1st Battalion of the 71st Regiment took a position across Brier Creek from the Americans. The battalion commander was Major Duncan McPherson, the 19th Chief of Clan McPherson. While the Americans watched that battalion, a force of nine hundred men made a fifty-mile march to come around behind the Americans. This force included the 2nd Battalion of the 71st Regiment – Aeneas Mackintosh's unit – under the command of Colonel John Maitland. About forty men of the 71st formed a dragoon company using cavalry equipment seized in Savannah. Sir James Baird, a Scottish baron, commanded two companies of light infantry. The force also included three companies of elite troops of the 60th Regiment, and fifty men of the Florida Rangers. The force crossed Brier Creek at Paris Mills, upstream of Ashe's army. The maneuver bottled up Ashe's army between Brier Creek, the Savannah River and the British force.

The British force attacked the American camp on March 3. Captain Baird's light infantry faced the American left flank along the Brier Creek swamp. The 2nd Battalion of the 71st occupied the center. North Carolina provincials and Florida Rangers faced the American right flank. Fifty loyalist riflemen took position to shoot down patriots attempting to flee toward the Savannah River. The grenadiers of the 60th Regiment and dragoons led by Thomas

Trawse were held in reserve. Prevost placed his five artillery pieces in the center, to the rear of the 2nd Battalion of the 71st.

The British advance took the Americans by surprise. As the Americans scrambled to take defensive positions, the British infantry advanced at the quick step and the British artillery opened fire. The confused Americans deployed with North Carolina militia from New Bern on the left beside Brier Creek, North Carolina militia from Edenton to the right toward the Savannah River swamp, and Georgia Continentals stationed between the North Carolina militia units. North Carolina militia from Halifax and Wilmington formed the second line.

The Georgia Continentals fired two volleys, and the British returned fire. Then, according to Ashe, the Georgians "advanced without orders a few steps beyond the line and moved to the left in front of the regiment from the district of New Bern, which much impeded their firing" (Heidler 328). The militia from Edenton moved slightly to the right. The combined movements of the Georgians to the left and the North Carolinians to the right created a gap in the American line. In the tradition of their Highlander forebears, the troops in the center of the British line launched a bayonet charge into the gap. Many of the American militiamen ran away without firing a shot. The Wilmington men and some of the New Bern men fired a few volleys and stood their ground waiting for reinforcements. The militia unit from Edenton fled from the British bayonets, and the rest of the North Carolina militia panicked and joined the flight (Heidler 328-29).

The battle gave the Highlanders of the 71st Regiment an occasion to avenge the death of Hugh MacAlister, the sergeant whose body had been hacked with hatchets in Augusta. Campbell, who received second-hand accounts of the battle, wrote in his journal: "...when the Light Infantry were running up in Line to charge the Rebels, one of the Highlanders called out – *Now my Boys, remember poor Macalister:* in Consequence of which, this Corps spared very few that came within their Reach" (Campbell 77).

John McIntosh taken prisoner

While the other Americans fled, Colonel Samuel Elbert and Lieutenant Colonel John McIntosh motivated a band of Continental troops and Georgia militia to keep fighting until they were killed, wounded, or captured. Legend has it that both Elbert and

McIntosh were spared through the last-minute intervention of British officers:

> The only ray of light that shone through the darkness of this sad defeat was shed by the bravery of Col. Elbert and his command. He fought until he was struck down, and he was on the point of being killed by a soldier with uplifted bayonet when he made the masonic sign of distress. An officer noticed it, responded instantly, stayed the soldier's arm, and saved Col. Elbert's life. As a prisoner on parole, in the British camp, he was treated with great respect and kindness. Honor and reward were promised him if he would join the British, but all such offers were promptly rejected.
>
> Col. McIntosh, the hero of Fort Morris, had stood his ground with Col. Elbert until nearly every man was killed, and then he was captured. As he was surrendering his sword, a British officer tried to kill him; and he was saved by the timely interference of his kinsman, Sir Aeneas McIntosh, of the British army. (Mitchell 75)

Americans flee through swamp

The entire battle lasted only about fifteen minutes, and most of the Americans fled within five minutes after the initial attack. When he realized the battle was lost, Ashe rode away from the battlefield, crossed the Savannah River in a rowboat and found refuge at Matthews Bluff.

The fleeing men were hemmed in by the confluence of the Savannah River and Brier Creek. Between fifty and one hundred men drowned. James Fergus, an American of Scotch-Irish descent, later submitted a pension application that described the desperate struggle:

> General Ashe rode a good horse, left his men, and got round the enemy and made to a ferry above, crossed, and escaped, while the rest of us were drove into the swamp between the creek and the river. The banks of these were so steep and deep that the horses that went in could not get out again, and some men would have been drowned had not canes been put into their hands and helped them out. We now got into a thick canebreak, and the enemy pursued us

no farther. This was late in the evening. Twelve of us got together, and, as it was moonlight in the night, we formed a small raft of driftwood in the mouth of a lagoon, on which three of us with danger and much difficulty got over the river, after being carried above a mile down before we landed (Dann 181).

As night fell on the battleground, the Highlanders set fires to flush out Americans hiding in the underbrush. Americans who were wounded too badly to flee perished in the fire (Howard 496).

The Americans who had not been captured or killed continued to suffer in the swamps. James Fergus, who had floated across the Savannah River during the night, recalled their plight:

We got out of the bottom and wandered up the river till daylight, and fortunately, in the mouth of a branch, we found a large periauger loaded with corn in the ear. Opposite to us on the other bank we discovered a great number of the North Carolina men. We quickly rowed over and took in as many as the boat would bear and caused them to throw out the corn while we crossed back. By this means we got all our men that were there off before the enemy came down to the river. …the next day the remains of our detachment got together and moved up the river to General Williamson's camp and joined the troops there. Many of our men were half-naked, having stripped to swim the river. The third of March we were defeated, and that night there was a light frost, and many suffered in the cold, having nothing on but a shirt or breeches. Here we lay, I know not how long (Dann 181).

American casualties were estimated from 150 to two hundred either killed in battle or drowned. One British officer and five privates died in the battle, and ten British soldiers suffered wounds.

Archibald Campbell – the commander of the 71st Regiment who had captured Savannah and had suggested the strategy for defeating General Ashe – left for England on March 12.

Americans lament loss

General William Moultrie of South Carolina wrote in his memoirs:

This unlucky affair at Brier-Creek, disconcerted all our plans, and through the misfortunes of Gen. Howe and Ash, the war was protracted at least one year longer, for it is not to be doubted that had we have crossed the river with our army, and joined Gen. Ash, which we were preparing to do, we should have had a body of 7,000 men; besides strong reinforcements were marching to us from every quarter sufficient to drive the enemy out of Georgia; and all the wavering, and all the disaffected would have immediately joined us; and it is more than probable that Carolina would not have been invaded, had this event taken place. (326)

Historian William Bacon Stevens of Georgia points out that Ashe commanded at Brier Creek only because Lachlan McIntosh had left Georgia for assignments in the North:

How unfortunate it was for Georgia that she should have had in her armies as her defenders such men as Howe and Ash, men totally incapacitated for the responsible duties, and whose errors and cowardice brought disgrace and ruin upon the State. Had not the wretched spirit of faction driven McIntosh from our borders, a different story might have been told of the British operations in Georgia.

The defeat of General Ash was very beneficial to the English. It opened to them the upper and back parts of the country and put them in connection with the Indian tribes; and their boast was that fourteen hundred of the inhabitants of these districts had given their adhesion to the crown, and had organized themselves into twenty companies of militia for the defence of their property against the incursions of the rebels from South Carolina.

To the Americans it was peculiarly disastrous. The well-laid plans of General Lincoln were thwarted, the spirit of the people depressed, and the gathering reinforcements of militia dispersed to their homes, more than ever impressed with the prowess of the British arms, and the hopelessness of the American cause. (197-98)

The British victory at Brier Creek completed the conquest of Georgia. On the day after the battle, British officials declared that Georgia was once again a royal colony. The victorious commander at Brier Creek, James Marc Prevost, took office as lieutenant governor of the colony.

Lachlan McIntosh calls on militia in emergency

From the Western Department headquarters at Fort Pitt, General Lachlan McIntosh sent George Washington a report dated March 12 on the situation at Fort Laurens:

> ... I am sorry to inform you, that contrary to my expectations, things have taken a turn here much for the worse, since I wrote you the 13th of January. The 30th of that month I rec[d] an express from Col Gibson, informing me that one Simon Girty, a renegade among many others found in this place, got a small party of Mingoes, a name by which the Six Nations, or rather Seneca Tribe, is known among the Western Indians and waylaid Capt. Clark of the 8th P[a] Reg[t] with a seargent and 14 privates, about three miles this side of Fort Laurens, as they were returning after escorting a few supplies from that post, and made Clark retreat to the fort again after killing two and taking one of his men with his saddle bags and all his letters.
>
> Upon hearing this unexpected intelligence, I immediately sent for Cols. Crawford and Brodhead to advise with them upon the best method of supplying that garrison with provisions, of which it was very short, and we had barely horses enough fit for service to transport a sufficient quantity of flour over the Mountains for our daily consumption, and scarce of forage for them, altho' thye were most worn down. It was therefore, thought most eligible upon that and other accounts to send a supply by water up Muskingum river by Maj. Taylor, who was charged with that duty. * * *
>
> The 26th of February a scalping party killed and carried off 18 persons, men, women, and children, upon the branches of Turtle Creek, 20 miles east of this, upon the Pennsylvania road, which was the first mischief done in the settlements since I marched for Tuscarawas, and made me apprehensive now that the savages were all inimically inclined, and struck

the inhabitants of Westmoreland with such a panick that the great part of them were moving away. While I was endeavoring to rouse the militia, and contriving by their assistance to retaliate, and make an excursion to some Mingo Towns upon the branches of Alleghany river who were supposed to have done the mischief, a messenger came to me the 3rd of March instant, who slipt out of Fort Laurens in the night of Sunday the 28th February – by whom Col^o Gibson would not venture to write, and informed me that the morning of Tuesday, the 23rd February, a waggoner who was sent out of the Fort for the horses to draw wood, and 18 men to guard him, were fired upon, and all killed and scalped in sight of the Fort, which the messenger left invested and besieged by a number of Wyandotts, Chippewas, Delawares &c.; and in the last account I had from them, which made me very unhappy, as they were so short of provision, and out of my power to supply them with any quantity, or, if I had it, with men for an escort, since Major Taylor went, who I thought now was inevitably lost; and if I had both, there were no horses to carry it, or forage to feed them, without which they cannot subsist at this season.

In this extreme emergency and difficulty, I earnestly requested the Lieutenants of the several countys on this side of the Mountains to collect all of the men, horses, provision and forage they could at any price, and repair to Beaver Creek [Fort McIntosh] on Monday next, the 15th instant, in order to march on that or the next day to Tuscarawas, and if they would not be prevailed on to turn out, I was determined with such of the Continental troops as are able to march, and all the provisions we have, at all events to go to the relief of Fort Laurens, upon the support of which I think the salvation of this part of the country depends.

I have yet no intelligence from the country, that I can depend on. Some say the people will turn out on this occasion with their horses; others, that mischievous persons influenced by our disgusted staff are discouraging them as much as possible. But I am now happily relieved by the arrival of Maj^r Taylor here, who returned with 100 men and 200 kegs of flour. He was six days going up about 20 miles of Muskingum River, the waters were so high and stream so rapid;

and as he had above 130 miles more to go, he judged it impossible to relieve Col. Gibson in time, and therefore returned, having lost two of his men sent to flank him upon the shore, who were killed and scalpt by some warriors coming down Muskingum river, and I have my doubts of our only pretended friends, the Delawares of Cooshocking, as none other are settled upon that water.

I have the honor to enclose you the last return from Col. Brodhead at Beaver Creek. (Kellogg 240-242)

Lachlan McIntosh postpones personal business

The emergency at Fort Laurens required McIntosh to postpone two undertakings that were deeply important to him personally. One was responding to complaints "in which I felt my reputation deeply concerned" being considered by Congress in Philadelphia. In a letter to his friend Henry Laurens dated March 13, 1779, he provided the same information he had given to Washington – but with a stronger tone of personal anguish – and slipped in a few comments about the political feud engulfing the Western Department:

> I had expected to have set off for Philadelphia before this time, but wishing to leave this Department in as good order as possible, and having some disagreeable intelligence, and unexpectedly, from Fort Laurens, determined me to wait the event...
>
> That garrison, so important to the Department, was unfortunately left short of provisions through the neglect of our Staff, which by some means the Indians must have been made acquaintance with. When I got flour over the mountains, the height of the waters, and scarcity of horses and forage, without which they cannot live in this season, obliged me to attempt sending a supply by water up the Muskingum, under the direction of Major Taylor. After he was gone, was informed by express from Col^o Gibson, which he slipt our of his Fort in the night, that on the 23^d February he sent out a waggoner for the horses and 18 men to guard them, who were all killed & scalped in their sight, and the express left the Fort besieged and invested by a great number of Wyandotts, Chippewas, Delawares &c

which gave me infinite concern on account of Taylor as well as Gibson, being out of my power to help either of them – and to add to it, all the discontented joined immediately in condemning the executing it, as much as they approved of it before, and particularly that poor Taylor was designedly sacrificed. And as he had 100 men with him & 200 Kegs of flour, which was all I had to spare, I had no other alternative left than calling on the militia for men, horses, forage and provision, but was at a loss in what manner. To press horses, &c would displease them, and give our staff a handle. To wait the tedious formality of draughting the men, &c as their laws direct, would take up too much time, and be too late for Gibson's necessity. Therefore I earnestly entreated the Lieutenants of the several counties to get as many men as they could voluntarily, with all the horses, provisions, & forage they could bring, at any price, and to be at Beaver Creek on Monday, the 15th instant, without fail, as later would be needless. I put them in mind of their continual boasts & desire of seeing the enemy who had repeatedly done them so much mischief to be revenged; that we could have no other chance of them equal to their being thus collected together, and would be far better to attack them in their own country than suffer them to come into our settlements. I urged the importance of Fort Laurens as a bridle to keep the Savages in their own country, as well as to facilitate our future operations. If they succeeded in taking, or they obliged us to evacuate it, they would impute it to our weakness, and unite to a man in routing all the inhabitants upon this side of the Mountains, and if we turned out cheerfully for once on this occasion to give them a scourging, and disappoint their first attempt, our business would be done in one stroke, the savages would see our superiority, and be obliged to treat on our terms, or remain on the other side of the Lakes, and leave all on this side to ourselves, as their towns would be exposed at all times to excursions from Fort Laurens.

I am informed from the country all these arguments will not prevail, nor the loss of so many of our brave country men, who suffer for the protection of this very people themselves. If it is so, I must attempt at all events with the few Continental troops I can make out, to save our brethren and fellow citizens, if I should be obliged for want of assistance or provision to evacuate that post... (Kellogg 249-51)

The other, and more distressing, personal matter involved the safety of Lachlan McIntosh's wife and younger children, who had been behind enemy lines since the British had conquered coastal Georgia. In his March 13 letter to Laurens, McIntosh said that he had just learned that his family in Savannah was trapped behind enemy lines. Perhaps because McIntosh and Laurens were partners in several business enterprises along the Georgia coast, McIntosh noted in his letter to Laurens that all of his property was under enemy control. Although McIntosh expressed a desire to be in the South to help his family, duty required him to respond to the emergency in the West (Kellogg 251).

Fort Laurens endures siege
A captain stationed at Fort Laurens later told a chronicler about his experiences. From his description it seems that unattended horses were equipped with bells so that the soldiers could find them in the forest:

He wished permission to go out with a party to get some horses the Indians had stolen, this Gibson peremptorily refused. "No, sir, attend to your command, when I want you I will tell you so." A party did go out – 16 in all – they heard what they thought were the bells in the bushes, thus decoyed by the Indians, and all, save one cut off * * * The siege lasted some 4 weeks, provisions exhausted; finally for 3 or 4 days had to live on *half* a biscuit a day -- then the last two days washed their moccasons and broiled them for food, and broiled strips of old dried hides. Two of the men in the fort stole out and killed a deer; and when they returned with it, it was devoured in a few minutes, some not waiting to cook it. (Kellogg 256-57)

Lachlan McIntosh leads relief mission
Lachlan McIntosh personally led a cross-country dash to Fort Laurens. He told George Washington of the mission in a letter dated March 19 at Fort McIntosh:

Sir:

I am just setting off for Fort Laurens with about two
hundred men I have collected of the militia, and better than
300 Continental troops from this garrison and Fort Pitt, but
unfortunately have not collected horses enough to carry the
quantity of provision I intended or would be necessary, and
as the time will not admit of an hour's delay to wait for any
more, I consulted the principal men from each county, with
all the field officers, who are unanimously of opinion that
Fort Laurens is a post of such consequence, that it should
not be evacuated by any means, if it can possibly be kept,
and that it may be defended by 100 men, if provisions cannot be carried for more. And indeed we are scarce enough
of it here – not above one month's provisions this side of
the mountains. The difficulty of getting it over, and the distance of carriage, is the grand objection to every enterprise
from this quarter.

I have thought it necessary to leave Col. Brodhead on
that account here, and use every exertion in getting further
supplies soon. Maj^r Taylor also is ordered down the country
for the same purpose, and to hurry the staff departments,
lest they disappoint us, and nothing can be had on this side.

I had some intelligence last night from Cooshocking,
which I have desired the Colonel to give you the particulars
of, as I have not time. It appears the Savages are all combined against us. (Kellogg 256).

Before the relief mission reached Fort Laurens, the siege had
been lifted. In a letter to "Brother McIntosh," Captain John Kill-
buck took credit for persuading the enemy to leave:

When I had heard some days ago that a large body of Warriors were going up the Tuscarawas to take that Garrison, I
immediately sent some of my wise Men to meet them, in
order to stop them from doing any mischief. These Men
with the help of those whom I had sent to that post some
time ago, had after much trouble and by frequent Speeches
to them the good luck in turning said Warriors back again.
(Kellogg 248)

When McIntosh's relief column arrived at Fort Laurens, the famished men inside the fort celebrated noisily, with the consequence of turning their brief sense of salvation into yet another cause for dismay. A soldier stationed at Fort Laurens and a soldier serving in the relief column later described the event from each point of view:

> … At length, the Indians left, and a convoy of packhorses arrived, guns fired for joy, horses scared, and run off scattering flour &c. This was gathered, and so incautious were many of the men that several made themselves sick with overloading their weak stomachs, and 3 died in consequence... (Kellogg 257)

> … I was an eye witness to the destruction of the provisions, when Gen[l] McIntosh arrived in view of the fort. It was late in the evening, when it happened, a great part of the flour was lost, a considerable part of next day was spent hunting horses, and the day following the troops Marched for fort M[c]Intosh, Maj[r] Vernon left to command the fort... (Kellogg 257)

McIntosh reported to Washington that the march out from Fort McIntosh to Fort Laurens took just over three days, but the march home took six days because the men and horses were so tired (Kellogg 270).

A publication of the Wisconsin Historical Society describes the siege of Fort Laurens, the relief expedition, and political squabbling among American officials on the western frontier:

> Meanwhile the [British] authorities at Detroit were making strenuous efforts to capture this handful of Americans defiantly planted in the heart of the Indian territory. Capt. Henry Bird was sent with a few British regulars to take post at Sandusky, there to stimulate successive attacks on the offending garrison. Bird carried with him large supplies of Indian goods and ammunition, and organized a party that laid siege to Fort Laurens and rendered Gibson's position desperate. A member of the garrison succeeded in stealthily

slipping out by night and hastened to Fort McIntosh to report the condition of the besieged. Gathering a relief party, the General marched out to Fort Laurens in three days, only to find that the besiegers had departed, leaving the garrison on the verge of exhaustion. The joy at McIntosh's arrival was marred by a stampede of the packhorses, which scattered through the woods the flour that had been taken to feed the starving men. (Kellogg 25)

…McIntosh, after the relief of Fort Laurens, was firmly resolved to push on at least to Sandusky and there establish the third in his chain of posts as a preliminary to a farther invasion of the enemy's territory…

But jealousy, lack of subordination in McIntosh's division, and the impossibility of coordination between the different expeditions [George Rogers Clark was on a separate expedition on the western frontier during the time of the McIntosh expedition] ruined this fair prospect. Col. George Morgan, who had arrived at Fort Pitt in early January, stirred the lurking dissatisfaction with McIntosh into severe opposition. As former Indian agent, Morgan persuaded the Delawares that they had been wronged by the treaty of 1778, and encouraged them to carry their protests to Congress in person. Morgan's friends and well-wishers in McIntosh's army opposed any farther advance, alleging difficulties which the latter's ignorance of the region rendered him unable to combat.

So in sadness and disappointment the General retired from Fort Laurens, taking with him the worn garrison of Gibson and leaving in its place a hundred fresher troops under command of Maj. Frederick Vernon of the Pennsylvania line. (Kellogg 26-27)

Violence lurks at Fort Laurens

The men of the new garrison at Fort Laurens did not suffer as much as the men of the first garrison, but they did experience some hostilities. The new commander at the post, Major Frederick Vernon, reported to McIntosh on March 28:

This morning I sent out a party of about forty men commanded by Ensigns Wiatt and Clark to bring in wood for the garrison. As Ensign Clark was placing the last centinel, he was fired on by a party of Indians (that lay concealed some small distance beyond where the centinel was placed), they killed him and the centinel, and scalped them, before the party could come to their assistance, as the greatest part of the men had got their loads and were on their way to the Fort. What few men had not got their loads up ran towards the Fort, expecting there was a large party of Indians. When this happened Mr Wiatt had not got up with his party as far as Mr Clark was. I immediately sent out three Indians to make a discovery how large the party was. They returned in a short time, and told me that party was not large, but they had discovered a number of tracks on the point of a ridge some small distance from where the Indians were that did the mischief. From their account, I think there were more parties than one. (Kellogg 263-64)

Lachlan McIntosh transfers to South

Lachlan McIntosh's feud with the Gwinnett faction in Georgia followed by his feud with factions in the West affected his appearance so much that an acquaintance who passed him on the street in the spring of 1779 did not recognize him (Lawrence, "Suspension" 121). McIntosh settled his feud in the West in roughly the same way he escaped his feud in Georgia; he requested a transfer to another military department. Congress had granted his request in a resolution dated February 20, 1779, and Washington had appointed Brodhead to succeed McIntosh in a letter dated March 5, but the letter did not reach Brodhead until weeks later (Kellogg 233, 238, 271).

A Wisconsin historian reports on the feud in the West:

> ... the representation of McIntosh's inefficiency made to Washington by the officers' clique had done their work, and his recall was determined upon. News from Georgia of a British invasion and his family's peril, as well as discouragement with western conditions, made the recall seem to the General a release from an intolerable situation. Nevertheless, stung by the misrepresentations of his conduct during the campaign, after his return to the main army he requested an official investigation. In view of the difficulty of

securing the attendance of witnesses from Pittsburgh and the need for his services in the South, McIntosh reluctantly abandoned the opportunity for exoneration, therein showing both good judgment and patriotism. (Kellogg 27)

... The question of McIntosh's successor agitated the advisers of Washington, who, nevertheless, decided that the only practicable thing was to choose one of the colonels then upon the Ohio frontier. To conciliate Pennsylvania interests Col. Daniel Brodhead was chosen, and on April 5, 1779, received notice of his appointment. Immediately McIntosh turned over the command to his successor and left for Philadelphia after but eight months active service on the western border. (Kellogg 28)

Although some officers who served with McIntosh were critical of him, others such as Lieutenant Colonel Benjamin Harrison supported him. McIntosh supplied a list of more than twenty witnesses on his behalf, including "Col^o John Gibson – Lt Col^o Campbell – Major Taylor with all the Officers of the 9th Virg^a & most of the 8th Pen^a" (Kellogg 330).

George Washington told Congress on May 11, "General McIntosh's conduct, while he acted immediately under my observation was such as to acquire my esteem and confidence; I have had no reason since to alter my good opinion" (Jackson 84).

"I wish matters had been more prosperously conducted under the command of Genl. McIntosh," Washington told Gouverneur Morris, "but during the time of his residence at Valley forge I had imbibed a good opinion of his good sense – attention to duty, and disposition to correct public abuse, qualifications much to be valued in a separate & distant command" (Kellogg 261-62).

A Pennsylvania historian concludes, "Long range appraisal of all the evidence available has vindicated McIntosh's military acumen and the wisdom of his policy. He has been vindicated in other ways from a stigma that attached to him and seemed never to have been dispelled during his lifetime" (Williams 162).

Armies on the march

In South Carolina and Georgia, American forces tried to regroup after the debacle at Brier Creek. British forces, meanwhile, tried to expand their control across the region. Continental General

Benjamin Lincoln prepared to attack the British forces in the Georgia backcountry. Lincoln led most of his army up the Savannah River and reached Augusta on April 22. A detachment under General William Moultrie stayed behind at Black Swamp to guard coastal South Carolina. Lieutenant Colonel Alexander McIntosh commanded a small force at the strategic location of Purrysburg on the Savannah River (Migliazzo 273).

The British commander in Georgia, Major General Augustine Prevost, took advantage of Lincoln's absence by invading South Carolina. When a few hundred British troops crossed the river at Purrysburg on April 29, Alexander McIntosh and his force fell back to Coosawhatchie. By May 2, Prevost was driving toward Charleston with three thousand men. Moultrie's force of twelve hundred men could not stop Prevost's army from reaching the peninsula above Charleston on May 10. The people of Charleston panicked, and South Carolina's governing officials wanted to make a deal. They proposed offering to remain neutral for the rest of the war if the British would leave Charleston in peace. They asked Lieutenant Colonel John Laurens to deliver the proposal to Prevost. Laurens, a fervent patriot, refused to carry a message like that. The message eventually was carried by Alexander McIntosh. General Prevost's brother Marc Prevost rejected the request.

Prevost's maneuver succeeded in drawing Lincoln out of Georgia. Lincoln hurried back toward Charleston with the main American army. Now outnumbered, General Prevost withdrew from the Charleston peninsula and began a return trip to Savannah along the sea islands. Lincoln followed Prevost. To enable the main British force to reach Savannah safely, the British rear guard had to fight a delaying action against the pursuing Americans.

Delaying Action at Stono Ferry: June 20, 1779

The rear guard was commanded by Colonel John Maitland of the 71st Regiment of Foot, also known as the 71st Highlanders. The force of five hundred men included the 1st Battalion of the 71st Regiment, part of a Hessian regiment, Provincial infantry regiments from South Carolina and North Carolina, and a small unit of artillery. The American army included Continental infantry, a North Carolina and South Carolina militia brigade, a Virginia militia brigade, a small group of horsemen from North Carolina led by William Richardson Davie, and Kasimir Pulaski's cavalry. The

American army outnumbered the British rear guard by seven or eight to one.

At Stono Ferry, the British built earthworks and an abatis. On June 20, two companies of Highlanders marched out of the defensive works toward the approaching American army. The Highlanders encountered the Continental infantry about a quarter of a mile away from the British fieldworks. "Though greatly inferior in numbers, the Scotsmen stood fast," writes historian Christopher Ward. When the Continental troops launched a bayonet attack, Ward writes, "a furious hand-to-hand fight ensued. With obstinate bravery the intrepid Highlanders maintained their ground until all but 11 of them had fallen" (686). All of the officers in the two companies were killed or wounded. The eleven surviving Highlanders fought their way back to the British defensive position.

The full force of the American army then attacked the British rear guard. When the Hessians on Maitland's left were pushed back, Maitland threw the 1st Battalion of the 71st Regiment from his right to the left wing to shore up the British line. The battle raged for nearly an hour. Lincoln then ordered cavalry to charge the British while the American army withdrew. The British soldiers drove back the American cavalry with volleys of musket fire and a line of bayonets. After the American reserve force came forward and fired a volley, the British crossed the Stono River. The rear guard had succeeded in delaying the American pursuit of the main British force, so there was no reason to continue fighting. Historian Henry Lumpkin writes, "the heroes of the day were the gallant Highlanders whose staunch fighting abilities undoubtedly saved Maitland from disaster" (32). American losses were 146 killed or wounded and 155 missing. British casualties were three officers and twenty-three men killed, ten officers and ninety-three men wounded (Ward 686).

The British withdrew in boats to Port Royal Island. Prevost returned to Savannah with the main body of British troops, leaving a garrison at Beaufort under Maitland's command (Migliazzo 274).

Lachlan McIntosh returns to Georgia

Lachlan McIntosh learned early in 1779 that the British had occupied Savannah, where his wife and younger children had stayed while he was serving first at Valley Forge and then in the Western Department. "I am lately informed my own country, all my family, and every thing of property I have in the world, are now in the hands of the enemy," he lamented on March 13. "I am exceedingly unhappy not to hear any thing from them. Desire to be there" (Kellogg 251). He may have heard reports such as the governor of Georgia delivered to Congress: "the spirit of Rapine Insolence and Brutality indulged in by the soldiery, exceeds Description... People who have got out of Town since the Action say [the British commanders] profess great humanity, and totally disavow many horrid Acts committed by their People... for my Part I wish to leave nothing to their Humanity and as little to their Justice" (Campbell 110). There were horror stories about British treatment of civilians in Savannah: "Robbery, incendiarism, rape and murder were the fruits of that unhappy day," wrote a witness to the British capture of Savannah (Lawrence, "Capture" 323).

McIntosh wanted to tend to his family affairs in Georgia and Washington's aide Alexander Hamilton said McIntosh would "be usefully serving the public to the Southward" ((Kellogg 233, 329). In late July, McIntosh arrived at Augusta, the largest town in Georgia controlled by American forces. McIntosh's command at Augusta consisted of a Virginia infantry regiment and a cavalry squad that had been sent south to Georgia, and whatever militia McIntosh could scrounge. "The Georgia Continental Line was now non-existent," says Savannah historian Alexander Lawrence ("Suspension" 121-22), after having been weakened by ill-fated invasions of British East Florida, then nearly annihilated by death or captivity when the British took Savannah, and finally mopped up in the debacle at Brier Creek. "The few Militia in this Corner who stick yet to their Integrity, and have not joined the Enemy, or shamefully left us altogether to ourselves, do not exceed six hundred men," McIntosh informed General Benjamin Lincoln, the commander of the Southern Department with headquarters in Charleston (Kennedy 128). McIntosh asked for help from South Carolina, but Lincoln could not spare any troops or supplies.

Allies plan attack on Savannah

In the summer of 1779, South Carolina Governor John Rutledge asked Count d'Estaing, the commander of a French fleet operating in the West Indies, to participate in an operation to recapture Savannah. The fleet sailed to the mainland, and an officer came ashore to inform General Lincoln that d'Estaing was prepared to support an attack on Savannah with his powerful fleet of thirty-three naval vessels and four thousand French troops. Lincoln, who was recovering from illness, ordered his Continental and militia regiments to prepare for battle.

Lachlan McIntosh marches toward Savannah

"I sent an express to General McIntosh who commanded the troops at Augusta," Lincoln wrote in his journal for September 4, "to march with the greatest dispatch with all the men he could collect in 24 hours after he should receive the information, to Ebenezer and to bring down a number of flats, which would facilitate his march as provisions might come in them" (Kennedy 121).

The next day Lincoln wrote, "I this day reiterated my orders to General McIntosh and urged him to the greatest exertions and dispatch as the Count could not remain long on the coast, and that if the infantry could not reach in time he must advance with the horse" (Kennedy 121). McIntosh apparently concentrated marching his troops to Savannah quickly, as urged in the second message, instead of sending flatboats downriver to Ebenezer, as requested in the first message.

The History of Georgia published in two volumes in 1811 and 1816 by Georgia's first historian, Captain Hugh McCall, gives information on the movements of Lachlan McIntosh that may have come from participants in the events. McCall worked not only from documents but also from personal experience as a child during the Revolution and from interviews with veterans and witnesses. McCall writes:

> … the command of the American cavalry had been confided in count Pulaski, who had taken post on the ridge, fifty miles north-east from Augusta… Pulaski was ordered to join general M'Intosh at Augusta, and M'Intosh was ordered to march with the infantry and cavalry, toward Savannah, in advance of the army under general Lincoln; to attack the British out-posts, and open a communication with the French troops upon the sea shore.
>
> General M'Intosh pressed forward on Savannah, and before the enemy was apprized of his approach, Pulaski cut off one of their piquets; killed and wounded five men, and captured a subaltern and five privates; he opened the com-

munication to the sea shore, and general M'Intosh advanced toward Ogeechee ferry. They had several skirmishes with the enemy's outposts, before they joined the French troops at Beaulieu. (430)

So soon as a body of the French troops had landed, general M'Intosh returned, and halted at Millen's plantation, three miles from Savannah, to wait the arrival of general Lincoln. (430)

On September 6, Lincoln led the march toward Savannah, leaving William Moultrie in command of the troops defending Charleston. As Lincoln approached the Savannah River near Purrysburg on September 9, he ordered Colonel John Laurens "to reconnoitre the ground, and provide boats to cross at Zubly's Ferry. Lest the boats from Augusta should not arrive in time he reported to me on my arrival towards night that he found one small canoe, a rowing boat and one flat which was sunk in the river" (Kennedy 122).

The effort of a large party of soldiers was unable to retrieve the sunken flat. On September 11, Lincoln "ordered a flat, partly built, to be finished and a raft made from the boards and timber of the buildings" (Kennedy 122-23). Lincoln's journal continued:

> 12th September. The troops began to cross in the morning. The raft sunk the first time the men attempted to cross in it. We were then left with one canoe which could carry three men, another about 15 and the flat which was now finished which would carry about 20. But before noon we procured another large canoe from McClay's Creek which would carry 30 men.
>
> … The troops were mostly thrown across and took post on the heights of Ebenezer. I crossed myself a little in the afternoon. (123)

Elderly Rory McIntosh jumps out window

While the Americans were crossing the Savannah River on September 12, the French were disembarking from their ships and setting up camp at Beaulieu, a plantation near the village of Thunderbolt. Rory McIntosh happened to be staying with friends at Thunderbolt. Rory, a cousin of General Lachlan McIntosh, was a loyalist who had moved from coastal Georgia to the British stronghold at St. Augustine early in the Revolution. He was in his mid to late sixties then. When d'Estaing's troops arrived at Thunderbolt, Rory jumped out a back window during the night and escaped to Savannah (White 473).

Generals McIntosh and Lincoln join forces

Lincoln recorded that September 13 was spent in getting the artillery and wagons across the Savannah River and repairing bridges over swampy streams at Ebenezer, "which General McIntosh crossed and joined us a little before night" (Kennedy 123). On September 15 the American army reached Cherokee Hill, ten miles from Savannah. The next day the Americans arrived at Savannah and encamped at Millen's plantation (Lawrence, *Storm* 157).

Maitland leads reinforcements to Savannah

On September 16, Count d'Estaing demanded that General Augustine Prevost surrender Savannah to King Louis XVI of France; d'Estaing's summons didn't even mention the Americans who were approaching the outskirts Savannah at that moment. General Prevost answered the summons according to formal European military etiquette, and asked for twenty-four hours to consider the terms of surrender. Count d'Estaing granted the request.

Prevost used the twenty-four hours to finish the fortifications around Savannah and to receive reinforcements who were on their way from Beaufort. Prevost praised officers of the 71st Regiment for preparations to defend Savannah: "Captain Moncrief, commanding engineer, but sincerely sensible that all I can express will fall greatly short of what that gentleman deserves, not only on this, but on all other occasions… We have been greatly obliged to Major Fraser of the 71st, and Quartermaster Jones for his zealous and indefatigable industry in landing and mounting upon the batteries the cannon, stores, etc., and constantly supplying all wants" (Kennedy 104).

Colonel John Maitland of the 71st Highlanders commanded the garrison at Beaufort, which included the 1st Battalion of the 71st. Although suffering a fever, Maitland evacuated Beaufort on September 12 and sailed across Port Royal Sound. He left convalescents suffering in the Southern climate on the southwestern side of

Hilton Head and transferred eight hundred relatively healthy soldiers from transport vessels to small boats.

Because the French fleet blocked the open waterway, Maitland had to find an alternate route to Savannah through what historian Hugh F. Rankin calls "a watery wasteland" (35). Maitland and the first group of his men reached Savannah at noon on September 16 and more men arrived in groups over the next two days.

The stuff of legend is included in descriptions of Maitland's exploits. Georgia historian Alexander A. Lawrence gives this version:

> ... If the lower South – if America itself was to be saved to the King – Maitland somehow had to get his troops through twenty miles of marsh and swamp that lay between them and beleaguered Savannah...
>
> At this crucial moment fortune threw some Negro fishermen in the path of Maitland. In their strange Gullah version of the English language they told the British about an obscure waterway behind Dawfuskie Island. In serpentining through the marshes a creek looped within a short distance of another. A shallow cut had been dug to connect the two. This passage, which was called Wall's Cut, could be used only at high tide. But once in the creek to which it led, the English with luck and hard work might get into the Savannah above the point to which the French vessels had advanced. ...an incredulous Charlestownian ...supposed that the British "must have plunged through swamps, bogs and creeks which had never before been attempted but by bears, wolves, and run-away Negroes."
>
> A long stretch of shoal creek lay between Wall's Cut and the Savannah. The men struggled through mud and marsh up to their waists. The boats were dragged through by main force. But suddenly the British were looking out upon the waters of a great river. Along the marsh-bordered banks of the Savannah one could see "multitudes of alligators lying in the mud like old Logs." That was all, for no enemy vessels were that far up the stream...
>
> The English are sometimes accounted an undemonstrative lot, but this was drama to warm the hearts of even the most reserved, the sight of these long-awaited reinforce-

ments – veterans of Brandywine, Fort Montgomery, Brier Creek and Stono Ferry – filing up the bluff and marching off to their posts in the lines. Even rough British tars were so moved that they gave three cheers... (*Storm* 49-51).

While cheers erupted from the British lines, dismay enveloped the besiegers. French commander Count d'Estaing added these notes to a journal of the siege kept by one of his officers:

> ...I went to Brewton Hill to confirm with my own eyes the report... We saw still crossing the river a string of small boats loaded with troops, a sight so vexatious that I began to bemoan bitterly the impossibility of stopping a reinforcement that was going to give the expedition extreme difficulty... (Kennedy 51)
> ... The Scotch troops, transferred from Beaufort and commanded by Colonel Maitland, were the ones the enemy always put in the fore... (Kennedy 73)

Alexander Garden – a patriot officer from Charleston who later wrote about the war – offers these anecdotes about Maitland:

> Every Avenue by which the Approach of Col. Maitland and his Highlanders could be looked for was closed; yet by unconquerable Industry, he discovered an obscure Creek, but little navigated; and, by dint of persevering Exertion, dragging his Boats through it, reached the Garrison before the Time allowed for Deliberation had expired. Entering the Council Chamber where Discussions were carrying on, he is said to have approached with hurried Step the Table, and, striking the Hilt of his Claymore against it, to have exclaimed, "the Man who utters a Syllable recommending Surrender makes me his decided Enemy; it is necessary that either *he* or *I* should fall." So resolute a Speech, at a Moment so critical, produced the happiest Effect on the Minds of all. Hope and Courage regained their Influence in every Mind; each Individual repaired to his Post with Alacrity and Confidence ... -- *Garden's Anecdotes of the American Revolution*, Brooklyn Ed. 1865, iii, 101. (qtd. in Hough, *Savannah* 63-64)

Once the reinforcements began arriving, Prevost ended the truce on the night of September 17 and defiantly rejected d'Estaing's terms of surrender.

American forces gather outside Savannah

General Benjamin Lincoln led the American army to join the French outside Savannah. Brigadier General Lachlan McIntosh commanded the 1st and 5th South Carolina Continentals and the Georgia regulars. Colonel Maurice Simmons commanded a Charleston militia brigade. A Charleston militia unit of light troops was led by Lieutenant Colonel John Laurens, son of Lachlan McIntosh's business partner Henry Laurens.

Brigadier General Isaac Huger commanded Continental troops from South Carolina. Huger's units included the 2nd Regiment, led by Lieutenant Colonel Francis Marion. Learning that d'Estaing had given Prevost a full day to prepare the British defenses, Marion flew into a rage. "My God!" Marion exclaimed. "Who ever heard of anything like this before? First allow an enemy to entrench, and then fight him!" (Rankin 35).

The allies besiege Savannah

As the twenty-four-hour truce ended, rain began to fall. Siege tactics, such as moving artillery forward, became more difficult on the muddy ground. On September 22, the French Army in three divisions moved into position east of the Ogeechee Road. The Americans encamped to the left of the French in positions reaching to McGillivray's Plantation on the Savannah River. Once the ground began drying, d'Estaing opened siege lines on September 23.

The British launched sorties to delay work on the siege approaches. A British journal gives an account of one of the sorties:

> Sept. 24th. At seven in the Morning, saw the Enemy very busy intrenching themselves to the Left of the Barracks. Three Companies of Light Infantry made a Sortie with great Spirit. The Enemy being too numerous, obliged them to retreat under the Fire of our Batteries, with the loss of 21 killed and wounded. Lieut. McPherson, of the 71st, was killed. It is supposed the Enemy suffered considerably... A

Flag was sent to bury the Dead, on both Sides... (Hough, *Savannah* 66)

The British journal writer was correct in supposing that his enemy suffered considerably. A French captain described the sortie from his viewpoint:

> ...They decided to make an immediate sortie against us, be-lieving there were few men there. They carried out their maneuver at 8 a.m. Three hundred men ambushed us when we least expected it. They were in front of our trenches be-fore we realized it, and we were caught by surprise. As soon as the enemy was spotted, all the soldiers got out of the trenches in attack formation because the trench's raised firing platform had not been built. The attack was on our left against three chasseur companies stationed there. They received the first enemy fire. I led my company to that point immediately and counterattacked furiously, making the English fall back. We pursued them back to their own lines; I made this charge with the Gatinois Company; we were not strong enough to go any further. M. O'Dunne, second in command, came out, stopped us, and ordered us to retreat, which we executed with the finest order. At that moment we were exposed to grapeshot charges which killed many of our men. Our two companies regrouped at our trench and the fighting stopped. If my company had not repelled the enemy with its first maneuver, a very large column, outfitted with tools to destroy our trenches, would have approached our right. But they were intimidated when they saw their men repelled and they withdrew.
>
> This skirmish, which lasted less than a half hour, cost us, and especially me, several grenadiers. I lost ten men killed and eleven wounded; my infantry lieutenant, named Blandat, was killed. That officer's death is a cruel loss. He was a 35-year veteran and was to be awarded the Cross of Saint-Louis on November 4th according to a letter of noti-fication from the minister. The Gatinois Company took losses almost as great as ours; its infantry lieutenant was al-so killed and three officers wounded, two of them serious-ly. Immediately after the skirmish the enemy sent out an

envoy to request a truce for picking up their wounded. It was granted. There was a two-hour cease-fire… Our losses totaled almost 100 men; for although the other companies did not attack, they lost men in cannonade.

After both sides had collected their wounded, we returned to our respective works, recommenced hostilities, and continued for the rest of the day. We lost several more men on the path leading to the trench; one of the enemy's batteries had it in range. I was quite happy to come out of the skirmish safe and sound; I looked forward to the hour when I would be relieved. We stayed there until eight o'clock that night and returned to our camp without experiencing a single cannon shot, much to our relief. (Kennedy 15-16)

Although the French captain perceived that he had been ambushed by three hundred British soldiers, the British commander reported that "97 rank and file" were sent out and the Highlanders were stationed behind the lines to support the rear flank of the attackers (Kennedy 97).

Another sortie three days later, writes historian Henry Lumpkin, "under Major Archibald McArthur of the 71st (Highland) Regiment, was carried out so adroitly that it accomplished its mission of disruption and also produced an exchange of fire between the French and American troops manning the lines" (34).

Raid on the Ogeechee

While the siege was underway, detachments from the American army harassed British troops who had not succeeded in getting into Savannah before the town was invested. Count Pulaski's cavalry attacked British and loyalist troops on the Ogeechee River on September 19. Many of them escaped the cavalry by boarding vessels and pushing away from land. They could not sail away, however, because the French fleet controlled the waters along the coast. On October 1, Colonel John White of the Georgia Line made a second raid on the five vessels sitting in the Ogeechee. White was accompanied only by Captain Etholm, three soldiers, and his servant. He lit a number of fires arranged to look like an army camp, and rode though the apparent camp giving orders in a voice loud enough to be heard by the troops on the vessels. He then went out to the vessels under a flag of truce and summoned the troops to surrender. The British commander, believing he was outnumbered, surrendered his troops, the crews of the vessels, and the vessels themselves, which were armed with fourteen guns. White told the commander that it would be difficult to protect the loyalists from vengeful patriot militiamen, so he would send three guides to lead the prisoners to Lincoln's encampment. The British commander readily agreed to the arrangement, knowing the loyalists were terrified of their fellow countrymen because patriots and loyalists had inflicted great cruelties on one another. White sent his three soldiers to guide the prisoners. (This tale is repeated on pages 151-153 of *The Siege of Savannah* edited by Franklin Hough and is attributed to *Bowen's Life of Lincoln*, Colonel Lee's *History of the War*, General Lincoln's private journal, a letter from Lincoln to Congress, a letter from White to Lincoln, and the original Articles of Capitulation signed by the British commander.)

McIntosh family endures bombardment

Lachlan McIntosh had returned to Georgia to protect his family, but the fighting at Savannah prevented a reunion. Writing just a few decades after the siege, Georgia's first historian, Hugh McCall, gives this report:

> On the 29th, general M'Intosh solicited general Lincoln's permission to send a flag, with a letter to general Provost, to obtain leave for Mrs. M'Intosh and his family, and such other females and children as might choose to leave the town during the siege, or until the contest should be decided. Major John Jones, aid to general M'Intosh, was the bearer of the flag and letter, and found Mrs. M'Intosh and family in a cellar, where they had been confined several days. Indeed these damp apartments furnished the only safe retreat, for females and children, during the siege. General Provost refused to grant the request, imagining that it would restrain the besiegers from throwing bombs and carcasses among the houses to set them on fire. (439)

McIntosh called the British decision an act of brutality (Lawrence, "General" 72). To McIntosh's dismay, the Americans resumed shelling on October 3. Witnesses reported "great Mischief both in town and in the enemy lines" (Jackson 98). During three days of bombardment, the McIntosh family "suffered beyond description" (Jackson 98). An account of their ordeal is recorded on a leaf of their family Bible:

> The British officers behaved with great attention and kindness toward Mrs. McIntosh and her children. During the siege, the British provided refuge in the cellar of a house where sick officers were quartered. Mrs. McIntosh nursed the convalescents despite the threat of cannon balls whistling around and perforating the abode. A shell fell into a well near the house and burst, destroying the well and alarming the family, but Mrs. McIntosh was above all fear. Her sons George, Henry and Hampden ran through the streets picking up spent cannon balls; they said they were going to send the ammunition to the Americans. ("Mackenzie Papers" 113-15)

Major John Jones – the aide to McIntosh who had visited Mrs. McIntosh on September 29 – wrote to his own wife Polly on October 4: "I feel most sincerely for the poor women and children! God only knows what will become of them" (Kennedy 131). On October 7 he wrote Polly, "a more cruel war could never exist than this. The poor women and children have suffered beyond description. A number of them, in Savannah, have already been put to death by our bombs and cannon. ...many of them were killed in their beds, and amongst others, a poor woman, with her infant in her arms, was destroyed by a cannon-ball. They have all got into cellars; but even there they do not escape the fury of our bombs, several of them having been mangled in that supposed place of security. I pity General McIntosh; his situation is peculiar. The whole family is there. We have burnt, as yet, only one house; but I expect this night the whole will be in flames" (Kennedy 132).

Jones was slightly inaccurate in saying "the whole family" was trapped in the besieged city. Lachlan and Sarah McIntosh had eight children, but only their five youngest were with Sarah in Savannah: daughters Hester and Catherine and sons George, Henry Laurens and John Hampden, called "Hampden," who was about 8 years old at the time of the siege of Savannah. Their three oldest sons are not mentioned in accounts of the siege.

The decision to reject Lachlan McIntosh's plea to remove women and children from the battleground would come back to haunt British General Augustine Prevost, whose own wife and children were in Savannah. Prevost noted in his journal entry for October 4, "At day light they open with nine mortars, thirty-seven pieces of cannon from the land side, and sixteen from the water. Continue without intermission 'till eight o'clock without other effect than killing a few helpless women and children and some few negroes and horses in the town and on the common" (Kennedy 99).

The colonial Chief Justice of Georgia described the plight of civilians in Savannah and mentioned the Prevost family:

> ... when all the women and children were asleep, the French opened a battery of nine mortars, and kept up a very heavy bombardment for an hour and a half, in which time those who counted shells found that they fired one hundred, which were chiefly directed at the town. I heard one of the shells whistle over my quarters, and presently afterwards I got up and dressed myself; and as our neighbourhood seemed to be in the line of fire, I went out with a view to go to the eastward, out of the way; but a shell that seemed to be falling near me, rather puzzled me how to keep clear of it, and I returned to the house not a little alarmed.
>
> I then proceeded to the westward, and then the shells seemed to fall around; there I soon joined a number of gentlemen who had left their houses on account of the bombardment, and, like me, were retiring from the line of fire to Yamacraw; here we stayed till between one and two in the morning, when the bombardment ceased...
>
> ...at five I was awakened with a very heavy cannonade from a French frigate to the north of the town, and with a bombardment and cannonade from the French lines in the south, which soon hurried me out of bed; and before I could get my clothes on, an eighteen-pounder entered the house, stuck in the middle partition, and drove the plastering all about.
>
> We who were in the house now found ourselves in a cross fire; and notwithstanding the rum in the cellar, we thought it less dangerous to descend there than to continue in the house, as the fall of a shell into the cellar was not so

probable as the being killed in the house with a cannon ball... After we had descended into it, some shot struck the house, and one passed through the kitchen... Whilst we were in the cellar, two shells burst not far from the door, and many others fell in the neighbourhood all around us. In this situation a number of us continued in a damp cellar, until the cannonade and bombardment almost ceased, for the French to cool their artillery; and then we ascended to breakfast.

...Mr. Pollard, deputy barrack-master, was killed by a shell in that house on the bay which was formerly inhabited by Mr. Moss; and the daughter of one Thomson was almost shot in two by a cannon ball, at the house next to where Mr. Elliot lived. I am told there were other lives lost... Fortunately for us, after breakfast, the town adjutant's wife and myself went over to Captain Knowles, who is agent for the transports, and to whose cellar Mrs. Prevost, the general's lady, and several gentlemen and ladies had retired for security. This house was directly opposite to my quarters, and about thirty or forty feet distant.

The general's lady and Captain Knowles invited us to stay there... and we continued in the cellar, with several others, as agreeably as the situation of matters would admit of, until three o'clock on Tuesday morning. During the whole of this time the French kept up a brisk cannonade and bombardment; the shot frequently struck near us, and the shells fell on each side of us with so much violence that in their fall they shook the ground, and many of them burst with a great explosion...

The guns seemed to approach on each side, and about three o'clock on Wednesday morning a shell whistled close by Captain Knowles's house. Soon afterwards another came nearer, and seemed to strike my quarters, and I thought I heard the cry of people in distress. We all jumped up... my quarters were so much in flames that I could not venture further than the door, for fear of an explosion from the rum... and as soon as the French observed the flames, they kept up a very heavy cannonade and bombardment, and pointed their fire to that object to prevent any person approaching to extinguish the flames.

I retired to Captain Knowles's... Being in the direction of the French fire, I was every moment in danger of being smashed to pieces with a shell, or shot in two with a cannon ball... I thought it safest to... retire to a place of safety...

I had some distance to go before I got out of the line of fire, and I did not know the way under Savannah Bluff, where I should have been safe from cannon balls; and therefore, whenever I came to the opening of a street, I watched the flashes of the mortars and guns, and pushed on until I came under cover of a house; and when I got to the common, and heard the whistling of a shot or shell, I fell on my face. But the stopping under cover of a house was no security, for the shot went through many houses; and Thomson's daughter was killed at the side opposite to that where the shot entered.

At last I reached an encampment made by Governor Wright's negroes on the common between Savannah and Yamacraw, and it being dark I fell down in to a trench which they had dug... I proposed to stop at a house... but a soldier, who was on guard at the Hessian hospital at Yama-craw... conducted me to the house of Mr. Moses Nones, at the west end of Yamacraw, which was quite out of the di-rection of the enemy's batteries.

This place was crowded, both inside and out, with a number of whites and negroes, who had fled from the town. Women and children were constantly flocking there, melt-ing into tears, and lamenting their unhappy fate, and the de-struction of their houses and property...

The appearance of the town afforded a melancholy prospect, for there was hardly a house which had not been shot through, and some of them were almost destroyed...

Many of the inhabitants went on board the ships in the river, and others retired to Hutchinson's Island, opposite the town, which... is a rice swamp, and very unwholesome, particularly in the fall.

I twice took a stroll to that island, and at Mr. McGillvray's rice barn the ladies told me there were fifty men, women, and children. Other places seemed equally crowded; but neither the ships nor island were places of security, for many shells fell into the river, and some into the shipping…

Most of the houses in the town had banks of earth thrown up, and those that had cellars secured them as well as circumstances would admit of. Captain Knowles, for the security of the ladies in his cellar, had in some places thrown up a bank of sand on the outside, and in other places put large casks filled with sand; he also propped up the floor over the cellar, and put such a quantity of sand on it that it was bomb-proof. (Kennedy 109-114)

On October 6 Prevost sent a letter to Count d'Estaing containing "Sentiments… of Humanity. The houses of Savannah are occupied solely by women and children. Several of them have applied to me that I might request the favour you would allow them to embark on board a ship or ships and go down the river under the protection of yours until this business is decided. If this requisition you are so good as to grant, my Wife and Children, with a few servants, shall be the first to profit by the indulgence" (Harden 218). In his journal, Prevost reported "After three hours and a great deal of intermediate cannon and shells, received an insulting answer in refusal from Messrs. Lincoln and d'Estaing conjunctly" (Kennedy 100).

Prevost correctly described the answer from Lincoln and d'Estaing as insulting – evidently d'Estaing remained angry over Prevost's previous stalling tactics:

CAMP BEFORE SAVANNAH, October 6th, 1779 – Sir: We are persuaded that your Excellency knows all that your duty prescribes. Perhaps your zeal has already interfered with your judgment.

"The Count d'Estaing in his own name notified you that you alone would be personally responsible for the consequences of your obstinacy. The time which you informed him in the commencement of the siege would be necessary for the arrangement of articles, including different orders of men in your town, had no other object than that of receiving succor. Such conduct, Sir, is sufficient to forbid every intercourse between us which might occasion the least loss of time. Besides, in the present application latent reasons might again exist. There are military ones which, in frequent instances, have prevented the indulgence you request. It is with regret we yield to the austerity of our functions, and we deplore the fate of those persons who will be victims of your conduct, and the delusion which appears to prevail in your mind.

We are with respect, Sir,

Your Excellency's most obedient Servants,

B. LINCOLN,

D'ESTAING. (Harden 219)

While each side blamed the other for the threat to women and children, the bombardment continued. A teenage woman whose relatives were loyalists gave an account of the events she endured:

The French and Americans were... constantly cannonading and throwing bomb shells. Fortunately, however, our men were encamped near the trenches, and these deadly shells went a distance over their heads. The streets being sandy and not paved, the shells fell and made great holes in the sand, which often put out the fuse and prevented explosion. Indeed, the colored children got so used to the shells that they would run and cover them with sand, and as we were rather scarce of ammunition they would often pick up the spent balls and get for them seven-pence apiece.

Soon almost every family was removed from the town to an island opposite, where they made use of barns, and taking their bedding and some furniture divided it by portions. In the barn where I was there were fifty-eight women and children, all intimate friends, and who had each one or more near relatives in the lines. My mother-in-law had two sons, I had my father and one very dear to me, my future husband. Only one male friend was with us, Dr. Johnston, too old to fight, though his whole heart was in the cause. Every other house and barn besides the one we occupied was full of females. The General sent a flag to Count D'Estaing to request that he would allow Mrs. Prevost and her children to go on board one of our ships to be in a safe place. The request was refused and she remained in a cellar in Savannah, which was made bomb proof with feather beds. Fortunately, though their hope was by the incessant fire to burn the town and force a surrender, a merciful God protected us and defeated their intention…

Our men, having few to relieve them, suffered from fatigue and want of rest… (Johnston 57-59)

Excerpts from a journal published in *Rivington's Royal Gazette*, a Loyalist newspaper published in New York, give an eye-witness account of the bombardment from the British viewpoint inside Savannah:

Oct. 3d. At 12 o'clock this Night, the Enemy opened the Bomb Batteries, and fired warmly into the Town, but none into the Field.

4th. The Enemy still continue their Fire from the Bomb and other Batteries. It was returned by us.

5th. The Enemy still cannonading the Camp and Town. At Night a House took fire, but it went out without communicating to any other Building…

6th. Enemy still firing on the Works, Camp and Town… The Cannonade and Bombardment continued all Night.

7th. Still continued Cannonading and throwing shells on both Sides; the Enemy throwing most of their Fire towards the Town, which suffers considerably… At 7 at Night the Enemy threw several Carcases into the Town, and burnt one House.

8th. The Enemy fired little this Morning, but during the Night cannonaded and bombarded the Town furiously. (Hough, *Savannah* 71-73)

Another eye-witness account of the bombardment was given by a British officer in a letter to his wife:

This morning… they opened one of the most tremendous Firings I ever heard; from 37 Pieces of Cannon – mostly 18-Pounders, and 9 Mortars, in Front, and sixteen Pieces of Cannon from the River, on our Left – mostly 24-Pounders. The Town was torn to Pieces, and nothing but Shrieks from Women and Children to be heard. Many poor Creatures were killed in trying to get to their Cellars, or hide themselves under the Bluff of Savannah River. The Firing lasted for some Hours, and a Flag was sent from us to Count d'Estaing, to allow Time for the Women and Children to go to an Island out of Danger. 'Twas savagely refused; and that Night they began to fire again, and heave Carcases and red Shot, which set two Houses on fire, and burnt them down; but some proper Persons being appointed to extinguish the Bombs, did it very effectually, and prevented any further Conflagration. (Hough, *Savannah* 84-85)

Women rely on French gallantry

While both Lachlan McIntosh's wife and Augustine Prevost's wife endured the bombardment, other women managed to escape British-occupied Savannah and seek asylum from the troops besieging the city. A French naval officer reported:

> Many women however, left the city and presented themselves of their own accord at the French camp. It was necessary for us to take good care of them as they were unwilling to return. General Prevost, whose generosity and humanity toward French prisoners have never been denied, had given them token of attention and goodness which could scarcely have been expected from an enemy. This conduct on his part was, without doubt, due in great measure to his wife, born French. It was jestingly remarked by a member of parliament that our gallantry could not be denied even in our manner of making war, and that the prettiest woman of the city came to test the effect of our bombs. (Jones 64)

Aeneas Mackintosh faces American attack

Although the siege was still in its early stages, d'Estaing became impatient and decided to launch an attack on Savannah. His strategy called on 3,500 French troops in three columns to lead the attack, supported by 1,500 American troops.

The plan called for the American and French allies to make a feint at the British left while making an all-out attack against the Spring Hill redoubt near the west end of the British line.

Count d'Estaing would personally lead the assault, while Lachlan McIntosh would command a second column designated to support the first assault.

The defenders of Savannah included – in addition to British army units – militia from Georgia, South Carolina, North Carolina, and New York, as well as armed black men. According to a French report, the defensive force totaled 7,165 men, including eighty Cherokees and four thousand black men from French colonies in the Caribbean.

A picket of the 71st was placed in front of the British lines on the eastern end of Savannah.

The 1st Battalion of the 71st, a unit that had come through a watery wasteland to reinforce the garrison in Savannah, anchored the east flank. Major Archibald McArthur commanded the battalion because Colonel Maitland, who had led the reinforcements from Beaufort to Savannah was given a greater responsibility.

Maitland, although mortally ill with a fever, was placed in charge of the entire force on the west of the lines. North Carolina loyalists were located on the extreme west flank of the British defenses with the Savannah River at their backs and Yamacraw Swamp to their right.

The Spring Hill redoubt on the west side of the lines was defended by British regulars of the 4th Battalion of the 60th Regiment – a regiment often associated with Roderick "Rory" McIntosh – and South Carolina Royalists. By special order the defenders at Spring Hill were all under the command of Captain Taws, who ordinarily served as an officer in the 71st Regiment. The 2nd Battalion of the 71st Regiment – Aeneas Mackintosh was a captain in that battalion – was positioned behind the Spring Hill redoubt under the command of Major M'Donald (Furneaux 299).

The positioning of the defending and opposing troops meant that South Carolina loyalists would face South Carolina patriots, and that British officer Aeneas Mackintosh would face Continental General Lachlan McIntosh as he led the second allied column toward Spring Hill redoubt.

A premonition of death

Major John Jones – an aide to General McIntosh – wrote frequently to his wife Polly. She was a refugee in Jacksonboro, South Carolina, because their plantation at Sunbury was behind enemy lines. Like most of their neighbors around Sunbury they were devout Christians who accepted Calvinist doctrine. In one letter he said, "believe that if it is my fate to survive this action, I shall; if otherwise, the Lord's will be done. Every soldier and soldier's wife should religiously believe in predestination" (Kennedy 131).

"Some of the Americans had a foreboding of disaster," writes Alexander Lawrence in *Storm over Savannah*. "Major John Jones and Lieutenant Robert Carnabie Baillie 'staggered' their friends, said James Jackson, by bidding them an affectionate farewell, each certain he would not survive" (95).

Bagpipes taunt d'Estaing

As the French and American allies gathered before dawn on October 9, d'Estaing knew he was in for a fight when he heard the bagpipers of the 71st Regiment located in the exact place he planned to attack. In his notes on the battle, he observed:

> The Scotch troops… evinced the most audacity during the siege. They ordinarily occupied the ground to the left of their barracks, as well as the front before which our siegeworks and batteries were located.
>
> Scotch Highland bagpipes, the saddest and most remarkable of instruments, was the usual band for this corps. Frequently our trench and even our camp heard the mournful harmony; it surprised me that it also taunted us on the day of the attack. At the very moment we came out of the marsh, we were given a serenade which issued from a place quite distant from the one this unit usually occupied. From it I concluded that the enemy was not only forewarned but also that he wanted to remind us that his best troops were waiting for us. Undoubtedly the soldiers felt inwardly as I did, for the sound of this band appeared to me to have made a profound impression on their morale. Certainly when I heard the unexpected sound of these peripatetic bagpipes, I would have decided to call off the attack had we not been so far advanced and had not had the Americans for companions, or rather, for masters. (Kennedy 73)

Just as the sun rose behind the British lines, firing began. The French troops swarmed out of the morning mist across open ground toward the British defenses. French grenadiers cut through the abatis with hatchets and broke the British line.

British and loyalist troops led by Thomas Tawse stubbornly defended their position on the Spring Hill redoubt. Their commander Augustine Prevost later wrote, "it is but justice to mention... those troops who defended it. They were part of the South Carolina Royalists, the light dragoons dismounted, and the battalion men of the 60th, in all about 100 men commanded (by a special order) by Captain Tawse of the dragoons (lieutenant of the 71st) a good and gallant officer who nobly fell with his sword in the body of the third he had killed with his own hand" (Kennedy 102).

Faced with such fierce resistance, the French retreated. D'Estaing rallied his men to charge once again. They became trapped in the entrenchments near Spring Hill redoubt and were cut to pieces by musket balls and grape shot. D'Estaing himself was wounded several times.

John Laurens' light infantry and Francis Marion's 2nd South Carolina Regiment – in which Alexander McDonald of the Darien district served – resumed the attack on the redoubt. Under heavy fire, Marion led his regiment across the moat and into the abatis.

Carrying the colors of the 2nd Regiment

Sergeant William Jasper of the 2nd South Carolina Regiment, who had distinguished himself in 1776 by rescuing the regimental flag at Fort Sullivan, suffered a mortal wound while trying to rescue the regimental flag in the assault on the redoubt at Savannah. Sergeant Allen McDonald, a Highlander from the Cross Creek country of North Carolina, carried another regimental flag. An American officer gave this account:

> Proud of the encomiums bestowed on their valour, encouraged by the animating address of the governor, to aim at the achievements of new honours, the feelings of the gallant second regiment, were sill more highly excited, when Mrs. Bernard Elliott, presenting an elegant pair of colours, thus addressed them:
> "Gentlemen Soldiers,
> "Your gallant behavior, in defence of your country, entitles you to the highest honours! Accept of these two standards as a reward justly due to your regiment, and I

make not the least doubt, but that under heaven's protection, you will stand by them as long as they can wave in the air of liberty."

Her anticipations were justified in the sequel. During the assault at Savannah, they were both planted on the British lines.

The statement which I am about to give of the event, differs widely from that which has been generally received; but that it is correct, cannot be doubted, as it was afforded me by Lieutenant James Legare, whose services and character, entitle him to all credit. He was present in the action and immediately in front of the colours at the time that the officers who bore them were killed. Lieutenant Brush, supported by Sergeant Jasper, carried the one, Lieutenant Grey, supported by Sergeant McDonald, the other. Brush being wounded early in the action, delivered his standard to Jasper, for its better security, who, already wounded, on receiving a second shot, restored it. Brush at the moment receiving a mortal wound, fell into the ditch, with the colours under him, which occasioned their remaining in the hands of the enemy.

Lieutenant Grey receiving a mortal wound, his colours were seized by McDonald, who planted them on the redoubt, but on hearing an order to retreat, plucked them up again, and carried them off in safety. (Garden 12-13)

Allies retreat

As the Americans of the 2nd Regiment carried their colors, a French soldier took the fleur-de-lis of France to the walls of the Spring Hill redoubt. The allies could not scale the parapet under fire, and were ordered to retreat.

Maitland – commanding the west side of the British lines – employed his reserve force. "At this most critical moment," General Prevost wrote, "Major Glasier of the 60th Grenadiers and the marines, advancing rapidly from the lines, charged, it may be said, with a degree of fury. In an instant the ditches of the redoubt and a battery to its right in rear were cleared, the grenadiers charging head long into them, and the enemy drove in confusion over the abatis and into the swamp. On this occasion Captain Wickham of the 2nd Battalion of 60th Grenadiers was greatly distinguished. On the advance of the grenadiers, three companies of the 2nd Battalion of the 71st ordered to sustain them, but tho' these lay at an inconsiderable distance, and advanced with the usual ardor of that corps, so precipitate was the retreat of the enemy, they could not close with him" (Kennedy 101).

Pulaski launches fatal charge

While Maitland was dislodging the attackers from the parapet, Casimir Pulaski, a Polish count serving with the Americans, led his cavalrymen on a dash between the British defensive works. Major Rogowski, one of Pulaski's officers, gives this account:

> Imploring the help of the Almighty, Pulaski shouted to his men "Forward," and we, two hundred strong, rode at full speed after him, the earth resounding under the hoofs of our chargers.
>
> For the first two minutes all went well. We sped like Knights into the peril. Just, however, as we passed the gap between the two batteries, a cross fire, like a pouring shower, confused our ranks. I looked around. Oh, sad moment, ever to be remembered! Pulaski lies prostrate on the ground. I leaped towards him, thinking possibly his wound was not dangerous, but a canister shot had pierced his thigh, and the blood was also flowing from his breast, probably from a second wound. Falling on my knees I tried to raise him. He said in a faint voice, Jesus! Maria! Joseph! Further, I knew not, for at that moment a musket ball grazing my scalp blinded me with the blood, and I fell to the ground in a state of insensibility. (Furneaux 300)

Lachlan McIntosh leads second column

Major Thomas Pinckney gave an account of Lachlan McIntosh's part in the assault on the defensive works around Savannah:

> By this Time the 2d American Column headed by Gen. M'Intosh, to which I was attached, arrived at the Foot of the Spring Hill Redoubt, and such a Scene of Confusion as there appeared is not often equaled. Col. Laurens had been separated from that Part of his Command that had not en-

tered the Spring Hill Ditch by the Cavalry, who had borne it before them into the Swamp to the Left, and when we marched up, inquired *if we had seen them.*

Count D'Estaing was wounded in the Arm, and endeavoring to rally his Men, a few of whom with a Drummer he had collected. General M'Intosh did not speak French, but desired me to inform the Commander-in-chief that his Column was fresh, and that he wished his Directions, where, under present Circumstances, he should make the Attack. The Count ordered that we should move more to the Left, and by no Means to interfere with the Troops he was endeavoring to rally; in pursuing this Direction we were thrown too much to the Left, and before we could reach the Spring Hill Redoubt, we had to pass through Yamacraw Swamp, then wet and boggy, with the Galley at the Mouth annoying our left Flank with Grape-shot. While struggling through this Morass, the firing slacked, and it was reported that the whole Army had retired.

I was sent by General M'Intosh to look out from the Spring Hill, where I found not an Assailant standing. On reporting this to the General, he ordered a Retreat, which was effected without much Loss, notwithstanding the heavy Fire of Grape-shot with which we were followed. (Hough, *Savannah* 167-68)

A Georgia historian gives the battle a romantic flair:

Troops the bravest, Soldiers the most disciplined, Hearts the stoutest, quailed before the Angel of Death, as he seemed to spread out his Wings upon that Blood-covered Plain. When the second American Column, under McIntosh, reached the Spring Hill Redoubt, the Scene of Confusion was dreadful. They marched up over Ground strewn with the Dead and Dying; and seldom has the Sun of a warm October Morning looked down upon a Scene so mournful and appalling. The Smoke of the Muskets and Cannon hung broodingly over the Place, gathering denseness and darkness from every Discharge; and the Roar of Artillery, the Rattling of small Arms, the calling Bugle, the sounded Retreat, the stirring Drum, and the Cries of the Wounded blended startlingly together.

Colonel Huger, marching through the low Rice Grounds, reached his appointed Post, and was received with Music and a brisk Discharge, which killed twenty-eight of his Men, and compelled him to retreat. Only the Column of McIntosh was now fresh and ready for Action. But the Fate of the Day was decided; the French and Americans had been slain and wounded by hundreds, and their Bodies lined the Redoubts and Ditches... For one Hour, they had stood gallant and undaunted before the murderous Cannonade, which struck down Rank after Rank, and sent Dismay, by its sweeping Fury, into every Column until, finding further Attempt but useless Sacrifice of Life, a Retreat was ordered, and the Remains of the gallant Army were drawn off the Field. – *Stevens's Hist. of Georgia*, ii, 217. (qtd. in Hough, *Savannah* 41-43)

The women and children who had sought refuge in barns on an island in the Savannah River heard the sounds of battle and saw clouds of smoke. A 15-year-old girl described her anguish as she pondered the fate of her father and fiancé, who were serving in the loyalist forces with the British defenders:

Alas, every heart in our barn was aching, every eye in tears!

... Our anxiety to hear about our friends may well be imagined, but we soon had great reason for gratitude and praise. None of our relatives and friends were killed or wounded, though all were much fatigued from many weeks' want of rest, and from that day's action. We had stock of all descriptions, and many a harmless animal and turkey was killed and prepared, to send over to our friends...

When we got into the town it offered a desolate view. The streets were cut into deep holes by the shells, and the houses were riddled with the rain of cannon balls. Winter was now approaching and many houses were not habitable, so Dr. Johnston with his family took a house out of town until his was repaired. (Johnston 61-63)

Aftermath of battle

Estimates of British casualties range from sixteen to forty killed and thirty-nine to sixty-three wounded. General Prevost reported that three officers of the 71st Regiment had been killed: Lieutenant Henry McPherson of the 1st Battalion on September 24; Captain-Lieutenant of Dragoons Thomas Tawse of the 1st Battalion on October 9; and Lieutenant of Dragoons Smollet Campbell of the 2nd Battalion on October 9.

A story on the siege of Savannah published two months after the battle in *Rivington's Royal Gazette* announced the death of Eneas McIntosh, Paymaster of the 71st Regiment, without specifying whether his death was a direct result of the battle. A correction in a subsequent paper gave the Paymaster's name as Angus McIntosh. Another officer named Eneas McIntosh was reported to be still at Savannah (Hough, *Savannah* 55). The other officer presumably was Aeneas Mackintosh, the 23rd Chief of Clan Mackintosh, who served throughout the war as a captain in the 2nd Battalion of the 71st Regiment of Foot.

The French had 521 men killed and wounded, and the Americans suffered 231 casualties. Historian Alexander Lawrence describes the grisly aftermath of the death of Major John Jones, an aide to Lachlan McIntosh: "Jones' body would be dumped into a burial pit so shallow a friend is said to have recognized his protruding hand and accorded his shattered remains a decent burial" (114). Jones had written his last letter to his wife Polly four days before the battle and she received it at her refuge in South Carolina after his death. "Adieu, my good wife," he had written, "and believe me to be, with sincerity, your ever affectionate, John Jones" (Kennedy 132).

About one-fourth of the South Carolinians engaged in the battle were killed. Two hundred bodies were buried around the Spring Hill redoubt. An American officer reported that the men of 2nd South Carolina Regiment, commanded by Francis Marion, "particularly distinguished themselves and suffered most" (Hough, *Savannah* 168). Two officers of the 2nd Regiment were killed and three were wounded.

While the French and Americans were burying their dead, the loyalist Rory McIntosh strutted about the battlefield and proclaimed, "A glorious sight – our enemies slain in battle!" (White 473).

Allies withdraw

Count d'Estaing raised the siege on October 18 and evacuated the French forces by sea. General Lincoln led the main American army back across the Savannah River on October 19 and returned to Charleston.

Lachlan McIntosh, still worried about his family in Savannah, made preparations to withdraw his Georgia troops. Many of his soldiers, however, disappeared into the countryside. Many others were sick or wounded. He had trouble finding enough able-bodied men to serve as guards. Leaving his family in enemy hands, he led the remnant of his force slowly back to Augusta.

Civilians suffer in Savannah

A British officer described conditions inside Savannah, where Lachlan McIntosh's wife and younger children remained:

> Poor Pollard, my Assistant, was killed the 4th of October by an 18-Pounder, my fine valuable Negro Carpenter the 7th, and a beautiful Mare that cost me 20 Guineas; my Store of Wine, all broke by Shot and Shells, and my Quarters torn to Pieces; but this is Neighbor's Fate, and the whole Town is in the same State. (Hough, *Savannah* 87-88)

Warriors die of wounds and fatigue

Sergeant Jasper, who had been wounded while carrying the 2nd South Carolina Regiment's colors, was put aboard a ship bound to Charleston and died at sea. Count Pulaski, who had been wounded in the thigh during a daring cavalry charge, was carried aboard the *Wasp*, an American brig, where he died despite the efforts of the most skillful surgeons.

Lieutenant Colonel Maitland of the British 71st Regiment, who had been suffering from a fever throughout the siege, died October 25 at Savannah. Noting that the "fatigues" of the siege damaged Maitland's health, Prevost described Maitland's death as "literally to have happened on Actual Service." Prevost said the loss of Maitland was "very much, and very justly regretted by all who knew him, both as a Gentleman, and as an Officer" (Lawrence, *Storm* 141). Maitland's eulogy was published in the *Royal Gazette*:

> The late Colonel Maitland was one of the most active Officers at the Commencement, and during the Progress of the present War. His Zeal and Gallantry were sufficient Incitements to lead him where Danger dignified and rendered a Post honourable. Though he possessed an early Fortune, had a Seat in the House of Commons, and was of an advanced Age, yet he never availed himself of such powerful Pretensions, or expressed a Desire of retiring from the Field of Honour. Unshaken Loyalty, genuine Patriotism, undaunted Bravery, judicious Conduct, steady Coolness, and unremitting Perseverance, constituted his Character as an Officer... His Country will feel the Loss of so accomplished a Chief; his Acquaintances long lament the Loss of so valuable a Friend; the Indigent search in vain for another so eminently Benevolent; and the Soldiers, long accustomed to his pleasing Command, lament his Death, and revere his Memory. (Hough, *Savannah* 110-12)

Flory McDonald sails homeward

Flory McDonald – the famed benefactress of Bonnie Prince Charlie – stayed with her husband Allan at his post in Windsor, Nova Scotia, for less than a year. She had broken an arm in a fall from a horse in North Carolina and during the summer she spent in Nova Scotia she suffered "ane accidental fall... dislockated the wrist of the other hand, and brock some tendons, which confined [her] for two months, altho [she] had the assistance of the Regimental Surgeon" (Toffey 134). She decided to return to Scotland while the Revolution continued to rage in America. "Flora departed for her homeland," American historian Bobby Gilmer Moss reports. "On the voyage the ship was attacked by a French ship-of-war and during the fight Flora fell down a flight of steps and broke her arm" (*Moores Creek* 33). Flory wrote:

> I fixed my thoughts on seeing my native Country, tho in a tender state, my husband obtained a birth in the Lord Dunmore, Letter of mark ship of 24 guns, I and three other young ladys and two gentlemen, sett sail in octr. But in our

passage spying a sail, made ready for action and in hurreying the Ladys below, to a place of Safety, my foot slipping a step in the trap, fell and brock the dislockated arm in two. It was sett with bandages over slips of wood, and keep my bed till we arrived in the Thames. (qtd. in Toffey 134)

Scottish biographer Alexander Macgregor adds some exciting embellishments:

Crossing the Atlantic, with none of her family… (for her five sons and son-in-law were actively engaged in the prevailing war), the gallant Flora met with the last of her adventures. The vessel in which she sailed was met by a French privateer, and a smart action took place. During the engagement, Flora refused to take shelter below, but prominently appeared on deck, where, with her wonted magnanimity, she inspired the sailors with courage, and assured them of success. Unfortunately her left arm was broken in the conflict, and she was afterwards accustomed to say that she had fought both for the House of Stuart and for the House of Hanover, but had been worsted in the service of each. (169)

Alexander McDonald re-enlists
Sergeant Major Alexander McDonald of the Darien district reenlisted in the 2nd South Carolina Regiment under Captain Thomas Dunbar on November 1, 1779.

Francis Marion's men suffer at Sheldon
When the main American army returned from Savannah to Charleston, the South Carolina regiments were stationed at Sheldon under the command of Lieutenant Colonel Francis Marion. In December, Marion reported in his rudimentary writing style "Distress of the Soldiers, for want of Shoes, they are without & doing Duty in the field, in Exceding Cold & frost" (Rankin 40). The men started taking apart the local church to use its bricks to build huts, but were stopped and had to settle for shelters of logs and earth.

The men celebrated Christmas day by firing their muskets, resulting in an angry reprimand from Marion for wasting ammunition.

Bandits attack Lachlan McIntosh

Nearly two years had passed since Lachlan McIntosh had seen his wife and youngest children. He had left them in Savannah while on assignment in the North and the West, and he had returned to the South because the British occupation of Savannah placed his family behind enemy lines. After the allied attack on Savannah failed, his family remained in British custody. In late December, he learned that the British were willing to release his family. At this point he put his family responsibilities ahead of his military duties, and he turned to a family member – his older brother – for help.

He hurried from Augusta to make the arrangements to free his wife and children. Because he was on a personal mission rather than a military campaign, Lachlan was accompanied only by his brother William and a few servants. Bitter winter weather slowed their progress.

As the coldest night of the year descended, the traveling party stopped at a hut beside the road. The men went inside to build a fire before unpacking the gear on their horses. Bandits stormed into the hut. One bandit pointed his gun at Lachlan McIntosh and pulled the trigger, but the gun misfired. Lachlan wrested the gun away. Lachlan then struck another gunman and deflected a shot overhead. Lachlan, William, and their servants fought their way clear of the bandits and escaped out the back door of the hut. The bandits plundered the baggage on the horses, taking not only supplies but also personal belongings and papers (Jackson 103-04).

George McIntosh dies

Not long after William and Lachlan McIntosh fended off the bandits, they learned that their younger brother George McIntosh had died. Lachlan had been especially close to George since the two of them had gone to Charleston when they were young. Political accusations against George had led to the duel between Lachlan and Button Gwinnett, which forever changed Lachlan's military career. George was just 40 years old when he died in December of 1779. He left his 7-year-old son John Houston McIntosh an orphan because his wife Ann Priscilla – sister of Sir Patrick Houston – had died in 1777. When Lachlan got the grim news, he set out from Augusta for George's plantation Rice Hope near Darien. Arriving several days after the funeral, Lachlan looked through George's papers and saved the grants and titles to George's land at the headwaters of the Sapelo River. Lachlan engaged a wagoner to carry a parcel of indigo from the plantation to Charleston, where it would be safe from the British forces occupying coastal Georgia. George's personal belongings were left in the care of the plantation overseer as Lachlan hurried to leave his family homeland that had become enemy territory ("Case" 187-88).

Flory McDonald bedridden

When Flory McDonald – famous for having rescued Bonnie Prince Charlie – arrived in London from Nova Scotia, she suffered from badly-healed broken bones and from a broken heart: Her son Alexander had died of complications of a wound presumably inflicted during the Battle of Moore's Creek Bridge. "To my great sorrow," she wrote, "on my landing, received the melancholy newes of my son Alex's death, Lieut. Of Light Infantry, being lost on his way home having got lieve on account of his bad state of health, an old wound constantly breaking out, from the fatigue of the light-infantry Service brought him very lowe." The news, she said later, "brought on a violent fit of sickness, which confined me to my bed" (Vining 185).

British fleet endures hellish voyage

Once the British held Savannah securely, they made plans to capture Charleston. Since General Augustine Prevost did not have enough men to hold Georgia and also take South Carolina, the British sent an army from New York. Sir Henry Clinton, the commander in chief of British forces in America, conducted the expedition himself. A hundred ships carrying 8,708 men weighed anchor on December 26 and almost immediately encountered winter storms. A Hessian officer reported: "On the 28th severe storms set in which scattered the fleet so widely that frequently we could not count over ten to twenty ships for several days, notwithstanding the fact that it numbered some hundred sail" (Uhlendorf 28).

Another Hessian officer gave a daily account of the voyage as the year 1779 came to an end:

> Dec. 28: A heavy sea and every indication of a storm… Our ship … pitched a good deal… Nothing remained in its proper

place unless firmly secured. It was impossible to cook anything, and the men had to be satisfied with biscuit and rum. Toward two in the morning an Anspach jager came rushing into the cabin with the report that one side of the ship was stove in and that some of the jagers had already been killed. It was pitch dark in the hold where they lay; the berths were arranged in two tiers and accommodated six men each. The rolling of the ship had caused four of the berths to come loose and collapse, so that the jagers in the upper berths had fallen, berths and all, upon those lying beneath. This crash had awakened the few still asleep. At this moment, with all wide awake and shouting, a big rude wave had rushed in through the opening above and a panicky, but easily excusable fear had spread over the entire ship.

By the light of the lamp the face of the frightened jager cheered up again.

Dec. 29: The storm continued through the whole forenoon, but the splashing of the waves showed us that it was beginning to slacken. Toward ten o'clock we sailed on again with an extremely high sea and a variable wind...

Dec. 30: ... The most unpleasant thing of all during a voyage in winter is, it seems, the necessity of having a fire in one's cabin, for the coal fumes impregnate the entire atmosphere with an everlasting disagreeable odor, affecting the windpipe and causing headaches and nausea.

Toward evening there was sheet lightning, in winter the certain forerunner of an approaching storm, and at two o'clock we had a violent squall with rain. We were in danger. Our ship was running before the wind, and the flagship, into whose course we were driven, was heading straight for us. Another moment and our ship would have been run down. However, the speed with which the man-of-war tacked saved us.... (Uhlendorf 111-15)

The British and Hessian troops would endure the hellish voyage down the Atlantic coast into the new year.

1780

American forces suffer from wintry weather, a British expedition endures storms at sea, and Lachlan McIntosh's family seeks refuge. Aeneas Mackintosh is among the British troops who capture Charleston, while Lachlan McIntosh and Alexander McDonald are among the American defenders. Aeneas Mackintosh serves in the British army under Lord Cornwallis that won the Battle of Camden. Rory McIntosh meets the Chief of Clan Mackintosh in Charleston. Allen McDonald distinguishes himself in combat under the command of Francis Marion.

Hellish voyage continues

Misery continued into the new year for 8,708 men in a British fleet of a hundred ships on a mission to conquer the South. The fleet sailed from New York on December 26 for what would ordinarily be a ten-day sail to Savannah. Storms lashed the fleet, however, and not only slowed the ships but also drove them into the northward-flowing Gulf Stream, which made their voyage southward seem interminable. The trip ended up taking five weeks. The hellish conditions affected men and beasts. Horses suffered injuries and death from being tossed around in the holds of the ships during vicious storms. When ships sank, horses sank with them. The water and feed that would have nourished horses during a ten-day trip ran out long before the five-week trip ended, and the sailors had no choice but to throw horses overboard. The army, which needed horses to pull heavy artillery, transport supplies, and mount cavalry, lost almost all its horses at sea.

Hessian officers described the voyage from New York to Savannah in their letters and diaries, written in German. An English translation of a letter from Captain Johann Ewald says:

> While on the open sea the Admiral was compelled several times to take troops from ships that had been badly damaged by constant storms and put them on board other vessels. Gradually the fleet assembled again. In spite of great adversity sixty-two vessels ran safely into the mouth of the Savannah River on the 2nd of February and anchored at Tybee,

where we found the greater number of the scattered ships already at anchor. The transports carrying the horses of the cavalry and artillery had been obliged to throw most of the horses overboard, an irreparable loss... (Uhlendorf 28)

The diary of Captain Johann Hinrichs describes the grueling voyage in gruesome detail:

Jan. 1: ... In the course of the afternoon it became gloomy and cloudy. In the evening it grew stormier and stormier, and during the night we had a real storm. Everything on board the ship was topsy-turvy; one sail after another was furled. The night was bad.

Jan. 2: And so was the following day... The storm seemed to be increasing every moment, and there was not the least prospect of the weather changing soon. – Indeed, it was no spring sun that smiled on us!...

Jan. 3: Today was no better than yesterday; in fact it was worse. Left to the fury of wave and wind, we drifted southward with helm lashed and before one sail...

Jan. 4: Last night was no better than the previous night, nor was the day any better – if anything, it was worse. It was so gloomy and dark that we lost sight of the fleet during the night. Hence, in spite of the abominable weather, we set four sails at eight o'clock in the morning. Toward noon we rejoined the fleet and then lay to again... The absence of the *Renown* allowed us to hope that the *Anna* transport, which was carrying Captain von Hanger's company of chasseurs and had lost her mainmast and mizzenmast in the first storm, was still afloat and the chasseurs alive, for she had been taken in tow by the *Renown* after the first storm.

Jan. 5: This morning we sailed for a few hours, but then the storm began to rage again so violently that toward noon it was necessary to lash the helm again and furl all the sails except one. The entire day and night one could see and hear nothing but the flags and shots of ships in distress. However, no one could go to their assistance. At noon our ship, too, sprung a leak below the cabin, near the helm. But it was easily stopped since one could get to it without trouble...

Jan. 6: Storm, rain, hail, snow, and the waves breaking over the cabin...

Jan. 7: Always the same weather!... The weather became thicker and thicker and the sea higher than at any time before...

Jan. 8: The wind was as violent as before...

Jan. 9: Up to midnight last night we had a SW. storm...

Jan. 10: In a short time the sea had become so calm and looked so innocent that one could almost come to love this treacherous element...

Jan. 11: This morning we had a head wind (SW.) and every inch we moved we went farther from our destination... In the afternoon there was a little mutiny among the crew, who complained to the ship's master about their rations. But everything was adjusted.

Jan. 12: The wind remained contrary... Toward afternoon, the weather became fairly good, though it was bitter cold. A strong gale and a heavy sea, tossing the ship a good deal.

Jan. 13: Everything the same! Still a westerly wind! We cruised up and down. Terrible weather! Snow, rain, hail, storm, foaming waves, and bitter cold!

Jan. 16: ... The weather was threatening, and the storm came quickly indeed. The ship had to withstand terrific pounding during the night.

Jan. 17: The sea was very rough and the wind was contrary...

Jan. 18: The same wind exactly and a swift current...

Jan. 19: A rather cold morning for this warm region, a cloudy sky, and always, always contrary wind... Toward noon the gale increased in violence... During the night the storm broke in all its fury. Never before had the wind and the water raged so; never before had the ship been battered as it was last night...

Jan. 20: This morning we still had the storm; by noon, however, it had abated...

Jan. 31: This was the forty-third day we have spent on board the ship, and the thirty-sixth day of our voyage. During these thirty-six days we had fifteen days of storm and twenty-five days of contrary wind. We have sailed 1,851 miles...

Feb. 1: ... we sighted Tybee Island ... and also the lighthouse...but who can foresee misfortune! Before we realized it we were aground on a sandbank...

Feb. 2: The ship heeled a good deal during the night... the tide set us free early in the morning... in the afternoon... we cast anchor in Savannah Sound, hard by Great Tybee Island. (Uhlendorf 117-43)

Archibald Campbell describes British strategy

Archibald Campbell – the commander of the 71st Regiment who had captured Savannah and had suggested the strategy for defeating the Americans at Brier Creek before returning to England – described the British plans in a letter to his son Hugh, who was still with the 71st Regiment in Georgia:

LONDON, 15th January, 1780

My Dear Hugh:

In my last, I informed you that the Defence of Savannah gave great Satisfaction here; and it has had a very good Effect upon the Minds of the People, whose Spirits were down on Account of the Length of Time which elapsed without any Effort even, to do Good. And though this was in some Measure no more than a gallant Defence, yet it made an Impression almost equal to what a Victory would have done.

The Plan which is now understood to be determined upon here for carrying on the War, is to take a certain Number of Posts in America, in such a Way as to command the Trade of the Country, and to have no other Object in America than the maintaining of these Posts, and the ruling of the Trade by our Fleets.

The Posts said to be fixed upon, are Halifax, Penobscot, New York, Portsmouth in Virginia, Charlestown, Savannah and St. Augustine. To accomplish which, we imagine that you are now employed in taking Charlestown, and establishing a Post at Portsmouth.

These Objects being accomplished, we understand 12,000 Men are to be detached to the West Indies, which is to be the active Seat of War against the French and Spaniards.

It is evident that unless we can carry on an active and defensive War against them abroad, we can never succeed or do well. Last Campaign we were all defensive, and every Thing went badly with us. I never wish to see such another Campaign.

We will be anxious, however, to know what our wise Heads in America will think of this plan for the American War. To be sure, the more Troops you can spare from thence to drub the common Enemies, the better. Yet I fear the Number mentioned is more than you can give, after putting the Posts mentioned in a proper Condition.

We have had Nothing new of any Moment going on since I wrote you. Indeed, Parliament has been adjourned all the Time, which prevents our furnishing so much as we otherwise do of the State Operations.

It is believed by many that there is an Alliance formed between us and Russia; and I am inclined to believe that that either is the Case, or that there is a Treaty in forwardness. They can very well spare us twenty Ships of the Line, which would enable us to detach a great Force to the West Indies. Indeed, it would completely restore us to the Superiority of the Seas. There is nothing settled yet between us and the Dutch, about our Right of searching their Ships. I expect our Court will persist in this Right, and I do not imagine the Dutch will chuse to go to War with us.

Farewell my dear Boy,
I ever am, unalterably yours,
A. Campbell.
Lieut., and Adjutant Hugh Campbell,
2nd Battalion, 71st Regiment, Georgia.
[Royal Gazette, June 17.]
(qtd. in Hough, *Charleston* 143-46)

Lachlan McIntosh's family freed

In early January, the British released Lachlan McIntosh's wife Sarah and their five youngest children from British-occupied Savannah. Lachlan McIntosh reported that his loved ones were "thrown over to Carolina with only the bare Clothes they had on" (Lawrence, "Suspension" 122). The family enjoyed only a short period together before Lachlan received orders to report to General Lincoln in Charleston.

Americans prepare for attack on Charleston

Fearing a British attack on Charleston, General Benjamin Lincoln called in the troops from outlying positions on January 31. Only a small force of light infantry and cavalry would remain in the field to observe British operations. A little over two hundred of the best men under Francis Marion's command at Sheldon would be chosen for the light infantry. Once Lieutenant Colonel William Henderson arrived to take command of the light infantry, Marion led the 2nd South Carolina Regiment – in which Alexander McDonald of the Darien district served – from Sheldon toward Charleston. By February 19, the men of the 2nd Regiment were working to strengthen fortifications at Charleston.

British army moves toward Charleston

The British fleet that transported Sir Henry Clinton's army from New York to Savannah was soon employed in an attack on Charleston. The ships left Savannah on February 9 and arrived the next day at the mouth of the North Edisto River, just south of Charleston. Troop transports carried most of the army into the inlet, where the men boarded longboats and were taken ashore. The fleet proceeded to blockade Charleston Harbor.

With Sir Henry Clinton in command and Lord Cornwallis as second in command, the army moved across Seabrook Island onto Johns Island. Boats in the Edisto and Stono rivers carried supplies for the troops on the island.

Lachlan McIntosh seeks refuge for family

Knowing that the British were on their way to Charleston, Lachlan McIntosh decided to take his wife and younger children to the relative safety of the backcountry of South Carolina. He recorded his experiences in a journal:

> Ponpon, Parsonage Saturday the 12th. Feby 1780
> Heard that between forty & fifty Sail of the Enemys Ships came in yesterday at No. Edisto Inlet, and were Landed in force upon Johns Island. Note, the British fleet arrived off Stonoe Inlet the 9th. Feby. (& alarm fired)
> Sunday the 13th February 1780

Set off this Day with my Family two wagons Northwardly, crossed ponpond river at Parkers ferry, & Lodged this night at Mr. J. McQueen's planta.

Monday the 14th. Feby.

… we crossed over Bacon Bridge & through Dorchester to Mr. Lartezettes at Goose Creek where we were detained this Night and all the next Day & Night. Sent letter to Genl. Lincoln & recd. an Answer giving leave to fix my Family.

Wednesday, the 16th. Feby. 1780

Met Genl. Huger with his Family at Monks Corner going up the Country – here we heard that Murray's ferry [was] impassable with Carriages which determined me to go higher up Santee River to put up this Night at Mr. Thos. Sabbs.

Thursday 17th. Feby.

Baited at Martins and put up this Night at Nelson's Ferry.

Friday the 18th. Feby.

Crossed the Ferry with much difficulty, and Lodged this Night at Colo. Sumpter's where we were weather bound all the next day and night and very genteely treated.

Sunday the 20th. Feby.

Put up this Night at Capt. Richardson's at the entrance of the high Hills.

Monday the 21st. Feby. 1780

Came to a house upon the high Hills belonging to Morton Wilkinson, Just Evacuated by a Capt. Chisolm, where we stayed till Sunday morning trying to get an empty House in this Neighborhood to no purpose.

Sunday the 27th. Feby.

Set off this Morning for Cambden & put up this night at one McCormicks a Little Inhospitable House over [blank] Creek.

Monday the 28th. Feby. 1780

Put up this Night at old payn's House upon Pine tree, or Town Creek in Sight of Cambden where we stayed all the next day& were visited by Messrs. Jo. Kershaw Jo. Habersham E. Telfair &ca.

Tuesday, the 29th. Feby. 1780

Moved this Evening to a Little Shop in Cambden which was the only Vacant House Colo. Kershaw could procure for me & was Lyable to be turned out every Hour, as it was engaged for Genl. Huger's Family if they came that Length.

My old Friend & acquaintance J. Kershaw was kind enough to promise he would Supply my Family with provision during my absence, & took the few Slaves I had Left to work with his own, upon Shares...

I Stayed here Settling these Matters, & my Family [for about a week] (96-97)

British troops approach Charleston

On February 28, the British army crossed the Stono River onto James Island across the harbor from Charleston. The 2nd Battalion of the 71st Regiment – in which Aeneas Mackintosh served – arrived from Savannah on March 3 (Uhlendorf 375). On March 7, the British constructed a bridge over Wappoo Cut so that the army could continue to advance. By March 9, two companies of the 71st were located at Hamilton's house and three companies of the 71st were placed on Lighthouse Island (Uhlendorf 199 - 203).

British gentleman describes situation

A British gentleman wrote a letter "dated at a Rebel house, 6 miles from Charleston, March 6, 1780" describing the political and military situation in Georgia and South Carolina:

Our passage, with very few Exceptions, was a long Series of blustering, disagreeable Weather, from the 26th of December, when we sailed from Sandy Hook, till the first of February, when the Fleet arrived at Tybee Island.

From our Arrival till the 9th, the General and many of the Principal Officers were at Savannah, when they returned and sailed, leaving one Battalion of the 71st, many Horses, Engineer's Stores, embarked to follow. General Patterson, with one Battalion of the 71st, a Hessian Regiment, and the Provincials, with Major Ferguson's Corps, are gone to Augusta. The Province of Georgia is in a State of perfect Security and Peace, and it is very probable the greatest Part of their Troops, after visiting their Friends on the Western Frontiers, may join the Army, not far from Charlestown (Hough, *Charleston* 35-37).

Lachlan McIntosh travels to Charleston

Having found refuge for his family in Camden, General Lachlan McIntosh traveled back to Charleston to report for duty. His journal describes his journey:

Wednesday the 8th. March, 1780

Sett off this morning with Lt. Colo. Hopkins (Just from Virginia) for Charlesto. – crossed the Wateree River at Cambden, & took up the Night at Mrs. McCords, Congree Ferry.

Thursday the 9th. March

Baited at fine Springs of Utaw, & Lodged the Night at [blank's] Tavern at Manigualt Ferry although my old friend & Country Man Wm. LeConte lived close by – here I met my Son Lackie going from Charlesto. to see his Mother at Cambden in his way to Augusta, & as the direct Road was not Safe traveling, which he experienced going there from ponpon when he Set off from the day we left it. (97)

Lachlan McIntosh reports for duty

Lachlan McIntosh had lived in Charleston as a young man, and he had married a South Carolina girl. The situation was vastly different in the spring of 1780 – his wife was a refugee in the backcountry and Charleston was under attack. McIntosh wrote a "Journal of the Siege of Charlestown" that describes his arrival:

Saturday the 11th March 1780

Heard Cannon all this Day as we rid along the Road, which made us impatient – that Genl. Moultrie who commanded the Horse at Bacon Bridge was taken Sick, & Gen. Huger Sent to take that Command in his room; -- it consisted of Bland's Boyler's Polaskys & Horrys Corps, with Some Voluntiers – altoge abot. 250 Horse; came to Charlestown in the Evening, & put up at Mrs. Minis's, tho' disagreeable upon Accot. Of some British Prisoners quartered at her House…

Sunday the 12th March

As I did not find Genl. Lincoln at home last Night I waited upon him this Morning, -- found the Enemy had possession of James Island since the latter end of Feby. &

were now errecting a work upon Bunkers Hill, behind Fort
Johnston. – We saw their Fleet, Transports, Store-ships,
Merchant Men &ca in Stonoe River, through Wappoe Cut,
from Fergusons House in Trad Street & some Men of War
over the Barr. – our Horse skirmished near Ashly Ferry.

Monday the 13th March

The Enemy burnt Fenwick's House on Wappoo Neck
(made a Pest House for the Small pox) & errected a Battery
of four *(six)* heavy Cannon, distance [blank] yds from
Town. I was ordered to take the Command of the So. Caro.
Country Militia. (98)

Lincoln posted most of the North Carolina and South Carolina
militia in batteries along the waterfront and put them under the
command of McIntosh. A muster record from the siege of Charleston shows a total of 1,231 men in the South Carolina and North
Carolina militia (Lumpkin 287). A contemporary newspaper account gives this information: "Brigadier General McIntosh's Brigade of Coventry, consisting of Militia – Col. Maybank's, Col.
Garden's, Col. Skirvin's, Col. McDougall's, Col. Giles's, Col.
Hick's, Col. Richardson's, Col. Kirshaw's, Col. Goodwyn's, Col.
Huntington's, Col. Tinning's" (Hough, *Charleston* 79).

McIntosh was reunited at Charleston with the Chevalier de
Cambray-Digny, an engineer who had laid out McIntosh's new
forts in the Western Department in 1778 and designed the defenses
of Charleston in 1780 (Williams 5-6). During their stint in the
Western Department, McIntosh had described Cambray as "a Gentleman of real Merit" (Kellogg 190).

McIntosh also was reunited with Colonel Thomas Clark, who
had served under McIntosh's command at Valley Forge and had
assumed command of the North Carolina Brigade when McIntosh
was appointed to the Western Department. Since then, Clark had
been deployed to the South and had been wounded at Stono Ferry
in June of 1779 before participating in the defense of Charleston
(Fitzpatrick 11: 388). As the siege progressed, McIntosh recorded
the details in a journal:

Tuesday 14th March 1780

The Enemy errected another Battery of two heavy
Cannon So. Side of Ashly River about Herveys above the

other, & a Bomb Battery upon a rising ground between the two Gun Batteries, the latter never played.

Wednesday the 15th March.

A Colonel's Command kept some time past at Ashley Ferry this Side were withdrawn this day & marched down to Gibb's, abot. 1½ Miles from our Lines, where we had a Picquett before. – only 25 Men for a Look out Left at the ferry.

Tuesday the 16th.

The Light Infantry of Hogans Brigade ordered to relieve the Command at Gibbes's – twelve Sail Shipping seen off of the Barr. (98-99)

Congress suspends Lachlan McIntosh

From Lachlan McIntosh's "Journal of the Siege of Charlestown:"

Friday the 17th March.

My Family, Servants, Horses, &ca. were moved yesterday to new quarters, Mr. Lowndes House where Genl. Hogun Lodged, near Ferguson's -- & early this Morning went to it myself. – rcd. Letter by Capt. Nash from president of Congress – date 15th Feby. (99)

In his journal, McIntosh understates the importance of the letter from Congress. McIntosh was never able to avoid Georgia politics, and on this occasion his political enemies hurt him deeply. Savannah historian Alexander Lawrence describes the situation:

On February 15, 1780, the Continental Congress without giving a hearing to Brigadier General Lachlan McIntosh abruptly relieved him of duty in the Southern Department of the army. By a vote of five states to three (with an even division in three others) it resolved "That a copy of the letters from the State of Georgia, as far as they related to General McIntosh, be transmitted to that officer, and that he be informed Congress deem it inexpedient to employ him at present in the southern army, and therefore, that his services in that department be dispensed with, until the further order of Congress."

Congress took this action on the basis of what McIntosh called "*ex parta* evidence," namely certain papers
which Governor George Walton transmitted to it. Among
the letters and documents sent from Georgia was an address
which purported to have been written "Pursuant to the
command of the General Assembly." It was signed "Wm.
Glascock." Glascock was Speaker of the Georgia Assembly.

The Address dealt with the urgent need for aid to the
State as a result of the British invasion. It contained a paragraph attacking General McIntosh who had returned to
Georgia in the summer of 1779 after military service at
Valley Forge and in the Western Department. A virtual exile from Georgia following his slaying of Button Gwinnett
in a duel, he had been transferred northward nearly twenty
months before.

The paragraph of the Address read: "It is to be wished
we could advise Congress that the return of Brigadier-
General McIntosh gave Satisfaction to either the Militia or
Confederals: but the common dissatisfaction is such, and
that grounded on weighty reasons, it is highly necessary
that Congress would, whilst that Officer is in the service of
the United States, direct some distant field for the exercise
of his abilities."

When Congress voted to dispense with the services of
General McIntosh it was unaware that someone else had
signed the Speaker's name to the Address of the Assembly
and that, so far from concurring with the portion relating to
that officer, Glascock vehemently denied any such attitude
existed in Georgia. "I do hereby most Solemnly declare to
congress," he protested on learning of the deception, "that
the above Extract is a flagrant forgery, of which I disclaim
all knowledge whatever, Either directly or indirectly."
McIntosh deserved, he said, "the greatest testimonials of
Publick approbation, instead of the malicious insinuations
of private Slander."

Quite naturally the victim of the "Address" looked upon Walton as the culprit. The Governor not only had transmitted the offensive paper to Congress but remarked at the
time that "he had made General McIntosh and he would be

Damned if he would not break him." (Lawrence, "Suspension" 101-02)

Throughout his career, McIntosh went into a rage whenever his honor was at stake, and this dishonor was especially hard to bear. His anger was evident when he showed the letter to General Lincoln – the commander of the American army in the South – and to South Carolina Governor Rutledge – the highest authority over the South Carolina militia units that McIntosh commanded at Charleston. After examining the letter and studying the political accusations that instigated it, they told him to remain at his post as long as the garrison was under siege (Jackson 105).

British fleet crosses the bar

While the British army marched toward Charleston, the British fleet maneuvered to clear the bar at Charleston harbor. The fleet contended against not only shifting sands, fluctuating tides, and fickle winds, but also the guns of Fort Moultrie and American warships.

To deprive the British of navigation markers, the Americans destroyed the beacon and lighthouse, blackened the towering steeple of St. Michael's Church, and removed buoys marking the channel.

The British responded by putting three companies of the 71st Highlanders and two cannon on Lighthouse Island to cover their ships while they located the channel and placed new buoys. The Highlanders assisted the sailors in unloading the lower tiers of guns and supplies from the ships and brought them to Lighthouse Island in two transports (Uhlendorf 209). The British fleet cleared the bar on March 20, and the next day the American warships withdrew into the Cooper River. On March 22 Clinton sent orders for the Highlanders to leave the harbor and reinforce the army marching toward Charleston.

British army reaches Charleston Peninsula

During the time that the main British force had been advancing on Charleston, a smaller force under General Paterson had marched from Savannah toward Augusta as a diversion. This smaller force included the 1st Battalion of the 71st Regiment and the American Volunteers, consisting of loyalists from the northern colonies led by Patrick Ferguson, a Scottish gentleman. After feinting toward Augusta, Paterson's force crossed the Savannah River at Ebenezer and marched toward Charleston. Banastre Tarleton, commander of mounted infantry and cavalry, joined Paterson's force near Jacksonboro on March 21, after taking horses from sea island plantations near Port Royal to replace the horses that died in the voyage from New York. Paterson's force joined the main British army at Rantowles on March 26; at this point, both the 1st and 2nd Battalions of the 71st were with the main body of troops.

By March 28, the British army was ready to cross the Ashley River, the last natural barrier separating the British from the Charleston Peninsula.

The Americans had posted a light infantry force to guard the Ashley River crossing at Bacon's Bridge and a slightly smaller force to guard Ashley Ferry. The British avoided the token American opposition by crossing at Drayton Hall. Longboats carried the first division of the British forces across the river at dawn on March 29. By afternoon the entire force, including the 71st Highland Regiment, was on the Charleston side of the river. The troops then moved into position to lay siege to the town.

John Laurens leads troops in skirmish

The Americans sent two hundred of their best men to impede the British advance. The light companies of the 2nd and 3rd South Carolina Regiments and the light companies of the North Carolina brigade were combined into a new light infantry brigade. The commander was Lieutenant Colonel John Laurens – the son of Henry Laurens, who was a longtime friend and business associate of Lachlan McIntosh. As the British marched toward Charleston, the brigade took position in a small fortification a mile outside of town. About a mile farther out of town, a detachment of riflemen hid in the woods alongside the road. When the British arrived at noon on March 30, the riflemen ambushed the lead column. The opening volley wounded Lord Caithness, an aide to General Clinton. The British counterattacked, driving the American riflemen down the road toward Charleston. A running battle continued for half an hour.

When the riflemen returned to their brigade, Laurens and Major Edward Hyne rode out of the fortification to reconnoiter. Hessian troops fired from a hidden position in the trees. Hyne was wounded and fell from his horse. Laurens drove off the riderless horse to keep the British from taking it, and helped Hyne back into the fortification. Lincoln sent orders to Laurens to abandon from the fortification. The opposing troops exchanged fire as the Americans withdrew. Hessians occupied the fortification

Late in the afternoon, Laurens ordered a counterattack. A bayonet charge drove the Hessians out of the fortification. After the attack, Laurens found a dead Hessian holding Hyne's hat. British light infantry drove the American brigade back out of the fortification. Skirmishing continued until evening. When darkness fell, the brigade was inside the American lines at Charleston. The rear guard of the British army that night consisted of the 71st and 33rd Regiments.

Besiegers summon Charleston to surrender

On April 2, the British broke ground on their siege works in front of Charleston. The besiegers and defenders began bombarding one another with cannon and mortars.

After dark on April 5, the British battery on Fenwick's Point and the galleys in Wappoo Cut opened fire on the town, damaging several houses. Observers in the British lines heard Charlestonians screaming and women wailing.

The next night the cannonade continued, killing a carpenter and doing mayhem. The bombardment hit close to home for Lachlan McIntosh: two cannonballs went through McIntosh's quarters, five balls struck Mr. Ferguson's house and outbuildings in front of McIntosh's quarters, and the shelling killed two of McIntosh's horses in the yard (Borick 126).

The British commanders, "regretting the effusion of blood, and consonant to humanity towards the town and garrison of Charlestown, of the havoc and desolation with which they are threatened from the formidable force surrounding them by land and sea," issued a summons on April 10. They gave the Americans a chance to surrender, offering the alternatives "of saving their lives and property contained in the town, or of abiding by the fatal consequences of a cannonade and storm" (Southern 59).

The summons warned:

> Should the place in a fallacious security, or its commander in a wanton indifference to the fate of its inhabitants, delay the

surrender, or should public stores or shipping be destroyed, the resentment of an exasperated soldiery may intervene; but the same mild and compassionate offer can never be renewed. The respective commanders, who hereby summons the town, do not apprehend so rash a part, as further resistance will be taken, but rather that the gates will be opened, and themselves received with a degree of confidence which will forebode further reconciliation. (Southern 59-60)

Lincoln, perhaps because the people of Charleston had vilified him for exposing their homes and property to risk in his campaigns of the previous year, notified Clinton he would not surrender. He still had the option of evacuating the American army by boat up the Cooper River toward Moncks Corner.

Marion breaks his ankle

Inside Charleston, Captain Alexander McQueen hosted a dinner party at his house on the corner of Orange and Tradd streets. Francis Marion of the 2nd South Carolina Regiment was among the guests. After dinner, McQueen locked the doors and proposed numerous toasts to liberty and victory. He was conforming to a local custom in which the host and the guests would drink very heavily. Marion felt the custom was more honored in the breach than the observance, so he jumped out of a second-story window. When his feet hit the ground, one of his ankles broke. On April 12, Lincoln ordered all officers who were unfit for duty to leave Charleston, and Marion was carried out on a litter. He planned to stay with relatives along the Santee River while he recuperated. British patrols forced him into hiding. He moved from house to house and occasionally hid in the forest.

Charleston endures siege

Lachlan McIntosh was in a unique position to chronicle the siege. As a former resident of Charleston, he was familiar with the people and places involved. As an experienced military officer he understood the intricacies of siege warfare, and he attended meetings of the American generals during the siege. His professional experience as a surveyor reveals itself when he records distances in chains. His journal mixes his personal observations with official information on the events of the siege of Charleston:

Monday the 10th April.

Sr. Henry Clinton & Admiral Arbuthnot sent in a Flagg Summoning the Garrison and Town to Surrender – to which Genl. Lincoln immediately, & without Consulting any one, Sent them for answer, that his Duty and inclination Led him to hold out to the last extremity. – this Evening Capt. Jno. Gilbank killed by accident in Bolton's Battery &ca. &ca.

Tuesday, the 11th.

The Enemy use double diligence now in Compleating their Works & Mounting their Cannon, whilst we ply them with our Cannon and Mortars as Usual, and they from their Gallies and Battery West side of Ashly River in return. – (Jno Houstoun went over)

Wednesday, the 12th.

The Same as yesterday on both sides, it is said some several flat bottomed Boats were hauled on Land by the Enemy across the Neck from Ashly to Cooper River. –

This Day Genl. Lincoln Sent for the General Officers to his Marque & presented a Letter to them directed to Govr. Rutledge which they all Signed Signifying their Opinion in Support of the Generals (already given) that the Governor & part of his Council at least ought to Leave the Garrison, for many Substantial Reasons. (McIntosh 99-100)

American officers realize their dire straits

From   Lachlan   McIntosh's   "Journal   of   the   Siege   of Charlestown:"

Thursday the 13th April 1780.

Between Nine & Ten this Morning The Enemy opened all their Gun & Morter Batterys at once (being the first time they fired upon the Town or our Lines upon the front) & continued a furious Cannonade & Bombarding with little intermissions till Midnight, their Batterys from Wappoo playing upon the Left flank of our Lines & the Town at the same time, & their Gallies from Wappoo Creek during the Night as usual, which we returned Smartly from our Lines, & we presume with good effect. – a Sergt. & private of No. Carolina Killed, & some Women & Children in Town, the Houses are

much damaged and two were burned down near Genl
Moultrie's, Anson bg. [bourough], by Carcases of which they
threw several from Ten Inch Mortars. – their Cannon are
chiefly twenty four pounders opposite our Lines & 36 pounders upon Wappoo their Morters from 5 ½ to 13. (*10*) Inches.

On Embrasure at Redan No. 7 destroyed, & also a twenty Six pounder in the flanking Battery on the right, & an
eighteen pounder in the Latter dismounted with some other
smaller damage.

All the General Officers were called by Genl. Lincoln to
his quarters this Morning where he gave us the *first* Idea of
the State of the Garrison, the Men, provisions, Stores Artillery &c in it – the little hopes he had of any succour of Consequence & the opinion of the Engineers respecting our Fortifications; that they were *only Field* works, or Lines, & could
hold out but few days more. – with every information he
could obtain of the Numbers & Strength of the Enemy &ca.
&ca. [he was compelled to] take up the Idea, & Consider of
the Propriety of evacuating the Garrison when without hesita-
tion I gave it as my own opinion that as we were so unfortunate as to suffer ourselves to be penned up in the Town, &
cut off from all resources in such Circumstances, -- we
should not loose an hour longer in attempting to get the Continental Troops at Least out, while we had one side open yet
over Cooper River, upon whose safety, the Salvation not only
of this State but some other will (*may*) probably depend &
which I think all the other Gentn. Seemd to acquiesce in.

The General said he only desired now that we should
consider maturely of the expediency & practicability of such
a Measure by the time he would send for us again & the Cannonade mentioned this Morning from the Enemy beginning
broke up the Council abruptly.

Governor Rutledge & part of his Council went over
Cooper River abt. 12 o'Clock this Day.

Friday the 14th April

The Enemy are approaching fast upon the right & keep
up an Incessant fire from their small Arms, Cannon, and
Morters.

A Sergt. Of No. Caro. Killed by a Cannon Ball – also
two Matrosses of So. Caro. & one of Militia Artillery by two

of our Cannon going off while they were Loading them Capt.
Hill says our Horse were surprised this Day at Monks Corner
– killed [blank] Men & an Officer with [blank] Horses taken
        Saturday the 15th April.

        The Enemy keep Approaching fast on our right. – our
Mortars are ordered to the Right to annoy them. – A continual fire of small Arms Cannon & Mortars from the Enemy

        A Battery of two Guns opened by the Enemy at Stiles's
place on James Island. – which played constantly on the
Town – distance across 82. Chain. – many of the Enemys
Boats hauled over the Neck into Town Creek. – two of them
mounted with brass Cannon came down the Creek this Morning & fired at the Ranger and Adventure. (100-01)

Shelling wreaks havoc

From   Lachlan   McIntosh's   "Journal   of   the   Siege   of
Charlestown:"

Sunday the 16th
        Two eighteen pounders, -- a quantity of Provisions, &
other Valuable Articles were got out of the Wreck of the
Vessel near Fort Moultrie. – It is said the Enemy attempted to
Land on Hobcaw Neck from two Gun Boats, but were prevented by Colo. Malmedy (*Capt. Theus*). – Cannonading
&ca. on both sides all day & Night as usual. the new Church
Steeple struck by a 24 lb. Ball from James Island Battery. –
pits arm broke off &ca. – Major Hoggwith detachment of
[blank] Men ordered over this night to Lampriers point. (102)

        The report "pits arm broke off" refers to damage inflicted on a
statue of English political leader William Pitt that stood in down-
town Charleston. The journal continues:

Monday the 18th say 17th April
        An Inhabitant of the Town killed, & a Woman wounded
in bed together. – the approaches continued to the Right. –
The Enemy advanced their Bomb Battery within 800. yds. of
our Lines.
        Note: Signed a Letter Genl. Lincoln brought to my qrs.
(102)

The British close the noose

From Lachlan McIntosh's "Journal of the Siege of Charlestown:"

Tuesday the 18th April

The Enemy continue Aproaching fast. – and firing from their Cannon Mortars & Small Arms. – We advanced a Breast Work nearly fronting the square redoubt for Rifle Men, to annoy the Enemy in their Approaches.

– Mr. Ph. Neyle A D C. to Genl. Moultrie killed by a Cannon Ball. – two Men killed by small Arms and three wounded by a Shell.

– a Soldier of Colo. Neville had an arm shot off by our own Cannon while he was Sentrie outside the Abbaties. – also two french Men wounded, one lost a Legg & the other an Arm.

a twelve pounder burst in the Horn Work by which two Men were much hurt. – the Enemy do not now throw large shells as they have done, but Showers of small ones from their Mortars and Howitzers, which prove very mischievous, especially on our right where one Man was killed & two wounded of the No. Carolinians.

We hear that our Cavalry under Genl. Huger were surprised near Monks Corner & have been totally defeated, that we lost between 20. & 30 killed & wounded, among there former Major Vernier of Pulaskis Legion -- & 150 Horses about forty of the Virginians got in last Night over Cooper River.

A Large party of the Enemy marched up the Country, crossed Wando River & took post at the Church, Hobcaw Neck.

– General Scott with the Light Infantry crossed over Cooper River, to Lampriers before day this Morning with private orders to secure Wapetaw or advantageous Bridge for the retreat of the army &ca. in order to keep open the Communication if possible, as any fresh provision we got was from that quarter.

– Lt. Colonels Webster, Tarleton & Robertson are said to have Commanded the Enemy's party who surprised our

Horse the 14th Inst. & gone over Cooper & Wando Rivers afterwards – they say 700 Infy. & 300 Horse (102-03)

The loss of Moncks Corner was disastrous to American forces in Charleston, because it cut off their route of escape across the Cooper River and also cut off food and other supplies coming from the backcountry. Patrick Ferguson and his American Volunteers were among the British troops attacking Moncks Corner.

Officials offend McIntosh's sense of honor

From Lachlan McIntosh's "Journal of the Siege of Charlestown:"

Wednesday the 19th April.

The Enemy continued their approaches to our right within 250. Yards of the front of the Square redoubt. – and began an approach from the Left Battery towards our advanced Redoubt or Half Moon Battery, & moved some of their Mortars into the Latter. – A Considerable party of them shewed themselves before our post at Lampriers this Morning, but soon retreated upon giving them some Cannon Shot. – our party there was too small to pursue them. – Genl. Scot mounted some Men upon his own & get intelligence, & then being sent for sett off for Town to a Council of War who (*which*) met this Morning at Genl. Moultries Quarters, having attempted it repeatedly before, at Genl. Lincolns, but as often interrupted so much, that we could come to no determination, or do any business; also to accommodate Colo. Lemoy [Laumoy] who was Sick. – besides the General Officers at this Council, Colo. Lamoy and Colo. Beekman were called to it to represent the Engineer and Artillery Departmts. & Colo. Simmons as Commdt. of the Town Militia when the subject first proposed to be considered on the 13th Instant, & several times since at our Meetings was again offered by Genl. Lincoln, & the Returns of the Army, Comissarys (*Provisions &ca. &ca.*) laid before the Council with a charge of the greatest Secrecy in that as well as any determination that may be taken. Some Gentlemen seem'd still inclined to an evacuation notwithstanding the difficulty appeared much greater now than when I formerly (*first*) Mentioned, which was my own opinion, also, & I proposed Leaving the Militia for the Guards &ca. in Garrison. – untill the Continental Troops Cleared themselves but was carried against us by the arguments of Colo. Lemoy and for offering Honl. Terms of Capitulation upon Hon. Terms fixed – in the Midst of our Conference the Lt. Governor Gadsden happened to come in whether by Accident or design is not known, & General Lincoln proposed he might be allowed to Sit as one of the Council, he appeared surprised & displeased that we had entertained a thought of Capitulation or evacuating the Garrison, and (*tho he*) acknowledged himself entirely ignorant of the State of the provisions &ca. &ca. before, but said he would Consult his Council & promised that if it was determined by us to Capitulate, he would Send such Articles as they required for the Citizens of Charlestown in an hour or two.

Adjourned in the Evening to Genl. Lincolns quarters where Colo. Lamoy representing the insufficienty of our Fortifications (if they were worthy of being called so) the improbability of holding out many days Longer, & the impracticability of making our Retreat good as the Enemy were now situated, carried it for offering (*trying first*) terms of Honle. Capitulation first ~~Unanimously in which I Joined after requesting to be the last Voice, as all the rest had been of that opinion~~. The Lt. Govr. with four of his Council Messrs. Ferguson Hutson Cattle & Dr. Ramsey in a Little after, Used the Council very Rudely, the Lt. Govr. declaring he would protest against our proceedings. – that the Militia were willing to live upon Rice alone rather than give up the Town upon any Terms. -- & that even the old Women were so accustomed to the Enemys Shot now that they traveled the Streets without fear or dread, but if we were determined to Capitulate that he had his terms in his pocket ready. Mr. Ferguson on the other hand said [illegible word] the Inhabitants of the Town observed several days (*some time*) ago the Boats Collected together to carry off the Continental Troops, but that they would keep a good Watch upon us the army & if it were attempted he would be among the first who would open the Gates for the Enemy and assist them in attacking us before we got aboard.

> After the Lt. Govr. & Counselors were gone some time, Colo. C.C. Pinkney came in abruptly upon the Council, & forgetting his usual Politeness, addressed Genl. Lincoln in great warmth & much the same Strain as the Lt. Governor had done, adding that those who were for business required no Councils & that he came over on purpose from Fort Moultrie to prevent any terms being offered the Enemy or evacuating the Garrison, & addressing himself to Colo. Lemoy, charged the Engineer Dept. with being the sole Authors & promoters of any proposals &ca. &ca.
>
> I was myself so much hurt by the repeated Insults given to the Commanding Officer in so public a Manner, & obliquely to us all through him, that I could not help declaring as it was thought impracticable to get the Continental Troops out I was for holding the Garrison to the last extremity, which we were already come to the last extremity, or if we were not of that opinion, desired to know what we called the last extremity. but it was carryed without other opposition to hold out & we parted this Night. – I desired a Letter Signed by Genl. Moultrie & myself the 17th might be destroyed which [was] done before us. (102-105)

McIntosh once again showed his extreme sensitivity whenever his honor was at stake when he wrote that he was "so much hurt" by the insults to Lincoln and "obliquely to us all."

When McIntosh proposed evacuating the Continental Army and leaving the militia to guard Charleston, he was offering to sacrifice his personal welfare for the good of the army. Since he had been placed in command of militia when he arrived in Charleston and since he had been suspended from service as a Continental officer, he presumably would have remained with the militia when the Continental troops retreated across the Cooper River.

The letter that McIntosh and Moultrie wanted destroyed was a written proposal for evacuating the garrison.

Council of War faces dilemma

When Lachlan McIntosh recorded his journal entry for Thursday, April 20, 1780, he wrote "June" instead of "April:"

This morning fourteen Sail of Shipping appeared off of the Barr said to be a Reinforcement to General Clinton, having a fine day, cold & windy. – two of our Magazines blown up by shells in Gibs Battery on the right; only one man hurt, but much other damage

This day General Lincoln called a Council of Warr again, same Members as yesterday. – and the same Subjects debated on. – Colo. Lamoy still insisting upon the Impossibility of holding out the Garrison much Longer, and a Retreat seeming to him impracticable, proposed, that the Honle. Terms of Capitulation should first be offered, which possibly might be accepted by Genl. Clinton, or, if it did not succeed that we might then attempt a retreat if we thought it could be accomplished.

The opposition now expected from the Citizens of the Town in evacuating it, in addition to the former obstacles we had in consideration Vizt. a Large party of Foot and Horse upon Wando Neck, & a number of the Enemys boats hawled aCross Charlesto. Neck from Ashly into Cooper River &ca. induced the whole Council to come into the Cornels [Colonels] proposal and make the Tryal. I requested to be the last in giving our Votes. – Upon which we parted.

The Enemys approach continues on our left, -- their Mortars moved from the left battery into their approaches. – an 18 pounder dismounted in Capt. Ballards Battery on our right. – four of the Enemy's Gallies that Lay in Wappoo Creek, & came in to Ashly River about every night since 4th Insta. went down abot. Nine o'Clock this night to their Shipping at Fort Johnston, under a very heavy firing from all our batterys West and So. of the Town. – The Enemy Retreated from Hobcraw across Wappetaw Bridge &ca. (105-106)

Colonel McIntosh regales besiegers

Two extraordinary visitors appeared at British headquarters on April 20. A journal entry by Hessian officer Johann Ewald identified one of them as "ein Chef der Niederen Creek Indianer" – a chief of the Lower Creek Indians – "Der Nahme des Indianers, war Konig Iacob" – whose name was King Jacob. Ewald described him as well-mannered and capable of speaking some English, and reported that he was a great warrior among the Creeks. Americans trying to turn the Creeks against the British had told King Jacob that the British army was not strong enough to take Charleston, and he had come to see for himself. The British led him through their entire camp and into the trenches (Uhlendorf 64-65).

King Jacob's companion, Ewald reported, was "einen 78 jahr: Schottish: Obristen Makendoslw" – a 78-year-old Scotsman, Colonel McIntosh. Although Colonel McIntosh was nearly 80 years old, he seemed to Ewald as robust as a man of 30 (Uhlendorf 64-65).

Ewald passed along the information that Colonel McIntosh had gone out with the Pretender to the British throne, Bonnie Prince Charlie Stuart, in the Rising of 1745. Like so many former Jacobites who had once tried to overthrow the reigning King of England, McIntosh was of the most faithful subjects of King George during the American Revolution. McIntosh had "lived among this nation" since 1748 (Uhlendorf 64-65).

Americans seek favorable terms of surrender

The Americans trapped in Charleston tried to negotiate an end to the siege under "honorable terms of capitulation." They wanted their army to be allowed to withdraw from town and live to fight another day. They also wanted security for the residents of Charleston and their property. Lachlan McIntosh's journal mentions the negotiations:

> Friday the 21st 1780. April
> A Flagg sent from us to Genl. Clinton, requiring a Truce for Six Hours, to consider upon Terms of Capitulation... which is granted ... & afterwards prolonged by Messenger. – The Articles proposed & Sent by Genl. Lincoln were made out by himself and Colo. Ternant, without his General Officers... – but they were called in the Evening to Genl. Lincoln's Tent, to consider upon Genl. Clinton & Adml. Arbuthnot's Reply... which after some hours spent in finding Copy of the Articles we sent out, was unanimously agreed to be a Rejection of the whole, & that a Messenger should be sent out to inform them they might begin firing again when they pleased – which they did immediately abot. Nine at night with greater Virilence & fury than ever, & continued it without intermission till day Light & was returned smartly from the Garrison.

The Enemy open'd two Embrasures against our battery No. 4 – a twelve pounder dismounted in Redan No. 7. the killed & wounded lately are so many they cannot be ascertained. – Colo. Tinning of No. Carol: with his Regmt. of Militia abot. 200 came over from Lampriers, & Joined my Brigade.

Saturday the 22d. April

Our Ration this day order'd to be reduced to ¾ lb. of Beef. – Lt. Colo. Laurens with his Lt. Infantry to return from Lampriers to Town & resume his former post...

The Enemy kept up a heavy Cannonade, & approach fast on our left in front of the advanced Redoubt or half Moon battery. – three men wounded &ca. – they made several Boyaux from their second parralell.

The 23rd April. Sunday

The Enemys approaches continually carrying on upon our Right & Left, those on our Right within 20. yds of our dam. – a Mortar moved from the right of Colo. Parkers Encampment. – abot. eight at Night two Deserters from the Enemy. – they confirm the report of a considerable Reinforcement from New York. – that they detached Ten Companys of Light Infantry to go over to Hadrells point. – and say the Enemy lost a Number of Men lately by our Shells.

Monday the 24th

A party of 200 Men detached from the Virginians & So. Caro: Lines under the Command of Lt. Colo. Henderson Sallyed out at day Light this Morng. opposite the half Moon or advanced Battery, upon the Enemy's approaches & compleatly Surprised them, in their trenches abot. fifteen of them were killed with the Bayonet in their ditches, & twelve Prisoners brought off. – Seven of whom were wounded. – the Enemy attempted to Support them, but were obliged to retreat upon our giving them some rounds of Grape Shot, the prisoners say Major Hall of the 74th Regt. Commanded them but no Officer was to be found. – Capt. Moultrie killed, & two privates wounded upon our side in our Retreat. – the whole was done in a few Minutes without our partys firing a Single Gun, & in the greatest order.

It is said Colo. C.C. Pinckney & Lt. Colo. Laurens assured Gen. Lincoln they could (keep the pass of Lampriers open, and) Supply the Garrison with plenty of Beef from Lampriers point upon which the Commissary was ordered to Issue a full allowance again as before the order of the 22d... but unfortunately the first, & only Cattle Butchered at Lampriers for the use of the Garrison were altogether Spoiled & useless through Neglect or Mismanagement before they came over. – these Gentlemen are said also to have some days past promised to keep the Communication open on the Cooper River Side, & besides Beef, to send a sufficient number of Negroes over to Town for the works which were much wanted. – (Kelly's).

Lt. Colo. Laurens with the Lt. Infantry, & Colo. C. C. Pinckney with the greater part (or almost the whole) of the 1st So. Caro. Regt. came into Garrison this Morning from Lampriers, & ordered into the Horn Work & to Mount the Port Guard. – Major Harris & 75 of his Regt. No. Caro: Militia ordered to Lampriers under the direction of Colo. Malmady, who with Major Hogg is left to Command that post. -- & Lt. Colo. Scott with [blank] of the 1st So. Caro Regm. & abot. [blank] Militia to Command at Fort Moultrie.

Colo. Parker of the Virginians killed abot. eight this Evening by a Rifle Ball looking over the Parapet of the half Moon battery. – two privates killed also & Seven wounded, with several others not known having kept an incessant Fire of Cannon, Mortars & small Arms on both Sides. (106-08)

McIntosh's matter-of-fact tone gives only a glimpse into the suffering of enlisted men such as Alexander McDonald of the Darien district, who served as a sergeant in the 2nd South Carolina Regiment. Historian John Ferling describes the situation:

...day after day, night after night, the city's residents and the American soldiers were subjected to a shuddering bombardment. The troops lived a miserable existence. Seven or eight soldiers were killed or wounded daily by artillery fire or enemy snipers. These men not only coped with ever-present fear, many lived in mire, occupying ditches filled with brackish water, and all suffered from both the high sun and the remorseless attacks from mosquitoes and sand flies. Hunger was their relentless companion as well, as rations were steadily reduced until nothing but a handful of rice remained in their diet. One officer claimed that "for want of sleep, many faces were so swelled they could scarcely see out of their eyes." Life was not much better for civilians. Some were plundered by famished soldiers who skulked about at night in search of food. Nor was anyone safe from the enemy. At any moment a cannonball might crash through the house, setting it ablaze or knocking it down. Over everything hung the terrible reality that if there was life after the siege, it would be filled with the hand-wringing uncertainty that always accompanies surrender and military occupation. (425-26)

Fog of war befalls the 71st Regiment

Like the Americans in Charleston, British besiegers such as Aeneas Mackintosh of the 71st Regiment endured roaring artillery exchanges, debilitating heat, irritating mosquitoes and enervating sleeplessness. Under these conditions it is not surprising that the fog of war befell the besiegers. One group of British soldiers mistook another group of British soldiers for American attackers and opened fire on their own comrades. A Hessian officer's journal entry for April 24 notes that the 71st Regiment was stationed in the British front line and suffered casualties. When the officer mentions "workmen" he means British soldiers assigned to build structures as part of the siege operation:

> The signal that the enemy was making a sortie along the whole line was a threefold "Hurray!" on our side – a fatal signal, indeed! About twenty to thirty of the enemy were seen at the gate-work. Our nearest infantry post on guard gave the signal and fired. Everyone repeated the signal; the workmen ran back; the second parallel saw them coming, heard the "Hurray!" believed they were enemies, and fired. Within a short time there was a tremendous fire of musketry, cannon, and shell on both sides. It was two o'clock in the morning before everyone realized that it was a mistake. We had an officer killed (71st) and more than fifty [men] killed and wounded. Besides, our working parties could accomplish little or nothing during the night. (Uhlendorf 265)

Another Hessian officer confirmed that one officer of the 71st Regiment was killed, and added that two officers of the 71st were wounded. About twenty noncommissioned officers and soldiers of the 71st were killed or wounded, he reported, two Hessian grenadiers were killed, and eleven Hessians were slightly wounded.

Without knowing what had happened in the British lines, Lachlan McIntosh referred to the incident in his journal entry for April 25:

> Between twelve & one this Morning a heavy fire of Cannon & Musketry, from our advanced redoubts & the right of our Lines, occasioned (it is said) by the Enemy's advancing in Collumn. – it is certain they gave several Huzzas, & abused us, calling us bloody Doggs, being upon duty myself & upon the Lines all the Night; but whether they were out of their trenches is not so clear. – it was forty or fifty Minutes before I could put a Stop to the waste of Ammunition untill we could make sure of a proper object. – the Enemy returned the fire Smartly & threw several Light balls & Carcasses into Town.
>
> about two oClock this Afternoon Lord Cornwallis with about 3000 Men took possession of Mount Pleasant, Hadrils Pt. abot. 2 oClock P.M. having crossed from Chas. Town Neck over Cooper River to [blank] last Night. (three men wounded J.H. [John Habersham]). (108)

Conditions deteriorate in Charleston

Lachlan McIntosh's journal describes the inexorable deterioration of the American defenses:

> Wednesday the 26th
>
> The small Ship Lord George Germaine & a Sloop Joined the Enemy's fleet near Fort Johnston after passing Fort Moultrie at a great distance with little or no damage. – some of the Enemy's Ships remain'd below in five fathom hole. -- & it was said two of 74. Guns Lay off the Barr. -- the Vigilant Capt. Brett at Beaufort. – The Enemy pretty quiet Yesterday and last Night: we suppose they are bringing Cannon into their third Paralel. – they are seen Strengthening their approaches. – and in Possession of Mount Pleasant.

Brigr. Genl. DuPortail arrived from Philadelphia which he left the 3d Insta. – where he says there was no Prospect of our getting any Reinforcement soon from our grand Army. – Congress having only proposed to G. Washington (then at Morristown) the Sending of the Maryland Line.

One Man killed, -- Capt. Goodwin of 3d. So. Carolina and one private wounded. (J.H.) [John Habersham]

(De Bra:) [Ferdinand de Brahm] the Enemy began their third parralel.

Thursday the 27th.

Last Night Colo. Malmady with his Detachmt. at Lampriers ferry retreated in great confusion across the River, after Spiking up four 18 pounders they left behind. – about one in afternoon four of the Enemy Gallies, and Armed Sloop, & a frigate moved down the River, and Anchor'd opposite, & near the Mouth of Hogg Island, after a very faint opposition from the Cannon of Fort Moultrie. – one of the Galleys got aground & was lost.

5 Militia Men of James Isld. (Capt. Stiles's) deserted last Night in a boat. (J.H.) one private killed & five wounded.

Tarr Bbs. ordered to be fixed before our Lines every Evening & burn all Night to prevent a Surprise, as the Enemy are close to the Cannal, & keep up almost a continued running fire of small Arms Night & Day upon us. – A pickett of a Field Officer & 100 Men of my Militia Brigade ordered every evening to Gadsdens old House, to Support a small Guard of a Sergt. & 12 Regulars upon the Wharf in case of an attack by the Enemy Boats upon that quarter. – Major Pinckney ordered out on some duty.

Friday the 28th

Two Deserters from the Enemy at Hobcaw brought over by our Troops. – we See the British flagg flying at our late post Lampriers. – Major Low and Several Supernumery Officers quitted the Garrison over Cooper River.

The Enemy very busy throwing up their third Paralel, within a few yards of our Canal, which in most places is above 100 yards from our breast work.

Our fatigue hard at work enclosing the Horn Work. – the few Negroes remaining in Town are obliged to be pressed daily, & kept under guard, as the masters as well as the

Slaves, were unwilling they should work. (J.H.) two privates killed. Lt. Campaign of No. Carolina & two privates wounded.

Saturday the 29th.

The Enemys third Paralel nearly finished, and a Redoubt begun toward the Middle of it. (deBra:) opposite the Gate & another towards our left (J.H.)

Our hands began a retired Redoubt on the right of the horn work. – General Lincoln informed the General Officers privately that he intended the Horn Work as place of retreat for the whole Army in Case they were drove from the Lines. – I observed to him the impossibility of those who were Station'd at the So. Bay & Ashly River retreating there in Such Case, to which he replyed that we might Secure ourselves as best we could.

A Heavy Bombardment from the Enemy during the Night. -- & small Arms never ceasing. –

A Deserter from them, Says, they are preparing a bridge to throw over the Canal.

Capt. Templeton of the 4th Geo. Regt. wounded by Shell.

Tattoo ordered not to beat.

Colo. Malmady ordered to deliver a written report of the Evacuation of Hobcaw, &ca. &ca.

Sunday the 30th:

General Lincoln received a Letter from Govr. Rutledge upon which he Congratulates the Army in Genl. orders for hearing of a Large Reinforcement that may open our Communication again to the Country, &ca.

The Deserters Yesterday tell us; the Huzzas which Occasioned the firing last Tuesday Morning were from the Enemy's working party, who thought we were Sallying. – the Engineers he Says ordered them when that happened to give three Cheers, & fall back upon their Covering party. – who not having been apprised of it, received them as an Enemy, in consequence of which a considerable Number of them were killed & Wounded. – he confirms the Account of their receiving a considerable reinforcement from New York, & says the last Detachmt. sent to Hobcaw Amounts to above two thousand, that they expect their Shipping up to Town every Night,

-- & are preparing a Large Number of faschines to fill up the Cannal.

Severe firing of Cannon, Mortars & Small Arms continued on both Sides. – Lt. Campen & Ensign Hall of No. Caro: wounded badly, & Lt. Philips of the Virginians. – privates killed and wounded not known there are so many.

I think it is this day that Genl. Lincoln called the Genl. Officers together at his Quarters, that Genl. duportail who had viewed our fortifications might give us his opinion respecting them, and the State of the Siege, which was in Substance much the Same as Colo. Lamoy repeatedly expressed before Vizt. that our works could only be called field Lines, & could hold out but very few Days &ca. &ca. – He brought the printed Resolve of Congress respecting me, which was laid before Council.

Monday the 1st May 1780.

Our Fatigue imployed errecting another Redoubt on the left of the horn work, & compleating these new works intended for a retreat in Case of Necessity.

The Enemy appear to be about another Battery in their third paralel, opposite No. 12 on our right. – five men deserted last Night, from the Gallie which yet remained in Wappoo Creek. – the many risques they run in the attempt is astonishing. – A very Smart Bombardmt. kept up during this day.

Capt. Mumford of No. Caro: wounded by a Muskt. ball. – and Mr. P. Lord a Voluntier killed yesterday by a Shell.

Tuesday the 2d. May.

Last Night the Enemy made a ditch on the right to drain our Cannal.

A Number of Men killed & wounded the last three or four days, which cannot be ascertained.

A General Monthly Return ordered to be made, with Accot. of the killed wounded & Deserted since 1st April:

A nine pounder burst in battery No. 12, -- and a quantity of fixed Ammunition blown up by accident in batterys No. 10 & 12.

It is said the Enemy throw Shells at us Charged with Rice & Sugar.

Lt. Colo. Smith of Town Militia with a party to press Negroes for the works – if possible.

Wednesday the 3d.

Cannonading, Bombarding & continual firing wth. small Arms as Usual on both Sides.

Our fatigue imployed fetching Picketts &ca.

Thursday the 4th

Lt. Gerrard wounded.

Our Rations reduced to 6 oz. of Meat, & bad enough. – Coffee and Sugar allowed the Soldiers with their Rice.

the Enemy appear to have possession of our battery on the end of Gadsden's Bridge Leading to Fort Moultrie. Fire from the Enemy's Cannon Slack but they do not spare shells & small Arms. – our Hospital Ship carryed away. (108-12)

Charleston surrenders: May 12, 1780

McIntosh did not continue his journal of the siege after his entry for May 4. At about that time, the British overran the batteries where McIntosh's militia brigade was posted, and he was taken as a prisoner of war (Jackson 110). McIntosh included in his papers a copy of a Subaltern's Journal that contains entries through May 16. This journal mentions negotiations between the American and British commanders over the surrender of Charleston and its defenders:

11th

Negociations continued the Soldiers not served with provision... The Butcher who destroyed the meat at Lampriers being somewhat insolent at Hopkin's Regiment was very roughly handled.

Hungry guts in the Garrison.

12th

Capitulation agreed on. Detachment of Grenadiers takes possession of the Horn Work at three o'Clock our troops march out and pile there Arms, they return and are dismissed to their Tents. The enemies Guard take possession of the town.

13th

At twelve this day ordered from the Lines – the Officers to empty houses and the Soldiers to the Barracks... no provision this day. (Hawes 121)

The terms of the surrender offered the Continental troops and sailors as prisoners of war and requested that the militiamen be allowed to return to their homes as prisoners on parole. The residents of Charleston also were considered prisoners on parole. The British took possession of the town, fortifications, artillery, public stores, and shipping at the wharves.

A captain in the 71st Regiment wrote to his father, "I have been an actor in two of the most obstinate and most successful contests that the British arms have experienced in this war, the defense of Savannah and the reduction of Charlestown" ("Message").

Aftermath of battle

American casualties during the siege totaled 89 killed and 138 wounded.

British casualties were 99 killed and 217 wounded. Among the officers of the 71st Regiment, Ensign McGregor and Ensign Cameron were killed and Captain M'Leod and Lieutenant Wilson were wounded. Among the rank and file of the 71st, six were killed, and fourteen were wounded (Hough, *Charleston* 120 - 21).

Five hundred militiamen and close to four thousand Continental troops surrendered. Most of the militiamen were given their parole within a week of the surrender and began walking home. More than two hundred Continental officers, including Lachlan McIntosh, resided in barracks at Haddrell's Point or in nearby houses while arrangements were made to exchange them for British officers.

Continental enlisted men and non-commissioned officers like Alexander McDonald of the Darien district were housed in barracks near the edge of town. Hundreds of them escaped individually or in groups as large as thirty. In August the British transferred the captives to prison ships in the harbor, where nearly four hundred sickened and died in unsanitary, crowded conditions. By the time prisoners were exchanged more than a year later, the number of enlisted men had been cut in half (Borick, *Relieve* 4-26; Borick, *Gallant* 223).

Buford's soldiers suffer 'Tarleton's Quarter'

General George Washington knew that the American army at Charleston faced a desperate situation in the spring of 1780. In April he sent Major General Johann de Kalb southward with three regiments and artillery. The regiments had reached North Carolina when Charleston fell.

When the British captured Charleston, nearly the entire Southern Department of the American army was taken prisoner. Scattered remnants of the American forces gathered at Camden, where South Carolina Governor Rutledge had gone to preserve the civil government while Charleston was besieged. After Charleston fell, the remnants of American forces retreated northward. A brigade of North Carolina militia headed for the Cross Creek country of North Carolina. About 350 Continental dragoons from Virginia set out for Hillsborough, North Carolina, under the command of Colonel Abraham Buford.

On May 18, six days after Charleston surrendered, General Charles Cornwallis led 2,500 infantry and mounted troops, including Banastre Tarleton's legion, from Charleston toward Camden. Cornwallis sent Tarleton to catch Buford. Along the way, Tarleton nearly captured Governor Rutledge at a house about twelve miles north of Camden; Rutledge was warned by his host and fled to Charlotte, North Carolina.

On May 29 in the community called the Waxhaws near the North Carolina border, Tarleton's legion charged Buford's dragoons. When the legion overran the American position, Buford raised the white flag of surrender and the Americans lay down their weapons. Tarleton's men did not give quarter as expected under the rules of war; instead, they butchered the Americans with swords and bayonets. More than a hundred Americans were killed and more than two hundred were wounded. Only five of Tarleton's men were killed in the battle and only fourteen were wounded.

The British occupy Augusta

While Lord Cornwallis was on his way to occupy Camden, British officials ordered loyalist Lieutenant Colonel Thomas Brown to take possession of Augusta, where Brown had been tortured and maimed by patriots at the beginning of the revolution. Departing from the British stronghold at Savannah, the King's Carolina Rangers and other loyalist units marched up the roads on the South Carolina side the Savannah River without resistance. As Brown approached Augusta, General Andrew Williamson led the patriot garrison of 364 men out of town without a fight. Brown established British control of Augusta on about June 10.

British forces also took Ninety-Six – a post in South Carolina within easy communication distance of Augusta – without resistance. The string of posts at Camden, Ninety-Six and Augusta strengthened the British grip on the South Carolina backcountry.

Flory McDonald goes homeward

Flory McDonald – famous for having rescued Bonnie Prince Charlie – had been terribly ill since her return to Britain from America. She described "a violent fit of sickness, which confined me to bed in London, for half a year, and would have brought me to my Grave, if under God's hands, Doctor Donald Munrow had not given his friendly assistance" (Vining 185). When she was well enough to travel, Flory left London and was in Edinburgh by May 17.

Flory's relatives serve in South Carolina

Two relatives of Flory McDonald served with British forces in South Carolina. Her son James, who had escaped into the swamps after the Battle of Moore's Creek Bridge, was serving in Tarleton's Legion by 1779. Her son Charles, who had entered the British service before she emigrated to America, commanded a troop of horse in 1780 and was with Tarleton's Legion by 1781. Her son-in-law Alexander MacLeod, who had gone from New York to London on military business, was serving with Cornwallis in the Carolinas by 1780 (Macgregor 171-72; Vining 182, 184).

Lachlan McIntosh repairs reputation

Lachlan McIntosh would never let an attack on his honor go unchallenged. Although he was held as a prisoner of war after the fall of Charleston, he continued to work ceaselessly to counter his political enemies who had caused him to be suspended from command by the Continental Congress. He turned for support to the officers the Georgia Line of the Continental Army, including his nephew John McIntosh and his son William. The officers remaining in the brigade – after it had been nearly annihilated in campaigns in Florida, the British capture of Savannah, and the Battle of Brier Creek – signed a declaration supporting their former commander:

Whereas it appears that Congress have received a Letter said to be from Wm. Glascock Esqr. Speaker of the House of Assembly in the State of Georgia, Containing the following paragraph, "It is to be wished that we could advise Congress that the return of Brigadier General McIntosh gave satisfaction to either the Militia or Confederates, but the Common dissatisfaction is such, & that founded on weighty reasons, it is highly necessary that Congress would whilst that Officer is in the Service of the United States direct some distant field for the exercise of his Abilitys." And also another Letter said to be from Governor Walton Containing the following paragraph "I am also ordered to apologise to Congress for the trouble given them respecting General McIntosh & to assure them that a General & settled aversion has & does prevail, I do not mean to suspect the Integrity of this Officer (for personally I am very much his friend) when I say it is the practice of Nations not to continue any Officer longer than he preserves the Confidence of the people."

We the Subscribers, Officers of the Georgia Continental Brigade think ourselves in honor bound to declare, that the said paragraphs, are in our opinions unjust, ungenerous, & malicious attacks upon the Character of General McIntosh who we think every way undeserving of such Aspersions, as from experience we have found him to be the brave, the humane, and the Circumspect Officer & the tenacious Citizen nor do we wish to be commanded by any Officer in the Contl. Line in preference to him, And we further declare that no opinions or assertions of ours could ever give sanction to the above paragraphs, for had our Ideas of General McIntoshs Conduct been consulted & followed they would have conveyed to Congress that Officers Character, in diametrically opposite Colours to what it has been by the said paragraphs.

Given under our Hands at Augusta, the 17th. Day of May 1780.

Jno. McIntosh Lieut Col. 3d Geoa. Regt.

John Lucas Captain 4th. Georgia Contl. Regt.

Geo. Handley Captain 1st. Geoa. Contl. Battn.

Natha. Pearre Lt 3 B.

Elisha Miller Capt. 2nd. Georgia Continl. Battn.
Patrick Walsh Capt. Georgia Cont. Dragoons
Fras. Tennill Lt. 2d Contl. Battn.
Patk. Fitzpatrick Capt. 4th. G. B.
Arthur Hays Lieutnt. 4th C. Battn.
Christopher Hillary Lieut. 4th. Geo. Battn.
Henry Allison Lieut. 2d C. Geoa. B.
George Melven Captain 4th Georgia Battn.
John Frazier Lt. 3 G B
Laban Johnson Lieut of the Artillery
John Peter Wagnon Lieut. 3rd Geo. Regt.
Thos. Glascock Lieut. 1st Geoa. Battn.
Jesse Walton Lieut. 1st G. Battalion
Wm. McDaniel Lt. G. Continental Lt. Dragoons
John Meanley Lt 3 G C Bt
Cornelius Collins Lieut. 2nd Geo. Cont. Battn.
Wm. McIntosh Captn. 1st Geoa. Regiment
Wm. Jordan Lt. 4th G. B.
 Brossard Captain in georgia line
 David Rees, Depy. Judge Advocate
 Wm. Matthews Comy of Musters

N. B. Those officers of the Georgia Line who have not signed this declaration respeg. General McIntosh are Prisoners in Charles Town, & on furlough in the State of Virginia. (Hawes, *University* 38-40)

Partisan bands roam the backcountry

On June 8, British commander in chief Henry Clinton returned from South Carolina to New York, leaving Lord Cornwallis in charge of operations in the South. By then, patriot militia groups and partisan bands had formed throughout the backcountry. One of the first forces that resisted the British occupation was led by Thomas Sumter, whose fierce fighting style earned him the nickname "The Gamecock."

Soldiers swelter in southern summer

British General Cornwallis sent out detachments to quell the disturbances in the South Carolina backcountry. Major Archibald McArthur was posted at Cheraw Hill on the Peedee River with the 71st Highlanders and a troop of dragoons (Landers 32). The regiment used St. David's Episcopal Church, report local historians, "as a hospital during a smallpox epidemic and a number of British soldiers who fell victim of the disease are buried in the old cemetery" (Julien and Chapman XLI).

South Carolina's midsummer weather and resulting bouts of fever debilitated McArthur's men. Since they were too ill to march back to Charleston, he sent ninety-six of them under the command of Lieutenant John Nairne down the Peedee River on flatboats. They were attended by a surgeon and escorted by loyalist militia led by a former doctor, Colonel Robert Mills. A partisan band ambushed the flatboats at Mars Bluff and captured the loyalists and the sick Highlanders as prisoners of war.

The Scottish soldiers were not the only ones to suffer in South Carolina's summer. Captain Johann Hinrichs, a Hessian serving with the British, became convinced that "June, July, August and September are unhealthy and frequently fatal to foreigners because of the excessive heat, suffocating electric storms and damp nights pregnant with fetid fogs."

In South Carolina, it seemed to Hinrichs, "the whole atmosphere" was filled with "unhealthy miasmas... All this insalubrity of the ground the sun causes to rise during the day, and in the night it descends again in mist and dew. Summing up all this, we shall have had by the end of the year one pleasant day for every fifteen bad ones and not a single healthy day, suitable to the needs of the human body."

Hinrichs described the "flat, marshy land" of coastal South Carolina in his German-language journal as "a habitat of snakes and crocodiles *(ein Wohnplaz von Schlangen und crocodillen)* strewn with bodies of stagnant water and covered with impenetrable woods." He emphasized his point by repeating, "snakes live in impenetrable marshes and swamps full of decaying brushwood." (Uhlendorf 335, 337)

Lachlan McIntosh's refugee family relocates
While Lachlan McIntosh languished as a prisoner of war at Haddrell's Point near Charleston, his family stayed on the move in search of refuge. Lachlan had escorted his wife Sarah and younger children to Camden before reporting to duty at Charleston. Soon after the British took control of Charleston, however, Camden became the center of British operations in the backcountry. Sarah had

already endured life behind British lines during the siege of Savannah, which may be why she decided to leave Camden. The McIntosh family may have left Camden at the same time when Colonel Buford withdrew and Governor Rutledge escaped. As Sarah sought refuge, her second-oldest son Lachlan, called Lackie, took responsibility for protecting the family. Lackie was a Major in the Continental Army, but apparently did not have an assignment at this time. A letter to Sarah from her husband in August of 1780 tells of the family's plight:

> ... I have kept my health pretty well since I have been a Prisoner, the Limit of the Genl. Officers is the Little Parish of Xt. Church opposite to Charlestown which we cannot complain of, & we must confess that we have hitherto had a Sufficient allowance of good Salt Provision, but cannot boast of any Luxury unless it is a Little Fish we catch at times ourselves, which Serves also for amusement & a necessary Exercise.
>
> I was very Uneasy that I could obtain no certain account for a Long time of the rout you had taken, all that I could Learn was that you Left Cambden, which I was sorry to hear, as you could not be much more injured than you have been already. Travelling near three hundred Miles from home with so large a Family, & Little or no Conveniency I thought sufficiently distressing without attempting to fly further. I am however so far happy now as to hear that your self & all the Children are well in health & fixed at Salsbury in No. Carolina, where if you can make it out tolerably I could wish you to remain until we see what time brings forth. Tell Lackie I charge him to Stay with you & give every assistance in his power to the Family an Indulgence which I think cannot be refused by any Officer who Commands the Southern Army. You & he may always inform me of your Situation by way of the Army Leaving your Letters open, & I am displeased that he has not done it before... (Hawes 41-42).

Lachlan McIntosh passed the time while a prisoner of war by working to refute the political allegations that had resulted in his suspension from command. Some of the officers who had served with McIntosh in Georgia in 1779 and had been taken prisoner at Charleston stated that they were highly satisfied with his leadership and that they had heard "the people in general make frequent public avowals of their good opinion of the General" (Lawrence, "Suspension" 131).

At this time following the American defeats at Brier Creek and Charleston both Lachlan McIntosh and his nephew Colonel John McIntosh were prisoners of war. As members of a family of warriors, their experience fell into a pattern. John Mackintosh Mor – father of Lachlan McIntosh and grandfather of Colonel John McIntosh – had been taken prisoner in a battle against Spaniards in Florida and while he was imprisoned in Spain his uncle Brigadier William McIntosh of Borlum was imprisoned in Edinburgh Castle as a leader in the Jacobite Risings. Lachlan McIntosh's experience as a father eerily resembled his experience as a child. While John Mackintosh Mor was imprisoned, Lachlan's mother sought refuge for herself and her children; she sent Lachlan and his sister to an orphanage for awhile. Similarly, while Lachlan was a prisoner of war, his wife and children roamed the war-torn land in search of refuge.

Rory McIntosh meets clan chief in Charleston

While the British held Charleston, Roderick "Rory" McIntosh had an opportunity to meet his clan chief. Rory was among the Mackintosh clansmen who had emigrated to Georgia, and during the American Revolution he remained loyal to the British crown. Aeneas the 23rd Chief of Clan Mackintosh was a captain in 71st Regiment and so was among the British forces that had captured Charleston. John Couper tells the following tale in a letter written many years later:

> I recollect seeing, in St. Augustine, on some public day, Rory, Colonel McArthur, and Major Small, Scotch officers, parading the streets in full Highland costume, attended by their pipers.
>
> After Charleston fell, Rory went there from Savannah, by land, particularly to visit Major Small. On meeting, Rory said: "I have traversed, at the risk of my life, the rebellious Province of South Carolina to see my friend, the famous Major Small."

"Welcome! Welcome! The brave Roderick McIntosh! I have heard his Majesty speak with kindness and respect of Roderick McIntosh."

"Spare me – oh, spare me!" said Rory, "his Majesty is too good;" and the two hugged each other.

"I can offer you," said Major Small, "no greater mark of respect than by ordering my pipers to attend you whilst in Charleston."

The 71st Regiment was then in Charleston. Sir Æneas McIntosh, the chief of the border clan, was a captain in it. Sir Æneas was a slender delicate gentleman, educated in France. Rory, who could broke no chief that was not a powerful man, was sadly disconcerted. Sir Æneas politely asked him to dine with him the next day on calf's head.

"Calf's head!" said Rory. "I feed my negroes on calves' heads."

Rory never afterwards noticed his chief, but observed that he was of a spurious race. (White 473)

Rory's description of Aeneas Mackintosh, like most of Rory's tales, cannot be taken as actual fact. A delicate man could not have withstood the rigors of campaigning with an elite regiment like the 71st, which saw action in many of the major battles of the Northern theater before fighting at Savannah, Brier Creek, and Charleston. The 71st continued to serve under Cornwallis until he surrendered at Yorktown. After Mackintosh returned to Scotland, he was a vigorous farmer who inspected his large estate by riding horseback through rugged terrain. His wife wrote that he had "the Patriarchal character of a Highland Chief" (Mackintosh 66).

Marion reports for duty

Francis Marion, recuperating from a broken ankle, still held rank as a Continental officer, but his soldiers of the 2nd South Carolina Regiment had been taken prisoner at Charleston. He led about twenty men, black and white, to a rendezvous with the Continental regiments encamped on Deep River in North Carolina. In early July, Continental General Johann de Kalb sent Marion and his volunteers to find supplies and seek information in the Peedee. Horatio Gates, designated by Congress to replace de Kalb, reached the encampment on Deep River on July 25. When Marion returned to camp a few days later, Gates' officers and soldiers laughed at the ragged volunteers.

Flory McDonald returns to Skye

Flory McDonald – famous for having rescued Bonnie Prince Charlie – spent two months in Edinburgh before departing for Skye in early July. As she rode horseback across the rough terrain of the Highlands, the poorly healed fractures in her arm and wrist ached. She wrote a friend:

> I arrived at Inverness the third day after parting with you in good health and without any accidents, which I always dread. My young Squire continued always very obliging and attentive to me. I stayed at Inverness three days. I had the good luck to meet with a female companion from that to Skye. I was the fourth day with great difficulty to Raasay, for my hands being so pained with the riding. I have arrived here [Dunvegan] a few days ago with my young daughter [14-year-old Fanny, who had remained in Scotland when Flory emigrated to North Carolina]. (Vining 187)

Flory chose Dunvegan as her first destination on Skye because her daughter Anne resided there at the time. Dunvegan was the seat of Clan MacLeod, and Anne's husband Alexander MacLeod was an uncle of the Chief of Clan MacLeod. The chief had gone to war in 1776 as a captain in Fraser's Highlanders – the regiment in which the Chief of Clan Mackintosh also served as a captain. Although Aeneas Mackintosh served in America throughout the war, MacLeod was transferred to India in 1781. Anne had returned from America to Britain in 1779 accompanied by her husband, who left her at Dunvegan when he went back to serve under Lord Cornwallis in the war in America.

After Flory and Fanny visited with Anne awhile, they traveled through the Hebrides visiting other relatives and old friends, including Flory's brother at Milton.

Americans trek through waste land

Before General Horatio Gates arrived to take command of the Continental army in the South, General de Kalb had planned to work southward through Salisbury and Charlotte, expecting the residents to be friendly and the food supply to be adequate for an army on the move. Gates, however, decided to take a direct route toward Camden. This route not only passed through the Cross Creek country – home of loyalist immigrants from the Scottish Highlands such as Flory McDonald's family – but also sent the troops through pine barrens where provisions were scarce. University of South Carolina history professor Henry Lumpkin describes the march:

> No food could be found except small herds of bony, stunted, half-wild cattle, a little green corn, and ragged peach or apple orchards. The officers even used their hair powder to thicken what little soup could be made from available rations. This adversity meant that it was a hungry, sick army that struggled along the sand roads and through the creeks and swamps. (59)

When they finally reached fertile farmland, the soldiers gorged on green corn, a recipe for digestive distress. The men frequently had to leave the line of march to relieve themselves. As the Americans advanced toward Camden, their army contained more than four thousand men, but only three thousand were fit for duty.

Francis Marion, meanwhile, learned that patriots in the Williamsburg District had requested that a Continental officer be detached to lead their militia. Marion asked Gates for permission to leave the army and take command of the Williamsburg militia. Gates gladly accepted the opportunity to rid his army of Marion and his little band of volunteers. Marion and his men parted company with the army on August 14 or 15, and Marion met up with the Williamsburg militia two or three days later.

The Battle of Camden, August 16, 1780

Lord Cornwallis was informed that the American army was on its way, and he hurried from Charleston to personally supervise the British forces stationed at Camden under Lord Rawdon. On the night of August 15, Cornwallis and Rawdon led more than two thousand British troops out of Camden in an attempt to surprise the American army. Gates, coincidentally, had ordered more than three thousand American troops on a night march to Camden in an attempt to surprise the British army. Early in the morning of August 16, the British advance party of horsemen under Banastre Tarleton ran into the American advance party of horsemen. The horsemen fired pistols and swung sabers in the dark until the Americans raced back to the protection of their infantry. The American infantry stopped Tarleton's charge. The British infantry moved up and engaged the Americans for half an hour. The American and British armies took up positions on both sides of the road.

Cornwallis placed the five companies of Highlanders from the 71st Regiment in reserve behind the center of the lines. At that time, according to a field return, the 1st Battalion of the 71st had two captains, four lieutenants, one ensign, an adjutant, a quartermaster, a mate, fourteen sergeants, six drummers, and 114 rank and file. The 2nd Battalion had one captain – presumably Aeneas Mackintosh – and three lieutenants, three ensigns, nine sergeants, and ninety-four rank and file (Tarleton 136).

"As the night gave way to the coming day out of the darkness appeared the dim visage of the ghostly armies," writes military historian Lieutenant Colonel H.L. Landers. "Every eye was strained to catch a movement of the enemy; every heart beat with fear of the unknown and hope of some advantage in troops and position" (45).

Dawn light revealed the colors of their uniforms as British soldiers cheered and moved forward in formation. The patriot militiamen ran away. As more than two thousand militiamen stumbled through the American ranks, they disrupted the Continental troops. General Horatio Gates – the commander of the American army in the South – spurred his racehorse into a gallop and rode full-speed sixty miles to Charlotte. Even after the patriot militia fled, the Continental troops stood and fought against the British. Colonel Landers describes the role of the 2nd Battalion of the British 71st Regiment – in which Captain Aeneas Mackintosh served:

> The regular troops, who had the keen edge of sensibility and fear rubbed off by strict discipline and hard service, saw the confusion with but little emotion. Some irregularity was created by the militia breaking pell-mell through the First Maryland Brigade, but order was restored in time to give the British a severe check, which abated the fury of their assault and obliged them to assume a more deliberate

manner of acting. The most severe part of the action occurred on the front of the Thirty-third Regiment, which advanced on the right of the road, and on the front of the Volunteers of Ireland, who went forward on the left of the road. The latter regiment, together with the Legion infantry and the militia and supported by the Second Battalion of the Seventy-first Regiment, engaged the Second Maryland Brigade and the Delaware regiment, which at the time were advancing to meet them. At the same time the right division, composed of the Thirty-third and Twenty-third Regiments and the light companies and supported by the First Battalion of the Seventy-first, having cleared the militia from its front, was now encountering Smallwood's brigade of Marylanders, which had moved up east of the road in line with Gist's brigade.

The disparagement in numbers of the two armies at this phase of the action was not so great, there being about 1,300 regular infantry of the British opposed to about 1,000 Continentals, but there was no way of checking the flanking movement which the British were making against the First Maryland Brigade. There were no more reserves, and the brigade was compelled to give ground. It fell back reluctantly and collectedly, and then a moment later, upon the rallying cry of some of its officers, it bravely returned to the fray. It was obliged to give way a second time and was again rallied and renewed the contest. Meanwhile the Second Brigade, fighting under the immediate leadership of De Kalb and Gist, was more than holding its own, inflicting heavy losses upon the Volunteers of Ireland.

There was now a distance of nearly 200 yards between the two Maryland brigades, and owing to the thickness of the air dependence had to be placed upon the hearing, and not upon the eyesight, to learn what was occurring on a different part of the battlefield. At this critical moment the deputy adjutant general, anxious that communication between the brigades should be preserved and hoping, in the almost certain event of a retreat, that some order might be sustained, hastened from the First to the Second Brigade and begged his own regiment, the Sixth Maryland, not to fly. He was answered by its commander, Lieutenant Colonel Ford, who said:

"They have done all that can be expected of them; we are outnumbered and outflanked; see the enemy charge with bayonets!"

General Cornwallis now had all of his regiments concentrated against these two gallant brigades. A tremendous fire of musketry on both sides was kept up for some time, with equal perseverance and obstinacy, until Cornwallis pushed forward a part of his cavalry under Major Hanger to charge the American left flank, while Lieutenant Colonel Tarleton led forward the remainder. The infantry, charging at the same time with fixed bayonets, put an end to the contest. The battle was terminated in less than an hour. The British victory was complete. All the artillery and a great number of prisoners fell into their hands. The dead and wounded lay where they fell and the rout of the remainder was thorough. General Gist moved from the battle field with about 100 Continentals in a body by wading through the swamp on the right of the American position. Other than this not even a company retired in any order; everyone escaped as he could. (47-49)

Casualties for the 1st Battalion of the 71st Regiment were: Lieutenant Archibald Campbell and four rank and file killed; Captain Hugh Campbell, Lieutenant John Grant, a sergeant, and twenty-two rank and file wounded. Casualties for the 2nd Battalion were: one sergeant and four rank and file killed; one sergeant and eight rank and file wounded.

Death of de Kalb

American Revolution authority Christopher Ward tells of Continental General Johann de Kalb's fate:

De Kalb's horse was shot under him. "Long after the battle was lost in every other quarter, the gigantic form of De Kalb, unhorsed and fighting on foot, was seen directing the movements of his brave Maryland and Delaware troops." His head had been laid open by a saber stroke…

The fighting was hand-to-hand, terrific in its fierceness. Sabers flashed and struck, bayonets lunged and found their meat, clubbed musket fell on cracked skulls...

Overwhelmed by numbers that almost entirely surrounded him, De Kalb called for the bayonet again. All together his men answered. De Kalb at their head, they crashed through the enemy's ranks, wheeled, and smote them from the rear. But ball after ball had struck their heroic leader. Blood was pouring from him; yet the old lion had it in him to cut down a British soldier, whose bayonet was at his breast. That was his last stroke. Bleeding from eleven wounds, he fell...

Prostrate in the field lay De Kalb. It was only when the Chevalier du Buysson, his aide, threw himself on his general's body, crying out his name and rank, that the thirsty bayonets were withheld from further thrusts into his body. Some of the enemy, British or Tory, carried him off and propped him against a wagon so that they might more easily appropriate his gold-laced coat. There he stood, gripping the wagon with both hands, his head in weakness bowed to his chest, bleeding to death from all his wounds, when Cornwallis came riding by, rescued him from the despoilers, and caused him to be cared for by the British surgeons. His great bodily vigor kept the life in him for three days before he died in Camden. (729-730)

South Carolina historian Henry Lumpkin gives this description of de Kalb's death scene:

...The wounded general was propped against a wagon wheel by his enemies... until Lord Cornwallis rode by and, recognizing the famous European soldier, had him carried into Camden on a litter and given the best possible medical treatment.

According to legend, and there is no reason to doubt it, Lord Cornwallis discovered that Johann de Kalb was a Mason, was he was himself. When de Kalb died with great courage and dignity three days later, Cornwallis had him buried with full military and Masonic honors. Cornwallis, Lord Rawdon, and all the British and Loyalist officers attended the funeral, a poignant note in an otherwise tragic and bloody affair. (66)

Fishing Creek: August 18, 1780

Soon after the Battle of Camden, British General Cornwallis sent a force of selected soldiers after patriot Thomas Sumter's partisans. British Colonel Banastre Tarleton led a hundred dragoons and sixty infantry north from Camden. In the relentless heat of August in South Carolina, Sumter's eight hundred men were resting on the banks of Fishing Creek or splashing in the water when the British picked force launched a surprise attack. The British killed 150 partisans and wounded many more. Sumter himself escaped. The raid recovered a supply convoy that Sumter's men had captured and rescued British prisoners of war.

One member of the 71st Regiment was killed at Fishing Creek. A letter to the father of Charles Campbell from Major Archibald McArthur says, "Capt. Campbell advancing at the head of his men with his usual intrepidity received a musquet ball in his breast & instantly expired, much regretted not only by the 71st Regiment, but by the whole Army as a very spirited and intelligent officer. He was decently interred that evening on the field of Battle" ("Message").

Marion frees Sergeant McDonald

About 150 Continental soldiers captured in the Battle of Camden were marched toward Charleston under escort. Along the way, they camped at Great Savannah near Nelson's Ferry on the Santee River. Francis Marion roused the Williamsburg militia before dawn on August 20 and rode rapidly toward Great Savannah. The British soldiers were sleeping inside a farmhouse and their weapons were stacked outside the front door. The patriot militiamen killed or captured the British soldiers without much of a fight.

Marion invited the Continental soldiers who had been captured at Camden to serve in his militia unit. Seventy Continental soldiers insisted on continuing to Charleston as prisoners of war. Another eighty-five of them either did not think militia duty was good enough for Continental soldiers or didn't want to fight any more. Only three of them, including Allen McDonald, accepted the invitation; McDonald later became known, wrote one of Marion's men, "for his daring spirit and address in single combat" (James 55).

Fearing pursuit by other British forces, Marion led his men more than sixty miles to Britton's Neck. Many of his men went home to harvest crops and take care of their families, but he recruited other patriots, including several former members of the 2nd South Carolina Regiment who had served with him before.

Ambush at Blue Savannah: September 4, 1780

Loyalists in the Britton's Neck area formed a militia regiment to oppose Marion's patriot militia. Marion awakened his men before dawn on September 4 and set forth in search of the loyalist militia. His advance guard of carefully selected horsemen was commanded by Major James, who rode a magnificent horse named Thunder. When a scout reported that the loyalists had blocked the road, James gave a cheer and led a charge. The loyalists fled. Major James pursued the loyalist commander, who joined a group of his men taking cover in a thicket. At this point, James realized that he had left his men behind and was facing the enemy alone. He looked back over his shoulder and shouted, "Come on my boys! Come on! Here they are! Here they are!" (Rankin 70). The loyalists, tricked into believing they would be attacked by a large force, rode off through the woods.

Marion then led fifty patriots toward a force of two hundred loyalists. When the loyalists formed battle lines, Marion withdrew. Marion halted at Blue Savannah and hid his men in the underbrush. The loyalist infantry set off in pursuit of Marion and walked into an ambush. Marion's men gave a battle cry and charged on horseback into the foot soldiers, cutting them down with pistols and sabers. After firing one volley, the loyalists fled into the Little Peedee swamp and the loyalist regiment dispersed.

Wahab's Plantation: September 21, 1780

Lord Cornwallis left Camden on September 8 on his way to North Carolina. His force of 2,200 men, including the 71st Regiment, camped at the Waxhaws for two weeks to give sick soldiers a chance to recover. One of the sickest soldiers was Banastre Tarleton, who suffered from a severe case of yellow fever. The army moved on into North Carolina and encamped at Wahab's Plantation on the Catawba River. The British Legion, commanded by

Major George Hanger while Tarleton was ill, camped on one side of the river and the 71st Regiment camped nearby on the other side. Patriot partisan William Richardson Davie with 150 men attacked the British Legion at sunrise on September 21. The British Legion was taken by surprise and fled in confusion. The Highlanders of the 71st heard the gunshots and moved quickly to counterattack Davie's men. As the Highlanders arrived at one end of the lane through the plantation, the Americans marched out the other end.

Greene temporarily commands main army

In the North, Continental Commander in Chief George Washington showed his trust in General Nathanael Greene by placing Greene in temporary command of the main American army. A biographer describes the circumstances:

> …because of expected further British attempts to wrest from the Americans control of the Hudson River, Washington suddenly moved part of his army nearer to West Point, key to the northern defense system. West Point already was stronger than Greene had envisioned it when he and Knox laid out the plans. Greene was left in New Jersey in command of the main army and the huge stores he had stockpiled as quartermaster general…
>
> When Washington departed on September 17 for a highly secret conference with Count de Rochambeau and Admiral de Ternay, he left Greene in command of the whole Army, with full authority to act in his absence. But Greene was under specific orders to march at once to Tappan, New Jersey, close by the Hudson. From there he could swing in any needed direction to meet a British threat.
>
> "I have such entire confidence in your prudence and abilities," Washington wrote, "that I leave the conduct of it to your discretion." Greene, nonetheless, was ordered not to "seek action, nor to accept one, but upon advantageous terms."
>
> Greene promptly instructed the men to "be in perfect readiness" and moved the troops to Tappan the next day.
>
> So secret was Greene's move that he posted picked riflemen to stop any deserters on the march so that they

could not carry news to the enemy. Greene's orders were to shoot to kill.

By nightfall the men were in camp at Tappan. (Bailey 74-75)

Encounter at Charlotte: September 26, 1780

In North Carolina, British forces including the 71st Regiment broke camp at Wahab's Plantation and marched toward Charlotte, forty miles away. William Richardson Davie's partisans beat the British to Charlotte and set up a defensive position around the courthouse. The British arrived on September 26. The British Legion, still led by Major Hanger while Colonel Tarleton recuperated from fever, served as the advance guard for the British army and so once again encountered Davie. The Legion charged. At sixty yards, Davie's men fired a volley that broke up the charge. The British infantry joined the battle, and Cornwallis personally came to the front lines and ordered the British Legion to charge once more. With no chance of halting the large British army, the small patriot band retreated in good order.

Major Wemyss lays waste to the land

As he led the main army toward North Carolina, Cornwallis sent hundreds of British troops and loyalist militia under Major James Wemyss to quell the rebellion in the Williamsburg and Georgetown districts. Wemyss not only burned more than fifty homes and plantations belonging to Marion's men and other patriots, but also burned a Presbyterian Church at Indian Town. He ordered his soldiers to destroy weaving looms, gristmills, and blacksmith shops. Any sheep and cattle not needed to feed his soldiers were stabbed with bayonets and left to rot. Loyalists plundered the property of their fellow Americans. Numerous patriots were hanged.

Wemyss ordered that Major James' wife and children be locked in their house. Captain David Campbell of Edisto secretly gave them food and water through a window. When Wemyss released the family from captivity, he burned the house and all of its contents.

Marion's men, faced with overwhelming odds, had gone into hiding at Great White Marsh in North Carolina. Mosquito-borne diseases inflicted fever, chills, sweats and nausea on the men. They rode south from Great White Marsh on September 24. Marion, who could not swim, crossed the Little Peedee by clutching his saddle as his horse churned through the dark water.

Battle of Black Mingo: September 28-29, 1780

Marion's next adversary was John Coming Ball, a prominent South Carolinian commanding loyalist troops stationed about twenty miles north of Georgetown. Ball's men dug trenches along Black Mingo Creek and set up camp near a tavern called the Red House. From that position, they controlled traffic on the post road and navigation on the creek.

On the evening of September 28, Marion advanced toward the loyalist encampment. Just before midnight, Marion's horsemen crossed an old bridge near the Red House. The rattle of hooves on loose planks alerted the loyalist sentry, who fired an alarm shot. Marion led his men at a gallop onto the post road, where he ordered most of them to dismount. A small group would act as cavalry while their comrades would attack the fortifications on foot. Ball deployed the loyalists in a field near the tavern.

When the patriot militia advanced through the dark night to within thirty yards of the loyalist line, Ball ordered the loyalists to fire. The patriots suffered casualties and fell back, but rallied and continued the advance under cover. A detachment of patriots attacked the loyalists' right flank.

Under attack from two sides, the loyalists fired once more and ran into the swamp. The fighting killed one patriot private and one officer, and wounded six privates and two officers. Three loyalists were killed, and thirteen were wounded or taken prisoner. The patriots captured muskets, ammunition, military baggage, and horses. Marion took a horse, saddle and bridle that had belonged to the loyalist leader – Marion named the horse Ball.

Despite his experience in conventional warfare as a Continental officer, Marion was learning the tactics and strategy of guerilla warfare on the job. One of the things he learned at Black Mingo was to cover a bridge with blankets before riding across it. Marion also appreciated the value of good horses – such as Ball and Thunder – in rapid raids and quick retreats. His reports included the number of horses killed or captured as well as the number of men killed, wounded, or captured (Rankin 298).

Battle of Kings Mountain: October 7, 1780

During Cornwallis' march into North Carolina, about nine hundred loyalists commanded by Patrick Ferguson covered his western flank. Ferguson was a Scottish gentleman with more than twenty years of military experience. Sir Henry Clinton promoted Ferguson to the position of major in the 71st Regiment, but Ferguson never served with the 71st as a regimental officer; his force consisted entirely of American loyalists.

In the autumn of 1780, frontiersmen from Georgia, South Carolina, North Carolina, and Virginia gathered to oppose Ferguson. Among them was Colonel William Campbell, a tall, redheaded Highlander who carried an ancestral weapon called a claymore, based on the Gaelic words for large sword. The patriot band swelled to more than 1,300 men. The officers picked 940 of the best riflemen and horsemen to close in on Ferguson.

Ferguson withdrew toward Charlotte and sought support from Cornwallis, whose army was thirty-five miles away from Ferguson's force. Cornwallis decided not to send the British Legion because Tarleton was still sick, and ordered Ferguson to rendezvous with the 71st Regiment at Arness Ford.

On October 6, Ferguson encamped at Kings Mountain to await the arrival of the 71st. On October 7, the picked force of patriot frontiersmen surrounded Kings Mountain and launched a surprise attack on Ferguson's loyalists.

Ferguson, wielding his sword, rode to the weakest points of the line to rally the loyalists. His horse was shot from under him. He mounted another horse, and it was shot. He mounted again, and again the horse went down. He mounted a gray horse and led a charge into the patriot line.

The frontier riflemen fired a dozen balls into his body. As he fell, his foot caught in the stirrup and he was dragged behind his horse. Within minutes, he was dead.

The patriots sought to avenge the murder of Buford's men at the Waxhaws by killing the defeated loyalists, although William Campbell tried to stop the slaughter. Patriot casualties totaled twenty-eight dead and sixty-four wounded, compared to 157 loyalists who were killed and 163 who suffered such severe wounds that they were left on the mountain to die; nearly seven hundred loyalists, many of them wounded, were taken prisoner.

Sergeant McDonald engages in single combat

Francis Marion attempted to free Georgetown, a strategically important town on the South Carolina coast, from British occupation. Historian Hugh F. Rankin describes the exploits of Allen McDonald, a redheaded Scot from the Cross Creek country, on that occasion:

> At Grimes Plantation, some sixty miles from Georgetown, [Marion] awakened his men early in the morning of October 8 and began riding hard for the coast. He sent ahead an advance guard under the command of Peter Horry and made up of Captain John Baxter, Sergeant McDonald and near thirty horsemen.
>
> As he neared the town, Marion sent in his advance party to draw the attention of the town's defenders. After this diversion had been established, he planned to circle around and hit the redoubt inside the town. About two miles from town the advance party met a group of Tory troopers under Major Ganey and Lieutenant Evans. The two groups came together in a clash of heaving horses, flashing sabers, pistol shots and the shouts and curses of angry men. Shortly after the shock of the first collision, Ganey's men wheeled and fled toward town, Horry's men in hot pursuit.
>
> Sergeant McDonald selected Ganey as the subject of his attention. For two miles they raced along, with neither the pursuer gaining nor the pursued pulling away. As they neared the village, still too far apart for McDonald to effectively use his sword, he lunged forward with his carbine and bayonet. He thrust into Ganey's back with such force that the bayonet penetrated the Tory leader's body, the point coming out through his chest. As the sergeant withdrew his weapon, the bayonet twisted loose from the gun. The bleeding victim still managed to maintain his seat as he fled into Georgetown. Horry broke off the pursuit; he had lost but one man. Among the Tory casualties was Lieutenant Evans, sprawled dead in the road. (Rankin 106-07)

William Dobein James, who served in Marion's band, wrote an eye-witness account of McDonald's single combat with Ganey.

When James wrote his memoirs many years after the war, he remembered the event as part of a running battle in January of 1781:

> A kind of savage warfare now took place in the woods, between the Sampit and Black river roads, during the whole morning. A party of Horry's was at one time seen advancing, and the tories retreating; then again the tories were advancing, and a party of Horry's retreating. At one time the commander was left as he thought alone, and Capt. Lewis at the head of a party was rushing on to shoot him down, when suddenly from behind a tree off went the gun of a boy by the name of Gwyn, and shot Lewis, whose party thinking more guns were behind the trees ran away. As Lewis fell his gun went off and killed Horry's horse. Finally the tories were routed. In this affair Serjt. M'Donald performed essential service; he singled out Ganey as his object of attack, and the latter fled from him. --- In going at full speed down the Black river road, at the corner of Richmond fence, M'Donald shot one of Ganey's men, and overtaking him soon after thrust a bayonet up to the hilt in his back; the bayonet separated from the gun, and Ganey carried it into Georgetown; he recovered, but tired of garrison life, after a few months he and his men deserted the British. (94)

When James looked back on his experiences with Marion, he recalled another tale of McDonald's valiant deeds:

> At the head of a party of this cavalry Col. Peter Horry had soon an opportunity to make a trial of his skill in cavalry evolutions. He met and charged a troop of British horse on Waccamaw neck, but by his own account he appears to have been rather worsted, for he was unhorsed himself and his life saved by Serjt. M'Donald... (92-93)

Attack at Tarcoat Swamp: October 25, 1780

Francis Marion was a moody man. When he called out the militia in early October and got little response, he fell into despair. He considered abandoning the South Carolina Lowcountry and resuming his career as a Continental officer with the Southern Army, which was at Hillsborough, North Carolina, at the time. Soon the militiamen began to come in from their homes and families, and Marion began to feel satisfied. As more men came in, he grew anxious for adventure. He was itching for a fight. His opportunity came when he learned that loyalist officers were recruiting in the forks of the Black River. His band of 150 men traveled hard for two days and approached the loyalist camp at Tarcoat Swamp. Marion's men awoke at midnight and prepared to attack early in the morning of October 26. They charged into the camp, and the loyalists fled into the swamp. Six loyalists were killed, fourteen were wounded, and twenty-three were taken prisoner. Some of the loyalists had been playing cards when the attack took them by surprise, and one of the casualties still held an ace, jack, and deuce of clubs in his dead fingers. None of the patriots were killed or wounded, but two of their horses were killed. Marion's men went through the loyalist camp and took eighty horses, saddles and bridles, muskets, ammunition, blankets, food supplies, and baggage.

British establish winter quarters at Winnsboro

The main British army pulled out Charlotte on October 14 and returned to South Carolina. Cornwallis established his headquarters at Winnsboro, a pleasant town not far from Camden. By November 1, Banastre Tarleton had recovered from yellow fever and was ready to once again lead the British Legion into combat. Because the supply routes from Charleston to Camden and Winnsboro were threatened by Marion's patrols, Tarleton was sent to seek and destroy Marion. Tarleton set forth with two artillery pieces, a hundred cavalrymen and three hundred infantrymen to crush Marion's force of about two hundred men.

Tarleton gives Marion a nickname

Starting from Brierly's Ferry on Broad River, Tarleton crossed the Wateree on November 3. Marion prepared to ambush Tarleton at Nelson's Ferry on November 5, but Tarleton took another route. Tarleton laid an ambush for Marion at Richardson's Plantation on November 7. Mary Richardson, the widow of patriot General Richard Richardson, resided in the plantation house and her son, paroled Continental Captain Richard Richardson, was hiding on the grounds. Mrs. Richardson sent Captain Richardson to warn Marion, who withdrew six miles to Richbourg's Mill Dam.

An escaped prisoner told Tarleton where Marion had gone, and Tarleton's dragoons struck camp before daylight and rode rapidly toward Richbourg's Mill. Marion's men also arose before daylight and sought sanctuary. Guided by local men, Marion's band scurried through the swamps of Jack's Creek, the Pocotaligo River, and the Black River. After traveling thirty-five miles, Marion took up a defensive position at Benbow's Ferry. Historian Hugh Rankin tells the tale:

> Tarleton kept up the pursuit "through swamps and defiles" for seven hours and twenty-six miles. When he came to Ox Swamp on Pocotaligo River, both his troopers and their mounts were too weary to attempt the foreboding wastes of the swamp. It is said that Tarleton, as he pulled up his jaded men, cried out, "Come my Boys! Let us go back and we will find the Gamecock [Thomas Sumter], But as for this damned old fox, the Devil himself could not catch him." The story spread and grew with each telling until the people along the Santee began to refer to the gimpy little colonel as the "Swamp Fox." (Rankin 113)

From Tarleton's perspective, Marion seemed "old;" Tarleton was 26 years of age and Marion was close to 50.

Tarleton led his men back to Richardson's Plantation. By this time he had been told that "a treacherous woman" had warned Marion of the planned ambush. On his return trip, he ordered that Mary Richardson be flogged. He also ordered that the body of her late husband, who had been buried on the plantation six weeks earlier, be dug up so he could look at the face of a brave man; apparently his true motive was a rumor that valuable family possessions had been hidden in the grave. He ordered that all the cattle, hogs, and poultry on the plantation be shut up in the barn where the plantation's harvested corn was stored; then his men set fire to the barn and let the animals burn alive.

Tarleton knew that Mary Richardson was not alone in supporting the patriots. To teach the local residents the error of their ways, Tarleton had thirty plantations burned and their food supply destroyed. The families were left without shelter in the November weather. When Marion wrote a report to General Gates, he mentioned seeing women and children sitting around a fire with nothing to ward off the chill except the clothes on their backs.

British attack Sumter's force

On November 9, a British force under Major Wemyss attacked Thomas Sumter's patriots at Fishdam Ford on the Broad River. Wemyss was wounded and taken prisoner. Sumter crossed the Broad River and threatened the British post at Ninety-Six. British commander Lord Cornwallis sent the 1st Battalion of the 71st Regiment under Major McArthur to protect Brierly's Ford on the Broad River. Cornwallis ordered Tarleton to drop the pursuit of Marion and to take up pursuit of Sumter.

Loyalists kill Marion's nephew

After eluding Tarleton, Marion moved toward Georgetown. On November 15, Marion sent out Captain Melton to reconnoiter along the Sampit Road leading into Georgetown. Marion's nephew, Lieutenant Gabriel Marion, volunteered to ride with Melton's men. Their route took them through a thick swamp, where they encountered a mounted force of loyalists commanded by Jesse Barefield. The loyalists and patriots opened fire on one another. Buckshot pierced Barefield's face and shoulder. The patriots wheeled around to ride away.

The loyalists shot at the patriots' horses, and Gabriel Marion's horse went down beneath him. He tried to flee on foot. The loyalists rode him down and clubbed him. He recognized one of the loyalists and, thinking his acquaintance would take mercy on him, he identified himself as Gabriel Marion. The other loyalists then realized that he was a member of Francis Marion's family. They warned Gabriel's acquaintance that both of them would be shot if they didn't put some distance between them. Gabriel clutched the saddle of his acquaintance until the loyalists pulled him loose. A loyalists shoved a musket into Gabriel's chest and fired a deadly shot.

Francis Marion mourned his nephew quietly. His men noticed a haggard expression on his face. Three days after his nephew died, Francis Marion told his men that Gabriel was a virtuous young man who had fallen in the cause of his country and that the mourning period was over.

Blackstock's Plantation: November 20, 1980

Banastre Tarleton's British force caught up with Thomas Sumter's patriot force near nightfall on November 20 at Blackstock's plantation on the Tyger River. In heavy fighting, Sumter was wounded. Darkness stopped the fighting, and both sides claimed victory.

Sumter's force suffered three killed and five wounded. Tarleton lost about fifty killed and wounded. Knowing that the 1st Battalion of the 71st Regiment was coming in support of Tarleton, Sumter withdrew across the Tyger River. Tarleton made his way to the British winter quarters at Winnsboro (Ward 746-47, Boatner 78-80).

The Swamp Fox finds a lair at Snow Island

As the coldest months of the winter approached, Francis Marion found a hiding place at Snow Island, a place named for the Snow family. Historian Hugh Rankin describes the legendary sanctuary:

> The low ridge that formed Snow Island was some five miles long and two miles wide, rising out of the water and boggy ground that formed its boundaries. On the east was the Pee-dee River, while Lynche's Creek lapped its skirts on the north before it emptied into the Peedee. Here the creek was wide and deep and well nigh choked with a great raft of a logjam. Clark's Creek, a deep stream, ran along the south and west. Snow's Lake also lay to the west, along with the turgid waters and marshy lands of Muddy Creek and the Sockee Swamp. (Rankin 127).

Marion's men enhanced the natural defenses of the island by tearing down bridges and removing boats.

Picked warriors square off for arranged combat

Marion's next target was a British column marching from Charleston toward Camden under the command of Major Robert McLeroth. Marion attacked McLeroth on December 13 at Halfway Swamp. During a lull in the fighting, a British officer approached Marion under a flag of truce. The officer complained that the Americans did not follow the rules of civilized warfare, and he challenged them to engage in a traditional military confrontation on open ground. Marion replied that the British also were guilty of violating the rules, and he accepted the challenge. They agreed that twenty of the best men on each side would face each other near an oak tree in the middle of a field. Marion wrote the names of the men he wanted to represent him on pieces of paper, and each man accepted the dangerous assignment. The twenty American riflemen and twenty British musketry marksmen marched out to face off. The Americans planned to begin shooting when the British were fifty yards away. Before they got that close, a British officer walked across the front of the British line and gave a command. The marksmen shouldered their muskets, performed an about-face, and quick-stepped back to the British defensive position. The whole thing had been a hoax to gain time for reinforcements to come to McLeroth's aid.

As the day came to an end, the British soldiers burned huge campfires and talked loudly late in the night. Then they stole quietly into the dark, leaving their heavy baggage behind. When dawn came, Marion found that McLeroth had tricked him a second time.

The wounded on both sides were taken to a tavern under a flag of truce. McLeroth not only left his own surgeon to take care of both the Americans and the British, but also paid the tavern keeper for feeding and sheltering them. McLeroth already had a good reputation among residents because he had refused orders to burn houses. The people appreciated his attempts to treat them equitably. They described him as being sweet-spoken, mild-looking and noble-spirited. The tavern keeper told Marion that it would be a burning shame to kill such a dear good gentleman as Robert McLeroth (Rankin 134).

Greene takes command in the South

The Continental Congress authorized General Washington to name a successor to Horatio Gates as commander of the Southern Department of the Continental Army. Washington chose Nathanael Greene, and Greene chose General Daniel Morgan as his second in command. Washington also agreed to Greene's request to assign Lighthorse Harry Lee's legion of horsemen and infantry to the Southern Department. Colonel William Washington's cavalry unit was already in the South, as were General Isaac Huger, General Andrew Pickens, and Colonel Otho Williams, along with partisan commanders Francis Marion and Thomas Sumter. Shortly after taking command of the Southern Department on December 2 at Charlotte, Greene sent a message to Marion asking for information on British operations. Marion reported that General Alexander Leslie had arrived at Charleston with British reinforcements on December 20 and was on his way to join forces with Cornwallis. Marion observed Leslie's progress across the swamps until, on Christmas Eve, Marion headed for his hide-away at Snow Island.

Greene moved the main force of his army down to the Peedee, where provisions were more plentiful, and sent a select detachment under Brigadier General Daniel Morgan toward Ninety-Six. Greene made camp on the Peedee on the day after Christmas.

As the year came to an end South Carolina Governor Rutledge promoted Marion from lieutenant colonel to brigadier general of South Carolina militia. Rutledge placed Marion in charge of regiments to the east of the Santee, Wateree and Catawba rivers, while Thomas Sumter was in charge of regiments farther inland. Marion learned of his promotion on New Year's Day of 1781.

1781

Aeneas Mackintosh, age 30, perseveres as his regiment suffers attrition in fierce fighting across the Carolinas and is taken prisoner at the Siege of Yorktown. Allen McDonald performs yet more feats of valor and earns a promotion to lieutenant shortly before dying in battle.

New strategies for a new year

As the year 1781 dawned, the British held South Carolina with a network of strategically located posts. Their administrative headquarters was at Charleston where the port provided for reinforcements and supplies to pour in from the sea. They also held the other ports in South Carolina, at Georgetown and Port Royal. In the backcountry, they established strongholds at Ninety-Six and Camden. Their large army under Lord Cornwallis was stationed at Winnsboro. They also controlled Georgia, and had posts on the South Carolina border at Savannah and Augusta.

Although the British army remained vastly superior, the Southern Department of the Continental Army was coming to life under the new leadership of Nathanael Greene and Daniel Morgan. In the swamps of northeastern South Carolina, Brigadier General Francis Marion continued to harass British outposts and supply trains. Because the British were unable to transport uniforms and other supplies to Winnsboro, the Highlanders of the 71st Regiment were "really quite naked" as the cold, wet winter set in (Wickwire 242).

Greene led half of his army from Charlotte to Cheraw, and sent Morgan with the other half toward Ninety-Six. Because British forces were tied up protecting lines of communication against Marion's raids, there were no troops to spare when the garrison at Ninety-Six requested reinforcements.

Gathering at the Cowpens

On New Year's Day of 1781, British General Cornwallis sent a detachment under Colonel Banastre Tarleton to drive Daniel Morgan's patriot troops away from Ninety-Six. The detachment numbered well over a thousand men, supported by artillery. The

British detachment included the 1st Battalion of the 71st Highlanders, an elite regiment that had distinguished itself in the fiercest fighting of the American Revolution in the North and the South.

The line companies of the 1st Battalion of the 71st Regiment in Tarleton's detachment had 249 men and fourteen officers; their commander was Major Archibald McArthur. Another thirty-five men from the 1st Battalion were assigned to a specialized light infantry battalion, along with thirty-four men from the 2nd Battalion of the 71st and specially selected men from other regiments.

Before dawn on January 16, Tarleton closed to within six miles of Morgan's camp. Morgan hurriedly broke camp and put some distance between him and Tarleton. Later that day, Tarleton's men took possession of Morgan's abandoned campground because, Tarleton observed, "it yielded a good post, and afforded plenty of provisions, which they had left behind them, half cooked, in every part of their encampment" (Tarleton 214). Tarleton's delight at finding Morgan's provisions implies that Tarleton's detachment was running low on food.

Morgan managed to move only twelve miles over rain-ravaged roads through the rough terrain of upstate South Carolina in midwinter weather.

Late in the afternoon, Morgan took a stand at a landmark known as the Cowpens. Patriot militia groups joined him at the traditional backcountry gathering place throughout the day and night; some of the men who joined Morgan had previously assembled at the Cowpens before proceeding to fight Patrick Ferguson's loyalist troops at Kings Mountain. As the backwoodsmen continued to arrive at the Cowpens, Morgan's force grew to somewhere between eight hundred and a thousand men.

Morgan conceives innovative plan of battle

With guidance from local men, Morgan surveyed the terrain of the Cowpens. Taking into account Tarleton's temperament as well as the lay of the land, Morgan decided on a disposition of his troops. He conceived a new way of using militia in battle, an innovation so successful that American commanders continued to take advantage of it for the rest of the war.

Morgan's innovation sprang from knowing the strengths and weaknesses of militiamen. Bitter experience had exposed their glaring weakness: they would not stand and fight against the bayonets of advancing infantry or against the sabers of charging cavalry. The most valuable strength of the backwoodsmen who gathered at Cowpens was their accuracy in shooting a rifle, honed from a lifetime of hunting, defending their homes from Indian raids, and choosing to participate in certain battles during the American Revolution, especially when war raged near their homes. To take advantage of their skill with a rifle, Morgan placed the best sharpshooters in the front lines. After aiming and firing, the sharpshooters would be free to run for cover behind the patriot lines.

Under Morgan's plan, the next line after the sharpshooters consisted of militia units commanded by Andrew Pickens, an elder in the Presbyterian church who had become one of South Carolina's best partisan leaders. The militiamen were instructed to fire two well-aimed volleys with their rifles or muskets. After that, they would not be expected to stand and face the British bayonet charge; they would withdraw in good order to safety behind the Continental infantry. The militia units were expected to regroup for further service as needed, but the men also knew where their horses were kept in case they felt obliged to flee. Morgan, however, knew there was no escape because the Broad River flowed behind the battlefield.

The next line in Morgan's plan consisted of Continental infantry, trained and experienced in fighting conventional warfare. Morgan's force included several hundred Continental soldiers who had fought valiantly under De Kalb at Camden. The force also had a couple of hundred veteran riflemen from Virginia.

As a reserve force, Morgan placed cavalry in a swale behind a low ridge. The force included a group of South Carolina horsemen led by James McCall and fewer than a hundred Continental dragoons. The reserve force was commanded by Continental cavalry officer William Washington, who was kin to George Washington.

Militiamen consider Morgan one of them

Morgan explained his plan to his troops in person. He fit right in with the militiamen; being a backwoodsman and former wagoner, he talked like them and acted like them, and they considered him to be one of them. Historian M.F. Treacy described Morgan as "the very figure of the culture hero, bellowing in his teamster's voice, laughing his deep-chested guffaw" (97).

Morgan was recovering from malaria when Greene sent him out with half the Southern army in cold, rainy, midwinter weather. His chronic sciatica flared up again, hurting him so badly that he could not ride his horse faster than a walk. As he visited with the soldiers at the Cowpens, he wanted to show them the scars on his back, but his rheumatism kept him from raising his shirt and he had to ask someone to raise it for him.

During the long, cold January night at Cowpens, Morgan moved through the camp, explaining his battle plan and exhorting the men to valor in battle. An eye-witness, teenage partisan Thomas Young of South Carolina, described Morgan's conversations with his men:

> ...It was upon this occasion I was more perfectly convinced of General Morgan's qualifications to command militia than I had ever before been. He went among the volunteers, helped them fix their swords, joked with them about their sweet-hearts, told them to keep in good spirits, and the day would be ours. And long after I had laid down, he was going about among the soldiers encouraging them, and telling them that the old Wagoner would crack his whip over Ben (Tarleton) in the morning, as sure as they lived. "Just hold up your heads, boys, three fires," he would say, "and you are free, and then when you return to your homes, how the old folks will bless you, and the girls kiss you, for your gallant conduct!" I don't believe he slept a wink that night! (Southern 181-82)

The Battle of Cowpens, January 17, 1781

At the British camp twelve miles away, Tarleton learned of Morgan's position. Buglers sounded reveille at two o'clock in the morning, and the British were marching toward Cowpens by three o'clock. Slogging across rain-swollen creeks and trudging along muddy paths, the British had to cross the same rugged terrain that Morgan's men had crossed earlier, but the British had to do it in the darkness of a midwinter night.

Scouts alerted Morgan that Tarleton was on the way. Knowing that the British had a long march ahead of them, Morgan let his men sleep awhile longer while he pondered and prayed.

At about an hour before sunrise, Morgan bellowed, "Boys, get up! Benny is coming" (Treacy 97). Morgan knew that Tarleton was still five miles away and there was time for the men to eat breakfast. When the men took their battle stations, Morgan shored up their resolve by going to their positions and speaking to them. Historian Don Higginbotham describes Morgan's exhortations to valor in battle:

> To the skirmishers in front of Pickens, he said, "Let me see which are most entitled to the credit of brave men, the boys of Carolina or those of Georgia." Moving to Pickens's militia, he delivered a fiery speech, pounding his fist into his palm as he spoke. He expected to see their usual zeal and courage, and he reminded them not to withdraw until they had fired twice at close range. His words to Howard's line were equally impassioned: "My friends in arms, my dear boys, I request you to remember Saratoga, Monmouth, Paoli, Brandywine, and this day you must play your parts for your honor & liberty's cause." Battlefield oratory was not uncommon in the eighteenth century, but it was seldom more effectively employed. Morgan struck a spark in his men. The often unpredictable militiamen were, as one American officer wrote, "all in good spirits and very willing to fight." (136)

The British arrived at the Cowpens around sunrise. Tarleton, as Morgan had predicted, immediately launched an attack. Fifty dragoons drew their sabers and charged the sharpshooters positioned in Morgan's first line. The riflemen aimed and fired, and fifteen dragoons fell from their horses; the survivors galloped back to the cover of the British infantry.

Holding the 1st Battalion of the 71st Regiment in reserve, Tarleton ordered the main body of his infantry to advance. The infantrymen yelled as they charged, prompting Moran to tell his men, "They give us the British halloo, boys, give them the Indian whoop" (Higginbotham 137).

When the British came within range, the militiamen with Pickens set their sights on the officers and sergeants, following Morgan's instructions to "Look for the epaulets! Pick off the epaulets!" (Commager 1153). The militiamen fired a volley. The advancing infantry slowed down but kept coming. The militia fired a second aimed volley, and withdrew as instructed by Morgan.

When Tarleton saw the units leave, he thought the militia had broken as it so often had in the past. He ordered fifty cavalrymen to pursue what he thought were panic-stricken men in flight. William Washington's horsemen drove Tarleton's cavalry away, and covered the withdrawal of the militia.

As Pickens and other officers tried to convince the militia units to regroup and reload, Morgan rode up, sword in hand, and shouted, "Form, form, my brave fellows!" (Buchanan 323).

The British infantry continued to advance, but because it had lost so many officers it did not stay in formation. The line of Continental infantry Morgan had placed near the crest of a ridge fired a volley that stopped the British in their tracks. The disciplined, veteran foes exchanged fire at point-blank range.

71st Highlanders enter the fray

Tarleton then called on his reserves, the 1st Battalion of the 71st Highlanders. Tarleton ordered the reserves to execute a flanking movement against Morgan's right. The battalion's bagpipers played a traditional march as the Highlanders entered the fray. The Highlanders fired a volley that created confusion among the Virginians on the right. The Scots of the 71st then charged in traditional Highland fashion, expecting to take advantage of the confusion.

Patriot officers ordered the Virginians to maneuver into position to oppose the flanking movement. In the confusion created by the Highlanders, some of Morgan's men misunderstood the maneuver, and soon the whole line was moving in order away from the British attackers.

The British assumed that Morgan's entire army was in retreat, and gave chase. Because they were charging at a run through a stand of trees, and because they had lost many of their officers, the usually well-disciplined British troops disintegrated into a mob as they pursued their foes. The British, however, did not overrun the Americans, perhaps because the British were physically exhausted. The Americans had rested throughout the previous night and had eaten breakfast, while the British had been on the march through the night in cold, wet weather across rugged terrain. The British not only did without breakfast but also had been on meager rations for several days. When the Highlanders had been called into action, they trotted three hundred yards uphill toward the American right flank. When the Americans withdrew, the Highlanders charged another hundred yards in pursuit. The Highlanders closed to within ten to thirty yards before the Americans turned to fight some more.

Morgan's men remained in formation as they marched toward the rear. Morgan picked a place to make a stand, and ordered them to halt. "Face about, boys!" Morgan told them. "Give them one good fire, and the day is ours!" (Buchanan 324). The Americans fired point-blank at their pursuers. Bodies of the killed and wounded covered the battlefield; among the casualties were nearly half the men of the 1st Battalion of the 71st Regiment. The Highlanders kept fighting hand-to-hand.

Continental infantry charged the 71st Highlanders with bayonets while Washington's horsemen attacked the Highlanders from their left flank and rear.

Pickens led his militia in a charge on the Highlanders' right flank. The Highlanders began to retreat; many of them ran for their lives. Surrounded and without hope of relief, the Highlanders surrendered. Of the sixteen officers of the 71st who fought at the Cowpens, six were taken prisoner, two were killed, and seven – including a lieutenant named Mackintosh – were wounded.

The only soldiers of the 71st who escaped from the Cowpens were a few who had been left behind to guard the baggage train.

Fearing reprisal

When the Highlanders surrendered, they expected their American captors to take revenge for Tarleton's numerous acts of cruelty. A high-ranking American officer, John Eager Howard, described a Highlander's apprehension:

> …In the pursuit I was led towards the right, in among the 71st, who were broken into squads, and as I called to them to surrender, they laid down their arms, and the officers delivered up their swords. Captain Duncanson, of the 71st Grenadiers, gave me his sword and stood by me. Upon getting on my horse, I found him pulling at my saddle, and he nearly unhorsed me. I expressed my displeasure and asked him what he was about. The explanation was that they had orders to give no quarter, and they did not expect any; and

as my men were coming up, he was afraid they would use them ill. I admitted his excuse and put him into the care of a sergeant... (Commager 1157)

Morgan proudly reported, "not a man was killed, wounded or even insulted after he surrendered. Had not the Britons during this contest received so many lessons of humanity, I should flatter myself that this might teach them a little" (Commager 1157).

Commander of 71st expresses bitterness

The 71st Highlanders boasted of a proud record of military prowess throughout the war until the Battle of Cowpens. Saddened by seeing so many of their comrades killed and humiliated by surrendering in battle, they vented their fury not on the Americans but on Tarleton. The commander of the Highlanders expressed his contempt of Tarleton to his captor, Colonel Howard:

> Major M'Arthur very freely entered into conversation, and said that he was an officer before Tarleton was born; that the best troops in the service were put under *"that boy"* to be sacrificed; that he had flattered himself the event would have been different, if his advice had been taken, which was to charge with all the horse at the moment we were retreating. (Henry Lee 98)

Horsemen fight hand-to-hand

Tarleton, watching his infantry surrender and most of his dragoons flee, rallied fifty loyal horsemen and led a last desperate charge. Washington's cavalry met the charge and drove off the British dragoons. Washington then took off in pursuit of Tarleton. Some people say that Washington and Tarleton engaged in single combat on horseback like knights of old. Washington was alone ahead of his men when Tarleton and a few of his horsemen turned to fight. In hand-to-hand combat, Washington broke his saber at the hilt. Washington's 14-year-old black servant raced to his rescue and shot Washington's opponent in the sword arm. Another British officer attacked Washington, but an American sergeant arrived in the nick of time and deflected the officer's sword. Tarleton himself charged in and swung his saber at Washington, who blocked it with his broken saber. Tarleton fired his pistol, but missed Washington while wounding Washington's horse. As Washington's cavalry caught up with him, Tarleton galloped away to fight another day.

Tarleton vents his wrath

Tarleton and the remnant of his command withdrew down the road to the place where the British baggage had been left with a small guard under Ensign Fraser of the 71st Regiment. Tarleton and Cornwallis claimed that a detachment of American troops had captured the baggage, and that Tarleton's dragoons "retook the baggage of the corps, cut the detachment who had it in possession to pieces, destroyed the greater part," and carried away the survivors as prisoners.

Roderick Mackenzie of the 71st Regiment disputed that story. When the British soldiers guarding the baggage learned that their comrades had been defeated, Mackenzie contended, Fraser destroyed the baggage that could not be carried off and retreated to Cornwallis' position with the baggage wagon and all the horses without ever seeing any American troops (Mackenzie 101-02).

Morgan reported that the British left behind thirty-five wagons filled with supplies. Morgan made no mention of Tarleton having retaken any baggage, and no American troops reported being attacked by Tarleton in an attempt to retake the baggage.

One American who had plundered the abandoned baggage earlier in the day was on his way to Cowpens when saber-wielding dragoons cut open his left hand, then disabled his sword arm, then sliced his forehead so that blood and loose skin blinded him, then stabbed both shoulders and took him captive (Babits 132-33).

Morgan sent a company of mounted infantry and cavalry commanded by Washington to pursue the remnants of Tarleton's detachment. Washington broke off the chase after riding twenty-four miles without overtaking Tarleton.

Morgan moves out

Morgan did not take time to savor his victory, because he knew the main British army under Cornwallis was a greater threat to his much smaller force than Tarleton's detachment had been. Cornwallis wanted not only to eliminate Morgan's division of the American army but also to free the British soldiers who had been taken prisoner at the Cowpens. Morgan explained the situation in a letter to Greene:

> ...As I was obliged to move off the field of action in the morning to secure the prisoners, I cannot be so accurate as to the killed and wounded of the enemy as I could wish. From the reports of an officer whom I sent to view the ground, there were one hundred non-commissioned officers and privates and ten commissioned officers killed and two hundred rank and file wounded. We have now in our possession five hundred and two non-commissioned officers and privates prisoners, independent of the wounded, and the militia are taking up stragglers continually. Twenty-nine commissioned officers have fell into our hands. Their rank, etc., you will see by an enclosed list. The officers I have paroled; the privates I am conveying by the safest route to Salisbury...
>
> Two standards, two fieldpieces, thirty-five wagons, a travelling forge and all their music are ours. Their baggage, which was immense, they have in a great measure destroyed.
>
> Our loss is inconsiderable, which the enclosed return will evince... (Commager 1159)

About a dozen Americans were killed in the fighting at the Cowpens. Reports of the number of Americans wounded range from sixty to more than a hundred.

The Battle of Cowpens started at sunrise and was over within an hour. By noon, Morgan moved out, and by nightfall his division had crossed to the north side of the Broad River. Before dawn the next morning, the division continued its rapid retreat and marched until sundown. Morgan detached a force to take the prisoners into Virginia, and led the rest of his division across the Catawba River. He had covered a hundred miles and crossed two rivers in six days.

Once encamped on the Catawba, Morgan stayed in bed in his tent, suffering from sciatica and a high fever.

Cornwallis destroys baggage

Cornwallis came up with a scheme to make his army mobile enough to keep up with Morgan. He ordered the destruction of cumbersome baggage, provisions, rum and personal possessions. Then he set out after Morgan as a light rain fell on the morning of January 28. The rain fell harder as the day went by and continued through the next day. By the time Cornwallis reached the Catawba, the river was too swollen to cross. As the army waited for the river to recede, the soldiers sought shelter under trees because their tents had been destroyed with their baggage.

Greene joins Morgan

General Greene, the commander of the Southern Department of the Continental army, had stayed with one division at Cheraw while Morgan led the other division. With Morgan on the run and Cornwallis in pursuit, Greene knew it was time to reunite the army. Greene instructed General Isaac Huger to lead the division from Cheraw to North Carolina, where the divisions would rendezvous. Greene himself set out on January 28 to join Morgan on the Catawba. With only a five-man escort, Greene traveled more than a hundred miles through no-man's land and arrived at Morgan's camp on January 30. Greene sent Morgan's division marching toward Salisbury, a major supply center, while a force of several hundred riflemen guarded the fords of the Catawba.

Before dawn on February 1, the British waded through chest-high water to cross the Catawba at Cowan's Ford while American militiamen fired upon them from the far bank. As Cornwallis rode across the river, his horse was hit by several musket balls but managed to carry Cornwallis across before collapsing. Once across the river, the British fired a volley at the militiamen. Most of the militiamen fled when their commander, General William Lee Davidson, was killed. British casualties, according to Cornwallis, were four killed and thirty-six wounded but, according to local residents, more than a dozen bodies of British soldiers washed downstream.

The two divisions of the American army met at Guilford on February 6, but the Americans were still outnumbered; Cornwallis led three thousand men, mostly British regulars, in pursuit of fourteen hundred Continentals and six hundred militiamen. Once the divisions had reunited, Morgan left the army in Greene's hands. Fighting and marching in cold, wet weather had aggravated Morgan's ailments so that he could no longer ride a horse. He was carried on a litter when he began his journey home to Virginia.

British chase Americans northward

Greene continued to withdraw before Cornwallis. The British and American armies marched northward for four days through cold rain and snow, skirmishing along the way. Greene had arranged for boats to be waiting at the Dan River, and during the night of February 13 the Americans crossed into Virginia. The British were close behind but could not follow the Americans across the river because there were no boats left on the bank. Cornwallis withdrew to Hillsboro, where his men could forage for provisions.

Historians Lawrence Babits and Joshua Howard describe the tortuous campaign from South Carolina to the Dan River:

> ...Cornwallis blamed his inability to intercept Greene on "defective" intelligence, "bad roads, and the passage of many deep creeks and bridges destroyed by the enemy's light troops." He had pursued Greene's army for three weeks, covering some 250 miles over muddy, frost-encrusted roads, in torrents of rain and sleet, crossed several major waterways, and fought numerous skirmishes. The Race to the Dan was over, and Nathanael Greene had won. (36)

On February 18, Greene sent a force back across the Dan to keep Cornwallis from consolidating British control of North Carolina, and two days later sent another force. Three days later, Greene led the Southern army back into North Carolina. Greene had been receiving reinforcements that boosted his army to more than four thousand men, including Continental infantry, Continental cavalry, Continental artillery, and militia units from Virginia and North Carolina. Many of the militiamen bore Scottish names such as McDowell, Stuart, and Campbell, and wore hats imported "from home," meaning from Scotland (Babits and Howard 67-68).

Two officers in the North Carolina militia had been at the Battle of Brier Creek: Brigadier General Thomas Eaton's only combat experience had been in the ignominious rout; his cousin Colonel Pinkatham "Pink" Eaton had been wounded while commanding a militia regiment at Brier Creek and had gone on to serve two years as a Continental company commander in George Washington's army. Another North Carolinian, Brigadier General John Butler, had served at the Battle of Moore's Creek Bridge and had earned distinction at Stono Ferry and Camden (Babits and Howard 59-60). An officer in the Virginia Continentals, 26-year-old Lieutenant Colonel Richard Campbell, had served under Lachlan McIntosh in the Western Department (Babits and Howard 73-74).

While the American army gathered reinforcements, the British army dwindled. Exhaustion and desertion – blamed partly on the lack of rum – reduced the British army to about two thousand men. The remaining British soldiers nearly starved. General Charles O'Hara wrote that the army was "completely worn out, by the excessive Fatigues of the Campaign in a march of above a Thousand Miles, most of them barefoot, naked and for days living upon Carrion… and three or four ounces of unground Indian Corn." A private reported having "but one pound of flour for six men per day with very little beef, and no salt the half of the time" (Babits and Howard 49).

Action at Wetzell's Mill: March 6, 1781

As the American and British armies maneuvered across North Carolina, American forces clashed with British forces including the 71st Regiment – in which Aeneas Mackintosh served – on March 6 at Wetzell's Mill on Reedy Fork. Historian Christopher Ward, referring to the 7st Regiment as Fraser's Highlanders, describes the action:

> Having arrived at the stream, Cornwallis ordered Webster's brigade – composed of the Royal Welch Fusiliers, the 33rd British Regiment, and Fraser's Highlanders, with a light company of the Guards in the lead. As they entered the water they were met by a heavy and well directed fire, and fell back in disorder. Webster, disgusted by their hesitancy, rode up, called them to account, and plunged into the stream. His men followed.
>
> When they gained the opposite shore, which lay under a high bank, the flanks of the American line drew in and formed behind the cavalry in the rear, while the center kept up a fire upon Webster's men clambering up from the water's edge; but there was no stopping them. The Americans retreated under heavy fire, and rear-guard action continued

for about five miles until the pursuit ceased... In the affair at Wetzell's Mill, the Americans lost about twenty killed or wounded. Tarleton admits a loss of twenty-one on his side.

A strange fact of this engagement was Webster's escape from death. Lee had posted twenty-five expert riflemen in a little log schoolhouse at the right of the ford. They all had participated in the King's Mountain affair and were reputed to be dead shots, and they had orders to concentrate their fire on the enemy's officers. Every one of them drew a bead on Webster, conspicuous as he was, and fired. Eight or nine of them tried a second shot, yet not a bullet touched him. (782)

Battle of Guilford Courthouse: March 15, 1781

On March 14, Greene prepared for battle at Guilford Courthouse. Greene stationed the militia in front of the Continental troops, similar to Morgan's disposition at the Cowpens. Greene, like Morgan, rode up and down the line inspiring the militiamen with themes of honor and liberty and asking them to fire two volleys and then withdraw from the front line.

In another echo of the Cowpens, the British awakened before dawn on March 15 and, without taking time to eat breakfast, marched twelve miles to confront the Americans. As the British neared Guilford, Tarleton's dragoons skirmished with American cavalrymen. Babits and Howard describe the approach of the British army: "By 10:00 A.M. the column had been on its feet for nearly five hours. The men were likely tired, definitely hungry, and probably well splattered with mud" (79).

At the time of the Battle of Guilford Courthouse, following the loss of the 1st Battalion of the 71st at Cowpens and attrition during the campaign across the Carolinas, the 71st consisted of one battalion with fewer than 250 men. The highest-ranking officers in the 71st at Guilford were three captains – including Aeneas Mackintosh. One of the captains, Robert Hutcheson, was in overall command of the 71st. Research indicates that the 71st was deployed in two wings, each commanded by a captain and each consisting of three companies led by lieutenants; in that case, Mackintosh was in command of one wing (Babits and Howard 86-88, 219).

At Guilford the 71st Highlanders were paired with a Hessian musketeer regiment called the Von Bose to form Leslie's brigade, under the command of Major General Alexander Leslie. Leslie's brigade was deployed in a wooded area on the British right; the 71st was on the south side of the main road to Guilford Courthouse and the Von Bose was farther to the right. On the north side of the road, the British left was held by Webster's brigade, under the command of Lieutenant Colonel James Webster, a son of a prominent Edinburgh minister. The 23rd and the 33rd regiments made up Webster's brigade. The 23rd Regiment, known as the Royal Welch Fusiliers, was across the road from the 71st, and the 33rd Regiment was on the British left flank farther from the road.

By noon the armies were exchanging artillery fire. In the early afternoon, Cornwallis deployed the British for battle. A nineteenth-century North Carolina historian rendered a romantic description of the scene:

> When they began to advance through the open fields at the distance of half a mile, they made a very gorgeous and imposing appearance. It was about noon and the sun was shining in its meridian splendor. The air was a little keen, but not piercing. Their scarlet uniforms, burnished armor, and gay banners floating in the breeze contrasted strongly with the somber and deathlike appearance of nature, as they advanced with firm and measured step to the work of human slaughter. (Caruthers 111)

The British soldiers beside the road moved out of the woods into a clearing, while the soldiers farther to the left and right remained in wooded terrain. Babits and Howard describe the scene:

> When the 23rd and the 71st reached the clearing, the sight before them must have been quite stunning. Four hundred yards away, across a recently plowed field, "wet and muddy from the rains which had recently fallen," were several hundred militiamen with "their arms presented and resting on a rail fence." The regiments would have to cross two fence lines before reaching the Americans, the first located on the western skirt of the clearing, and then a second fence roughly 200 yards from the American line north of the road, and 150 to 175 yards south of the road. The 33rd Foot and Von Bose likely saw very little to their respective

fronts other than thick woods... Despite the obvious psychological, physical, and geographical difficulties before them, the veteran British and Hessian soldiers wasted no time advancing toward the North Carolina militia with "steadiness and composure." The attack on the American first line had begun. (96, 99)

As the British attackers approached, American riflemen in flanking parties picked their targets, particularly British officers. Lieutenant Archibald McPherson of the 71st was leading his men with his sword drawn when he was killed by rifle fire. When the British reached the "killing range" of a musket, American militiamen in the front line fired a volley. The 71st lost as many as thirty men in the assault, reducing the regiment to fewer than two hundred men.

The British returned fire as they continued to advance – the American who had killed Archibald McPherson was wounded in the thigh and abdomen. Threatened by the onrushing British line of bayonets, most of the American militiamen ran for their lives. As the British overran the American position, they bayoneted the man who had killed McPherson.

As the British pursued retreating Americans, a gap opened between the 71st and 23rd regiments; Cornwallis sent reserves to fill the gap. The battle broke up into various encounters spread across a long front through woods and across ravines. Cornwallis himself led a charge on the north side of the road; his horse was shot from under him, and soon afterwards the replacement horse also was shot from under him.

The Highlanders continued to advance on the south side of the road; the British artillery moved forward on the road beside the Highlanders, followed by cavalry. Babits and Howard describe the situation when the Highlanders reached the second line of American defenders:

Fighting along the road became intense, Col. Otho Holland Williams recalled: "The Virginia Brigades of militia commanded by Generals Stevens and Lawson gave the enemy so warm a reception, and continued their opposition with such firmness ... during which time the roar of musquetry and cracking of rifles were almost perpetual and as heavy as any I ever heard." Coming from a veteran of several of the war's most ferocious engagements, Williams's comment about the noise is testimony to the volume of fire along the second line.

Near the center of the line, an equally vicious battle erupted between Nathaniel Cocke's and George Moffett's regiments and the 71st Foot. Thomas Anderson of Cocke's regiment stated that he fired his gun until the barrel became "so hot that he could scarcely hold it." ... Anderson's statement corroborates fellow militiaman Isaac Grant's claim that he "fired his musket six or seven times." Several American officers were shot down... Cocke himself had his horse killed and he nearly died when a British musket ball knocked his hat from his head. The fire was too much for Maj. John Williams, as Samuel Houston noted: "Our brigade major, Mr. Williams, fled." (125)

... Exactly what took place near the road is impossible to know; however, the very fact that ... Cornwallis, O'Hara, and Stevens were present indicate something dire happened there. The latter two being wounded and the former having two horses killed underneath him indicates that a ferocious fight took place. (126)

Research by Babits and Howard gives details of the wounds inflicted by the Highlanders on American enlisted men. A musket ball lodged in a man's right shoulder. Another man was captured after a ball bored all the way through his body. Another got his first wound when he was shot in the thigh and got a second wound when a Highland officer sliced him across the face with a broadsword. A sergeant was wounded in both thighs. Two men survived being shot in the neck. Another survived after a ball went in his head and came out in front of his nose. The researchers estimate that the 71st suffered several casualties in the fighting on the second line (125-26).

The Virginia regiments held their ground until one of their commanders, Brigadier General Edward Stevens, was wounded and gave the order to retreat. Hard fighting continued to the south of the Highlanders' position, and the British formations continued to be stretched farther southward. "The end result of the second line fighting," write Babits and Howard, "was that tired, numerically weakened British battalions with diminished ammunition supplies, and most important, fighting as individual units, came upon fresh Continental infantry. The result had the potential for a British disaster" (128).

The 33rd Regiment was the first British unit to attack the American third line. Continental infantry and artillery drove the 33rd back to a strong position on high ground. The 2nd Battalion of Guards attacked next, routed their Continental opponents, and captured the American artillery. Other Continental units counterattacked. In hand-to-hand fighting, Continental Captain John Smith killed British Lieutenant Colonel James Stuart, the son of a Scottish lord. In an exchange of volleys, British Brigadier General Charles O'Hara was shot in the chest, the second wound he suffered during the battle, and fell from his horse. Continental and state horsemen including Colonel William Washington's light dragoons supported the counterattack and took back the American artillery pieces. The 71st Highlanders were among the last British troops to reach the American third line, because they had to maneuver in heavily wooded, deep ravines while exchanging fire at close range with Americans taking cover behind trees.

Many published accounts claim that Cornwallis ordered Lieutenant John McLeod's Royal Artillery section to fire grapeshot into the middle of the battle, knowing that both American and British soldiers would be struck down; the Americans withdrew out of the path of the grapeshot, and the British officers re-formed their battalions. The legend was first published in Henry Lee's *Memoirs*:

> Stuart fell by the sword... his regiment driven back with slaughter, its remains being saved by the British artillery, which, to stop the ardent pursuit of Washington and Howard, opened upon friends as well as foes; for Cornwallis, seeing the vigorous advance of these two officers, determined to arrest their progress, though every ball leveled at them must pass through the flying guards... (280)
>
> ... Cornwallis, seeing the discomfiture of one battalion of the guards, repaired in person to direct the measures for the recovery of the lost ground... It was on this occasion he ordered his artillery to open through his flying guards, to stop Washington and Howard. Brigadier O'Hara remonstrated, by exclaiming that the fire would destroy them-

selves. "True," replied Cornwallis; "but this is a necessary evil which we must endure, to arrest impending destruction." (283)

Apparently Lee did not let the facts get in the way of a good story. Historical research debunks the tale:

> The image of a draconian Cornwallis ordering his guns to cut down his own elite Guards over the pleas of his courageous, wounded subordinate became legendary in the annals of Guilford Courthouse, despite the fact that neither Cornwallis nor O'Hara, nor for that matter any actual participant in the event, actually recorded its taking place...
>
> ... What most likely happened was that Cornwallis ordered his guns to fire on Washington's cavalry and break up the attack, which they did... In the process a number of the fleeing Guardsmen were possibly hit by grapeshot from their own guns. (Babits and Howard 162)

Cornwallis himself reported, "the enemy's cavalry was soon repulsed by a well-directed fire from two three-pounders just brought up by Lieutenant Macleod, and by the appearance of the grenadiers of the guards, and of the 71st regiment, which having been impeded by some deep ravines, were now coming out of the wood on the right of the guards, opposite to the courthouse" (Babits and Howard 161).

With the British pressing the American third line, General Greene decided it was more important to save his army than to win the battle. He ordered the Americans to withdraw from the field with one regiment of Continentals covering the withdrawal.

The 71st Highlanders and the 23rd Royal Welch Fusiliers emerged from the ravines and came out of the woods opposite the courthouse as the Americans were leaving. As at Cowpens, fatigue became a factor. The British, who had not eaten anything all day, had been fighting for nearly seven hours counting the skirmishes on the march toward Guilford Courthouse. Since their arrival at Guilford Courthouse, they had advanced uphill and had engaged in combat for more than two hours. Under these conditions, an army could collapse. "Instead," Babits and Howard point out, "Cornwallis's men persevered with the kind of courage and tenacity that did them great honor" (218). Cornwallis acknowledged in his reports that the Highlanders were exhausted:

> Such men of the fusiliers and 71st as had strength remaining were ordered to pursue the dispersed enemy. This they did in so persevering a manner, that they killed or wounded as many as they could overtake, until, being completely exhausted, they were obliged to halt, after which they returned as they could to rejoin the army at Guildford Court House. (Babits and Howard 167)

While the main battle was underway along the road to the courthouse, a battle within a battle was being fought on the southeastern flank. The battle within a battle began as the British encountered the American second line and continued to rage even after the main battle had ended on the American third line.

Early in the combat on the southeastern flank, Captain Augustus Maitland of the 1st Guards was wounded, had the wound dressed, and returned to the battle. Maitland's second in command, Ensign John Stuart, was wounded in the groin and abdomen.

The Hessian unit positioned to the south of the Highlanders engaged in close-quarter combat with riflemen commanded by Colonel William Campbell; the Hessians and Virginians exchanged gunfire that set the woods ablaze and burned wounded soldiers to death. Colonel Banastre Tarleton led his dragoons into the fray and was shot in the right hand. Chased by Tarleton's dragoons, the Americans fled for cover in dense woods.

Cornwallis claimed victory because he held the field at the end of the day, but victory came at a terrible cost. He had lost at least a fourth of his army. He reported casualties of ninety-three killed and 439 wounded, while Greene believed that seventy-eight British officers had been killed and 183 British officers had been wounded. Tarleton's wounds resulted in the amputation of his fore finger, his middle finger, and part of his right hand.

Three ensigns in the 71st Regiment were killed at Guilford Courthouse: Malcolm Grant, Archibald McPherson and Donald McPherson. Total casualties of the 71st were thirteen killed and fifty wounded (Babits and Howard 224). Ensign Dugald Stuart of the 71st later sent a letter to a relative in Guilford County to dispel an assumption that the regiment suffered most of its casualties while fighting Continental troops on the American third line. In fact, Stuart reported, half of the casualties were inflicted by Scots-Irish militiamen deployed on the American first line:

> In the advance we received a very deadly fire from the Irish line of the American army, composed of their marksmen, lying on the ground behind a rail fence. One-half of our Highlanders dropped on that spot. There ought to be a very large tumulus on that spot where our men were buried. (qtd. in Schenck 349-50; Babits and Howard 108)

American casualties at Guilford Courthouse were seventy-nine killed and 184 wounded. More than a thousand Americans were reported missing, but they were mostly militiamen who had simply gone home.

The British, still lacking the tents they had destroyed with their baggage, suffered through the night. A veteran of the battle reported:

> The night succeeding this day of blood was rainy, dark and cold; the dead unburied, the wounded unsheltered, the groans of the dying and the shrieks of the living shed a deeper shade over the gloom of nature. The victorious troops, without tents and without food, participated in sufferings which they could not believe.
>
> The ensuing morning was spent in performing the last offices to the dead and in providing comfort for the wounded. In executing these sad duties, the British general regarded with equal attention friends and foes... All his wounded incapable of moving (about seventy in number) he left to the humanity of General Greene. (Commager 1166)

Armies go their separate ways

Cornwallis had commanded more than 3,200 men in January, but his command had dwindled to about 1,400 by the end of March. He withdrew toward the coast of North Carolina, where he could count on British ships to bring badly needed supplies and reinforcements to his army. He planned his route through the Cross Creek country, where emigrants from the Highlands of Scotland maintained allegiance to the king. Tarleton's memoirs described the reception the Highlanders gave to the weary British army:

> Notwithstanding the cruel persecution the inhabitants of Cross creek had constantly endured for their partiality to the British, they yet retained a great zeal for the interest of the royal army. All the flour and spirits in the neighborhood were collected and conveyed to camp, and the wounded officers and soldiers were supplied with many conveniences highly agreeable and refreshing to men in their situation. After... some wagons were loaded with provisions, Earl Cornwallis resumed his march for Wilmington. (281)

The British army rested at Wilmington for nearly three weeks. Then Cornwallis marched his army into Virginia, reasoning that if the British conquered Virginia they would exert control over all the southern colonies. Cornwallis expected Greene to pursue him into Virginia.

Greene, reasoning that other departments of the Continental army could deal with Cornwallis in Virginia, returned to South Carolina. He knew that the British outposts in South Carolina had been left vulnerable when Cornwallis departed.

Partisans keep up pressure in South Carolina

While Greene and Cornwallis were maneuvering in North Carolina, bands of patriot partisans continued to operate in South Carolina. Thomas Sumter and Francis Marion led men who came and went as the fighting waxed and waned.

Sergeant McDonald rescues Colonel Horry

When Marion sent Lieutenant Colonel Peter Horry and Sergeant Allen McDonald out with a foraging party, the party encountered a larger patrol of the Queen's Rangers.

Horry was riding a beautiful horse that he had found in the swamp the day before. Gunfire spooked the horse and Horry was thrown. While he was trying to catch his horse, his men fled the scene because they were outnumbered.

Sergeant McDonald gave his own horse to Horry. McDonald ran into the swamp as Horry rode away.

Officers support Lachlan McIntosh

General Lachlan McIntosh remained a prisoner of war at Haddrell's Point near Charleston through the first half of 1781. He continued to try to restore his reputation from political attacks that led Congress to suspend him from command early in 1780. Having already procured a declaration of support from the officers of the Georgia line, he next turned to officers who not only had served under him in the Western Department and had later served in Georgia but also had become fellow prisoners of war with him after the surrender of Charleston. They declared:

> The Officers of the Battalion late Colonel Parkers with Such of Blands as are present, do declare, that they Served the most of the Campaign of 79 under the command of Brigadier General McIntosh; that they neither publickly, privately, Generally or individually, ever Manifested or express'd to the executive Council of Georgia or any other publick body's or Individuals, the most distant dislike to General McIntosh as a gentleman or disapprobation to his Comand as an Officer, but had every reason to be highly Satisfied with both.
>
> That they had during their Service in Georgia been Acquainted with its most respectable Citizens, who together with the people in General made frequent & publick avowals of their Good opinion of the General; and appeared by their alertness to take the field when-ever the General directed, to place in him the Greatest Confidence as an Officer.
>
> In justice to themselves they are obliged to declare, that so much of the letters addressed to Congress from Mr. Walton, Govr. & Mr. Glascock Speaker, of Georgia as mentions or comprehends the Continental Troops "Generally having a Settled aversion to General McIntosh" are with respect to themselves utterly false & are convinced were dictated from principles that have produced the Highest Injustice to the General
>
> The Officers Subscribed are with Great Esteem & regard the Generals
>
> Mo. Obt. Hble. Servants (Hawes, *University* 42, 45)

British major named McIntosh opposes Sumter

In February, General Thomas Sumter laid siege to Fort Granby on the Congaree, but called off the siege when British reinforcements arrived.

Sumter went downstream and stormed an outpost called Belleville, but was forced back by fierce defenders. He left a detachment to watch Belleville, and led most of his band to the Santee. A British major named Alexander McIntosh marched out of Camden and chased the patriot detachment away from Belleville.

Sumter next launched an unsuccessful assault against Fort Watson and suffered serious casualties.

Sumter then withdrew to the safety of the High Hills, carrying his ailing wife and young son with him.

On March 6 Sumter's band ran into the Loyal South Carolina Regiment, commanded by Major Thomas Fraser; fierce fighting left ten of Sumter's men dead and forty wounded before Sumter retreated.

Combat at Wiboo Swamp: March 6, 1781

With Sumter subdued, the British turned their attention to Francis Marion. Lord Rawdon, in command of British forces since Cornwallis had departed, sent Lieutenant Colonel John Watson and Colonel Welbore Doyle to trap Marion between their forces. On March 6, Marion laid an ambush for Watson on a causeway through Wiboo Swamp, but Watson anticipated Marion's tactic and ordered a loyalist cavalry troop to dash down the causeway. Peter Horry led his mounted troops out to meet them. Tarleton Brown, a young soldier who was serving under Marion at the time, wrote in his memoirs what happened next:

> Col. Horry stammered badly, and on this occasion he leaned forward, spurred his horse, waved his sword, and ran fifty or sixty yards, endeavoring to utter the word *charge*, and finding he could not, bawled out, *"Damn it, boys, you, you know what I mean, go on!"* (19)

Historian Hugh Rankin describes the battle:

> The two groups clashed, fought briefly in a rattle of sabers, and then fell back to their own lines. As Marion deployed

the remainder of his troops across the road Horry was once again ordered to charge. Watson's musketry and fire from his two artillery pieces sent them reeling backward. Taking advantage of the situation, Watson ordered forward Major Samuel Harrison and his loyalist dragoons.

As they sped across the causeway, one man stood in their path. Gavin James of Horry's light horse regiment, a giant of a man both in size and courage, sat on his great gray horse. He fired his musket; a Tory horseman spun from his saddle. The enemy fired a volley; James was unhurt. A trooper darted forward, swinging his saber and was spitted on James's bayonet. The third who came charging up saw this same bayonet redden with his own blood. As he fell he grasped James's musket, and as the husky man retreated the last fifty yards to his own lines, he dragged the dying trooper behind him, still tightly clinging to the weapon.

As Harrison's horsemen made their way across the causeway, Marion sent out the remainder of his cavalry under the commands of Captains Conyers and McCauley. They sent the Tories scampering back to their own lines. In a personal duel on horseback, Conyers mortally wounded Major Harrison.

Watson now ordered his infantry forward. They trotted across the causeway, bayonets at the ready. Feeling that his men, few of whom had bayonets, could not stand up to regulars, Marion ordered a retreat. (166)

McDonald's treetop marksmanship

Over the next several days, Watson followed Marion and there were several skirmishes. While Watson was camped on John Witherspoon's plantation, Sergeant Allen McDonald climbed up a tree and fired down into the camp. Historian Hugh Rankin relates this version of the tale:

> Redheaded Sergeant McDonald climbed high in the branches of one of the huge oaks bordering the lane leading to the Witherspoon house. There, from his lofty perch, and at a distance estimated to have been three hundred yards, he

put a rifle ball through the knee of Lieutenant George Torriano of the Sixty-Fourth Regiment. (170)

A young member of Marion's brigade, William Dobein James,
mentioned the incident in his memoirs: "To increase the panic of
the British, Serjt. M'Donald, with a rifle, shot Lieut. Torriano
through the knee, at a distance of three hundred yards" (James
103).

Colonel Peter Horry also recorded the event, and Parson
Weems fashioned Horry's recollection into this version of the tale:

> ...Macdonald, as usual, was employing himself in a close
> and bold reconnoiter of the enemy's camp. Having found
> out the situation of their sentries, and the times of relieving
> them, he climbed up into a bushy tree, and thence, with a
> musket loaded with pistol bullets, cracked away at their
> guard as they passed by; of whom he killed one man and
> badly wounded the lieutenant, whose name was Torquano;
> then sliding down the tree, he mounted his swift-footed
> Selim, and made his escape.
>
> ...[Torquano] was a young Englishman, who had been
> quartered in Charleston, at the house of that good whig la-
> dy, Mrs. Brainford and her daughters, whom he had treated
> very politely, and often protected from insults.
>
> ... On repassing Black river in haste, Macdonald left
> his clothes behind him at a poor woman's house, where the
> enemy seized them... [Macdonald] sent word to colonel
> Watson, that if he did not immediately send back his
> clothes, he would kill eight of his men to pay for them.
>
> Several of Watson's officers who were present when
> the message was delivered, advised him by all means to re-
> turn his clothes, for that they knew him to be a most des-
> perate fellow, one who would stop at nothing he set his
> head upon; witness his late daring act of climbing like a
> cougar, into a tree, to kill his passing enemies. Watson sent
> him back his wallet of clothes. (Horry and Weems 167-68).

Action at Sampit Bridge

On March 28, Marion attacked Watson's force as it crossed
the Sampit River near Georgetown. During the fighting, Watson's

horse was shot from under him. When Watson ordered his gunners to fire grapeshot, Marion's men broke off the fight. Watson's casualties were about twenty killed and enough wounded to fill two wagons.

Moods possess Marion

While Watson pressed Marion from one direction, Doyle came from the other direction. With Marion away from his base camp at Snow Island, Doyle's force overwhelmed the camp's small guard, burned the buildings and destroyed the supplies.

In this desperate situation, Marion's moodiness manifested itself. His men were equally dejected. He bolstered their spirits with a speech declaring the reasons they fought, although the speech was tinged with thoughts of death. He said, "I would die a thousand deaths, most gladly would I die them all, rather than see my dear country in such a state of degradation and wretchedness" (Rankin 178).

Marion stirred into action and led his band toward Doyle's force.

During a hazardous crossing of Lynche's Creek, the current pushed horses and men downstream and carried away weapons and equipment. The crossing is described in the memoirs of Colonel Peter Horry, as rewritten by Parson Weems:

> ...as we were borne along down the stream in the dark, my horse and I were carried under the limb of a tree hung thick with wild vines, which soon caught me by the head like Absalom, and there held me fast, dangling in the furious flood, while my horse was swept from under me. I hallooed ... without getting any answer... ...as I was near giving out, a bold young fellow of the company overheard me bawling, and having the advantage of a stout horse, dashed in and took me safely off.
>
> I was afraid at first that my horse was drowned – but sagaciously following the rest of the horses, he made his way good, but lost my saddle, great coat, and clothes. But what grieved me most of all was the loss of my holsters, with a pair of elegant silver mounted pistols, a present from Macdonald, and which he had taken from a British officer whom he killed near Georgetown. (176-77)

Marion's brigade was spared the hazards of battle when Doyle was ordered to Camden. The British needed a strong force to defend Camden against Nathanael Greene's oncoming army.

Although Doyle was out of the way, Watson remained a threat to Marion. Watson waited in Georgetown with nearly a thousand men. Only five hundred men were in Marion's brigade, and they had only two rounds of ammunition apiece.

Thoughts of death again preoccupied Marion. Military historian Hugh Rankin writes:

> Another of his dark moods began to cloud his mind. He entertained the idea of throwing over the business in the low country and taking to the hills from where, from time to time, he could sally down and harass the enemy until either the British had left the country or he was killed. (182)

Siege of Fort Watson: April, 1781

Marion's mood improved when he learned that Greene had sent Continental reinforcements. Henry Lee's legion was on the way. Boats that Marion had hidden along the Peedee were used to ferry the legion to Marion's side of the river. Lee's legion joined with Marion's brigade on April 14.

Lee and Marion decided to attack a British fort on the Santee. Watson had built the fort a few months previously and had named it for himself. Fort Watson, situated atop an ancient Indian mound overlooking Scott's Lake, held such a strong position that an attack by Sumter in February had failed.

Because Lee and Marion did not have artillery, they needed a new strategy to take the fort. A member of Marion's brigade, Hezekiah Maham, suggested building a tower tall enough to allow riflemen to fire down into the fort.

The patriots built the tower at night, and at dawn the riflemen opened fire while foot soldiers rushed the fort. The garrison surrendered on April 23.

"Maham's Tower" proved to be so successful that it was used in subsequent campaigns. Marion expressed his gratitude not only to Lee and Maham but also to Allen McDonald, who had recently been promoted from sergeant to lieutenant.

John McIntosh returns to service

John McIntosh, whose life had been spared by Aeneas Mackintosh at Brier Creek in 1779, had been held as a prisoner of war for more than a year.

He was exchanged for a British officer, John Harris Cruger, in the fall of 1780. Although he was a Continental officer, he volunteered to serve with the Georgia militia through the campaign of 1781. For a time he was an aide to General Thomas Sumter, whom he would have known from the time when Sumter's regiment of horse was stationed on the Altamaha River in Georgia in 1777 (R.J. Massey 243; Boatner 692; Hawes, "James Jackson" 19; Searcy 88-89).

Legendary deeds were ascribed to the dashing young officer:

> ...McIntosh, when a Lieutenant Colonel in the army of the Revolution, during the war became acquainted with Miss Sarah Swinton, of South Carolina, of Scottish descent, and whose father, a patriot of those times, was killed in battle by the British at Stono. Her form was light and delicate. Possessed of a well-cultivated and discriminating mind, with a rare faculty for conversation and argument, and although of retiring manners, she espoused with an almost imprudent zeal the cause of freedom, in a part of the country infested by Tories, and marauding bands of British troops. To this lady he was engaged to be married; and in one of his excursions to the neighbourhood in which she resided, he was informed that Captain Elholm, a Polander in the American service (Lee's Legion), had acted oppressively towards some of the inhabitants, and on remonstrating with him on the injustice and impolicy of his conduct, a quarrel quickly ensued, and which, it was promptly determined, should be settled by the arbitrament of the sword.
>
> ... Both were young, resolute, active, and powerful men, and it was thought that one or both would certainly be killed in the contest; and as the parties were moving to the place of combat, Miss Swinton requested to see for an instant her intended consort... He called on her, and was met with serious distress, and after a little conversation, she observed, "If you are, then, inviolably pledged to meet this man, and feel that your honour is dearer than life, what

shall I do?" ...[She soon] fled to her room, to conceal there her agitation and the anguish of a devoted heart.

The hostile parties met under a large oak... At the word "Ready," they drew, and, advancing with sharp and glittering swords, commenced the battle in good earnest, with firm hearts and sturdy arms. In a little time the right arm of Captain Elholm was nearly severed from his body, and fell powerless by his side. ...His sword was dexterously transferred to his left hand, which he used with great effect; and the blows came so awkwardly, that they were not easily parried by his right-handed antagonist. Both were in a few moments disabled in such a manner, that the friends present felt it proper to interfere, and end the bloody conflict.

They carried to their graves the scars, and deeply furrowed cheeks, as evidences of a once terrible struggle. Miss Swinton was not long in suspense; the combatants were soon taken from the field, disfigured by many deep and dangerous sabre wounds, of which, in due time, they both recovered; and the Colonel often remarked that he was more indebted to the tender attentions of Miss S. for his restoration to health than to the management or skill of his surgeon...

A little time after this occurrence, Colonel McIntosh brought his young and patriotic wife to Georgia, his native State... (White 547-48)

Lachlan McIntosh's family assisted in Virginia

Lachlan McIntosh's wife and younger children roamed the South seeking refuge while he was a prisoner of war near Charleston. They were "drove," he said, "from place to place before the enemy many hundred miles, without any means to convey them... and obliged to exist on the bounty of such as might wish to assist."

In 1781 they were stranded at Hillsboro, North Carolina, "in very great distress." Lachlan's fellow prisoners included officers from Virginia who petitioned Virginia Governor Thomas Jefferson to assist the McIntosh family. The officers reminded Jefferson that McIntosh had commanded the Western Department that included "the western part of our state" and that "the good effects" of his command "are still felt and acknowledged by our back inhabitants." As a result of the officers' petition, the Virginia Assembly appropriated funds to assist the McIntosh family. "The seasonable releif which my distressed famely has lately received… will contribute to clothe and support us for some time," Sarah McIntosh wrote Jefferson on April 23, 1781. She assured him that she would "consult all possible Oeconomy in its expenditure" (Lawrence, "Suspension" 132-33).

Battle of Hobkirk Hill: April 25, 1781

General Nathanael Greene led the Southern department of the Continental army from North Carolina back into South Carolina in April, and took up a position on Hobkirk Hill, north of Camden. With Lord Cornwallis on the move from North Carolina into Virginia, Lord Rawdon led the British and loyalist troops at Camden out to attack the Greene's army. A biographer of Greene describes intense action in the midst of the battle:

> …The Fifth Virginia was ordered to cover a general withdrawal, and [a] company of Marylanders tried desperately to protect the three American cannon. Rawdon's dragoons overran them, sabering the gunners down…
>
> For the moment Greene was dismayed by the rout of his veteran Continentals, but he was determined to save not only his army but also his precious cannon. Utterly disregarding the pleas of his officers, he galloped into the heaviest musket fire, rallied what men he could, and… personally led them into the melee of fleeing Americans and attacking British cavalry around the three vitally needed guns. When his men hesitated, Greene jumped from his horse and, with the bridle rein in one hand, seized a cannon's rope and helped to drag the heavy gun out of danger. Greene's voice and his example revived the courage of his gunners. The general shouted for camp guards to help pull the guns farther away from the British dragoons and Rawdon's onrushing, bayonet-thrusting infantrymen.
>
> Colonel Washington's cavalry appeared just in time to dispute the field with the British dragoons… (Bailey 157-58)

The battle reached a stalemate when the Americans formed a new line near the crest of Hobkirk Hill. Lord Rawdon returned to

Camden and Greene withdrew so that his men could recuperate. American casualties were 19 killed and 136 missing; British casualties were 38 killed and 220 wounded and missing (Dupuy and Dupuy 411).

> "We fight, get beat, rise, and fight again." Thus Greene, writing of his campaign to date, summed up his efforts in what might have been the official record of the whole war. Time after time, the Americans seemingly had been beaten. Only, much to the disgust of the British generals, they didn't seem to think so. (Bailey 159)

Patriots control Camden and Orangeburg

British and loyalist troops abandoned Camden on May 10, leaving several burning buildings and carrying off hundreds of slaves.

The next day, patriots led by Thomas Sumter captured the British garrison at Orangeburg.

McDonald dies in battle at Fort Motte

While Nathanael Greene put pressure on the main British army at Camden, Francis Marion and Henry Lee continued their assault on British outposts strung between Camden and Charleston. Their next target after Fort Watson was a fortification overlooking the Congaree near the junction with the Wateree that forms the Santee. The fortification was built around the plantation home of Rebecca Motte and was called Fort Motte. Anticipating an attack, the British asked Mrs. Motte and her family to move out of the plantation house. The family moved into a nearby farmhouse that was part of the property.

When the American forces arrived on May 6 to besiege Fort Motte, Lee's Legion encamped on the northwest side around the farmhouse. Mrs. Motte not only invited Lee to use the house as his headquarters but also provided his officers with meals and "the best wines of Europe" (Robert E. Lee 347; Smith 24).

While the Continental officers enjoyed Mrs. Motte's hospitality, Marion and his militiamen camped on the southeast side of Fort Motte. In those circumstances, Marion decided to resign as a South Carolina militia commander and resume his service as a Continental officer. On the day he arrived at Fort Motte, Marion wrote

Greene a letter asking permission to seek a Continental Army assignment in Philadelphia.

The Americans set up positions surrounding Fort Motte and riflemen opened fire on the garrison from a distance of about two hundred yards. Allen McDonald of Marion's Brigade, renowned as an expert marksman and daring fighter, must have been among those riflemen. William Dobein James, a young soldier in Marion's brigade who chronicled the adventures of Allen McDonald in his memoirs, reported McDonald's death at Fort Motte:

> At the commencement of this siege, Serjt. M'Don-ald, now advanced to a lieutenancy, was killed. He was a native of Cross Creek, in North-Carolina, and his father and other relations had espoused the opposite side of the cause. Lieut. Cryer, who had often emulated M'Donald, shared a similar fate. (121)

An authority on the life of Francis Marion calls the battle of Fort Motte "costly for Marion. He lost one of his bravest men, Lieutenant Allen McDonald, who had been with Marion at least since the attack on Savannah in 1779" (Smith 26-27).

The soldiers set in for a siege, and slaves from local plantations began digging saps toward the fort. The Americans offered the garrison an opportunity to surrender, but the commander, Lieutenant McPherson, chose to keep fighting.

Three days after Marion had written for permission to go to Philadelphia, Greene wrote a reply. Greene tried to cheer up Marion by praising his "important services to the public with the Militia under your command," and offering to meet with him. "I shall be always happy to see you at head Quarters," Greene wrote, "but cannot think you can seriously mean to solicit leave to go to Philadelphia" (Smith 32). Marion wrote a response on May 11:

> I assure you I am very serious in my intention of relinquishing my Militia Command; not that I wish to Shrink from fatigue or trouble, or for any private Interest but because I found Little is to be done with such men as I have, who Leave me very Often at the very point of Executing a plan & their Late infamous behavior in Quiting me at a time which required their service must confirm me in my

former Intentions. If I cannot act in the militia I cannot see any service I can be, to remain in the state & I hope by going to the Northward to fall in some employ where I may have an Opertunity of serving the United States, in some way that I cannot be in this Country. (Smith 32-33)

During the time that Fort Motte was under siege, Lord Rawdon's British forces pulled out of Camden and marched toward Charleston on a route that would pass near Fort Motte. Marion and Lee realized that they had to take Fort Motte before Rawdon reached the vicinity. They decided to force the garrison to abandon the fortified house by setting it afire. When they informed Mrs. Motte that they planned to burn her house, according to Lee, she declared "that she was gratified with the opportunity of contributing to the good of her country, and that she should view the approaching scene with delight" (Robert E. Lee 347; Smith 24)

Most versions of the tale, including a report by Lieutenant McPherson, say that fire arrows were shot from a bow onto the roof of the house. Some versions say that Mrs. Motte herself provided a bow and some arrows that were among her family keepsakes, and that she ordered one of her slaves to shoot the flaming arrows onto the roof of her house.

Another version says that Mrs. Motte provided the arrows and a private in Marion's brigade launched the arrows from the barrel of a gun, either a rifle or musket.

The memoirs of William Dobein James say that a private in Marion's brigade made up a ball of rosin and brimstone, set it afire, and slung it onto the roof of the house (120-21).

The flaming arrows (or fiery brimstone) landed on the roof at noon on May 12. When the roof was afire, the garrison surrendered. The soldiers from both sides worked together to extinguish the fire on the roof and save the house.

That evening, Mrs. Motte invited the British and American officers to a dinner party in a brush arbor in front of the farmhouse where she had been staying. Arrangements were made for the British officers to be paroled and for the British Army soldiers to be exchanged, and the next day they marched out to join Rawdon at Nelson's Ferry.

The spirit of brotherhood among the American and British regular army personnel did not extend to the local patriots and loyalists. Vengeful patriots hanged a loyalist prisoner on Mrs. Motte's gate. Then the patriots hanged another loyalist. The next morning they hanged another. A fourth loyalist had the noose around his neck when Marion rode up, went into a rage, wielded his sword, cursed the lynch mob, and rescued the loyalist.

Cornwallis invades Virginia

Lord Cornwallis based his decision to invade Virginia on rigorous strategic reasoning. Not only was Virginia the home of staunch revolutionaries such as Thomas Jefferson and George Washington, it also was an indispensable source of soldiers and supplies for the patriot forces in South Carolina. Cornwallis could count on the support of British troops operating out of Norfolk, and his battered army could receive supplies and reinforcements by sea through the ports of coastal Virginia.

Cornwallis led his army, including the 71st Regiment in which Captain Aeneas Mackintosh served, on a 225-mile march across North Carolina in twenty-five days. Cornwallis reached Petersburg on May 20, 1781, and assumed command of British forces in Virginia.

Greene gives assignments to Marion and Lee

In South Carolina, Continental General Nathanael Greene, traveling with a small escort, came to Fort Motte to meet Francis Marion in person for the first time. He must have soothed Marion's hurt feelings, because Marion did not pursue his earlier request to leave South Carolina.

Although Henry Lee's legion had been supporting Marion's operations, Greene felt the time had come to give Marion and Lee separate assignments. Marion followed behind the British troops under Lord Rawdon to make sure they continued on their way to Charleston without doubling back. Lee besieged Fort Granby – a British post built around a large house – on a hill near where the Saluda and Broad rivers flow together to form the Congaree. The loyalists garrisoning Fort Granby surrendered on May 15.

Marion followed Lord Rawdon to Moncks Corner, and then ventured off toward the British post at Georgetown, on the coast north of Charleston. Marion had attacked Georgetown in November of 1780 and again in January of 1781, and he was determined to keep trying until he succeeded. In late May, Marion began digging in for a siege. The garrison boarded boats in the night and sailed to Charleston.

Patriots retake Augusta

Meanwhile, patriots under Andrew Pickens – who had commanded the militia at Cowpens – and partisans from Georgia led by Colonel Elijah Clarke had been besieging Augusta on the Savannah River. Greene sent Lee's legion and other troops to assist the patriots. The garrison of 330 loyalists and three hundred Creek Indians fought fiercely under the leadership of Lieutenant Colonel Thomas Brown before finally surrendering on June 6.

Siege of Ninety-Six

General Greene himself, meanwhile, had begun siege operations against the last British post in the interior of South Carolina, the "star fort" at Ninety-Six. The garrison put up a stubborn defense, devising a counter-move for each of Greene's tactics. Lee's legion reinforced Greene on June 8, and then Andrew Pickens arrived. But by then Lord Rawdon was on the march out of Charleston to relieve the garrison. Greene tried to take the fort quickly by ordering a direct assault, which caused heavy casualties but failed to overrun the defenses. Greene broke off the siege on June 20 and withdrew toward Charlotte. Rawdon reached Ninety-Six the next day, destroyed the fortifications, and brought the garrison along with his army. The fierce midsummer heat killed fifty of Rawdon's men on the march back to Charleston.

During the heat wave, Greene's army rested at the High Hills of Santee, an area east of the junction of the Wateree and Congaree rivers that was known for its relatively healthful environment. Rawdon returned to England due to illness, and his successor, Lieutenant Colonel Alexander Stewart, stationed the British army on the Santee River near the location where Fort Watson had been.

71st refuses to go out under Tarleton's command

In Virginia, Lord Cornwallis sent 250 cavalry and mounted infantry under Lieutenant Colonel Banastre Tarleton to disrupt a meeting of the Virginia General Assembly at Charlottesville in early June. Virginia Governor Thomas Jefferson escaped from his home Monticello near Charlottesville five minutes before British soldiers arrived; the soldiers drank some of Jefferson's wine in a birthday toast to their king (Meacham 140).

The initial plan for the raid on Charlottesville provided for Tarleton's force to include the 71st Regiment. The Highlanders, however, had not forgiven Tarleton for leading their comrades to death or capture at Cowpens. An officer who served with Cornwallis reported that when the 71st received the order to accompany Tarleton to Charlottesville, "the officers drew up a remonstrance, and presented it to Lord Cornwallis, stating their unwillingness to serve under Tarleton, from a recollection of his conduct at the Cowpens, where the other battalion of the 71st was taken by Morgan. In consequence of this remonstrance, the 71st regiment was attached to colonel Simcoe" (Stedman, 387).

The Highlanders never relented in their resentment; Roderick Mackenzie, who had been wounded at Cowpens, later wrote a book ridiculing Tarleton's claims of military expertise. Mackenzie wrote:

> The first error of judgement to be imputed to Lieutenant Colonel Tarleton, on the morning of the 17th of January, 1781, is, the not halting his troops before he engaged the enemy. Had he done so, it was evident that the following advantages would have been the result of his conduct. General Morgan's force and situation might have been distinctly viewed, under cover of a very superior cavalry; the British infantry, fatigued with rapid marches, day and night, for some time past ... might have had rest and refreshment; a detachment from the several corps left with the baggage, together with batt-men, and officers' servants, would have had time to come up, and join in the action. The artillery all this time might have been playing on the enemy's front, or either flank, without risque of insult; the commandants of regiments, Majors M'Arthur and Newmarsh, officers who held commissions long before [Tarleton] was born, and who had reputations to this day unimpeached, might have been consulted, and ... time would have been given for the approach of Earl Cornwallis ...
>
> The second error was, the un-officer-like impetuosity of directing the line to advance before it was properly formed, and before the reserve had taken its ground; in

consequence of which, as might have been expected, the attack was premature, confused, and irregular.

The third error in this ruinous business was the omission of giving discretional powers to that judicious veteran M'Arthur, to advance with the reserve, at the time that the front line was in the pursuit of the militia, by which means the connection so necessary to troops engaged in the field was not preserved.

His fourth error was, ordering Captain Ogilvie, with a troop, consisting of no more than forty men, to charge, before any impression was made on the continentals, and before Washington's cavalry had been engaged.

The next, and the most destructive, for I will not pretend to follow him through all his errors, was in not bringing up a column of cavalry, and completing the rout, which, by his own acknowledgment, had commenced through the whole American infantry... (Mackenzie 107-10)

Because Tarleton had accused the 71st Regiment of "total misbehavior" at Cowpens, Mackenzie recounted the regiment's distinguished history:

The first battalion of the 71st regiment, who had landed in Georgia in the year 1778, under the command of Sir Archibald Campbell, had established their reputation in the several operations in that province, at Stono Ferry, at the sieges of Savannah and Charlestown, and at the battle of Camden. Now ... they were led by an officer of great experience, who had come into the British service from the Scotch Dutch brigade: Out of sixteen officers which they had in the field, nine were killed and wounded.

The battalion of light infantry had signalised themselves separately on many occasions. ...those of the seventy-first regiment were distinguished under Sir James Baird at the surprise of General Wayne in Pennsylvania, of Baylor's dragoons in New Jersey, at Briar Creek in Georgia, at the capture and subsequent defence of Savannah, and at the battle near Camden under Earl Cornwallis...

Such were the troops whom [Tarleton] has so severely stigmatised. Few corps, in any age or country, will be found to have bled more freely... I am not without my feelings as an individual for so wanton an attack on characters and entire corps, whose conduct had been, till then, unsullied. There is not an officer who survived that disastrous day, who is not far beyond the reach of slander and detraction; and with respect to the dead, I leave to Lieutenant Colonel Tarleton all the satisfaction which he can enjoy, from reflecting that he led a number of brave men to destruction, and then used every effort in his power to damn their fame with posterity (Mackenzie 111-12, 118).

Mackenzie blamed the loss of the war on Tarleton, reasoning that if Tarleton had not lost a division of the British army at Cowpens, then Cornwallis not only would have crushed the American army at Guilford Courthouse but also would have prevented the blockade at Yorktown (Mackenzie 88-89).

The Battle of Green Spring: July 4, 1781

Lord Cornwallis was at Williamsburg when he received orders from Sir Henry Clinton, the commander of British forces in America, to send units from the army in Virginia to reinforce British headquarters at New York. Cornwallis felt that he could not defend Williamsburg with his smaller army, and made plans to establish a post at Portsmouth, where his army could be supported by the British navy. The British army left Williamsburg on July 4 and camped near a plantation called Green Spring. The Marquis de Lafayette, commander of the American army in Virginia, attacked the British camp. The Americans advanced along a causeway through marshes toward the British position on high ground. The British used their advantageous position to inflict about three hundred casualties on the Americans while suffering only seventy-five casualties themselves. The next morning, Cornwallis crossed the James River and marched toward Portsmouth.

Heavy casualties at Quinby Bridge

In South Carolina, partisan leader Thomas Sumter got permission from General Nathanael Greene in July to combine forces with Francis Marion and Henry Lee for an attack on the British garrison at Moncks Corner. The garrison withdrew toward Charleston. Lee's cavalry caught up with the British at Quinby

Bridge on the morning of July 18. The British took position behind plantation buildings and fences. When Marion arrived, he and Lee agreed that the British defenses were too strong for an attack to be successful. Later in the afternoon, Sumter arrived and overruled them. The Americans attacked, suffered heavy casualties, and retreated. Marion and Lee wanted nothing further to do with Sumter; Marion took his men to an encampment on the Santee while Lee joined Greene at the High Hills.

Congress repeals suspension of Lachlan McIntosh

Brigadier General Lachlan McIntosh, who had been taken prisoner when the British captured Charleston in the spring of 1780, was paroled in the summer of 1781. A document dated July 18, 1781, at the American War Office in Philadelphia lists McIntosh among Continental officers who had been paroled and had gone from Charleston to Philadelphia under flags of truce (Hawes, *University* 45).

Still seething with resentment over being suspended from Continental command because of baseless accusations cooked up by his political enemies, he went before Congress and stated his case. "The soldier who stood up to misfortune so stoutly" Savannah historian Alexander Lawrence writes, "found a sympathetic audience in Congress. The censorious action taken seventeen months before was quickly rescinded. McIntosh was reinstated" ("Suspension" 132).

Ambush at Parkers Ferry

In August, Colonel William Harden's militia operations south of the Edisto River were threatened by large bands of loyalists supported by British dragoons under Major Thomas Fraser. Francis Marion moved south stealthily and reached Harden at the Round O without being detected by the British.

On August 29, Marion prepared an ambush along a causeway leading to the Edisto River at Parkers Ferry. Fraser's dragoons were caught in the ambush, and those who were not killed fled. The main body of British, Hessian and loyalist troops exchanged fire with Marion's men for three hours. With his men growing hungry and their ammunition running low, Marion withdrew through the river swamp.

Battle of Eutaw Springs: September 8, 1781

While Francis Marion was operating near the Edisto River, Nathanael Greene was marching toward the British position at Eutaw Springs. After the battle at Parkers Ferry, Marion moved north to Henry Laurens' plantation seventeen miles from Eutaw Springs. Greene arrived at Laurens' plantation on September 7 and blended Marion's band in with the Southern Department of the Continental army.

Because Lord Rawdon had returned to England due to illness, Lieutenant Colonel Alexander Stewart commanded British forces in South Carolina. The British and American armies clashed early in the morning of September 8 and fought hard for four hours.

Colonel William Washington was wounded while leading a cavalry charge and was taken prisoner. Colonel Richard Campbell – who had served with Lachlan McIntosh in the Western Department – bravely led the Continentals in a charge and was killed in battle (Williams 284).

By the time Greene withdrew from the battleground, the Americans had suffered casualties of 139 killed and 375 wounded. Eighty-five British soldiers were killed, 351 were wounded and 430 were missing (Dupuy and Dupuy 420).

British confined to Charleston

Nathanael Greene took his army back to the High Hills, while Francis Marion and Henry Lee pursued the British forces withdrawing from Eutaw Springs toward Charleston. As autumn set in, Greene came down from the High Hills and blockaded Charleston, the only place in South Carolina still occupied by the British. Greene kept the British in check by establishing winter quarters about forty miles from Charleston at a place called the Round O.

Yorktown: September 28-October 17, 1781

In Virginia, British units bound for New York boarded ship at Portsmouth, but did not depart because a new order from British commander in chief Henry Clinton told them to stay with Lord Cornwallis – the troops under Cornwallis had fought their way across South Carolina and North Carolina before invading Virginia. Clinton instructed Cornwallis to establish a post that could protect British naval vessels anchored at Hampton Roads in Chesapeake Bay. Cornwallis chose to fortify Yorktown and Gloucester on opposite banks of the York River.

Unfortunately for Cornwallis, the fleet that entered Chesapeake Bay on August 20 was not British. It was French. When the British fleet arrived outside the entrance to the bay on September 5, the French sailed out to do battle. The naval action inflicted 346 British casualties and two hundred French casualties. The French fleet sailed back into Chesapeake Bay. The British fleet sailed for New York on September 9. Cornwallis was isolated in Yorktown, with the French fleet preventing relief from the sea and the Marquis de Lafayette's Continental troops cutting off escape routes over land.

Meanwhile, General George Washington led an allied army on a march from near New York to Virginia. By September 24, Washington commanded a force of 7,800 French troops, 8,845 Continental soldiers, and 3,200 Virginia militiamen gathered at Williamsburg, in addition to the French naval personnel in the fleet blockading the bay. The American and French allies commenced a siege of Yorktown on September 28. The superintendent of materials in the trenches was Colonel Samuel Elbert – who together with Colonel John McIntosh had fought valiantly at the Battle of Brier Creek in Georgia.

Also among the Americans at Yorktown was Lieutenant Colonel John Laurens – the son of Lachlan McIntosh's friend Henry Laurens. Colonel Laurens, along with McIntosh, had been on the losing side of the siege of Charleston and had been captured with the garrison; after Laurens was exchanged, he rejoined George Washington's command. At Yorktown, Laurens served as Washington's aide-de-camp and commanded the 3rd Battalion of the 2nd Brigade, which mustered two hundred men.

Major General Benjamin Lincoln – who had commanded the Southern Department of the Continental Army during the siege of Charleston – commanded a division at Yorktown (Lumpkin 308; Hilborn 212).

Lachlan McIntosh stays in barracks

Lachlan McIntosh was living in an army barracks in Philadelphia during the fall of 1781 while Yorktown was under siege. Lachlan's strength in the face of adversity impressed Aedanus Burke, who in October of 1781 wrote Lachlan a letter saying:

"When I see a man surrounded with what the world calls more than difficulties: Exile from country, splendid fortune, from family, with wants of almost every kind into the bargain, when such a man bears all this not only with constancy, but laughs at it with gaiety, you must not blame me if I envy him, when I see myself and see most of the World besides me incapable of it." (Lawrence, "Suspension" 131-32).

The 71st Regiment endures siege

In Virginia, Lord Cornwallis commanded about seven thousand British troops in Yorktown, and a smaller British post across the river at Gloucester. The 71st Regiment of Foot, commanded by Lieutenant Colonel Duncan MacPherson, was among the British forces in Yorktown (Lumpkin 311). Aeneas Mackintosh – a captain in the 2nd Battalion of the 71st Regiment – had endured the siege of Savannah from the inside and the siege of Charleston from the outside. Once again he was subjected to incessant cannonading, nerve-wracking periods of enforced inactivity, and scarcity of provisions.

During the siege, a remarkable reunion occurred. It involved a boy who had served as a drummer in the 71st Regiment until he was captured at Cowpens. He subsequently joined the American army. When his unit was positioned outside Yorktown, he escaped and made his way to the British lines. As fate would have it, the 71st Regiment was maneuvering on the front lines at the time, and the boy found refuge in the piquet commanded by his father (Babits 144).

The 71st Regiment lost three officers at Yorktown: Lieutenant Angus Cameron, Lieutenant Thomas Fraser, and Ensign John Grant. (Mackenzie 102, Babits and Howard 188). Other casualties in the 71st at Yorktown were nine soldiers killed, nineteen soldiers wounded, and three drummers wounded (MacLean 35).

Siege warfare intensifies

At Yorktown, the British had run out of feed for their horses by the beginning of October and were forced to kill the animals or turn them loose in the no-man's land between the besiegers and the besieged. Facing the same shortages across the river at Gloucester, the garrison commanded by Lieutenant Colonel Banastre Tarleton killed more than a thousand horses, a decision that destroyed the capacity of the British to conduct cavalry maneuvers.

An observer reported that the sky blazed the entire night of October 11 while French and British artillery exchanged continuous cannonades.

On the night of October 15, Colonel John Laurens led a detachment that helped capture a British redoubt.

A British sally before dawn on October 16 caused seventeen casualties among French and American troops, but failed to stop the allied advance. Later that morning, the allies came within rifle range of the British lines, and marksmen exchanged fire throughout the day. The allies placed howitzers on captured redoubts and inflicted close-range shelling on the British garrison.

Cornwallis decided to evacuate the garrison by boat across the river to Gloucester, starting late in the night of October 16. While the evacuation was underway, a storm arose and stopped further attempts to cross the river. When the weather improved, the troops that had landed in Gloucester were recalled to Yorktown.

The besiegers opened fire at daylight October 17 with more than a hundred pieces of artillery. The British responded feebly because most of their artillery had been damaged and they had exhausted their supply of shot and shell. Cornwallis realized that he had to surrender. During the morning of October 17 he sent a message to Washington asking for a cease fire while terms were negotiated (Lumpkin 234-45).

British army surrenders

Two British officers negotiated the terms of surrender with a French officer and Continental Colonel John Laurens. British naval personnel would become prisoners of the French, while British soldiers would become prisoners of the Americans. British officers would keep their side arms, and individuals would keep their private effects.

The British army surrendered on October 19. The soldiers march out of Yorktown as their musicians played "The world turned upside down." Led by Brigadier General Charles O'Hara, they proceeded along a road lined with French soldiers on the west and Continental soldiers and patriot militiamen on the east. Approaching Continental Commander in Chief George Washington, O'Hara said that he represented Lord Cornwallis, who was too ill to attend. Washington, aware of rank and status, asked O'Hara to deal with General Benjamin Lincoln. As a result, the general who had surrendered an American army at Charleston was the general who accepted the surrender of a British army at Yorktown.

The British continued marching into a field surrounded by French hussars on horseback. Many of the humiliated British soldiers cursed, and a few cried, as they laid down their weapons. Captain Aeneas Mackintosh and the men of his company in the 71st Regiment would be prisoners of war for two years (Lumpkin 234-45; Mackintosh 65).

1782-1791

Aeneas Mackintosh sails home to Scotland after nearly two years as a prisoner of war. "Colonel Anne" Mackintosh dies. Lackie McIntosh dies on his way home to Georgia. Rory McIntosh dies on his way home to Scotland. Flory McDonald dies and is given a heroine's burial. Lachlan McIntosh is regarded as an elder statesman in Georgia; during President George Washington's Southern Tour, Lachlan McIntosh shows Washington around Savannah.

Fighting continues in the South

The capture of Lord Cornwallis's army at Yorktown crippled the ability of the British to wage war, but the war was not over. The British still had two armies in America, and occupied New York, Wilmington, Charleston and Savannah (Ward, 837).

At the beginning of 1782, more than three thousand British soldiers and a large force of loyalists held the city of Charleston, while American forces controlled the territory around the city. The Southern Department of the Continental Army, commanded by General Nathanael Greene, was camped about forty miles from Charleston at the Round O, a pleasant locality where the patriots filled their cooking pots with rice, game, waterfowl and fish.

Two thousand Continental troops who had participated in the victory at Yorktown marched from Virginia to South Carolina as reinforcements for Greene's army. When they set out, their provisions included a herd of four hundred cattle. The men and cattle trudged along ruined roads in rainy, frigid midwinter weather. They forded streams and waded through swamps where mud rose to their knees. As the Continentals passed through North Carolina, the British feared an attack on Wilmington and, therefore, evacuated the garrison to Charleston. The Continentals reached the Round O on January 4, 1782.

Some of the Continentals, commanded by General Anthony Wayne continued marching southward to Georgia, and crossed the Savannah River on January 12. South Carolina militiamen and Georgia volunteers joined forces with Wayne. The patriot force subdued loyalist bands in the Georgia backcountry and stopped reinforcements from reaching Savannah.

Meanwhile, Lee's legion and Marion's brigade patrolled near Charleston, trying to keep British foraging parties from scouring the countryside to provide food for the Charleston garrison. Colonel Henry Lee proposed attacking Johns Island, where the British kept cattle to provide beef for the garrison in Charleston. General Greene assigned Colonel John Laurens and some of the newly arrived reinforcements to assist Lee's legion in the attack. Some of the attackers got lost in the dark of night, and the attack was called off when a rising tide prevented the troops from fording the streams around the island.

Wounded soldiers restored by Healing Springs

As partisan fighting raged on in the backcountry of South Carolina, nearly two hundred loyalists slaughtered sixteen patriots. In the days before the attack, "Bloody Bill" Cunningham led 150 loyalists on an expedition toward Ninety-Six. Other loyalists commanded by Colonel Hezekiah Williams joined Cunningham's troops along the way. The combined force traveled along an Indian trail near the South Edisto River. Meanwhile, a small band of patriots led by Captain Benjamin Odom made camp north of the junction of Windy Hill Creek and Sheepford Branch. The loyalists attacked the encampment before daybreak and killed all the patriots.

An Indian girl ran from the scene and told of the bloody deed. Relatives of the patriots came and buried the bodies on the third day after the massacre. The battleground became known as Slaughter Field.

About half a dozen loyalists suffered what seemed to be mortal wounds in the fighting. Rather than let them die alone, the loyalists left two men to tend to them during their final hours. Compassionate Indians led the wounded men to Healing Springs, a sacred place of restorative waters. The men who had been left for dead were alive in Charleston six months after the battle (Boylston 75-76).

South Carolina legislature meets

The South Carolina Assembly convened January 8, 1782, at Jacksonboro, just thirty miles from the British stronghold at

Charleston. Greene's army posted at the Round O and Marion's brigade patrolling the Lowcountry kept the British army in check while the legislature met. Because Francis Marion had been elected to represent St. John's Parish, Berkeley, he appointed Lieutenant Colonel Peter Horry to command the brigade while he served in the senate. Horry headed homeward because of illness on February 24 and entrusted command of the brigade to Colonel Adam McDonald.

British detachment ventures out of Charleston

While the South Carolina Assembly was meeting, a detachment of the British army at Charleston mounted an offensive. The British force of five hundred infantry, two hundred mounted troops and two artillery pieces routed patriots at Mepkin Plantation on February 24. The British then attacked a camp at Wambaw Bridge, where the fleeing patriots ripped planks off the floor of the bridge to slow the British pursuit; Major John James escaped British pursuit only because his horse leaped twenty feet across the gap in the flooring of the bridge.

When news of the British offensive reached Jacksonboro, the Assembly allowed Francis Marion to depart from the senate in order to return to his brigade. As he rushed northward, a band of dragoons joined him.

Marion's brigade and the dragoons were in camp at Tydiman's Plantation when the British attacked before dawn on February 26. Some of the dragoons attempted to flee across the Santee River; several drowned and British marksmen shot others in the water. After Marion rallied his men, the British withdrew. Marion's losses were humiliating: eight men killed, seven men wounded, forty horses captured, and his own tent, canteens and baggage taken.

Nathanael Greene's wife joins him

While General Nathanael Greene – commander of the Southern Department of the Continental army – was camped at the Round O about forty miles from Charleston, his wife Caty joined him in late March of 1782. She left their four young children with friends and relatives up north. George Washington personally selected the officers who escorted her to South Carolina. A biographer describes Caty and Nathanael's reunion:

Greene quickly found that life had taken on new zest and meaning. For Caty soon was the center of what social life was possible in the camp and on those neighboring plantations that still could offer hospitality after going through the devastating ravages of war. Some of the other officers' wives joined their husbands for the duration of the Charleston siege. Caty made many friends among the mothers and daughters of neighboring planters, some of whose relatives still were serving with Washington in the North, and others of whom were in Greene's army.

...She rode horseback with the general in the lush countryside. She was gay, although not always in the best of health... (Bailey 195)

Flory McDonald's family scattered

In Scotland, 60-year-old Flory McDonald – famous for having rescued Bonnie Prince Charlie – missed her husband Allan, who was stationed in Nova Scotia with the Royal Highland Emigrant Regiment. She worried about her sons, who were scattered around the world: Johnny had received a cadetship in the Bombay Infantry in 1780; Charles and James served in the British army in America; Alexander, called Sandy, had died on a voyage from America to Britain but she had heard rumors that he might be still alive. She wrote to a friend in 1782 with news about her family and other acquaintances:

I return you my most sincere thanks for your being so mindful of me as to send me the agreeable news about Johny's arrival, which relieved me of a great deal of distress, as that was the first accounts I had of him since he sailed. I think, poor man, he has been very lucky for getting into bread so soon after landing. I had a letter from John which, I suppose, came by the same conveyance with yours. I am told by others that it will be in his power to show his talents, as being in the engineer's department. He speaks feelingly of the advantages he got in his youth, and the good example show'd him, which I hope will keep him from doing anything that is either sinful or shameful.

I received a letter from Captain Macdonald, my husband, dated from Halifax, the 12th Nov. '81. He was then recovering his health, but had been very tender for some time before. My son, Charles, is captain in the British Legion, and James, a lieutenant in the same. They are both in New York. Ranald is captain of Marines, and was with Rodney at the taking of St. Eustati. As for my son Sandy who was amissing I had accounts of his being carried to Lisbon, but nothing certain, which I look upon, on the whole, as a hearsay; but the kindness of Providence is still to be looked upon, as I have no reason to complain, as God has been pleased to spare his father and the rest. I am now in my brother's house, on my way to Skye, to attend my daughter, who is to ly-in in August. They are all in health at present. As for my health at present, it's tolerable, considering my anxious mind and distress of times. (Macgregor 172)

Flory later received the news that her son Ranald had died when the ship he was aboard sank after a naval battle (Vining 190).

The death of Rory McIntosh
Roderick "Rory" McIntosh – who had remained loyal to his king and had fought for the British against his kinsmen Lachlan McIntosh and John McIntosh – knew that the war was going badly for his side by the time Cornwallis surrendered at Yorktown. Rory decided to return to Scotland, the land of his birth and boyhood. He survived the voyage across the Atlantic but before he reached Scotland he died aboard ship at Gravesend, England, in 1782 (Gladstone).

Lachlan McIntosh returns to Georgia
The British garrison at Savannah evacuated on July 11, 1782, leaving Georgia in possession of the patriots. Lachlan McIntosh's older brother William McIntosh was elected to the Georgia Assembly and served on a committee negotiating a cessation of raids back and forth across the border with Florida, which remained a British colony. This negotiation was important to the McIntosh brothers because their plantations were just north of the border. William had been involved in raids and counter-raids across the border since his childhood, when Florida was Spanish territory, and continuing during his service as a patriot officer during the

American Revolution. With the Revolution coming to a close, he was ready for peace.

Lachlan McIntosh, who had been a prisoner of war for almost two years, was exchanged for Brigadier General Charles O'Hara, who had been captured at Yorktown when Cornwallis surrendered (Jackson dissertation 203; "Case" 139). After being exchanged in February of 1782, Lachlan went to see his wife and children in Virginia, where they had ended up after enduring "a pursuit by the enemy of seven or eight hundred miles" ("Case" 137). He decided to send them to Camden, South Carolina, where friends would take care of them. He himself planned to return to Georgia "to try if I can to pick up any of my Wreckt property" (Lawrence, "Suspension" 132).

Lachlan McIntosh returned to Georgia in August of 1782. He found his plantation at Darien in ruins and his finances in shambles. His house at Savannah had not only been damaged during the siege but also had been sold during the British occupation, and he had to take legal action to get it back. His wife and younger children, meanwhile, remained in exile. A deposition noted that Lachlan "returned to this State after an absence of near five years" – counting his service at Valley Forge and in the Western Department as well as his time as a prisoner of war – "his family then in Virginia and his affairs much deranged by the War which required all his attention, in his advanced stage of life" ("Case" 139).

At age 55 in 1782, Lachlan had been wounded in battle and in a duel, had endured sultry weather on the southern frontier and frigid weather at Valley Forge and in the West, had fended off fierce political feuds and slurs on his honor, and had suffered "Severe Imprisonment" for more than a year (Lawrence, "Suspension" 131).

A letter from his sister's husband Robert Baillie, who was a loyalist, sums up the situation facing Lachlan's extended family:

> I saw William & his family a few days ago... This cursed War has ruin'd us all, however, I still flatter myself it will soon be at an End, and that we shall again be able to return to our Plantations and live peaceably together which I assure I most sincerely wish for... We are very anxious to hear where Mrs. McIntosh & the children are. I hope you will now be able to have them with you... (Sullivan 35)

John Laurens dies in combat: August 27, 1782

Both Lachlan McIntosh and his longtime friend and business partner Henry Laurens endured hardships as the war dragged on. The British had burned Laurens' home at Mepkin during the occupation of Charleston. Laurens himself had been imprisoned in the Tower of London for more than a year before being exchanged for Lord Cornwallis after the siege of Yorktown. He suffered from gout so severely that he could not walk out of prison and was carried in a sedan chair. He continued his diplomatic service in Britain and Europe through the remainder of the war.

Henry Laurens' daughter Martha, called Patsy, had left South Carolina before the war with her sister Mary Eleanor, called Polly, and their aunt and uncle James Laurens. In the summer of 1782 they were residing at Vigan in France. Martha, age 22 in the summer of 1782, had been "preparing herself for meeting the contemplated loss of her father, brother, and fortune by the events of the war, and at the same time doing every office of love to her afflicted uncle" (Ramsay 19). Martha was known "to live a life of prayer, for she incorporated it with her daily business, and was so habituated to its constant practice, that prayers frequently constituted a part of her dreams" (Ramsay 30).

Colonel John Laurens, age 27 in the summer of 1782, had returned to South Carolina after the siege of Yorktown. Like many British and American soldiers in the Lowcountry during the summer of 1782, Laurens suffered from a fever. He arose from his sickbed when he learned that the British had sent a small fleet from Charleston on a foraging raid to plantations along the Combahee River. Laurens asked for command of a breastwork overlooking the river at Tar Bluff on Chehaw Neck, manned by fifty troops, including artillerymen with a howitzer. On August 27, a force of about 150 British soldiers came ashore and took up a position along the road to Chehaw Neck. Laurens led a charge towards the position despite being outnumbered three to one. British volleys killed Laurens and two other officers, and wounded nineteen enlisted men. The survivors retreated, abandoning the howitzer.

The British returned to their ship in the Combahee River with losses of one dead and seven wounded (Gregory Massey 223-31; Hilborn 219-20; Kelly 336-38). A wound suffered by British officer John McDonald – a veteran of the Battle of Moore's Creek Bridge – made his left arm permanently useless (Moss 37).

The memoirs of William Dobein James declare that Laurens "fell in the flower of his youth, and yet had long been the admiration of both the contending armies. In history the parallel to his character is perhaps to be found only in that of the Chevalier Bayard: the knight without fear and without reproach" (158).

Nathanael Greene wrote, "Poor Laurens is fallen in a paltry little skirmish… I wish his fall had been as glorious as his fate… The love of military glory made him seek it upon occasions unworthy of his rank. The state will feel his loss; and his father will hardly survive it" (qtd. in Gregory Massey 228).

Laurens was the only member of General George Washington's staff to be killed in the war. Washington wrote, "Poor Laurens is no more. He fell in a trifling skirmish in South Carolina, attempting to prevent the Enemy from plundering the Country of rice" (Gregory Massey 230).

In France, Martha Laurens had a supernatural experience concerning John Laurens' death. "It is remarkable, that from and after the time col. John Laurens was killed in South Carolina, August 27th. 1782, his sister… never put up a prayer for him, though she was previously in the habit of praying frequently for him; and his death was unknown to her for two or three months after it had taken place. She mentioned the fact, without pretending to account for it, and added, that she several times wondered at her omission of that usual part of her duty, and resolved to retire for the purpose of praying for her brother; but that in every such case, some sudden call or other unexpected event interposed to prevent her doing so" (Ramsay 29).

John Adams sent the news of John Laurens' death to Henry Laurens in England, writing "Our Country has lost its most promising Character" (Gregory Massey 231).

Henry Laurens reported that he was "in deep mourning for that brave honest man, that good soldier and good Citizen, that dutiful son and sincere friend, the dear object of my present woe" (Gregory Massey 231).

Marion fights once more: August 29, 1782

As the war waned, Francis Marion's brigade dwindled. Marion sent a regiment to protect Georgetown, and led his little brigade back and forth across the Lowcountry, stopping loyalist risings and responding to reports of British excursions from Charleston.

On August 29, Major Thomas Fraser led more than a hundred British dragoons against Marion's camp at Fair Lawn. Marion reported that one of his men was wounded and three were captured, while six British dragoons were killed and fourteen were wounded. The engagement was Marion's last battle.

William Dobein James, a young soldier serving with Marion, described the scene in his memoirs:

> ...there stretched toward the road an extensive avenue of old cedar trees. The trimming of which had been neglected for some years; and their long boughs now descended nearly to the ground. While encamped in this situation, Gen. Marion heard of the approach of Major Fraser with the British cavalry, towards the Santee, in his rear. On this side there was nothing but an open old field for a mile. None but the officers now had horses, and he immediately ordered out a party of these, under Capt. Gavin Witherspoon, to reconnoiter the enemy. They had advanced but little way in the woods beyond the old field, when the reconnoitering party were met by Major Fraser at the head of his corps of cavalry, and were immediately charged. A long chase commenced, which was soon observed by Marion, and he drew up his men, under the thick boughs of the cedar trees. As the chase advanced towards him it became more and more interesting. When in full view, either Witherspoon's horse had failed him, or he fell purposely in the rear to bring up his party, and a British dragoon was detached to cut him down. He advanced until nearly within his sword's length, and was rising in his stirrups to make sure of his blow, but Witherspoon had eyed him well, and at the instant, Parthian like, he fired the contents of his gun into his breast. The good omen excited much animation, and the British, still advancing, attempted to charge upon the left, but were received on that side with a well directed fire, which caused them to break and fly in great disorder. Had Gen. Marion's cavalry been present they might now have been cut to pieces; but scarcity of forage had induced him to quarter them at the distance of six miles. The enemy ral-

lied and manoeuvered about in the old field for an hour, making several different feints of charging, but never coming in reach of Marion's fire, whose men stood firm at their post...

Here ended the warfare of Marion. Its close was as the last ray of the setting sun; in his progress through the day, at times shining brightly; at others clouded with darkness: but at eventide descending with cheerful brilliancy. (James 169-70)

British evacuate Charleston: December 14, 1782

British forces evacuated Charleston on December 14 and returned to England. A biographer describes Nathanael Greene's triumphant entry into the city:

> ...announced by the blare of a trumpet, General Nathanael Greene, mounted on a superb charger and in full Continental uniform, escorted by Governor Mathews of South Carolina, rode to the statehouse through lines of American troops at present arms. General William Moultrie and General Mordecai Gist came next in line, followed by prominent citizens and Greene's principal officers. Behind the soldiers were the populace, most of them wild with joy. The Tories stayed glumly indoors with their windows shuttered... although they had been told... that Greene would treat them generously.
>
> There was a brilliant ball that evening. Decorative paper magnolia leaves hung in graceful festoons overhead in the big ballroom... Caty Greene, at her husband's side, was the center of attraction. (Bailey 203)

Francis Marion returns home

South Carolina militiamen were released from duty after the British left Charleston. Marion told his men he would "always consider them with the Affection of a Brother" and wished them "a long Continuance of happiness and the Blessings of Peace." Historian Hugh F. Rankin describes the Swamp Fox's homecoming:

> Francis Marion didn't have much to come home to. Pond Bluff was in ruins. Unfortunately, his farm was but a mile

off the highway over which the British had marched many times; both friend and foe had pillaged and despoiled his belongings; his personal possessions were missing, his furniture was destroyed and his house burned. His cattle had been driven off, his horses stolen, and at least half of his slaves either taken up by the enemy or run away. [Ten slaves remained at Pond Bluff.]

As did many of his friends and neighbors as well as a number of his former enemies, Marion had to begin again almost from scratch... He did have his land and the remaining slaves with which to work it. He had been without pay for almost three years but hoped to be pensioned on half-pay. He was not. Somehow he managed to acquire seed, feed, and tools as well as food and clothing [for his slaves]. (289)

Lachlan McIntosh restores his honor

In Georgia, Lachlan McIntosh continued to refute the claims of his political enemies who had caused him to be suspended from command. Many of the officers who had served under his command declared that he was one of the best commanders they knew, both as a gentleman and an officer.

On February 1, 1783, the Georgia Assembly adopted a resolution stating that the letter to Congress that resulted in McIntosh's suspension from command was "a forgery, in violation of law and truth." The Assembly expressed "abhorrence" of attempts "to injure the character of an officer and citizen of this state who merits the attention of the Legislature for his early, decided and persevering efforts, in the defence of America" (Lawrence, "Suspension" 137).

Georgia authorities, meanwhile, denounced McIntosh's political enemies. On one occasion in early 1783, his son William attacked a political enemy with a horsewhip. Also in 1783, William attained the rank of Major (Hawes, *University* 6, 60).

Fate buffets Lachlan McIntosh yet again

Just when things seemed to be going his way, Lachlan McIntosh suffered a devastating personal loss. His second-oldest son, Lachlan McIntosh Jr., died on February 15, 1783, at the age of 25, while escorting Sarah McIntosh and the younger children on their journey home. Harvey H. Jackson, a historian who wrote a biography of Lachlan McIntosh, describes how the son's death affected the father:

> ...he wanted simply to gather his scattered family and return to the life he had known before. But that, too, was denied him, for early in 1783 his beloved Lackie had taken ill and died in Camden. Always his father's favorite, the young man's sense of responsibility and attention to duty made it appear that once again a second son would emerge as family leader. With Lackie gone, much of the warm, human side of the general seemed to fade. His concern, of course, was for the living, but it is doubtful if he ever fully forgot the dead. (128)

Savannah historian Alexander A. Lawrence calls Lachlan McIntosh "a man of larger mould than has been supposed. The trials and tribulations he underwent in the American Revolution would have broken a less indomitable spirit" ("Suspension" 104).

George Washington rallies his officers

Although the fighting was over, George Washington kept his army on stand-by in case the peace negotiations broke down. The idle soldiers grumbled about broken promises from the Continental Congress. Washington put down two uprisings among the enlisted men and personally rallied his disgruntled officers.

He called a meeting at noon on March 15, 1783, in the Temple of Virtue, a building that was used for church services, dances and Masonic meetings. In his address to his officers, Washington appealed to their patriotism, pointed out that he had been their faithful friend since the beginning of the war, and promised to ask Congress to treat them fairly. Biographer Ron Chernow describes the scene:

> It was an exemplary performance from a man uncomfortable with public speaking. He had castigated his officers but also lifted them to a higher plane, re-awakening a sense of their exalted role in the Revolution and reminding them that illegal action would tarnish that grand legacy. For all his eloquence, Washington achieved his greatest impact

with a small symbolic gesture. To reassure the men of congressional good faith, he read aloud a letter from Congressman Joseph Jones of Virginia and tripped over the first few sentences because he couldn't discern the words. Then he pulled out his new spectacles, shocking his fellow officers: they had never seen him wearing glasses. "Gentlemen, you must pardon me," he said. "I have grown gray in your service and now find myself growing blind." These poignant words exerted a powerful influence. Washington at fifty-one was much older and more haggard than the young planter who had taken charge of the Continental Army in 1775. The disarming gesture of putting on the glasses moved the officers to tears as they recalled the legendary sacrifices he had made for his country. When he left the hall moments later, the threatened mutiny had ended, and his victory was complete. The officers approved a unanimous resolution stating they "reciprocated [Washington's] affectionate expressions with the greatest sincerity of which the human heart is capable." (436-37)

Nathanael and Caty Greene return home

In Charleston, General Nathanael Greene received orders in the spring of 1783 to dismiss the troops serving under him in the Southern Department of the Continental Army. The men from North Carolina and Virginia began walking homeward. The men from Maryland and Pennsylvania waited until July while a fleet of ships assembled in Charleston to take them home by sea.

Caty Greene boarded the first ship bound for Philadelphia. Gathering her children from the homes of friends and relatives who had been entrusted with their care while she was in South Carolina, she returned to Rhode Island.

Nathanael Greene remained in Charleston through early August to arrange for the management of two plantations that had been given to him by the grateful legislatures of South Carolina and Georgia.

Biographers describe his homeward journey:

Crossing the Brandywine northward, he reflected that he had traveled down the same road in the opposite direction nearly three years before, on his way to take command of

Gates's army. Word of his approach had spread into Philadelphia, and officers and citizens drove out to meet him and
escort him to the door of his tavern, when a shout of "Long
life to Greene!" rang out as he left his carriage, much
moved by his reception.

[Greene proceeded to Princeton, where Congress was
in session and where George and Martha Washington were
staying,]

…His welcome from the Washingtons and his former
comrades was as warm as he could have wished. He lingered at Princeton, hearing all the Northern news and
bringing Washington up to date on the state of the country
as revealed by his recent journey from Charleston through
North Carolina and Virginia. (Thane 271)

[Greene] visited for a last time with George Washington, his friend and former commander in chief. The trip was
a triumphal procession for the hero of the Carolinas and
Georgia. He was not completely happy, however, until he
[arrived in Rhode Island] and for the first time saw Caty
and their four children together.

There was a big celebration in East Greenwich in
Greene's honor. The Kentish Guards… turned out on parade in smart new uniforms. Cannon boomed, and martial
music blared under the stately elms along Main Street. The
General Assembly… came down to Kent County, meeting
in grand committee in the courthouse to pay special honor
to the state's most distinguished son. (Bailey 204)

The nations establish peace

Although the war had been winding down ever since Lord
Cornwallis had surrendered at Yorktown, the political process of
peacemaking had been progressing slowly. British and American
leaders had agreed to conduct peace negotiations in Paris. American commissioners Benjamin Franklin, John Jay, John Adams and
Henry Laurens – the friend and business partner of Lachlan McIntosh –had signed preliminary peace terms on November 13, 1782.

Martha Laurens departed from her invalid uncle's residence in
another part of France to be with her father, who himself was ill.
"[After] a separation of seven years, she joined him in Paris, and

presided over his domestic concerns, while he assisted in the nego-tiations which terminated in peace and the acknowledged inde-pendence of the United States. The transition from the nurse's chamber, in a remote country place, to the head of the table of a minister plenipotentiary in the metropolis of France, was great and sudden. Amidst the gayeties of Paris, in which she occasionally indulged, her bible was her companion and counsellor. She read it by day, and meditated on it by night. It had taught her to bear ad-versity with patience, resignation, and happiness" (Ramsay 23-24).

The final peace treaty between Great Britain and the United States of America was ratified in September of 1783. British troops left New York on November 25, 1783.

The officers and men of the 71st Highlanders were released and sent to Scotland. The regiment disbanded at Perth. Captain Aeneas Mackintosh returned to the seat of Clan Mackintosh at Moy.

George Washington resigned his commission as Continental Commander in Chief at noon on December 23, 1783. He told the Continental Congress assembled at Annapolis that he was "Happy in the confirmation of our Independence and Sovereignty, and pleased with the opportunity afforded the United States of becom-ing a respectable Nation" (Sobol 163-64).

Aeneas Mackintosh resumes role as clan chief

Aeneas Mackintosh returned to Scotland in 1783, resuming his role as the 23rd Chief of Clan Mackintosh and managing the farms and forests on his estates. His wartime experience became part of clan folklore repeated two hundred years later by an 84-year-old storyteller:

> Now, when the American War of Independence was being fought around 1776, the chief of the Mackintoshes was first and foremost to help with the American War of Independ-ence – to keep it for the British, of course.
>
> And you know, he mustered 500 clansmen. They were made up of Mackintoshes and MacQueens and McPhersons and MacBains and, of course, there were Smiths among them because they were on his estate. They went across to America, and I think that they had a pretty hard time of it on their voyage: I think there were pirates and all.

They were there under the command of Lord Cornwallis and the army opposing the Americans was mostly English. But Lord Cornwallis was defeated severely by the Americans, of course, and that finished the campaign. (Larimer 61)

The death of Colonel Anne: March 2, 1784

Not long after he returned to Scotland from the war in America, Aeneas Mackintosh mourned the death of his aunt Lady Anne Mackintosh – the renowned "Colonel Anne" of the Rising of 1745.

"It is with pain that I am to acquaint you," he reported in a letter, that Lady Anne died "after suffering much by five months illness, which she bore with becoming fortitude, retaining her reason to the last, and leaving the world without a sigh."

In another letter, he remarked, "You, I, and the whole Clan have lost in Lady Mackintosh a steady and sincere friend, and I fear it will be difficult to find her like" (McGillivrary, "Colonel Anne" 79; MacKintosh, "Lady" 49).

Clan historian Angus MacKintosh writes, "Thus passed away a lady who made for herself an abiding place in the hearts of Clan Chattan, to whom her name is synonymous with all that is loyal, unselfish, gentle, and brave" ("Lady" 49).

Another clan historian, Robert McGillivray, points out that Aeneas the 23rd Chief of Mackintosh had a close relationship with his aunt Lady Anne:

> Much of what is known about Anne and the events around Moy, is contained in a manuscript written by Sir Aeneas Mackintosh, nephew of Anne's husband and subsequently 23rd Chief, who spent a good deal of time with her in later years…
>
> …Sir Aeneas wrote "The people of England and the soldiers were prepossessed with a notion that Lady Mackintosh was a woman of a monstrous size, had always rode at the head of her regiment, and that she charged with it in the battle of Culloden, fully accoutered and mounted upon a white horse; but this was far from the truth, for she was a very thin girl, never saw the men but once, and was at her own house the time of the action." ("Colonel Anne" 73)

Notes by a Highland Chief

Aeneas Mackintosh kept notes on a tour of his estates during seven weeks in September and October of 1784. His notes focus on his agricultural enterprises, and they also provide glimpses into the social and economic conditions in the area near Inverness. He was disturbed to discover that while he was fighting in America other landowners had infringed on his fishing rights:

> Salmon this far, till the Duke of Gordon shut up the mouth of the rivers at the Castle of Inverlochy by cruives (by what right to be enquired into) – fine meadow ground and corn field wants enclosing and a few belts of planting. No stones but out of the rivers, the moss close to the place – the Spean is the march betwixt the Duke of Gordon and me, and the Roy boundary twixt it and Achaderry. A fine bank of young oak fronting Keppoch extends for a mile and a half which can be easily enclosed – the Spean running the whole length... and the Roy the whole breadth, so that a straight line of a sunk fence faced with stone or a double turf dyke such as at Moy would do. Near the end of the oak there commences a birch and other wood tolerably high. The part of the oak wood near Spean can be cut in ten years.
>
> Achlochrich – A fine fall of water called a linn stops the salmon from getting further up the country. If people of the Duke had not stopped up the river would willingly be at the expense of blowing this linn. The farm a fine, flat, green hills but no wood – here is the burial place of the former family of Keppoch and Chapel built by one of the Lochiels, being one of seven built by him in order to pacify the Pope (by whom) for his great wickedness he had been ex-communicated.
>
> Murlagan – A bulwark necessary to be built in front of the house.
>
> Tullich and Dulderig – Fine flat corn country. The Charters relative to the Lochaber to be very pointedly examined with respect to the Proprietor's title and right of fishing, as for a few years past the same is totally monopolized by the Duke of Gordon's having quite shut up the

mouth of the river with cruives and other engines wholly to prevent a single fish getting up the river. (*Notes* 2)

The notes describe the hazards of riding horseback through the rough terrain of the Scottish Highlands. "It rains very heavy in the afternoon," he observed on September 7, and when he resumed his journey, "Before we proceed two miles it turns dark and rains and blows." The next day, "Did not breakfast till ten, and it was twelve before I could get on horseback" (6).

> 8th (Sept.) Set off by seven, breakfast at Dalwhily, a farm possessed by Parson Robert Macpherson, and dine at Banchor. Proceeding from thence in the evening to Dunnaughtane, very near falling from my horse, but my servant prevents it. However, hurt my thigh very much. Was afraid I had dislocated my haunch bone; confined to bed several days. D. Stewart and Mr Grant attend me.

> On the 15th proceed in a Post Chaise to Moy. (7)

Aeneas, who was in his early thirties and had recently returned from seven years of warfare and imprisonment, paid close attention to the pretty women he met during the tour. During the first part of the tour, he noted, "I and company retired early to a party of ladies assembled at Miss Mally McIntosh's, where we danced and supped" (5).

The next day he observed, "upon entering a neat house, found the Landlady a very agreeable young woman at the tea table to entertain us. She is Sister to Fassifearn" (5).

Two weeks later, although still recovering from a riding accident, he enjoyed the social life of Inverness:

> 17th (Sept.) Asked to dine at Provost Chisholm's, but Lord Hinderland asks us off to dine with some ladies. Accordingly attend him. There were present Lady Jannett Train, lately married to the Sheriff-Depute of Caithness, a very handsome, polite young lady; Mrs Forbes, Culloden, and Miss Grant, Dalvey. In evening all hands go to Mr Pierson's concert. Several young lassies sing and perform well on the Spinette.

See some pretty girls... Miss Dallas, daughter to the late Professor of Cantrae, lately from Aberdeen, a showy girl, and has the appearance of a woman of fashion. Miss Campbell, daughter to the late Governor of Fort-George, promises to be pretty. (7)

... 20th (Sept.) All the gentlemen who had been scholars to Mr Hector Fraser, late schoolmaster, dine together, and gave a ball to the ladies... The number of gentlemen was 50 and 100 ladies, well dressed, and a few well looked girls... (7)

The notes show that Aeneas, like his kinsman Roderick Mackintosh who emigrated to coastal Georgia, was an avid sportsman:

23rd (Sept.) The Colonel goes ashooting. Out of compliment I attend him on horseback through a rough moor to the west of the house covered with birch wood and shrubs. See from a dozen to 15 black game, of which he kills one, but by four, being tired and my leg very uneasy, return and obliged to wait dinner till seven in the evening.

24th (Sept.) The Colonel having applied for leave to shoot a roe buck, send my servant to attend him, and go myself to visit my farms in the neighborhood, which I frequently do. Return by four, when I understand that Thornton had killed a doe giving suck. I in consequence entertain him very coolly, and form in my mind that it was the first and last he should kill any time he should be at my house...

25th (Sept.) From irregular hours and my chagrin at Thornton's behavior, obliged to lie in bed longer than usual. Thornton goes to Inverness and carries the doe with him... The Colonel makes present of the deer at Inverness instead of leaving her with me.

... 8th (Oct.) Go afishing for the last time this year. The fish rise fast but don't fix firmly. (8)

Petition rests on Mackintosh lore

The journal *Clan Chattan* tells a tale titled "Sir Aeneas Mackintosh and Allan McDonald:"

> Allan held a farm from Sir Aeneas in the Braes of Strathdearn, but owing to Allan not paying his Rent regularly, he was turned out, and went to reside in a small Hut at Tordarroch. Allan was however very anxious to get back his possession from Sir Aeneas and he got a friend to write a Petition to the Laird, setting forth his claims, which rested principally upon the following story.
>
> When the Chiefs of Mackintosh resided at Dunachton, one of them had a large family of grown up sons. Upon a certain occasion some of the Ross-shire Gentry happening to be passing through Badenoch, a scuffle ensued regarding some cattle which they were driving north, and in the affray several of the Ross-shire people were killed. For this, a son of Mackintosh was tried, found guilty, and condemned to be hanged in Edinburgh. Young Mackintosh was much beloved by his Clan and kinsmen, and his approaching fate created a great sensation among them. At last, as the day for his execution was approaching, a predecessor of Allan came forward and volunteered his services to go to Edinburgh to suffer upon the scaffold instead of his Chief's son. He was accordingly dressed in such a manner as to resemble young Mackintosh, sent off for Edinburgh and was hanged in his stead.
>
> After Sir Aeneas read the Petition and recollecting that he had heard something of the grounds upon which it was founded, in his younger days, he granted Allan the lands as long as he could pay a reasonable rent for them. But Allan's means were soon gone, and at last he died in poverty. (242)

Flory McDonald's husband returns

Flory McDonald – legendary for having rescued Bonnie Prince Charlie – lived with relatives in the western isles of Scotland while her husband Allan was stationed in Nova Scotia with the Royal Highland Emigrant Regiment during the last years of the

American Revolution. They were reunited when he returned to Skye in 1784 ("Flora MacDonald").

Flory has become both a participant in history and a heroine of folklore. In the fairytale version of her adventures, she lived happily ever after:

> When peace was eventually restored, Flora's husband... made as little delay as possible in returning to Skye, as Captain on half-pay. On his arrival at Portree, he was met by his affectionate wife, and a numerous party of friends, to welcome him. He made no delay in reaching Kingsburgh, which, during his absence in America, was left open for his return. ...Flora and her husband lived comfortably and happily in their old residence... (Macgregor 173)

In the historical version, Flory suffered the slings and arrows of outrageous fortune resulting in the heartache and the thousand natural shocks that flesh is heir to. Allan didn't actually return to Skye without delay; he accepted a grant of three thousand acres in Nova Scotia and cleared the land for farming. After about a year, he went to London to seek reimbursement for the losses he had incurred during the war. Only then, after a separation of six years, did he join Flory at Skye. They stayed with relatives, because Kingsburgh had not actually been left open for his return; it had been acquired in 1774 by a man named William MacLeod who continued to occupy it after Allan returned to Skye (Vining 190-92).

Rather than living comfortably, Flory suffered from badly-healed bones broken in falls in America and aboard ship on her voyage home, while Allan suffered from injuries incurred when he had marched as a prisoner of war from North Carolina to Pennsylvania. Flory wrote:

> The cast in both my arms are liveing monuments of my sufferings and distresses. And the long Gaol confinement which my Husband underwent has brought on such disorders that he has totally lost the use of his legs. So that I may fairly say we both have suffered in our person, family and interest, as much as if not more than any two going under

the name of Refugees or Loyalists, without the Smallest recompense. (Vining 194-95)

The deaths of her sons Alexander and Ranald while serving in the British military forces continued to have consequences for Flory. She pointed out that if the two sons had survived they "with God's assistance, might now be my support in my old age."

She did have two sons in Skye: Charles was married to a daughter of the MacDonalds of Aird; James and his wife Emily lived at Flodigarry, where Flory and Allan had lived as newlyweds (Vining 192-93).

Her son John was in the British service in Sumatra (Vining 185).

Martha Laurens has supernatural experience

Martha Laurens – daughter of Lachlan McIntosh's friend Henry Laurens – had a supernatural experience in 1774 resembling the one she had experienced two years earlier upon the death of her brother Colonel John Laurens.

"When Mr. James Laurens died in Vigan, [a place in France], his niece Martha Laurens was with her father in England. She started out of bed, and pronounced that her uncle was dead; and at her request the day and the hour was committed to writing, by Miss Futerell. In the ordinary course of the posts between the two countries, intelligence of his death arrived, and the day and hour of it precisely corresponded with what had been recorded as aforesaid in England" (Ramsay 19).

Life goes on for Lachlan McIntosh

In Georgia, Lachlan McIntosh resumed his role as a member of the coastal land-owning aristocracy. His social activities included serving as president of Savannah's Society of St. Andrew, which celebrates Scottish ancestry. Turning his attention from warhorses to race horses, he became an officer in the Liberty County Jockey Club. In political matters, he was appointed to several commissions and served a term in the Georgia Assembly.

Lachlan's sons George and Henry Laurens, like Lackie, died unmarried. The surviving children established families of their own and gave Lachlan and Sarah a dozen grandchildren, including a grandson named John Lachlan, another named Lachlan, and two granddaughters named Sarah (Britt 113-15; Wightman and Cate 63). Surely General Lachlan McIntosh and his wife Sarah enjoyed spending time with their grandchildren and namesakes.

Their first-born child John, who had returned from Jamaica after the war, helped Lachlan with farming and business matters, and provided aid to his parents during a severe winter following poor harvests (Jackson 147, 149).

Lachlan and Sarah McIntosh lived in the Savannah area after the war and established a plantation on Skidaway Island (Jackson 130, 135). Sarah became known in Savannah as a "truly respectable old Lady" ("Cemetery Guide").

Although he lived in Savannah, Lachlan still owned property in the Darien area and maintained a business partnership with Henry Laurens involving land along the Altamaha. McIntosh County historian Buddy Sullivan reports on Lachlan's struggle to restore his war-ravaged property:

> After the Revolution, in 1785, with McIntosh and Laurens having sustained serious financial setbacks as a result of the war, it was McIntosh who averted further disaster when the two planters came very near to losing their Altamaha rice islands. McIntosh learned that since General's and Broughton islands had not been properly registered after the war, both were on the verge of being declared vacant. McIntosh, after considerable legal maneuvering, managed to acquire renewal certificates and thus preserve ownership of the land. This proved to be one of the last business dealings in the "long and amicable relationship" between Lachlan McIntosh and Henry Laurens. (Appendix 1)

Along with his political duties and social activities, McIntosh enjoyed associating with military veterans. Shortly after the war, officers who had served in the Continental Army formed the Society of the Cincinnati. When the Georgia chapter of the Cincinnati was founded, the officers who had served under McIntosh showed their respect for McIntosh by choosing him as their president. He made his priorities clear in 1784 when he was elected to Congress but he did not go to Philadelphia to take his seat because at the time he was involved in an effort to obtain land in Georgia for his fellow war veterans (Jackson 132-44).

In February of 1784 Congress praised McIntosh as "a worthy and brave officer who has served the United States with great reputation for near eight years" and promoted him to Major General (Lawrence, "Suspension" 139). Four years after he had been suspended from command, McIntosh's wounded pride had been restored.

Francis Marion marries: April 20, 1786

In South Carolina, Francis Marion – "The Swamp Fox" of the American Revolution – married his first cousin Mary Esther Videau on April 20, 1786. He was 54 years old and she was 49. He built a cypress house at Pond Bluff to replace the building that had been destroyed during the war. He resumed life as a planter and his family prospered. Historian Hugh F. Rankin reports:

> Francis Marion never erased the excitement of the war years from his mind... When his memories became too overpowering, he would pack his camp equipage on two old sumpter mules, and, with Mary and the faithful Oscar in attendance, he would wander over the High Hills of the Santee, visiting old haunts and reliving the past with those he had led along the road to adventure.
>
> Many of those who had followed him in the field still looked to their old general for advice and guidance...
>
> Francis Marion grew old gracefully, something of a folk hero in his own time. He was a good citizen, performing those tasks in the community for which he felt he was qualified. Time after time the voters of St. Johns Parish returned him to the senate of the South Carolina Assembly. He was a hardworking though not particularly skillful politician, nor did he exhibit political ambitions. Most of his interests were concentrated on local problems or were related to the militia.
>
> He did, however, demonstrate more than a passing interest in public education, perhaps because of his own rather vague and inadequate preparation... It was his feeling that an educated citizenry was South Carolina's best defense against ambitious political demagogues...
>
> In 1790 he spent twenty-five days as a member of the convention that drew up a new South Carolina constitution.

After its completion and acceptance, he withdrew from active political life. In his personal politics he remained a Federalist, although not a dogmatic one.

Most of his time during his later years was devoted to the improvement of the militia. He commanded a brigade and spent more time in training than did the average militia officer of his day... (294-96)

The death of Nathanael Greene: June 19, 1786

After returning to Rhode Island when the war ended, Nathanael and Caty Greene had stayed in a rented house at Newport. He had gone alone to Charleston in July of 1784 to attend to the plantations that had been given to him by the legislatures of South Carolina and Georgia. He had sold the plantation on the Pon Pon in South Carolina and had settled on Mulberry Grove on the Georgia side of the Savannah River. During 1785 he had traveled back and forth from Georgia to Newport, where he had been elected head of the Society of the Cincinnati in Rhode Island. Biographers describe the untimely end of Greene's life:

> In the autumn of 1785 the Greenes gave up their pleasant town house on Mill Street in Newport and became year-round residents of the extensive Mulberry Grove plantation in Georgia. With Louisa, the newest arrival, there now were five children. Neighbors within easy riding distance of Mulberry Grove included General Anthony Wayne, who had become a Georgia planter, too...
>
> Greene quickly adjusted to the life of a Southern planter and apparently enjoyed every hour of the remaining months of his life... Mulberry Grove was a big plantation, and it had escaped most of the ravages of war. The flower garden was restored to its former beauty, his fields and orchards were in such good shape that, under his personal supervision, they soon would yield better crops than he had dared to hope.
>
> "The prospect," Greene wrote to a friend in the North, "and the house are delightful. He joyed in the fact that he had a "fine smokehouse," a coach house, stables with good riding horses, an outkitchen, and a pigeon house that would accommodate up to one thousand pigeons. He and Caty

spent many happy hours riding over the estate and the
countryside. Soon the Greenes were as popular with neighboring planters as they had been in Coventry and Newport.

The following spring Greene wrote exultantly that he
had "green peas almost fit to eat, and as fine lettuce as you
ever saw." He had apples, pears, peaches, apricots, nectar-
ines, plums, figs, pomegranates, and oranges in his orchards. "And we have strawberries which measure three
inches around," he added, with pardonable pride.

On June 12, 1786, Greene went to Savannah with Caty
[on business]. They... started home the next day in the cool
of the morning, expecting to reach Mulberry Grove well
before the day became hot. But Greene's enthusiasm as a
planter led him to stop on the way back at a neighboring
plantation to examine the rice fields. He spent several hours
in this interesting task, but he failed, unlike his host, to carry an umbrella to protect himself from the sun. While he
was driving home that afternoon, his head began to ache.
Next day the pain was intense, and his forehead was badly
swollen. (Bailey 210-12)

The children were sent away to a neighboring plantation and retained all their lives a memory of the darkened
house and their mother's tears. [Anthony] Wayne arrived in
great anxiety to find his friend in a stupor from which he
was never to be roused, and watched, weeping, by the bedside until the heavy breathing ceased. "I have seen a great
and good man die," he wrote sadly to one of their former
comrades.

Sunstroke, they said. But after all that campaigning in
the summer heat of the war years, and considering a constitution that had withstood fever, bad food, and perpetual
lack of sleep, a more likely diagnosis today would be a
sudden heart failure...

Savannah heard the news of his death with incredulity.
His friends had seen him there, only a few days before, in
perfect health. He was only forty-four years of age. He was
beginning a new chapter in his life, like a bridegroom, with
everything to live for...

The body was taken by water to Major Pendleton's house in Bay Street in Savannah for the last honors – the same house he had left for the visit to Gibbons's rice plantation less than a week before. Minute guns were firing as the coffin was carried ashore, and a large crowd of citizens and militia were gathered to receive it. The streets were empty and silent, the shops were closed, the flags were at half-mast. Troops with reversed arms and muffled drums led the procession from the Pendleton house to Christ Church while a band played the Dead March from *Saul*. A vault had been hastily opened. In the absence of a clergyman, Judge William Stephens read in a voice trembling with emotion the funeral service of the Church of England. The coffin was placed in the vault, the artillery fired thirteen rounds, and with trailed arms the troops withdrew slowly, followed by a silent, weeping crowd. (Thane 278-79)

When George Washington learned of his friend's death, he urged that widowed Caty and her fatherless children be given adequate financial support. He offered to provide the oldest child, George Washington Greene, with the finest education available in North America and to "bring him up to either of the genteel professions that his friends may choose or his own inclinations shall lead him to pursue, at my own cost and expense" (Thane 279-80).

The death of Flory McDonald: March 5, 1790

The people of Scotland continued to treat Flory Macdonald as a heroine as long as she lived and much, much longer. An early biographer describes the communal mourning that followed her death:

On the 5th of March, 1790, the ever-memorable Flora departed this life. She died of a short illness, nearly two years before her husband. She retained to the last that vivacity of character, and amiableness of disposition, by which she was all her life-time distinguished.

Her death did not take place at her own residence at Kingsburgh, but at Peinduin, a friend's house on the sea coast, about three miles further north. She went thither in her usual health, to pay a friendly visit to the family at Peinduin, where she was taken suddenly ill with an inflammatory complaint, which refused to yield to all the medical skill available at the time. She possessed all her mental faculties to the very last, and calmly departed in the presence of her husband and two daughters...

Flora's remains were shrouded in one of the sheets in which the Prince had slept at the mansion of Kingsburgh. With this sheet she never parted in all her travels. It was religiously and faithfully preserved by her in North Carolina, during the Revolutionary War. She had it in safe keeping even when her own person was in danger. At length the purpose she intended it for was accomplished, when all that was mortal of herself was wrapt in it by her sorrowing family. Her remains were conveyed under shade of night from Peinduin to Kingsburgh. The coffin was carried shoulder-high by a party of stalwart youths procured for the purpose...

The night was pitch-dark, except when the frequent flashes of lightning spread a momentary gleam over the scene. The thunder rolled with terrific peals; the rain fell in gushing torrents. It would seem as if the ghosts and hobgoblins had that night left their dark abodes to take a "dander" abroad, to lash up the elements into a perfect fury!

...When the funeral party arrived at the river of Hinisdale, about half the journey, it was swollen from bank to bank. The usual ford was impracticable, while higher up it was, if possible, worse.

Some proposed to return, while others objected, stating that she whose body they carried never flinched when alive, from any duty which she had undertaken, neither would they flinch from performing their last duties to her mortal remains.

After due consultation, it was agreed to attempt crossing by the strand near the sea beach, which was fortunately effected in safety. Shortly [afterward] they reached Kingsburgh, where the body lay in state for nearly a week.

At length the funeral day arrived. The procession started at an early hour, as the distance between Kingsburgh and the place of burial was about sixteen miles. The body was interred in the churchyard of Kilmuir, in the north end of Skye, within a square piece of course wall, erected in 1776, to enclose the tombs of the Kingsburgh family. The spot is about a mile and a half from the rock called Gailico, near Monkstadt, on which the Prince landed in Skye from the Long Island.

The funeral cortege was immense – more than a mile in length – consisting of several thousands of every rank in Skye and the adjacent Isles.

Flora's marriage and funeral, between which there was an interval of forty years, were the most numerously attended of any of which there is any record as having taken place in the Western Isles. Notwithstanding the vast assemblage present, all were liberally supplied with every variety of refreshment. Of genuine "mountain dew" alone upwards of three hundred gallons were served. About a dozen of pipers from the MacCrimmon and MacArthur colleges in Skye, and from other quarters, simultaneously played the "Coronach," the usual melancholy lament for departed greatness.

It must, no doubt, have been consonant with Flora's feelings to have spent her latter years, and breathed her last moments, in that romantic Isle where she had found shelter for her wandering Prince, and where she had passed so many of her juvenile years, in the enjoyment of its sublime scenery. (Macgregor 175-76)

A twentieth-century biographer challenges some of the details of the early account. Flory and Allan did not live at Kingsburgh after their return from America. Alexander MacDonald of Cuidrich acquired Kingsburgh in 1790, however, and Allan lived there as Cuidrich's guest after Flory died. Allan's daughter Fanny also lived there awhile; a few months after Flory's death, Fanny married Donald MacDonald, a son of Cuidreach who had served in Tarleton's Legion in the war in America (Vining 196).

Flory could not have been buried in the sheets in which Bonnie Prince Charlie had slept, because in 1756 the sheets had been buried with Allan's mother, the lady of the house at the time Prince Charles stayed at Kingsburgh (Vining 70, 126).

Captain William McIntosh claims plantation

Captain William McIntosh – a British officer who served as an emissary to the Creek Indians during the American Revolution – came to live among his kinsmen and former enemies. He had gone to England after the Revolution and placed his claim to Mallow plantation, which originally had been granted to his father John – a grandson of Brigadier William Mackintosh of Borlum. Mallow occupied a beautiful location on a bluff above the Sapelo River near Darien. At Mallow, Captain William McIntosh married Barbara, a daughter of Colonel William McIntosh of neighboring Fair Hope plantation – and so the former opponents in the war on the southern frontier became in-laws as well as blood relatives. Captain William's aunt Winnewood and uncle Roderick "Rory" McIntosh had lived at Mallow while their brother John had been living in Indian country a decade before the Revolution. Rory – a loyalist officer during the Revolution – died on his way to his homeland in Scotland in 1782. Winnewood died in 1786 at Mallow, and "William McIntosh of Mallow qualified as executor, 8 December 1791" ("Captain William McIntosh;" Sullivan 34-37).

Creek uncles redeem Captain McIntosh's son

A story involving Captain William McIntosh resembles another story in which young brothers William and Lachlan McIntosh sneaked onto a ship bound for England in order to join Bonnie Prince Charlie's glorious cause, but General Oglethorpe convinced them to stay in Georgia with their family. *The Georgia Historical Quarterly* tells Captain William McIntosh's tale:

> [Creek Indian leader William] McIntosh was born to a woman of the Wind clan and a Tory soldier [Captain William McIntosh] in Coweta, a Lower Creek town, in 1778. According to several accounts, his parents... tried to raise their offspring according to two differing cultural standards. In matrilineal Creek society, both men and women played the crucial parenting roles. Maternal uncles taught young boys how to hunt, participate in ritual ceremonies, and otherwise be a man. McIntosh's British father, however, would not dissolve himself of his own parenting responsibilities. Despite a Creek custom which excluded biological fathers from raising their children, Capt. William McIn-

tosh taught his offspring to speak English, trade deerskins, and participate in worldly affairs. Eventually, however, the two systems of child raising came into conflict. One story recounts that when Captain McIntosh suggested that his two sons leave the Creek Nation for schooling, he met with resistance from his wife and her kinsmen. Her brothers, acting on their traditional responsibilities to raise and protect their sister's children, rejected the captain's proposal to take the boys to Scotland for an education. Captain McIntosh ignored this outright refusal and offered a compromise. He promised that he and his children would return to Georgia… However, this did not appease worried [Wind] clan members. Still, Captain McIntosh stubbornly went ahead with his plans. While waiting for a Scotland-bound boat to leave the Savannah port, the maternal uncles successfully thwarted what they saw as a breech of Creek etiquette. They snuck onto the vessel and "redeemed" the children. Family legend states that while the boys rested from the long journey to reach Savannah, their father had "joined the other passengers in the lounge area. Later in the evening when the Captain returned to his stateroom, the two boys were missing… Nothing could be done now for the ship was at sea and the Captain was taking the trip alone." William and his brother remained within the Wind clan's pervue and lived on Creek lands for the rest of their lives. (Frank 26)

George Washington's Southern Tour: 1791

In the United States, George Washington decided to visit each of the thirteen states to see for himself how the new nation had recovered from war and developed under the federal government. He was inaugurated as the first President of the United States in April of 1789 and after Congress adjourned in the fall he set out from the federal capitol in Philadelphia on a tour of the northeastern states. In the spring of 1991 Washington toured the southern states.

In preparing for the southern tour, Washington chose four matching horses, reddish-brown with black manes, to pull a custom-made traveling coach that would become known as his "white chariot" (Lipscomb 3). The chariot was driven by a Hessian coachman, which is interesting because Washington's most celebrated victory – when he crossed the Delaware at midwinter – was an attack on Hessian mercenaries. Realizing that the roads would be treacherous in springtime, the coachman added another pair of horses.

Washington brought a horse to ride when he wasn't in the chariot, described in *South Carolina in 1791: George Washington's Southern Tour* by Terry W. Lipscomb:

> In keeping with his stately concept of the presidential office, Washington always rode a white horse with a silver-mounted saddle, a leopard-skin housing and a gold-trimmed saddle cloth. He chose a magnificent milk-white charger named Prescott as his saddle horse on the southern tour. Preston was his parade horse; he was dignified, showed no skittishness under musket and cannon fire, and was one of two white horses Washington kept in his Philadelphia stable. (3)

Washington's traveling companions were his pet dog, a greyhound named Cornwallis, and his secretary, Major James Jackson, who had served in South Carolina during the war. Four servants and a slave driving the baggage wagon completed the entourage.

Washington departed the executive mansion in Philadelphia on March 21 and spent a week at Mount Vernon, his plantation in Virginia. On April 24 he arrived at Wilmington, near the Cross Creek country settled by Scots Highlanders such as Flory McDonald – legendary for her adventures in Scotland – and Allen McDonald – legendary for his exploits while serving with Francis Marion. The chief town of the Cross Creek country, Fayetteville, was described to Washington as a "thriving place" (Freeman 311).

In northeast South Carolina, Washington's route ran along the beach beside the Atlantic Ocean for sixteen miles. Lipscomb describes the scene:

> On a clear day, the traveler had an immense view of the ocean often with one or more sailing ships on the horizon. Washington's cavalcade would have made the scene even more picturesque – especially since Washington, who usually took his morning exercise on horseback, was probably

galloping down the beach, mounted on his white horse, with his pet greyhound running alongside. (9)

Washington spent a day and night at William Alston's plantation near Georgetown. Alston, who had served in Peter Horry's light horse regiment, probably told Washington about the Revolution in the Georgetown area and the genius of Francis Marion. While at the Alston plantation, Washington was welcomed to South Carolina by a reception committee: William Moultrie, a war hero and former governor; John Rutledge Jr., son of the wartime governor; and William Washington, who not only was a celebrated cavalry commander who contributed to the crucial victory at Cowpens but also was George Washington's cousin. Alston served on the board of Charleston's horse-racing track with Moultrie and William Washington; since George Washington also was an avid fan of horse racing, the men presumably toured Alston's stable of thoroughbreds (Lipscomb 11).

The next morning, a flotilla ferried the presidential party and its vehicles down the Waccamaw to Georgetown, a port that had been bitterly contested during the war. Washington rode in an "elegant painted boat" rowed by seven sea captains uniformed in blue coats, white jackets and hats trimmed with gold lace. In Georgetown, fifty ladies entertained Washington at a tea party. Women at a grand ball wore bandeaus inscribed with the sentiments "Long life to the president" and "Welcome the hero" (Lipscomb 11-14).

Early on the morning of May 1, honorary oarsmen rowed Washington across the Sampit River, and an escort of men from Georgetown and Charleston accompanied the presidential party to the Santee delta. Crossing the delta was a complicated process, involving the North Santee ferry, a mile-long causeway across a marshy island, and the South Santee ferry.

Washington ate breakfast and dinner at Hampton Plantation, where his hostesses were Harriott Pinckney Horry, widow of Colonel Daniel Horry, and her mother, Eliza Lucas Pinckney (Lipscomb 14-17).

Washington spends a week in Charleston

At about noon on May 2, Washington reached the ferry landing at Haddrell's Point, the place where Lachlan McIntosh had been held prisoner after the British captured Charleston. Washington boarded a custom-fitted barge flying the standard of the United States on a ground of blue silk, and displaying the South Carolina coat of arms and the motto "Long live the president." Thirteen sea captains manning the presidential barge were dressed in blue silk jackets, black breeches, white silk stockings, shoes with blue silk bows, and black round hats with blue silk sashes. More than forty boats escorted the presidential barge across the Cooper River to Charleston, including two boats carrying choirs, soloists and instrumentalists who filled the air with music as the flotilla crossed the water. Spectators viewed the presidential crossing from the decks of merchant ships anchored in the river.

In Charleston, throngs of spectators filled the streets, peered through windows, looked down from balconies, and perched on rooftops. After experiencing more than an hour of water-borne pageantry, Charlestonians welcomed Washington ashore with voices shouting, church bells pealing, and artillery firing a fifteen-gun federal salute (Lipscomb 21). Washington marched in a grand procession of civic leaders, clergymen, former Continental Army officers, and enthusiastic citizens of the new nation. They processed from the shore to the Exchange Building, where Washington ascended to the front porch and reviewed the parade as artillery continued to fire salutes. He then resumed his march through the streets toward the house where he would stay while in Charleston. He passed the statue of William Pitt that had been damaged by a ball fired from a British ship in the harbor, as Lachlan McIntosh had noted in his journal. Charleston's most influential men and most respectable ladies lavishly entertained Washington during the next seven days.

On May 4, Washington rode out on his white horse early in the morning for a battlefield tour. Veterans of the siege of Charleston, including William Moultrie and Washington's private secretary William Jackson, guided their commander in chief around the battleground. The *City Gazette* reported that Washington praised "the very gallant defense that had been made by the garrison during the siege" (Lipscomb 30).

Later that day, Washington socialized with his Masonic brethren. Washington was a longtime Mason who had remained involved in the fraternal organization even while serving as commander of the Continental army. Masonic affiliation was a trait shared by many American and British officers, and legend has it that at the Battle of Brier Creek a British officer saved the life of Colonel Samuel Elbert when Elbert gave a Masonic sign of distress.

That evening, Washington dined with the Society of the Cincinnati. Historian Terry Lipscomb tells the tale:

> The Continental army's officer corps had organized the Society of the Cincinnati in 1783 as America's first veterans' association. Washington had served as president general since the founding of the order, and the members of the South Carolina society were eager to honor the head of their national organization.
>
> ... Among the Cincinnati members, Washington saw several familiar faces. Two of his morning tour guides – William Moultrie and Charles Cotesworth Pinckney – served as president and vice-president of the South Carolina society, and Masonic Grand Master Mordecai Gist belonged to the organization as well.
>
> Only at official Cincinnati functions like this dinner did members wear the badge of their order – a golden eagle hanging from a blue-and-white ribbon, with a cameo of the Roman hero Cincinnatus affixed to the eagle's breast. When Washington attended meetings of the society, he usually wore his blue-and-buff military uniform and his personal membership insignia – the diamond eagle. In 1784, Count d'Estaing and the officers of the French navy had given him this jeweled version of the Cincinnati badge.
>
> The dinner at McCrady's followed a typical pattern. A choral group performed, and after dinner, the guests toasted the members of Washington's cabinet. In deference to the French and Spanish diplomats present, they also drank to the foreign military allies who had helped America during the Revolution. Washington proposed a toast to "the memory of... all those officers who fell in defence of America."
>
> The Charleston Artillery must have set up its field pieces in the tavern courtyard, for the gunners fired a volley after each of the fifteen toasts. (32-33)

The next morning, Washington went on a boating excursion to inspect the defenses of Charleston Harbor and visit the ruins of Fort Moultrie, where the 2nd South Carolina Regiment won distinction in the summer of 1776. One of his hosts was Henry Laurens, Jr. – a brother of John Laurens, the only one Washington's aides to die in the war, and a son of Henry Laurens, who had served as president of the Continental Congress and who had been Lachlan McIntosh's longtime friend.

On Sunday, Washington attended the morning services at St. Philip's and the afternoon services at St. Michael's. The rectors at both churches were veterans of the American Revolution and members of the Society of Cincinnati; Dr. Henry Purcell of St. Michael's had served as chaplain to the 2nd South Carolina Regiment.

Washington mounted his white horse early Monday morning, May 9, and rode out of Charleston with an escort including the Cincinnati and the officers of the Charleston militia. As Washington's party rode by, the Charleston Artillery and the German Fusiliers fired ceremonial volleys.

William Washington hosts George Washington

George Washington continued his southward travel and spent Monday night at the home of his cousin, William Washington. President Washington explained, "My going to Colo. Washingtons is to be ascribed to motives of friendship and relationship" (Lipscomb 47).

During the war, William Washington had distinguished himself as a cavalry commander. His horsemen had played a major role in the American victory at Cowpens, and legend has it that Colonel Washington and British Colonel Banastre Tarleton had fought like knights in individual combat as Tarleton withdrew from Cowpens.

The Washington cousins were Virginians, but William Washington relocated to South Carolina when he married Jane Reilly Elliott of South Carolina in 1782. Mr. and Mrs. William Washington took up residence at Sandy Hill, the Elliott family mansion south of Charleston. The former cavalry commander became a member of the South Carolina Jockey Club and installed a racecourse at Sandy Hill. Although his neighbors let their horses roam the woods, he confined his fine thoroughbreds to grassy fields.

As sportsmen, the Washingtons loved race horses and, as planters, they needed animals such as draft horses and oxen. For years, George Washington had been experimenting at Mt. Vernon with jackasses and mules. He was given a large, powerful jackass by the king of Spain that he named Royal Gift. While President Washington was at Sandy Hill, William Washington and other South Carolina planters asked him to loan Royal Gift to them and he agreed.

President Washington continues toward Savannah

George Washington continued southward Tuesday morning and crossed the Edisto River at Pon Pon or Jacksonboro, where the South Carolina Assembly had met in 1782 while the British still occupied Charleston. On Wednesday morning he crossed the Combahee River at Saltketcher, where a ranger named Aeneas Mackintosh had commanded a colonial fort in 1733. Washington soon reached Pocotaligo, the location of Fort Balfour during the American Revolution and also the site of a Yamassee town where Thomas Nairne had been killed at the outbreak of the Yamassee War in 1715. Local planters welcomed Washington with a formal dinner at the tavern in Pocotaligo. They drank to the memory of Colonel John Laurens, who had fallen in a skirmish near Pocotaligo in 1782.

On the morning of May 12, President Washington arrived at Purrysburg on the South Carolina side of the Savannah River. Lachlan McIntosh and four other men met Washington at Purrysburg with a flotilla of boats and an eight-oared presidential barge to transport the presidential party to Savannah.

On the way downstream, they stopped at Mulberry Grove, the plantation given to Nathanael Greene by the state of Georgia. Greene had died young, but his widow Catherine remained at the plantation. Washington and Greene had served together from the beginning of the American Revolution in the summer of 1775 and had grown to like and respect one another; when their wives joined the generals in winter quarters, Martha Washington and Caty Greene became friends. Nathanael and Caty named a son George Washington Greene and named a daughter Martha Washington Greene. During his visit to Mulberry Grove, Washington surely dwelt on Greene's role in winning the war. Washington had picked Greene to succeed Horatio Gates in command of the Southern Department, and Greene had risen to the occasion brilliantly. Greene had severely weakened the British army under Lord Cornwallis in a series of battles across the Carolinas. As a result, Cornwallis had withdrawn to Virginia, where Washington had led French and American forces that entrapped the British army at Yorktown. Once Cornwallis had surrendered, the British government's decision to end the war had become inevitable.

After a brief visit with Caty Greene, Washington resumed his journey downriver. He noted in his diary that it was a difficult voyage: "The wind and the tide being both against us, it was 6 o'clock before we reached the City where we received every demonstration that could be given of joy and respect. We were Seven hours making the passage which is often performed in 4" (Henderson 207).

The Georgia Gazette published this account of Washington's arrival:

> Within ten miles of the city they were met by a number of gentlemen in several boats, and as the President passed by them a band of music played the celebrated song, "He comes, the Hero comes," accompanied with several voices. On his approach to the city the concourse on the Bluff, and the crowds which had pressed into the vessels, evinced the general joy which had been inspired by this most beloved of men, and the ardent desire of all ranks and conditions of people to be gratified by his presence. Upon arriving at the upper part of the harbor he was saluted from the wharves and by the shipping, and particularly by the ship Thomas Wilson, Capt. White, which was beautifully decorated with the colours of various nations. At the foot of the stairs where the President landed he was received by Col. Gunn and Gen. Jackson, who introduced him to the Mayor and Aldermen of the city. The Artillery Company saluted him with 26 discharges from their fieldpieces, and he was then conducted to a house prepared by the Corporation for his accommodation, in St. James's Square, in the following order of procession: Light Infantry Company; Field Officers and other Officers of the Militia; Marshall of the City; Treasurer and Clerk; Recorder; Aldermen; Mayor; President and Suite; Committee of Citizens; Members of the

Cincinnati; Citizens two and two; Artillery Company. (qtd. in Henderson 208)

McIntosh shows Washington around Savannah

Lachlan McIntosh participated in most of the events Washington attended during three days in Savannah. McIntosh and Washington held long-standing respect for one another. McIntosh had served with Washington during the terrible winter at Valley Forge. Then Washington had assigned McIntosh the difficult, if not impossible, task of pacifying the northwest frontier. When McIntosh had endured censure from his political enemies, Washington had not wavered in his regard for McIntosh.

As a member of the Cincinnati, McIntosh was invited to dine with Washington and other dignitaries on the evening Washington arrived in Savannah. The men drank fifteen toasts, including one to the memory of General Nathanael Greene, and the artillery company fired field pieces after each toast. Washington then retired for the evening, and the Georgians drank one more toast to the President of the United States.

The next day, a committee including McIntosh presented an address to Washington:

Sir,

When, having accomplished the great objects of a war, marked in its progress with events that astonished while they instructed the world, you had again returned to the domestic enjoyments of life... there was little probability... that the People of Georgia, however ardently they might desire, should ever be indulged, the happiness of a personal interview with you – but summoned again, as you were, from your retirement, by the united voice and the obvious welfare of you country, you did not hesitate to furnish one more proof that, in comparison to the great duties of social life, all objects of a private nature are with you but secondary considerations; And to this your ruling passion of love for your country it is that we owe the opportunity now offered of congratulating you on your safe arrival in the City of Savannah...

History furnishes instances of some eminently qualified for the field, and of others endued with talents adequate to the intricate affairs of state; but you, Sir, have enriched the annals of America with a proof... that... the virtues and talents of soldier and republican statesman will sometimes dwell together, and both characters derive additional luster from a subserviency to the precepts of Religion...

You have now, Sir, an opportunity of viewing a state which, from its exposed situation, has been peculiarly affected by the calamities of war, but which, under the influences of a happy Government, will rise fast to that rank of prosperity and importance to which her natural advantages so justly entitle her, and which will enable her to reflect back upon the Union all the benefits derived from it...

We make it our prayer to Almighty God that you may be long continued to your country her Ornament and Father, and that it may be more and more exemplified in you, Sir, that to know how to conquer, and to improve the advantages of conquest into blessings to a community, are faculties sometimes bestowed on the same mortal...

> N.W. JONES
> LACH. M'INTOSH
> JOSEPH CLAY
> JOHN HOUSTON
> JOSEPH HABERSHAM (Henderson, 212-13)

In his reply, Washington observed that Georgia was "no less distinguished by its services than by its sufferings in the cause of freedom" (Henderson 214).

Later in the day, Washington dined with the Georgia chapter of the Cincinnati, and proposed a toast to "The Members of the Society of the Cincinnati throughout the globe."

That evening, as Washington noted in his diary, he attended "a dancing Assembly at which there was about 100 well dressed handsome ladies" (Henderson 218).

Washington tours battleground

While Washington was in Savannah, he saw first-hand the sites associated with the American Revolution. British forces commanded by Archibald Campbell of the 71st Highlanders had captured Savannah in 1778. Lachlan McIntosh had been on assignment in the North at the time, but his wife and younger children had remained in Savannah.

Washington had given McIntosh permission to return to the South, where he had taken part in a joint French and American effort to recapture Savannah in 1779. Because McIntosh had failed to persuade the British to send his wife and children out of harm's way, they had endured bombardment while he had participated in laying siege to the city. The siege had ended in a disastrous assault against British fortifications.

Washington's diary entry for May 14 says: "… in Company with Genl. McIntosh, Genl. Wayne, the Mayor and many others (principal Gentlemen of the City,) I visited the City, and the attack & defence of it… Dined to day with a number of the Citizens (not less than 200) in an elegant Bower erected for the occasion on the Bank of the River below the Town. – In the evening there was a tolerable good display of fireworks" (Henderson 220-21).

A chronicle of Washington's Southern Tour reports: "As it fortunately chanced, General McIntosh had been second in command to General Lincoln at the time of the storming of the works; and gave the President a detached and lively account of the principal events of interest which happened during the siege and attack of the city" (Henderson 220).

Charles C. Jones, Jr., a nineteenth-century historian from Georgia, gives this account of Washington's sight-seeing excursion:

> Upon the occasion of President Washington's visit to Savannah in May, 1791, he was attended by General McIntosh when he inspected the lines constructed by the British in 1779 for the defence of Savannah, and the approaches and batteries then made by the Allied Army.
>
> Having himself participated in the siege and in the assault of the 9th of October, General McIntosh was able to convey to the President full information touching the whole affair.
>
> The earth mounds covering the slain, the lines of circumvallation, the sand parapets and gun chambers, had not then yielded to the influences of time and an encroaching population. The scars of the siege were still upon the bosom of the plain, and some of the houses within the limits of

the city bore the marks of the lethal missiles which were then hurled. About him stood those who had passed through that baptism of fire.

The President exhibited a deep interest in everything he then saw and heard. (153-54)

The President pronounces a benediction

When Washington returned from the tour of the battleground at about noon, the Mayor and Aldermen of Savannah presented an address to the President. Washington replied:

> While the virtuous conduct of your citizens, whose patriotism braved all the hardships of the late war, engaged my esteem, the distress peculiar to the state of Georgia, after the peace, excited my deepest regret.
>
> It was with singular satisfaction I perceived that the efficacy of the General Government could interpose effectual relief, and restore tranquility to so deserving a Member of the Union. Your sentiments on this event are worthy of citizens, who, placing a due value on the blessings of peace, desire to maintain it on the immutable principles of justice and good faith. (Henderson 223)

George Washington, first President of the United States, concluded with a benediction upon Lachlan McIntosh and his neighbors, "May you individually be happy."

THE END

BIBLIOGRAPHY

Agnew, Daniel. *Fort McIntosh: Its Times and Men. "Fort Pitt" and Its Times. "Logstown,"on the Ohio.* 1893-1894. Normal, Illinois: Normal Warfare Publications, 2007.

American Revolution Roster: Fort Sullivan (later Fort Moultrie), 1776-1780. Charleston: Fort Sullivan Chapter of the Daughters of the American Revolution, 1976.

Babits, Lawrence E. *A devil of a whipping: The Battle of Cowpens.* Chapel Hill: University of North Carolina Press, 1998.

--- and Joshua B. Howard. *Long, obstinate and bloody: The Battle of Guilford Courthouse.* Chapel Hill: University of North Carolina Press, 2009.

Barthorp, Michael. *The Jacobite Rebellions, 1689-1745.* London: Osprey, 1982.

Barton, John. "The Spey – From Source to Sea." *Clan Chattan: The Journal of Clan Chattan* XII.4 (2010): 241-243.

"Battle of Moore's Creek Bridge." *Learn NC.* 26 June 2013. <http://www.learnnc.org/lp/editions/nchist-revolution/4267>

Bingham, Caroline. *Beyond the Highland Line: Highland History and Culture.* London: Constable, 1991.

Boatner III, Mark M. *Encyclopedia of the American Revolution.* New York: David McKay Company, 1976.

Bodle, Wayne. *The Valley Forge Winter: Civilians and soldiers in war.* University Park: The Pennsylvania State University Press, 2004.

Borick, Carl P. *A Gallant Defense: The Siege of Charleston, 1780.* Columbia: University of South Carolina Press, 2003.

---. *Relieve us of this burthen: American Prisoners of War in The Revolutionary South, 1780-1782.* Columbia: The University of South Carolina Press, 2012.

Boswell, James. *The Journal of a Tour to the Hebrides with Samuel Johnson, LL.D.* 1785. Boston: Houghton Mifflin, 1965.

Britt Jr., Albert S., and Lilla M. Hawes, eds. "The Mackenzie Papers, Part II." *Georgia Historical Quarterly* LVII.1 (1973): 113-115.

Campbell, Colin, ed. *Journal of an expedition against the rebels of Georgia in North America under the orders of Archibald Campbell Esquire Lieut. Colol. of His Majesty's 71ˢᵗ Regimt. 1778.* Augusta, Ga.: Richmond County Historical Society, 1981.

"(Captain) William McIntosh." *Ezell Family Tree.* 2 July 2013. <http://ezell.familytreeguide.com/getperson.php?personID=I 10838&tree=T1>

"Case of George McIntosh." *Georgia Historical Quarterly* 3.3 (1919): 131-45.

Cashin, Edward J. *Lachlan McGillivray, Indian Trader: The shaping of the Southern Colonial Frontier.* Athens: University of Georgia Press, 1992.

--- *William Bartram and the American Revolution.* Columbia: University of South Carolina Press, 2000.

--- and Heard Robertson. *Augusta and the American Revolution: Events in the Georgia Back Country, 1773-1783.* Augusta, Ga.: Richmond County Historical Society, 1975.

Cate, Margaret Davis. *Our Todays and Yesterdays.* 1930. Spartanburg, S.C.: The Reprint Company, 1972.

"Cemetery Guide." City of Savannah Department of Cemeteries. 9 May 2011 <http://www.savannahga.gov/cityweb/cemeteries web>

Chernow, Ron. *Washington: A life.* New York: Penguin Press, 2010.

"Col. David Gregg McIntosh: Clan Chattan Heroes of the American Civil War." *Clan Chattan: The Journal of Clan Chattan.* Ed. Robert McGillivray. XII.3 (2009): 164-169.

Coleman, Kenneth. *The American Revolution in Georgia.* Athens: University of Georgia Press, 1958.

"Colonel John McIntosh laid to rest for the third time in McIntosh Co." *The Darien News* 28 Oct. 2010: 1+

Colonial Records of the State of Georgia (CRG), 28 vols. 1904-10. New York: AMS Press, 1970.

Coulter, E. Merton. *Georgia: A short history.* Third Edition. Chapel Hill: University of North Carolina Press, 1960.

Dann, John C. *The Revolution Remembered: Eyewitness accounts of the War for Independence.* Chicago: University of Chicago Press, 1980.

Davis, Burke. *George Washington and the American Revolution.* New York: Random House, 1975.

Davis Jr., Robert Scott. *Encounters on a March Through Georgia in 1779: The Maps and Memorandums of John Wilson, Engineer, 71st Highland Regiment.* Sylvania, Ga.: Partridge Pond Press, 1986.

---. *Georgians in the Revolution: At Kettle Creek (Wilkes County) and Burke County.* Easley, S.C.: Southern Historical Press, 1996.

Dobson, David. *Directory of Scots in the Carolinas, 1680-1830.* Baltimore: Genealogical Publishing, 1986.

---. *Scottish Emigration to Colonial America, 1607-1785.* Athens: University of Georgia Press, 1994.

Dupuy, R. Ernest and Trevor N. Dupuy. *The Compact History of the Revolutionary War.* New York: Hawthorn Books, 1963.

Edgar, Walter. *South Carolina: A History.* Columbia: University of South Carolina Press, 1998.

Fitzpatrick, John C. *The Writings of George Washington from the Original Manuscript Sources 1745-1799.* 39 vols. Washington: United States Government Printing Office, 1931-44.

"Flora MacDonald." *Wikipedia.* 26 June 2013. <http://en.wikipedia.org/wiki/Flora_McDonald>

Frank, Andrew K. "The Rise and Fall of William McIntosh: Authority and Identity on the Early American Frontier." *Georgia Historical Quarterly* 86.1 (Spring 2002): 18-48.

Furneaux, Rupert. *The Pictorial History of the American Revolution as told by Witnesses and Participants.* Chicago: JG. Ferguson (distributed by Doubleday), 1973.

Galbraith, Dr J.J. "The Battle of Glenshiel, 1719." Presented to the Gaelic Society of Inverness, Nov. 23, 1928. Rpt. Bruceton Mills, W. Va.: Unicorn Limited, c. 1994.

Gellhorn, Martha. "Introduction, 1967." *The face of war.* London: Sphere Books Limited, 1967. 11-12.

Gladstone, Mattie. Notes, manuscripts and photocopies related to McIntosh genealogy. The Ridge, Darien, Georgia: unpublished, personal communication, 1980 - 2002.

---. Family Group Record for John Mor McIntosh. Copies may be available at the McIntosh County Historical Society office at Fort King George Historic Site at Darien, Georgia.

---. Genealogical chart showing descendants of William Mackintosh, 3rd Proprietor of Borlum. Copies may be available at the McIntosh County Historical Society office at Fort King George Historic Site at Darien, Georgia.

Hamer, Philip M., ed. *The Papers of Henry Laurens*. 9 vols. Columbia: University of South Carolina Press, 1968-81.

Harden, William. *A History of Savannah and South Georgia*. Vol. 1. Atlanta: Cherokee Publishing Company, 1969.

Harrington, Peter. *Culloden 1746: The Highland Clans' Last Charge*. London: Osprey, 1991.

Hawes, Lilla M., ed. *Collections of the Georgia Historical Society Vol. XII: The Papers of Lachlan McIntosh, 1774-1779*. Savannah: Georgia Historical Society, 1957.

---, ed. "The Papers of James Jackson 1781-1798." *Collections of the Georgia Historical Society Vol. XI*. Savannah: Georgia Historical Society, 1935.

---, ed. *University of Georgia Libraries Miscellanea Publications, No. 7: Lachlan McIntosh Papers in the University of Georgia Libraries*. Athens: University of Georgia Press, 1968.

Henderson, Archibald. *Washington's Southern Tour, 1791*. Boston: Houghton Mifflin Company, 1923.

Holland, Marcus. "Famous duel between Gwinnett, McIntosh to be played out again." *Savannah Morning News* 15 May 1996: 1A+

Howard, Joshua B. "'Things here wear a melancholy appearance:' The American defeat at Briar Creek." *Georgia Historical Quarterly* 88.4 (Winter 2004): 477-98.

Hough, Franklin B., ed. *The Siege of Charleston by the British Fleet and Army under the command of Admiral Arbuthnot and Sir Henry Clinton which terminated with the surrender of that place on the 12th of May, 1780*. 1867. Spartanburg, S.C.: The Reprint Company, 1975.

---, ed. *The Siege of Savannah by the Combined American and French Forces under the command of Gen. Lincoln and the Count d'Estaing in the Autumn of 1779*. 1866. Spartanburg, S.C.: The Reprint Company, 1975.

Hunter, James. *A Dance Called America: The Scottish Highlands in the United States and Canada*. Edinburgh: Mainstream Publishing, 1994.

Ivers, Larry E. *British drums on the Southern Frontier: The military colonization of Georgia, 1733-1749.* Chapel Hill: The University of North Carolina Press, 1974.

---. *Colonial Forts of South Carolina 1670-1775.* Columbia: University of South Carolina Press, 1970.

Jackson III, Harvey Hardaway. *General Lachlan McIntosh, 1727-1806: A Biography.* Diss. University of Georgia, 1973. Athens: University of Georgia, 1973.

---. *Lachlan McIntosh and the politics of revolutionary Georgia.* 1979. Athens: University of Georgia Press, 2003.

James, William Dobein. *A sketch of the life of Brig. Gen. Francis Marion and a history of his brigade from its rise in June 1780 until disbanded in December, 1782, with descriptions of characters and scenes not heretofore published. Containing also an appendix with copies of letters which passed between several of the leading characters of that day, principally from Gen. Greene to Gen. Marion.* Marietta, Ga.: Continental Book Co., 1948.

Jamie, Kathleen. "The Way We Live." *A Poem a Day.* Ed. Karen McCosker and Nicholas Albery. South Royalton, Vermont: Steerforth Press, 1994.

"John McIntosh." *GlynnGen.com Coastal Georgia Genealogy & History.* 10 March 2011 <http://www.glynn gen.com/military/amrev/glynn/mcintoshjno.htm>

"Johnnie Cope." *Rampant Scotland.* 29 Jan. 2014. <http://www.rampantscotland.com/songs/blsongs_cope.htm>

Johnson, Dan. "Battle site rarely gets recognition," *The Sylvania Telephone,* 9 Aug. 1996, 1-2.

Johnson, Samuel. *A Journey to the Western Islands of Scotland.* 1775. Boston: Houghton Mifflin, 1965.

Johnston, Elizabeth Lichtenstein. *Recollections of a Georgia Loyalist.* 1836. Spartanburg: The Reprint Company, 1974.

Johnstone, James. *Memoirs of the Rebellion in 1745 and 1746 by the Chevalier de Johnstone.* 1820. Rpt. in *Culloden 1746: The Last Highland Charge.* Stratford-upon-Avon: Cromwell Productions, 1993.

Jolly, William. *Flora Macdonald in Uist: a Study of the Heroine in her Native Surroundings.* Appended to *The Life of Flora Macdonald* by Alexander Macgregor. Stirling: Eneas Mackay, 1932.

Jones Jr., Charles C., ed. *The Siege of Savannah by the Fleet of Count D'Estaing in 1779*. 1874. New York: The New York Times & Arno Press, 1968.

Julien, Carl and Chapman J. Milling. *Beneath so kind a sky*. 1947. Columbia: University of South Carolina Press, 1969.

Kellogg, Louise Phelps, ed. *Frontier Advance on the Upper Ohio, 1778-1779*. 1916. Charleston, S.C.: Bibliolife, 2011.

Kennedy, Benjamin, ed. *Muskets, Cannon Balls & Bombs: Nine narratives of the Siege of Savannah in 1779*. Savannah: The Beehive Press, 1974.

Kerber, Linda K. *Women of the Republic: Intellect and Ideology in Revolutionary America*. New York: W.W. Norton, 1986.

Landers, H.L. *The Battle of Camden, South Carolina, August 16, 1780*. Washington: United States Government Printing Office, 1929.

Lane, Mills, ed. *General Oglethorpe's Georgia: Colonial Letters. 1733-1743*. 2 vols. Savannah: The Beehive Press, 1975.

Larimer, Charlie Fraser, ed. *Tales of Dunlichity: The Stories of Willie MacQueen*. Chicago: Sigourney Press, 2001.

Lawrence, Alexander A. "General Lachlan McIntosh and His Suspension from Continental Command During the Revolution." *Georgia Historical Quarterly* 38.2 (1954): 101-141.

---. "General Robert Howe and the British Capture of Savannah in 1778." *Georgia Historical Quarterly* 36.4 (1952): 303-327.

---. *Storm over Savannah: The story of Count d'Estaing and the Siege of the Town in 1779*. Athens: University of Georgia Press, 1951.

Lenman, Bruce. *The Jacobite Clans of the Great Glen, 1650-1784*. 1984. Aberdeen: Scottish Cultural Press, 1995.

Lewis, Bessie. *They Called Their Town Darien*. Darien, Ga.: The Darien News, 1975.

Lockhart, Paul. *The Drillmaster of Valley Forge: The Baron de Steuben and the Making of the American Army*. New York: Smithsonian Books, 2008.

"Lt. Benjamin McIntosh." *The Briskey Crossroads.* 10 March 2011 <http://briskeycrossroads.com/McIntosh. html>

Lumpkin, Henry. *From Savannah to Yorktown: The American Revolution in the South*. Columbia: University of South Carolina Press, 1981.

Macdonald of Castleton, Donald J. *Clan Donald*. Loanhead, Mithlothian, Scotland: Macdonald Publishers, 1978.

MacDonald, Norman H. *The Clan Ranald of Knoydart & Glengarry: A history of the MacDonalds or MacDonells of Glengarry*. Edinburgh: Norman H. MacDonald, 1979.

MacDonell, Alexander R. "The Settlement of the Scotch." *Georgia Historical Quarterly* 20.3 (1936): 250-62.

Macgregor, Alexander. *The Life of Flora Macdonald*. 5th ed. Stirling: Eneas Mackay, 1932.

MacKintosh, Angus. "Brigadier MacKintosh of Borlum." *The Celtic Monthly* Jan. 1903: 73-75.

---. "How the feud between the Camerons and Mackintoshes was ended." *The Celtic Monthly* Apr. 1903: 122-24.

---. "Lady MacKintosh of the '45.'" *The Celtic Monthly* Dec.1902: 45-49.

Mackintosh of Mackintosh, Margaret, revised by Lachlan Mackintosh of Mackintosh, 30th Chief of Mackintosh. *The History of Clan Mackintosh and Clan Chattan*. Edinburgh: The Pentland Press Limited, 1997.

Maclean, Fitzroy. *Highlanders: A History of the Scottish Clans*. New York: Penguin, 1995.

Maclean, J.P. *Flora MacDonald in America*. Lumberton, N.C.: A.W. McLean, 1909.

MacLean, John. *Historical and Traditional Sketches of Highland Families and of the Highlands*. 1848. 24 June 2013. <http://www.electricscotland.com/books/ highlands8.htm>.

Massey, Gregory D. *John Laurens and the American Revolution*. Columbia: University of South Carolina Press, 2000.

Massey, R.J. "John McIntosh." *Men of Mark of Georgia Vol. I*. Ed. William J. Northen. Atlanta: A.B. Caldwell, 1907. 241-45.

McCall, Hugh. *The history of Georgia : containing brief sketches of the most important events, up to the present day*. 2 vols. 1811-16. Atlanta: A.B. Caldwell, 1909.

McGillivray, Robert. "A Tribute to Virtue." *Clan Chattan: The Journal of Clan Chattan* XII.5 (2011): 269-271.

---. "Colonel Anne of the '45." *Clan Chattan: The Journal of Clan Chattan* XI.2 (2002): 70-79.

McGuire, Thomas J. *Battle of Paoli*. Mechanicsburg, Pa.: Stackpole Books, 2000.

McIntosh, Lachlan, "Journal of the Siege of Charlestown, 1780." *University of Georgia Libraries Miscellanea Publications, No. 7: Lachlan McIntosh Papers in the University of Georgia Libraries.* Ed. Lilla Mills Hawes. Athens: University of Georgia Press, 1968. 96-122.

McLynn, Frank. *The Jacobites.* London: Routledge & Kegan Paul, 1985.

Mealing, Isobel Thorpe. Personal correspondence Jan. 2, 2002, Darien, Ga. She provided photocopies of her research on our ancestors Alexander McDonald and his son Alexander. She grew up on a McDonald plantation at Harris Neck in McIntosh County and lived in Darien during the last years of her long, active life. Copies of some of her records may be available from the McIntosh County Historical Society or from Jim McDonald of Savannah, the genealogist of Clan Donald USA.

Meldrum, E. Alexander. "Loch Moy and its Islands." *Clan Chattan: The Journal of Clan Chattan* XII.5 (2011): 264-268.

"Message depicts S.C. in Revolutionary War: Columbia museum buys rare British letter describing Charleston in 1780." *The State* 30 Nov. 2008: B6. (Reprinted from *The Post and Courier* of Charleston, S.C.)

Migliazzo, Arlin C. *To make this land our own: Community, identity, and cultural adaptation in Purrysburg Township, South Carolina, 1732-1865.* Columbia: University of South Carolina Press, 2007.

Mitchell, Frances Letcher. *Georgia Land and People.* 1900. Spartanburg, S.C.: The Reprint Company, 1974.

Moncreiffe of that Ilk, Sir Iain and David Hicks. *The Highland Clans: The dynastic origins, chiefs and background of the Clans and of some other families connected with Highland history.* 1967. New York: Bramhall House, 1977.

Moss, Bobby Gilmer. *Roster of the Loyalists in the Battle of Moore's Creek Bridge.* Blacksburg, S.C.: Scotia-Hibernia Press, 1992.

---. *Roster of South Carolina Patriots in the American Revolution.* Baltimore: Genealogical Publishing, 1983.

Moultrie, William. *Memoirs of the American Revolution.* 1802. New York: The New York Times & Arno Press, 1968.

Murray, Patrick. "Memoir of Major Patrick Murray, who served in the 60th from 1770 to 1793." *The Annals of the King's Royal Rifle Corps. Volume 1: The Royal Americans.* Lewis Butler. London: Smith, Elder & Co., 1913. 288-319.

Notes by a Highland Chief in 1784: Notes by Sir Aeneas Mackintosh of Mackintosh. Bruceton Mills, W.Va.: Scotpress/ Unicorn Limited, 1997.

"North Carolina." *Clan Chattan: The Journal of Clan Chattan* XII.5 (2011): 284.

"Oglethorpe's Treaty with the Lower Creek Indians." *Georgia Historical Quarterly* 4.1 (March 1920): 3-16.

Parker, Anthony W. *Scottish Highlanders in Colonial Georgia: The recruitment, emigration, and settlement at Darien, 1735-1748.* 1997. Athens: University of Georgia Press, 2002.

Piechocinski, Elizabeth Carpenter. *The Old Burying Ground: Colonial Park Cemetery, Savannah, Georgia 1750-1853.* Savannah: The Oglethorpe Press, 1999.

Pottle, Frederick A. and Charles H. Bennett, eds. *Boswell's Journal of A Tour to the Hebrides with Samuel Johnson, LL.D. Now First Published from the Original Manuscript.* New York: Literary Guild, 1936.

Ramsay, David. *Memoirs of the life of Martha Laurens Ramsay, who died in Charleston, S.C., on the 10th of June, 1811, in the 52nd year of her age,* 2nd edition. Charleston: Samuel Etheridge, Jun'r, 1812.

"Ranger's Report of Travels with General Oglethorpe in Georgia and Florida, 1739-1742." *Travels in the American Colonies.* 1916. Ed. Newton D. Mereness. New York: Antiquarian Press, 1961: 215-36.

Rankin, Hugh F. *Francis Marion: The Swamp Fox.* New York: Thomas Y. Crowell Company, 1973.

Redfearn, Daniel Huntley. *Alexander McDonald of New Inverness, Georgia, and his descendants.* Miami: Daniel Huntley Redfearn, 1954.

"Reinterment of Major General John McIntosh, Oct. 23, 2010." [DVD] Brunswick, Ga.: Dale Leonard Productions, 2010.

Rogers Jr., George C. "A Tribute to Henry Laurens." *South Carolina Historical Magazine* 92.4 (1991): 269-276.

Rose, D. Murray. *Historical Notes or Essays on the '15 and '45.* Edinburgh: William Brown, 1896.

Ross, William Fraser. "Family of Mackintosh of Borlum." *Clan Chattan* I.6 (1939): 180-90.

Rowland, Lawrence S., Alexander Moore and George C. Rogers Jr. *The History of Beaufort County, Volume I, 1514-1861.* Columbia: University of South Carolina Press, 1996.

Scarlett, James D. "Another Highland Road." *Clan Chattan: The Journal of Clan Chattan* XII.5 (2011): 290-297.

Schafer, Elizabeth D. "MacDonald, Flora (1722-1790)." *The American Revolution 1775-1783: An Encyclopedia.* Ed. Richard L. Blanco. New York: Garland, 1993.

Scheer, George F. and Hugh F. Rankin. *Rebels and Redcoats.* New York: The World Publishing Company, 1957.

Seton, Bruce. "Dress of the Jacobite Army." Rpt. Bruceton Mills, W. Va.: Unicorn Limited, c. 1994.

Seymour, William. *Battles in Britain 1066-1746*, v. 2. London: Sidgwick & Jackson, 1989.

"Sir Aeneas Mackintosh and Allan McDonald." *Clan Chattan: The Journal of Clan Chattan* X.4 (1998): 242.

"Skye Boat Song." *Rampant Scotland.* 8 Jan. 2014. <http://www.rampantscotland.com/songs/blsongs_skye.htm>

Smurthwaite, David. *The Ordnance Survey Complete Guide to the Battlefields of Britain.* London: Webb & Bower, 1987.

Spalding, Thomas. "Lachlan McIntosh, 1725-1806: Soldier." *The National Portrait Gallery of Distinguished Americans*, v. 3. 1867. New York: Arno Press and The New York Times, 1970: 99-110.

---. "Sketch of the life of General James Oglethorpe presented to the Georgia Historical Society." *Collections of the Georgia Historical Society* v. 1. Savannah: Georgia Historical Society, 1840: 240-95.

Stewart, David. *Sketches of the character, manners and present state of the Highlanders of Scotland; with details of the military service of the Highland Regiments.* Vol. 2. 1822. Edinburgh: John Donald Publishers, 1977.

Stokes, Thomas L. *The Savannah.* 1951. Athens: University of Georgia Press, 1982.

Sullivan, Buddy. *Early Days on the Georgia Tidewater: The story of McIntosh County & Sapelo.* Darien: McIntosh County Board of Commissioners, 1990.

--- . Supplemental Appendixes. *Early Days on the Georgia Tidewater: The story of McIntosh County & Sapelo*. 1991.

Thane, Elswyth. *The Fighting Quaker: Nathanael Greene*. New York: Hawthorne Books, 1972.

Toffey, John J. *A Woman Nobly Planned: Fact and Myth in the Legacy of Flora MacDonald*. Durham, N.C.: Carolina Academic Press, 1997.

"Traditions of the Mackintoshes of Borlum." *The Celtic Monthly* v.? (d.?): 165-68, 187-89. Rpt. in *Mackintosh Family History*. Bruceton Mills, W. Va.: Unicorn Limited, c. 1994: 165-68, 187-89.

Uhlendorf, Bernard A., trans. and ed. *The Siege of Charleston with an account of the province of South Carolina: Diaries and letters of Hessian officers from the von Jungkenn Papers in the William L. Clements Library*. Ann Arbor: University of Michigan Press, 1938.

Vining, Elizabeth Gray. *Flora: A biography*. New York: J.B. Lippincott, 1966.

Ward, Christopher. *The War of the Revolution*. 2 vols. Ed. John Richard Alden. New York: Macmillan, 1952.

White, George. *Historical Collections of Georgia*. 1855. Baltimore: Genealogical Publishing Company, 1969.

Wightman, Orrin Sage, photographer, and story by Margaret Davis Cate. *Early Days of Coastal Georgia*. St. Simons Island, Georgia: Fort Frederica Association, 1955.

Wilson, John. *The Gazetteer of Scotland*. 1882. Lovettsville, Va.: Willow Bend Books, 1996.

Williams, Edward G., ed. "A Revolutionary Journal and Orderly Book of General Lachlan McIntosh's Expedition, 1778." *The Western Pennsylvania Historical Magazine* 43 (1960): 1-17, 157-77, 267-88.

Young, Peter and John Adair. *From Hastings to Culloden (Battlefields in Britain)*. Kineton: The Roundwood Press, 1979.

DIRECTORY

MACDONALD, FLORA, SEE **McDONALD, FLORY.**

MACKINTOSH, AENEAS, 22nd Chief of Clan Mackintosh, sometimes called by the Gaelic name Angus. He was related to the McIntosh men in Georgia through the 16th Chief of Clan Mackintosh.

He served in the British army in colonial America, was commissioned lieutenant at the Palachacola ranger fort on the Savannah River in 1732, and was one of twenty-five men who accompanied Oglethorpe on a visit to the Creek nation in 1739.

In 1740, he returned to Scotland, and succeeded as the Chief of Clan Mackintosh when his older brother died. He married Anne Farquharson in 1741.

In the Rising of 1745, he served in the government army while his wife raised the Mackintoshes for the rebels. He surrendered to rebel forces at Dornoch in March of 1746. He was set free when the Rising ended with the Battle of Culloden in April of 1746, and managed to save the Mackintosh estate at Moy from destruction.

He died in 1770 and was succeeded by his nephew, also named Aeneas.

MACKINTOSH, AENEAS (1751-1820), 23rd Chief of Clan Mackintosh. He succeeded as Chief when his uncle died in 1770.

When the American Revolution began, he raised a company for the 71st Regiment of Foot and was given the rank of captain. His regiment fought in the campaigns across New York, New Jersey and Pennsylvania in 1776 and 1777.

In 1778 he participated in the capture of Savannah. In 1779 he fought in the Battle of Brier Creek and helped defend Savannah against an assault by American and French forces.

In 1780 he participated in the capture of Charleston and the Battle of Camden.

As one of only three captains remaining in the 71st Regiment in March of 1781, he commanded a wing of the regiment at the Battle of Guilford Courthouse (Babits and Howard 86-88, 219).

He was taken prisoner when Cornwallis surrendered at Yorktown in October of 1781.

He returned to Scotland in 1783 and managed the farming and forestry operations on his estates. An accidental fire destroyed the Mackintosh manor house, and he constructed the fourth building known as Moy Hall in 1800.

King George created Aeneas a baronet in 1812, and he became known as Sir Aeneas.

The fact that he and his wife Margaret did not have any children became woven into a legend. Morrit of Rokeby wrote a poem titled "The Curse of Moy" that was published in *Minstrelcy of the Scottish Border* in 1802. According to the legend, a distraught woman put a curse on the Mackintosh chiefs that prevented them from having sons to succeed them. Sir Aeneas was the fourth chief who had no son to succeed him, and the next chief also was childless (Mackintosh 66-68).

When Sir Aeneas died, his widow had a tribute to his character inscribed onto a seventy-foot granite obelisk:

Sacred to the memory of Sir Aeneas Mackintosh Baronet
Captain of Clan Chattan
Who died at Moy Hall on 21st January 1820 in the 69th year
of his age
Having in youth after the example of his forefathers served his
country in war
He retired to this ancient seat of his family
And married Margaret, youngest daughter of Sir Ludovic
Grant of Dalvey Baronet
And grand-daughter to Sir Patrick Grant of Dalvey Bart. and
Sir James Innes of Bahennie Bart.
Without relinquishing the Patriarchal character of a Highland
Chief
He combined it with an exemplary observance of all the
duties of civilised society
And with the exercise of every domestic and social affection
His charities were extensive, unostentatious, and
discriminating

His hospitality and Kindness were peculiarly felt
By all those whom the Remains of the Ancient Usages and
feelings of his country recommended to his Protection
His Paternal Regard to his Tenants displayed itself in a
spontaneous remission of a third part of their Rents
During the general Distress which prevailed in the last years
of his life
And it may be truly said of him
That it was his constant and earnest desire
To do Justice, to love Mercy, and to walk humbly
with his God.

THIS MONUMENT IS ERECTED BY HIS WIDOW,
DAME MARGARET MACKINTOSH
(Mackintosh 65-66)

MACKINTOSH, ANNE (1725–1784), known as Colonel Anne, married Aeneas the 22nd Chief of Clan Mackintosh on January 14, 1741. She was the daughter of John Farquharson of Invercauld, the chief of that branch of Clan Chattan. John Farquharson had fought under the command of Brigadier William Mackintosh of Borlum in the Rising of 1715 and had been taken prisoner with the other Clan Chattan soldiers at Preston.

In the early stages of the Rising of 1745, Aeneas raised a company of militia for the government. His wife Anne, at the age of 20, raised the clan for the Jacobites without any hindrance from him.

Lady Anne Mackintosh hosted Prince Charles and a few attendants at Moy, home of the Chief of Clan Mackintosh, on February 16, 1746. A government attempt to capture the Prince was thwarted in the Rout of Moy.

When Aeneas surrendered to Jacobite forces, according to the official clan historian, Prince Charles sent Aeneas Mackintosh to Moy to be held prisoner by his wife Lady Anne Mackintosh.

On April 17, a detachment of government troops was sent to Moy to bring in all the cattle and another detachment was sent to take Lady Anne Mackintosh to Inverness.

She remained in custody at Inverness for six weeks.

In 1748, Lady Anne Mackintosh visited London and attended a ball given by William Augustus, the Duke of Cumberland.

When her husband Aeneas died in 1770 and was succeeded by his nephew Aeneas, Lady Anne Mackintosh moved to Edinburgh. She died on March 2, 1784.

MACKINTOSH, ANGUS. SEE **MACKINTOSH, AENE-AS**, 22nd Chief of Clan Mackintosh.

MACKINTOSH, BENJAMIN, the natural son of Brigadier William Mackintosh of Borlum. He was one of the founders of Darien led by his cousin John Mackintosh Mor in 1736. He was the father of Roderick "Rory" McIntosh, John McIntosh, Winnewood McIntosh, and others. He was the grandfather of William McIntosh, a British emissary to the Creek Indians, and the great-grandfather of Chief William McIntosh.

He moved from Darien to Charleston in October of 1740.

MACKINTOSH, JOHN (1698 or 1700-1761), known as John Mackintosh Mor, teenage soldier in the Jacobite Rising of 1715, leader of the colonists at Darien in 1736, father of Colonel William McIntosh, General Lachlan McIntosh, and others.

He was taken prisoner in the invasion of Florida in 1740 and held in a Spanish jail.

He was released in 1743 and returned to his family in Georgia.

He died in 1761 at his farm near Darien and was buried in the old city cemetery in Darien.

MACKINTOSH, MARJORY FRASER (1701-?), wife of John Mackintosh Mor. She was born in 1701 at Boleskine, a daughter of John Fraser of Garthmore and Elizabeth Fraser of Errogy. She married John Mackintosh on March 4, 1725 (Gladstone, Family Group Record).

After her husband was taken prisoner in the Battle of Mosa in 1740, Marjory took three of their children to Palachacola and sought refuge from John Mackintosh, a ranger captain who was distantly related to her husband.

Based on the scant source material available, biographer Harvey H. Jackson concludes that Marjory reunited with her husband after he was released from prison in Spain. After reporting that Marjory "returned to Darien to await her husband's release" (4), Jackson reports: "Sometime between 1744 and 1748 John McIntosh was released and the family reunited... During the next four years Lachlan McIntosh remained with his family at Darien..." (5).

Family genealogist Mattie Gladstone records Marjory's date of death as "after May, 1741" the place of death as Darien and the location of the grave as the old city cemetery in Darien.

MACKINTOSH, WILLIAM (c. 1663-1743), Jacobite officer in the Risings of 1715 and 1719. William Mackintosh was the great-grandson of the founder of the Mackintosh of Borlum family. He was often referred to as Borlum, although in 1715 he was technically the younger of Borlum because his father was still alive. The lands of Borlum were on the River Ness about five miles to the southwest of Inverness. William Mackintosh possessed the estate of Raits in Badenoch.

William Mackintosh was born around 1663. He received a Master of Arts at Kings College and was considered a man of polite education and good knowledge. In 1686 he became the father of a natural son, Benjamin.

He received military training in France and in the Guards of King William and Queen Anne. While in England, he married Mary Reade of Ipsden, Oxfordshire. Before their marriage in 1688, she had been a Maid of Honour to Princess Anne, later Queen Anne.

The couple had five children: Lauchlan, 5th of Borlum; Shaw, 6th of Borlum; Winwood; Maria Forbes; and Helen.

William Mackintosh became a Jacobite agent and was sent on a mission to James Edward Stuart's residence at Bar-le-Due in Lorraine. By the time William Mackintosh returned to Scotland in 1714, he was an experienced soldier in the French service.

Brigadier William Mackintosh of Borlum remained in Scotland after the Battle of Glenshiel in 1719. He was imprisoned in 1729 for his part in the Rising of 1715. He refused to take an oath of allegiance to the king, and spent his last fifteen years as a prisoner in Edinburgh Castle. He died January 7, 1743, at the age of about 80 (Mackintosh; MacKintosh, "Brigadier;" Moncreiffe; Rose; Sullivan).

McDONALD (also spelled MacDonald, Macdonald, M' Donald, McDonnell, and other variants), a very common name in Scotland and America. *Roster of the Loyalists in the Battle of Moore's*

Creek Bridge lists twenty-seven men named McDonald (Moss 31-39). Coincidentally, *American Revolution Roster Fort Sullivan* also lists twenty-seven people named McDonald (238-40).

People named McDonald are generally assumed to be part of Clan Donald, but the name was so common that it appears among other clans as well. A footnote to "Sir Aeneas Mackintosh and Allan McDonald" in the journal *Clan Chattan* says:

> This tale is a reminder of those MacDonalds who were faithful followers of the Mackintoshes... Sir Aeneas Mackintosh of Mackintosh in his memoirs written about 1780 says that "the hereditary standard-bearer to Mackintosh is Macdonald whose descendants live in Glenroy and speak nothing but Gaelic." In an "Obligation and Declaration" dated 1727 Angus MacDonald of Muirlaggan refers to himself as Ensign and Banner Bearer to the Captain of Clan Chattan and says his predecessors had held this position for 300 years and upwards. It is also a reminder that surname alone does not always indicate one's clan. (242)

McDONALD, ALEXANDER, common name in Scotland and America. For example, *American Revolution Roster Fort Sullivan* lists four soldiers named Alexander McDonald (238-40). *Roster of the Loyalists in the Battle of Moore's Creek Bridge* lists five men named Alexander McDonald (Moss 31-39). "Alexander" is commonly used as the English version of the Gaelic name "Alasdair" and variants such as "Alistair" and "Alister."

There were several men named Alexander McDonald in colonial Georgia.

McDONALD, ALEXANDER (c. 1715-1771), emigrant from Scotland to Darien, soldier in the regiment at Frederica, ancestor of the author.

Marriage records of the Kingussie Parish Register, Invernesshire, indicate that "Alex McDonald in Riatt and Mary Gordon in Laggan" had been married for three years when the *Mary Ann* set sail (Mealing).

I have been unable to find any mention of a place named Riatt and assume the scribe misspelled Raits, a place in Mackintosh of Borlum territory where John Mackintosh Mor lived for awhile. A subsequent owner renamed the estate Belleville, apparently because the Gaelic name Raits reminded him of the English word rat. Isabel Mealing found a source explaining that Raits comes from the Gaelic Ràt meaning a stone circle. Another place called Rait is a ruined ancient castle on the east side of the River Nairn, two miles south of the town of Nairn, which is near Inverness (Wilson 382).

Alexander McDonald was one of five recruits for the Independent Company of Foot who sailed to Georgia aboard the *Mary Ann* in the summer of 1737. His wife Mary accompanied him (*CRG* 21: 443). Their son Alexander was born in 1750. The elder Alexander McDonald was granted a tract of land in 1751 in recognition of his service in the regiment at Frederica (*CRG* 6: 413).

McDONALD, ALEXANDER (1750–1844), soldier in the 2nd South Carolina Regiment during the American Revolution, ancestor of the author.

Alexander McDonald Jr., as he is called in family histories, was the son of Alexander McDonald, who had emigrated from Scotland to Darien and had served in the regiment at Frederica.

Records of the American Revolution show that Alexander McDonald enlisted November 4, 1775, as a sergeant in the 2nd South Carolina Regiment, was promoted to sergeant major on November 16, 1778, and re-enlisted on November 1, 1779. Based on this information, he apparently participated in the defense of Fort Sullivan, the siege of Savannah, and the encampment at Sheldon. He could have been among the soldiers captured when the American army surrendered at Charleston.

Alexander McDonald Jr. married Christine McLeod, daughter of Scottish emigrant Murdoch McLeod, who was a loyalist during the Revolution. Murdoch McLeod's property was confiscated by an act of Georgia made at Augusta in 1782.

Alexander and Christine had three known children: Alexander; William (1772-1844); and Daniel (1777 or 1778-1856).

Alexander McDonald Jr. died in 1844 at the age of 94 (Moss, *South Carolina* 615; Redfearn 28, 29, 31, 77).

McDONALD, ALLEN, a sergeant in the 2nd South Carolina Regiment and later in Marion's brigade. He carried a regimental flag during the assault on Savannah in 1779.

He was among patriot prisoners being marched under guard toward Charleston when Francis Marion's band attacked the guard on August 20, 1780, and freed the prisoners. From that time on, he served in Marion's partisan band.

He distinguished himself in marksmanship, horsemanship and extraordinary bravery in the autumn of 1780.

He died in battle during the siege of Fort Motte in the spring of 1781.

McDONALD, FLORY (1722–1790), legendary Highlander who rescued Bonnie Prince Charlie in 1746.

Although her name is usually spelled Flora MacDonald or Macdonald, her wedding contract uses the spelling Flory McDonald. In her native language her first name may have been Floraidh – the Gaelic equivalent of Flory – and her first name is known in legend as Fionnghal – a Gaelic term meaning "the fair one" (Toffey 34-35; Vining 103).

She emigrated to North Carolina in 1774. Her husband and sons were officers in loyalist and British military units during the American Revolution and fought in the Battle of Moore's Creek Bridge on February 27, 1776.

She returned to Scotland in 1779, although her husband remained in the British army in Canada and her sons were scattered among various posts.

She died on March 5, 1790, and was given a heroine's burial.

McINTOSH, first name not recorded, a British or loyalist officer whose visit to the British lines outside Charleston in 1780 is recorded in the German-language journal of Johann Ewald, in which he is identified as "Obristen Makendoslw" (Colonel McIntosh). Perhaps the visitor actually was a 78-year-old veteran of the Battle of Culloden who had emigrated from Scotland to America in 1748, as Ewald recounts.

Bernard Uhlendorf, who translated and edited Ewald's journal, believes the visitor was Captain William McIntosh even though Uhlendorf points out several discrepancies in a footnote on page 65:

Captain (not Colonel) William McIntosh was an Indian agent for the Southern Department, whose family had lived in

Georgia for some time. The McIntoshes played important roles in the rebellion of 1715 and that of 1745, but the McIntosh mentioned here did not fight in the interest of the Stuarts…

Captain William McIntosh does not fit Ewald's description of a 78-year-old Scotsman. He was only about thirty-five years old in 1780, and he was not a native of Scotland, having been born about twelve years after his father immigrated to Georgia. But it is logical for Uhlendorf to deduce that Captain William McIntosh would be accompanying a Creek chief. He had grown up among the Creeks at his father's trading post above Mobile. Remaining loyal to Britain during the American Revolution, Captain William McIntosh made military recruiting visits to Creek towns and commanded a contingent of Creek allies.

Perhaps Ewald's visitor was Rory McIntosh, who not only fits the description pretty closely but also was present at the siege of Charleston, according to his friend John Couper. Rory fits the description because he was born and raised in Scotland and he was about sixty-eight years old in 1780. Rory had come to Georgia in 1736, among the founders of Darien. Although Rory was in America during the Jacobite Rising of 1745 in Britain, he was fond of toasting "the Young Gentleman," Bonnie Prince Charlie.

Regardless of whether Ewald's visitor was William, Rory, or someone else, the left wing of the Jacobite forces at Culloden was not commanded by a Mackintosh. The Mackintosh clansmen who fought at Culloden were led by Colonel Alexander MacGillivray and they were stationed in the center of the lines. The left wing was commanded by the Duke of Perth. But there is a famous Jacobite commander in the Mackintosh family tree: Brigadier William Mackintosh, who figured prominently in the Risings of 1715 and 1719. Ewald could have attributed the exploits of the Brigadier to his grandson Rory McIntosh or his great-grandson Captain William McIntosh.

McINTOSH, ALEXANDER (died November 18, 1780), officer in both the South Carolina line of the Continental Army and the militia. He was appointed the rank of major in the 2nd South Carolina Regiment on June 15, 1775. He was promoted in July to Lieutenant Colonel of the 3rd Regiment, which was a Rangers unit.

Early in 1776, the South Carolina legislature elected McIntosh as second in command of the First Rifle Regiment. After other American officers refused to do it, he delivered an offer to surrender from the civic officials of Charleston to British General Prevost in May of 1779. He was married to Eleanor James (*American Revolution Roster Fort Sullivan* 242; Moss, *South Carolina* 630).

From *Pioneers of Wiregrass Georgia*, v. 6: Col. William McIntosh's second son Lachlan married "1st. Catherine McIntosh, cousin, dau. of Gen. Alexander McIntosh of Cheraw Dist. S.C." (182).

A family historian gives this account:

> ...By that year [1756] two brothers, John McIntosh the older, and Alexander McIntosh the younger brother, had settled in South Carolina. These two brothers may have emigrated from Scotland sometime after the reverses suffered at the Battle of Culloden...
>
> The younger brother, Alexander McIntosh, settled on the east side of the Pee Dee River a few miles below Long Bluff, also in the Welch Neck section. He had three children, Catherine, John and Eleanor. By his marriage he acquired considerable property and subsequently amassed a substantial fortune and was prominently associated with the history of South Carolina in civil and military affairs. He is described as a handsome and commanding person and possessed of a better education than was usual in his day.
>
> His public career may be described as beginning when, in 1761, he was appointed to the earliest list of Justices of the Peace. In 1765 he was commissioned a Captain in the King's Service to help fight the Indians...
>
> ...He appears as a member of the Grand Jury of Cheraw, S.C., in 1773 and 1774 and he was elected one of the representatives of St. David's Parish to the Provincial Congress of 1775.
>
> ...Soon after the resolution for raising the regiments was passed [by the South Carolina legislature in 1775], a ballot for officers was held and Alexander McIntosh was elected Major of the Second Regiment in June 1775. It is said of him that his decision and energy with a commanding person and ample fortune gave him a peculiar fitness

for the position. Thus began a brilliant career in the defense of his new homeland.

...In the year 1778 he was elected President of St. David's Society of the Welch Neck community, an organization for the promotion of learning in St. David's Parish which he helped to found.

...When the enemy evacuated Augusta, Georgia, Lt. Col. McIntosh was detached to command a company of regulars, with a party of militia under Col. Howard, ordered to follow and harass the enemy. He continued to serve extensively in Georgia where he gained the confidence and respect of General William Moultrie, his commander.

As a result of the regulations promulgated under the Militia Act of 1778 he was appointed to command a brigade of militia embracing the eastern part of the State of South Carolina. This position he maintained with the rank of Brigadier General until his death on November 18th, 1780.

It is written of him that "in every relation of life, this patriotic and honoured citizen had ever maintained the most exemplary character. It was his happiness to fill every position to which he was called with fidelity and honor. Of superior mental endowments – he was enabled to exert a degree of influence beyond most of his contemporaries in the service of his country."

Capt. Alexander McIntosh, nephew and namesake of Gen. McIntosh was... the eldest son of the older brother John McIntosh. Capt. McIntosh also served actively and with honour in the American Revolution. He served in the campaigns of South Carolina under Col. Lemuel Benton... Once when his brother was wounded, he was excited to such an extent that he killed every Torie that he caught. He is described in the local history as a man of large size and extraordinary strength and activity. Legend has it that once when hotly pursued by the Tories he leaped his horse across Black Creek, which is almost impossible to believe... (McIntosh, J. Reiman. "The McIntoshes of South Carolina, U.S.A." *Clan Chattan: The Journal of Clan Chattan* VII.1 (1977): 4-10.)

McINTOSH, GEORGE (1739-1779), youngest son of John Mackintosh Mor.

He accompanied his brother Lachlan to Charleston in 1748 and they lived there together until 1756.

George married Ann Priscilla Houston, a member of one of Georgia's most prominent families. George became a successful planter and established Rice Hope at the head of the Sapelo River.

As the American Revolution approached, George participated in the patriot movement with his brothers and in-laws. In March of 1777 Georgia President Button Gwinnett accused George of selling rice to the British, charged him with treason, and had him put in chains in the common jail. His family arranged for him to be released on bail, and he set out for Philadelphia to state his case before the Continental Congress. By the time the guards who were supposed to escort him caught up with him he was in North Carolina. The charges infuriated his brother Lachlan, who fought a duel with Gwinnett, resulting in Gwinnett's death.

Congress dismissed the charges against George McIntosh for lack of evidence.

His wife died in 1777, so when George died in 1779 at the age of 40 his estate passed to his 7-year-old son John Houston McIntosh.

McINTOSH, JOHN, known as John McIntosh Mohr, SEE **MACKINTOSH, JOHN,** known as John Mackintosh Mor.

McINTOSH, JOHN (c. 1712-1780), British deputy to the Chickasaws during the American Revolution (Cashin, *Bartram* 254).

He was a son of Benjamin McIntosh and, therefore, grandson of Brigadier William Mackintosh of Borlum and a brother of Roderick "Rory" McIntosh. He was the father of Captain William McIntosh, British deputy to the Creeks during the American Revolution, and, therefore, grandfather of Chief William McIntosh.

McINTOSH, JOHN (1755-1826), Continental officer. John McIntosh was a son of William McIntosh, who was a son of John Mackintosh Mor, who was the leader of the Highlanders who founded Darien, Georgia.

John McIntosh became a captain in the 1st Georgia Regiment on January 7, 1776, under the command of his uncle Lachlan McIntosh. On April 1, 1778, John McIntosh was promoted to Lieutenant Colonel at age 23.

He earned the nickname "Come and take it" for his defiant defense of the fort at Sunbury in November of 1778.

According to published accounts, he was rescued at the Battle of Brier Creek in March of 1779 by Aeneas Mackintosh of the 71st Regiment; both Aeneas Mackintosh and John McIntosh were descendants of the 16th Chief of Clan Mackintosh.

After his surrender at Brier Creek in March of 1779, John McIntosh remained a prisoner of war for more than a year before being exchanged for a British officer. McIntosh continued in service until the end of the war. Although he was a Continental officer, he volunteered to serve with the Georgia militia through the campaign of 1781 and for a time was an aide to the South Carolina partisan leader General Thomas Sumter.

While serving in South Carolina, he met Sarah Swinton and married her. John brought Sarah home to Fair Hope on the Sapelo River near Darien. John's father William had built the house at Fair Hope and had given the plantation to John before the war. Fair Hope was next to Mallow, the plantation home the branch of the McIntosh family that included Rory McIntosh. John and Rory had been neighbors before the war, but were not neighbors after the war. Rory, a loyalist, chose to return to his native Scotland.

John established himself as a prosperous planter and leading citizen in the community that became McIntosh County. Later, John and Sarah McIntosh moved to the St. Johns River in Florida. During their residence in Florida, Sarah lost her eyesight in an accident. John was arrested on suspicion of activities against the Spanish government, and was imprisoned first at St. Augustine and then in Havana for a year. After his release, John and Sarah returned to Georgia.

Sarah died in 1799 on St. Simons Island. John later married a widow, Agnes Hillary, and John's son William married the widow's daughter, Maria.

During the War of 1812, John McIntosh served as a Major General of militia, commanding three regiments of infantry and a battalion of artillery assigned to protect coastal Georgia. When the British threatened the Gulf Coast, McIntosh led his force through the Southern wilderness to Mobile. When the war ended, the Mayor of Savannah and the City Council declared their gratitude for his gallant service (White 548-50; "John McIntosh." *GlynnGen.com*).

John returned to Fair Hope and resumed his role as a leading businessman and planter. He served as a ruling elder in the Darien Presbyterian Church until his death (Sullivan 35-36).

He died at Fairhope in 1826 and was buried in the family cemetery on the plantation. Two decades later, a storm washed his coffin out of the grave. The family reburied his body in a prestigious type of coffin that had not been invented at the time of his death. The new Fisk coffin was made out of iron and cost a hundred dollars, while a wooden coffin cost only a dollar at that time. In 2006 a workman trimming bushes for a new owner of Fair Hope found the rusted iron coffin on the bank of the river. Evidence proved that the coffin held the remains of John McIntosh. One clue was that the coffin was unusually long and John was known to have been more than six feet tall, unusually tall for a man in the 1700s. Billy McIntosh of Savannah, a descendant of John McIntosh, arranged for John to be buried a third time, and this time farther from the river. John would be buried in the McIntosh cemetery at Mallow, the final resting place of several of Rory McIntosh's family members.

Billy McIntosh scheduled the third burial of John McIntosh for October 23, 2010. *The Darien News* reported the event:

> On that beautiful October Saturday afternoon, a horse-drawn hearse carried "Col. John" only a mile between his first and second resting place at Fair Hope and what will hopefully be his last, at Mallow.
>
> The glass carriage arrived under a canopy of moss-draped oaks, kicking up dust, as the Savannah Pipe and Drum played "Going Home" on the bagpipes...
>
> Beginning with Billy, the ceremonial shoveling of dirt into the grave began. In the Scottish tradition, flasks containing Scotch whisky were brought out, at which time swigs were taken prior to the pouring of the Scotch over the casket... ("Colonel John McIntosh" 17, 19).

It was a proud moment for Billy McIntosh, but it didn't exactly bring what his generation might call closure. "The McIntoshes are so stubborn," Billy McIntosh told the newspaper. "He doesn't want to stay in the ground. This may not be the last!" ("Colonel John McIntosh" 17).

McINTOSH, JOHN (born 1757), called Jack, eldest son of Lachlan and Sarah McIntosh.

In 1773 Jack accompanied the naturalist William Bartram on a trek through Creek and Cherokee territory.

Jack enlisted in the Continental army early in 1776 along with his father, brothers, uncle and cousins, but before November of 1776 he left Georgia to stay with his uncle John Mackintosh in Jamaica for the remainder of the war.

He returned to Georgia after the war and helped his father restore the family's farming and business operations.

McINTOSH, LACHLAN (1727-1806), Continental General. He was born in Scotland, on March 5, 1727, in Achugcha, near Raits in Badenoch, the second son of Marjory and John Mackintosh Mor.

When Lachlan was eight years old, his father led a group of Highlanders who sailed to America and founded the town of Darien, Georgia.

In February of 1740 13-year-old Lachlan and his sister Ann went to the orphanage at Bethesda, near Savannah. Lachlan joined the regiment at St. Simons as a cadet shortly before the Battle of Bloody Marsh at St. Simons in 1742.

When Lachlan McIntosh turned 21, he asserted his independence by moving away from his family in the Darien district. Bringing his younger brother George with him, he moved to Charleston and stayed there nearly eight years.

While living in South Carolina, Lachlan McIntosh met Sarah Threadcraft of Williamsburg. He married her on New Year's Day of 1756, and they relocated to the Darien District later that year. Lachlan experienced success as a rice planter and made joint investments with Henry Laurens in various enterprises in coastal Georgia.

Lachlan and Sarah's first child was born early in 1757 and was named John after his grandfather John Mackintosh Mor.

Their second son – named Lachlan and called Lachlan Jr. or Lackie – was born about a year later. In 1759 their third son was born and was given the esteemed family name William. Over the years, their marriage would produce five more children: daughters Hester and Catherine and younger sons George, Henry Laurens and John Hampden, called Hampden.

In 1770, Lachlan McIntosh was elected as a delegate to the Commons House.

Lachlan McIntosh offered his hospitality to roving naturalist William Bartram in the spring of 1773, and they continued to correspond throughout their lifetimes.

In January of 1775, Lachlan served as leader of the Darien Committee, which issued a declaration against slavery.

Georgians opposed to British rule called a Second Provincial Congress in the summer of 1775. Lachlan McIntosh remained the leader of the Darien Committee that elected delegates to the Provincial Congress. The committee selected Lachlan, his older brother William, and his younger brother George as delegates. On July 4, 1775, the Provincial Congress declared its support for the Continental Congress and established itself as Georgia's revolutionary government.

Congress elected Lachlan McIntosh to lead the first Continental battalion in Georgia in January of 1776. He held the rank of Colonel and his teenage sons William, Lackie, and John were subalterns. His brother William McIntosh led a troop of Light Horse. William's son John McIntosh, who had become an officer in the Continental army in 1775 at age twenty, was promoted to the rank of captain in the 1st Georgia Regiment.

Early in 1776, Lachlan commanded the patriot forces in the Battle of the Riceboats on the Savannah River. Lachlan was promoted to Brigadier General on September 16, 1776.

Lachlan became embroiled in a political feud with Georgia's civilian leader Button Gwinnett. On May 16, 1777, Lachlan killed Gwinnett in a duel.

Lachlan's old friend and business partner Henry Laurens, who held a powerful position in the Continental Congress, arranged for Lachlan to report to General George Washington for reassignment.

Lachlan and his son Lackie reported for duty at George Washington's notorious winter encampment at Valley Forge. Washington assigned McIntosh to command the North Carolina Brigade and assigned Lackie to serve as an aide to Major-General Baron von Steuben, renowned as the Drillmaster of Valley Forge. Lachlan McIntosh made a favorable impression on Washington, who always spoke highly of him.

In May of 1778, Washington placed Lachlan in command of the Western Department of the Continental army with headquarters at Fort Pitt. He was responsible for suppressing loyalist and Indian raids on settlements along the Western frontier.

Lachlan pushed the American military presence farther into the wilderness by building Fort McIntosh on the Ohio River thirty miles from Fort Pitt and building Fort Laurens on the Tuscarawas River a hundred miles from Fort Pitt.

Early in 1779 McIntosh learned that the British had captured Savannah, where his wife and younger children were living. McIntosh requested permission to return south to protect his family. Congress granted his request and turned over command of the Western Department to one of Lachlan's most vociferous critics, Daniel Brodhead.

Lachlan resumed command of the scant Continental troops remaining in Georgia after the British conquest of the state. He marched his troops from Augusta to join the allied American and French attempt to take back Savannah. He failed to convince British officials to release his wife and younger children from captivity in Savannah, and worried about their safety as the allies bombarded the city. He was the second-highest-ranking Continental officer during the disastrous allied assault on the British defenses in October of 1779.

Lachlan endured one heart-rending episode after another. Shortly after the ill-fated assault on Savannah, and in the midst of Lachlan's efforts to remove his wife and children from behind enemy lines, Lachlan learned that his younger brother George had died.

After painstaking negotiations, Lachlan freed his wife and children from British control and escorted them to relative safety in the South Carolina backcountry. Then he reported for duty in Charleston just as the British moved in to capture the South's most important city. In Charleston he learned that his political enemies in Georgia had caused Congress to suspend him from command. He stayed at Charleston, however, and commanded militia units rather than Continental troops. He was captured when Charleston capitulated in May of 1780 and was held as a prisoner of war at Haddrell's Point on the east bank of the Cooper River.

Lachlan was released as a prisoner of war on parole in the summer of 1781. Still seething with resentment over being suspended from Continental command because of baseless accusations cooked up by his political enemies, he went to Philadelphia and stated his case. McIntosh convinced Congress to repeal the resolution suspending him from command. He was living in the American barracks in Philadelphia during the fall of 1781 while Yorktown was under siege. By February of 1782, McIntosh had been exchanged.

The British garrison at Savannah evacuated on July 11, 1782, leaving Georgia in possession of the patriots. Lachlan McIntosh returned to Georgia in August of 1782. He found his plantation at Darien in ruins and his finances in shambles. His wife and younger children, meanwhile, remained in exile under the protection of Lachlan's son Lackie.

Lachlan continued to refute the claims of his political enemies who had caused him to be suspended from command. Many of the officers who had served under his command declared that he was one of the best commanders they knew. Georgia authorities, meanwhile, denounced his political enemies. On one occasion in early 1783, his son William attacked a political enemy with a horsewhip. McIntosh felt that his wounded pride had been restored when Congress promoted him to Major General in January of 1783.

Just when things seemed to be going his way, McIntosh suffered a devastating personal loss. His second-oldest son, Lachlan McIntosh Jr., died on February 15, 1783, at the age of 25, while escorting Sarah McIntosh and the younger children on their journey home.

Lachlan resumed his role as a member of the coastal land-owning aristocracy. In political matters, he was appointed to several commissions and served a term in the Georgia Assembly. Officers who had served under McIntosh in the war chose him as the founding president of the Georgia chapter of the Society of Cincinnati.

When President George Washington toured the southern states in the spring of 1791, Lachlan escorted him into Savannah and showed him around the town.

Lachlan died at his house in Savannah on February 20, 1806. He was buried at the old Christ Church cemetery, now named Colonial Park.

McINTOSH Jr., LACHLAN (1757-1783), called Lackie, second son of Lachlan and Sarah McIntosh.

He was about 19 years old when he enlisted in the Continental army early in 1776 along with his father, brothers, uncle and cousins. He commanded a company protecting the plantations in the Darien area and assumed responsibility for the safety of his mother and younger brothers and sisters while his father was based in Savannah.

He accompanied his father to join George Washington's army at Valley Forge in the winter of 1777-78 and served as an aide to Major-General Baron von Steuben, the famed Drillmaster of Valley Forge who is credited with shaping the American army into a well-trained, well-disciplined, formidable fighting force.

When Washington appointed General Lachlan McIntosh to command the Western department at Fort Pitt, Lackie went with his father. On October 11, 1778, General McIntosh appointed his son Lackie to serve as the Deputy Adjutant General for the Western Department.

Lackie returned to the South while his mother, sisters and younger brothers were refugees. When General McIntosh was taken prisoner at the siege of Charleston in 1780, Lackie once again assumed responsibility for protecting the family during its wanderings.

After the British evacuated Savannah in the summer of 1782, the family trekked homeward. They were in Camden when Lackie, age 25, died on February 15, 1783.

McINTOSH, RODERICK (died 1782), known as "Rory." He was in his late teens or early twenties when he emigrated from Scotland in 1736 with his father Benjamin, brother John and sister Winnewood. Their family was among the group of Highlanders – led by Benjamin's cousin John Mackintosh Mor – who founded Darien on the Georgia coast.

Rory fought at the Battle of Mosa in Florida in 1740. Conditions deteriorated in Darien following the debacle at Mosa, and Rory's father was among the discontented Highlanders who left

Darien in the 1740s. Rory's brother John became an Indian trader on the southern frontier. Roderick and his sister Winnewood remained on the family's plantation, Mallow, near Darien. Rory became a legendary character.

Remaining loyal to Great Britain during the American Revolution, Rory found refuge in the British territory of East Florida in 1777.

While in St. Augustine, Rory engaged twenty fellow loyalists who had evacuated from the Darien district to serve as mariners on a privateer ship.

Rory accompanied the British troops that invaded Georgia and, legend has it, confronted his relative John McIntosh at Sunbury in 1778. He was in Savannah when Lachlan McIntosh and Aeneas Mackintosh fought on opposing sides in 1779. Legend has it that Rory dined with Aeneas the Chief of Clan Mackintosh at Charleston in 1780.

After the war ended badly for his side, Rory decided to return to Scotland. He survived the voyage across the Atlantic but before he reached his boyhood home he died aboard ship at Gravesend, England, in 1782.

McINTOSH, WILLIAM (1726-1801), eldest son of John Mackintosh Mor, brother of General Lachlan McIntosh and father of Colonel John McIntosh. He fought in the Battle of Mosa in 1740 and the Battle of Bloody Marsh in1742.

He married Mary Jane Mackay. William became a successful planter at Fair Hope on the Sapelo River and participated with his brothers in political activities.

As the commander of a troop of light horse in the opening period of the American Revolution, he conducted campaigns on the southern frontier.

His daughter Margery married James Spalding and lived on St. Simons Island; her son Thomas Spalding recorded the history and legend of his family in early Georgia.

McINTOSH, WILLIAM (died 1794), son of John McIntosh, who was a son of Benjamin McIntosh, who was a natural son of Brigadier William Mackintosh of Borlum. He served as a British officer operating among the Creek Indians during the American Revolution. In about 1775 he fathered a Creek son who would become known as Chief William McIntosh. Captain William McIntosh recruited Creek Indians from the Chiaha and Hichata bands in August of 1778 to reinforce the British at St. Augustine. American allies among the Cussita band of the Creeks issued threats against McIntosh personally and against loyalist settlers in the Pensacola area.

After the war, he reclaimed his family's plantation, Mallow, near Darien. He married Barbara McIntosh, a daughter of William McIntosh, who was the eldest son of John Mackintosh Mor.

McINTOSH, WILLIAM (c. 1775-1825), known as Chief William McIntosh. His mother was a member of the powerful Wind Clan of the Creek Indians and his father was Captain William McIntosh, a British officer operating among the Creeks. Captain William McIntosh was a great-grandson of Brigadier William Mackintosh of Borlum.

Chief William McIntosh served as a major in the United States Army during the Red Sticks War in 1813. His prowess in battle earned the praise of General Andrew Jackson. He was later promoted to brigadier general.

After he signed the Treaty of Indian Springs in 1825, a war party of Crecks opposed to the treaty attacked his house and killed him in battle.

In the ensuing Indian Removals, often called the Trail of Tears, his sons led the Creeks to Oklahoma. Their descendants are known as the McIntosh Creeks.